THE COURT of APPEAL for SASKATCHEWAN

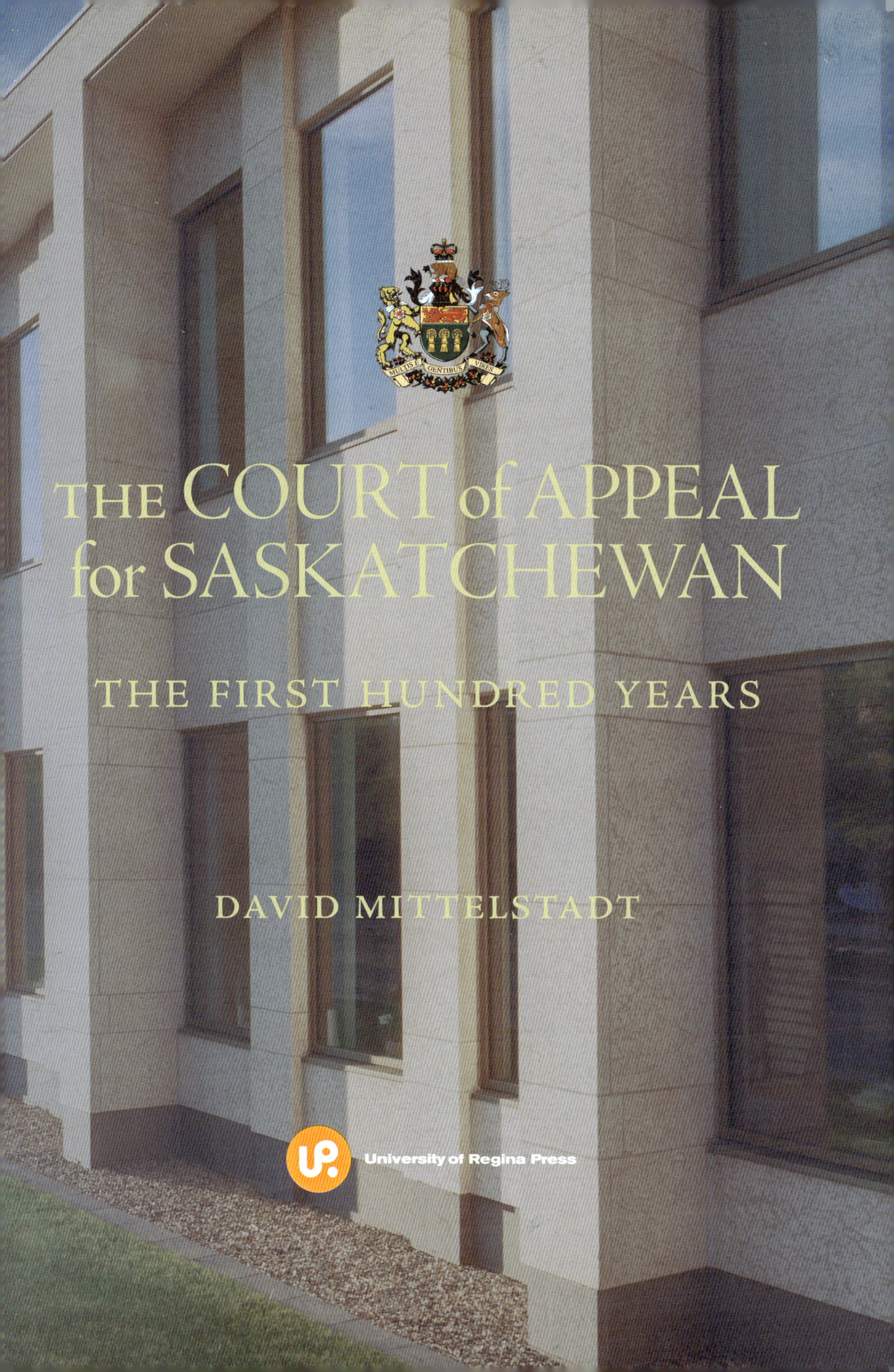

THE COURT of APPEAL for SASKATCHEWAN

THE FIRST HUNDRED YEARS

DAVID MITTELSTADT

University of Regina Press

Printed and bound in Canada at Marquis. The text of this book is printed on 100% post-consumer recycled paper with earth-friendly vegetable-based inks.

Copy editor: Alex Schultz
Proofreader: Kristine Douaud
Indexer: Judy Dunlop
Designer: Duncan Campbell, University of Regina Press
Cover and title page photo: Patricia Holdsworth

Library and Archives Canada Cataloguing in Publication

Mittelstadt, David, 1966-, author
The Court of Appeal for Saskatchewan : the first hundred years / David Mittelstadt.

Includes bibliographical references and index.
Issued in print and electronic formats.
ISBN 978-0-88977-569-5 (hardcover).—ISBN 978-0-88977-570-1 (PDF).
—ISBN 978-0-88977-571-8 (HTML)

1. Saskatchewan. Court of Appeal—History. I. Title.

KES535.2.M58 2018 347.7124'0309 C2018-903903-5
KF8764.ZB6M58 2018 C2018-903904-3

10 9 8 7 6 5 4 3 2 1

U OF R PRESS

University of Regina Press, University of Regina
Regina, Saskatchewan, Canada, S4S 0A2
TEL: (306) 585-4758 FAX: (306) 585-4699
WEB: www.uofrpress.ca

We acknowledge the financial support of the Government of Canada. / Nous reconnaissons l'appui financier du gouvernement du Canada.

Canada

CONTENTS

INTRODUCTION

SIR FREDERICK HAULTAIN, THE CHIEF JUSTICE OF SASkatchewan, was not pleased. Haultain had been a judge for nearly twenty-five years. He had once travelled the length and breadth of the province conducting trials and for nearly twenty years had been the head of the province's Court of Appeal. There wasn't much he hadn't heard or seen in a courtroom. Haultain was a gentleman, affable and approachable, but even his patience had worn thin. Justice Percy Gordon, one of the other judges hearing the appeal before the court, was never known for patience, nor was Justice H.V. Bigelow, a trial judge sitting temporarily on the Court of Appeal. The judges were irritated by the arguments of Peter Makaroff, the maverick Doukhobor lawyer who had taken on the unpopular task of defending the men charged after the Regina Riot in 1935. Downtown Regina had been left in shambles when police clashed with unemployed men on their way to Ottawa to protest conditions during the Great Depression. More than two dozen men were convicted of assault and other charges, and on a June morning in 1936 Makaroff was appealing the convictions and sentences of eight of them.

Haultain believed fundamentally in doing justice, and though he had little sympathy for the rioters he also considered his personal feelings to be beside the point. But Makaroff was leaving no stone unturned, and the chief justice thought that his arguments had veered into the irrelevant and the unimportant. "Generalities of that sort are no good," Haultain chided counsel at one point. Later, as Makaroff challenged the identification evidence, the chief justice exclaimed that his arguments were "an absolute absurdity." What really annoyed Haultain were Makaroff's constant challenges of the jury's findings of fact on the evidence. It was a basic legal principle that a court of appeal would not interfere with such findings unless they were clearly in error and unsupported by the evidence. Makaroff should have known better. "The appeal court does not conduct retrials," the chief justice said. He dismissed the two appeals of conviction that Makaroff had argued. Knowing he was fighting a lost cause, the lawyer withdrew the five other conviction appeals and concentrated instead on challenging his clients' sentences.

Haultain's criticism of the arguments Makaroff presented to his court was a little harsher than one would hear in a modern courtroom, but it captures an important aspect of how appeals work in Canada. Appeals are not new trials or hearings but challenges to the outcome of a trial, a chambers motion, or a board hearing. Appeals focus on purported errors, most usually in how the law has been interpreted and applied but also, on occasion, in the findings of judge or jury on the evidence, the facts of the case as judicially determined. The hearing of an appeal is very different from a trial. A panel of three judges, sometimes more on very important appeals, hears the case. The dynamic environment of witnesses, objections, and cross-examinations found at a trial is replaced with the calm, focused arguments of counsel, interrupted from time to time when judges want a point clarified or a line of argument expanded or abandoned. There are few if any spectators; there are no dramatics; there is no theatre. Yet the arguments of the lawyers and the judgment of the court can have widespread ramifications, leading to major changes in the law that have profound consequences for society at large. What happens in the Court of Appeal can matter a great deal to people who never set foot in a courtroom and only have a hazy idea of what an appellate court does.

The appeals of the Regina rioters are a few among the thousands the court has decided over the last one hundred years, part of a vast tapestry of the law in the province. This book is a history of the Court of Appeal for Saskatchewan, conceived and written to celebrate its centennial. In 1918, the government of Saskatchewan put into effect legislation, proclaimed three years before, to set up separate appeal and trial courts, replacing a single court that combined both functions. The Court of Appeal is the highest court in the province, with the power to review, reverse, or affirm the decisions of the province's trial courts and administrative boards and tribunals, which must follow the appeal court's pronouncements on the law. The modern Court of Appeal answers only to the Supreme Court of Canada, the court of "last resort" for Canada. But since the Supreme Court only hears a very small number of appeals, usually dealing with matters of national reach and significance, the Court of Appeal has the final say on the law in the province in nearly all instances, a tremendous responsibility.

The decisions of Saskatchewan's Court of Appeal are regularly scrutinized by lawyers who need to know what the court has decided on a point of law, and by academics and other commentators eager to understand why the court decided one way or another and what that might say about the development of the law and the relationship of the law to society. Yet for all that, the Court of Appeal as an institution has not been studied in any comprehensive fashion. A little has been written on the judges who have sat on the court over the years, but almost no attention has been paid to the full story: the court's origins; how it has developed as an institution; the judges who have served, their background and predilections, and how they have influenced both court and law; and, most importantly, the court's contributions to the development of the law in the province and the nation.

It is a story that needs to be told. Courts are the forum for disputes between individuals, between individuals and the state, and between governments over their respective legislative powers. They are fundamental to the rule of law and the functioning of democracies, a bulwark of the state and society. They are also the counterweight against the power of the state, the protectors of individual rights and liberties. Canadian courts have a long-standing tradition of judicial independence that makes it possible for judges to take on both roles. The vital importance of the courts means that understanding them is crucial, and history is an excellent route to this understanding. This history looks at the three elements of the court and its history: the jurisprudence the court has produced, the judges who have made up the court, and the court's institutional development.

Jurisprudence is the most important and complex branch. The Court of Appeal has two equally important roles. The first, and more prosaic, is error correction and likely accords closest to the public's understanding of what appeal courts do. The court considers claims that the trial court judge has made errors by misunderstanding, misinterpreting, or misapplying the law, by making findings on the evidence that are incorrect, or by not properly explaining the law and evidence to a jury. Most appeals are error correction, but this is not necessarily easy or simple. The second role is developing the law. This involves properly interpreting a statute, particularly if the statute is ambiguous or unclear, and declaring how statutes should be correctly applied. It includes constitutional adjudication. It requires applying, distinguishing, and creating the case law that is the common law, the underpinning of Canada's legal system. The two functions are not always clearly separated; an appeal might be mostly error correction but also lead to development of the law, perhaps correcting a common mistake of trial judges on a point of law, perhaps reconciling different views of different judges on an issue, perhaps because a new wrinkle surfaced in the trial, a situation where it was not clear how the law should best be applied. The Court of Appeal is expected to supply the answer.

The role of the "intermediate appellate courts"—in Canada, the provincial and territorial courts of appeal and the Federal Court of Appeal—in developing the law is also both constrained and expansive. Until 1949, there were two higher courts that could overrule a provincial appeal court: the Supreme Court of Canada and the Judicial Committee of the Privy Council, which was established in 1837 as the highest court of appeal for British colonies and dominions. There were limitations on what could be appealed to either court and also the intrinsic limitation of the time and expense needed to appeal to these courts. This meant that the vast majority of cases were already settled in the provincial courts. After the end of Privy Council appeals in 1949, only the Supreme Court of Canada could overrule a provincial court of appeal. After 1975, the Supreme Court took control of its docket with a requirement for leave of the court for the majority of appeals, allowing the court to concentrate on cases with national importance. This made provincial appeal courts effectively the court of last resort in about 99 percent of litigation.

Saskatchewan has punched above its weight in many forums. Provincial politicians were cherry-picked to serve as federal cabinet ministers, and an exodus of civil servants to Ottawa created a "Saskatchewan mafia" that played a key role in establishing Canada's health-care system and social safety net. And the decisions of the Saskatchewan Court of Appeal, whether upheld or overturned in the Supreme Court of Canada or the Privy Council, have been very influential. *John East Iron Works* in 1947 greatly influenced the way Canadian courts dealt with administrative law, with Saskatchewan's Court of Appeal acting as a guardian against the extension of significant powers to unaccountable boards and tribunals.

Canadian Industrial Gas and Oil and *Central Canada Potash* were major constitutional cases from the 1970s that led to an amendment in the *Constitution Act, 1982* regarding provincial control and taxation of natural resources. Saskatchewan was particularly bold with the *Charter of Rights and Freedoms*. RWDSU *v Saskatchewan* was a critical decision on the *Charter* and the rights of labour to collectively bargain and strike. The Supreme Court overruled the Court of Appeal in 1987, but nearly thirty years later, in another appeal from the province, *Saskatchewan Federation of Labour*, the high court reversed its previous precedent and acknowledged that Saskatchewan's judges got it right the first time. These are just a few examples.

The jurisprudence of the court is one branch of its history. The second is the biographical. The judges are the court and the court is the judges. Indeed, for much of the court's history, the judges, the court's registrar, and one or two clerks were the entire complement of Court of Appeal personnel. The background, professional qualifications, judicial philosophy, character, and personalities of the judges are all grist for the mill. Part of the evolution of the Canadian judiciary over the last hundred years has been the growing awareness of the influence of factors like background and possible bias, both conscious and unconscious. While judges in the common law tradition strive to be objective and impartial, they still bring their life experiences with them to the bench. It is important to know who becomes a judge and how their background might influence them. Judges in Canada start out their careers as lawyers and are drawn from a small professional elite that even today is not representative of society at large. But within this homogenous group—for many decades, white middle-aged males of Anglo-Scottish descent—there is still a range of personalities, backgrounds, and perspectives.

Personalities also play a role in the function of a court of appeal. Unlike trial courts, appellate courts are collegial, meaning that the judges work together to decide appeals. Collegiality is of particular importance at the appellate level, as courts strive to achieve consistency and clarity in judgments even though the judges are equally empowered, acting independently of another, to arrive at their own conclusions in any given case. The role of collegiality is often somewhat intangible, difficult to quantify and articulate but still an element of how courts function. Or don't. There have been instances of judicial rivalries on Canadian courts sometimes detrimental to their function. The Saskatchewan Court of Appeal has been largely free of these problems but not without the occasional clash of personalities and disagreements of principle, sometimes fundamental, sometimes pointed.

Then there are the individual judges, their personalities, their quirks and idiosyncrasies. Although some might protest that personal stories about the judges are irrelevant to what really matters—the jurisprudence—they can give insight. And sometimes they are just good stories. The frontier judges played poker until all hours when they met to decide appeals. Saskatchewan's first chief justice didn't hesitate to bodily remove a stopping-house drunk who was interfering with his sleep and once gave a bar admission exam over a glass or two of whiskey. The second chief justice was a towering figure in the history of Western Canada who led the fight for provincial autonomy that created Saskatchewan and is sometimes called the forgotten Father of Confederation. Two judges became diplomats during the Second World War, one while still a member of the court and never actually sitting on an appeal. One particularly outspoken and opinionated judge had the premier of the province call him out in the legislature, suggesting he run for office if he wanted to express political opinions. Yet another chief justice was practically a one-man court, reputed to have personally heard every appeal of sentence that came before the court and never increased a stay in jail. Stories like these are amusing and interesting, but it is also important to remember that judges are human beings, and their experiences and personality, professional and personal, shape how they approach the law.

One relevant and interesting question is how judges got their appointments. Ability is one answer, but political patronage and partisanship have influenced judicial appointments in Canada from Confederation. Patronage can be mostly innocuous; lawyers historically were disproportionately involved in politics, and holding public office was a mark of ability and a valuable experience. It was consequently not surprising to see many politician-lawyers later named to the bench. In Saskatchewan, no fewer than five attorney generals went to the Court of Appeal as well as two premiers, one of the province and one of the North-West Territories. But there have been questions historically about the influence of political considerations in appointments and concern that judgeships were handed out as rewards for political services rendered.

Saskatchewan was long understood to be a province where the connection between politics and judicial appointments was strong, especially in the province's first few decades, when the federal and provincial Liberal parties were intertwined. This relationship greatly influenced who was appointed to the courts. The first serious reforms of the federal judicial appointment system, in the 1970s, ensured appointees were well qualified but did not necessarily remove the political dimension as to who exactly got appointed. Saskatchewan was also where the tensions intrinsic to the divided jurisdiction over superior courts—with the provinces responsible for the constitution and administration of the superior courts and the federal government for appointments to the same courts—came to the fore. The federal government had no duty to consult with provinces over appointments, and this bred resentment. After the historic victory in Saskatchewan of Tommy Douglas and the Co-operative Commonwealth Federation (CCF) in 1944, there was a strong disconnect between federal and provincial governments and a great deal of tension over judicial appointments. The CCF threatened several times in its first two decades in power to reduce the size of the province's superior courts to protest their lack of say over appointments, a strategy revived by a Conservative provincial government thirty years later. The appointment process in Saskatchewan is extensively explored in this book, providing a detailed picture of the experience in one province.

The third branch of the history of the court is its development as an institution. In many respects this is perhaps the simplest. For much of its history, the court consisted of the judges, a registrar, and perhaps two or three registry staff, who also covered the filings for the trial courts. Judges did not even have secretaries, as judicial assistants were called. They wrote their own letters and answered their own phones. The court and the senior trial court were both housed in one Regina courthouse, and they still are. Until the 1980s, there were only five judges of the court. They determined their sitting schedules and the rules of court, which set the procedures for filing and hearing appeals. For over forty years, this was the institutional history of the court.

The first significant evolution came in 1961, when the court started holding sittings in Saskatoon. In the 1970s, the court's caseload steadily increased, and the institutional story became interesting. The chief justice of the time, the storied E.M. Culliton, found himself locking horns with the provincial Department of the Attorney General over the court's lack of resources, whether it was office equipment, clerical assistance, or the complement of judges. This corresponded with increasing awareness among the judiciary across the country that the executive's direct administration of the courts raised uncomfortable questions about judicial independence on top of pragmatic issues like convincing ministers to increase budgets and hire more help. Some jurisdictions saw considerable conflict, and the judiciary even lobbied to take direct control of court administration, which was in the hands of the executive.

In Saskatchewan, some minor clashes reflected this larger picture, but for the most part executive and judiciary maintained cordial, co-operative, and respectful relations. The Saskatchewan court's efforts to adopt technology, an Achilles' heel for other Canadian appellate courts, were in part successful due to its relationship with government.

Each chapter of the book covers a decade or so of the court's story. Within each chapter, the judges joining the court are profiled, institutional changes are chronicled, and a selection of case studies gives a flavour of the jurisprudence, connected to a larger theme derived from the social, economic, and political developments of the time. Accounts of judges, legal philosophies, practices of the court, and jurisprudence carry over between chapters, as Saskatchewan's court often had long periods of stability, with long-serving judges and chief justices, which don't fit neatly into an arbitrary scheme of decades. The history of the court touches on many aspects of the larger history of the province, stars a group of talented, ambitious individuals who in the execution of their duty directly affected their society in numerous ways, and includes many important and even dramatic appeals that sometimes touched the life of the nation. As befits a centennial, this history is a celebration of the people and the institution and honours their service to the people of Saskatchewan, and it is also a fascinating story.

CHAPTER I

THE NORTH-WEST TERRITORIES

JUDGE HUGH RICHARDSON HELD THE FULL ATTENTION OF the hushed courtroom in Regina as he pronounced sentence in what was to become perhaps the most famous trial in Canadian history.

> Louis Riel, after a long consideration of your case, in which you have been defended with as great ability as I think counsel could have defended you with, you have been found by a jury who have shown, I might almost say, unexampled patience, guilty of a crime the most pernicious and greatest that man can commit. You have been found guilty of high treason. . . .
>
> For what you have done the law requires you to answer. It is true that the jury in merciful consideration have asked Her Majesty to give your case such merciful consideration as she can bestow upon it. I had almost forgotten that those who are defending you have placed in my hands a notice that the objection which they raised at the opening of the court must not be forgotten from the record, in order that if they see fit they may raise the question in the proper place. That has been done.[1]

Richardson would finish by telling Riel his fate: to be hung by the neck until dead. But before that, almost as an afterthought, he hinted at a recourse: the objection his counsel had made and that they could "raise the question in the proper place." That place was a court of appeal.

The story of the Court of Appeal for Saskatchewan truly begins thirty-five years before the province was founded in 1905. Before the Court of Appeal came the Supreme Court of Saskatchewan, and before that came the Supreme Court of the North-West Territories, and before that a stipendiary magistrate's court. What began as a court of limited jurisdiction for the frontier, primarily establishing law and order, evolved into a superior court the equal of any in Canada, which then bequeathed experienced judges and a body of law to the province and courts of Saskatchewan. The stipendiary magistrates and the Supreme Court of the North-West Territories were important antecedents to the Court of Appeal. The development of a court system in the Territories also began not long after the modern appellate court was established in Canada. Appeals in the Territories reflected this, and development of appellate procedure during the territorial period had a lasting influence on Saskatchewan.

IN THE BEGINNING . . .

IN 1870, THE fledgling government of the Dominion of Canada took possession of a new hinterland christened the North-West Territories. Two years earlier, the Hudson's Bay Company (HBC) had agreed to sell the new nation the area known as Rupert's Land. The company had generously interpreted its original 1670 grant to include the entire drainage basin of Hudson Bay. The British also ceded to the Dominion the lands in the west the HBC did not control, long known as the Indian Territories and then the North-Western Territory. In the wake of the Red River Resistance, a new province, Manitoba, was created in 1870, encompassing a small square of territory around the Red River Settlement. The North-West Territories included everything else up to the Continental Divide, including the high Arctic and what would later be the northern parts of Ontario and Quebec.

On inception, the North-West Territories lacked a judicial system aside from the traditional practices of the Indians. The HBC's charter had empowered the company to constitute courts and administer the laws of England as they might apply.[2] The company did not exercise its prerogative

HUGH RICHARDSON

Born in London, England, in 1826, Hugh Richardson was just five when his family immigrated to Canada. The family settled in London, Ontario, where Richardson's father was a bank manager.[1] Richardson was admitted to Osgoode Hall in 1842 and articled with John Wilson, a prominent London lawyer and politician who had the dubious distinction of killing a man in what is reportedly the last duel in Upper Canada. Richardson was called to the bar in 1847 and set up practice in Woodstock. He served as the Oxford County Crown attorney from 1856 to 1862. Active in the militia, Richardson was one of the organizers of the Oxford Rifles and commanded the garrison at Sarnia during the Fenian troubles, ending his militia career with the rank of lieutenant colonel.

In 1872, Richardson left practice in Woodstock for an appointment as chief clerk of the Department of Justice in Ottawa, and was at times acting deputy minister. As such, he was involved in the formation of the NWMP and was credited with drafting the *North-West Territories Act*. This may have played some part in his 1876 appointment as a territorial magistrate. When the Supreme Court of the North-West Territories was formed in 1886, Richardson brought his decade of experience in the Territories as a magistrate and legislative draftsman to the new bench. His reported decisions reveal a solid

Justice Hugh Richardson after his retirement, c. 1905. (Provincial Archives of Saskatchewan R-B7409)

if unimaginative jurist, and he was respected as fair and impartial. His colleagues considered Richardson the chief justice of the court, although he never officially bore the title.

Richardson retired in 1903. He returned to Ottawa and died there in 1913.

until taking control of the Red River Settlement, rechristened Assiniboia, in 1835. There had been little need; the factors in charge of the fur-trading posts disciplined employees without resorting to formal courts, and the HBC generally did not try to exert legal authority over the Indians and Métis in Rupert's Land unless there was a conflict with the company and its employees.[3]

Violence between rival fur traders in the Indian Territories led to the *Canada Jurisdiction Act* of 1803, which gave the courts of Upper and Lower Canada jurisdiction in the area. After the merger of the HBC and the North West Company of Montreal in 1821, the jurisdiction of the Upper Canada courts was extended to Rupert's Land. The General Quarterly Court, established by the HBC in Assiniboia in the 1830s, also claimed jurisdiction throughout Rupert's Land and the Indian Territories, but this was disputed. In any event, the reach of any court into the west was very limited. There was no law enforcement or court officials outside of Assiniboia, and even when wrongdoers were brought to Canada for trial, the jurisdiction of the courts was almost always challenged and lack of evidence usually meant acquittals.

All this changed in 1870. The Indians and Métis, by far the majority of the population of the Territories, were now subjects of the Crown. The first lieutenant-governor for the North-West Territories, Adams Archibald, commissioned army captain William Francis Butler to undertake a fact-finding tour.[4] Butler later turned the report of his journey, undertaken in winter, into the classic book *The Great Lone Land*. The report vividly described the lawless condition of the Territories, including the depredations of American whiskey traders and wolf hunters on the plains tribes. Butler recommended the appointment of resident magistrates and the formation of a mounted constabulary to keep the peace and establish Canadian sovereignty over the North-West Territories.

THE STIPENDIARY MAGISTRATES

THE GOVERNMENT WAS slow to act on Butler's recommendations even with fears of American annexation of the Territories. As one historian wrote, "A spirit of procrastination and delay pervaded the actions of the Dominion government in its dealings with the Prairies."[5] This was certainly the case with the administration of justice of the North-West

Territories. The federal government remained largely in charge of the territorial judicial system until Alberta and Saskatchewan were created as provinces in 1905. Whether passing legislation, appointing judges, or building courthouses, the Dominion government tended to sit on its hands, especially when expenditure was involved. Tardy judicial appointments were a legacy for the future province of Saskatchewan.

In 1873, the John A. Macdonald government passed the *Act respecting the Administration of Justice, and for the establishment of a Police Force in the North West Territories*.[6] Following Butler's recommendations, the statute allowed for the establishment of a mounted police force and the appointment of three stipendiary magistrates. In addition, the *Act* made the officers of the police force justices of the peace and, in an amendment, gave the force's commissioner the same judicial powers as those of the stipendiary magistrates. The *Act* thus made the proposed police force prosecutor, judge, and jailer for many offenders. Although unprecedented in the common law world, giving the police judicial powers served the frontier conditions.[7] Three magistrates could not cover all of the Territories, and there were few residents suitable or available to be justices of the peace. The police would otherwise have to transport the accused great distances or keep them locked up for long periods awaiting trial. The system, once it got going, seemed to work reasonably well, and police reports showed surprisingly high rates of acquittals and abuses appeared minimal.[8]

The Cypress Hills Massacre, in the summer of 1873, forced the government to act on its legislation. American wolf hunters looking for a stolen horse attacked an encampment of the Assiniboine people near the international border in present-day Saskatchewan and left more than twenty dead. The North-West Mounted Police (NWMP) was quickly formed and, after training in Winnipeg through the fall and winter, proceeded into the Territories in 1874.

Macdonald did not name the first magistrates until the beginning of 1876. A journalist before joining the bar, Matthew Ryan was a Montreal lawyer who had worked in the civil service.[9] He came west in 1875 to serve as an enumerator of the Métis. Lieutenant Colonel James Farquharson Macleod of the NWMP was the second appointment. Macleod had been the assistant commissioner of the police. Shortly after his judicial appointment, Macleod was made commissioner, but he continued as a stipendiary magistrate as well. In 1880, he resigned once more from the police to sit full-time as a judge. The third magistrate, Hugh Richardson,

JAMES FARQUHARSON MACLEOD

One of the best-known pioneers of the Canadian West, Colonel James Macleod was born on the Isle of Skye in 1836. His family immigrated when he was nine years old, settling on a farm north of Toronto.[2] Macleod attended Upper Canada College and later Queen's College, in Kingston, where he graduated in 1854 with a degree in classics and philosophy. Pushed into law by his father, Macleod twice failed the Osgoode Hall entrance exams before finally gaining admission in 1856, articling in Kingston in the office of Alexander Campbell, John A. MacDonald's one-time law partner, and spending his spare time with the local militia.

Justice James Farquharson Macleod, c. 1890. (Glenbow Archives, NA-2258-1)

Joining the bar in 1860, Macleod practised law in a desultory fashion while dreaming of a military career. He joined the Wolseley expedition against Louis Riel's provisional government with a commission as a brigade major and, like Richardson, rose to the rank of lieutenant colonel in the militia. While in England, hoping to further his military career, Macleod was offered a commission as a superintendent with the NWMP. He was quickly appointed assistant commissioner but resigned to take his judicial post due to tensions with his superior, Commissioner George French. French's abrupt departure brought Macleod back to the NWMP as commissioner. Four years later, he finally left the police and became a full-time magistrate.

Macleod was widely respected among Indian leaders for his honesty and fairness. He was well liked as a judge. The rigours of his life on circuit likely led to his early death, in 1894, due to Bright's disease. ❧

was appointed in July 1876. Richardson had practised law in Woodstock, Ontario, before joining the Department of Justice in Ottawa. The magistrates were stationed, respectively, in Qu'Appelle, Fort Macleod, and Battleford, the territorial capital after 1878, and went on circuit to other points in their districts. Their respective judicial districts were known initially as Qu'Appelle, Bow River, and Saskatchewan.[10] Qu'Appelle was the southeast area of the Territories; Bow River covered the south as far east as Swift Current; and Saskatchewan was the northern district, stretching from the British Columbia border to what would be the border of Ontario, encompassing Edmonton and Prince Albert.

The stipendiaries initially had a limited criminal jurisdiction, trying summary charges alone and indictable charges requiring penitentiary sentences with a justice of the peace or another magistrate. Under the 1873 *Act*, capital crimes were to be tried in Manitoba Court of Queen's Bench and judges from that court had jurisdiction in the Territories. The Dominion gradually increased the magistrate's criminal jurisdiction over the first few years of their tenure. By 1880, the stipendiaries could try nearly every offence alone or with a jury and capital crimes sitting with a justice of the peace.

The government gave the stipendiary magistrates civil jurisdiction from the beginning. *The North-West Territories Act, 1875* (NWT *Act*) enabled the lieutenant-governor in council to make provisions for the administration of justice, setting up civil courts for the magistrates and determining judicial districts and sittings.[11] Hugh Richardson has been credited with drafting the NWT *Act*, one of his last assignments at the justice department.[12] He was not finished with drafting statutes. The stipendiary magistrates were also members of the Territorial Council, which advised the lieutenant-governor. The combination of judicial and executive duties was not that unusual and reflected Canada's recent colonial past. The magistrates were legal advisers but also drafted legislation on behalf of the lieutenant-governor and council. Richardson, based in the capital, did the lion's share of the work and is credited with drafting most of the early territorial ordinances.[13] This included the judicature ordinance that set out civil procedure, which was adapted from the rules of court of England to apply to the local conditions.

By territorial ordinance of 1878, the magistrates were styled Judges of the District Court, with regular civil and criminal sittings at important locations within their districts.[14] It was declared a court of record, and

North-West Territories Executive Council Meeting, Regina, NWT, 1884, with Judge Hugh Richardson and Colonel James Macleod in attendance. The meeting table, used by the Fathers of Confederation in Quebec in 1864 and brought west by Lieutenant-Governor Edgar Dewdney, is now in the Legislative Library in Regina. (Glenbow Archives, NA-3668-1)

provision was made for the appointment of district sheriffs and clerks of court. Another ordinance in 1885 made the stipendiaries judges of the "High Court of Justice."[15]

"Judge of the High Court" sounded grand, but the stipendiaries had a hard life. On circuit, court was held in whatever building was available, usually the police post, if there was one, and, if not, in a schoolhouse, a church, the storeroom of a trading post, or even a tavern. The judges rarely had access to any library and, in the absence of a clerk, frequently had to keep the record of the proceedings in longhand. The travel conditions were daunting. In summer, the magistrates travelled by horseback or wagon over the rough trails or on water with canoe or York boat, and in winter by sleigh or dog team. Hotels and stopping houses were few and far between, and it was often necessary to camp, even in frigid temperatures.[16] It was not uncommon for travellers in the Territories to come to grief in winter blizzards. In letters to his wife, Colonel Macleod described violent windstorms threatening his encampment and nights huddled by a fire.

Government building and courthouse, Regina, NWT, 1885. (Glenbow Archives, NA-3205-6)

The distances were significant. Richardson faced a journey of almost four hundred kilometres from Battleford to Edmonton. He would go there and to Prince Albert in the dead of winter. Macleod faced an even longer journey from Fort Macleod to Swift Current.

The difficulties they faced raise the question of why men like them would have wanted the position, far from familiar surroundings and comforts of Eastern Canada. Richardson was already in his forties, with a career in the civil service. In that era, the practise of law was not always lucrative, and the salary of three thousand a year was attractive. There was also a great deal of prestige to a judicial appointment, which was hard to come by in the established provinces. And there was the siren call of opportunity in the North-West, even for judges. Richardson had a major impact on the law established in the Territories, likely far beyond what he might have achieved professionally if he had remained in Ottawa.

Of the first three magistrates, Ryan did not prove satisfactory. Macleod noted after his first Territorial Council meeting with Ryan and Richardson that "the two first do not speak to each other and Ryan does not speak to me. I have proposed a triangular duel to address the matter."[17]

The stipendiaries served "at pleasure"—meaning they did not have tenure—and Ryan was relieved of his post in 1881 after an investigation into reported erratic behaviour on the bench. Charles Borromée Rouleau, a lawyer from Aylmer, Quebec, who had been a police magistrate for the Ottawa district before his new appointment, replaced Ryan in 1883.[18] He was based in Battleford, with Richardson moving to the new territorial capital, Regina.

After much local lobbying, a fourth magistrate was appointed in 1885 to sit at Calgary. Jeremiah Travis was a New Brunswick lawyer with an exaggerated reputation as an expert in constitutional law. Macleod thought Travis was a political hack. A temperance supporter, the humourless Travis almost immediately alienated most of the town with his campaign to strictly enforce territorial Prohibition, which had been put in place to end the whiskey trade with the Indians. Travis eventually exceeded his powers when he disallowed the results of a municipal election that brought his nemesis, Mayor George Murdoch, back into office. Travis was suspended and Rouleau took his place.

The Territories also had a court of appeal: the Court of Queen's Bench of Manitoba. After 1878, Queen's Bench judges no longer had trial jurisdiction in the Territories but still exercised appellate jurisdiction. Criminal appeals to the Queen's Bench were limited to capital offences, which reflected the very limited right of appeal in Canadian criminal law of the time. All civil judgments could be appealed, but few were. The expense of taking an appeal to Manitoba was such that only very determined litigants did so, and this was a point of dissatisfaction in the Territories.[19]

THE TRIAL OF LOUIS RIEL

THE MOST SIGNIFICANT appeal heard in the Court of Queen's Bench from the Territories was for Louis Riel's conviction on the charge of high treason. Riel's politically charged trial and execution was a test of the magistrate's court and remains one of the most controversial events in Canadian history. Hugh Richardson was the judge, sitting with Justice of the Peace Henry LeJeune and a jury of six. The Dominion government sent prominent Ontario lawyers Christopher Robinson and B.B. Osler to prosecute, while Charles Fitzpatrick and François-Xavier Lemieux, future chief justices of Canada and Quebec, acted for Riel. Two Regina counsel,

D.L. Scott and T.C. Johnstone, were junior members of the prosecution and defence teams respectively. Both were later named to the Supreme Court of the North-West Territories.

Richardson's conduct of the trial has been heavily criticized, both at the time and by many historians since. Fitzpatrick appealed the guilty verdict to the Manitoba court.[20] He cited as grounds the constitutionality and jurisdiction of the magistrate's court, the lack of a grand jury indictment as usual in the common law, the small size of the jury, the manner in which the trial was recorded, and, finally, the evidence that Riel was legally insane.[21] The panel of three Manitoba judges made short work of these points, affirming the verdict. The objectivity of Manitoba judges might be questioned, given memories of Riel in that province, but the Judicial Committee of the Privy Council in England, at that time the highest appeal tribunal for former colonies like Canada, refused leave to hear the case, stating that the decisions of the lower courts had been reviewed and no fault found. Historians continue to debate whether Riel really had a fair trial.

Richardson also tried a number of Indian leaders for their part in the rebellion, including Big Bear and Poundmaker, on a charge of treason-felony, a lesser charge than high treason. They were convicted and given short prison sentences. Richardson's conduct of these trials has also been soundly criticized, including the fact that the Indians received harsher sentences than did many Métis followers of Riel.[22] In other rebellion trials labelled by one historian as a mockery of justice, a vindictive Rouleau sentenced to death six Cree and two Assiniboine braves involved in the Frog Lake Massacre.[23] Unlike Riel, they had no benefit of an appeal or, in some cases, legal representation at trial.

The injustices of Canadian government policies imposing an alien legal system on the Indians and Métis are well-documented. The stipendiary magistrates shared many of the prejudices of the time, and Richardson and Rouleau's conduct of the rebellion trials throws doubt on their objectivity and even competence. Yet there is also evidence that the judges tried to give Indian and Métis offenders the benefit of so-called British justice. Macleod was known for his fair and often lenient treatment of Indians.[24] Sitting with a jury, he acquitted the Kainai brave Star Child of the murder of a mounted police officer for lack of evidence. Recent scholarship contends that Indians also received generally fair treatment from Richardson and sometimes successfully prosecuted whites in his court.[25] Even Rouleau,

CHARLES BORROMÉE ROULEAU

Charles Borromée Rouleau was born in 1840 at L'Isle-Verte, Quebec, a small town on the St. Lawrence.[3] Graduating from École Normale Laval in 1859, Rouleau then obtained a teaching certificate and taught in Aylmer. He was appointed inspector of schools for the Ottawa district in 1861, a post he held for the next twelve years. He studied law on the side and was called to the Quebec bar in 1868. Active in the Conservative Party, Rouleau also took a stab at office, running unsuccessfully for the Legislative Assembly in 1875. The next year, he received an appointment as a police magistrate for the Ottawa district.

Justice Charles Borromée Rouleau, n.d. (Legal Archives Society of Alberta, acc. 2007-28)

Rouleau replaced Matthew Ryan as a stipendiary magistrate in 1883 and was stationed in Battleford. The year before the North-West Rebellion, to deal with the growing unrest, Rouleau had told the government to settle Métis land claims and ensure the Cree had adequate supplies for the winter. He was later forced to flee Battleford with his house in flames. He was moved to Calgary and remained there as the resident judge after the rebellion, replacing the ill-fated Jeremiah Travis. Rouleau used his position on the Territorial Council to advocate for Catholic education and French language rights in the Territories and was largely responsible for the creation of a dual school system. He served on the territorial board of education until 1892 and was very vocal in his criticism of the removal of French language rights in the Territories, much more than would be seemly for a modern judge.

A bon vivant, Rouleau built a rather grand mansion on the outskirts of Calgary, and he and his wife were known for lavish entertaining. He also made many ill-advised investments in real estate and gold mining and left an indebted estate when he died in 1901.

who contemporaries criticized as being harsh with Indians, supposedly told an Assiniboine man convicted of murdering an Indian farm instructor, "If the instructor had done you any wrong, you could have come to me and I would have given you redress. I am here for that purpose."[26]

There is evidence as well that the magistrates disliked adjudicating the punitive provisions of the *Indian Act* and resisted political pressure to bring their court into line with government policy.[27] If true, this assertion of judicial independence was in the best tradition of the common law and spoke well of judges like Macleod and Richardson. The rebellion trials suggest, however, that the court of the stipendiary magistrates was still frontier justice, with obvious limitations.

THE SUPREME COURT OF THE NORTH-WEST TERRITORIES

BY 1886, WHATEVER their other failings, the stipendiary magistrates were clearly no longer sufficient for the North-West Territories. There were now too many people and too much legal business in such a vast area for three judges of limited jurisdiction. Much had changed since 1870. The settler population was nearly fifty thousand, double that of the Indians and Métis.[28] The Canadian Pacific Railway was complete, opening up the Territories to more immigration. The federal government had surveyed the Territories and was granting homesteads. There was now a number of substantial towns—Regina, Moosomin, Prince Albert, Edmonton, and Calgary, to name the most important—and many smaller settlements.

The Territories had also started down the road to responsible government. A lieutenant-governor had administered the Territories with an appointed council since 1876. As the population increased, so did demands for participation in local government. The Territories first gained representation in the House of Commons in 1886, with four ridings. In 1888, an elected assembly was created for the Territories, although the lieutenant-governor still exercised executive power with an advisory council chosen from the assembly. Frederick W. Haultain, a lawyer from Fort Macleod, led a somewhat bitter fight to wrestle control of federal grants to the territorial government away from the lieutenant-governor, Joseph Royal. This culminated with an amendment to the NWT *Act* in 1891, which allowed the assembly to choose an executive council. Haultain was the chair. In 1897, the *Act* was further amended to introduce fully representative government, with Haultain becoming the first, and only, territorial premier. With limited powers of taxation and a small tax base, the territorial government remained heavily dependent on Ottawa for funds.

With the Territories' growth and development, the magistrates were stretched very thin. The inadequate number of court sittings and consequent delays for litigation, and cases of the criminally accused being released for want of prosecution, raised a growing chorus of complaints. Appeals were another problem. A delegation representing the NWT's governing council had travelled to Ottawa in February 1885 with a long list of resolutions. The ninth read,

> That owing to the great expense now attending Appeals to the Court of Queen's Bench of Manitoba, and the rapid settlement of the country, and increase of Litigation in the Territories, this Council recommends the establishment of a Territorial Supreme Court of Appeal for the North-West Territories.[29]

In the wake of the rebellion, it was clearly time to replace the magistrates with a properly constituted superior court. Prodded into action, the Dominion government created the Supreme Court of the North-West Territories with *An Act to further amend the law respecting the North-West Territories*, passed by Parliament on June 2, 1886, and coming into effect in February 1887.[30] The territorial Supreme Court was to "possess all such powers and authorities as by the laws of England are incident to a superior court of civil and criminal jurisdiction."

The new bench consisted of five *puisne* justices with no chief justice. Five newly constituted judicial districts each had a resident justice. The districts were Eastern Assiniboia, with the judge resident at Moosomin; Western Assiniboia, with the judge resident in Regina; Saskatchewan, with the judge resident in Prince Albert; Northern Alberta, with the judge resident in Calgary; and finally Southern Alberta, with the judge resident in Fort Macleod. There were no restrictions on the jurisdiction of the court or judges. Like other provincial superior courts in Canada, the federal government appointed the judges, a power reserved under section 96 of the *British North America Act* (BNA *Act*). The judges served "at good behaviour," meaning they had tenure and could only be dismissed for serious dereliction of duty or criminality, involving a hearing in both houses of Parliament.

The new court was the equal in independence, jurisdiction, and inherent powers to superior courts in the provinces, but with one vital difference: it was established by federal statute. Although the NWT *Act* had given the lieutenant-governor in council authority to constitute courts of criminal and civil jurisdiction, it was beyond the council's limited legislative ability to create a superior court. The Dominion also appointed the sheriffs and clerks, and created the judicial districts and designated the headquarters of said districts. The territorial government set civil procedure and could legislate regarding the operation and maintenance of the court, as long as this was consistent with the provisions of the enabling act. It was a shadow of the provincial powers, given in section 92 of the BNA *Act*, for the administration of justice, and remained the case even with the arrival of responsible government in the Territories.

The Supreme Court of the North-West Territories was also the appellate court for the Territories, replacing the Manitoba Court of Queen's Bench. The sections of the *Act* regarding appeals were short. The court was to sit *en banc*—literally, "in bench," meaning with the whole court—at the seat of territorial government or as the lieutenant-governor and council decided. The senior judge was to preside, with three judges sufficient for a quorum. The court *en banc* was to

> hear all and determine all applications for new trials, all questions or issues of law, all questions of points in civil or criminal cases reserved for the opinion of the court, all appeals or motions in the nature of appeals, all petitions and all other motions, matters or things whatsoever which may be lawfully brought before it."[31]

The territorial *Judicature Ordinance* of 1886 laid out the basic procedure for bringing civil appeals and further expanded on the appeal court's powers and jurisdiction.[32] The trial judge's leave was required to appeal if the matter under litigation concerned a sum less than $200, unless it involved real estate or affected substantive rights. The court had the power to hear further evidence if it wished, make inferences of fact if warranted, and give judgment or make orders as necessary. In addressing the appeal, the court could vary the original judgment, substitute a new judgment, or order a new trial.

For criminal appeals, the court followed the procedure the Dominion government set under its exclusive power to legislate in relation to the criminal law. Before the *Criminal Code* was introduced in 1892, the right to appeal, based on the English *Crown Cases Act* of 1848, was very limited.[33] Counsel for the accused could request that the trial judge reserve his decision, at his sole discretion, for the consideration of a higher court on points of law. The original verdict could be affirmed or quashed. Similar statutes were adopted in the Canadian colonies, and in Canada West (which became Ontario) the reviewing court could order a new trial. The procedure for reserving a case for review survived in a more restricted form in the criminal law statutes after Confederation, and after 1875 such cases could be further appealed to the new Supreme Court of Canada.

The *Criminal Code* created substantially more appellate review of criminal decisions but fell short of a full appeal.[34] Both prosecution and defence could request that the trial judge reserve his decision. The judge was to "state the case" for review, giving his findings of fact and the disputed rulings on law. The court of appeal dealt directly with reserved cases from the superior trial courts. A single superior court judge reviewed summary convictions by justices of the peace and police magistrates, with a further appeal possible. A trial judge could refuse to reserve his decision, but the parties could apply to the reviewing court to order the trial judge to do so. Considering the reserved case, the reviewing court could decide to affirm or quash a conviction, modify the verdict, or order a retrial. This would be more or less the procedure for criminal appeals until the 1920s.[35]

The court's enabling act also set July 15, 1870, as the date for the reception of English law into the North-West Territories. This was a vital reference point. Under the accepted doctrine in common law, when an English colony was established, it adopted—received—English law as it existed at that moment, with the exception of laws which clearly had no local application.[36] The law in that colony was then developed by statute and judicially by the colonial courts to suit conditions in that colony, although in practice subsequent English case law was treated as authoritative and even binding.[37] The Territories benefited from having a relatively contemporary start for its common law. Some older provinces in fact adopted through statute a later date of reception to acquire some desirable case and statute law. The question of whether a particular English law applied in the Territories was a frequent subject of deliberation by the judges on the NWT court.

The fact that the trial judges sat together to decide appeals rather than having a separate appeal court was not at all unusual for the time. The Manitoba Court of Queen's Bench also sat *en banc* for appeals, as did most of the provincial superior courts. In 1886, only Ontario and Quebec had separately constituted appeal courts. In part, sitting *en banc* reflected the fact that in many places the population and legal business did not require a dedicated appeal court. On Prince Edward Island, the superior court sat *en banc* until 1987. Much more striking to modern sensibilities is that until 1893 the territorial judges sat on appeals of their own trial decisions at the court *en banc*. There is even one reported decision where the trial judge changed his mind and overruled himself on appeal.[38]

Limited criminal appeals and judges reviewing their own decisions and sitting *en banc* reflected the fact that in 1886 appeal courts and comprehensive appeals were relatively new things. There had never been a right of appeal in the common law; the king's justice was God's justice and not lightly questioned. At one time, the only "appeal" was a petition to the monarch if a party had not had satisfaction in his courts.

Eventually, mechanisms evolved to review trial decisions, at least in civil litigation. In the common law courts, the writ of error allowed for a review of mistakes found in the formal record of a trial.[39] More useful for litigants was a challenge of a verdict at the courts at Westminster before it was formally recorded, when a litigant could point out errors and ask for a new trial on grounds of inadmissible evidence, misdirection of a jury, or irregularities in the proceedings. This was done before the full court. In Chancery, the court of equity, which itself had originated through litigants seeking redress unavailable in the common law courts, appellants could ask for a review in the form of a rehearing "in similar spirit to a modern appeal."[40] This review, initially by the lord chancellor and later moved to the House of Lords, became very expensive and time-consuming.

By the nineteenth century, judicial reform brought about broad-based appeals and created dedicated appellate courts. Cumulative reforms in England finally resulted, with the 1873 *Judicature Act*, in the establishment of a court of appeal, with wide-ranging powers of review except for criminal appeals. The zeal for reform was seen earlier in the colonies and former colonies of England, which were less bound by tradition and vested interests. Quebec had something resembling a modern appeal court as early as the 1820s. Ontario established a Court of Error and Appeal in 1848, with judges from the different trial courts sitting on appeals, replaced in

Supreme Court of the North-West Territories, Regina, NWT, c. 1890. *From left:* Sheriff James H. Benson, Justice E.L. Wetmore, Colonel James F. Macleod, Justice Hugh Richardson, Justice Charles B. Rouleau, Justice Thomas H. McGuire, "Dixie" Watson, clerk of the court. (Glenbow Archives, NB-16-239)

1876 with a Court of Appeal partially staffed with permanently assigned appeal judges.[41] The previous year, the federal government had acted on its ability under the BNA *Act* to establish a general court of appeal. As a Dominion, Canada was not fully independent, so the Supreme Court of Canada still answered to the Judicial Committee of the Privy Council, which had been established in 1833 to hear appeals from colonial courts.

Several important principles had also been established for common law appellate courts. Judges sat in panels or as the whole court to hear an appeal, as had been done with reviews for error in the common law courts. By convention, appeals were not supposed to be new trials, but in 1886 English and Canadian appellate courts generally had the power to review and overrule any aspect of the trial decision, as the territorial Supreme Court's *Judicature Ordinance* clearly stated. Even so, another convention had formed that appellate judges should primarily review points of law and avoid rehashing the evidence and the findings of fact from trials. This restraint recognized that judges and juries had advantages in weighing evidence first-hand, such as witness testimony. This was good practice, but nineteenth-century appeal courts still frequently substituted their own conclusions on the evidence. Appellate courts also took on a central role in judicial lawmaking where decisions settling the interpretation or application of law became the precedents judges subsequently followed on that point. As the higher, reviewing court, with several judges contributing to the decision and having the benefit of focused argument from counsel, the appeal court's view on the law was authoritative. The Supreme Court of the North-West Territories *en banc* inherited a fully formed appellate process quite recognizable to lawyers now.

THE TERRITORIAL JUSTICES

THE THREE STIPENDIARY magistrates appointed to the new Supreme Court were Hugh Richardson, Charles Rouleau, and James Macleod. Richardson was the senior judge and considered head of the court but never had the title of chief justice. Conveniently headquartered in Regina, he looked after the administration of the court, such as it was.[42] Macleod was headquartered in the town named after him and where he had been stationed as a magistrate. He was junior to Richardson despite his earlier appointment as a stipendiary due to the four years he spent as commissioner of the NWMP. Rouleau remained in Calgary. The two other judges added to bring the number to five were Edward Ludlow Wetmore, of New Brunswick, and Thomas Horace McGuire, from Kingston, Ontario. They sat at Moosomin and Prince Albert. The judges had regular circuits within their assigned districts, but all sat on appeals and thus were part of the legal inheritance of Saskatchewan.

Over the twenty-year span of the court, new judges replaced those who died or retired and others were added as the court expanded. Macleod was moved to Calgary in 1894 to help Rouleau with his heavy workload but died shortly afterward. A prominent citizen of Regina, David Lynch Scott, was his replacement. Scott had special significance as the first territorial lawyer to be named to the court. He joined Rouleau but was later moved to Edmonton to be the first resident judge there. James Emile

EDWARD LUDLOW WETMORE

When Edward Wetmore joined the judges on the Supreme Court of the North-West Territories, it was the start of a remarkable twenty-five-year career on the bench, the last five as the first chief justice of Saskatchewan. Born in Fredericton, New Brunswick, in 1841, Wetmore was the son of a lawyer.[4] After school in Fredericton and Gagetown, Wetmore earned an honours bachelor of arts degree from King's College, later the University of New Brunswick. He entered articles in Fredericton with John Campbell Allen, later chief justice of New Brunswick, joining the bar in 1864. Wetmore practised in the town of Sussex for five years before returning to Fredericton to join Fraser and Winslow, considered the leading legal partnership in the province, and becoming a leading barrister.

Justice Edward Ludlow Wetmore, n.d. (Provincial Archives of Saskatchewan, R-A624)

Instead of joining the militia like Richardson and Macleod, Wetmore was drawn to politics. He was the mayor of Fredericton for two years and then went into provincial politics, winning election to the House of Assembly in 1882 as the member for York. A Conservative, Wetmore became leader of the opposition the following year, but lost his seat in 1886. Education was another interest: Wetmore was a member of the senate of his alma mater and he was later chancellor of the University of Saskatchewan. Made a Queen's Counsel in 1881, Wetmore also served as a commissioner in the consolidation of the statutes of New Brunswick. Such were his accomplishments that the question is raised as to why he would go to the North-West Territories. One biographer states that Wetmore took the post at the personal request of Sir John A. Macdonald, likely to ensure the court would have a jurist of stature.[5]

Wetmore was stationed at Moosomin, headquarters of the new judicial district of Eastern Assiniboia. He spent ten years there before moving to Battleford for the rest of the territorial period. A stern Victorian, Wetmore was no shrinking violet. While on circuit, he once physically ejected a drunk from a stopping house who was disturbing the judicial party sleeping on the floor.[6] Moosomin was known as a peaceable, law-abiding town during his tenure.

THOMAS HORACE MCGUIRE

Thomas Horace McGuire was assigned to the district of Saskatchewan and based in Prince Albert. McGuire was from Kingston, Ontario, where he had been born in 1849 to Irish immigrants.[7] He attended Queen's University and graduated in 1870 at the top of his class, with numerous scholarships and prizes in subjects ranging from mathematics to classics. McGuire practised in Kingston after joining the bar in 1875. He was also editor of the Kingston *Daily News*, served as an alderman for five years, and was on the separate school board as well as being a member of various charitable groups and the local Conservative Party association.

A contemporary described McGuire as a "fine-looking man," tall and masculine, and suggested he likely came west for the adventure of it.[8] McGuire spent a year in the Klondike to establish the Yukon Territorial Council before taking up his duties again at Prince Albert in 1898. A gifted writer, he was liable to quote Shakespeare or a classical philosopher in correspondence or even his judgments and was known for the occasional witticism from the bench.

McGuire was on good terms with Richardson. They corresponded frequently and McGuire invariably addressed Richardson as "My Dear Chief."[9] This made McGuire's appointment as chief justice quite poignant; Richardson was allegedly very bitter about being passed over. McGuire lasted less than two years before retiring,

Justice Thomas Horace McGuire, c. 1902. (Legal Archives Society of Alberta, acc. 2007-28)

perhaps because he had been moved to Calgary. He returned to practice in Prince Albert and was appointed in 1906 to the commission to consolidate the ordinances and statutes for the Province of Saskatchewan. McGuire served on other commissions, lectured students at the University of Saskatchewan's law school, and drafted legislation to revamp the provincial school system, the last shortly before he died in 1923.

Moosomin Courthouse, Justice Wetmore's judicial headquarters, c. 1890s. (Provincial Archives of Saskatchewan R-A19051)

Pierre Prendergast came from the Manitoba County Court in 1902 to replace Rouleau, who died in 1901. Prendergast was joined by McGuire in Calgary, which was the busiest centre in the Territories and required two judges. McGuire was also made the first chief justice of the court, despite Richardson's seniority.

McGuire's appointment as chief justice was likely due to Richardson's age; Richardson was approaching eighty and retired in 1904. Henry Newlands replaced him. McGuire then left the court after only two years as chief. Arthur L. Sifton, of Calgary, replaced McGuire as chief justice in 1903. Horace Harvey was appointed in 1904 to expand the court, as were Charles A. Stuart and T.C. Johnstone in 1906, a year after the creation of Saskatchewan and a year before the territorial Supreme Court ended. Sifton, Scott, Harvey, and Stuart went to the Alberta courts while Prendergast, Newlands, and Johnstone joined Wetmore on the first bench of the Supreme Court of Saskatchewan. Newlands and Johnstone are profiled in the next chapter.

Apart from Prendergast, every appointment to the court after the original five came from the territorial bar. But all the judges were from Eastern

JAMES EMILE PIERRE PRENDERGAST

James Prendergast had a somewhat unique judicial career.[10] His first appointment was to the County Court of Manitoba in 1897, and after five years on the NWT bench and three more on the Saskatchewan Supreme Court, he returned to Manitoba and ended his career as the chief justice of Manitoba. Over a span of forty-five years, Prendergast served on five different courts in two provinces and one territory.

Prendergast was from Quebec and replaced Rouleau as the bilingual judge on the bench. Born in Quebec City in 1858, Prendergast was educated at Laval, where he earned a bachelor of arts in 1878 and a law degree in 1881. He practised only briefly in his home province before relocating to Winnipeg in 1882 and practising for the next five years with Nicholas Beck. Prendergast entered politics in 1886 with a seat in the provincial legislature and served as provincial secretary before crossing the floor when the Greenaway government abolished separate schools. He served as an MLA until his judicial appointment and was also elected mayor of St. Boniface in 1893 and 1896 and served on the provincial board of education.

Prendergast likely took the NWT appointment to join a superior court. He sat in Calgary with McGuire to help service the busy courts there. One authority argued that Prendergast had little impact on the *en banc* deliberations of the territorial Supreme Court, mostly dissenting and rarely writing.[11] His time on the Saskatchewan courts was also brief. He would, however, serve twenty-five years on the Manitoba Court of Appeal, his last three as chief justice.

Justice James Emile Pierre Prendergast, n.d. (Archives of Manitoba, A2000)

Canada: Richardson, Macleod, Scott, and McGuire from Ontario; Rouleau and Prendergast from Quebec; Wetmore from New Brunswick; and so on. All were educated, and in most cases had a substantial number of years of practice, in their birth provinces. Only one had a formal law degree, which is a comparatively modern invention. The rest learned their law primarily through long articles, augmented with courses from their law society in the case of those who entered Osgoode Hall in Toronto. The appointments of Rouleau and Prendergast indicated that the Dominion cabinet wanted a French-speaking judge in the Territories, which would also mean a Catholic appointment. This was an important concern; there was a convention that every superior court in Canada outside Quebec should have at least one Catholic judgeship. Of the original five justices, only Wetmore was a leading member of the bar in practice. Contemporary observers agreed, however, that they acquitted themselves as competent judges.

THE SUPREME COURT OF THE NORTH-WEST TERRITORIES AT LAW

THE FIRST SIX judges of the court—Richardson, Macleod, Rouleau, Wetmore, McGuire, and Scott—served the longest and had the most impact on the development of the law of the Territories. Before turning to the court's legal decisions, a few words can be said about the traits of the judges. The Macdonald government had seen fit to promote the three stipendiary magistrates—Richardson, Macleod, and Rouleau—but there seems little doubt that the appointment of Wetmore and Maguire was intended to bolster the new court. As a contemporary remembered, "Justices Wetmore and McGuire were at each end of the bench . . . [and] led the discussions. They were the 'end men.' How were the end-men going? That was the question."[43]

In the opinion of C.C. McCaul, a frontier lawyer from Fort Macleod who appeared frequently at *en banc* sittings, Wetmore was "quite the strongest member of the court."[44] Wetmore was thought stern but fair.[45] He was a stickler for proper decorum and was quite prepared to reject submissions and applications that had minor errors. Wetmore made many rulings on civil procedure and was clearly the authority on the court, although the other judges also engaged the topic.[46] Wetmore's decisions, both at trial and appeal, dominate the territorial law reports. He was a careful and

DAVID LYNCH SCOTT

David Lynch Scott was born in Brampton, Ontario, in 1845 and received his education there before entering Osgoode Hall. He articled with his brother Alexander back in Brampton and was called to the bar in 1870.[12] He later moved to Orangeville, where he was mayor from 1878 to 1880. Scott was another militiaman, serving as a private during the Fenian invasions and later attaining the rank of lieutenant colonel.

In 1882, Scott moved to Regina and partnered with William Cayley Hamilton. He was the first lawyer enrolled as a territorial advocate under the *Legal Profession Ordinance* of 1885. Scott also became the Crown counsel for Western Assiniboia, and as such was the junior prosecutor for the trials of Louis Riel, Poundmaker, and Big Bear. Although Scott's performance in the rebellion trials was not considered distinguished, his career subsequently flourished. He was made a legal adviser to the lieutenant-governor, and his name was seen frequently in the territorial law reports, often on appellate cases. Scott served as the first mayor of Regina when it was incorporated in 1884.

Although Scott had his detractors—Nicholas Flood Davin, a political enemy, called him a "conceited flabby mass of mediocrity"—he was generally considered a good judge and was chief justice of Alberta when he died in 1924. He was charismatic, sociable, and involved in cultural circles wherever he resided.

Supreme Court of the North-West Territories trial sitting, Fort Macleod, NWT, 1896. *Standing, from left:* C.F.P. Conybeare, M. McKenzie, Patrick Jason Nolan, T. Dixon. *Seated, from left:* D.J. Campbell, Judge David Lynch Scott, unknown. (Glenbow Archives, NA-2380-8)

conservative jurist and typically gave an extensive recital of the facts in an appeal, often shot through with his observations of their significance. He may have questioned the conclusions of his brethren at trial, but Wetmore did not unduly interfere with their findings.

McGuire had some Irish mischief about him. He occasionally indulged in witticisms from the bench, even at the expense of his chief.[47] Some of that wit carried over into his written judgments, which frequently had allusions and quotations from prose and poetry and the occasional pun. In one *en banc* decision, McGuire inserted a passage (which he did not expect to survive the reports editor) in which he joked about the philosophical proclivities of a litigant:

> I do not know that Mr. Bannerman is a logician, or if so, to what school he belongs; whether to an ancient or modern school; whether he is to be classed as an Aristotelian, an Epicurean, or a Heraclitic-Protagorean . . . or is he, like so many in these Territories, a lover of *Bacon*?[48]

McGuire took a special interest in appeals from the justices of the peace, usually involving *certiorari* applications and stated cases. He produced a handbook for the justices, who were laymen and often mounted police officers, to help them avoid common mistakes. On the bench, McGuire was quick to grasp arguments and was very thorough in his judgments, tending, like Wetmore, to rather long recitations of the facts at trial, although he became noticeably more concise over time.

Rouleau was in some ways the most scholarly of the early judges. According to McCaul, he shared with Macleod strong common sense on bench but also delighted in parsing the law.[49] Rouleau had what was probably the finest private law library in the Territories and meticulously researched his decisions. He was well versed in the common law in addition to his early training in the Quebec *Civil Code*. McCaul said that Rouleau took great pleasure in listening to argument, no matter how long and convoluted, and took careful notes. He would invariably reserve decisions so that he could consult the case law and authorities and work out the guiding principles. While respecting the rule of *stare decisis*, or precedent, Rouleau was the most likely to depart from existing case law, often arguing that the particular conditions of the Territories required a different approach and appealing to the court's original jurisdiction. As he said himself, "To use the language of Mr. Justice Gwynne . . . I am not concerned to seek whether or not any reported case can be found in which the Court of Chancery has interfered in the manner in which this Court may interfere here."[50] Perhaps because of this, Rouleau was by far the most appealed of the territorial justices, although he was usually sustained by his brethren.[51]

Of all the early territorial judges, Macleod was not particularly suited to appeal work. As McCaul later remarked, Macleod "did not profess to be a very well-read lawyer. In fact the nicer distinctions and subtleties of the law did not appeal to his type of mind at all. He possessed, however, a solid sense of justice and a fund of common sense, and above all, he was a gentleman and very human, the best of all qualities in a judge."[52] Macleod, it must be said, was also seldom reversed by his colleagues. He only authored one reported *en banc* judgment but did participate in discussion and research with his brother judges. Prendergast similarly rarely wrote, but his contributions, too, may have come through discussion in hearings and toiling over judgments.

Macleod's successor, David Lynch Scott, has been called "a master of short judgments with incisive summaries of legal issues." Reading his decisions bears this out. Scott kept meticulous notebooks and wrote quite frequently at trial, second only to Wetmore, but much less so on appellate decisions. In his trial decisions, Scott frequently made distinctions about the law in the Territories to highlight the different statutory regime and local circumstances. In one very interesting trial decision, Scott acquitted a woman acting as a midwife of a charge of practising medicine without a licence, distinguishing between the law of Ontario and that of the Territories.[53]

As for Richardson, his decisions were workmanlike, and in hearings he was known to be somewhat ponderous and pompous, though he was less prolix than Wetmore or McGuire. He wrote frequently on appellate decisions, particularly in criminal appeals. Richardson's main contribution to territorial law, however, was with legislation. He and McGuire provided the Department of Justice with considerable suggestions for a revision of the territorial *Real Property Act*, and although the judges no longer acted as official legal advisers after 1891 or drafted territorial ordinances, he carried out major consolidations of the Territories statutes in 1888 and 1898, the latter with Wetmore and McCaul.[54]

THE TERRITORIAL SUPREME Court greatly influenced the subsequent Saskatchewan court's practice and procedure. The *Judicial Ordinance* of 1886 and later amendments laid out the procedure for bringing appeals to the court *en banc*, and this was adopted by the province and not replaced with new rules of court until 1912. But the judges also had additional informal practices for conducting appeals. By and large, these were common to most appellate courts, but some reflected the different conditions of the Territories. More importantly, most of these practices carried over to the courts of Saskatchewan.

Appeal books and factums were part of NWT civil appellate procedure as early as 1895.[55] Factums are a written presentation of the appeal, laying out the grounds of appeal, a brief argument and authorities, and the case law, while appeal books contained the trial judgment, the relevant evidence, and transcripts of testimony, such as might exist. Standard now, factums were unusual in Canada at the time, at least in provincial appeal courts. The territorial judges usually emulated Ontario or English practice, but factums and appeals books were not part of English practice.[56] Judges in England heard each appeal with no prior knowledge, thus, it was thought, avoiding any bias. Most Canadian courts followed this tradition. British Columbia did not require factums until the 1930s,[57] and Ontario did not use them until 1972.[58]

The Supreme Court of Canada, however, did use factums. This was likely because Quebec, with its civil law tradition, used a form of factum. Another possible influence was the United States. American courts had early adopted the practice of preparing a "brief" to provide judges with a precis of the appeal and their argument.[59] Why the court decided on factums in the Territories is not known, but they were in use. The judges may have decided that the Supreme Court of Canada should set Canadian procedure. Another possibility was that factums allowed the judges to get the gist of the appeal before the hearing and thus focus on the arguments and save time, which was the American rationale.

Justice Macleod's correspondence and a surviving hearing transcript give insight into how the judges heard appeals. Even with factums, the hearing was the heart of an appeal in the Territories, as it was in all Canadian courts. Counsel gave their arguments for and against the appeal before the court, and the judges also asked questions of counsel in sometimes

Benchers of the Law Society of the North-West Territories, 1902. *Standing, from left:* James McKay, Norman MacKenzie, W.B. Willoughby, H.C. Taylor, C.H. Bell. *Seated, from left:* C.F.P. Conybeare, Edward L. Elwood, N.D. Beck, James Muir, James A. Lougheed. McKay and Elwood were later on the Saskatchewan Court of Appeal. (Provincial Archives of Saskatchewan R-D1403)

spirited exchanges. There were no time limits on the hearing; tradition was to allow counsel as much time as they felt they needed. As Macleod wrote, "I expect we will get through the arguments tomorrow night but very likely it will take until Monday evening—if then. We have two Calgary lawyers here who talk and talk until I am inclined to choke them."[60]

The practice of the court was to prepare judgments immediately after hearing arguments and give them before departing Regina at the end of the sitting. On one occasion, Macleod wrote to his wife, Mary, "We got thro' all the arguments this fore noon and are now deep in settling our judgments. The others are deep in Reports and I am letting Smith walk."[61] And on another occasion, "Well we have been at it all the week sitting till after 5 every day. We got through with the arguments yesterday and probably judgments will be delivered tomorrow at 4 o'clock, in which case

I expect to leave here on Tuesday afternoon and get home on Wednesday by the Calgary train."[62]

There were practical reasons to do judgments immediately. Once the sitting was over, the judges returned to busy circuit work and might not see each other again for six months, making further discussion impossible. Time and a decent library, or any library, were scarce resources. The judges needed to write while the appeal was fresh in their minds and there were reference works available. The territorial bench was diligent in reviewing the law. "We spent the whole day yesterday wrestling with law books from 10 in the morning till 10 at night. In the evening we met at R's house and gave the old lady a dose of Law," Macleod wrote to Mary.[63] The working habits of the judges were collegial and collaborative, out of necessity.

The lack of proper libraries for researching case law and authorities was a sore point. The situation became even worse when the Regina law library was lost in the courthouse fire of 1895. Wetmore registered his disgust in one decision, writing,

> I must again express my regret that in forming my judgment with respect to the questions of law . . . I have had to rely largely on textbooks and digests. Now I have not even the benefit of a library at Regina. I do not suppose that there is a Superior Court in the Dominion of Canada so awkwardly placed in this respect as the Supreme Court of the Territories.[64]

The lack of decent law libraries also accounts for the judges' practice of reserving decisions for the consideration of the full court. These were not stated cases but instances where at trial the judge was uncertain about a point of law and, with no library available on circuit to consult, brought it instead to the attention of his brother judges. Such references to the full court became less common as the court's jurisprudence grew and as the libraries in the judicial districts improved. The establishment of the Law Society of the North-West Territories in 1897, which took over responsibility for the libraries, no doubt helped.[65]

The pressure of time also influenced how the court wrote their judgments. The common practice of the day was for appeal courts to present judgments *seriatim*, meaning each judge gave reasons either concurring or dissenting. In contrast, many reported judgments in the territorial reports had just one author, with the other judges simply registering their

Regina Courthouse, Victoria Avenue. Completed in 1894, this was the home of the Court of Appeal until 1961. (Provincial Archives of Saskatchewan, R-A5534)

concurrence. It is tempting to conclude that the judges divided the writing after the hearings to get them done quickly. The earlier judgments of the court tended be *seriatim*, but their number dwindled over time, reflecting a growing case load and less time for writing. More likely than not, if there were concurring reasons, it was McGuire or Wetmore's doing. Both also frequently wrote spirited dissents.

A surviving transcript from an 1896 hearing showed the court at work. The hearing dealt with several criminal and civil matters, including discipline of a lawyer, which under the terms of the profession's regulating statute was in the hands of the court *en banc*. The lawyer in question did not attend the hearing. The judges were annoyed at this, but they were reluctant to proceed on the application to disbar without him present, being uncertain whether the court had the power to do so under statute.[66] As an aside, the judges felt keenly the responsibility of disciplining the profession. *Re: Forbes*, as the 1896 hearing was reported, was the first application to strike an advocate from the rolls. As Richardson pronounced in later disbarring the lawyer, "However . . . disagreeable it may be personally to the members of this court," to protect "the public interest" and to uphold "the honorable profession of advocates in the Territories," striking him off was "a duty from which they will not certainly in clearly established instances as this shrink from making."[67]

On the other appeals, much time was spent discussing procedure. The court was still wrestling with the introduction of the 1892 *Criminal Code*. On the appeal of *R v Brewster*, the judges and counsel became immersed in discussing whether the Code eliminated a judge's power to reserve a case at any point in the trial. Wetmore tended to lead the discussions, but other judges contributed. The exchanges with counsel were also instructive: on some matters they were testy, but on others there was downright collaborative discussion on points where no one was sure of the correct answer. It showed a court that was both self-confident but also still finding its jurisprudential feet.

The twice-yearly journey to Regina for *en banc* sittings was a burden for judges who had large circuits and continued to travel and hold court in primitive conditions. But Regina had its compensations. Macleod's letters home detailed the social whirl of life in the capital. Richardson often had the visiting judges to his house for dinners, as did the lieutenant-governor. There were sometimes dances and even formal balls. Macleod recounted that he was the only judge who showed up for work the day after one boisterous dinner party.[68] Cards were popular, and the poker games sometimes went all night. On another occasion, Macleod wrote his wife that "Poor old Rouleau was pretty bleary this morning" after the latter had fallen in with two friends and "had a regular jamboree till about 4 this morning."[69]

Sittings in Regina may have been a chance to socialize for judges often on circuit, but they also meant long hours hearing arguments and then crafting judgments for the more difficult appeals, which slowly but surely developed the law of the Territories.

ALTHOUGH SOMEWHAT NEW in the common law, appellate courts immediately became the authoritative voice on the law. Often, cases came before an appeal court because of a difficult legal question. An intermediate appellate court like the territorial Supreme Court *en banc* did not necessarily have the final word. The Supreme Court of Canada and the Judicial Committee of the Privy Council, which remained the highest court of appeal for Canada, as it was for other British colonies and dominions, were above the territorial Supreme Court in Canada's judicial hierarchy. But as with the other provincial appeal courts, many appeals never went any further, and the decisions of the court created a body of case law for the Territories.

One historian of the territorial Supreme Court has claimed that "the justices' decisions emphasized finding new rules of law, fashioned for the new communities and novel situations of the Territories, while remaining true to English common law."[70] There was some truth to this characterization. The justices of the court understood that part of their responsibility was to develop the law, part of the centuries-long common law tradition of judicial lawmaking. But by the late nineteenth century, statute law—government-drafted laws passed in legislatures—had become the primary instrument for changing or creating law. Increasingly, the work of the judges was to interpret statutes and fill in the deficiencies, and also to reconcile new statutes with the doctrines and principles of common law and equity that still governed most private law.

The vast majority of appeals the court heard were prosaic—correcting errors rather than developing the law. Many involved well-established case law and legal principles and were not particularly difficult. Others were trickier and brought the court into uncharted waters. For the Territories, the amount of recently created statute law, both territorial ordinances and Dominion statutes, meant a great deal of interpretation was necessary in their implementation, primarily in decisions that decided whether and how statutes replaced or modified accepted common law. It is not necessary to discuss the court's jurisprudence at length, but two examples give a flavour of the legal problems the court faced and where the judges had to exercise some creativity.

Pacific Investment Co. v Swan is one.[71] Charles Rouleau had granted an injunction to prevent the receivers for the Quorn Ranch Company from

Justice Henry Newlands in a courtroom of the Regina Courthouse, c. 1900. (Provincial Archives of Saskatchewan, R-B655)

liquidating the ranch's assets and paying them to the defendant. David Scott subsequently removed the injunction on the defendant's application and the plaintiff appealed. At issue was whether the territorial *Judicature Ordinance* and *Ordinance No. 6* (1897) allowed a creditor to obtain such an injunction—to prevent a debtor from potentially putting money beyond its reach—before judgment in an action. This could not be done in England, even if a debtor could then defraud the creditor.

On the appeal of Scott's order, Rouleau argued that the ordinances did make this possible: "The conditions in the North-West Territories are entirely different. A creditor here can attach any debts due or to accrue due to the defendant, if the debtor has attempted to sell or dispose of his personal property with intent to defraud his creditors generally, or the plaintiff in particular."[72] Rouleau thought that the court's equitable jurisdiction justified this interpretation of the governing ordinance. His brethren did not agree. Writing for the court, Edward Wetmore thought that the plaintiff did not place sufficient evidence the defendant might defraud him in front of the court to keep the original injunction.

But Wetmore also thought the legal question should be answered. He wrote, "This appeal however was brought with a view of having the question of the abstract right to have an injunction order issued in such cases and a receiver appointed, and it would be a matter of some regret if that question was not settled."[73] On the point, Wetmore argued that the proper construction of the statutes did not allow for Rouleau's broader interpretation and that invoking equity did not allow the court to go beyond the intent of the legislature. Generally, although the territorial justices were sensitive to the fact that the territorial ordinances and different conditions might mean accepted doctrine elsewhere might not apply in their bailiwick, they were careful not to interpret statutes too broadly. Rouleau was a maverick in this regard.

At other times, a new statute changed a particular area of law so much that the question might be whether any older common law doctrines still applied. The same year the territorial Supreme Court was established, the North-West Territory *Real Property Act* was passed. The Dominion statute established a Torrens land titles registry in the Territories. Under the Torrens system, named after the premier of South Australia, a duplicate of the title for a piece of real property was kept at a central registry, and all liens, caveats, mortgages, and so on against the property were registered on the title. A registry simplified land transactions, and certifying the title also helped to limit fraud, a frequent problem with title deeds under the common law. With one piece of legislation, most existing real property law was made obsolete in the Territories.[74] Inevitably, the application of the Torrens system threw up problems, some unique, where the judges of the court had to exercise creativity in the absence of precedents.

Jellett v Wilkie in 1895 was one such case.[75] Jellett, a creditor of the Edmonton and Saskatchewan Land Company, obtained a court order (then called a writ of execution) to seize and sell lands of the company, which was registered against the title. As it turned out, some of the land had been sold, but the owners had not yet registered their titles, and the registrar refused to accept the transfers and issue titles due to the order. The putative owners of the land in question challenged the registrar's stance in the matter, but Rouleau dismissed their action.

Thomas McGuire, writing for the court, reversed Rouleau. He argued that the long-established equitable principle that the title of a bona fide purchaser of land was protected from a claim like Jellett's still operated in the Territories notwithstanding the *Real Property Act*. The rule had been part of English law in 1870 and came into the Territories, where it was still applicable unless changed by statute. Jellett's counsel contended that section 94 of the *Act*, which dealt with the sheriff's execution of orders affecting titles, did just that. McGuire disagreed; he thought the proper interpretation—or construction, to use the legal term—of the section was obviously that an order such as Jellett's was intended to act as caveat against a subsequent purchase from the debtor and couldn't apply to a prior purchase even if unregistered. This was also consistent with the fact that the *Real Property Act* preserved other equitable remedies.

The Supreme Court of Canada agreed with McGuire, and a point of law with great import was settled. One authority called *Jellett v Wilkie* "a leading case."[76] And *Jellett* remained "good law" for decades, followed in Saskatchewan until the 1940s and in Alberta until the 1970s. It was an example of how the court, even with due deference to the legislature, had to interpret the action of a new statute and, in this case, also reconcile the law with accepted common law principles and thus further develop the law for the Territories. The Territories were the first jurisdiction in Canada to use the Torrens system, and other decisions of the court helped establish a functioning registry. The judges exercised initiative and creativity dealing with the issues the registry created, using Australian decisions and digests in the absence of relevant English or Canadian case law to help solve problems.

These two decisions, and many like them, paint a picture of a lively court with several strong judges, as well as a maverick in Rouleau. In settling the law for the Territories, the primary challenge was to interpret a new statutory regime which although based on familiar laws from the rest of Canada and England also had differences, sometimes marked. The judges had a good sense that the different conditions of their frontier society might require development of the law to reflect this. They were, however, generally cautious in nudging the law along. As statute law continued to replace as well as supplement the common law, the Canadian judiciary increasingly saw its role as interpreter, clearing confusion and removing ambiguity, rather than as lawmakers, leaving that to the various legislatures. This outlook crystalized as legal formalism, a philosophy that is explored in subsequent chapters, as it greatly constrained appellate judges in their approach to the law.

CONCLUSION

THE SUPREME COURT of the North-West Territories continued until 1907, allowing the provinces of Saskatchewan and Alberta time to establish their own courts. This made the territorial Supreme Court *en banc* quite literally the first appellate court of Saskatchewan. Most important was the continuity between the old court and the new. With their decisions, the judges of the court created a body of law specific to the Territories, establishing precedents that they cited in subsequent cases and which became part of the law of the two new provinces. The decisions of the court were one of several bequests to Saskatchewan. The first judges of the provincial superior court came direct from the territorial predecessor, and brought practices, procedures, and their wide experience of a society transforming from frontier to something more settled but still different from its Eastern Canadian roots.

CHAPTER 2

THE SUPREME COURT OF SASKATCHEWAN

"WE HAVE COMPLETED PROVINCIAL AUTONOMY with the assembling of this court."[1] So Edward Ludlow Wetmore, the newly appointed chief justice of the Supreme Court of Saskatchewan, told those assembled for the opening of the court's first sitting on October 8, 1907. The Supreme Court of the North-West Territories was finally supplanted two years after the province of Saskatchewan was established. The *Regina Leader* would later note that "no longer is Saskatchewan dependent for the administration of the law upon a body with jurisdiction outside her borders."[2]

Frederick Haultain, formerly the territorial premier and recently returned to the practise of law, gave an address that sketched the evolution of judicial institutions in the West up to the auspicious moment at hand. After more speeches, presentations of patents for King's Counsel, and the admission of new lawyers—including the aptly named George Herbert Barr—the court got down to business. The judges sat *en banc,* exercising their appellate jurisdiction and authority. Justices Henry Newlands, T.C. Johnstone, and newly appointed John H. Lamont joined Wetmore, while their colleague James Prendergast toiled in Prince Albert on a contentious by-election appeal.

These five judges were the start of the evolution of the law of Saskatchewan. Over the next decade, the court interpreted and set that law. It was not an easy task. The court was nearly overwhelmed in the face of ever-mounting case lists that reflected the province's rapid development. The first ten years moulded the character of Saskatchewan's appellate court. It was a court that hewed to the orthodoxies of the times, applying and interpreting the law carefully and with great restraint so as not to invade the prerogatives of the legislature.

SASKATCHEWAN RAMPANT

SEPTEMBER 4, 1905, was a day of celebration in Regina with the official inauguration ceremony ushering in provincial status. Three days before, the new provinces of Saskatchewan and Alberta had been established. The short wait for Prime Minister Wilfrid Laurier to arrive from Edmonton had not dampened the mood. It was a propitious time to achieve provincial autonomy. The severe depression that plagued the world economy through the 1890s had ended with the new century. A flood of settlers and investment to the Prairies created a decade-long boom that saw Saskatchewan's population grow to a half million. It was a time of boundless optimism, spectacular growth, and runaway speculation that transformed the province.

Saskatchewan's birth was not without intrigue. As territorial premier, Frederick Haultain had led the drive for provincial autonomy. He had envisioned one province encompassing much of the former Territories. This did not fit the plans of Prime Minister Wilfrid Laurier and the federal Liberals. Laurier wanted two provinces to avoid creating too strong a counterweight to Central Canada. Haultain and Laurier also clashed over education rights as Laurier sought to restore the broad education rights francophones and Catholics had at one time enjoyed in the Territories, and over Laurier's insistence on maintaining Dominion control over natural resources in the new provinces. Consequently, Laurier discarded any thought of appointing Haultain, who was resolutely non-partisan in conducting territorial affairs but leaned Conservative, as provisional premier of either of the new provinces.[3] Walter Scott, a Regina newspaperman and until autonomy the Liberal member of Parliament for Assiniboia West, became the provisional premier of Saskatchewan. Haultain became leader of the Provincial Rights Party, dedicated to recovering control over Saskatchewan's natural resources. Scott and Haultain faced off in the first election, in December 1905, with Haultain losing to his Liberal rival.

William Melville Martin, MP (*left*), and Premier Walter Scott, Swift Current, c. 1908. Martin later became premier and then chief justice of Saskatchewan. (Provincial Archives of Saskatchewan, R-A12113)

Laurier wished to keep federal control over public lands in part to support his government's immigration policy. The great influx of settlers that drove Saskatchewan's boom was primarily due to Clifford Sifton, Laurier's first minister of the interior. Sifton aggressively sought settlers for the West, and the trickle of newcomers at the beginning of the century became a flood of land-hungry immigrants. From 1901 to 1911, the population of the province jumped from under 100,000 to nearly 500,000. Towns became cities, villages became towns, and new settlements sprang up to service the homesteaders. By 1911, Regina had a population of 30,000, a fifteen-fold increase in a decade.[4] Saskatoon, which had a mere 311 souls in 1901, grew to 12,000, and the other principal towns and cities of the province, such as Prince Albert, Moose Jaw, and North Battleford, saw similar expansion.

The thousands of homesteaders were initially focused on survival, proving up their claim and supporting themselves with mixed, often subsistence, farming. It was not long, however, before more and more farmers concentrated on growing a cash crop, specifically wheat. By the 1910s, wheat had taken its place at the centre of the province's economy,

HENRY WILLIAM NEWLANDS

Henry Newlands was born in Dartmouth, Nova Scotia, in 1862 and subsequently educated in nearby Halifax.[1] After public school, he went straight into articles with the prominent firm of Thompson, Graham and Tupper. Charles Hibbert Tupper was son of Sir Charles Tupper, one of the Fathers of Confederation and prime minister of Canada in 1896.[2] Newlands was called to the Nova Scotia bar in 1883 and immediately moved to Winnipeg, joining the firm of William Johnston Tupper, another son of Sir Charles. After three years, Newlands moved to Prince Albert and joined the territorial bar.

Justice Henry Newlands as lieutenant-governor, 1929. (Artist: Philip de László. Provincial Archives of Saskatchewan, R-B746)

After practising for a short time in Prince Albert, Newlands decamped to the United States, practising law in Boston and Chicago before returning around 1895.[3] He did not stay long in Prince Albert, taking the position of inspector of land titles in Regina in 1897. Clearly an adventurous sort, he went to the Yukon in 1901 as the legal adviser to the Territorial Executive Council and was acting commissioner for several months. Although associated early in his professional life at law firms aligned with the Conservatives, Newlands later gave his allegiance to the Liberal Party.[4] He returned to Regina in 1904 as the replacement for Hugh Richardson on the territorial Supreme Court.

Newlands also served on several royal commissions, including the 1906 and 1918 commissions to consolidate the statutes of Saskatchewan. Named to the new Court of Appeal in 1918, Newlands resigned three years later to become Saskatchewan's fourth lieutenant-governor. He served for ten years, resigning short of completing his second term due to ill health.[5] He then lived for another twenty-three years, dying in St. Thomas, Ontario, in 1954 at the age of ninety-two. Newlands cut an active figure in Regina public life, becoming president of the Regina chapters of the Canadian Club in 1908 and the Society for the Advancement of Art, Science and Literature in 1910.

THOMAS COOKE JOHNSTONE

T.C. Johnstone was a fixture of the bar in Regina, which was barely a hamlet when he arrived as a homesteader in 1882.[6] Johnstone soon opened a law office, making him one of the first practising lawyers in the North-West Territories. Born in Brant County, Ontario, around 1850, Johnstone articled with a lawyer in Brantford before going to Toronto to finish his studies at Osgoode Hall. Called to the bar in 1876, he subsequently practised in Toronto until deciding to head west. The local member of Louis Riel's defence team in 1885, he made his reputation in criminal law. He was the Crown prosecutor for the District of Assiniboia for many years, as well as Regina's city solicitor. Around Regina, Johnstone was known as a cricketer as much as a lawyer. He played for many years and then sponsored a trophy, the Judge Johnstone Shield, for the local cricket league.

Johnstone was appointed to the bench in 1906, in the twilight days of the Supreme Court of the North-West Territories. He served on Saskatchewan's court until 1913, when he retired due to poor health and moved to California. He suffered a severe stroke some eighteen months before his death in 1917. He had been twice widowed. Married originally to a woman from Cobourg, Ontario, Johnstone then married his first wife's sister, who predeceased him in 1913.

Justice Thomas Cooke Johnstone, c. 1907 to 1913. (Provincial Archives of Saskatchewan, R-B1404)

establishing a boom and bust cycle that would continue for decades as prices rose and fell. Wheat prices were good in the first part of the century and even better during the First World War, helping drive Saskatchewan's boom. Wheat and agriculture generally dominated Saskatchewan society, especially politics. The Liberal Party established a near lock on power in the province largely due to its deep support among farmers. These same farmers, disgruntled with the elevator companies and grain dealers, also established a thriving co-operative movement that strongly influenced political culture in the province.

Sifton had cast his net wide, and his policies created a diverse society on the Prairies. Earlier immigrants to the North-West Territories had been primarily from Eastern Canada and the British Isles, but the flow from these sources was not enough, and Sifton turned to Central and Eastern Europe. He wanted "stalwart peasants in sheepskin coats," self-reliant, land-hungry, and used to farming in difficult conditions. The policy was a great success, but it also created tensions in a fragile new society between the Protestant Anglo-Scottish majority and newcomers with alien cultures, languages, and faiths. Many of the new immigrants were Catholic, re-stoking conflict over language and education rights that had been a continual source of dissension in the Territories. If immigrants from Eastern Europe were regarded with suspicion, it was much worse for the tiny non-Caucasian, generally Asian, population. The province's Indian and Métis inhabitants, meanwhile, confined on reserves, many of which were remote, became almost invisible, a demoralized remnant of the proud cultures that had bargained as near equals with fur traders.

By 1913, the great expansion slowed as the political situation in Europe deteriorated, and the outbreak of war a year later dried up the stream of immigrants and investment from overseas. In Saskatchewan, wartime demand for the province's main commodity, wheat, cushioned the blow. Farmers put more and more acreage under till and started to mechanize. The good times ended only when recession and drought struck after the end of the war. Until then, the breakneck development of the province and consequent legal business threatened to overwhelm Saskatchewan's new court system, established in 1907 to replace the Supreme Court of the North-West Territories.

A COURT DELAYED

THE PEOPLE OF Saskatchewan had welcomed provincial autonomy with great enthusiasm, but an enormous amount of work awaited Scott's provisional government after the celebrations. There was a rudimentary civil service, a legacy of Regina's status as the territorial capital, but Scott's administration had to create the statutory framework for government, prepare for an election, and embark on major public works projects. Under the circumstances, Saskatchewan was content to continue the Supreme Court of the North-West Territories despite the fact that the court remained a creation of the Dominion government and subject to its executive and Parliament. The territorial court was well-respected, and the appointment of two judges in 1904 and two more in 1906 helped address the most common complaint, that there were not enough sittings.

The Supreme Court of Saskatchewan was in nearly all respects a direct continuation of its predecessor. Four of the first five judges of the court had been on the territorial Supreme Court. Saskatchewan continued to use the territorial rules of court until 1912, and the new rules then greatly resembled the old. Saskatchewan's court also sat *en banc* for appeals. As an appellate court, in terms of statutory powers, procedures, and judicial outlook, the provincial Supreme Court was much like the territorial Supreme Court, evolving a distinct character over the next decade until replaced with the Court of Appeal for Saskatchewan.

THE STATUTORY BASIS OF THE COURT *EN BANC*

AN ACT RESPECTING *the establishment of a Supreme Court in and for the Province of Saskatchewan* was a fair mouthful, and mercifully the short title of chapter 8 of the Statutes of Saskatchewan, 1907, was the *Judicature Act*.[5] Given royal assent on March 8, 1907, the statute laid out the form of the new court. There were four *puisne* judges and a chief justice, styled the chief justice of Saskatchewan. All the judges would reside in the capital, Regina, where the court sat *en banc* unless directed otherwise by the lieutenant-governor in council. For trials, the judges went on circuit to specified points in the province's judicial districts, newly established under the *District Court Act*. The statute gave the new court the same authority, jurisdiction, and powers the Supreme Court of the North-West Territories had possessed, as well as the original jurisdiction of the common law courts of England prior to the passing of the *Judicature Act* of 1873.

The province also established a superior court of lesser jurisdiction, the District Court of Saskatchewan.[6] This followed the model seen in Ontario, British Columbia, and other provinces. Each judge of the court had jurisdiction throughout the province but was assigned to a judicial district. The District Court provided a more accessible local court for small claims and minor litigation and tried criminal offences of a less serious nature that were beyond the jurisdiction of local magistrates. It was also the court of revision for municipal assessments and election results, and the judges acted as local masters for the Supreme Court. Eight districts were established in 1907.[7] There was constant demand for more judicial districts and judges, and by 1923 the province had twenty-one districts and seventeen judges to serve it.[8]

Finding qualified judges for the District Court was a problem. Like Supreme Court judges, they were appointed by the federal government, but they were paid considerably less than a Supreme Court justice and the appointment was less prestigious. No shortage of lawyers were interested in the position, but it was difficult to get men of ability. Four of the five candidates initially sounded out by Premier Scott politely declined.[9] Some appointments reflected patronage over merit, as was often the case in other provinces, and the quality of judges was uneven. One of the early District Court judges was a disaster, opening court while intoxicated, and he quickly resigned.[10] When legal business dropped off sharply between the two world wars, some judges had very little work. Eliminating districts and reducing the roster of judges would, however, prove very unpopular.

THE SUPREME COURT *EN BANC*

APPEALS FROM THE District Court went to the Supreme Court *en banc*. Appeal sittings were held in Regina three times a year, with three judges as quorum. *The Judicature Act* declared that the powers of the court *en banc* were the same as those of the Supreme Court of the North-West Territories, or as otherwise possessed by superior courts of England as of 1898. This minor change made the *Act* consistent with the territorial *Judicature Ordinance*. For appeals, the major substantive change was the addition of rules for District Court cases. The court's appellate powers

The Barr, Sampson and Stewart law office in Regina, c. 1915. George Herbert Barr was admitted to the bar at the first sitting of the Supreme Court of Saskatchewan. His office was typical for the period. (Provincial Archives of Saskatchewan, R-B1325)

in civil matters continued to be very broad. Jurisdiction and procedure remained the same for criminal appeals, as Ottawa had not made any substantive changes to appeals under the *Criminal Code*.

A comparison of *The Judicature Act* with its Alberta equivalent, the *Supreme Court Act*, is instructive. The draftsmen of the respective acts consulted the judges of the NWT court. Wetmore and Horace Harvey of the Alberta Supreme Court, a former territorial deputy attorney general, reviewed *The Judicature Act*. The content of each province's act was quite similar but ordered differently. *The Judicature Act* expansively defined the court's equitable powers and put into the statute some rules that in Alberta were left to the case law. The Saskatchewan statute also arguably made a more explicit connection to the predecessor court in the manner of drafting and enumeration of powers and jurisdiction, particularly the court's ability to review fact findings from trial.

JOHN HENDERSON LAMONT

Born a farmer's son in Dufferin County, Ontario, in 1865, John Henderson Lamont ascended to the Supreme Court of Canada. He was the first judge from Saskatchewan,

Justice John Henderson Lamont as attorney general, c. 1907. (Provincial Archives of Saskatchewan, R-B3204)

the second from the Prairies, and only the third from Western Canada to serve on the nation's highest court.

After beginning his education in a small rural school, Lamont attended high school in Brampton and Orangeville, Ontario.[7] He then taught school near Brampton to save money for university. Lamont was the second member of the Saskatchewan judiciary with a law degree, graduating from the University of Toronto in 1893. The Law Society of Upper Canada did not recognize the upstart law program at the university until well in the 1950s, and Lamont had almost three years of articling and course work through Osgoode Hall before he could join the bar in 1895.

Lamont practised briefly in Toronto but came west in 1899 in search of more opportunity and landed in Prince Albert. He was appointed Crown prosecutor for the Saskatchewan district in 1903 and partnered with a young New Brunswick lawyer, W.F.A. Turgeon. Lamont began his political career in 1904 as the Member of Parliament for the District of Saskatchewan. He resigned his parliamentary seat to become the province's first attorney general and was duly elected as the member for Prince Albert in the first provincial election.

As attorney general, Lamont skillfully executed the mammoth task of setting up his department while simultaneously preparing legislation establishing the machinery of government. He oversaw the creation of the Supreme Court of Saskatchewan in September 1907, to which he was immediately named as a judge. Lamont was a strong jurist and was appointed to the Court of Appeal in 1918. In 1927, he became a *puisne* judge of the Supreme Court. He died in Ottawa in 1936 after two years of failing health. Shortly before his death, Lamont supposedly said, "My memorial is in the Saskatchewan Law Reports."[8]

The Judicature Act was proclaimed in March 1907, but the judges of the court did not receive their patents until the following September and were sworn in, with some ceremony, by Lieutenant-Governor Amédée Emmanuel Forget on September 19, 1907.[11] The date was coordinated with Alberta to allow the NWT court to be disestablished and pass into history as the provincial courts took up their duties.[12] The court then sat *en banc* for its first sitting on October 9. All the appeals on the sitting's list were from trial decisions of the territorial Supreme Court, as might be expected, but this underlined the continuity of one court to the next.

THE JUDGES OF THE COURT

FOUR OF THE five judges of the new court were sitting members of the Supreme Court of the North-West Territories. The eight-judge territorial bench was simply split between Alberta and Saskatchewan. The judges residing in each province went to the respective superior court, with the exception of James Prendergast, who left Calgary for Regina.

Premier Scott favoured the appointment of the four NWT judges, and the Dominion cabinet followed his advice in choosing Edward Ludlow Wetmore as Saskatchewan's chief justice.[13] Wetmore was the most senior judge of the territorial Supreme Court, but this was no guarantee that he would be the chief. Hugh Richardson had been passed over in 1901. Wetmore's age and previous connection to the Conservative Party were not in his favour, as judicial appointments of the time involved patronage and were very partisan. It was a testament to Wetmore's stature that his elevation was greeted as a foregone conclusion. At Wetmore's swearing-in as chief justice, Lieutenant-Governor Forget commented that the appointment transcended partisanship. Wetmore graciously replied that he had, as befitted a judge, left politics behind many years before.[14]

Edward Ludlow Wetmore, 1914. (Artist: Inglis Sheldon-Williams; photo: Mark Greschner. Court of Appeal.)

Henry Newlands and T.C. Johnstone were the other NWT judges on the new court. Newlands was appointed in 1904 to replace Richardson in Regina after Richardson retired. The Nova Scotian had practised in Prince Albert before becoming inspector of land titles in the territorial capital. Newlands later served as Saskatchewan's fourth lieutenant-governor. T.C. Johnstone was a true Western pioneer, coming to Regina from Ontario in 1882, and was likely the first lawyer to practise there. He was appointed in 1906 and placed in Moose Jaw, which had lobbied hard for a resident judge.[15] Walter Scott had opposed Johnstone's appointment for political reasons,[16] but whatever Johnstone's sins, the problem was resolved to Scott's satisfaction.

A new appointment was necessary to complete the five-judge bench. The province's first attorney general, John Henderson Lamont, filled the berth. Scott had recommended Lamont, writing, "It is with no little regret that I contemplate the loss of Mr. Lamont as a colleague but our loss as a Government will be the gain of the Supreme Court. My knowledge of Mr. Lamont enables me to predict with confidence he will make an excellent judge."[17]

The Prince Albert lawyer, originally from Ontario, had supervised the creation of the court he now joined. Lamont's appointment was well merited: he would later be the first appointment from Saskatchewan to the Supreme Court of Canada. It also set something of a precedent for the province, where several times an attorney general moved directly from politics into a vacancy or new position on the courts.

Politics, partisanship, and patronage have played a central role in Canadian superior court appointments.[18] Lawyers have always been prominent in the nation's public life: seventeen prime ministers out of twenty-three have been lawyers or have earned law degrees. The connections and skills developed in legal practice translate well to politics. It is not surprising that many judges had political as well as legal careers. Holding political office, especially a cabinet post, showed ability as well as interest in public service and was relevant experience for the judiciary. But in Canada, judicial appointments were also a reward for political service and strongly partisan. With few exceptions, new judges came from the ranks of supporters of the party in power federally. Sir John A. Macdonald had memorably stated, "Whenever an office is vacant, it belongs to the party supporting the government."[19] Patronage was expected, and this remained true well into the twentieth century. An appointment like Wetmore's, seen as being across party lines, attracted much comment.

As long as judges were well qualified, patronage was not necessarily a problem, but that was the rub. The legal profession became increasingly critical of the role patronage played, fearing that political calculations took priority over ability and that excellent lawyers were being overlooked because they had little involvement in politics or were opposition supporters. In the nineteenth and early twentieth centuries, critics derided a number of appointments to the Supreme Court of Canada as blatant patronage, with the implication that competence was an issue.[20] The appointment process, done in the federal cabinet, was also opaque, with ministers who were not lawyers often wielding great influence over appointments in their home province. Another issue with partisanship was the tension between provincial and federal governments of different political convictions. By 1918, the profession's grumblings about the quality of appointments solidified into Canadian Bar Association resolutions calling on the federal government to consult with the provincial law societies and bar associations on appointments.[21] Saskatchewan earned a reputation as a jurisdiction where politics played an especially acute role.[22]

This was true of the first new appointment to the court in 1910. Prendergast had somehow finagled an appointment to the Manitoba Court of King's Bench—no small accomplishment, as provinces expected appointments to come from the local bar, although Prendergast could claim to be

JAMES THOMAS BROWN

Born in Huntingdon, Quebec, in 1871, J.T. Brown grew up on the family farm.[9] After graduating from the Huntingdon Academy, Brown attended McGill and earned a bachelor of arts with honours in philosophy. He relocated in 1893 to Winnipeg, where he had articles and joined the Manitoba bar in 1896. He then moved almost immediately to Moosomin, headquarters of the judicial district of Eastern Assiniboia.[10] He was appointed the district's Crown prosecutor in 1904 and was considered a leader of the territorial bar. Brown was made a King's Counsel in 1907. Active in politics, he was elected in 1905 to represent Souris in the provincial legislature, running for the Provincial Rights Party. He then tried for Parliament in 1908 under the Liberal banner but was defeated.

Justice James Thomas Brown, c. 1932. (Provincial Archives of Saskatchewan, R-A7888(1))

When the Court of King's Bench was established in 1918 as the trial court to replace the Supreme Court, Brown was named chief justice. He remained on the bench until his death in 1957 at the age of eighty-six, one of many long-lived Saskatchewan jurists. Aside from his judicial duties, Brown headed *the Farmers' Creditors Arrangement Act* board for the province during the Depression. He also served on several prominent commissions, the first in 1916, with Justice Elwood, to investigate charges of corruption against the Scott government, and then the Royal Grain Inquiry Commission, from 1929 to 1931.[11] Most famously, Brown and Justice W.M. Martin of the appeal court were appointed to the commission investigating the Regina Riot of 1935. Their report exonerated the police of any wrongdoing.

The many tributes to Brown painted a picture of a warm, humorous man who brought a human touch to the bench and was respected as a jurist.[12] Outside of his profession, Brown was involved in his church and a founder of the Regina Music Festival, serving as festival president and contributing a trophy. He was a keen golfer, tennis player, and hunter. Brown was widowed late in life but remarried a few years before his death.

originally a Manitoba lawyer and had sat on the province's county court. His successor was James Thomas Brown, who began a forty-seven-year career in the Saskatchewan judiciary. Brown had been a Moosomin lawyer for many years, the senior partner of Brown, Wylie and Mundell. He had just moved to Regina when his appointment was made.[23] Moosomin, Wetmore's seat as a territorial judge, had not lived up to its early promise and by 1910 was clearly destined to be a minor centre.

Brown's appointment was problematic. Lamont's successor as attorney general, W.F.A. Turgeon, strongly recommended Brown with the backing of Premier Scott. But Brown had political baggage: he had run successfully for the Provincial Rights Party in the first provincial election but later changed his allegiance to the Liberals.[24] The switch left bad blood. Rumours of Brown's impending appointment caused consternation among federal and provincial Liberals in the province. Saskatchewan MP J.G. Turriff told Scott that "the north members and senators have been particularly strong against Brown."[25] But aside from Turgeon's endorsement, Brown had enough political friends that Scott feared the cost of not appointing him.[26]

Brown is an example of how politics influenced judicial appointments in Saskatchewan: a qualified appointment might have been derailed due to considerations that had nothing to do with merit. Interestingly, Brown's appointment meant the Saskatchewan Supreme Court did not have a Roman Catholic judge. This violated an unwritten but accepted principle

Frederick Haultain (*centre*) with the North-West Territories attorney general's staff, n.d. (Provincial Archives of Saskatchewan, R-B3874)

in Canada that superior courts needed at least one Catholic judge, which remained a consideration until the 1960s. Laurier had proposed appointing Turgeon in 1910 in part because he was Catholic. Scott had said no, needing his very able attorney general in government.[27] Brown was the next best choice. The lack of a Catholic judge attracted little comment at the time, which was surprising given the province's relatively large Catholic population and the sectarian politics of the time.

A NEW CHIEF

AFTER FIVE YEARS as chief justice, Edward Wetmore decided to step down, officially resigning on October 15, 1912.[28] His letter of resignation had been in Ottawa for some time, awaiting the return of the minister of justice from England.[29] He was only seventy-one, at a time when appointments were for life and judges often died in office, but he had been on the bench twenty-five years. Wetmore's wife had died in an accident in 1905, and after retiring he moved to Victoria, where his son and his family lived. H.A. Robson, a one-time Moosomin lawyer, after seeing Wetmore with his grandsons on a ferry to Seattle, said that "he seemed more happy presiding over that company than I had seen him anywhere else."[30] Wetmore returned to Saskatchewan in 1916 to head the royal commission investigating corruption in government road building contracts. When he died in 1922, he was interred beside his wife in Moosomin, his funeral attended by the premier and nearly the entire judiciary of the province.[31]

Even before Wetmore announced his retirement, rumours were flying that Prime Minister Robert Borden's government would name Frederick Haultain as the next chief justice. Haultain has been called Saskatchewan's "forgotten Father of Confederation."[32] He fought for responsible government in the North-West Territories and served as the first and only territorial premier, subsequently leading the charge for provincial autonomy. Haultain then found himself contesting Saskatchewan's first election as leader of the opposition, suffering the first of three defeats at Scott's hands. After his third defeat in 1912, he decided to retire from politics, and he returned to the practise of law with the Regina firm of Haultain, Cross and Jonah.

Speculation was immediate that Haultain was destined for the bench, a reward for his years of political service,[33] and the announcement that he was replacing Wetmore was no surprise, although James Mackay, of Prince Albert, appointed to the court two years later, was a potential candidate.[34] Haultain's appointment was greeted with general approval, even in the province's very partisan Liberal press.[35] Robert Borden's government was almost certainly going to appoint a Conservative. Haultain was respected, and his strong feelings on the evils of partisanship—which had hampered him as a politician—made him a palatable choice for provincial Liberals. The new chief took up his duties on October 30, 1912, before his commission had even arrived from Ottawa.[36] Lamont, Newlands, and Brown began the November *en banc* sittings with Haultain expected to participate on the appeals once he was finally sworn into office.

BY THE TIME of Brown's appointment in 1910, it was clear that five judges were no longer enough. The growth of the bar matched the growth of the province; legal business burgeoned, and lawyers came from Manitoba, Ontario, Quebec, and the Maritime provinces to meet the demand. It added up to ever-increasing court lists.

Chief Justice Wetmore first raised the question of a sixth judge with Turgeon, the attorney general, at the beginning of 1911.[37] Turgeon and Wetmore discussed increasing the jurisdiction of the District Court, but Wetmore thought that would merely burden the lower court and that the better solution was an additional Supreme Court judge. He thought this would improve the operations of the court *en banc*. With five judges, the court often had to sit as a panel of three, as it was common, due to illness, leave, commission work, or delays on circuit, to be a judge short. Wetmore deemed a panel of three insufficient for proper consideration of an appeal, but his primary concern was trial sittings. He rejected Turgeon's suggestion that the province set up a court of appeal. Wetmore preferred *en banc* sittings, feeling that sitting on both trials and appeals helped vary a judge's work. He also felt the number of appeals did not yet merit a separate court and cited Manitoba, where the appellate judges took trials to fill their time.

Wetmore's successor was not so phlegmatic. By the time Haultain became chief justice, the court lists had increased greatly, particularly the *en banc* workload. Haultain lost no time requesting another judge.[38] Turgeon obligingly introduced an amendment to add another judge to the court at the beginning of January 1913, but the appointment only materialized in September. Edward L. Elwood, acknowledged as a leading counsel, and another recent transplant from Moosomin to Regina, was finally named to the position.[39]

Haultain was not satisfied that a sixth judge was enough; in the nine-month wait for Elwood's appointment, the lists had swelled further. In Haultain's view, another judge was desperately needed, and he wrote Turgeon in December 1913 to press the case. Haultain thought that he could manage until the next summer vacation, but the situation, he said, was growing critical. The court's appeal work was particularly affected. The chief justice wrote,

> The court is not large enough to attend to the ordinary trial work and at the same time to admit of a sufficient interval for the proper performance of its appellate work. . . . Our appeal list is getting bigger all the time. We heard 26 appeals at the sitting beginning October last and only had four or five days after hearing the last appeal in which to consider our judgements before having to leave for the regular courts elsewhere.[40]

To underline the point, Haultain finished his letter by telling Turgeon, "I should have written about this earlier in your session but I have just returned from four weeks work at Saskatoon where I encountered a non-jury list of 170 cases."

Turgeon's response, almost a week later, was not helpful. With the legislature in session, he may have fallen behind on his correspondence, but his reply was curiously lackadaisical. He politely but briefly stated that the government had considered whether to add a judge to the court and decided against it and that it was too late in the present session to reconsider.[41] He reminded Haultain that the government had reduced the quorum for the court *en banc* back to three after raising it to four and said he hoped this would offer "some measure of relief."

Haultain soon had only five judges, including himself, to cover the sittings. Johnstone's health was poor, and in 1914 he decided to retire early.[42] His replacement, James McKay, was not named until December 16, 1914. McKay's forebears were Hudson's Bay Company fur traders and the family had been in Canada since the eighteenth century. A Prince Albert lawyer and the Conservative MP for the riding, McKay was considered an excellent appointment, but the court was left short-handed for nearly a year.

The delay was symptomatic of how Canada's division of powers over the administration of justice created ongoing issues for superior court appointments. Under section 92(14) of the *British North America Act* (now known as the *Constitution Act, 1867*), the provinces established and administered the courts, including determining their size, but under section 96 the federal government made appointments to the superior courts and, most importantly, paid the salaries. Provinces could expand a court, but they had to wait for the federal government to make appointments. More judges meant more expenditure, and Ottawa tended to delay appointments, sometimes for years, a problem which has by no means vanished.[43]

Partisanship complicated the process, especially when the provincial and federal administrations were of different political stripes. This was the case for Saskatchewan after the victory of Robert Borden's Conservatives in the 1911 federal election. There was no guarantee of co-operation between the two levels of government, but ties between the federal and provincial wings of political parties, which were particularly strong at the time, could be helpful. Premier Scott had the ear of Laurier. With Borden in power, Scott now had much less influence over appointments, which were almost certainly going to go to Conservative supporters. It was a disincentive to pursue appointments aggressively, although both levels of government were mindful of complaints about overburdened courts.

Saskatchewan also had a much harder time than neighbouring Alberta did persuading Ottawa to make judicial appointments, even though they both had Liberal governments. Both provinces, struggling to keep up with the growth of judicial work, had seen similar increases in the court lists. But Alberta was able to expand its superior court bench much faster, with a sixth judge in 1910, a seventh in 1912, and three more in 1914, which allowed the formation of a full-time appellate panel of four judges. Saskatchewan struggled along with six judges, even though its population was considerably bigger.[44] Political factors were again likely in play. Support for the federal Conservatives was much higher in Alberta, with very prominent Conservative lawyers and politicians such as R.B. Bennett likely making the difference.

The other factor in Saskatchewan was lack of aggressive action on the part of the Scott administration and Attorney General Turgeon. As Turgeon told Haultain, the provincial cabinet had debated adding a seventh judge to the Supreme Court and decided against it. Turgeon may have been giving the District Court priority. The province was quickly expanding the number of judicial districts, with a total of seventeen by 1912 with more to come.[45] Alberta had nine. Pursuing District Court appointments likely made it harder for Turgeon to procure more judges for the Supreme Court. Another explanation was that Turgeon had in mind a court of appeal.

A COURT OF APPEAL?

BY 1912, THE legal profession in Saskatchewan was not satisfied with the existing *en banc* arrangement. In response to the government's 1913 amendment to appoint a sixth judge, Moose Jaw lawyer and leader of the opposition W.B. Willoughby called in the legislature for the creation of a court of appeal.[46] The Law Society of Saskatchewan appointed a special committee of benchers in 1914 to discuss establishing a court of appeal with the provincial bar.[47]

Turgeon's reluctance to push for more Supreme Court appointments was calculated to establish a court of appeal sooner rather than later. During their 1911 discussion about appointing a new judge, Turgeon had told Wetmore that the government wished to establish a court of appeal soon and argued that appointing more judges to the Supreme Court would make this difficult.[48] Turgeon's logic was curious, as there was no apparent reason why increasing the existing court in the interim would interfere with later creating a new court. But Turgeon made the same argument in the Legislature in 1915 when introducing a bill for a court of appeal. Citing the "experience of the other provinces," he stated that the government "had thought it better . . . that the extension of the judiciary should take place in this manner, rather than by merely appointing new Supreme Court judges."[49] Events would prove otherwise.

The Court of Appeal Act and *The King's Bench Act* were introduced to the legislature on June 4, 1915.[50] The statutes were to end the existing Supreme Court, replacing it with a four-judge court of appeal and a six-judge trial court, with the judges ex officio members of the other court and able to substitute for trials and appeals in certain circumstances.[51] As was practice in Canada, the chief justice of the appeal court was the chief justice of Saskatchewan, with the provision that the sitting chief justice of the province would retain the title, whether assigned to the appeal court or trial court.

Establishing the new courts required three appointments, but none were forthcoming from Ottawa. Turgeon had proceeded without any firm agreement with the Borden government. The attorney general had met with the minister of justice, Charles Doherty, in the spring of 1915 to discuss Saskatchewan's dire need for more superior court judges.[52] Doherty told Turgeon that he could make no appointments until Parliament was

SIR FREDERICK WILLIAM GORDON HAULTAIN

Born near Woolwich, England, in 1857 to a military family of long standing, Frederick Haultain came to Ontario in 1860. His father was a retired colonel of the Royal Artillery who chose to homestead near Peterborough. The Haultains counted among their neighbours Susanna Moodie, the famed pioneer writer.[13] Colonel Haultain was a member of the Legislative Assembly of the Province of Canada.

Frederick Haultain studied classics at the University of Toronto, graduating with honours in 1876. Haultain then took up law and was called to the Ontario bar in 1882. After a short period of practice in Toronto and Kingston, Haultain heard the call of opportunity in the West and arrived in Fort Macleod in 1884. He hung his shingle in the cattle town and enjoyed telling stories of ranching clients, the bulk of his business, who would hand over their revolvers to him for safekeeping before heading to the saloon.[14] Haultain partnered with barrister C.C. McCaul and was Crown prosecutor for the district.[15] Active in local affairs, Haultain was the editor of the Fort Macleod newspaper for a time.

Haultain soon entered politics and was elected to the Territorial Assembly in 1887. At the time, the Assembly had little power, and Haultain turned his energy to achieving responsible government. He prevailed in an acrimonious confrontation over control of territorial funds with Lieutenant-Governor Joseph Royal. As the premier of the North-West Territories after 1897, Haultain concentrated on building the civil service, a structure for local government, infrastructure, and the school system, accomplishing a great deal with relatively little revenue.[16] He felt partisanship was corrosive and did his best to govern with the confidence of the whole Assembly. A noted orator with a tremendous grasp of language, Haultain was favourably compared by his contemporaries with his bombastic political rival Nicholas Flood Davin.[17]

Haultain's personal life was not a happy one. Long a bachelor, he secretly married Marion St. Clair Castellain in 1906. He had first met the twice-divorced Marion as the daughter of Lieutenant-Governor Charles Mackintosh.[18] Marion suffered from mental illness, and Haultain financially supported her and her daughter for many years before their marriage. Her mental health further deteriorated until Haultain had no choice but to institutionalize her. Amazingly, throughout his public life, Haultain kept his marriage a secret. Widowed in 1938, he remarried at the age of eighty, just before he retired from the bench to live out his last years happily in Montreal.

Haultain had also succeeded Edward Wetmore as chancellor of the University of Saskatchewan, a post he held until his retirement. His ashes were later interred on the campus in Saskatoon. Education had always been a passion for Haultain, although he had not supported separate schools while territorial premier. He was knighted in 1916 for his many years of public service, the first resident of Saskatchewan so recognized.

Haultain lived at the Assiniboia Club in Regina, where he often entertained friends. He held a convivial birthday supper every year, usually with about twenty-five guests. Haultain did not hold grudges; even bitter political rivals such as Davin or Walter Scott were counted as friends. He had a fine sense of humour and a quick wit, which sometimes was heard on the bench. Haultain could also be reserved, in the manner, according to some, of an English gentleman, but one biographer claimed he felt right at home with Prairie farmers, who knew him as Fred. Haultain loved to shoot, and fall assizes usually included some hunting. His retirement in 1938 and death in 1942 attracted massive press coverage in Saskatchewan, but some historians contend that Haultain has since been largely forgotten.

Frederick Haultain, c. 1904. (Provincial Archives of Saskatchewan R-B3200)

Banquet for law students and young lawyers joining the military, Regina, c. 1915. (Provincial Archives of Saskatchewan, R-B4519)

in session and the *Judges Act* amended, but that he would take it up at the first opportunity. That was the extent of his commitment.

By the end of November, Ottawa had taken no action. Turgeon wrote Doherty to impress upon him the urgency, enclosing statistics to show that from 1908 to 1914 the work of the court had increased threefold. Echoing Haultain two years before, Turgeon told Doherty that the court sat for a full month hearing arguments and then had only one week to prepare forty judgments. He sent a newspaper clipping reporting that Haultain had informed the bar that judgments from the fall sitting would not be available until the New Year because the panel did not have time to finish them before going on circuit. "I know by personal observation," Turgeon added, "that our judges are probably the hardest worked men in the Province. They have to take up all their spare time including their nights and their holidays in an endeavor to keep their work from falling behind."[53]

Doherty's reply was not promising. He somewhat disingenuously claimed that he could do nothing until the Saskatchewan court acts were proclaimed but promised again to give the matter his "best consideration."

Turgeon was a year late. If the attorney general had hoped that introducing the new court acts would force Doherty to act, he was disappointed. The federal government had other concerns in the autumn of 1915. The war was not going well for Canada and its allies, and the needs of the Saskatchewan judiciary were a low priority. The nation's resources were being mobilized for the war effort and austerity was the order of the day.

Turgeon was forced to leave the statutes un-proclaimed and in legislative limbo. This left the Saskatchewan court short-handed with no immediate relief in sight. The situation would not improve until 1918, when the Court of Appeal was finally established.

Turgeon was also left waiting for his own judicial appointment. He had expected to join one of the new courts, as Lamont, his predecessor, had. F.W. Halliday, a Prince Albert lawyer, wrote Turgeon to say he had heard rumours that the attorney general was eyeing the bench and passed on the news that an appointment was Turgeon's for the taking, as a Roman Catholic judge was needed.[54] Turgeon replied that, confidentially, the matter was all arranged. He was not appointed until 1921.

The judges who had been appointed to the Saskatchewan Supreme Court were a fairly homogenous group, primarily Anglo-Scottish and Protestant. Prendergast was the token Catholic, and after he left, Saskatchewan went eight years before it had another. Not surprisingly, nearly all were born and raised in Eastern Canada. Wetmore and Newlands were from New Brunswick and Nova Scotia respectively; Brown and Prendergast were from Quebec; and Elwood, Haultain (born in England), Johnstone, and Lamont were from Ontario. McKay was the first judge of the court who was born and raised in Western Canada, fully a generation before the next. Family backgrounds varied: Lamont and Brown came from the farm; Haultain was the scion of an old English military family. In age, the judges ranged from thirty-nine (Brown, a very youthful appointment) to fifty-six (Johnstone). The average age at appointment was around forty-seven.

Almost all judges had their legal training through articles. Only Prendergast and Lamont had law degrees, although Johnstone and Haultain had some of their legal training through Osgoode Hall.[55] For that generation, university-based legal training was still a novelty, and law degrees were very uncommon. Newlands and Elwood had no university degree of any kind. Lamont and Brown were low in seniority for a judicial appointment—the former had been at the bar twelve years, the latter fourteen—but the others had between twenty and thirty years' practice under their belts. Wetmore and Prendergast had come to the NWT court after spending their years at the bar elsewhere, but the other appointments to the Saskatchewan court had practised primarily in the Territories and then Saskatchewan. The time had passed when a judicial appointment could come from outside the provincial bar. Premier Scott had firmly refused when the justice minister suggested some Ontario lawyers for the District Court.[56]

It would be some time before the first native-born son of the province was appointed, but it was very much a Saskatchewan court, with judges who had long experience at the bar and on the bench in the North-West Territories and subsequently the new province. Wetmore, Prendergast, Newlands, and Johnstone had already contributed to the law of the province as territorial judges, and they and the first group of judges appointed to the Supreme Court of Saskatchewan now set the law for the first decade of the province.

THE SUPREME COURT *EN BANC* AT LAW

THE SUPREME COURT of Saskatchewan was established at a time when the dominant philosophy in common law countries was legal formalism, which had been born from the legal reforms and modernization that began in the late eighteenth century and picked up momentum in the nineteenth. Formalists believed that the common law embodied logical principles that could be brought to bear to solve nearly any legal problem. Formalism, in line with the increasing prevalence of statute law, sought to rationalize the application of law for greater consistency and certainty and tame the vagaries of judge-made case law. A fundamental aspect of legal formalism was judicial restraint in interpreting and applying the law.

The restraint took several forms. In England and Canada, judges saw policy—how the law affected and served society, and particularly how it should affect society—as the realm of the legislature. Under the doctrine of parliamentary supremacy, judges strove for literal statutory interpretation, only inferring the intent of the legislature when a statute was ambiguous. As Wetmore put it, "The question is, not what may be supposed to have been intended, but what has been said."[57] The doctrine of *stare decisis*, the application of precedent, became relatively rigid as judges sought clarity and consistency.[58] When developing case law, judges were cautious and conservative, departing from existing precedents only reluctantly. Along with the long-held recognition of the binding nature of decisions of higher courts, many appellate courts felt compelled always to follow their own decisions on a point of law.[59] Some judges even felt that decisions of courts of "coordinate jurisdiction"—such as other provincial appellate courts in Canada—if not strictly binding should still be followed. These were the widely accepted orthodoxies of the time.

The decisions of the Saskatchewan Supreme Court *en banc* reflected this outlook. The judges of the court had a strong sense of justice, but they hewed to the "black letter" of the law, as formalism came to be characterized, seeking well-established precedents and principles. For most decisions, many of which were simple error correction, this sufficed and gave litigants clear, predictable outcomes. But in some instances, such as *R v Quong Wing*, which dealt with a law prohibiting the hiring of white female employees by Chinese businessmen, judicial restraint meant the court could not address a manifest injustice. Yet in two appeals involving separate school funding, long a contentious issue in Saskatchewan, the formal approach allowed the court to avoid being drawn into a political maelstrom.

PRACTICE AND PROCEDURE

THE SUPREME COURT *en banc*'s practice and procedure changed little from the territorial court. Until 1912, the court followed the territorial rules, and when new rules were introduced they mostly refined existing appellate procedure. Appeals from the District Court, which were new, used the same procedures with one major exception. Under the 1912 rules, factums were not necessary, but the appellant was required to obtain from the District Court judge a signed copy of his notes to submit with his judgment and the original pleadings.[60] The 1912 rules also gave District Court appeals priority at hearing.[61] Generally, appeals were heard in the order the appeal books were filed, but District Court appeals were heard before Supreme Court appeals.

The court also decided informally to use smaller panels for District Court appeals.[62] *The Judicature Act* had initially set quorum at three for the court *en banc*. The amendment that added a judge in 1913 increased the quorum size to four. Wetmore had favoured sitting as a full court for appeals to have a more definitive statement of law, which was likely also the attitude of the bar, but the drawback of a larger quorum on a small court was little flexibility. Turgeon changed the quorum back to three to help Haultain. To conserve some manpower, the court often used a panel of three for District Court appeals and four or five for Supreme Court appeals.

The court presented most judgments immediately after a sitting, continuing the territorial practice. The tradition was to read the judgments in open court, as was done in England, a week or so after the last hearing, and the court rarely reserved a decision longer.[63] But as Haultain complained to Turgeon, the long lists made it challenging to finish judgments quickly, and the court was not always able to manage it. The practice meant frenetic work for the judges after the sitting if they wanted to finish writing while the appeals were fresh in their minds and before departing on circuit.

The volume of appeals meant the Supreme Court *en banc* practised an economy of effort. Written judgments were generally short, which was also the style of the day. The court adopted an informal practice of a single writer for most District Court appeals unless there was a dissent, and a single judge often authored Supreme Court decisions. Concurring opinions were more common for the latter, but the court never fully adopted the *seriatim* style of judgment. There was still a large measure of collaboration, as in the territorial days. Judges frequently mentioned that they had read a colleague's draft before writing their own. Dissents and concurrences were frequent enough to demonstrate a lively engagement with the issues, but no judge stood out as a contrarian. The press of business no doubt discouraged extraneous writing.

Prendergast and Johnstone wrote relatively little. Wetmore was very prolific and dominated the early jurisprudence of the court, but Lamont and Newlands were also energetic writers. Lamont soon emerged as the strongest judge of the Saskatchewan Supreme Court. In Haultain's time, with Elwood, Brown, and McKay on the court, the judges shared the writing duties fairly equally, with some variation reflecting time away serving on royal commissions or for illness or leaves of absence.

Regina Law Student Society executive with Chief Justice Wetmore, c. 1908. *Standing, from left:* R.E. Turnbull, J.M. Hanbidge, C.W. Hoffman, A.S. Trotter. *Seated, from left:* R. Hogarth, R.D. McMurchy, Chief Justice Wetmore, F.W. Turnbull, T.B. Hooper. (Provincial Archives of Saskatchewan, R-B3908)

TWO CHIEF JUSTICES

A CHIEF JUSTICE is often assumed to be the leader of the court. The reality is somewhat more complex. Then as now, a chief justice is first among equals, and in their adjudicative role every judge is independent, free to decide matters without interference, including from other judges. The chief justice might not even be the best lawyer on his court. The bar hoped for a chief justice who was a strong judge and for judgments of the court that clearly set out the law and gave satisfaction to litigants, but there were limits to how much a chief justice could influence the work of his brother judges. The chief justice was generally responsible for administration of the court. This was not a great burden in the early twentieth century, especially for a small court. Determining the sitting schedule was the main chore, complicated in Saskatchewan by the long trial lists. At the same time, the character of the chief justice could play a large role in the function and character of a court.

Chief Justice Wetmore was greatly respected, by his colleagues on the bench, by the bar, and by the public, and in his five years put a lasting stamp on the court. He was long considered the most able judge on the Supreme Court of the North-West Territories. Becoming chief justice of Saskatchewan was the culmination of a long career. Wetmore was an orthodox judge, but he was admired for his grasp of the law and careful reasoning. One legacy from his days on the territorial court was an appetite to delve into the facts and evidence of an appeal, often coming to conclusions that differed from those of the trial judge. Wetmore had a reputation as a stickler for form in the courtroom, and it is easy to imagine that *en banc* sittings were conducted with great decorum. But the chief justice was also very human. One of Wetmore's appealing qualities was that he cheerfully admitted when he was wrong. As he wrote in one judgment,

> I have stated that the learned trial Judge *seems* to have based his judgment on *res ipsa loquitur*, but on a close reading of the judgment I have reached the conclusion that his idea of *res ipsa loquitur* and mine may be quite different, and if it is, his idea may be right.[64]

There is a charming story that captures Wetmore the man. Murray McIntyre, a long-time member of the Saskatchewan bar, recalled moving to Regina as a green lawyer from Manitoba.[65] He called the courthouse to arrange his bar exam with the chief justice. Wetmore answered the phone himself and gruffly advised McIntyre that he had court but would come to McIntyre's hotel after four o'clock. Wetmore arrived hot and perspiring and asked the lawyer if he had anything to drink. The young man had bought a bottle of Scotch that afternoon and poured two generous tots. Wetmore then exclaimed that he had arranged to meet Newlands after court. He stepped into the hall and telephoned his brother judge, who came to the hotel with another colleague. The whisky bottle quickly emptied. Wetmore then remembered he had a dinner engagement and the judges took their leave. McIntyre, taken aback, stammered, "But sir, my exam . . ." Wetmore replied, "Son, you passed as soon as you brought out the bottle of Teacher's."

Frederick Haultain came to the court as a public figure of stature and was a fixture for two generations of Saskatchewan lawyers. On his retirement, he was lauded for his sagacity and learning as a judge, and he had a reputation as an expert on constitutional law, partly gleaned from his political experience. Colleagues spoke glowingly of Haultain's personal qualities and the collegiality of the court during his long tenure. In jurisprudence, however, he did not cut the same figure as Wetmore. He had revived his legal practice after many years in politics and while still engaged as leader of the opposition. Haultain was named chief justice "off the street," direct from practice. He was a little rusty and it showed. His jury charge in a trial for attempted rape was surprisingly inept: the chief justice told the jury that, "As soon as there is sufficient evidence before you which would tend to point to the guilt of the accused, then the presumption is on the other side."[66] It scarcely needs to be said that this was at odds with accepted criminal law on the onus of proof. On appeal, Brown ordered a new trial and tactfully did not name the trial judge. More surprisingly, the attorney general's office fielded several complaints from counsel about long-overdue trial judgments from Haultain. His tardiness could be blamed on the ridiculous workload the judges faced.[67]

Haultain frequently wrote for the court, and his judgments were clear and cogent, characterized by a great regard for the common law. But some of his brother judges, particularly John Lamont, overshadowed him. Lamont has long been considered one of the province's great jurists. He wrote with a distinct intellectual quality. His decisions incisively stated the main points or questions of the appeal and then elaborated, sometimes at length. He did not suffer fools and poor argument, writing on one occasion,

> The evidence further shews that from November 16th, 1907, until May 14th, 1909, a year and a half, the plaintiffs took no steps in the matter, and it was only when the provincial university was being located in the vicinity, and as a result property in that neighbourhood increased in value, that the plaintiffs tendered the defendant the balance of the purchase price. How under these circumstances it can be seriously contended that equity demands a return of the moneys paid by the plaintiffs passes my comprehension.[68]

One authority described Lamont as an "able if traditional jurist who tended to assess legal issues narrowly."[69] He was restrained and careful, the very picture of an appellate judge of the era.

The same could be said for Brown, Elwood, and McKay. Brown's judgments have been called incisive, economical, concise, and lucid.[70] A wry sense of humour was evident in one of his decisions, involving a suit for breach of promise:

> I might add that the plaintiff apparently never dreamed of bringing this action until the defendant very ill-advisedly, I think, had caused a solicitor's letter to be sent to her demanding a return of the engagement ring. Being the first to invoke the aid of a solicitor, he cannot very well complain under the circumstances if she has retaliated in kind. I would have thought it better policy on his part, and less expensive, to have purchased another ring if he was really again in need of one.[71]

Elwood was a workhorse, writing often for the court. McKay was the most concise of all the judges, coming to the point quickly and avoiding excessive recitations of facts and the long quotes from the case law that cluttered many judgments of the time. The veteran Newlands was also an energetic writer, direct and blunt-spoken. He was independent and opinionated, dissenting and concurring more than his brother judges. Newlands had a strong sense of equity and sometimes invoked "natural justice" in his decisions. Newlands, Brown, Elwood, and McKay were practical judges, most concerned with just outcomes for litigants and exercising a great deal of common sense, drawing on their experience and understanding of a still raw society.

It is important to note that judicial conservatism was something different from political conservatism. A judge could be labelled conservative or liberal, traditional or progressive, restrained or activist, depending on how they interpreted statute law, applied precedent, and created new case law, not on their personal politics or the end result of their judicial rulings. The prevailing judicial philosophy of the time strongly encouraged judges to be restrained and cautious in interpreting and developing the law, but within this some judges or even courts might be bolder or more deferential. Thus it is possible to speak of an appellate court having a certain character, even given the prosaic nature of most of the appeals heard in an intermediate court.

SASKATCHEWAN'S APPELLATE COURT was very orthodox. The judges of the court assessed and applied case law strictly, and they consistently and explicitly warned against considering policy or straying into legislating.[72] The court also considered itself bound by its own decisions.[73] Wetmore, who set the tone of the court, gave the "greatest respect" to the decisions of both the English courts and other Canadian appellate courts.[74] The Supreme Court was not a court of bold jurisprudence, in an age which did not encourage bold jurisprudence. But it was not "hidebound," as courts that were excessively mechanistic and unimaginative in interpreting and applying law were often called. And on one point, the review of fact findings, the court set a somewhat different course.

Appellate courts had early recognized that trial judges and juries had advantages in weighing evidence and particularly in assessing witnesses and that appeal courts should be deferential to their findings on the evidence as to the facts of a case. On appeal, the determination of facts could still be challenged as not being supported by the evidence, but if the trier of fact was not obviously wrong, appeal judges were discouraged from overturning findings merely because they disagreed. This deference was not necessarily formalism, but it was another aspect of appellant restraint, which had the immense practical value of limiting appeals and reflected the veneration of the trial process and the fact that appeal courts were relative latecomers in the common law. By 1907, the principle of deference was well established but not necessarily rigorously observed, as appellate judges sometimes could not resist the temptation to meddle.

Wetmore noted the change towards more restraint. As he stated, a little skeptically, "It also seems to me that the trend of recent decisions in the Supreme Court of Canada is in the direction that the Court of Appeal ought not, and will not, interfere with the findings of the trial Judge on a question of fact."[75] Saskatchewan's *Judicature Act*, however, had given the Supreme Court broad and explicit powers to review fact findings, powers that went further than they did in neighbouring Alberta. Wetmore likely had a role in this when the statute was drafted. And in a 1911 decision, *Coventry v Annable*, Wetmore further established a tradition of robust appellate intervention in Saskatchewan.

A central point in the appeal was whether the defendant had fraudulently obtained a transfer of title to two quarters of farmland and largely came down to the testimony of the witnesses. Wetmore did not agree with the trial judge's finding that he believed the defendant's version. The important question was whether, given the general deference to a trial judge's view of the evidence, especially witness testimony, the court could overturn his findings. Delving into recent English case law, Wetmore concluded that in trials by a judge alone, the English courts took the position that, while acknowledging the advantages of a trial judge in weighing evidence, there was room for appellate intervention. The most deference was owed to the trial judge's assessment of witnesses, as they had significant advantages in this regard, but not to further inference or deductions from the evidence. Here, the appeal court was "in as good a position for arriving at a correct conclusion."[76] This left many fact findings open to appellate scrutiny.

The Supreme Court of Canada upheld Wetmore's judgment and did not contradict his view on an appeal court's ability to review and overturn fact findings, and Wetmore's conclusions in *Coventry* would later be enshrined in *The Court of Appeal Act*. Interestingly, Wetmore was much more interventionist than his fellow judges. Johnstone dissented in *Coventry*, arguing that if there was any evidence to support the trial judge's view, it should be followed. In an earlier case, *Davis v Burt*, Lamont had only very reluctantly agreed with Wetmore that the trial judge had been wrong to accept testimony of a key witness, even though the testimony was ludicrous.[77] And Newlands stoutly defended the trial judge. He and McKay consistently refused to review fact except in the clearest cases of error. Paradoxically, while the Saskatchewan court had broader explicit powers to intervene in this area than other courts did, most of the judges exercised more restraint.

The *Coventry* decision dealt with the findings of trial judges, not juries. The court was consistently respectful and restrained towards jury verdicts. This deference was the accepted norm for common law appeal courts, reflecting that the jury trial was a hallowed tradition. Interestingly, due to the small population in the North-West Territories, juries were just six men and were used infrequently for civil trials. Alberta continued to use juries of six until the 1960s and has always had a weak jury tradition, even in criminal trials. Saskatchewan chose to follow the rest of Canada and instituted twelve-person juries that featured regularly in civil trials. Jury findings could be challenged on appeal as unreasonable and against the evidence, but the court was rigorous in their review and showed great deference.

Allan, Gordon and Gordon law office in Regina, c. 1914 to 1918. Percy Gordon later served on the court. (Provincial Archives of Saskatchewan, R-B3639)

It was not always easy for the judges to show restraint, particularly Wetmore. Negligence cases involving injured railway workers were common, and juries consistently found in favour of plaintiffs and gave large damage awards. In *Gordon v Canadian Northern Railway*, the jury had awarded more than $10,000 in damages for injuries to an employee after finding the company negligent.[78] In Wetmore's view, the jury award came under appellate scrutiny as unreasonable, and he dissented, stating, "I am of opinion that the damages are outrageously excessive."[79] The jury, he suggested, had used the wrong principle in calculating the award, namely that the railroads could afford to pay large amounts:

> I am now about to speak merely from conjecture, but at the same time as the result of experience, and I have no hesitation in stating that if the conductor and the engineer, the parties so actually guilty of the negligence, had been the defendants in the place of the railway company, the jury would have hesitated before giving

> a verdict for half the amount which they did give in this case. This is the first opportunity that I have had of putting my opinions upon record in a question of this character, and having done so, as a matter of course, I will hereafter feel myself bound, as I must be, loyally to follow the judgment of the majority of this Court.[80]

In a number of similar appeals, the court supported the findings of judges and juries as to both negligence and damages.

The reported judgments of the court were primarily civil law, in part reflecting the fact that criminal appeals were still restricted. The civil appeals of the court covered the usual range of actions, torts, contracts, and so on, with a definite air of country life. As in the territorial days, many of the appeals involved land, primarily farmland but also, as the province's cities and towns expanded, urban property. Land transactions could be quite complex, particularly with contracts and mortgages that involved payment in the form of crops. Promissory notes circulated freely, sometimes assigned two or three times over and often secured against crops. Appeals of interpleader orders were frequent as sheriffs tried to determine priority among creditors and interested parties appealed seizures and judicial sales. Even with the territorial decisions on land titles, the court dealt frequently with appeals regarding the registration of various instruments on titles, including appeals from the master of titles—the registrar for land titles—refusing or granting titles, depending on the circumstances.

The purchase of farm implements, especially the newfangled powered tractors, generated a great deal of litigation, with disputes on terms of contracts and frequent attempts to claim under warranties as machinery broke down or did not function properly. Arguably, the court took the view that some protection of the public was necessary, giving the benefit of the doubt, at trial and appeal, to farmers who claimed that implement dealers or their agents misrepresented contracts or made false claims about the performance of machinery. The legislature took notice and in 1915 passed the first *Farm Implement Act*, the subject of another chapter.

Very much more could be said about the court's decisions. To sum up the entirety of ten years of appeals even for a small court like Saskatchewan is difficult. Three appeals that involved public policy illustrate the court at law. These decisions further demonstrate the court's formalist character but also the advantages and disadvantages of the judicial restraint this entailed. The appeals discussed below, *R v Quong Sing*, *Regina Public School v Gratton Separate School*, and *McCarthy v City of Regina*, at their heart all deal with rights but expose the limitations faced by Canadian judges attempting to adjudicate on these questions, first and foremost the belief that their role in determining and protecting rights was very circumscribed.

R V QUONG SING AND *QUONG WING*

IN *R V QUONG SING*, the Supreme Court *en banc* had to decide between two precedents of the Judicial Committee of the Privy Council, and the choices were revealing. One would make a Saskatchewan law that banned Chinese employment of white women invalid, the other valid. The Saskatchewan decision and Supreme Court of Canada decision in these cases illustrate the limitations of the courts in this era to deal with a case of overt racism and denial of civil rights. The neutral stance of the court, disavowing policy and giving complete deference to the legislature, allowed a law to stand that, even at the time, some saw as an injustice, and that there was a choice of precedents to follow, throws some doubt on whether the hands of the judges were tied.

In 1912, the Saskatchewan Legislature passed the *Act to Prevent the Employment of Female Labour in Certain Capacities* (*Female Employment Act*).[81] The statute's main provision stated,

> No person shall employ in any capacity any white woman or girl or permit any white woman or girl to reside or lodge in or to work in or, save as a bona fide customer in a public apartment thereof only, to frequent any restaurant, laundry or other place of business or amusement owned, kept or managed by any Japanese, Chinaman or other Oriental person.

In response to protests from the government of Japan, Saskatchewan amended the statute in 1913 to strike out the reference to Japanese employers but, despite strong opposition from Moose Jaw's Chinese business community, the province's largest, refused to rescind the law. A $100 fine waited for anyone convicted under the statute's provisions.[82]

Canada's history with Chinese immigration is an unsavoury one. Racism was endemic in Canada in the nineteenth and early twentieth centuries—not universal but acceptable in polite society. The Chinese in particular were viewed as alien and lacking in moral character. There was strenuous opposition to Chinese immigration, but economic imperatives such as the building of the Canadian Pacific Railway sometimes took priority, and Chinese labourers were allowed into Canada. After the railway was finished, the federal government imposed an oppressive fee known as the head tax on the Chinese before finally bowing to public pressure and ending all Chinese immigration in 1923.

The Chinese population in Canada was overwhelmingly male, thanks to the head tax, and largely consigned to ghettos called Chinatowns in larger cities, though they also lived in small numbers in Prairie towns and villages along the rail lines. Many urban Chinese opened small businesses, particularly laundries and restaurants. While some gained a measure of acceptance and even respect in their community, as a group the Chinese were subject to discriminatory provincial laws and local bylaws even after becoming naturalized.

Saskatchewan's 1912 law reflected the near hysteria over the perceived threat of Chinese men towards women. Already associated in popular sentiment with gambling and opium use, the men were suspected of being "white slavers," luring women into prostitution.[83] In one of history's poignant ironies, many of the women's groups fighting for female suffrage also campaigned against Asian immigration.[84] Iconic feminist, journalist, and magistrate Emily Murphy sensationalized these fears in her book *The Black Candle*.[85] *The Female Employment Act* was intended to prevent white women from being placed under the influence of Chinese men. The fact that the legislation was also deeply sexist did not feature in the appeal and indeed may not have occurred to anyone at the time.

The Chinese community in Moose Jaw—Saskatchewan's largest, with about 270 individuals in the city and surrounding district[86]—fought back against the new law through the courts. Two naturalized immigrants, Quong Wing, proprietor of the CER Restaurant, and Quong Sing, who ran the Royal Restaurant and Rooming House, declined to forgo their white employees. They were soon charged, and on May 27, 1912, they were convicted in the Moose Jaw police court. The Chinese community raised funds to pursue an appeal.

In *Quong Sing*, counsel for the appellant, W.B. Willoughby, challenged the conviction on the grounds that *The Female Employment Act* was *ultra vires* because the statute trespassed on federal powers over naturalization and immigration in section 91(25) of the BNA *Act*.[87] In the era of the *Charter of Rights and Freedoms*, it is hard to believe that the law was not attacked for its obvious racism. At the time in Canada, some civil liberties were ensconced within the common law, often referred to as "the traditional rights and freedoms enjoyed by British subjects." But many rights that have subsequently been codified and defined, like racial equality, did not have any legal existence. And under the doctrine of parliamentary supremacy, legislation could supersede even age-old civil liberties.

There was not much recourse to the courts; in common law, judges had little scope to review properly passed statutes.[88] But the division of powers in Canada between federal and provincial governments under the BNA *Act* created a basis for review of legislation in the courts on the grounds that a statute trespassed on an area where one level of government or the other had exclusive power to legislate. The division of powers was sometimes an indirect way to challenge a statute repugnant for another reason, but the strategy had the obvious drawback that the court was deciding on the basis of the division of powers, and the actual issue, such as the discrimination in *Quong Sing*, was not necessarily relevant to the outcome.

Haultain, Lamont, Brown, and Newlands heard the appeal at the spring sittings in 1913. The court affirmed the magistrate's conviction, with Haultain dissenting.[89] *Quong Sing* was not the first challenge of a Canadian law aimed at the Chinese. The court split over which decision of the Judicial Committee of the Privy Council—*Union Colliery v Bryden* or *Cunningham v Tomey Homma*, both Canadian cases—was the precedent that governed the appeal.

In *Union Colliery*, the Judicial Committee had declared a British Columbia law outlawing Chinese labour in underground mines *ultra vires* because it interfered with the federal power over immigration and naturalization. The committee had deemed the "pith and substance," or true intent, of the law was not mine regulation but to discourage Chinese settlement in British Columbia by preventing a common type of employment. This clearly interfered with immigration and naturalization, in the committee's view, because only the Dominion government could decide on the rights and privileges given to aliens and naturalized aliens if such rights affected their naturalization. In *Tomey Homma*, the committee upheld a BC law preventing Chinese from registering and voting in elections. Distinguishing the circumstances from *Union Colliery*, the committee held that naturalization did not automatically grant the franchise, and the law did not prevent Chinese immigrants from enjoying "ordinary rights," such as earning a living and settling in the province, that directly affected their ability to immigrate and be naturalized.

To Haultain, it was clear that *Union Colliery* determined the appeal. He read *The Female Employment Act* in the same way the Judicial Committee had read the BC mining law. The *Act* did not regulate white female labour in a general way; it was aimed at Chinese business owners and hampered their ability to operate their businesses. As he wrote,

> The regulations which are here impeached are not really aimed at the regulation of restaurants, laundries, and other places of business and amusement or of the employment of female labour, but were devised to deprive the Chinese, whether naturalized or not, of the ordinary rights of the inhabitants of Saskatchewan. The right to employ, the right to be employed, the right to own property and to own, manage or conduct any business without being subjected to unequal and discriminatory restrictions, are just as truly ordinary rights of the inhabitants of Saskatchewan as the right to work.[90]

Haultain implied that the violation of what were considered "ordinary" civil rights was important in itself and distasteful. More to the point, it also interfered with the Chinese business owners' ability to support themselves. The parallel to *Union Colliery* seemed exact.

In Lamont's view, the violation of rights was not relevant. The effect of the law was only important in how it touched upon the division of powers. For Lamont,

> All argument, therefore, as to the wisdom or unwisdom, the justice or injustice, of provincial legislation, or the fact that it discriminates against one person or set of persons and in favour of another person or set of persons is excluded from our consideration. The only matter for inquiry is as to the legislative competence of the provincial legislature to pass the Act impeached.[91]

EDWARD LINDSEY ELWOOD

Edward L. Elwood was born in Goderich, Ontario, in 1868.[19] He did not attend university but instead entered into articles in Goderich in 1884 and was called to the bar in 1890.[20] Before establishing a practice in Oxbow, Saskatchewan, he spent two years practising in Washington State. In 1897, he moved to Moosomin and became a partner in White, Elwood and Gwillim.

Elwood ran a solo practice for several years after 1900 and then had a succession of different partners. A leader of the bar, Elwood was a bencher and president of the Law Society of the North-West Territories and was the first president of the Law Society of Saskatchewan when it was formed in 1907.[21] Like his colleague J.T. Brown, Elwood moved to Regina, where he became the senior partner of Elwood, Embury, Scott and Graham shortly before his appointment to the bench in 1913.[22] Elwood was a frequent visitor to the Supreme Court *en banc* while in practice.

Elwood ran unsuccessfully for the Conservatives in the 1912 provincial election and served as mayor of Moosomin. An Anglican, he was chancellor of the Diocese of Qu'Appelle. Elwood was a great one for fraternal orders, belonging to the Masons, the Order of Foresters, and the Ancient Order of United Workmen. He was grand master of the Masonic Order in Saskatchewan.

Elwood was appointed to the Court of Appeal when it was established in 1918, but his career was cut short by cancer. He died in 1921.

Justice Edward Lindsey Elwood, c. 1912. (Provincial Archives of Saskatchewan, R-A28211)

His funeral procession in Regina was a spectacle, attended by over a thousand Masons and nearly every member of the Saskatchewan judiciary and many prominent members of the bar.[23] The chief justice and his brother Wilmot Haultain were among the pallbearers. Both Haultain and Newlands spoke of their close friendship with Elwood and his ability as a judge.

Lamont followed *Tomey Homma,* as did Brown in a concurring judgment. Lamont started his analysis by first determining if *The Female Employment Act* was within the competence of the provincial legislature under the provincial powers in the BNA *Act*:

> The right to employ white women in the conduct of the businesses referred to in the Act is a civil right, and legislation affecting that right comes within the class of subjects enumerated in sub-sec. 13 of sec. 92, namely, "Property and civil rights in the Province."[92]

The next step was determining if the law then also came under the purview of the federal power over immigration and naturalization. Lamont argued that *Tomey Homma* determined the answer. As he understood it, the immigration and naturalization power was "the exclusive legislative right of saying what shall constitute alienage and what shall be the conditions upon which an alien may become a naturalized British subject, but it does not include the consequences flowing from either alienage or naturalization."[93] Essentially, a law was *ultra vires* if it interfered substantially with the immigration of an alien or the process of their naturalization, but once that person was naturalized, legislation could affect them in the same way it did any other British subject.

Lamont argued that the true aim of *The Female Employment Act* was to protect the morals of white women, not to prevent immigration. While the statute undoubtedly affected the rights of Chinese business owners and imposed extra burdens on them, it did not make it impossible to carry on a business or prevent residing in Saskatchewan. Brown agreed with Lamont, also making the point that the morality of the statute was not the question for the court. As he wrote, "We of course have nothing to do with the policy or impolicy of the legislation; that is a matter entirely for the legislature."[94]

The court decided the question on narrow legal grounds, which was consistent with good appellate practice at the time. The choice to follow *Tomey Homma* over *Union Colliery* may not have been really so free of policy or morality, however. One authority has argued that on the merits, following *Union Colliery* made more legal sense.[95] Another scholar has argued that despite the disavowal of policy, choosing *Tomey Homma* as the less suitable precedent demonstrated the influence of underlying beliefs about the Chinese.[96] In this view, given a way to do so, the court upheld an unjust law. This conclusion may be unfair to Lamont, Brown, and Newlands, as the choice of precedents to follow was not clear cut, deference to the legislature was very strong, and it is difficult to account for unconscious biases or remove individuals from the context of their own times.

The battle of the precedents continued at the Supreme Court of Canada, where the *en banc* decision was upheld four to one. The Judicial Committee denied leave to appeal further. At the Supreme Court, Justice John Idington dissented. He agreed with Haultain's judgment and also had this to say:

> The highly prized gifts of equal freedom and equal opportunity before the law, are so characteristic of . . . all British modes of thinking and acting . . . that they are not to be impaired by the whims of a legislature; and that equality taken away unless and until forfeited for causes which civilized men recognize as valid. . . .
>
> This legislation is but a piece of the product of the mode of thought that begot and maintained slavery; not so long ago fiercely claimed to be a laudable system of governing those incapable of governing themselves.[97]

Idington's words demonstrate that while racism in that era was rampant, it was not universal. One judge was prepared to advance the argument that rights should not be subject to whims of the legislature, moving beyond the strictures of formalism and anticipating modern conceptions of human rights.

REGINA PUBLIC SCHOOL V GRATTON SEPARATE SCHOOL: EDUCATION POLICY IN THE COURT *EN BANC*

PROTECTION OF INDIVIDUAL liberty was the rallying cry for one side in two appeals that dealt with funding separate schools in Saskatchewan. There had been decades of controversy over denominational schools in Manitoba and the North-West Territories. The Manitoba Schools Question in the 1890s created a constitutional crisis after separate schools were eliminated in that province and left behind bitter feelings in Quebec and on the Prairies. The broad minority language and religious education rights—generally French and Catholic—in the North-West Territories eroded in the wake of the Manitoba controversy, although separate schools representing either the Protestant or Catholic minority in a school district remained. The question of separate schools had plagued the autonomy talks leading up to Saskatchewan's creation in 1905. Laurier's initial insistence on restoring French language instruction caused consternation, while Haultain's opposition to separate schools cost him dearly.[98] The continuation of the territorial system in Saskatchewan gave the Liberals a lock on the Catholic vote but provoked strong opposition from the Protestant majority, which degenerated into bigotry.[99] The fact that many new immigrants to the province were Catholic added fuel to the conflict over education rights.

Under Saskatchewan's system, the schools serving the religious majority in a given district were the public schools, schools serving the minority the separate schools. A separate school was created if the majority of ratepayers belonging to the religious minority in the district voted for it. In most districts, the public schools were Protestant and separate schools Catholic, but in a small number of districts the opposite was true. Once a separate school was founded, the taxes of a ratepayer in the district were allotted to the school that reflected their religion. The province's *School Act* was not explicit on whether this was compulsory, but this was the assumption.[100]

In 1911, a decision of Judge E.A.C. McLorg of the Saskatoon District Court reopened the debate over schools. McLorg's decision, which was never appealed, held that individual ratepayers could support whichever school system they wished.[101] This created a great deal of uncertainty about funding. Another difficulty arose with the school taxes assessed from businesses. Under section 93 of *The School Act*, which was identical to a provision found in the territorial ordinances, companies with separate school supporters among the shareholders could declare that some or all their assessment should go to the separate school, in proportion to the number of shareholders. Companies generally didn't bother about their assessment, and by default the funds went to the public boards and the separate boards lost revenue.

The government responded to the McLorg decision and complaints from separate school trustees about business assessments with amendments to *The School Act*, given royal assent in January 1913. One of the amendments, section 93(a), addressed the business tax issue. The amendment allowed the separate board to notify companies that they had to specify where their assessment should go; if the company subsequently did not do so, the assessment was to be split between the two school systems in proportion to the number of Catholics and Protestants among ratepayers.

The amendments were soon challenged in court. In 1913, 159 companies in the Regina school district gave no direction about their assessment after receiving notice from the separate school trustees. The public school board trustees claimed all the money, the separate board trustees part of the money, and the City of Regina, which had collected the assessment, asked the Supreme Court of Saskatchewan what it should do with the funds.[102] Brown heard the interpleader application and ruled that the funds should be paid to both boards in proportion to the number of ratepayers of each faith in the district, as per section 93(a).

The public school district appealed. The district's argument turned on two points. The first was that, as sections 93 and 93(a) were drafted, only companies with separate school supporters could get notice from the separate board trustees and potentially have their school taxes given to the separate school. The appellant contended that section 93 barred a business without separate school supporters from directing that any of its assessment go to the separate board. It made no sense for separate school trustees to give these companies notice asking for their intentions under section 93(a). The second argument was that section 93(a) was *ultra vires*. Although the BNA *Act* gave legislative authority over education wholly to the provinces, the statute stated that any education rights in existence when a province entered into Confederation had to be maintained and not interfered with in any way. The appellant argued that section 93(a) prejudiced the rights of the majority in a school district because the separate district might receive funds from companies that did not have to pay for separate schools.

Writing for the majority, Lamont dismissed the appeal. He quickly disposed of the constitutional argument, holding that the limitation on the province's ability to legislate on education, found in both the BNA *Act* and *The Saskatchewan Act*, only existed to protect the rights of a religious minority to have a separate school. The public school supporters had no rights to a separate school and there could be no discrimination. The limitation only existed to protect the minority education rights.

Lamont thought that the appellant's other argument also failed. Although the amendment had confusing wording, the context made it clear that section 93(a) was intended to apply to all companies, not just

JAMES MCKAY

Justice James McKay, n.d. (Provincial Archives of Saskatchewan, R-B2802)

James McKay had been considered a possible candidate to succeed Wetmore as chief justice of Saskatchewan. He was born in Fort Ellice, Rupert's Land, in 1862, the eighth of ten children, and spent some of his childhood there and at Fort Pelly before his father sent the family to Manitoba for the education of his many children. The McKay family had been in Canada since the eighteenth century, working as traders for the Hudson's Bay Company. His father, William, and his grandfather John McKay had been company factors, running the far flung northern trading posts. McKay had an Aboriginal ancestor on his paternal side, a Cree woman named Titameg, making him the first judge of the court to have Aboriginal heritage.[24] He was quite proud of the fact. He attended school in Winnipeg before entering the University of Manitoba, earning a bachelor's degree in 1882 with honours in Greek and Latin.

McKay entered into articles with the Winnipeg firm of Blain, Blanchard and Mulock. While articling, he volunteered during the North-West Rebellion and fought at the battles of Fish Creek and Batoche. Later he raised and led a unit of volunteers in the 1897 manhunt of Almighty Voice, a Cree warrior from Duck Lake wanted for killing a NWMP officer. Admitted to the bar in 1886, McKay practised in Winnipeg for just a year before going to Prince Albert. He practised both in partnership and alone and was the senior member of McKay, Adam, Beattie and Fear when he was appointed. Considered a leading member of the territorial bar, McKay was the Crown prosecutor for the Saskatchewan district for a decade and was made Queen's Counsel in 1891. He was also a bencher of the Law Society of the North-West Territories.

McKay began his political career as an alderman in Prince Albert. He made his first run at Parliament in 1896, narrowly losing to Sir Wilfrid Laurier, who ran in the Saskatchewan district as well as in Quebec to guarantee a seat in the house. He campaigned again in 1904 and 1908 but was not elected until 1911, when Robert Borden swept Laurier and the Liberals from power. He was appointed to the bench on December 13, 1914. McKay was initially assigned to the Court of King's Bench in 1918 but moved to the Court of Appeal in 1921 to replace Elwood. He was still on the court when he died, in December 1931, in Toronto, where he had gone to seek medical treatment.

Outside of the law, McKay served as president of Prince Albert's Victoria Hospital and was involved in the Boy Scouts. An Anglican, he was at one time chancellor and registrar for the Diocese of Saskatchewan. An avid Mason and member of the Assiniboia Club, McKay enjoyed curling, golf, tennis, and hunting. At his funeral, his colleagues spoke of his dedication and rigorous attention to detail. He was described in one tribute as a calm, polite presence on the bench who was especially encouraging to young counsel.[25]

those with minority supporters. The amendment was obviously intended to address the problem that companies didn't make a declaration about their assessment and deprived separate schools of funds. The amendment did not instruct the separate board to identify and give notice to only the companies required to pay them, and the amendment only made sense if applied to all companies. In Lamont's view, to give sections 93 and 93(a) the appellant's interpretation made the statute absurd and violated a basic rule of statutory interpretation. As he summarized,

> If we construe the section as applying to all companies whatsoever, we are giving to it an interpretation consistent with the literal meaning of the words "any company" in the first line of the section, and an interpretation which remedies the defects found in the prior legislation, and which provides an easy working basis by which the municipality can distribute the taxes.

> The whole scope of the legislation seems to me to be an application by the legislature, in matters over which it has absolute jurisdiction, of the principle laid down in sub-sec. (2) of sec. 17 of the Saskatchewan Act as to the appropriation of public moneys, namely, that as between the two classes of schools recognized by the constitution of the province there shall be no discrimination. That sec. 93*a* is not well drawn cannot be denied. But, although the matter is not free from doubt, I think that, from the language used in the section and a consideration of the evil sought to be remedied, an intention that it should be applied to all companies is sufficiently indicated.

Haultain and Elwood concurred with Lamont. Newlands dissented in part. He disagreed with Lamont on his construction of sections 93 and 93(a). He held that section 93(a) should be interpreted literally as drafted, and thus could only apply to companies that had separate school supporters, not all companies.

Lamont was reversed at the Supreme Court of Canada three to two.[103] The dissenters, Chief Justice Charles Fitzpatrick and Justice Francis Anglin, more or less agreed with Lamont. Justices Louis Davies and Lyman Duff ignored the whole constitutional argument but agreed with Newlands. John Idington, meanwhile, decided that the *ultra vires* argument held water. The somewhat incoherent judgment may explain why the decisions of the Supreme Court in that era were not held in high esteem.[104]

The reversal at the Supreme Court was not immediately a political bombshell for the Scott administration, but it fuelled the ongoing controversy over schools. The 1913 amendments caused consternation among opponents of separate schools, who accused the government of trampling on freedom of conscience and rued the fact that the amendments shored up funding for separate schools. Scott's own pastor, the Reverend Murdoch MacKinnon, was one of the more outspoken separate school opponents, and relations between the two became strained. Responding to the Supreme Court, the government revised *The School Act* in 1915, moving the sections on assessment for school funding to *The School Assessment Act*.[105] The revisions angered Scott's opponents even more, and the premier ended up in a very public spat with MacKinnon at the end of 1915.[106] MacKinnon denounced Scott from the pulpit, accusing the government of suppressing civil liberties. Scott counterattacked in the legislature, but in an attempt to appease more moderate opponents, he also repealed some of the amendments intended to protect separate school funding, calling them "no longer necessary."

The repeal led to a sequel that finally addressed the point in Judge McLorg's 1911 decision. In 1917, the Supreme Court of Saskatchewan *en banc* considered *McCarthy v City of Regina*, an appeal from the Local Government Board, which was acting as the appellate tribunal of the court of revision.[107] Two ratepayers in the Regina school district had successfully switched their assessments at the court of revision to the school opposite from their religious denomination. Another ratepayer in turn successfully challenged these decisions at the Local Government Board, which held that ratepayers were obligated to support the school reflecting their religious denomination. The City of Regina and the public school board appealed. All six judges heard the appeal, with Haultain giving judgment for the court and Lamont and Newlands penning concurring opinions.

The appellants advanced two arguments, similar to *Gratton* but based on different legislation. The first argument was that section 39 of *The School Act*, which regulated the establishment of separate school districts, did not mandate that all members of the religious group only support that school and that reference to ratepayers establishing a separate school only meant those who voted in favour of such a school. Otherwise, it was a matter of individual conscience. The other argument was that section 39 was *ultra vires* because of limitations on the provincial legislature regarding the education rights found in section 17 of *The Saskatchewan Act*, which affirmed and expanded on the protections in section 93 of the BNA *Act*. In a new twist, the appellant argued that if section 39 was valid, then section 17 must be *ultra vires* as not conforming to the BNA *Act*. This argument turned on the fact that when the North-West Territories became part of Confederation in 1870, there were no denominational schools, indeed no taxpayer-supported schools, and thus the bare language of section 93 of the *BNA Act* should stand without the later embellishments of section 17.

Haultain chose to refute the first point by analyzing not just section 39 of *The School Act* but other sections of the statute and other legislation, such as *The City Act* and *The School Assessment Act*, which also dealt with ratepayer support for schools. The language of the other statutes, he contended, directly or indirectly supported the interpretation of section 39 that all ratepayers belonging to a religious minority had to support a separate school if one was founded. As Haultain put it, "All, in my opinion, point conclusively to an intention of the legislature to establish majority rule within a minority, either Protestant or Roman Catholic, establishing a separate school."[108] Lamont and Newlands proceeded on narrower grounds. Lamont argued that "ratepayers" should be understood consistently and that in section 39 the first usage clearly included all potential separate school ratepayers.

All the judges were a little mystified at the second, constitutional, argument. Counsel for the appellant abandoned the contention that section 39 was *ultra vires* and instead tried attacking section 17 of *The Saskatchewan Act,* because it expanded on section 93 of the BNA *Act,* which provided for protection of denominational schools. The chief justice was intrigued: Haultain wrote that whether Parliament could, under the BNA *Act,* establish a province with restricted or different powers than others was "perhaps debatable."[109] But he could not see how this idea applied in the case at hand. In the absence of any legislation about the schools in the North-West Territories in 1870, there was, in his opinion, a clean slate for subsequent legislation. Newlands agreed. Lamont further argued that even if the contention about section 17 was true, section 39 was consistent with the BNA *Act* provisions about education and would still stand as valid. He suspected that the appellant was actually advancing "a rather far-fetched argument" that, in the absence of any school legislation, a resident of the Territories in 1870 would not have been compelled to pay taxes to support separate schools, and this created a right not to pay such taxes subsequently. As he said, scathingly,

> How an exemption from taxation, when there was no law imposing taxation, can be said to be a right or privilege with respect to denominational schools which a class of persons had *by law,* passes my comprehension.[110]

Brown and Elwood concurred with the chief justice. This time, a further appeal was taken directly *per saltum* to the Judicial Committee, which could be done with leave of the court. The committee denied the appeal in a very short decision, commenting that the Local Government Board "delivered a most careful and reasoned opinion . . . confirmed by equally careful and elaborate opinions delivered by the learned Judges of the Supreme Court."[111] This ended legal challenges to separate school funding. Opposition to denominational schools in Saskatchewan moved back to the political arena and fed the rise of the Ku Klux Klan in the province in the 1920s. Finally, the James Anderson government's 1930 amendments to *The School Act* banned religious emblems and garb in public schools and ended primary school French language instruction.

As politicians, Lamont and even more so Haultain had been involved in separate school debates. Haultain had never favoured denominational schools and allowed significant erosion of educational rights in the Territories. During the provincial autonomy talks, he had even espoused a constitutional argument similar to that in *McCarthy*.[112] He left behind these personal convictions after donning judicial robes, but the court's narrow approach to the problems in school funding also served to keep it aloof from the hornet's nest of sectarian education. The judges consistently upheld the right of religious minorities to have denominational schools, on the basis of their best interpretation of the relevant statute and assiduously avoiding any policy dimension. The Supreme Court *en banc* decisions did not create controversy or even get much notice. Judge McLorg's decision, which was not challenged at appeal and had little authority as a statement of law, played a far larger role in this contentious chapter of Saskatchewan's history.

CONCLUSION

AS WETMORE SAID, Saskatchewan's Supreme Court was another step in achieving provincial autonomy. The new court seamlessly took the place of its predecessor under the tutelage of a chief justice who had been a leading member of the territorial bench. The appointment of a new chief justice, Frederick Haultain, marked the beginning of a half decade where the court was under increasing pressure to meet the needs of a burgeoning society that at times nearly overwhelmed its judges. What seemed a lukewarm and ineffectual response from the provincial government to this crisis in turn set the stage for the creation of a Court of Appeal for Saskatchewan in 1918. Until then, the judges made do as best as they could, through unceasing work.

As the judges went about adjudicating trials and then appeals, the Supreme Court *en banc* built up a body of law for Saskatchewan. Their approach was very "black letter," applying well-established precedent and principles and taking a very restrained approach to judicial lawmaking, with great deference to the legislature. Even by the constrained standards of the time, it was a conservative court. There was much to recommend this judicial conservatism. With the school funding decisions, the court upheld the government's support of minority education rights, but the judges explicitly limited their analysis to the letter of the law and avoided as much as possible any pronouncement on public policy. They were neutral arbitrators on a contentious issue. But *Quong Sing* showed that there were also manifest limitations to such judicial orthodoxy. The judiciary had only limited means to deal with an injustice, and at the very least this supported the status quo.

CHAPTER 3

THE COURT OF APPEAL FOR SASKATCHEWAN

FOR MANY OF THE LAWYERS AND JUDGES GATHERED AT the Regina courthouse on a morning in early March, 1918, it must have been *déjà vu*. They were there to inaugurate the Court of Appeal for Saskatchewan, in the same courtroom where, just over a decade previously, they had gathered to mark the first sitting of the Supreme Court of Saskatchewan. They were a decade older, greyer, and in some cases on the bench rather than in the audience. Instead of speaking in welcome to the new court, Sir Frederick Haultain received the congratulations and felicitations of the bar as first chief justice of the Court of Appeal.

Mr. J.A. Allan, KC, spoke for the Saskatchewan Bar Association. Allan doubtlessly meant no slight to the newly sworn judges when he awkwardly stated, "Press of work and the time given for the consideration of cases was such that the courts felt that they did not have the full opportunity for consideration of cases and the performance of their duties that they should have had."[1] He was merely reminding those assembled of the difficult conditions the judges had faced for years. Haultain in his reply could not resist reminiscing again about the territorial days but ended his speech with a patriotic reminder that the war raging in Europe was to defend "British justice and British liberty." Chief Justice James Brown of the Court of King's Bench then added some levity to the ceremonies. Among other humorous asides, he remarked that the new court of appeal was weakened by the fact that the two hardest-working members of the court *en banc*, namely himself and Justice James McKay, had been assigned to the trial court.

When the celebrations were over and court resumed that afternoon, Haultain announced that only motions, District Court appeals, and criminal appeals would be heard. Civil appeals from the Court of King's Bench—the trial court replacing the Supreme Court—would be held over to the next sittings. The Court of Appeal was overwhelmed at its first sitting. A cynic might have said that nothing had changed. Yet a court of appeal was another necessary step in the evolution of Saskatchewan's justice system.

SASKATCHEWAN AFTER THE WAR

NOT LONG AFTER the court's inauguration, the newspapers were full of reports of Allied reverses in France. On March 21, 1918, the Germans launched an offensive that took them almost to Paris. But their subsequent retreat was the beginning of the end, and seven months later the guns fell silent. Private George Price of Moose Jaw was the last Canadian soldier to die in combat in the war.[2]

In Saskatchewan as elsewhere in Canada, the armistice was greeted with jubilation, but it was short-lived. Even before the war's end, the Spanish Flu epidemic had begun. It reached Saskatchewan in October 1918 and soon spread through the province, killing thousands, with outbreaks lasting into 1919.[3] It would eventually kill more people worldwide than had died in the war. The cost of living had risen greatly due to wartime inflation, and with the end of war production the Canadian economy went into deep recession. Many veterans returned home to unemployment and few immediate prospects.

Saskatchewan was hit particularly hard by a precipitous decline in the price of wheat on top of a worsening drought. It was a taste of what was to come ten years later. The war had shifted farming from subsistence homesteading to commercial agriculture, and many farmers had prospered. But the provincial economy had become dependent on wheat. Saskatchewan had grown up to 60 percent of the nation's wheat crop during the war.[4] Spurred on by the war effort and taking advantage of high wartime prices, farmers pushed more and more land into production. Farmers had also started mechanizing, buying the latest tractors, cultivators, and other equipment, sensible enough with wartime labour shortages and high wages but leaving many overextended.[5] In a bitter irony, the soldier settlement scheme, a major federal program for veterans, provided land and low interest loans to encourage veterans to homestead. But on the Prairies, the good land was long taken, and Saskatchewan veterans using the program ended up on marginal farms, struggling to make ends meet.

The difficulties facing farmers, combined with perennial grievances such as tariffs and freight rates, put a great deal of pressure on the Liberal government of Premier William Melville Martin. A Regina lawyer and long-time member of Parliament, Martin had taken over the leadership of the Liberal Party when Walter Scott, plagued by ill health, resigned in 1916. A year later, Martin gave the Liberals, now in their second decade of power, their biggest majority to date, with fifty of fifty-nine seats. He continued the Scott legacy of moderate and progressive government, providing competent administration, farm-friendly policies, and socially progressive legislation. Martin ably handled controversies over sectarian education and made provincial control over natural resources a priority. He extended the provincial franchise to women, which helped the Liberals at the ballot box. Martin also held a provincial referendum on the prohibition of alcohol and passed *The Saskatchewan Temperance Act* in 1917.

By the time of the provincial election in 1921, farm organizations across Canada had entered the political arena, establishing parties that brought down Ontario's long-standing Conservative government in 1919 and Alberta's venerable Liberal administration in 1921. Helped by rivalry among different Saskatchewan farmers' groups, Martin adroitly aligned his party with rural interests, distanced the provincial Liberals from their federal counterparts, and won another comfortable majority. He then lost the confidence of farmers when he campaigned in the federal election on behalf of Liberal candidates facing the new Progressive Party, a loose coalition of farmers and labour.[6] Fifteen of sixteen federal ridings in Saskatchewan went Progressive. To save provincial Liberal fortunes, Martin stepped down and was replaced by Charles A. Dunning, who had been a homesteader and then worked for farmer co-operatives and was the general manager of the Saskatchewan Co-operative Elevator Company. Dunning led the Liberals to another electoral success before Mackenzie

King persuaded him to go into federal politics. Dunning handed the reins over to James G. Gardiner and decamped to Ottawa and the King cabinet as finance minister in 1926. To Gardiner fell the dubious distinction of overseeing the end of the Liberal dynasty in Saskatchewan in 1929.

Gardiner had presided over a rebounding economy before his electoral defeat as the '20s finally started to roar in Saskatchewan. The post-war recession ended by 1924, and good weather returned the following year.[7] The province had a record wheat crop in 1928. Prices had greatly improved, and farmers had also formed the Saskatchewan Wheat Pool to better market their produce. With money coming in, more farmers could again afford the ever-improving tractors and a new innovation, the combine. Regina became the largest distribution centre of agricultural machinery in Western Canada.[8] Imperial Oil expanded its Regina refinery, first opened in 1917. General Motors opened an assembly plant that was greeted as much-needed diversification in an economy dependent on agriculture. The

Canadian Bar Association annual banquet, Hotel Saskatchewan, Regina, 1928. (Provincial Archives of Saskatchewan, R-D1428)

return of prosperity brought something of a building boom, including road construction to serve the increasing number of automobiles. The provincial government built a number of fine courthouses among other public works. By the time of the 1931 census, the province's population had grown to 922,000, nearly 200,000 more than neighbouring Alberta. Saskatchewan was considered the third wealthiest province in Canada, with one of the lowest levels of public debt.[9] The future in 1929 looked very bright.

The increasing use of machinery in agriculture had inspired the passing of *The Farm Implement Act* in 1915 to give equipment purchasers more protection, an example both of the importance of the farmer to the political fortunes of any political party in Saskatchewan and the progressive legislation of the Liberals. With more farmers buying more equipment, the *Act* would get a thorough working-over in the new Court of Appeal.

The first few years of the court also coincided with Prohibition in Saskatchewan. *The Saskatchewan Temperance Act* was the product of several decades of campaigning against the social ills of alcohol use. Flawed, and representing a significant intrusion of the state into the affairs of citizens, the *Temperance Act* was another statute that tested the province's new appellate court.

A COURT OF APPEAL AT LAST

THE COURT OF Appeal did not have an easy birth. The Saskatchewan legislature passed the court's enabling statute in 1915, but the federal government made the necessary appointments only in 1918. Until then, the legislation gathered dust. Meanwhile, the six judges of the Supreme Court of Saskatchewan remained swamped. By the end of 1917, there was a sense of crisis among the provincial bar. The Saskatchewan Bar Association passed a resolution in December 1917, which read in part:

> This Association deeply regrets that no effective action has been taken since the last meeting of the Association to bring into force the Acts respecting the Court of King's Bench and the Court of Appeal, which Acts have been on the Statute Books for almost three years. . . . This regret is not lessened by a consideration of the facts respecting the present sittings of the Court en Banc, at which there are forty-two cases set for hearing with a period of only three weeks to allot to the hearing and two weeks for consideration and giving of judgment, and also the circumstances of the preceding Court when it was found impossible by reason of the necessity of the Judges going on circuit to hear all eighteen cases set for hearing at that Court and to deliver judgment in two others then heard.[10]

The resolution ended with a fine flourish predicting the direst consequences for the administration of justice in the province.

The bar association was not telling Premier Martin and W.F.A. Turgeon, the attorney general, anything new. Turgeon had been working at the problem, but progress was frustratingly slow. In April 1917, much less provide for the Court of Appeal, the department of the solicitor general in

Ottawa was still drafting an amendment to the *Judges Act* to add another judge to the Supreme Court of Saskatchewan.[11] The Justice ministry finally started preparing amendments for the new court in the fall, only to be delayed again when the draftsman discovered he did not have copies of the Saskatchewan statutes establishing the Court of Appeal and the Court of King's Bench. It was November before this was sorted out and the amendments ready.

The next hurdle was scheduling near-simultaneous proclamations of Saskatchewan's court statutes and the amendments to the *Judges Act*. The timing was important: the Court of Appeal and Court of King's Bench disestablished the existing court and even the sitting judges required new letters patent. The province hoped for January 1, 1918, but the date was moved to March 1. A flurry of panicked telegrams still ensued as March 1 approached and there was no official announcement. On February 28, the local Saskatchewan papers reported on the new courts and the new appointments. The judges, new and old, were still waiting for their patents.[12]

THE STATUTORY BASIS OF THE COURT

AN ACT RESPECTING *a Court of Appeal for Saskatchewan*, having received royal assent on June 24, 1915,[13] finally took effect on March 1, 1918, without amendment. The statute created a four-judge court, with a chief justice who was also the chief justice of Saskatchewan and three *puisne* judges. The court sat at Regina four times a year. The March term began on the first Monday of the month, the June term on the second Monday, and the September and November terms on the last Monday. Sittings lasted two weeks. The judges could extend or adjourn sittings as necessary and set up special sittings "as the business of the court requires."[14] The court set the day, to come within three weeks from the end of a sitting, when judgments were given.

Quorum for the court was three, and the chief justice could ask for a judge of the Court of King's Bench to sit ad hoc if needed. King's Bench judges could hold chambers for the appeal court, and the appeal judges could return the favour. The appeal judges were ex officio members of the trial court and were initially required to sit on criminal trials in Regina, Saskatoon, and Moose Jaw as part of their usual duties. The chief justice of the King's Bench could also request that an appeal judge take other trials.

WILLIAM MELVILLE MARTIN

Born in Norwich, Ontario, in 1876, Martin was the son of a Presbyterian minister. The family moved to Exeter, Ontario, and Martin received his early schooling there. He later attended the Clinton District Collegiate Institute in nearby Clinton.[1] He studied classics at the University of Toronto, graduating with honours in 1898. Martin then obtained a teaching certificate and was a high school teacher for two years to earn money for law school. Entering Osgoode Hall in 1901, he earned a scholarship and in 1903 began articles with the legendary criminal lawyer T.C. Robinette.[2]

After articles, Martin decided to head west for better prospects. Young lawyers in Toronto, he later recalled, were only earning about $50 a month. A cousin, James Balfour, had established a thriving practice in Regina and Martin joined him. He gained notice almost immediately with his defence of notorious horse rustler Edward Shoefelt. Martin, alone and unarmed, visited the outlaw in his hideout in the hills outside the hamlet of Willow Bunch and escorted him to his preliminary hearing. Shoefelt was later convicted.

Balfour introduced Martin to Liberal politics, and Martin was asked to stand for the 1906 federal by-election for Walter Scott's vacant riding. He declined, being more interested in growing his practice and getting married. Two years later, he reluctantly agreed to be the fed-

Justice William Melville Martin, n.d. (Provincial Archives of Saskatchewan, R-B747-2)

eral Liberal candidate for Assiniboia and was duly elected, retaining the seat until 1916. As a parliamentarian, Martin was respected if not especially prominent, but pre-eminent Saskatchewan jurist Emmett Hall was convinced that Martin could easily have won the leadership of the federal Liberals in 1919 instead of Mackenzie King, Canada's longest-serving prime minister.

By 1919, Martin was well ensconced as Saskatchewan's second premier, also holding the portfolio of minister of education and later attorney general. He decided to retire from politics in 1921 and was appointed to the Court of Appeal. Martin was made chief justice in 1941 with the resignation of W.F.A. Turgeon. Martin's judicial career lasted a remarkable thirty-nine years, ending only with the introduction of mandatory retirement in 1961. On his retirement, one newspaper article claimed he had turned down an appointment to the Supreme Court of Canada to stay in Saskatchewan.[3] He lived downtown near the courthouse, and lawyers frequently encountered the retired chief justice.

Martin and Chief Justice Brown of the Court of King's Bench were the commissioners for the Regina Riot Inquiry Commission in 1935. During the Second World War, Martin served as custodian of enemy property and set up the rent control board in Saskatchewan. In 1949, he chaired the commission charged with reforming the *Criminal Code*.[4] Martin was also provincial president of the Red Cross and headed a cancer fund drive for the Canadian National Institute for the Blind. He was a lifelong Mason and grand master for the province. Martin died in 1970, at the age of ninety-three. He was praised for his courtesy, for his kindliness to young and inexperienced lawyers, and for the dignity and decorum of his court.

The Court of Appeal Act explicitly gave each judge of the appeal court "all the jurisdiction, both civil and criminal, possessed by the judges of any court in Saskatchewan, under any statute of Canada or of this province."[15]

The court had a registrar, appointed by the lieutenant-governor, and deputy registrars at the headquarters of other judicial districts, usually King's Bench officials doing double duty. The registrar supervised the filing of appeals but also had judicial powers like the master of chambers of some Canadian trial courts, exercising the same jurisdiction as a judge of appeal in chambers. Within this jurisdiction, the court could grant the registrar further powers to transact any business provided for in the rules and other practice and procedure the judges might set.

The Court of Appeal exercised the same broad jurisdiction as its predecessor. The founding statute stated that the court was vested with "all the rights, powers and duties" that previously applied to the Supreme Court of Saskatchewan *en banc* under *The Judicature Act* and "any other statute in force in this province." The court could

> hear and determine all applications for new trials, all questions of issues of law, all questions of points reserved for the opinion of the court, all appeals or motions in the nature of appeals respecting any judgement, order or decision of any judge of the Court of King's Bench or respecting any judgement or decision of any judge of a court of inferior jurisdiction where an appeal by any Act, all petitions, and all other motions matters or things whatsoever which might have been brought before any divisional court of the high court of justice in England . . . where not specially changed altered or provided for by this or any other Act of Saskatchewan.[16]

Essentially, the court could hear an appeal of anything a trial judge did, except where a statute limited the court's jurisdiction. The section was similar to the enabling statutes of other provincial appellate courts.

Two clauses specifically addressed the court's powers regarding the fact findings of trial judges. Section 8 of the *Act* stated that a party could appeal against the verdict or finding of a trial judge, his view of the evidence, sufficiency of the evidence, or any award of a jury. Section 9 specified that the court was not obligated to adopt the trial judge's view of any evidence but that "the court shall act upon its own view of what the evidence in its judgment proves, and the court may draw inferences of fact and pronounce the verdict, decision or order, which in its judgment the judge who tried the case ought to have pronounced." The two sections incorporated the court's *Coventry v Annable* decision in explicit statutory language and extended the court's power to review fact and evidence in the previous *Judicature Act*. The unusual drafting even caught the attention of the press. The *Leader* noted that "this court will not be bound by the view of the evidence taken by the trial judges."[17] The express ability of the court to review fact findings exceeded that of any other appellate court in Canada.[18]

The two sections had lasting significance. Nearly a century later, the court's interpretation of its powers to review fact findings was at odds with the Supreme Court of Canada's direction to appellate courts on standards of review. It turned into an unequal jurisprudential battle which the Saskatchewan court only reluctantly conceded.[19]

One other clause of *The Court of Appeal Act* was more important than it might seem from a cursory glance. Section 3(3), stated that the sitting chief justice of Saskatchewan would retain that title even if not appointed to be chief justice of the Court of Appeal. After the incumbent's death or retirement, the head of the appeal court would become the chief justice of the province. Federal control over judicial appointments made the clause necessary. The province could not designate which judges might be appointed to which court, and the chief justice of the Supreme Court of Saskatchewan might not necessarily become the head of the appeal court. The clause, similar to ones used in British Columbia, Manitoba, and Ontario, avoided the possibility that the sitting chief justice of the province might be in effect demoted. This was not an academic question. In Alberta, the statute establishing a separate appellate court was not clear on this point, with the result that the sitting chief justice was assigned to the trial court and lost his title as chief justice of Alberta, which went to the head of the new appeal court. The resulting litigation went to the Privy Council, much to everyone's embarrassment.[20] Sir Frederick Haultain was guaranteed to be spared such ignominy.

THE JUDGES OF APPEAL

AS SOON AS it was known that the new courts would be established in March 1918, speculation began as to where the Supreme Court judges would be assigned and who would be appointed from the bar. Some judges were clearly better at appeal or at trial, and they had their own preferences, but there was potential for wounded pride, as the appeal court had greater prestige. Another complication was Ottawa's Union Government, comprised of Conservatives and Liberals, formed to better prosecute the war. This changed the usual patronage dynamic. The easy solution for the four new judges was to have two Conservatives and two Liberals. But partisanship also mattered in the assignments of the sitting judges.

Turgeon had his own ideas. He exchanged correspondence in January with J.A. Calder, formerly a provincial cabinet minister and Scott's right hand, now minister of immigration in the Union cabinet and the

Frederick Haultain, c. 1918. (Provincial Archives of Saskatchewan, R-A3572)

Saskatchewan voice on judicial appointments. Turgeon suggested Hector Y. McDonald and J.F. Frame of Regina as the Liberal choices, with Frame going to the appeal court. Frame had lobbied assiduously for the position, preparing a brief for the attorney general on the desirability of appointments direct from the bar to appellate courts. Turgeon thought this a good idea. As he put it, "Another consideration is the feeling there should be some new blood on the Court of Appeals on account of habits which the present Judges have acquired, through necessity no doubt, but which do not make for efficiency."[21]

More surprising was that Turgeon was leaning towards appointing John Lamont, the strongest appellate judge, as chief justice of the Court of King's Bench. This was not Lamont's choice. In a subsequent discussion with Turgeon, Lamont and Henry Newlands made clear their preference was the Court of Appeal.[22] Newlands was flexible, as long as he was made chief justice of the King's Bench and an ad hoc member of the Court of Appeal, giving him precedence after Haultain. Turgeon thought this was a reasonable request. His final recommendation to Calder for the appeal court was Haultain as chief justice with Lamont, Frame, and a Conservative candidate. Calder consulted further with Arthur Meighen, a Conservative cabinet colleague. His final recommendation to Charles Doherty, the minister of justice, was Haultain, Lamont, and Edward L. Elwood for the Court of Appeal with one new appointment.[23] For the King's Bench, Newlands was to be chief justice with Brown, McKay, and three new appointments completing the bench.

On February 27, 1918, the appointments were finally announced.[24] Haultain, as expected, was chief justice of the Court of Appeal, joined by Lamont, Elwood, and Newlands. Brown was made the chief justice of the Court of King's Bench, joined by McKay and the new appointments, H.Y. McDonald, Henry V. Bigelow, John F.L. Embury, and George E. Taylor. The first three were from the Regina bar, and Taylor, the youngest appointment to date, from Moose Jaw. Frame, the putative candidate for the appeal court, was offered a position on the King's Bench, which, as he had warned Turgeon, he turned down.

THE FIFTH MAN

NEWLANDS STAYED ON the court for only three years. Rumours spread that he was going to be named lieutenant-governor shortly before the official announcement on February 18, 1921.[25] This created a small crisis, as it meant the court was effectively down to two judges. Elwood, ill with cancer, had managed the November sitting but shortly afterward was in hospital and not expected to leave. With the March sittings about to open, the court had no quorum, and a list of sixty-three motions and appeals was waiting. Chief Justice Brown sat ad hoc for the motions, but court was then suspended as he had trials scheduled.[26]

The judges of appeal were as overloaded as ever. In 1920, the court issued over one hundred reported judgments, a number impressive even to modern judges, and the pace did not let up for several years.[27] The situation forced the federal government to make a quick decision.[28] W.F.A. Turgeon joined the Court of Appeal on March 12, 1921. The opportunity was a timely one. Turgeon had spent fourteen years as attorney general and later confessed he had grown weary of politics. He even contemplated leaving Saskatchewan for Montreal, feeling that he needed to be in a major city to progress in private practice.[29] He had previously wanted an appointment to the court but had to wait several years. With Turgeon's appointment, the Court of Appeal had its first Roman Catholic and francophone.

The addition of Turgeon gave the court a quorum for a particularly heavy June sitting, with the new judge doing much of the writing. Elwood had died in May, but the federal government did not move with the same alacrity in naming his replacement, and it was not until the fall sittings that Justice McKay was moved to bring the court back to full strength.

The experience made it clear that a bench of four was not sufficient. Early in 1922, the court met with Premier Martin, who was also holding the portfolio of attorney general in the wake of Turgeon's appointment,[30] and called on him to add another judge to the Court of Appeal.

The long lists facing the court and the danger of being short a man were the main rationales for another position, but a shift in general appellate practice played a part too. Many judges and members of the bar in Canada no longer thought that even-numbered courts, relatively common in the nineteenth century, were still appropriate. Such panels had previously been viewed as more respectful of a trial judge's decision, since an evenly split court meant dismissal of an appeal and it was harder to overturn a decision.[31] But this view was no longer popular. Haultain wrote, "It is also desirable that an Appellate Court should consist of an odd number of Judges. The dismissal of an appeal on account of an equally divided Court is an unsatisfactory disposition of the case from every point of view."[32]

Martin agreed to add a judge. One reason he was amenable was that he planned to be the fifth man. Martin had come to Saskatchewan as a young lawyer in 1903 from Ontario. Elected to Parliament in 1908, he had been in politics for thirteen years, and his star had suddenly dimmed after his last electoral success. Now a potential liability to the provincial Liberals, Martin decided to step down with a judicial post in mind. The same day he received Haultain's official request, Martin wrote to Prime Minister Mackenzie King, a university classmate as well as a parliamentary colleague. His letter left no doubt that Martin expected King to grant him the appointment, although he put it diplomatically: "I write you simply to advise you in advance, so that as other applicants materialize you will know the situation."[33] Martin took the opportunity to hint he would be happy to join the Supreme Court of Canada, given that there had not yet been an appointment from Saskatchewan, but acknowledged that a vacancy was unlikely in the near future. King responded with a veiled assurance: "I thank you for writing me as you have with respect to your intentions and wishes, and when the right moment comes shall be only too happy to see that they are made known in a manner which I hope may prove of service to you."[34]

The appointment did not immediately materialize. Martin hoped to have it in hand before he resigned but by March felt he had to leave soon to make room for his successor. He wrote King again to inform him and, he hoped, speed up the appointment. Martin waited several anxious months after stepping down in April. The necessary amendment to the *Judges Act* had been bundled with other legislation, and the package was stalled in the Senate.[35] On July 21, the appointment was finally announced, ending speculation among the Saskatchewan bar and press as to whether Martin would fill the position he had created.

The appointment was not popular in all quarters. Franklin W. Turnbull, a prominent Regina lawyer, had written a scathing letter in April 1922 to Arthur Meighen, the federal Conservative leader, about the rumoured appointment. Turnbull said that the public in Saskatchewan saw it as blatant patronage and that Martin's qualifications were rather thin. He further maintained that there was "a good deal of objection here to this appointment" among members of the bar and that "there are twenty within the province, or more, of more outstanding ability than Mr. Martin."[36] Turnbull was a prominent Conservative and no friend of Martin, but others did share his opinion. He suggested that J.F. Frame was an outstanding candidate and a Liberal as well, and he questioned whether a fifth judge was necessary. He claimed that the appeal courts had no arrears of judgments and suggested that the additional judge was desired simply to create an odd-numbered court. Meighen replied that he agreed and thought that three judges would probably suffice for the workload in Saskatchewan.[37]

Martin nonetheless was appointed, and he proved his detractors wrong. He was a strong judge. His career on the Court of Appeal spanned thirty-nine years, and from 1941 to 1961 he was chief justice. The former premier, for his part, later said that the court he joined—Haultain, Lamont, Turgeon, and McKay—was the best the province ever had.[38]

John Lamont, who was largely responsible for the Court of Appeal's excellent reputation, left for the Supreme Court of Canada in 1927, the first appointment to the court from Saskatchewan. His replacement was Justice Philip Edward Mackenzie of the Court of King's Bench. Mackenzie was the first appointment to the court from the Saskatoon bar, where he had practised since 1903 and subsequently sat as trial judge after his appointment to the King's Bench in 1921.[39] Like Elwood, he had not held any significant political office. Mackenzie brought to the court a strong background in criminal law from nearly twenty-five years as a Crown prosecutor, shortly after a major change took place in the right of criminal appeal.

The new judges—Turgeon, Martin, and Mackenzie—were very much of the same mould as the earlier appointees to the courts. They were born in Eastern Canada and had had their legal education there, coming

Justice John Henderson Lamont, c. 1935, on the Supreme Court of Canada. (Library and Archives Canada, PA-804781)

west early in their practices. All three had a university education, and Martin and Mackenzie had both earned law degrees, but parchment was not yet ubiquitous: Turgeon learned his law through articles. Turgeon and Martin continued the strong association in Saskatchewan between holding high political office and appointment to the Court of Appeal.

The Regina bar, while the largest in the province, did not dominate appointments to the superior courts, whereas in Alberta the appeal court came entirely from the Edmonton and Calgary bars until the 1990s. Appointments to the Saskatchewan Supreme Court had been calculated to avoid stacking the courts with Regina lawyers, and if anything the city was under-represented.[40] Province-wide representation was a consideration for the new courts. Liberal grandees felt there was a potential problem that three of the new King's Bench judges had come from the capital.[41] Regina lawyers certainly did not dominate the Court of Appeal. Turgeon recounted that he would tell Haultain that the chief justice was not qualified for the court because Haultain didn't come from Prince Albert, where Turgeon , Lamont and McKay had all practised.[42] The Regina and Saskatoon bars contributed the majority of future appeal judges, but appointments were made from Moose Jaw, Prince Albert, and even Moosomin.

THE COURT OF APPEAL AT LAW

THE COURT OF Appeal for Saskatchewan was a new court with a new name, but continuity was its defining quality. The first draft of judges were old hands at appellate work. The judges who joined the court in the first few years—Turgeon, Martin, Mackenzie, and McKay—did not greatly alter the orthodox character of the court and its careful, even narrow, approach to law. But there were also signs of change. Turgeon was a breath of fresh air, and Lamont, his former law partner, demonstrated a new flexibility in his jurisprudence. It was likely not coincidence, as the tide of formalism was starting to recede in the 1920s.[13] The shift was subtle and did not change the basic tenets of jurisprudence in Canadian appellate courts, but there was perhaps more regard for the effect of a law as well as the letter.

During the Court of Appeal's first decade, two statutes produced numerous appeals and tested the court's deference. The first was *The Saskatchewan Temperance Act*, which established Prohibition in the province from 1917 to 1924. The other was *The Farm Implement Act*, first passed in 1915 and extensively revised in 1917, which regulated the sale of agricultural machinery to producers. These two quite different statutes had a major impact on society in Saskatchewan and changed established law and challenged long-held legal principles. The *Temperance Act* was a regulatory statute that mimicked criminal law but without the same enshrined degree of protection for an accused. *The Farm Implement Act* replaced the law of contracts with a statutory regime for the sale and purchase of expensive farm equipment. The court strove to interpret and apply the statutes with the legislative intent in mind, but even a deferential court found the task difficult. The court's judgments interpreting the two statutes were not landmark decisions, but they are illustrative of the interplay between legislature, court, and society.

PRACTICE AND PROCEDURE

THE COURT OF Appeal's practice and procedure was a continuation from the predecessor court. In 1921, the judges undertook a revision of the rules of court, and separate rules were established for the Court of King's Bench and the Court of Appeal respectively. The new appellate rules had only minor amendments from the 1912 rules. The court ended the practice of using a smaller panel on District Court appeals and sat as a full court whenever possible, which was not that often. Three-judge panels remained common, as one judge or another was often absent, either with illness or on commissions. The court continued to have one judge give the judgments for District Court appeals unless there was a dissent, and extended the practice to criminal appeals. This anticipated an amendment to the *Criminal Code* in 1923 that directed courts of appeal to provide *per curiam*—as one opinion—judgments in the absence of a dissent.[44]

The court gave appeals from the King's Bench greater consideration. Judgments were often *seriatim*, with each judge writing an opinion. Martin was especially diligent. Newlands, Elwood, Lamont, and Turgeon frequently wrote concurring judgments, but Haultain and McKay much less so. The multiple judgments were often repetitious, and the court eventually seemed to come to the same conclusion; the number of concurring opinions noticeably dropped over the first decade. Concurring judgments also became better focused, featuring a different emphasis or alternate reasoning and not repeatedly reciting the facts, and simple concurrences were more common. As Haultain wrote in a dissent,

> During the course of the argument I formed the impression, which a subsequent consideration of the evidence has strengthened, that the defendant had established its defense of contributory negligence. As, however, the other members of the Court have come to the opposite conclusion, no useful purpose will be served by anything more than the bare expression of my dissent.

On the subject of dissents, there were remarkably few on Haultain's court. This likely reflected a great deal of collaboration and like-mindedness. The justices frequently exchanged drafts, as they had done for years. There was also some appetite to dig down into appeals. Factums and appeal books were not just for show; counsel would have been gratified to know the judges used the books extensively, reviewing the evidence. On one appeal, Elwood commented that he had looked up other relevant cases counsel had not used.[45] How often the judges did additional research on the law is not known and likely varied from judge to judge.

Strong bonds existed to begin with between the Court of King's Bench and the Court of Appeal. Elwood once had a question about a point in an appeal, so he simply found McKay, now on the King's Bench, and asked him.[46] The trial judges that sat ad hoc fully participated on appeals, often writing in concurrence or in dissent.[47] After a fifth judge was appointed, the court needed ad hoc judges much less, but the King's Bench still helped out from time to time in the 1920s. The reverse was also true: there are reported judgments where the Court of Appeal reviewed a trial or chambers decision of one of their own.

Turgeon was an outstanding judge. He had a deep understanding of an appellate court's role, a subtle grasp of law, and a strong measure of pragmatism and sympathy for litigants. He possessed a fine analytical mind, and his writing mixed economy and exposition. Unlike many contemporaries, Turgeon avoided long recitations of the facts in appeal, often referencing the appeal book, and the lengthy quotes from case law that often cluttered judgments, especially in support of basic and well-known propositions of law. His style anticipated modern appellate writing. He did not stint with his analysis, fully canvassing the issues and the pertinent law. Turgeon's experience in drafting legislation was apparent: he was adroit in discussing legislative background of statutes and had the advantage of being intimately familiar with much of the province's statute law. He did not use his inside knowledge to infer legislative intent, stringently applying the rules of statutory interpretation. He was also skilled at tracing the development of case law. In a mechanic's lien case, he deftly explored the relationship between Canadian and American law with lien legislation in pursuit of good law to apply to the appeal at hand.[48]

Martin was industrious and diligent. As mentioned, he almost always prepared a judgment rather than simply concur. Like Haultain, he was initially a little rusty. His early efforts were derivative, essentially duplicating other judgments and rarely attracting concurrences. But as he settled onto the bench, his decisions became more distinct. Within a few years, Martin wrote important decisions that were the judgment of the court. "Diligent" also describes his style: Martin's decisions could be relied on to give a complete background to an appeal. But his exposition was clear and direct and well-organized. His take on the law was orthodox but intelligent.

Mackenzie was a good appellate judge, conventional in his approach to law but producing strong, pragmatic judgments that reflected his seven years on the trial court. He was in the same mould as Brown, Elwood, and McKay, generally to the point, much like Brown had been on the court *en banc*. He had a reputation for incisiveness as a counsel and was very experienced in criminal law, and may have been chosen for the appeal court because of this background. He was not intimidated by appeal work, putting pen to paper immediately.

WILLIAM FERDINAND ALPHONSE TURGEON

Originally from New Brunswick, W.F.A. Turgeon had a remarkable public career, encompassing law, politics, and the diplomatic service. He was born in 1877, in Bathurst, New Brunswick, but largely grew up in New York City, where the family moved when Turgeon was seven, returning to Canada when he was sixteen.[5] His father, Onésiphore Turgeon, was a journalist who later started his own paper in Bathurst but was better known for politics, serving twenty-two years in the House of Commons and another twenty-two in the Senate. Turgeon's brother was another notable politician, serving in the Alberta legislature, the House of Commons, and then the Senate. At one time, all three were sitting in a legislature.[6]

Justice William Ferdinand Alphonse Turgeon, n.d. (Provincial Archives of Saskatchewan, R-B4041)

Turgeon worked briefly as a reporter before attending Laval University in Quebec, studying classics and taking a bachelor's degree before returning to New Brunswick to study law with articles in Saint John.[7] He qualified for the bars of Quebec and New Brunswick in 1902. He interviewed in Montreal with a friend of his father, Sir Charles Fitzpatrick, later chief justice of Canada, who advised Turgeon to go west. Turgeon started practice in Prince Albert in partnership with John Lamont. Turgeon was the Crown prosecutor for the Saskatchewan judicial district and Prince Albert's city solicitor. After Lamont went to the bench in 1907, Premier Scott asked Turgeon to join his cabinet as attorney general. Turgeon proved an invaluable lieutenant and personally drafted much of the government's legislation until 1912.[8] As a Roman Catholic and francophone, he ensured the loyalty of a significant voting bloc for the Liberals.

Turgeon was interested in the bench as early as 1915, when *The Court of Appeal Act* was first introduced. He was appointed in 1921 to replace Newlands. Turgeon was a popular choice for commissions of inquiry, reputed to have served on more royal commissions than any other individual in Canada by the time he retired. His first royal commission after his judicial appointment examined the grain trade, and he helped draft the *Canada Grain Act*.[9] His commissions looked at subjects as diverse as the textile trade, railway transportation, the Saskatchewan coal industry, and financial problems at the University of Manitoba.

Despite his frequent absences on commissions, Turgeon was a stalwart of the court, and it was no surprise he was chosen as chief justice in 1938. He only served three years before Prime Minister Mackenzie King personally asked him to join the diplomatic service, where many personnel had left positions vacant when they joined the military. Originally destined for Japan, he was sent to South America to counter German influence there. He spent fifteen years as a diplomat, serving as Canada's ambassador to Argentina, Chile, Mexico, Belgium, Ireland, and Portugal.[10]

After leaving the diplomatic service, Turgeon returned to Prince Albert. His last royal commission, from 1957 to 1958, examined Manitoba's workers' compensation program. He died in 1969 at the age of ninety-three. Fluently bilingual, Turgeon was known for his wit and charm.

As the first chief justice of the court, the seasoned Haultain wore the mantle well. He was not the strongest judge on his court—Lamont and Turgeon overshadowed him in jurisprudence—but Haultain had his strengths. He showed a particular interest in estates, matrimonial law, and constitutional law. The chief justice wrote a fine dissenting judgment in *Gutschenritter v Ball*, where the court split in an appeal concerning land titles.[49] Haultain analyzed the historical development of the law around reservations on titles to argue that such reservations had to be clearly stated in contracts for sale, as there were too many exceptions to allow assumptions on the state of titles.

Haultain had other qualities beyond his knowledge of the law. He cut a fine figure as the chief justice and was held in high esteem among members of the bar and in Saskatchewan more widely. The court was pleasant to appear before and was collegial in the broader sense, with the judges enjoying camaraderie and friendship as well as good working relationships. As chancellor of the University of Saskatchewan, the chief justice had a keen interest in the law school, knew the promising students, and kept an eye on them as young lawyers.[50] Emmett Hall recalled that his first appearance as a young lawyer at the Court of Appeal did not go well. The court had given him a good grilling and he lost the appeal. Hall was surprised when Haultain followed him to the robing room and commiserated with him on the lost appeal. As Hall related it, Haultain told him, with a twinkle in his eye, to "be sure and come back and he wouldn't treat me as badly next time."[51]

The Court of Appeal's jurisprudential character remained very much the same as the Saskatchewan Supreme Court *en banc*. It was a conservative and orthodox court, conforming to the dominant formalist approach of the time. Through the 1920s, the court largely reaffirmed these tenets in their decisions: strong deference to legislatures, avoidance of judicial legislating, a narrow approach to issues, and strong adherence to *stare decisis*, including treating the court's previous decisions as binding authority. The court was not rigid or doctrinaire, however, and showed greater flexibility and creativity in its approach to law than did the Supreme Court *en banc*. This may in part reflect the fact that a dedicated appellate court, even if busy, had more time to spend on crafting judgments and considering the development of the law.

Turgeon had significant influence. While generally orthodox, he had a keen eye for where the law was not settled and was not timid about making law.[52] In one appeal, he held that a magistrate's negligence without malice could create grounds for an action, contradicting *Halsbury's Laws of England*.[53] Turgeon noted that the claim that malice had to be shown was not grounded in any authority but seemed simply the opinion of *Halsbury's* editor. On another point in the appeal, Turgeon decided that the authority cited was neither conclusive nor binding and dismissed the argument, being of the opinion that the proposition involved was unreasonable. In another appeal, a resettled soldier tried to repudiate a land purchase on the grounds that it was illegal, violating the terms of the *Soldier Settlement Act* and therefore against public policy.[54] Turgeon noted that the appeal was a novel situation created by a new statute but that the courts were very reluctant to invoke public policy. In the case of the appeal, Turgeon held that the circumstances of the contract did not merit a consideration of larger policy, as the existing laws of contract sufficed to settle the matter.

Turgeon's broader approach may have influenced Lamont. In a 1924 decision, he wrote very critically about a notorious Privy Council decision, *Victorian Railway Commissioners v Coultas*, which held that an accident victim could not claim damages for mental suffering unless the suffering was directly connected to a physical injury.[55] Lamont pointed out that modern medicine and psychology, and especially the experience of war veterans, showed that mental trauma was real and was as debilitating as a physical injury. The jury had found for the plaintiff, who had been knocked down by a streetcar and, while not injured, had seen her daughter run over and killed. The trial judge, in his charge, had told the jury that as the nervous system was physical, a shock to the nerves could be considered physical injury. This was a dubious argument under the *Coultas* precedent, but Lamont upheld the jury verdict on the basis that there was evidence that allowed them to come to their conclusion and he should not interfere.

In another appeal, dealing with dower rights, Lamont made some *obiter* comments that openly flirted with policy. Lamont raised the possibility that a woman, if her husband was open to damages for breach of contract that had occurred because he had not obtained her consent to sell property considered exempt, would feel great compulsion to then give her consent, undermining her free will. "To put this species of compulsion upon a wife seems to me to be entirely inconsistent with the spirit of the Act," he wrote.[56] The point was not essential to decide the appeal at hand, but Lamont raised it anyway. While this did not necessarily mean Lamont thought the point had to be resolved judicially (he may have flagged it for possible legislative action), the commentary was a departure for a judge who had, in earlier decisions, been very clear about avoiding policy and liked to decide appeals on narrow grounds.

Given that *The Court of Appeal Act* created great latitude for the court to review fact findings, the judges were almost perversely rigorous in deferring to trial judges, going beyond mere expressions of judicial piety. The court consistently made it clear that it would not intervene unless a judge was manifestly in error, a position quite close to the restrictive modern standard for appellate review. One of Turgeon's early decisions spelled it out, listing the decisions where the court had stated how fact findings would be approached and the large degree of deference that would be shown to trial judges.[57]

DISCIPLINE

ONE OF THE responsibilities of the Court of Appeal was the discipline of the profession. Under *The Legal Profession Act*, the court was the disciplinary tribunal for the province's lawyers. The benchers of the Law Society investigated and initiated proceedings, but the court decided on sanctions, including disbarment, and also controlled readmission, as had been the case in the North-West Territories. The court provided less formal discipline by admonishing the profession on poor practice.

One major point of irritation was lawyers not following the rules of court, especially providing inadequate factums and appeal books. As Turgeon wrote in one instance,

> I think the Court has some reason to complain of the paucity of the material submitted. . . . We are left to our own surmises on many important matters, and the trial Judge was in the same state. Apparently the parties were content to leave the case in this position, and to ask us to adjudicate upon whatever hypothesis we may deem it right to construct upon the "facts," such as they are.[58]

In an appeal dealing with timber leases, the court was forced to secure information on the leases from the land titles office and the Department of the Interior after counsel failed in their undertaking to provide it.[59] On another occasion, the problem was not incomplete but unusable appeal books. Turgeon made his displeasure very clear:

> Before leaving this case, I wish to say that the solicitors responsible for the typing of the appeal book deserve severe censure, to say the least, for the condition of the book as presented to the members of the Court. The book contains 500 pages, and over four-fifths of it is typed on thin onion-skin paper in such indistinct type that it cannot be read without imposing a severe strain on the eyesight. There is no excuse for such a thing. . . . This offence has been committed on several occasions in recent months. The Registrar has been directed to reject, in future, all appeal books and factums which are not set up on substantial paper, in distinct and easily legible type.[60]

In one instance, Justice Mackenzie issued a reprimand to a lawyer who did not appear to argue in front of the court; the lawyer had sent word that his argument was in his factum and he had nothing further to say. With great forbearance, the court dealt with the appeal, but Mackenzie clarified matters for that counsel and others tempted to do the same: "The practice of this Court requires that appeals be presented orally by counsel engaged therein. Factums are designed to assist counsel in submitting their arguments, but cannot be accepted by the Court in substitution for the oral presentation of an appeal."[61]

The court also had to warn against the practice of counsel appearing as witnesses for their clients in proceedings, stating that it was to be avoided unless absolutely necessary.[62] And when the chief justice discovered that solicitors were charging large fees to estates for advice given to executors, he left no doubt about his view on the practice:

> This is another of those cases in which an outrageous fee under the name of "counsel fee on passing accounts" was allowed to the solicitor. That any fee at all was allowed was due to a prevailing practice which has since been declared wrong, but even then I can find no justification for the amount allowed.[63]

Haultain was outraged that the lawyer's fees came to nearly $1,500 on a simple estate worth $13,000. In another judgment, the court made clear that assistance given to executors should be charged to the executors as clients, not the estate.

It is no surprise that the court had to issue such reprimands. Saskatchewan's profession had grown in leaps and bounds in the boom years, with young and inexperienced lawyers setting up offices in small towns and practising in relative isolation. A few likely came west because they had acquired reputations that made practice back east untenable. Law societies did not provide as much guidance or enforce professional standards to the same degree as they do now. Yet it is also true that the Court of Appeal rarely heard formal disciplinary matters.

The court could be forgiving. In one judgment, it decided an appeal although technically the trial judgment shouldn't have been given. As Turgeon noted,

> It is quite true that the pleadings do not in all strictness lay the foundation for such a judgment, but we have to deal here with a small debt case where expert and accurate pleading should not be too strictly insisted upon, and, as I think the judgment provides a common sense solution for a difficulty which the defendants brought upon themselves by their neglect, I would dismiss their appeal with costs.[64]

Like any appellate bench, the judges of the court sometimes had to give some direction to the profession and were occasionally impatient. The Saskatchewan judges were more inclined to forbearance, as with the timber lease case, where the court obtained the necessary information rather than simply throwing the appeal out. Unlike other appellate courts of the time, where judges could be harsh and arbitrary, Saskatchewan had a gentlemanly bench that reflected the kindly and dignified chief justice.[65]

THE EXPANSION OF CRIMINAL APPEAL

IN 1923, FIVE years after the Court of Appeal was established, the federal government undertook the first major revision of the right of criminal appeal since 1892. It was long overdue. The appeal provisions of the *Criminal Code* had been substantially broader than the equivalent in England under the 1848 *Crown Cases Act*.[66] That changed in 1907. After public outcry in England over several wrongful convictions, the *Criminal Appeals Act* established a court of criminal appeal for England and Wales and replaced the reserved case with a right of appeal of both conviction and sentence. The *Criminal Appeals Act* inspired the 1923 expansion in Canada of the appeal provisions of *Criminal Code*, although it took over fifteen years for the Canadian government to act, and it was not until 1930, after more tinkering, that the right of appeal took the form it would have until 1955.[67]

The 1923 amendment considerably broadened the right of appeal for conviction and sentence. An accused could appeal on any point of law, and with leave, mixed law and fact (essentially how the law was applied to the facts), or any other grounds the Court of Appeal deemed sufficient. The court could also allow an appeal on the grounds that a verdict was unreasonable or not supported by the evidence or that there had been a miscarriage of justice. The reverse was also true: an appeal could be dismissed if the court deemed the error did not sufficiently undermine the verdict. Allowing an appeal, the court could quash the conviction and enter an acquittal or direct a new trial. With leave, a sentence could be appealed unless the term was fixed by law. The court could reduce or increase a sentence or substitute a different sentence as it saw fit, within the limits for the offence set forth in the *Code*.

The 1923 statute also laid out further appeal to the Supreme Court of Canada. The affirmation of a conviction could only be appealed if a judge dissented and only on questions of law. Initially, overturning an acquittal could be appealed on any grounds, but after 1935 only on a point of law. One odd result of the 1923 amendment was that the Crown's right to appeal was inadvertently eliminated.[68] Another amendment in 1930 finally returned appeals on the law to the Crown. There was also a short-lived requirement for a court of appeal to present a judgment *per curiam* unless there was a dissent. Haultain's court already followed this practice, with the chief justice, or the senior judge in his absence, giving the judgment of the court.

Prior to the amendments, the Court of Appeal saw relatively few criminal appeals, perhaps one for every twenty civil appeals, and this did not change immediately after 1923. The only significant jump was for sentence appeals, which had been very rare under the limited provision previously available. Sentence appeals soon became commonplace but were not numerous until the 1960s.

The court made its first significant judgment on sentence in 1924. When an accused, who had been charged with stealing two sets of books, failed to appear in court for his sentencing, the trial judge changed his mind about imposing a suspended sentence and instead gave the accused four years' hard labour. The court allowed the appeal. Justice Martin wrote *R v Finlay*, which established that the court would sharply scrutinize sentence appeals and freely intervene, and which remained the approach for decades.[69] Martin took his cue from English case law, arguing that section 1013 of the *Code*, governing sentence appeals, was very similar to the corresponding section in the 1907 English *Criminal Appeals Act* and that English decisions formed a good grounding. In his view, the English courts preached restraint but freely intervened with sentences. The principle in the case law was quite deferential: an appellate court should only step in if it was clear a sentence was obviously incorrect, decided on a wrong principle, or improperly weighed evidence, and not merely because the court might have given a different sentence. But Martin found that the English courts scrutinized sentence appeals very closely and frequently allowed them. This struck him as a good approach. "The conclusion," he wrote, "to be reached from the English practice is, that the circumstances of each case are very carefully taken into account in every instance, and that any mitigating circumstances or otherwise are given the fullest consideration."[70]

Martin acknowledged the principle that trial judges always had an advantage due to their direct contact with an accused, but he argued that Parliament would not have given Canadian courts the broad ability to review and vary sentences if it had not intended these courts to do so. Implied, though not stated, was the fact that with the liberty of an individual involved, the court should take extra care. In the first two sentence appeals the court heard, sentence was significantly reduced.[71] This liberality was characteristic of the court. *Finlay* established a lasting tradition of appellate intervention in sentencing in Saskatchewan.

The stance the court took on sentencing fit with its approach to criminal justice, which took seriously the jeopardy of an accused and the grave responsibility of deciding their fate. The appeal court treated due-process rights with great respect and carefully scrutinized the exercise of jurisdiction, procedural mistakes, and the admittance of evidence and jury charges in conviction appeals. In a case deciding whether a private prosecutor could be considered an agent of the attorney general, Lamont wrote,

> The Crown does not desire to secure a conviction unless the evidence establishes that the accused has been guilty of the offence charged. The duty of counsel for the Crown is to bring out and place before the Court all the evidence, whether such evidence be in favour of or against the accused. It is because the Crown has no private ends to serve, no private feelings to satisfy, that counsel representing the Crown is in a position to act with the utmost impartiality, and with an eye single to the ends of justice.[72]

Lamont's paean to prosecutorial neutrality suggests that the court saw itself, in the context of the times, as the protector of the rights of an accused. In this light, *The Saskatchewan Temperance Act* presented a challenge. The *Temperance Act* was a regulatory statute that looked like criminal law but was not criminal law and used measures that flew in the face of long-held principles like *mens rea*, meaning a guilty mind, or intent to commit crime. The court was caught between proper deference to the legislature and the desire to see justice done.

THE TEMPERANCE ACT

THE PROHIBITION ERA in Saskatchewan, from 1917 to 1924, was a colourful chapter in the province's history. Canada had long had a liquor problem, at least in the eyes of the temperance movement, Victorian reformers who saw in alcohol the source of many social ills: crime, poverty, and domestic abuse, as well as general moral decay. They were not far wrong. In the Prairies, with a large population of young, single men, public drunkenness was endemic.[73] Despite this, the temperance movement made only slow progress in the West. Until 1891, the North-West Territories was under Prohibition to control the whiskey trade. The policy was deeply unpopular with white territorial residents, widely flouted, and a policing nightmare.[74] The North-West Mounted Police had all but stopped enforcing the law shortly before repeal.

The experience of territorial Prohibition left a mark. Saskatoon may have been founded as a temperance colony, but the movement faced an uphill battle in Saskatchewan. The province had a large population of immigrants from Central and Eastern Europe—generally Catholic, and Liberal voters—who regarded alcohol more positively. There was a strong racist element to calls for Prohibition, with the Anglo-Saxon majority in support and immigrant Catholics and Orthodox worshippers much less so.[75] Although personally favouring the measure, Premier Scott refused to consider Prohibition in 1911.[76] Temperance advocates reorganized, rallying behind the slogan Banish the Bar and seizing on the war effort to promote temperance, equating Prohibition with patriotism. Many advocates of women's rights were also temperance enthusiasts, and the province's suffragists lent their voice to the campaign.

Scott saw how the wind was blowing and closed the bars and taverns in 1915, despite fierce opposition from hotel owners who relied on bar profits to keep their businesses afloat.[77] But the premier did not implement Prohibition. In a canny compromise, the 1915 *Sales of Liquor Act* created a system of government liquor stores in Saskatchewan, but within two years the stores were also closed. The implementation of full Prohibition in Alberta and Manitoba put pressure on Saskatchewan to follow suit. The new premier, W.M. Martin, a devout Presbyterian, agreed to a referendum at the end of 1916, which went in favour of Prohibition. *The Saskatchewan Temperance Act* was proclaimed on March 10, 1917.

The *Temperance Act* was in many respects quite strict, but it was also riddled with loopholes that seriously undermined its effectiveness.[78] The statute banned all sales of liquor within the province, all public consumption of alcohol, and the storage of alcohol in any business or public premises, but people could still possess and consume liquor in their homes. Doctor's prescriptions were another major exception: many physicians still thought alcohol had medicinal properties, so doctors could prescribe it and druggists could fill the prescription. Despite stringent record-keeping requirements, prescriptions were widely abused.[79]

The *Act* could not close breweries, distilleries, or liquor wholesalers as long as the product was for export to other provinces or international destinations, due to the federal power to regulate trade and commerce and license alcohol production. This had the somewhat bizarre consequence that it was perfectly legal to mail-order booze from another province for private consumption in Saskatchewan, and vice versa in other provinces. Export warehouses leaked large quantities of booze to the local bootleggers.[80] The federal government was not very co-operative about ending the trade. There was an export ban from 1918 to 1919 for the war effort, but the ban lapsed in the face of strong opposition from Quebec, where support for Prohibition was low and most of the country's distilling industry was located. The federal government finally brought in a law allowing provinces to end the local export trade after a popular plebiscite, which took effect at the end of 1921.

The export loophole allowed Saskatchewan entrepreneurs to develop a booming trade, most prominently the Bronfman family, hoteliers in Saskatchewan and Manitoba who became liquor exporters and distillers. The trade became more lucrative when the United States enacted Prohibition in 1920. Soon, powerful cars, modified to carry as much booze as possible, prowled the dirt roads of Saskatchewan after dark, picking up their loads legally from the export warehouses before crossing back over the border. Notorious American gangsters such as Dutch Schultz, Diamond Jim Brady, and Al Capone allegedly visited the province to make deals. In contrast to the violence in the United States, only one murder in Saskatchewan was ever linked to the liquor trade, that of Harry Bronfman's brother-in-law.

PHILIP EDWARD MACKENZIE

Born in 1872, Philip Mackenzie received his education in London, Ontario, attending the Collegiate Institute, the city's original high school.[11] He graduated with a bachelor's degree from the University of Toronto in 1893. He earned a law degree from the university in 1895 and after a mandatory year at Osgoode Hall joined the bar in 1896. Mackenzie moved soon after to Kenora, Ontario, near the Manitoba border, and in 1903 was appointed Crown prosecutor for Kenora and district. In 1910, he decided to relocate to Saskatchewan and settled in Saskatoon, going into partnership with George E. McCraney, a former classmate. He was appointed Crown prosecutor for Saskatoon in 1911 and made a King's Counsel in 1913. Mackenzie was president of the Law Society of Saskatchewan in 1916.

In 1921, Mackenzie joined the Court of King's Bench. In a departure for the court, he remained in Saskatoon along with Justice Douglas Maclean despite efforts of Chief Justice Brown to keep the trial court judges centralized in Regina.[12] On Mackenzie's promotion to the Court of Appeal, the Saskatoon *Phoenix* noted that the trial court "loses one of its keenest intellects. In his years at the bar, his lordship was noted for his searching methods of examination that made him one of the provinces' noted prosecuting barristers."[13]

Mackenzie had been a noted rower in his youth and later became an avid golfer, a member of clubs in Saskatoon and Victoria. He also belonged to the Baconian Club of London, Ontario, for legal, educational, and literary gentlemen, and the Royal Colonial Institute (now the Royal Commonwealth Society) in London, England, an educational society that promoted links to the United Kingdom. Mackenzie was a member of the Regina bastion of business and the professions, the Assiniboia Club. Keenly interested in higher education, he was on the board of governors of the University of Saskatchewan from 1920 to 1940 before succeeding Haultain as the university's chancellor. He died suddenly in 1946.

Justice Philip Edward Mackenzie, n.d. (Provincial Archives of Saskatchewan, R-B4536)

With the export law about to change, the Bronfmans wound up their business, going to Montreal and buying the Seagram distillery.

Considering the exceptions that undermined the *Temperance Act*, the statute gave authorities somewhat draconian powers for enforcement.[81] Peace officers and liquor inspectors could, without warrant, search hotels, restaurants, cafés, and other places of business if they believed liquor was present. Private and commercial vehicles could also be searched without warrant. If a person was convicted under the *Act*, the house they lived in was no longer considered a private dwelling house for purposes of the *Act*, meaning no booze could be kept or consumed there, and could be searched without a warrant. Many of the provisions also had a reverse onus: the burden of proof was on the accused. Mere possession of alcohol except as allowed in the *Act* was sufficient proof of violation. The occupant of premises where liquor was found was deemed to be keeping it for sale unless they proved otherwise. Simply possessing equipment or fixtures that could be used to make or serve alcohol meant, in the eyes of the authorities, that an individual was making or serving alcohol.

The reverse onus found throughout the *Act* was contrary to a basic principle of criminal law, where the prosecutor, with some exceptions, has the burden of proof. The *Act* also explicitly and implicitly did not require proof of *mens rea*, or intent, another central principle of criminal law. But the *Temperance Act* was not criminal law, although it greatly resembled it. The *Temperance Act* was a provincial regulatory statute, and so the province did not necessarily have to observe the same niceties that existed in criminal law and create what are known as "strict liability" offences, in which simply committing the act was sufficient proof of guilt. The *Temperance Act* was an early example of a regulatory statute which had extensive enforcement measures—that allowed for arrests, convictions, fines, and jail time—but unlike many such laws, enforcement was a major part of the operation of the *Act*. In the 1970s, there was considerable division of powers jurisprudence as to whether such statutes should be considered criminal law.

With the liberty of subjects at some jeopardy in liquor prosecutions, the form of enforcement did not necessarily sit well with judges, including those on the Court of Appeal. But the prevailing judicial tenets meant that even in outrageous cases the appeal court had little ability to strike down statutes properly passed.

This could be seen in *R v Ping Yuen*.[82] The accused had a grocery store in Moosomin and had bought a stock of "soft drinks"—which included beer with a very low alcohol level—from a wholesaler under the assumption that the drinks were legal. A police constable took a random sample of five bottles for analysis, and it was found that three contained more than the legal amount of 1.13% alcohol, the exact amount varying from bottle to bottle. Ping Yuen was charged and convicted under section 35 of the *Temperance Act*, which specified that vendors of soft drinks found with liquor in their stock were guilty of an infraction, although the magistrate held that the accused had honestly believed the soft drinks were legal. Ping Yuen's initial appeal at the King's Bench was dismissed, and the matter then came before Haultain, Lamont, and Turgeon. The appeal was dismissed again, with Lamont dissenting.

Turgeon, writing for the majority, boiled the appeal down to one question: Was Ping Yuen guilty under the *Temperance Act* when he had no intent, "that usual (but not invariable) element of guilt which is known as *mens rea*"?[83] The rule, as Turgeon defined it, was that *mens rea* applied to all penal statutes, whether provincial or federal, unless the statute explicitly or necessarily excluded its application. Finding that recent Canadian decisions on the subject were confused and not authoritative, Turgeon reached back to an 1846 English decision that dealt with a statute prohibiting adulterated tobacco. The accused had purchased tobacco from a reputable wholesaler and assumed it was legal. When tested, the tobacco proved adulterated, and the tobacconist was convicted despite having no *mens rea*. Under that statute, the simple possession of the tobacco was proof of guilt, and the decision had held that the aim of the statute would be seriously impaired if guilty intent had to be proved.[84]

Turgeon thought the analogy was perfect and that while the result was not fair, it was in the public interest. Haultain agreed that the court's conclusion was regrettable: "This is a case of great hardship, because there is no doubt that the defendant purchased the goods in question in good faith and had no knowledge of a violation of the law."[85] The situation was, in both judges' opinion, a matter for the legislature to correct.

Lamont dissented. He agreed that a legislature had the competence to define an offence such that knowledge or intent was irrelevant. But as *mens rea* was so fundamental, he argued, a statute had to be very specific; otherwise, the court had a duty to analyze the statute's intent, scope, and object, and the nature of the offence and punishment, to decide if *mens rea* was needed. Lamont distinguished the appeal from Turgeon's English case, where the tobacconist could theoretically have tested the tobacco's purity, because the soft drinks would have become unsuitable for sale if tested. Furthermore, the statute put no duty on the vendor to test the drinks. Lamont argued that the vendor was left in an unreasonable position, and under the accepted rules of construction this could not be the intent of the statute. And, he added, the statute actually said something different: "I would have expected the section to make it an offence for a vendor to have soft drinks in his possession containing alcohol in excess of the percentage permitted. That, however, is not the prohibited act. The offence is 'keeping liquor with his soft drinks.'"[86]

Lamont argued that the potentially heavy penalty further militated against ignoring *mens rea*:

> Can it reasonably be supposed that the Legislature intended to impose a fine and imprisonment upon a vendor of soft drinks because the manufacturer from whom he purchased his stock either by accident or design permitted a fraction more alcohol to get into the soft drinks than the law allows, when the vendor was totally ignorant of the fact and had purchased the stock in good faith and when there was no way in which he could ascertain it without destroying his entire stock? It would take much clearer language than I find here to lead me to the conclusion that such was the legislative intention.[87]

In Lamont's estimation, with the liberty of an accused at stake, the intent of a statute had "to be expressed in much clearer language than has been used here."[88] Insisting on very clear statutory language was one strategy that judges, in the age of parliamentary supremacy, used to attack legislation that was unjust.[89] Lamont's dissent, while carefully argued and specific to the appeal at hand, revealed his discomfort with provisions of the *Temperance Act*.

The court decided differently about *mens rea* in another case, argued at the same sitting as *Ping Yuen*. The decision unintentionally helped protect the export liquor trade that was also blamed for providing much of the booze for bootleggers. In *R v Busy Bee Wine and Spirit Importers*, an employee at a mail-order business was found to have sold a bottle to an individual within the province.[90] The manager of the company swore that the employee had not received permission to do so, that he had no idea the employee had done so, and that the company did not receive the money from the sale. The company was found guilty and failed in an attempt to quash the conviction with a writ of *certiorari*. At the Court of Appeal, the question was whether the company, in the person of the manager, had to have *mens rea* for a conviction.

The crucial difference with the *Ping Yuen* case was that *Busy Bee* involved the law of master and servant as well as the *Temperance Act*. Sorting through a morass of decisions, Turgeon found that under a penal statute a master could be liable for an act of their servant without regard to *mens rea*, but the servant had to have acted in the course of their duties. Aside from the testimony of the manager, Turgeon thought it was unreasonable to assume that the employee was selling liquor on the side as part of their duties, as that exposed the employer to the seizure and forfeiture of stock and other severe penalties. This had to be proved, and the onus was on the prosecution. Turgeon seemed to contradict his view on *mens rea* in the *Ping Yuen* appeal, but he distinguished between the two appeals because of the extra dimension involving the employee. The principle, however, seemed identical to Lamont's view in *Ping Yuen*: that it was unreasonable for the employer to be assumed guilty unless the statute explicitly stated they were responsible for the illegal acts of employees.

According to one popular history, the Bronfmans were quick to structure their mail-order and export empire so that they could disavow the actions of any local manager caught selling to bootleggers.[91] And in another appeal shortly after *Busy Bee*, Haultain applied Turgeon's logic in a case where a company had stored a stock of liquor at another company's warehouse, which was seized when the latter firm was convicted of illegally selling liquor. Haultain quashed the conviction of the appellant company and the seizure of its stock. The attorney general, seeing how this decision on the heels of *Busy Bee* was going to make enforcement very difficult, then took the step of applying for leave to appeal to the Privy Council, which the Court of Appeal denied.[92] But this was largely because the legislature had already acted, amending the *Temperance Act* to create a new reverse onus. Employees selling liquor were assumed to be acting as part of their employment unless proved otherwise.

Like Lamont's dissent in *Ping Yuen*, Turgeon's short decision in *Busy Bee* was narrowly focused but had major implications, and revealed disquiet at the circumventing of *mens rea*. And in one final case, *R v Richardson*, Haultain levelled strong criticism at the *Temperance Act*. The chief justice allowed an appeal of the conviction of a drug store owner on the charge of having alcohol for sale on the premises. The store owner claimed it was for personal use, pointing to the small amount as proof of this. As Haultain wrote,

> Counsel for the prosecution contended that the defendant's unsupported testimony should not be held to be sufficient for that purpose. That contention, if well founded, would, in most cases, make it impossible for an accused person to get rid of the statutory presumption, although the possession of liquor, especially in very small quantities, would in many cases, apart from the statute, much more reasonably presume a keeping for private use rather than for sale. No general rule can or should be laid down. Every case must be decided on its own facts. The bare denial by the defendant may not be sufficient in every case, but to say that it is never sufficient would be to have the effect of taking away in very many cases the only means an accused person would have of defending himself when charged with an offence he never committed, and which can only be attributed to him by a statutory presumption. When a man who has committed a minor offence thereby becomes by statutory presumption *prima facie* guilty of a more serious offence, he should not be confronted, in making his defence, with the almost insuperable obstacle contended for by the prosecution in this case.[93]

Given the judicial restraint of the times, the judges of the Court of Appeal were unlikely to denounce the *Temperance Act* overtly as a violation of individual liberty, as anti-Prohibition forces such as Saskatchewan's Moderation League were doing. The Privy Council had ruled that statutes like the *Temperance Act* were not criminal law, which meant judges could not unreservedly apply the accepted norms of that law.[94] There was ample evidence this did not necessarily sit well with the judiciary in Saskatchewan, but their hands were tied.

Ironically, Saskatchewan's court, like others in Canada, stymied provincial attempts to control the export trade that made a mockery of Prohibition. A 1917 decision, *Hudson's Bay Co. v Heffernan*, had struck down as *ultra vires* an attempt by the province to ban liquor export.[95] In a later decision, *Canada Drugs v Saskatchewan*, the government had some success when a split court upheld the restriction of export warehouses to

Regina, Saskatoon, and Moose Jaw, which was designed to make it much easier to police the trade.[96] But the same decision also declared *ultra vires* sections of the statute that restricted the transportation of alcohol to the rail companies as well other licensing and inspection requirements, severely undermining the new law's effectiveness. In both cases, it was clear that the division of powers and federal control over exports impugned the statutes.

The export business in Saskatchewan ended in 1921 with federal legislation that allowed provinces to decide whether to allow such traffic. A referendum the year before had reaffirmed the provincial government's commitment to Prohibition. But public support quickly waned, and enforcement was always difficult, with Saskatchewan's provincial police force, formed in 1917 to replace the North-West Mounted Police, lacking the manpower and resources to tackle the monumental task. In 1924, Premier Charles A. Dunning reinstated a system of government-run liquor stores for Saskatchewan. With that, a difficult law-enforcement problem effectively disappeared. Government liquor inspectors chased after country stills, but the big bootleggers were out of business. Yet for all the faults and short life of the *Temperance Act*, Prohibition was credited with ending the scourge of public drunkenness and changing drinking culture in Saskatchewan for the better. The worldly Haultain, fond of a glass of whiskey and having endured two spells of Prohibition, likely drank a toast with his colleagues.

THE FARM IMPLEMENT ACT

VOTERS CONSIDERED THE *Temperance Act* progressive legislation, intended to tackle a serious social problem and popular at least for a time. The Saskatchewan *Farm Implement Act* was another example of the provincial Liberals' progressive agenda, a statute intended to protect farmers as they made major capital investments to further their livelihood and contributed to the war effort. *The Farm Implement Act* imposed a statutory regime in the place of long-established contract law. While honouring the intent of *The Farm Implement Act*, the court also used the common law to return what the judges saw as a measure of fairness between the parties so as not to unduly favour the purchaser.

The advent of gas- and diesel-powered agricultural machinery—tractors, separators, balers, and combines—started a revolution in farming.

Machinery made large-scale commercial agriculture possible, and wheat production was well suited to mechanized farming. But mechanization was a mixed blessing: machinery was expensive, and the early versions of many implements, some of which used steam power rather than petroleum, were unreliable. There were many complaints in Saskatchewan about the aggressive sales tactics of the implement companies. Turgeon explained clearly the reasons why the government passed a statute to regulate the sale and purchase of farm machinery:

> We know, then, that all matters pertaining to the sale of farm implements, and particularly of "large" farm implements, such as traction engines, grain separators, engine ploughs and engine discs, have been for many years matters of great concern to the people of this province, on account of the paramount importance of the farming industry and of the great importance in the business and home life of the average farmer of any contract whereby he undertook to purchase such an implement. Case after case came before the Courts wherein it was made evident that the provisions of *The Sale of Goods Act* and of the common law were inadequate to establish an equitable basis of contract between the farmer and the vendor, on account of the great difference in education, business training, and legal knowledge which existed between the parties. The result was that a great number of these large gasoline and oil engines, still in their experimental stage, were sold to farmers under contracts which put all the risks involved in the experiment upon the farmer and none upon the vendor. For an example of the conditions which I am now describing, I may refer to the remarks of Idington, J. and of Brodeur, J. of the Supreme Court of Canada. . . . The remarks of Brodeur, J. are practically a suggestion that the Legislature should intervene in this matter as it had done in other cases, as, for instance, in the case of insurance contracts. As a result of the situation known to exist, the Legislature of Saskatchewan adopted the present law in 1915.[97]

Turgeon was writing in *Murdoch v Minneapolis Threshing Machine Co.*, an important judgment of the court in 1921 on *The Farm Implement Act*. Before the *Act*'s passage, the courts saw numerous lawsuits of farmers who had purchased expensive machinery that did not work as expected, usually on terms that were not to their advantage. Claims of misrepresentation were common, for the performance of the machinery, the terms of warranties, and financing. As Turgeon wrote,

> The result was that, in many cases, the farmer was left with an implement on his hands which did not suit his purposes, which he would gladly have returned, but which on account of his contract he had to keep and pay for; his sole remedy, if any, being a doubtful suit for damages. There is no doubt, in my opinion, that the main object of the Act was to remedy this situation by stipulating, in express terms, what conditions should prevail between the parties in regard to this most important purchase.[98]

The Farm Implement Act was short but far-reaching. In Haultain's words, "The statute in question very considerably changes and modifies the general law relating to the sale of goods in many important respects."[99] The legislation required vendors to file annually a list of the implements they sold and the repairs they performed, with prices. The statute created three contracts: one for large implements, such as tractors; one for small implements; and one for used implements. The contracts were standard forms that specified the terms of sale and payment, a trial period during which the purchaser could return the implement as unsatisfactory, the warranties, and the terms for the return of the implement. The statute also required that the purchaser clearly understood the contract and if the purchaser could not read English that it was explained in a language that they understood. Haultain summed up the effect of the *Act*: "In view of all these special provisions, I am of opinion that the effect of the statute with the forms is to exclude the application of the general law in *pari materia*, and to state exclusively the respective rights and liabilities of the purchaser and vendor."[100]

This was the crux of the *Murdoch* appeal. A farmer had purchased a fifteen-horsepower motor intended for ploughing, considered a large implement. The motor had not performed satisfactorily, and after the vendor tried unsuccessfully to repair it, the purchaser returned the motor as per the terms of the statutory contract. When the vendor did not return his money and promissory notes, the purchaser sued and also claimed substantial damages, his losses for being unable to cultivate and put in a crop. The vendor at trial admitted liability under the contract and agreed to return the purchase money including shipping costs. The trial judge then withdrew the other damages from consideration of the jury, holding that *The Farm Implement Act* removed the purchaser's right to pursue these under *The Sale of Goods Act*, another codification of the common law. The plaintiff purchaser appealed. The question was whether *The Farm Implement Act* eliminated the plaintiff's ability to claim damages aside from those specified in the *Act*.

Haultain, Turgeon, and Lamont dismissed the appeal, holding that a purchaser's redress was limited to the statute. As Turgeon wrote, under the common law, the purchaser was entitled to return the motor, demand his money back, and sue for additional damages. *The Farm Implement Act* had replaced these remedies because farmers often did not get adequate compensation with a lawsuit. Turgeon argued, however, that *The Farm Implement Act* was a trade-off. The duties and responsibilities of vendors were clear, and they were relieved of the possibility of facing additional damages. The judges on the panel agreed that the statutory language, by specifying some redresses and not others, implied that only the former applied. As Turgeon put it,

> The provision as a whole is substantially in favour of the purchaser, as it alters very considerably the conditions which existed during the time that freedom of contract prevailed and the contracts entered into were prepared solely by the vendor. And the same may be said of the statute in its entirety. It is reasonable to assume, therefore, that the Legislature, in imposing such a contract upon the vendor, intended at the same time to limit his obligations by express words.[101]

The panel voiced no qualms about the fact that *The Farm Implement Act* had replaced long-established common law and imposed a fairly constrained framework for the sale of an important commodity. The replacement and codification of common law in statute was commonplace by 1921. As Turgeon pointed out, *The Sale of Goods Act*, another codification, would have otherwise applied to an implement sale contract. *The Farm Implement Act* was legislation that the members of the panel likely supported, as former legislators of a province heavily dependent on agriculture. As Turgeon had implied, farmers had long felt that the implement dealers took advantage of them. Haultain and Lamont had seen many lawsuits in the courts as a result, and Turgeon had been deeply involved in writing the law.

Murdoch, however, shows that the court, while approving the general thrust of *The Farm Implement Act*, also saw a need for balance between vendor and consumer. The language of the statute may have inevitably led to the court's conclusion anyway, but several minor decisions made it obvious that the court decided there should be a quid pro quo. In a 1917 trial decision, Lamont had held that when a farmer had continued to use a machine after the statutory return period had expired but the contract was subsequently declared void , the vendor had an equitable right to demand any profits from the use of the machine.[102] Martin, writing in a later appeal, endorsed Lamont's conclusion, and in several other decisions after *Murdoch*, the court allowed compensation to vendors for excessive wear and tear or damage to returned equipment.[103] Superficially, it contradicted *Murdoch*'s conclusion that *The Farm Implement Act* defined the redresses available, but the statute was silent on the exact point. The court invoked equity to prevent vendors from suffering loss when a purchaser had use of machinery for some time but then was able to repudiate the contract.

The court further explored the balance between giving the intent of *The Farm Implement Act* "full expression" and considering the position of the parties in *Advance Rumely Thresher Co. v Yorga*.[104] The appeal dealt primarily with a provision in *The Farm Implement Act* that exemplified the statute's intent. Section 18 required a vendor to verify that the purchaser had read and understood the contract and if the purchaser did not read English ensure that the contract was fully explained to the purchaser in a language they understood. The protection of illiterate and non-English-speaking farmers was a primary goal of the *Act*, but the statute had not specified what happened if section 18 was not fulfilled. This was the main issue in *Yorga*.

The facts of the appeal were simple. The implement company had sued the purchaser, a farmer of Romanian origin, for payment on a tractor. The tractor had been sold as new but was an older model that had been inventory for several years and was substantially discounted. The contract was read to the purchaser in English, with several sections explained in Romanian when the purchaser said he did not understand. The defendant then signed the contract and took delivery. He used the tractor for his threshing, but when pressed for payment he rejected the contract on the grounds the engine was used, not new, and did not perform properly. At trial, the defendant amended his statement of defence to allege that he

Sir Frederick William Gordon Haultain, 1914. (Artist: Inglis Sheldon-Williams; photo: Mark Greschner. Court of Appeal.)

had not understood the contract when it was explained to him in English and only partly in Romanian. The trial judge found for the plaintiff, holding the evidence showed that the defendant regularly carried out business in English and had understood the terms of the contract.

Haultain, Lamont, McKay, and Martin heard the appeal, with Lamont and Martin writing opinions and the other two judges concurring with Martin. There were two grounds of appeal: that the engine was not new as called for in the contract, and that section 18 of the statute had not been fulfilled. Martin quickly disposed of the first ground, agreeing with the trial judge's finding the engine was new. He was quite clear about the appellant's objective: "There is no doubt, in my opinion, but that the defendant knew he was getting an old model, and he must pay for it, unless he can be excused by reason of the second ground of appeal."[105]

Despite his suspicions, Martin held that section 18 had not been fulfilled. The language of the statute, in his opinion, was clear and imperative and required that the contract be read in its entirety to the purchaser in a language he understood if he did not read English. Martin argued that section 18 had to be interpreted in this fashion to give full force to the legislative intent. As Martin put it,

> In the present case a great deal of evidence was given to show that the defendant understood English, the object being to prove that he had been accustomed to transact his business in English, and knew sufficient of the language to understand the

> contract in question: and it was argued that the defendant had a sufficient understanding of the English language to understand the contract, and that, in any event, the parts which he did not understand in English were explained to him in Roumanian [sic], and that, therefore, the section had been complied with.
>
> If this interpretation is to be placed upon the section, then, in every case where the question is raised there will be a contest as to whether or not the defendant is sufficiently conversant with the English language to understand the terms of the contract in question, and, in order to determine this, it would be necessary to relate the evidence to the date of the contract which conceivably might be several years before the trial. I cannot think that it was the intention of the Legislature to leave it to be determined in every case, from evidence adduced, whether or not a defendant who cannot read English is sufficiently conversant with English that he must be held to have understood the contract. Evidence in such a matter would of necessity be of a very unsatisfactory character, and any decision on the subject would always be open to doubt. The test in the section is, "reading" English, not "understanding" it. The object of the legislation was to protect the non-English people in the province, and, in order to carry out such intention on the part of the Legislature, it must be held that, when the purchaser cannot read English, the contract must be read over and explained to him in a language with which he is familiar, and that, of necessity, must be his own language.[106]

Without full compliance with section 18, Martin held the contract was void and directed the appellant return the engine in return for his promissory notes. The respondent had asked, in this eventuality, for the defendant to account for any benefit he received by using the engine. Martin agreed, following the previous decisions of the court. Despite his skepticism over the true motivations of the appellant in invoking section 18, Martin felt it was more important that the section be applied without reservation.

Yorga was further appealed to the Supreme Court of Canada after receiving special leave of the Court of Appeal. The court in Ottawa dismissed the appeal three to two. Chief Justice Francis Anglin, for the majority, held that the Saskatchewan court had correctly interpreted section 18. Justice Edmund Newcombe dissented vigorously, arguing that the trial judge's finding that the farmer understood English should stand, and that section 18 did not specify a penalty for a violation, unlike other sections of the *Act*, implying that the legislature intended no penalty. Underlying Newcombe's dissent was the opinion that in trying to solve one problem—the exploitation of farmers—the statute had created a new problem by allowing farmers to avoid their obligations. The court in Saskatchewan arguably also found some issue with the balance in *The Farm Implement Act*. The court's strong deference to the legislature and penchant for strict reading of statutes was evident, but so was a desire to make certain, as much as was reasonable, that no one had an unfair advantage.

CONCLUSION

THE ESTABLISHMENT OF the Court of Appeal ended the evolution of judicial institutions in Saskatchewan that had begun in the North-West Territories over forty years earlier. Saskatchewan's rapid development as a province had quickly shown the inadequacy of using one court to cover both trials and appeals. A full-time appeal bench was necessary. With the Court of Appeal, Saskatchewan had a fully formed court system that would remain largely unchanged until the 1970s.

The new court, still nearly overwhelmed by the press of business, had an awkward start, but within just a few years an additional judge put it on firm footing. The jurisprudence of the court was orthodox in character, no surprise given the strong continuity between the court *en banc* and the Court of Appeal and the temper of the times. The primary challenge for the Court of Appeal was interpreting and applying politically and socially charged statute law that was not in accord with previous common law. The judges of appeal navigated *The Saskatchewan Temperance Act* and *The Farm Implement Act* adroitly but with reservations. As the court moved into its second decade, no one could imagine the social and economic upheaval to come.

CHAPTER 4

THE COURT OF APPEAL AND THE DEPRESSION

"THE CLASS IN LAW OF 1929 IS GRADUATING AT A TIME when the tide of Canadian business prosperity is at a higher point than it has been since 1913. Indeed in the opinion of our financial nestors, the tide is not yet at flood and we are promised for a reasonable time in the future a continuance of this prosperity." So wrote Arthur Moxon, the dean of law at the University of Saskatchewan, in the 1929 edition of the *Greystone*, the university's yearbook.[1] Black Friday, the stock market crash in the United States that signalled the start of the Great Depression, was just months away, as was the disappointing 1929 harvest in Saskatchewan. Within a year, Dean Moxon's sentiments rang very hollow. But Moxon did not just send the university's newest law graduates into the world with high hopes. He left teaching and went back into practice. It was a decision which, at least in shorter term, he might well have regretted.

A justice of the Saskatchewan Court of Appeal did not need to worry about his livelihood, but the court, too, had to confront the Great Depression. Riots in the streets led to arrests, trials, and appeals. In the struggle to cope with an unprecedented economic crisis, governments turned to unorthodox legislation. Some of it replaced and undermined time-honoured common law, interfering with contract and property rights that were a basis of capitalism. Inevitably, this legislation was tested at the Court of Appeal. Although dismayed at the tragedy unfolding around them, the judges of the court could only respond within the relatively narrow bounds allowed in the jurisprudence of the times.

THE DEPRESSION AND SASKATCHEWAN

IT IS NOT easy to capture in words the dislocation and despair of the Great Depression in the 1930s. One historian dubbed it "ten lost years."[2] Saskatchewan was possibly the worst affected region of Canada.[3] The collapse of international grain prices devastated the economy. Drought blasted large areas of the province's south and in 1937 hit the moister parkland regions, leading to an almost complete crop failure. Saskatchewan endured the punishing dust storms that stalked the central plains of North America along with plagues of grasshoppers. Thousands abandoned their farms and tried to start over on the northern margins of the fertile belt in Saskatchewan and Alberta or moved to the towns and cities to find work. But work was in short supply: unemployment in parts of the province reached 40 percent. Losing much of their farm trade, businesses in the small towns failed. The bigger cities were not much better off. In Regina, the General Motors plant closed.[4] Many who kept their jobs had their hours and wages cut drastically. No account of the Depression would be complete without mentioning a common sight in rural Saskatchewan: Bennett buggies, horse-drawn cars and trucks with their engines removed because their owners couldn't afford to run them, named after Canada's millionaire Conservative prime minister R.B. Bennett, who had the bad luck to win the 1930 election.

In Saskatchewan, a rookie government confronted the immense challenges of the Depression. James Anderson, a former educator who had authored a controversial report on education for the Martin administration in the early 1920s, had become leader of the provincial Conservative Party. In 1929, he managed to bring down the Liberal dynasty with an unwieldy alliance of Conservative and Progressive members of the legislature. Anderson had run a divisive campaign (including an unhealthy connection to the Ku Klux Klan), playing on the fears of the province's Anglo-Saxon, Protestant majority about education, immigration, and the threat of "foreign" elements, but in government he adopted a conciliatory and non-partisan style that made his coalition work.[5]

Anderson tried hard to deal with the mounting problems. The Co-operative government, as it was called, a coalition of the Conservative and Progressive parties, reformed the civil service after decades of Liberal patronage. Anderson established a provincial commission to ensure equitable distribution of relief funds, as welfare was then called, and passed laws to provide debt and tax relief and slow down the sale of land for tax arrears.[6] One of these statutes, *The Debt Adjustment Act*, aimed primarily at massively indebted farmers, created a framework for renegotiation of debts and limited the ability of creditors to turn to the courts. Prime Minister Bennett would later bring in similar legislation, *the Farmers' Creditors Arrangement Act*, to help keep Canadian farmers on their land.[7] Anderson also led the effort to bail out the Prairie wheat pools, and in 1931 his government introduced legislation to form a province-wide compulsory pool. While the statute was withdrawn for constitutional reasons, the law foreshadowed the national compulsory pool that became the Canadian Wheat Board. Anderson's greatest accomplishment was finally convincing Ottawa to transfer control of Saskatchewan's natural resources back to the province.

Anderson's efforts, while salutary, were inadequate to the scale of the Depression. Governments across Canada expected, as with past recessions, that the economy would soon revive. The instinct of most politicians was to tighten belts and cut expenditures, which made the downturn worse. And when the scope of the challenge became clear, there was no money. Government revenues tumbled, credit dried up, and the lack of funds hamstrung municipal and provincial governments. By 1935, Saskatchewan teetered on the edge of bankruptcy. Providing relief and other support was a tremendous financial burden: nearly one in five Saskatchewan households was dependent on social payments.[8] The federal government was forced to step in. Bennett also undertook public works projects to address the widespread unemployment. Less beneficent were the work camps set up for unemployed single men, which seemed calculated simply to get them off the streets. Only in his last year in power did Bennett make a concerted effort to tackle the Depression, imitating President Franklin D. Roosevelt in the United States with a slate of "New Deal" statutes establishing unemployment insurance, old-age pensions, a wheat board, and other measures, most of which the courts declared *ultra vires*.

The end result was parsimonious support for the unemployed and destitute. Saskatoon was notorious for the intrusive and petty administration of relief. Many people suffered in silence, but there was also protest, sometimes violent, against niggardly relief funds, conditions in work camps, or the state of society. Saskatchewan witnessed some of the most violent unrest in Canada, and the response of authorities who saw unrest as the work of communist agitators and a presage of revolution was often heavy-handed. The RCMP shot three striking coal miners in Estevan in 1931. An attempt to transfer "troublemakers" in a Saskatoon work camp to another more remote work camp resulted in a riot and a dead Mountie. These incidents paled in comparison to the Regina Riot of 1935. Protesting work-camp strikers travelling in the On to Ottawa Trek to take their grievances to the capital were stopped in Regina. After several weeks, Regina police and RCMP moved in to arrest the leaders during a peaceful rally, resulting in a pitched battle and two deaths.[9]

Anderson's provincial Conservative-Progressive coalition paid the price for taking power at the beginning of the Depression, just as R.B. Bennett did federally. James Gardiner swept back into power in 1934, and in 1935 Mackenzie King was again installed in Ottawa. Gardiner then went into federal politics and became King's minister of agriculture and Prairie czar. The competent but colourless William Patterson became premier in Gardiner's stead. Patterson pursued a progressive legislative agenda and practised fiscal probity, introducing a sales tax, extending benefits, making concessions to labour, and laying some of the foundations for public health care, while trying his best to balance the budget and maintain the province's credit.[10] Returned to power with a healthy majority in 1938, the provincial Liberals looked once again unassailable. But a new party, first called the Farmer-Labour Party and then the Co-operative Commonwealth Federation (CCF), formed the official opposition in 1935 with five members. In 1938, the CCF doubled its take of seats while openly advocating socialism. A new player had arrived on Saskatchewan's political scene.

The Depression's grip on Canada and Saskatchewan loosened at the end of the 1930s, but it was the Second World War that dug the nation out of its economic malaise. Within two years, as men enlisted and war production started, a labour shortage replaced chronic unemployment. The war arguably gave a demoralized nation a new sense of purpose. Like a miracle, the drought ended in Saskatchewan, and the province soon had bumper crops. In fact, with European markets gone, there was a glut of wheat. Aided by government programs and price supports, farmers turned to other cereal crops, dairy, and livestock to supply Britain and the war effort. The biggest problem for Saskatchewan farmers was soon lack of manpower. With the nation focused on winning the war with Germany and Japan, the nightmare of the Depression faded, but it left an indelible mark on a generation.

HARD TIMES

THE DEPRESSION AFFECTED lawyers in Saskatchewan much as it affected the rest of society: some still prospered, many hung on, sometimes barely, and some succumbed. Well-established members of the bar, representing the banks, mortgage companies, railways, insurance companies, and implement dealers, managed just fine. There were foreclosures, bankruptcies, and seizures to keep some fees coming in the door. Legislation to help mortgaged farmers took away some of this work but also provided fees for lawyers representing creditors and debtors in front of debt adjustment boards. John Diefenbaker, later prime minister of Canada, was primarily a criminal defence lawyer in Prince Albert in the 1930s but still managed to earn a healthy income.[11] A classmate of Diefenbaker's from the University of Saskatchewan, Emmett Hall, later chief justice of Saskatchewan, had a brother who managed an insurance company office and always had a steady stream of insurance claims to pay the rent.[12]

Others were not so lucky. A great deal of legal work disappeared as the economy ground to a halt. One lawyer, later a judge, recalled that people stopped filing for probate or letters of administration due to the court fees.[13] People started to turn to non-professionals for many types of routine legal work. Insurance agencies, justices of the peace, commissioners for oaths, notary publics, and even municipal officials engaged in conveyancing and drew up wills, agreements, and chattel mortgages using standard forms available from stationers and charging much less than lawyers. One Battleford lawyer claimed that amateurs may have performed between 25 and 50 percent of the solicitor work in the depth of the Depression, and he knew at least two people who built up tidy businesses "without ever having attended a law lecture."[14]

The same Battleford lawyer also recalled that two other lawyers in town lost their houses to foreclosure for unpaid taxes.[15] Others remembered lawyers in the province taking relief or eating at soup kitchens. Young lawyers and rural practices were the worst hit. Law students articled for no pay, and it was very difficult to find a position subsequently or open an office. Lawyers in smaller towns, reliant on the farming community for clients, carried accounts or took payment in the form of produce.[16] One lawyer remembered getting a pig, others received chickens, turkeys, or

The Law Society of Saskatchewan's first annual general meeting, Saskatoon, 1936. (Provincial Archives of Saskatchewan, R-D658)

even borscht.[17] In the areas of the province worst affected by drought and grasshoppers, not even this exchange was possible. No one kept statistics, but very likely the Depression was the end of many small-town practices and budding careers in law.

The *Saskatchewan Law Reports* ceased publishing in 1932, a clear indication of the difficulties facing the profession. Saskatchewan cases, particularly decisions of the Court of Appeal, could still be found in the *Western Weekly Reports* and the *Dominion Law Reports*, but it was yet another sign of how the Depression was affecting the practice and the business of law in the province. Mulling over his future in 1938, Thomas Clayton Davis, the provincial attorney general, doubted he could earn a living if he returned to practice.[18]

Not surprisingly, the lists at the Court of Appeal dwindled rapidly in the 1930s. Statistics from the attorney general showed the decline.[19] In 1931, the court heard 110 civil appeals, about the same as in 1929, but by 1936 the load has shrunk by more than half. In 1938, the court heard around forty appeals, the same number on the docket for one sitting a decade or so before. The litigation that reflected Saskatchewan's robust agricultural economy, from thresher's liens to implement purchases to the often complex land dealings, simply vanished. Only criminal appeals showed little change, making up perhaps 20 percent of appeals at the beginning of the 1930s and averaging about twenty-five a year through the decade.[20]

The reduced lists were a relief for the judges, who had been overworked for years, but the court was almost always short-handed in the 1930s. W.M. Martin and James McKay were on a commission in 1931, and Martin subsequently conducted the inquiry into the Regina Riot of 1935 with Chief Justice James Brown of the Court of King's Bench. Martin was later absent for a year when he chaired one of the two boards of review set up under *the Farmers' Creditors Arrangement Act*. W.F.A. Turgeon was once again on a royal commission, this one, in 1936 and 1937, regarding the marketing of grain. Frederick Haultain was on sick leave several times and took a leave of absence for most of 1938. And for almost four years, the court had an empty seat.

BENNETT'S LONE APPOINTMENT

AT THE BEGINNING of December 1931, the court lost Justice McKay. He had been in Toronto for the treatment of an undisclosed illness and had undergone surgery. It was initially deemed successful, but he died a month later. His colleagues were a court of four until 1935.

The economic conditions were largely responsible for the long wait for McKay's replacement. Although it had been over a decade since a Conservative government had been in power federally and had a hand on the lever of patronage, the administration of R.B. Bennett was in no hurry to take advantage of the Saskatchewan vacancy. By 1932, the Depression had fully set in and, with court lists rapidly shrinking, there was not the usual pressure to fill the post, and it saved the federal government another salary.

Bennett also had strong feelings about patronage and the quality of judicial appointments. The prime minister had been a leading barrister and solicitor in Western Canada. His law practice and subsequent business dealings made him rich, but Bennett had also taken great pride in his courtroom ability. A prized possession was a note from Lord Macnaghten complimenting him after a hearing at the Privy Council.[21] Bennett had appeared in courts across Canada, including Saskatchewan, and was not overly impressed with the calibre of judges, for which he blamed patronage. As leader of the opposition and as president of the Canadian Bar Association, Bennett had called for appointments to be made solely on the basis of merit.[22] As prime minister, he stated bluntly in 1932 that "there has been too much political patronage concerned in appointments to the Bench," adding the acid observation that "the test [of] whether a man is entitled to a seat on the Bench has seemed to be whether he has run an election and lost it."[23] Privately, however, he admitted it was almost impossible to keep patronage out of judicial appointments.[24]

This was demonstrated with his only appointment to the Saskatchewan Court of Appeal, Percy Gordon. With the writing on the wall for the Conservatives, Gordon was one of a number of judicial appointments Bennett and his cabinet made shortly before the 1935 election, including five District Court appointments in Saskatchewan rushed through at the last minute.[25]

Gordon was not Bennett's first choice. That honour had gone to Murdoch A. MacPherson. Originally from Nova Scotia, MacPherson was a Dalhousie graduate who had started practising in Swift Current in 1913 and then begun over again in Regina after serving in the First World War. MacPherson was elected to the legislature in 1925, defeating Liberal attorney general James Cross, and became attorney general himself in the Anderson government. MacPherson had gone to Ottawa in 1934 to draft *the Farmers' Creditors Arrangement Act*. Bennett promised him a seat on the Court of Appeal and had the requisite order-in-council drawn up in June 1935.[26]

Bennett's Saskatchewan lieutenant, agriculture minister Robert Weir, of Melfort, strongly objected to MacPherson's appointment and

PERCIVAL HECTOR GORDON

Percy Gordon was the first appointment to the Court of Appeal who can be called a native son of Saskatchewan, born at Qu'Appelle in 1884. His family had emigrated from Scotland the previous year.[1] Gordon did not have the easiest childhood. His father, also a lawyer, died in an influenza epidemic in 1890. When he was fifteen, Gordon suffered a terrible misfortune, losing his right arm when a shotgun was accidentally discharged. Amazingly, he was a trophy-winning athlete in high school and university, competing in tennis, fencing, and track and field. Thanks to a wealthy relative, he attended Trinity College School in Port Hope, Ontario, and then the University of Toronto, where he excelled in classics.

Justice Percival Hector Gordon, n.d. (Provincial Archives of Saskatchewan, R-B7261)

After graduating in 1905, Gordon returned to Saskatchewan, entering articles with his older brother, A.T. Gordon.[2] After three years, he was ready for his bar exams and started practice. A number of other prominent lawyers joined the brothers to establish one of Regina's larger firms. A.T. Gordon retired in 1922 due to heart problems, but by the late 1920s the firm numbered some fifty staff and Percy Gordon was reputed to be earning nearly $30,000 a year.[3] George Curtis, later dean of the University of British Columbia law school, was a prominent firm alumnus. Gordon represented the federal government on the Saskatchewan Relief Commission and acted for the provincial government before the Royal Commission on the Natural Resources of Saskatchewan, known as the Dysart Commission. Despite his position as a leading counsel in Regina, Gordon moved to Toronto in 1934. He returned to Saskatchewan to take his seat on the Court of Appeal.

Gordon was an independent and outspoken judge. His comments from the bench regarding the Labour Relations Board created a major political flap in 1956, and he had a reputation as being hostile to organized labour.[4] He was also known as a difficult judge for counsel in hearings. He was the Martin court's authority on practice.[5]

Gordon was forced to retire in 1961 after the Diefenbaker government amended the *Judges Act* to make retirement mandatory at seventy-five. Typically, he publicly criticized the new policy. He raised eyebrows by returning to practice with Noonan, Embury, Heald, Molisky and Gritzfeld after retirement and even appeared before the Court of Appeal. As counsel, Gordon acted for physicians, challenging the province's health-care act in 1962. Upon retirement from the court, he had said, "There is nothing I'd rather do than work on a lawsuit."[6]

Law was very much Gordon's life, but he was also involved in the Anglican Church and was chancellor for the Diocese of Qu'Appelle. During the war, he was chairman of the Red Cross national executive. He had several hobbies, including gardening, and was a noted breeder of lilies. Widowed before his retirement, Gordon died on April 6, 1975, at the age of ninety-one. He received the Order of Canada in 1968.[7]

put forward Gordon's name.[27] Some contemporaries thought that Gordon, who had been managing director of a Saskatoon paper Bennett owned, called in a favour from the prime minister.[28] Gordon was not even practising in Saskatchewan when he was appointed, having gone to Toronto to try his luck. MacPherson had thought the appointment was his and never knew why Bennett changed his mind.[29] After an unsuccessful bid for the federal Conservative Party leadership, MacPherson returned to practice, establishing the firm now known as MacPherson, Leslie and Tyerman, the largest in the province.

The profession might have regretted Gordon's appointment over MacPherson. Percy Gordon was a leading counsel and very able, but he was one of the more outspoken and impatient judges to sit on the court and was known for his dim view of Tommy Douglas and the CCF. In fact, Gordon had the dubious honour of having Douglas single him out for criticism in remarks to the legislature.

Gordon was a singular character. A year after his appointment, he made headlines for suing the government over unpaid legal fees.[30] He had acted for the province before the commission tasked with fixing compensation for natural resources alienated before the transfer of control in 1930, but when he presented a bill of over $30,000, the province offered $11,000, and the matter headed to court. Gordon later raised eyebrows by returning to practice after his retirement in 1961, which included appearing at the Court of Appeal.

A SUCCESSION OF CHIEF JUSTICES

BENNETT HAD ALSO come into office determined to impose mandatory retirement for federally appointed judges. Elderly judges were a problem. So-called section 96 judges had tenure for life on "good behaviour." The removal of a judge required a hearing in both houses of Parliament, something that had never happened, although several had resigned instead of facing proceedings. Canadian superior court judges received a pension of two-thirds of their salary, but judicial salaries were not very high. A chief justice earned $10,000 annually and a puisne justice $9,000, much less than a prominent counsel could earn, even in the Depression. Whether due to the pension or other factors, few judges chose to retire, staying instead on the bench until they were too ill to function or died in office.

The prime minister certainly had a strong case. In almost every provincial judiciary there were members who suffered physical and mental infirmities yet stubbornly refused to retire. Many stories circulated about deaf judges, senile judges, absent judges, and cantankerous and difficult judges. Ontario was particularly badly served. One Ontario appeal panel was known as "murderer's row," and few counsel appearing before that particular combination of judges escaped unscathed.[31] Appeal courts were in many ways the worst off, as appointees to the trial courts had to be able to withstand the rigours of circuit work. Older and less hardy candidates might go to the appeal court, where the physical demands were much less onerous.

Bennett thought no individual should receive an appointment after the age of sixty and even claimed that this was an unwritten rule.[32] After fruitless consultation with the judiciary, Bennett attempted to unilaterally force retirements with an amendment to the *Judges Act* in 1933. Judges who did not retire at seventy-five would only draw a salary equivalent to their pension. Bennett hoped that, while it was not quite mandatory retirement, this would be an incentive for elderly judges to step down. The stratagem provoked outrage among the judiciary, who questioned the constitutionality of the measure. The amendment was defeated in the Senate, and one historian has suggested that the senators realized Bennett's logic applied equally to them.[33]

Bennett's defeat left the problem of elderly judges unresolved. Emmett Hall had a classic Saskatchewan story.[34] He was at the appeal court with John Diefenbaker, appearing before Haultain, Mackenzie, and McKay. Diefenbaker, acting for the appellant, led off with his address. Chief Justice Haultain soon nodded off, his glasses sliding off his nose. Diefenbaker continued. When Haultain woke up more than an hour later, Diefenbaker had begun his summary, returning to his opening remarks. Haultain exclaimed, "Half past three! Mr. Diefenbaker, have you made no progress at all?"

In the chief justice's defence, the appellate courtroom in the old Regina courthouse (which dated from 1894) had a row of big west-facing windows and in the afternoon was often hot and stuffy. He was not the only judge who nodded off during hearings. The story also shows that time had not dulled Haultain's wit. The chief justice was sensitive about his age, however; one counsel remembered Haultain giving him a severe lecture after he suggested advanced years might affect a testator's competence in making a will.[35] And in the end, Haultain had the grace to retire. The chief justice was too ill to attend hearings for several extended periods in the 1930s, and he wrote almost no judgments in his last years. He took a leave of absence for the first six months of 1938, which may have made up his mind. Turgeon later recalled how he discovered Haultain was stepping down:

> So one day [Haultain] came in to see me. We were working in the same old Court House down in Regina there.
>
> "Well," he said, "you know I'm going to have a birthday now in a few days. . . . The 14th of November is my birthday and I'm doing two things." He had a letter in his hand, a letter that he had written and sealed.
>
> He said, "I'm going to mail this letter now, here at the door. That's my resignation."[36]

Turgeon asked why Haultain was resigning, to which the chief justice replied, "'Well,' he said, 'I'm eighty-one years old.' He went on to tell me then he thought he should resign, and 'the second thing I'm going to do is I'm going to get married.'"

Haultain's first wife had died. His new bride was a widow, Mrs. W.B. Gilmour, and Haultain spent his remaining years with her in Montreal. He publicly announced his resignation at a Regina Bar Association dinner given in his honour on October 27, 1938, but it was already well known he was leaving, and the banquet was really a farewell. In his remarks, Haultain gave some sound advice for any lawyer aspiring to his office: "Each one of you is entitled to believe he is the best man for the job, but remember, the best horse does not always win the race."[37]

Turgeon had almost certainly known that Haultain was resigning long before their courthouse conversation. The Justice Department, and more importantly Jimmy Gardiner, now ensconced in Ottawa as minister of agriculture but considered the de facto premier of Saskatchewan and in charge of patronage, had known of Haultain's intention as early as September 1938, and discussion had begun about his successor.[38] The logical choice was Turgeon. He was the senior judge of the court and considered the strongest jurist in the province. One lawyer told Gardiner that the profession in Saskatchewan considered Turgeon the "greatest judge we have ever had in Western Canada."[39]

The only difficulty with Turgeon's promotion was that Mackenzie King had already sounded him out to join the diplomatic service as Canada's envoy in Paris or Brussels. [40] King thought the cultured and bilingual Turgeon was ideal for the position. Turgeon was very interested, but the appointment was contingent on the retirement of Dr. Philippe Roy, who had long served as Canada's representative in the French capital. While Roy did retire late in 1938, the offer of chief justice came first, and Turgeon elected to accept the promotion.[41] Turgeon seemed destined, however, for the international stage. In 1939, he was Canada's nominee for the International Court of Justice in The Hague, a forerunner to the present court.[42] The war began before the new slate of judges was chosen, and whether Turgeon would have gone to The Hague is speculation, but it was a mark of distinction to be considered.

Turgeon's elevation to chief justice created a vacancy on the court that Mackenzie King filled on June 30, 1939, with Thomas Clayton Davis, of Prince Albert, the province's attorney general. It had been assumed for

Justice W.F.A. Turgeon with his father, Senator Onésiphore Turgeon, and brother, J.G. Turgeon, March 9, 1936. (Library and Archives Canada, E11045833-SI)

some time in Saskatchewan political and legal circles that T.C. "Tommy" Davis was the most likely candidate. The attorney general had asked that the appointment be delayed at the behest of Premier Patterson, who wanted Davis to stay in government for one more legislative session.[43] Davis's family was Prince Albert royalty. His father, Thomas Osborne Davis, had been a pioneer businessman, an MP, and a senator. Tommy Davis was born in Prince Albert, making him the second Saskatchewan-born appointment to the Court of Appeal. He followed his father's footsteps and entered politics at a young age, first at the municipal level in Prince Albert and then as the legislative member for the district. Davis had served as attorney general in the Dunning, Gardiner, and Patterson administrations and was close friends with Jimmy Gardiner.

Davis had made it very clear that he expected an appointment to the bench. He had considered vying for the leadership of the Liberal Party in 1938 but stepped aside for Patterson. He remained in cabinet but thought he had reached the peak of his political career. Writing to Gardiner in 1938, Davis laid out his case for a move to the bench.[44] His doctor had told him he was developing a heart problem from overwork. "It is therefore necessary," he wrote, "that I get into something where I have more leisure and not so much intense work and such long hours." Years in politics had also exacted a financial cost, leaving him, he said, without enough to live on. Returning to the practice of law was not much of prospect, he told Gardiner: "The legal profession in this province as you know is in a serious condition." He had relinquished his Prince Albert practice to his brother, Clifford Sifton Davis, and felt that the business could not support them both. To Davis, the best prospect for his future was the bench, an appointment he believed was his due. "I feel that I have earned something from the party and I would like to get it when the party is in a position to give it to me."

Davis's letter makes clear two things. The first is that an extended political career carried a high cost for lawyers, preventing them from building a practice. The second is that the judiciary was regarded as a reward for political service and as a refuge from the difficulties of practice, almost to the extent of being semi-retirement. In the case of Davis, the appointment could be defended on merit. Turgeon thought Davis would be a fine appellate judge, an opinion shared by M.A. MacPherson, who sat on the other side of the legislature. But the primacy of patronage and the role of considerations aside from ability were clear.

The opposition in the legislature exploited the Davis appointment for its own ends. A CCF member, Tom Johnson, introduced an amendment to *The Court of Appeal Act* to eliminate a position on the court. He argued that the court was no longer busy enough to require a fifth judge, illustrated by the fact that judges were serving on commissions or on *the Farmers' Creditors Arrangement Act* (FCAA) boards. Davis had been expecting the move and had little doubt it was being done chiefly to embarrass him in revenge for his attacks on the CCF in the recent election.[45] He waxed indignant at the idea of reducing the court for simple economic expediency.

The opposition Conservatives declined to support the CCF motion and the amendment died on the order paper.

With more than a little irony, Davis had the dubious distinction of never sitting on an appeal.[46] He was appointed during the court's summer break in 1939. War broke out a week before the fall sittings were scheduled to begin, and the day court was to open Martin was summoned to Ottawa to take up the office of custodian of enemy property. Effective immediately, Davis replaced Martin on the FCAA review board. In 1940, Davis in turn went to Ottawa to become the deputy minister of the Department of War Services. When his stint as deputy minister ended in 1942, he intended to return to Saskatchewan but was sent instead to Australia as the high commissioner for Canada. In 1945, he was again intending to take his seat on the appellate court when Mackenzie King asked him to go to China. He remained an absentee judge until 1948, when he finally resigned after settling a dispute over his pension. And bizarrely, he was not the only Saskatchewan appellate judge to serve in the diplomatic corps.

MARTIN BECOMES CHIEF

THE REDOUBTABLE TURGEON was not chief justice of Saskatchewan for long. In 1941, he was in Prince Albert to attend a function for Mackenzie King. The prime minister summoned the chief justice to his private railway carriage and asked him to become ambassador to Japan, where Canada needed a reliable diplomat. Turgeon gladly acceded to King's request. Japan declared war before Turgeon could get there, but he was subsequently dispatched to South America.

Turgeon had no choice but to remain with the diplomatic service; he had resigned his judicial post. The position of chief justice devolved almost automatically on Martin. The former premier had long ago silenced any doubts about his ability and was a very capable judge, second only to Turgeon. Chief Justice of Saskatchewan was not Martin's first choice for further advancement; he had hoped to go the Supreme Court of Canada. Martin had angled for a position after John Lamont died in 1936 and Saskatchewan was no longer represented on the court. An appointment did not materialize before Turgeon's resignation, and Martin did not hesitate to take the offer of chief justice. In a later letter to King, Martin admitted that after spending two years in Ottawa on war duties, he was glad he had

THOMAS CLAYTON DAVIS

T.C. "Tommy" Davis was the scion of Prince Albert's most prominent political family. The Davis clan were Irish Protestants who immigrated to Quebec in the 1840s. Tommy's grandfather had taught at Trinity College, Dublin, but was an alcoholic and reduced the family to penury. Thomas Osborne Davis, Tommy's father, received little education and left home as a teenager to become a vaudeville singer in the United States.[8] He returned to Canada and joined a surveying party bound for the North-West Territories in 1879. This brought him to the Prince Albert area, where he opened a general store with his brother around 1880. T.O. Davis prospered as a freighter and later branched out into other businesses, including real estate. He became a prominent Liberal, elected as MP for Prince Albert in 1896. T.O. Davis was later appointed to the Senate.

Justice Thomas Clayton Davis, c. 1934. (Provincial Archives of Saskatchewan, R-B8266)

Thomas Clayton Davis was born in Prince Albert in 1889. He went to St. JoÚ's College in Winnipeg (now part of the University of Manitoba) for his initial university education. Senator Davis pressed his son to take law and in 1909 Tommy Davis dutifully entered Osgoode Hall. After graduating in 1913, Davis returned to Prince Albert and entered practice with Frank Halliday. He also went into politics. As Davis told it, he encountered the president of the local board of trade, who took him by the arm, introduced him to several cronies as an ideal candidate for alderman, and whisked him to City Hall to file the nomination papers.[9] Elected as alderman in 1916 at twenty-seven, Davis became mayor in 1921.

Davis entered provincial politics in the 1925 election and the following year was made minister of the new portfolio of municipal affairs as well as provincial treasurer. In 1927, Premier Jimmy Gardiner made him attorney general, a position he held in subsequent Liberal administrations. He survived the defeat of the Liberal government in 1929 and practised law while sitting in opposition. A tall, handsome man, Davis was a skilled debater with a sharp wit and could be a fiery opponent. Davis and John Diefenbaker, who had emerged as a political rival in Prince Albert, heartily detested each other. When Diefenbaker took the reins of the provincial Conservative Party, Davis wrote a letter to his friend Jimmy Gardiner that described the new leader in most uncomplimentary terms. Davis got on well with other Conservatives, such as M.A. MacPherson, who supported his appointment to the bench.

Much like Lamont and Turgeon before him, Davis had an excellent reputation as attorney general. Two highlights of his political career were attending George VI's coronation in 1937 as Saskatchewan's representative and presenting the province's submission to the Rowell-Sirois Commission, which laid the foundation for equalization payments between the federal and provincial governments. Davis unsuccessfully ran against William Patterson for the leadership of the provincial Liberals in 1935 and continued to serve as attorney general under his rival. After his FCAA and war services work, Davis subsequently had a fascinating career in the diplomatic service. Following his assignment as high commissioner in Australia, he served successively as ambassador to China, Germany, and Japan. Davis retired in 1957 to Victoria, BC, where he died three years later at seventy.

not been given a berth on the Supreme Court. "I fear I am something of a confirmed Westerner," he wrote.[47]

With both Gordon and Davis seconded to war-related duties, keeping quorum required an immediate appointment. Turgeon and Martin strongly recommended Hector Y. MacDonald of the Court of King's Bench. MacDonald was a 1918 appointment and one of the most respected trial judges in the province. Martin claimed that the profession would certainly approve of the promotion and would likely be hostile towards anyone of lesser experience.[48] MacDonald had sat a number of times ad hoc and had written more than a few judgments on appeals.

Justice William Melville Martin, n.d. (courtesy Martin family)

The fact that MacDonald was Catholic sealed the decision. It was an unofficial but well-understood policy that there should be a least one Catholic seat on the provincial superior courts. This was doubly true in Saskatchewan, where language added another dimension. Gardiner claimed that Haultain and Turgeon, while still attorney general, had agreed that there should be one Catholic on the appeal court and one on the King's Bench.[49] More problematic was whether there should be French-speaking judges. In Saskatchewan, francophones were still a vocal minority with political influence and some recognition as having special constitutional status. A French-speaking District Court judge, Thomas Gallant, was appointed in part to appease francophones, and Turgeon's ascension to the appellate court had greatly pleased the community.

As soon as it was known that Turgeon was stepping down, francophones agitated for another bilingual appointment.[50] Gardiner listened: he initially suggested that Adrian Dorion, of Humboldt, a respected barrister, be named to the Court of Appeal rather than MacDonald. He bowed to Martin and Turgeon's wishes, but Dorion was named to the King's Bench, a move that pleased francophones and the profession praised. Dorion was later considered as a possible candidate to be chief justice of the trial court. Appointing French-speaking judges as a matter of policy opened a

Pandora's box, inviting demands from other significant linguistic minorities such as Germans and Ukrainians, and in fact Gardiner engineered several District Court appointments to keep these important Liberal supporters happy.[51]

Martin, Mackenzie, and MacDonald were essentially the Court of Appeal for the rest of the war. Gordon sat occasionally and did write judgments but was usually busy with Red Cross work. Davis was entirely absent. Ironically, given how often the court struggled with its workload while short-handed, the three judges were up to the task. The court lists remained short through the war, even shorter than in the darkest years of the Depression. In 1942, the court only issued twenty-nine reported decisions; in 1944, thirty-four. With millions in uniform, including many lawyers, and so much economic activity directed towards the war effort, there simply wasn't much legal business. Across Canada, judges were seconded to war work in part because they were available. The nation had other priorities.

THE COURT AT LAW IN THE DEPRESSION

GOVERNMENTS PASSED ALL manner of legislation to address the Depression and its consequences. Some of these laws, such as debt relief legislation and other public welfare statutes, drastically interfered with long-established commercial relationships—the "sanctity of contract" as some put it. Other statutes stepped over the boundaries of the division of powers as the provincial and federal governments both tried to deal with the Depression, the provinces locally, Ottawa for the nation. The radical Social Credit government of Alberta saw a raft of its legislation sent to the Supreme Court of Canada where it was overturned as *ultra vires*. Bennett's own "New Deal" package of statutes, passed in the twilight of his tenure, was in turn disallowed on reference to the Supreme Court and the Privy Council.

The courts in Canada thus played a consequential role in efforts to deal with the Depression, and Saskatchewan was no different. The court ruled on legislation to create a province-wide wheat pool, considered whether Saskatchewan's debt reduction statute was constitutional, and pondered the operation of similar federal legislation. Within the strictures of statutory interpretation of the time, the judges tried to give effect to this legislation as best they could, understanding the need but limited in what they could do. But when dealing with violent protest, the court was the stern upholder of order.

PRACTICE AND PROCEDURE

THE DEPRESSION IN Saskatchewan was a time of shrinking lists and absent judges, but there was little change to the court's procedures and practice, and it was business as usual through the 1930s. The court sat as full court, although in practice this was often the minimum of three for quorum, and with the reduced number of appeals, sittings in some years were cut back to just three. It was well-established practice that the court usually issued just one opinion for District Court appeals and criminal appeals in the absence of a dissent.

Notwithstanding the much slower pace in the courtrooms, a revision of the rules of court was begun in 1939 and finished in 1941. It had been twenty years since the last overhaul, and the trial court rules had accreted many amendments. Some housekeeping was in order. Davis, still attorney general when the revision began, also wanted to reduce the cost of litigation, especially for the appeal court.[52] He hoped the revisions would accomplish this goal. A committee was struck—comprising Gordon; Justice Percy M. Anderson of the King's Bench; District Court judge Alex Ross; Arthur Moxon, former dean of law at the university; and F.L. Bastedo and Frank Mulcaster—to revise the rules for the Court of Appeal and the Court of King's Bench.

Fees were indeed cut, but otherwise the revisions to the appeal rules were not very consequential. The time limits for appeals of motions, applications, and so forth were expanded, and the requirements for appeal books and factums received minor changes. One new rule allowed the appellate judges to inspect a location or property if that property had been viewed by the trial judge or a jury. This clearly supported the court's powers to review fact and evidence. The one important substantive addition was rules for sentence appeals. The *Criminal Code* only specified somewhat bare-bones procedures, and the rules promulgated for Saskatchewan provided more detailed instructions for sentence appeals.

THE ADDITION OF Gordon and MacDonald, and the loss of McKay and Haultain, did not change the basic character of the court. It remained deferential and restrained, rigorous in statutory interpretation and in applying precedent, quite in character with other Canadian appellate courts of the time. The court's veterans, Haultain, Turgeon, and Martin, did not demonstrate any noteworthy shifts in their perspectives. Overall, the judges wrote a little less, with fewer concurring opinions. Haultain, often absent in the 1930s, wrote less and less as he approached retirement. Mackenzie was clearly considered the court's criminal expert and frequently gave the opinion of the court in criminal appeals.

Gordon was an outspoken and opinionated judge who didn't suffer fools and did not hesitate to interrupt counsel, often peremptorily. Emmett Hall, one of the leading counsel of the time, thought him rude and disrespectful. Although Gordon didn't often formally dissent, following a tradition of the court, he was independent and frequently had a different view on a point of law. Not surprisingly, he wrote often, which was often true of new judges on the appeal court. His early judgments were not models of brevity. Gordon was thorough, even exhaustive, in parsing the factual background as well as the statute or case law involved in an appeal, but he was a clear, organized writer. One affectation in his early judgments was a courtly deference to his colleagues, particularly "My Lord the Chief Justice," even when he disagreed with them.

One of these occasions was his dissent in a 1936 appeal, *Hackworth v Baker*.[53] The question had been whether a transfer of land was fraudulent when the defendant knew there was an unregistered interest in the property. Gordon thought it was a form of passive fraud. He later recounted that he believed he was in the majority with Martin and Haultain up until the judgments were read in court, at which point Martin read a different opinion than the one Gordon had earlier seen. Martin had changed his mind after reading Turgeon's judgment but had never informed Gordon, who kept his copy of Martin's original judgment for posterity.[54]

Gordon quickly became the court's authority on practice and procedure and later wrote a paper on appellate practice in Saskatchewan that was the guide for several generations of lawyers. An early judgment demonstrated his proclivities. *Saskatchewan Farm Loan Board v Tomlin* dealt with the Saskatchewan courts' long-standing practice of appointing an administrator

William Ferdinand Alphonse Turgeon, 2016. (Artist: Iris Hauser; photo: Mark Greschner. Court of Appeal.)

ad litem—a temporary administrator to deal with litigation involving estates without executors—for a foreclosure action.[55] Conforming to a trend in other provincial courts, Justice Taylor of the King's Bench had questioned whether he had the jurisdiction to continue the practice. Following Taylor's lead, the local master had refused to appoint an administrator and was upheld at the King's Bench. Gordon allowed the further appeal. He thoroughly canvassed the practice from the territorial period onwards, before concluding that "I do not think that after a practice has been established and followed for so long a period it should be abruptly terminated without a change in the Rule or in the statute."[56] Given the hundreds of orders that had been made the previous way, Gordon pointed out that changing now "would cause serious legal repercussions."

MacDonald had sat a number of times as an ad hoc judge on the Court of Appeal. He had shown no hesitation in participating on appeals, even dissenting in one of his first sittings. Whether years as a trial judge had honed his skills or it was just his nature, MacDonald tended towards brevity and a plain-spoken, common-sense style, although he was not quite as to the point as Mackenzie. MacDonald knew his law, and his decisions surveyed the authorities extensively. He was competent and conventional. Given his reputation as trial judge for interrupting and arguing with counsel, MacDonald was probably vocal in appeal proceedings, but Gordon likely stole much of his thunder.

Saskatchewan's court may have been quite orthodox, but it was never doctrinaire or inflexible. In a 1934 workmen's compensation appeal, *Wolfe v Canadian National Railways*, Turgeon declined to follow a previous decision from 1918.[57] But he hastened to say that the judgment in question was an anomaly which did not conform to the decisions of the court before and after on the same point. Discarding a previous decision was bold, especially given the court's rigorous adherence to *stare decisis*. Turgeon's decision was not licence to challenge the court's previous decisions except in exceptional circumstances, but it showed a certain flexibility and realism.

THE REGINA RIOT

COURTS ONLY DEAL with matters brought before them. In this sense, the Saskatchewan Court of Appeal was in many ways remote from the realities of the Depression. A perusal of the reported judgments shows a mix of appeals: the usual torts, frequently dealing with automobile accidents; divorce and support matters; more appeals involving wills and estates as the population aged; a smattering of litigation involving real property and contracts; and criminal appeals, mostly of sentences. The Depression could be seen mostly in the *absence* of appeals, such as the litigation involving farming that used to swamp the court lists. Relatively few appeals resulted from seizures and foreclosures. With people walking away from their farms and businesses, sometimes leaving the province entirely, and with legislation effectively limiting litigation on debt, this is actually not that surprising. And though times were desperate, there was little increase in crime. The court did consider appeals in several cases involving relief fraud, one of which involved a large-scale fraud perpetuated by a storekeeper and relief official.[58]

The Depression was, however, marked by protests, strikes, and other unrest. One of the most famous incidents of civil unrest in Canada occurred in Saskatchewan during the Depression: the Regina Riot of 1935. There were hundreds of arrests, scores of charges, several dozen trials, and eventually a few appeals. These amply demonstrated that the Court of Appeal acted primarily as the upholder of order in the face of civil disobedience.

The story of the Regina Riot has been well told.[59] Hundreds of men in work camps through the BC interior went on strike and descended on Vancouver. Once there, the strikers decided to take their grievances to Prime Minister R.B. Bennett in Ottawa. The On to Ottawa Trek, as it became known, numbering over a thousand men, began to travel east from Vancouver on freight trains, but much to the indignation of Premier Gardiner, a force of Mounties stopped the protesters in Regina. A deputation of strikers, led by Arthur "Slim" Evans, continued to the capital for a meeting with the prime minister that ended with a shouting match between Bennett and Evans. The deputation returned to Regina, and a tense impasse took hold. The police thwarted the strikers' attempts either to continue the trek or return to Vancouver, and the strikers refused to leave Regina to be processed at a work camp in Lumsden. On July 1, a force of RCMP and Regina Police descended on a public rally of strikers to arrest the leaders, resulting in a pitched battle in the streets of downtown Regina, with two deaths, scores of injuries, and thousands of dollars' worth of damage.

There were also many arrests and subsequent charges. The trials of the accused, delayed three times, finally took place in April 1936, by which point charges had been dropped against many rioters, including charges against Arthur Evans and other trek leaders of being members of an unlawful association. Thirty-three were eventually tried for assault and rioting. Peter Makaroff, a lawyer of Doukhobor heritage, along with rising legal talent Emmett Hall, of Saskatoon, defended the strikers. The depth of feeling against the strikers was such that the Regina legal establishment roundly snubbed the two lawyers during the trials.[60] Hall later remembered the tense and hostile atmosphere as he and Makaroff contested each trial. Justice MacDonald presided, and sparks flew between the outspoken judge and Makaroff as the lawyer hammered away at police complicity in the violence. At one point, MacDonald threatened Makaroff with contempt of court. Most of Makaroff and Hall's clients were convicted.

Meanwhile, Premier Gardiner had ordered a commission of inquiry into how the police had handled the riot. The government appointed Justice Martin of the Court of Appeal, Chief Justice Brown of the Court of King's Bench, and Judge A.E. Doak of the District Court to investigate the circumstances of the riot. The inquiry was thorough, with Doak travelling to Vancouver and Calgary to take evidence on the march's origins and progress to Regina. The commissioners heard from hundreds of witnesses, including Arthur Evans and many strikers as well as ordinary citizens who had been caught up in the events. Evans prodded and provoked the commissioners and did not help the cause much by proudly proclaiming himself a communist at the onset.[61]

The 331-page report of the Regina Riot Inquiry Commission was released four days after the last trial. It amounted to a whitewash of the police. The commissioners had accepted with little skepticism the testimony of the police and government officials and discounted testimony regarding incidents of police brutality, only lightly reprimanding the mounted police for their timing in arresting the trek leadership.[62] The commissioners also accepted the police claim that the protest leaders were essentially communist agitators looking to cause trouble.

Although the commission's report must have given him pause, Makaroff appealed the assault convictions and sentences of eight of the trekkers. Hearings began on June 15, 1936, in front of Haultain, Gordon, and Justice Henry Bigelow of the Court of King's Bench, sitting ad hoc, and lasted two days. The hearings did not go well for the accused. The court dismissed the first three conviction appeals, and Makaroff abandoned the rest and concentrated on sentences. He was only able to obtain a small reduction for one striker. Haultain was tetchy with Makaroff throughout, exclaiming at one point, "Are you going through all this evidence with a microscope?"[63] The chief justice called some of Makaroff's arguments an "absolute absurdity" and bemoaned the pointless expense of the appeals. Haultain's irritation may have been due in part to the fact that Makaroff's argument challenged the trial judge's fact findings, which was an uphill battle at best and not something that would endear him to the appeal judges.[64] He got no sympathy from the other panel members. Bigelow considered the accused lucky that riot charges had been withdrawn at trial and they were convicted only of assault. Gordon pronounced, perhaps sarcastically, "These men were given a wonderful trial, a wonderful defense."

Haultain did show some understanding of the strikers' plight. After giving the judgment of the court on the last five sentence appeals, he said, "We have every sympathy for the men and the conditions they find themselves in."[65] In his opinion, the strikers had allowed themselves to be misled by agitators. But he left no doubt where the court stood. After stating that the accused had been leniently treated, he concluded, "Men will get nothing in this country by force and violence."[66]

The Regina Riot commissioners. *From left:* Justice W.M. Martin, Chief Justice J.T. Brown, Judge A.E. Doak, c. 1935. (Provincial Archives of Saskatchewan, R-B2800)

Haultain's sentiments and the conduct of the appeals made it clear that the Court of Appeal was not inclined to leniency towards civil unrest. This was the attitude of Canadian courts generally, which saw themselves as bulwarks of order during the Depression.[67]

The Regina Riot was not the only time the Depression came into the courtroom in Saskatchewan. The Court of Appeal dealt with several pieces of legislation aimed at addressing the desperate circumstances of the province's farmers: *The Grain Marketing Act*, *The Debt Adjustment Act*, and *the Farmers' Creditors Arrangement Act* of 1934.

GRAIN MARKETING ACT, IN RE

IN 1931, THE Anderson government tried to address the precipitous plunge in grain prices with legislation to create a compulsory marketing pool for all grain grown by Saskatchewan farmers that would replace the voluntary, farmer-run, Saskatchewan Wheat Pool. The idea of a monopoly marketing agency had been around for some time. The only things most farmers disliked more than the railroads were the elevator companies and the grain dealers. Farmers blamed the dealers for fluctuating prices and greatly resented their lack of bargaining power and the extra costs of dealing with a middle man. Saskatchewan farmers had founded their own co-operative marketing organizations, but farm activists also lobbied for years for either the provincial or federal government to create a single grain marketing agency.[68] Lobbyists argued that, aside from having greater clout, such an organization would eliminate speculation, reduce costs for producers, and guarantee them a price for their crop, especially if the government provided backing. The federal government had done so as a wartime measure and extended the monopoly through 1919, but it then expired. Grain prices had immediately plummeted, and while this had little to do with the end of the pool, the timing fed rural resentment in Saskatchewan.

The new *Grain Marketing Act* created a corporation called the Saskatchewan Grain Co-operative comprising all grain producers in the province, with a board of directors elected from the membership.[69] The new co-operative was to take over the Saskatchewan Wheat Pool and its assets, such as its large elevator network. The statute made it compulsory for grain producers to join the new co-operative and to sell it all their produce except what might be kept for seeding or personal consumption. The co-operative undertook to store, transport, and sell the grain on behalf of its members and pay out the proceeds to them. The statute established stiff fines for producers who sold their grain independently and draconian powers of inspection, including the requirement that elevator companies, warehouses, and the railroads and other carriers produce documentation that showed all grain purchases and shipments. *The Grain Marketing Act* essentially made belonging to and selling to the co-operative mandatory for all Saskatchewan grain producers with the purpose of obtaining wider markets for the province's grain.

It did not take a legal genius to see that the legislation might trespass on the federal government's control of trade and commerce set out in section 91(2) of the *British North America Act* (BNA *Act*) and the provisions of the federal *Canada Grain Act*, which comprehensively regulated the grain trade based on that power. The Anderson government accordingly sent the legislation to the Court of Appeal on a reference, asking the court to rule on whether the statute was legal and within the legislature's competence. Saskatchewan, like other provinces, had legislation allowing the government to make such references; the federal government could likewise send a reference to the Supreme Court of Canada.[70] References were opinions and not strictly speaking binding decisions, but they were usually treated as such. True to the adversarial system, other interested parties could ask for leave to participate and submit arguments to the court on the reference.

The reference on *The Grain Marketing Act* was heard on April 9, 1931, at the spring session of the court. The hearing took three days—a long duration by the standards of the time—and was front page news. The *Regina Leader-Post* carried extensive coverage, including lengthy exposition of the positions put forward by the counsel.[71] The private grain marketing interests and elevator companies were well represented at the hearing, with a number of leading counsel arguing against the compulsory pool. Isaac Pitblado, of Winnipeg, and C.E. Gregory acted for the Winnipeg Grain Exchange and the Northwest Grain Dealers' Association, while Percy Gordon represented the "Association Opposing Compulsory Pool" with former attorney general James Cross. The federal government was not represented at the hearings.

Haultain was away on sick leave, leaving Turgeon, McKay, Martin, and Mackenzie to hear the reference. The court ruled unanimously that the statute was *ultra vires*. The problem was simply that *The Grain Marketing Act*, by mandating how grain grown in Saskatchewan would be sold outside of Saskatchewan, interfered with the federal power over trade and commerce. Counsel opposing *The Grain Marketing Act* had advanced a number of arguments attacking the form of the new co-operative, its monopoly over grain marketing, and the compulsory membership for producers. This was all, in the opinion of the court, quite legal, if perhaps draconian in regards to property and commercial rights. As Turgeon wrote in disposing of these arguments,

When pursuing the accomplishment of an object within its jurisdiction the Legislature can set aside the common law and interfere as it may deem advisable with the property and civil rights of individuals. . . . Appeals to the Court on compassionate grounds must go unheeded because the Courts have nothing to do with the reasonableness, the wisdom, or the justice of otherwise competent legislation. . . . Objections of this nature must be addressed to the Legislature itself, or to the electorate. . . . So, although the legislation, while speaking of a company and of the common-law rights of corporations, creates in fact a monopoly and interferes seriously with the property and contractual rights of individuals, it would not be invalid for those reasons alone, if it were confined to a subject wholly within the limits of the jurisdiction of the Legislature.[72]

Turgeon's statement made it very clear that the court was concerned only with the competence of the legislature to pass the statute, not whether it was a desirable policy in terms of meeting the crisis facing the province's agriculture.

It was abundantly obvious to the panel that *The Grain Marketing Act* was intended to regulate the trade in Saskatchewan grain outside of the province. The vast majority of Saskatchewan's crop was exported, and the point of the new company was to expand the markets where the grain could be sold, which obviously did not mean within Saskatchewan. The preamble of the *Act* itself made the "true nature and character" of the law, the "pith and substance," apparent. As McKay put it,

As already stated, the main object of the Act in directing the delivery of the grain grown in Saskatchewan, available for sale to the company, is that the company may sell the same beyond Saskatchewan, thus depriving thousands of grain growers of the right to the possession of their grain, and their right to export and sell it beyond the province, and interfering with interprovincial and international trade and commerce on a large scale, as by far the larger portion of the grain grown in Saskatchewan is exported and sold in other provinces and countries. . . .

There is no doubt that, had the Legislature confined the Act to the incorporation of this company for handling and marketing

> grain within the province for local purposes, it would have power to enact that all grain grown in the province be delivered to said company. For instance, if there was a scarcity of grain in the province and such grain was required for seed and consumption in the province, such legislation would come under the above heads of 11, 13 and 16. But such is not "the true nature and character" of the Act, as it gives a monopoly to the company to deal not only in the local trade of grain grown in Saskatchewan, but in the external trade thereof as well, the latter trade being the main object of the Act.[73]

The opinion of the court raised the question why the provincial government thought the legislation could possibly be valid. The government had put its hopes on a line of argument which held that the federal power to regulate trade and commerce had limitations that saved *The Grain Marketing Act*. Counsel arguing for the statute contended that the Privy Council had long held that federal trade and commerce power could not regulate civil rights within a province, because this made the reach of the power so broad that it would allow the federal government to interfere with all manner of activity. Several more recent Privy Council decisions had supposedly developed a doctrine that the federal government could only invoke the regulation of trade and commerce in support of exercising another of its enumerated powers under the BNA *Act*. In the case of the proposed *Act*, the federal government could not use its trade and commerce power to prevent the monopoly pool from selling grain, as that would interfere too much with property and civil rights.

The court did not agree, holding that a very recent Judicial Committee decision, *Re: Combines Investigation Act*, explicitly repudiated this supposed doctrine. In addition, *Lawson*, a Supreme Court of Canada decision concerning a British Columbia fruit and vegetable marketing agency, made it clear that the federal government could make substantive laws to regulate interprovincial and international trade. This could incidentally impose on property and commercial rights within a province, just as other federal powers did, such as those governing banking or bankruptcy. To the court, the analogy seemed exact. In essence, the province could legislate to regulate grain marketing in any way it wished within the province, but as soon as this affected interprovincial or international trade, the federal government had control, even if this limited the province's ability to legislate in its spheres of competence.

The decision of the Anderson government to formulate legislation and then use a reference to test its legality may have been a purely political strategy. Even at the time, references were criticized as a way for politicians to avoid making controversial decisions and shifting the responsibility to the judiciary. This same charge can be heard today. Anderson may have taken the opportunity to be seen to be taking action on a common demand knowing full well the proposed solution was not feasible. While this is speculation, Mackenzie King referred a number of Bennett's "New Deal" statutes to the Supreme Court of Canada and thence to the Privy Council almost certainly as a way to rid the government of laws it did not want to implement.[74] While Mackenzie King may well have been that Machiavellian, Anderson seems to have been more sincerely interested in helping farmers and may have hoped there was a chance the grain marketing statute would stand.

The court had decided the reference as a question of the division of powers. The policy dimensions were not examined, as was characteristic of the "black letter" approach to law of Canadian courts in the era. The decision was not hostile to the statute but was restricted to relatively narrow grounds. Counsel for the government had tried to provide a route to validate the statute, but it never held much promise of success. The hard reality was that the court had little choice but to declare the statute *ultra vires* even if *The Grain Marketing Act* was in the best interests of the province's farmers.

THE DEBT ADJUSTMENT ACT: MALEY V CADWELL

THE COURT'S SCRUPULOUSLY formal stance could also support contentious and controversial legislation. The provincial *Debt Adjustment Act* was later criticized as inadequate, but in the context of the early 1930s the statute was a radical assault on the sanctity of the contract.

As the title suggests, the aim of the statute was to allow for the reordering of debt to relieve some of the pressure on the province's highly indebted farming community. The statute skated close to the line in regards to division of powers, as the BNA *Act* assigned bankruptcy and insolvency law

HECTOR Y. MACDONALD

Justice H.Y. MacDonald retired in 1951 after thirty-two years on the bench, yet another of many long-lived and long-serving Saskatchewan judges. MacDonald was born in Margaree, Cape Breton, Nova Scotia, in 1875.[10] His family lineage was Highland Scots. After attending St. Francis Xavier University in Antigonish, MacDonald earned a law degree at Dalhousie Law School. In 1906, he joined the westward flow of lawyers from the Maritimes and tried practice first at Prince Albert and then Moosomin before taking a position in 1908 with the Attorney General's Office in Regina. Two years later, MacDonald became the first full-time city solicitor for Regina but resigned after six months to join the Mackenzie and Brown firm, where he made a name for himself as a litigator.[11] He later briefly practised with Percy Gordon.[12] MacDonald was offered a seat on the Court of King's Bench in 1918, making him one of the few early appointments to the Saskatchewan superior courts without substantial political experience.

Justice Hector Y. MacDonald, n.d. (Provincial Archives of Saskatchewan, R-A25016)

MacDonald was widely praised for his sagacity, common sense, and legal ability. One failing was his tendency to interrupt counsel, especially in criminal trials. John Diefenbaker, often the victim of MacDonald's interventions, nonetheless thought he was an excellent judge.[13] MacDonald was known for his dry, sometimes acerbic, wit. He seemed a natural for promotion to the appellate bench in 1941, bringing even more trial experience than Mackenzie. He also served as chairman of the board of governors of the University of Saskatchewan and received an honorary doctorate in law in 1950 from the university. He was a grand knight of the Knights of Columbus, a Catholic service organization, and a member of the Regina Golf Club. He retired to the coast, where he lived eighteen years before his death in 1969 in Vancouver.

to the federal government. The Saskatchewan statute created a board to which debtors could apply for protection from seizures and foreclosures. The board also controlled almost all civil litigation regarding debtors, as creditors had to apply for permission to start an action in court. Under the statute, after holding a hearing with the debtors and creditors, the board could recommend a measure of debt relief, including debt forgiveness or a sustainable repayment schedule. Saskatchewan's *Debt Adjustment Act* was not unique: Alberta and Manitoba had similar legislation designed to prevent mass foreclosures on farmers, and other provinces brought in general debt adjustment statutes. First introduced in 1931, the Saskatchewan statute was significantly amended and the powers of the board greatly increased in 1933 and 1934.

The Debt Adjustment Act was bound to produce litigation. *Maley v Cadwell* started as a minor and quite prosaic lawsuit, and the validity of the *Act* was not the central point in the original litigation. A lawyer had asked for a trial date in a lien action a day before the statute passed and, as the law applied to any action not yet in court, subsequently tried to obtain a board certificate. When he did not receive the certificate, the lawyer applied to declare the suit a nullity. The defendant's solicitor, however, told the judge his client was prepared to defend the suit, and the application was denied. The District Court judge then declared that *The Debt Adjustment Act* was *ultra vires* for trespassing on bankruptcy law and that section 11, which laid out the permit system for litigation, could not "prevent the Courts of the Province from functioning."[75] On appeal, there were three issues: whether the trial judge should have allowed the lawsuit to go forward; whether the trial judge could, without it being argued, decide that a statute was *ultra vires*; and whether the *Act* was indeed illegal.

The court, with Haultain, Turgeon, Martin, and Mackenzie, overturned the decision. The panel agreed that the suit was illegal under the statute and the defendant could not give a waiver. Haultain also stressed that under *The Court of King's Bench Act*, a judge could not raise the constitutional validity of a statute on their own accord: this had to be argued, and if a constitutional issue was raised, notice had to be given to the provincial and federal attorney generals to allow them to intervene. *The District Court Act* did not contain such a provision, but as Haultain noted, "In my opinion, it is highly undesirable that an important constitutional question should be decided in the District Court without notice to the Attorney-General; and it is particularly undesirable that it should be decided, as it has been in the present case, where it was not raised or argued."[76]

Haultain and Mackenzie still addressed the trial judge's ruling that *The Debt Adjustment Act* was *ultra vires*. The main issue was whether section 11, which gave the board the power to restrict legal actions, had made the original suit a nullity, but counsel for the original defendant had seized upon the trial judge's ruling that the whole statute was invalid. As Mackenzie put it,

> He argues that sec. 11 is really part and parcel of a general statutory scheme devised by the provincial Legislature for the administration of bankrupt or insolvent farmers' estates which, by virtue of such provisions, is a compulsory one. He therefore contends that those provisions clearly constitute an infringement upon the explicit authority granted to the Parliament of Canada.[77]

The chief justice and Mackenzie disagreed and held that section 11 of the *Act* was "severable" from the parts of the *Act* that laid out the mechanism for a debt adjustment. By this, they meant that the section was within the jurisdiction of the legislature and could function without reference to the rest of the statute even if the other sections were found *ultra vires*.

Haultain argued that section 11 came solidly under the purview of the province's power over property and civil rights and also within its control over the administration of justice and the constitution of the courts. Under this power, the province "bestows and prescribes their jurisdiction, and may at any time enlarge or circumscribe, or otherwise alter their jurisdiction."[78] The legislature could take matters out of the hands of the courts, notwithstanding the courts' original jurisdiction. The legislature also could curtail civil litigation regardless of the common law.

Mackenzie and Haultain also pointed out that *The Debt Adjustment Act* was essentially a moratorium, with the legislature reconsidering the statute every three years. The statute only temporarily restricted, not eliminated, a creditor's rights to sue. Mackenzie thought the fact that *The Debt Adjustment Act* was a moratorium avoided infringement of bankruptcy law. The statute delayed the payment of debts but did not settle them permanently as in the *Bankruptcy Act*. This observation and the finding that section 11 was severable did not address whether *The Debt Adjustment Act* otherwise infringed on federal bankruptcy law. Haultain believed this was irrelevant to the appeal because that question had not been argued. As he put it,

> The learned trial Judge holds that the greater part of the Act is *ultra vires* because it infringes on the exclusive legislative authority of Parliament in relation to banking, bankruptcy, and bills of exchange and promissory notes, but does not specify the parts of the Act which have that effect, except as above mentioned or the provisions of the federal Acts which are so affected.
>
> As I have already pointed out, we are not called upon on the present occasion to consider that finding except in so far as it relates to the particular provisions in question in this case. Those provisions obviously relate to property and civil rights in the province and are *intra vires* of the Legislature except where they are not applicable by reason of their conflict with statutory provisions which are properly ancillary to bankruptcy and other federal legislation. An Act may be both *intra vires* in part and *ultra vires* in part *and that can only be determined by a consideration of the applicability of the part in question to any given object* or purpose [italics in the original]. It will be quite time enough to discuss the applicability of the other numerous provisions of *The Debt Adjustment Act, 1933*, to actions and proceedings authorized by the *Bankruptcy Act*, R.S.C., 1927, Ch. 11, and other federal Acts when the question, if ever, is raised.[79]

The court had studiously avoided consideration of debt adjustment mechanisms in the statute. This was consistent with its traditional restraint but had the benefit of not disallowing legislation to help many citizens of the province and support a crucial industry. Perhaps because of *Maley*, no further challenge to the constitutionality of the statute was mounted before the federal *Farmers' Creditors Arrangement Act* came into effect in 1934. This legislation had similar but more extensive provisions for the reorganization and retirement of debts. *The Debt Adjustment Act* was later amended to remove the sections on debt restructuring, although the board continued to act as gatekeepers for litigation. By that point, the Depression was over.

THE FARMERS' CREDITORS ARRANGEMENT ACT

THE SCOPE OF the problem of farm debt and the limitations for provincial statutes eventually led to federal legislation. In 1934, R.B. Bennett introduced *the Farmers' Creditors Arrangement Act* (FCAA).[80] The FCAA differed from existing bankruptcy law in important ways. The statute imposed a regime for renegotiating and reducing debts but did not seek to liquidate assets; the point was to keep farmers farming. There was no cost for debtors' or creditors' use of the statute. Farmers who could not meet their obligations submitted simple proposals for the restructuring and repayment of their debts to "official receivers" appointed in farming communities. A receiver convened a meeting with creditors and assisted with negotiating an agreement, which in Saskatchewan was registered with the District Court. If the parties couldn't come to an agreement, the receiver submitted the matter to a review board for the province. The board held a hearing to ascertain the facts and adjust the proposal, and if creditors continued to reject an agreement, the board formulated a settlement binding on all parties. The chair of each review board was a superior court judge with jurisdiction in bankruptcy, with two additional commissioners representing the interests of creditors and debtors.

Saskatchewan eventually had two review boards. Chief Justice Brown of the Court of King's Bench chaired the first board and remained its chair until well into the war years, to the exclusion of most of his other judicial duties. Demand was so great that a second board was set up in 1939, with first Martin and then Tommy Davis as chair. Interestingly, the FCAA did not produce much litigation in Saskatchewan until late in the 1930s. It likely reflected the end of the drought and the budding economic recovery; until then, both creditors and debtors were probably happy with what they could get from the FCAA.

There was no challenge in the Saskatchewan courts to the constitutional validity of the FCAA. The statute was one of the few measures of the Bennett government's "New Deal" legislation that was upheld in references to the Supreme Court of Canada and the Privy Council.[81] Two appeals, however, provide some insight into how the Saskatchewan Court of Appeal interpreted the FCAA. The court was deferential to the legislature's aims and intent but also rigorously applied the rules for the interpretation of statutes to limit the reach of the law due to its radical nature.

This was apparent in *Prudential Insurance Co. v Berg* in 1940. The creditor was trying to foreclose, as the debtor had not made the payments fixed in his 1937 FCAA arrangements. The debtor relied on a clause in the agreement imposed by the review board that relieved him of making scheduled payments if he suffered a crop failure. The sheriff of the judicial district was given the responsibility of deciding if the defendant had a failure and issuing a certificate to this effect. The plaintiff argued that the review board did not have the jurisdiction to make the crop failure clause.

The court agreed. Chief Justice Turgeon held that the FCAA gave the court only very limited power of review over proposals. Unlike agreements under the *Bankruptcy Act*, FCAA agreements did not require approval of a court. A court of appeal could not review the proposal on grounds of reasonableness or fairness but only whether the board had the jurisdiction to make an order under the statute. As Turgeon wrote, "I think, with great deference to the Board of Review, that such is the case here." This was an emerging principle of administrative law when statutes limited appellate review of the decision of a tribunal. A court might not be able to review the merits of a decision but could inquire if the board had jurisdiction.

As Turgeon interpreted the terms of the FCAA, the agreements were similar to those used in bankruptcy in having definite terms for repayment and discharge of debts. More importantly, the review board could not change the terms of a proposal once it was registered. The crop failure clause made repayment of the debt "contingent, uncertain and indefinite." This was particularly true given that the local sheriff, with no firm rules or criteria to guide him, decided whether a crop failure had occurred. Martin came to the same conclusion. In his view, the order of the board was final even for the board. The clause in question allowed further possible extensions of time for future contingencies, but the review board had no jurisdiction to do so if the FCAA did not explicitly say so. As Martin put it,

> Had Parliament intended to confer power upon the Board of Review to provide for contingencies which might arise at some time in the future it would have conferred such power in unmistakable terms. As *The F.C.A. Act, 1934* empowers the Board of Review to take away rights which existed before the statute was passed and to alter the effect of written instruments, it should be the subject of strict construction.[82]

The court reinforced this view of the statute in a 1941 appeal, *Carney (Re)*, arising from a creditor's application for a writ of *certiorari* to quash the order of the review board formulating and confirming a proposal. The plaintiff argued that the board lacked jurisdiction because there was no proper proof the debtor was a farmer or was insolvent, in part because the statutory declaration of these facts was not provided on the proper standard form. The court denied the application. Turgeon and Martin noted that the court could issue a writ of *certiorari* but only to determine whether the review board was within its jurisdiction, not to examine the terms of a proposal. Turgeon reiterated that the FCAA did not allow appeal of questions of law or fact from a decision of the review board, and a litigant could not use *certiorari* to get around this fact.

On the question of whether the board had exceeded its jurisdiction by ordering a proposal without properly sworn evidence, the court held that the board did not require such evidence. As Turgeon wrote,

> The Board of Review is a body which, having regard to the nature of its work, must conduct its proceedings with a minimum of formality. It does not usually take evidence under oath since such a course would not be practical, and since there is nothing in the Act or in the rules of procedure made by the Governor in Council which makes it necessary; it is directed by the Act (sec. 12 [4]) to "consider representations on the part of those interested" and these representations may be made by the parties conversationally and in discussions in which all parties join including members of the Board; and no doubt in the course of these discussions many questions having to do with the position of the debtor are clarified by means of question and answer. But no record is made or kept, by shorthand or otherwise, of all that takes place. In this case we find the Board saying in its proposal: "The Board finds that the debtor is entitled to the benefits of the Act." This must be taken in the circumstances to include the finding that the debtor is a legally qualified farmer within the meaning of the Act and unable to meet his liabilities as they become due.[83]

In light of this, Turgeon helpfully pointed out, concerned parties should "exercise vigilance while their interests are before the Official Receiver and later on before the Board." Martin elaborated further to say that if it was intended for the board to act as a court, with evidence taken formally under oath, Parliament would have made this clear in the *Act*. More importantly, the fact that board hearings were of a legally informal character made a review of the record via *certiorari* of little utility even if it was permitted, as there might not be much to review. Mackenzie pithily observed that the plaintiff presumably had ample opportunity to challenge the proposal and ask for proof that the debtor was eligible during the meetings with the official receiver and then again with the board. The plaintiff had not done so, which Mackenzie thought should preclude him from trying to do it afterwards with his application.

Gordon agreed that the application should be dismissed and that the plaintiff had acquiesced to the board's findings by not challenging the debtor's bona fides earlier. But he was not willing to concede that the review board's informal operation was sufficient. "The Board of Review is a Court possessed of extraordinarily wide powers," he wrote. "The statutory requirements are so simple that anyone should be able to follow them exactly. In my view they should be followed strictly to confer jurisdiction on the Board."[84]

Gordon signalled that he was uneasy with the broad powers granted to the FCAA boards when these bodies did not have to observe the same rules as courts of law. Gordon's judgment foreshadowed the court's view of the Labour Relations Board, established after the war by the CCF government of Tommy Douglas. It also underscored a development that had been well underway but which picked up momentum in the 1930s and snowballed during and after the Second World War: the formation of administrative boards which were not courts but acted like them, and had founding statutes like the FCAA that greatly limited appellate review and supervision.

Gordon was not the only judge who had misgivings about legislation like the FCAA. Davis, who had headed one of the two boards of review, had a marked change of heart. Initially, he had been enthusiastic, moved by the stories of privation and desperation that his board heard. He felt that farmers wanted nothing so much as to meet their debts and was critical of the mortgage companies. He wrote to Gardiner,

> This year, 1939, there has been a crop and the reaction of the farmer has been remarkable. It is plainly evident that he wants to pay and to treat his creditors fairly and equitably. This can be taken as an absolute fact from my experience. On the other hand,

L.W. Brockington, special advisor to Mackenzie King, Major General L.R. LaFlèche, minister of national war service, and Justice T.C. Davis speak at a Victory Loan rally, Supreme Court of Canada, c. 1942. (Library and Archives Canada, PA-113177)

> there is a tendency on the part of the loaning institutions to apply the heat and by what are, on the face most generous concessions, get a third share of the crop and in a good many cases more than that. I am very much afraid that they have taken so much money that by next Spring you are going to find a lot of people looking . . . for relief.[85]

Yet only a few years later, with his strong dislike of the CCF government and its various boards perhaps colouring his memories, Davis complained to Gardiner that farmers used the FCAA and other legislation to avoid paying their rightful debts. He suggested that their settlements were in many cases fraudulent because their insolvency claims were not put to rigorous test. His change of view is perhaps not so much of a surprise. As attorney general, Davis had sounded off about the increasing usurpation by boards of the prerogatives of the courts, even suggesting that this was responsible for the diminished case lists of the trial and appeal courts.[86]

Davis never wrote a judgment dealing with any debt relief statutes. The sitting judges of the court did not show, in their decisions, any strong bias against the legislation.[87] This may reflect the background of judges like Haultain, Turgeon, and Martin as politicians. Their interpretation and application was consistent with the court's many past decisions on legislation, showing strong deference to elected lawmakers, scrupulous avoidance of policy, but also a narrow reading of statutes when legislation impacted on traditional common law rights.

CONCLUSION

THE GREAT DEPRESSION was like a natural disaster, unfolding such that almost no one really understood the scope of the problem until it was overwhelming. There had been recessions and depressions before but nothing that caused so much misery and materially contributed to the horror of a world war. Ironically, for Canada and Saskatchewan, war was the catalyst that jumpstarted the economy and led to new prosperity.

No one looked to the courts to provide solutions for the problems of the Depression. If anything, elites and average citizens alike looked to the judiciary to maintain order in the face of unrest and possible revolution. To those in distress, the courts may have seemed like another agent of oppression, as foreclosures, repossessions, seizures, and evictions multiplied. The misery affected judges, but the predominant judicial philosophy was to apply the law as written. The legislature, not the courts, was responsible for solutions. In Saskatchewan, the Court of Appeal dealt with legislation to address the Depression as the judges saw their duty: to decide what was lawful and not to get pulled into debates about what was best in terms of policy. The court flatly ruled against *The Grain Marketing Act*, may have fudged a little with *The Debt Adjustment Act*, and blended deference with rigour in interpreting the FCAA. And faced with those fomenting unrest, the judges were stern.

In the post-war era, expectations for judges and how they interpreted and applied the law would start to change, largely due to the progressive political agenda that dominated in North America, but not without some resistance from the judiciary. The election of North America's first openly socialist government in Saskatchewan in 1944 would bring this tension to the fore in the province somewhat earlier than it was felt in the rest of Canada.

CHAPTER 5
TOMMY DOUGLAS VERSUS THE COURT OF APPEAL

NO ONE SITTING DOWN TO LISTEN TO PREMIER Tommy Douglas's radio broadcast on a cold night in January 1948 likely had any idea they would be hearing a declaration of constitutional war. Listeners certainly got an earful.

> Let no one imagine that I am making any attack on those who preside in our courts. Most of them are men of honor and integrity. It is also true, however, that most of them are either defeated candidates or former members of parliament or the legislature. They represent the point of view of those who believe in our monopoly-capitalistic system. Many of them as lawyers have represented large corporations for years before going on the bench. What is more natural than that they should feel the status quo must be maintained even when it is in conflict with basic human liberties?
>
> The time has come when some government—acting for the people—must challenge the right of the courts to frustrate the will of the electorate.[1]

The premier had thrown down the gauntlet before an unexpected foe: the superior courts of the province. Was it a sign that the revolution was indeed coming?

Some may have thought that Douglas was finally showing the true colours of the CCF, but the premier was expressing a frustration that other legislators in other provinces likely felt at seeing statutes declared null and void in the courts, as had happened to several key pieces of CCF legislation. Douglas's remarks also raised questions about the courts and their role in post-war Canadian society. His government would further question the process of judicial appointments and the impartiality of the judiciary, commonplace now but near heresy then. Much of Douglas's displeasure revolved around how the Court of Appeal dealt with the CCF's labour legislation and appeals from the new Labour Relations Board, part of a larger issue of how courts viewed administrative tribunals in the post-war era.

POST-WAR MIRACLES

THE END OF the war was in sight when Saskatchewan went to the polls in 1944. The result of the provincial election, nine days after the Allies invaded France, reverberated across the nation. The voters of Saskatchewan had elected North America's first openly socialist government. The long-dominant Liberals had faced the CCF, an alliance of labour and progressive farm interests active both federally and provincially, which espoused socialism as the means to address the many inequities in Canadian society. In Saskatchewan, the party had a new leader, Thomas Clement Douglas. Imbued with the social gospel and working as a Baptist preacher in Weyburn, Saskatchewan, Tommy Douglas had become active in leftist politics after experiencing first-hand the devastation of the Depression. He served eight years in Ottawa as a CCF member of Parliament before heading the provincial party. Douglas was a force of nature: an outstanding orator, outgoing and approachable, and with a genius for connecting with voters.

Premier William Patterson and the Liberals had taken the unpopular step of extending the government's term for a year by legislative fiat, citing the exigencies of the war effort.[2] Ironically, this was a gift to Douglas and the CCF, who had another year to organize. With the war economy humming, the return of a measure of prosperity aided the CCF message of reform and reconstruction.[3] Many voters no longer relied on government handouts to survive, and the mood had changed. Douglas tapped into the frustration of voters and their appetite for social and economic progress. Many feared that a recession or depression would follow the war, as had happened after the First World War. And the war effort had made people think differently about the role of government. As one historian put it, "The reputation of government as a social and economic manager was at an all-time high."[4] Douglas promised an activist government dedicated to making people's lives better. The result was a Liberal rout, with the party reduced to five seats. The CCF took forty-seven seats, inaugurating a remarkable twenty consecutive years in power.

The novice government hit the ground running, passing more than 190 statutes in its first sixteen months.[5] Belying Douglas's populist style and the CCF's roots in Christian socialism, the party brought modern, technocratic government to the province. The civil service was modernized and professionalized. Douglas and his cabinet brought in outside experts and consultants to advise on policy and help implement new programs. Their ambitious legislative agenda included statutes to encourage unionization, help the province's still highly indebted farmers, protect civil liberties with Canada's first bill of rights, and institute a health insurance scheme to make hospital care more affordable. Working to undo the damage of ten years of depression, the government launched ambitious infrastructure projects, encouraged more co-operative enterprises, and employed a new tool, Crown-owned companies, to diversify the economy. While many measures were not particularly radical—the Patterson government had introduced progressive policies as well, such as public care for cancer and tuberculosis patients—the scale was something new.

It was possibly too much too soon. The opposition Liberals compared the CCF to the planned economy of Soviet Russia, which struck a chord. After a sizeable drop in support in the hard-fought 1948 election, the CCF adopted a more measured pace of change. The premier and his advisers, after some key pieces of legislation were declared *ultra vires*, realized that implementing a truly socialist system was beyond the powers allocated to a provincial government.[6] Douglas was also very much a pragmatist and in spirit a reformer rather than a dogmatic socialist.[7] The premier and Clarence Fines, his remarkable finance minister, concentrated on improving the economy, reasoning that prosperity would allow the CCF to undertake an ambitious social agenda. Towards that end, Fines imposed stringent fiscal discipline on the CCF and brought in sixteen consecutive balanced budgets.[8] While continuing to support co-operatives and actively participate in the economy through Crown corporations, the CCF government also courted private investment. When oil and gas companies, already fearful of expropriation, deserted Saskatchewan for Alberta after Imperial Oil struck it big in Leduc, Douglas personally assured the industry that the province was open for business.[9] Touting the new business-friendly policies during the 1948 election campaign, John W. Corman, the attorney general, quipped that the voters could choose between capitalist free enterprise and CCF free enterprise.

The province undeniably prospered in the 1950s, although the CCF could not necessarily take the credit. Like the rest of Canada, Saskatchewan experienced a post-war boom as government programs to help veterans—such as access to education and cheap financing for homes—added to pent-up consumer demand from years of rationing and enforced savings. The economic boom also created a new resource economy in Saskatchewan to augment agriculture. Substantial oil and gas reserves were discovered in the province, with heavy oil near Lloydminster and lighter crude in the Williston Basin in the southeast. With the ushering in of the nuclear age, the uranium deposits of Northern Saskatchewan became valuable. The provincial government established Uranium City in 1952 as a service centre for the mines in the Beaverlodge area.

Uranium would later pale in importance compared to potash, used in making fertilizer. Oil exploration had discovered Saskatchewan's massive potash deposits in the 1940s. But potash's riches remained more of a promise in the 1950s due to the technical challenges of mining it, and the first large-scale mine did not open until 1962.

The CCF actively encouraged potash exploitation with an attractive royalty regime and subsidies. But not all the party's economic initiatives bore fruit. In the party's first mandate, Joe Phelps, the minister of natural resources, went on a buying spree of small manufacturing concerns in an ill-considered bid to encourage industry in the province. Almost all turned into money-losers. The government had more success with Crown-owned utilities such as Saskatchewan Power and Saskatchewan Government Telephones. These companies made substantial profits and provided two vital components of the modern age—electricity and telecommunications—for the province's residents.

Despite the party's rural roots, the CCF struggled with agricultural policy. Wartime demand and good growing conditions had brought the province's farmers back from the brink, but the post-war boom did not necessarily mean prosperity. The decade after the war saw major fluctuations in grain prices, even with the Canadian Wheat Board now a permanent fixture. The provincial government could do nothing about grain prices and, no longer seeing Saskatchewan as a stronghold, the federal Liberals were increasingly unresponsive to Prairie farmers.[10] Farming became almost entirely mechanized after the war, which drove up operating costs. Low prices and higher costs put a great deal of pressure on small family farms. Size increasingly mattered. Larger-scale farmers could turn a profit when small farmers couldn't, and could absorb losses better. The number of farms in the province shrank steadily through the 1950s even as the size of the annual crop increased. The provincial government tried to protect farmers from bankruptcy problems through more debt legislation, which was then declared *ultra vires*, but there was even less the province could do about the price of wheat.

Larger farms contributed to rural depopulation after the war. Saskatchewan remained predominantly rural in the 1950s, but urbanization gathered momentum. The government became concerned as early as 1953 about the decline in rural Saskatchewan.[11] Another force driving the shift was demographic: young people did not want to stay on the farm. Many who had left during the war did not return, as veterans took advantage of educational opportunities and the rapidly expanding economy. Their younger siblings followed. Meanwhile, telephones, vehicle ownership, and good roads helped ease the isolation of life on the farm but sounded the death knell for many small villages and towns. The major cities and larger towns grew at the expense of smaller centres, which saw their commercial life siphoned off. Too many customers preferred to drive a little further to a larger centre for their needs. The CCF had no answer for this structural change, which would pick up speed in coming decades and is still taking place.

The Douglas government had little success in addressing the dire circumstances of the province's Indigenous peoples. Life on Saskatchewan's reserves and in the province's Métis communities had gone from bad to worse in the Depression. Previous Liberal and Conservative provincial governments had taken sporadic notice of their plight but done little to help, and they had sometimes pursued policies that made things worse, such as developing a commercial fishery in the north that interfered with traditional practices. The Douglas government also ran into the same roadblock met by earlier administrations: federal jurisdiction over Aboriginal affairs. The CCF advocated transferring jurisdiction to the province, and Douglas encouraged Métis and Indians to organize. But in the end, the well-intentioned CCF Indian policy suffered from the same problems as federal policies: it was paternalistic and didn't consult the people it hoped to help. It aimed for cultural assimilation and did not really address in any meaningful way the needs of Indians for education and economic opportunities, or the intense racism of mainstream society.

This history is not the place to enumerate different measures of progress in Saskatchewan in the post-war years, which included new schools; rural electrification; the construction of all-weather roads and highways; a hospitalization insurance program, the forerunner of national medicare; popular, no-fault, government-run insurance; and so on. Greater prosperity, education, and the shift towards a more urban society also helped dissipate the tensions between ethnic groups and the major Christian faiths that had still greatly marked Saskatchewan society in the 1920s and 1930s. The second and third generations of immigrants had grown up and were educated together and had served together during the war. As one historian put it, "Gesiorowski, Hounjet, Pasqualoto and Syroteuk were just as much Saskatchewan family names as Barnhart and Brennan."[12]

Douglas and the CCF provided good government and generally competent administration. Confronted with the realities of governing, Douglas and the CCF were not the socialist radicals that their political opponents liked to portray. The government's activist and sometimes overreaching legislation, however, was bound to eventually spill into the courts, where it did not always fare well. This ignited a confrontation between government and courts that raised questions about the relationship of judiciary and legislature, the judicial appointment process, and the role and responsibility of judges, questions that still have not been fully answered.

THE MARTIN BENCH

DURING CHIEF JUSTICE Martin's twenty-year tenure, the personnel of the appeal bench changed substantially. By 1951, William Martin and Percy Gordon were the veterans of the court. MacDonald had just stepped down. E.M. Culliton, a practitioner from Gravelbourg, was plucked "from the street" (and the legislature) to join the court. Mackenzie died in 1946. His replacement, Percy M. Anderson from the Court of King's Bench, served only two years before he also died, leading to the appointment of Donald A. McNiven, another trial judge. The four-man bench finally became five again when Tommy Davis relinquished his position in 1948 and Arthur Thomas Procter of Moosomin, another Liberal politician, replaced him. Procter's appointment very nearly did not happen. No sooner had a position opened on the court than Tommy Douglas, in a fit of pique, threatened to eliminate it, angered by the judiciary's treatment of several key statutes and by the provincial government's lack of influence in the appointment process.

William Melville Martin, 2016. (Artist: Iris Hauser; photo: Mark Greschner. Court of Appeal.)

It was perhaps inevitable that there would be conflict over who became judges. The victory of the CCF meant that, for the first time in the province's history, there was a complete decoupling of the provincial government and the federal government. This created a novel situation in Saskatchewan for judicial appointments. For much of the Saskatchewan's history, the provincial government usually had a strong influence or even the final say on who was appointed to the courts thanks to the links between the major federal and provincial political parties. The CCF had no friendly ears in the federal cabinet and virtually no say in who was appointed to the province's superior courts.

Lawyers were also very much under-represented in the ranks of the CCF. Douglas had reached beyond the party before the 1944 election and persuaded John W. Corman, a Moose Jaw lawyer, long-time Liberal stalwart, and one-time Social Credit candidate, to run for the CCF, dangling the promise of a cabinet seat as attorney general.[13] John "Jack" Corman would serve as attorney general for twelve years before retiring in 1956 and introduced much of the CCF's signature legislation, such as *The Trade Union Act*, *The Farm Security Act*, and *The Saskatchewan Bill of Rights Act*. Corman had a weekly radio broadcast, which he often used as a pulpit for explaining CCF policies. Douglas also recruited CCF-leaning lawyers from Ontario, such as F.A. Brewin, the drafter of *The Trade Union Act*. One of Douglas's hires was Dr. Morris Shumiatcher, a brilliant young lawyer from Alberta, as a special legislative adviser. Along with working on legislation, Shumiatcher was the government's counsel for some of the contentious labour appeals.

None of this changed the fact that the CCF government lacked intimate connections with the legal profession and the judiciary of the superior courts. It is fair to say that the profession viewed the CCF with suspicion, while the party rank and file in turn regarded lawyers as part and parcel of the established political and business elites. For the first decade or so of CCF rule, there was no significant cadre of lawyers active in the party. More importantly, there was almost no chance a lawyer with CCF sympathies would find their way onto the superior courts. Until 1957, Liberal patronage remained the deciding factor for appointments to the Court of King's Bench and the Court of Appeal. After 1957, it would be Conservative, something discussed in the next chapter. But it was not CCF. This was a major factor in the contretemps between Douglas and the courts.

In the eyes of Douglas and the CCF, former premier Jimmy Gardiner was the villain. As the political minister from Saskatchewan, he had immense influence on appointments, although his advice was not always followed.[14] Gardiner consulted with Martin and W.F.A. Turgeon—good Liberals—and other trusted members of the profession as to the suitability of candidates, but it was clear that legal excellence was not necessarily his first concern. On the eve of his own resignation, Tommy Davis pressured Gardiner to appoint his brother, Clifford Sifton "Hully" Davis, to the King's Bench. Davis even went so far as to say that he was finally resigning in part to "free up" a spot on the judiciary for his brother, "to get him into a position of security," and allow Hully to educate his three children.[15] Martin thought that Hully Davis was not King's Bench material. Turgeon, overseas but still consulted, was of the opposite opinion.[16] Despite the optics, in the end Gardiner engineered the appointment, clearly influenced by his close friendship with Tommy.

Gardiner's cavalier attitude towards qualifications carried over to Court of Appeal appointments, not all of whom had exemplary practices.[17]

Anderson and McNiven were leading counsel, but the same could necessarily not be said of Procter or Culliton. They practised in Moosomin and Gravelbourg respectively, and while Procter had some experience at the appeal court and as assistant counsel at the 1925 Royal Grain Inquiry Commission, Culliton was a country lawyer. But all four appointees had been politically prominent, especially Procter and Culliton, who were in the Patterson cabinet and then continued in opposition. Both were also veterans, Procter in the First World War and Culliton in the Second. Gardiner wrote about Procter:

> The chief reason why it has been found possible to make an appointment is Procter's condition. Everyone agrees that Procter should be appointed to the bench. In the first place, he is a returned soldier with a first-class record overseas and injuries received which have made it most difficult for him to carry on. In spite of that he has given very fine service as a member of the House and a member of the Government. It so happens that he is now in the House and we do desire to create a vacancy. Procter cannot possibly be appointed to the King's Bench as he could not stand the travelling about the province involved in that appointment. When he is appointed it must be to the Appeal Court.[18]

Gardiner captured the attitude that the bench was a sort of retirement home for lawyers no longer up to the rigours of practice as well as a reward for political service. One prominent Tory MP and lawyer, Robert Hanbidge, had some reservations about Culliton's qualifications.[19] Culliton later privately confided that he worked very hard after his appointment and remarked in a speech that his colleagues "did everything possible to assist me—and assistance I did need."[20] Ironically, Culliton became one of the strongest jurists the province ever produced.

It was not surprising that the Douglas government had problems with the prevailing method of choosing judges. One day, Procter and Culliton were hammering government policies as members of the opposition, and the next were on the province's highest court and ruling on CCF legislation. The premier's 1948 radio address made clear that he thought such appointees might prove unable to set aside partisanship. The concern about patronage went beyond CCF circles. While defending the judiciary after Douglas's 1948 speech, a contributor to the *Leader-Post* did say, "Admittedly

PERCY MCCUAIG ANDERSON

Percy Anderson had the unfortunate distinction of having one of the shortest tenures on the appeal court. Appointed in 1946 at the age of sixty-seven, he died unexpectedly just two years later. He had spent his last day on the job working in his office but later that evening was taken to hospital, where he died the following evening.[1] His colleagues were shocked at his sudden death.

Justice Percy McCuaig Anderson, n.d. (Provincial Archives of Saskatchewan, R-A689)

Anderson was an Ontario transplant. He came to Regina in 1909 after taking his law through articles in Winnipeg at the firm of Aikins, Robson and Co.[2] Born in Paisley, Ontario, near the Bruce Peninsula in 1879, he started school in Uxbridge, near Toronto, but attended high school in Belleville, not far west of Kingston, graduating at the top of his class. He then attended Kingston's Queen's University, graduating with honours in political science and history.

Anderson initially practised with Mackenzie, Brown and Co. in Regina but left in 1912 to found a new firm, Anderson, McNiven, Fraser and Rose, with Donald McNiven. Anderson was a successful litigator and was made a King's Counsel in 1919. He frequently appeared at the appeal court in Saskatchewan as well as the Supreme Court of Canada and made two appearances at the Privy Council. As befitted a prominent lawyer, he was involved in the community, serving as the president of the Regina Board of Trade in 1920 and 1921. Anderson was a founding member of the Regina Kiwanis Club, its president in 1919, and later the club's district governor for Western Canada. He was also a Mason, a member of the Assiniboia Club, and a member of the Wascana Country Club. He was chancellor for the Anglican Diocese of Qu'Appelle and chairman of the board for the Grey Nuns Hospital.

Like many in the Saskatchewan judiciary, Anderson took on extra duties during the Second World War, heading the Saskatchewan war mobilization board. He succeeded Justice John Embury as head of the board in 1943 and inherited a minor controversy regarding the deferment of military service of John Makaroff, son of prominent Doukhobor lawyer Peter Makaroff, to continue his medical studies.[3] Embury, a brigadier general in the First World War, had arbitrarily categorized Makaroff as a conscientious objector and sent him to an alternative service camp and eventually a rock quarry. Anderson reversed Embury's decision, stating that Makaroff had been "singled out for discrimination and persecution." For his trouble, Anderson was roundly criticized by the Canadian Legion and other members of the board. It was an example of Anderson's even-handedness and sense of fairness.

Heavily involved in the Liberal Party both federally and provincially, Anderson was on the executive of the association for his federal constituency and served as president. He ran successfully for the provincial legislature in 1934 and was re-elected in 1938 but resigned when he was appointed to the Court of King's Bench at the beginning of November. He was known as a quiet, courteous judge.

our present system of appointing judges is not good: the premier's point there is well taken."[21] Within a year of Douglas's radio address, the Law Society of Saskatchewan called for consultation with provincial chief justices and law societies for judicial appointments.[22] The Canadian Bar Association—which had often disparaged patronage—took up the cause with a similar resolution. The association president repeated the call for reform a few years later.[23] There was little sign of change.[24]

THE 1948 AMENDMENTS

SOME URGENCY ACCOMPANIED Procter's appointment. Douglas's frustration with appointments, and the Court of Appeal's perceived obstruction of the democratic will, prompted the CCF to retaliate with amendments to *The Court of Appeal Act* and *The Court of King's Bench Act* to reduce the size of the courts.

In its first term, the CCF had passed a blizzard of statutes, putting in motion an activist, reform agenda. Inevitably, some of this legislation was challenged in the courts as being beyond the competence of the provincial government. *The Farm Security Act* was disallowed on a reference to the Supreme Court of Canada. It was not unprecedented. William Aberhart and the Social Credit Party had experienced the same difficulty in Alberta in the 1930s, particularly as the party's monetary theories could not be implemented without running afoul of federal control of banking. And the Anderson government had seen *The Grain Marketing Act* declared *ultra vires*.

The Court of Appeal's decision in *Labour Relations Board v John East Iron Works* was the last straw for Douglas. The court's decision (discussed in detail below) declared *ultra vires* a crucial section of *The Trade Union Act*, which gave the Labour Relations Board its enforcement powers. This came after several board orders had been quashed on appeal. Douglas was infuriated and he took to the airwaves to vent his anger—and did he vent. His speech on January 14, 1948, claimed that judges, as part of the existing political and economic elite, had an intrinsic, albeit possibly unconscious, bias. He criticized the courts for their narrow and legalistic interpretations of legislation, implying that judges were being obstructionist and "anti-democratic" by frustrating the legislature and not considering the broader aims and social good intended. It was not clear exactly what Douglas thought the CCF should do about it, but it was clear that he intended to do something.

Reaction to Douglas's radio talk was muted at first, but the storm soon broke. The premier's remarks attracted widespread condemnation from the opposition benches, from the legal profession, and from the press, no friends to the CCF. The Law Society was near apoplectic. Douglas was accused of maligning the judiciary and undermining the administration of justice. Walter Tucker, the leader of the Liberal opposition, professed himself "shocked" and immediately invoked patriotic sentiment: "I think of the people who lost their lives fighting to establish our rights. Surely we aren't going to throw all this away."[25] Others, like Rupert Ramsay, leader of the provincial Progressive Conservatives, asked whether Douglas wanted to get rid of an independent judiciary.[26] Some lectured Douglas on constitutional law and the role of the judiciary. And critics defended the courts for doing their duty: the fault was with the CCF in passing laws that exceeded the province's legal powers. As one editorialist wrote, "Mr. Douglas enumerated a number of instances in which the legislation of the CCF government has failed in the courts. In these cases, it was not because such legislation was 'socialistic' in character but because the province was trying to stretch its authority beyond its constitutional limits."[27]

The last criticism was quite on point. Under the doctrine of parliamentary supremacy, judges had little ability to disallow a statute. The major exception was the division of powers, which had assigned some legislative areas to the provinces and some to the federal government. There was no doubt that some CCF legislation, like statutes of previous Liberal and Conservative governments, had strayed into federal areas of competence and the courts had no choice but to declare them void. But there was still a certain amount of leeway in judicial interpretation, so this did not necessarily fully answer the premier.

As a parliamentarian of long standing, Douglas understood the constitutional issues involved. While sincere in its sentiments, his speech was likely very calculated. Douglas almost always consulted his cabinet colleagues before making major decisions, and Jack Corman was one of his closest advisers. "Run it by Jack" was the premier's refrain when a new policy was under consideration.[28] Corman may well have had a hand in the speech. According to his biographer, Corman "believed that legal practices should be based on current realities and democratic needs rather than ancient precedents and legal technicalities."[29] This might be translated as frustration with the constrained approach of the courts to interpreting and applying the law. Douglas's speech in fact foreshadowed the frustration that developed in the 1960s with the Canadian judiciary, which was increasingly seen as being out of touch and unresponsive to modern society.[30] Corman was also known in CCF circles for his shrewd reading of the voting public.[31] Douglas's speech was aimed at this public, not the legal profession or the judiciary. His remarks fitted into the CCF's narrative of reform and standing up for the average citizen against established interests. Casting aspersions on the judiciary had an additional advantage: judges, by tradition, could not publicly answer back.

Despite the storm of criticism, the premier did not back down. Douglas and Corman next aimed a volley back at the Law Society of Saskatchewan. Douglas slyly took the society to task for misrepresenting him when it claimed he had said some judges were not men of integrity when in fact he had said most judges were men of integrity, which of course had the same implication. The premier and attorney general then criticized the Law Society for distributing to its membership a chamber of commerce pamphlet attacking socialism, asserting that this was evidence

John W. Corman, taking the oath at the swearing-in of the first CCF cabinet, July 10, 1944. *Seated to Corman's left:* Finance Minister Clarence Fines and Premier T.C. Douglas. (Provincial Archives of Saskatchewan, R-B10956)

of the suspected bias. As Douglas quipped, "The lawyer of today is often the judge of tomorrow."[32] A month later, at a candidates' forum, Clarence Fines, the finance minister, reiterated the premier's points. According to the *Leader-Post*, Fines stated bluntly in reply to a question, "There is no doubt that there have been judges appointed more on account of their political service than because of their judicial ability."[33] Fines went further, saying "that there were judges in the courts which were not in favour with modern social legislation." In his opinion, appointments were required that represented a better cross section of viewpoints.

The CCF was not content simply to make speeches. In February 1948, as the legislature reconvened, on the order paper were amendments to *The Court of Appeal Act* and *The Court of King's Bench Act* that reduced the courts from five to four and seven to five judges respectively. The government had been toying with the idea for over a year, but the timing spoke for itself.[34] Corman presented the amendments as an economy measure, arguing that the courts did not require so many judges as case lists were light. No one was fooled, either in Regina or Ottawa. James Ilsley, the federal justice minister, refused to comment, but there were plenty who had no compunctions inside and outside of his department. A former Regina journalist, Chester Bloom, reported from Ottawa that according to ministry insiders, "The Saskatchewan government does not want the federal government to fill existing vacancies with trained legal talent who may not happen to see eye to eye with the provincial government's economic and political theories."[35] His sources also thought it clear that the CCF, with a dearth of legal talent in its own ranks to put forward for the bench, did not want any new appointments.

The amendments never reached a vote. Point made, the government seemed content to await further developments. As Tommy Davis later said, the CCF had left the amendments "to hang over the head of the Govt at Ottawa."[36] The federal Liberals rushed to make two appointments to the King's Bench and put Procter in at the Court of Appeal.[37] And then the controversy faded away, at least for the moment.

The reaction of the sitting judges of the Court of Appeal to the amendments and public posturing is not known. In his correspondence with Gardiner, Tommy Davis seemed more resigned than outraged and said he thought the amendments typical of "that gang." The court was now in an unenviable position where any ruling against the government could be seen by some to confirm the premier's thesis, and a ruling that pleased the government could be seen by others as obsequious. And in 1950, with the issue of judicial bias still simmering in the background, the court found itself in the very awkward position of hearing an appeal in a slander lawsuit between Walter Tucker, the Liberal leader of the opposition, and Premier Douglas.

At a public forum during the 1948 election campaign, Douglas claimed that Tucker, a lawyer in Rosthern, had been involved in a shady land deal. During the subsequent legal proceedings for fraud, the master in chambers had adjourned while he considered a motion to strike out the statement of claim, an adjournment that the premier claimed conveniently coincided with the election. An outraged Tucker sued, and the slander action was dismissed at trial. The Court of Appeal directed a new trial because the jury charge had been defective. Douglas then appealed to the Supreme

Court of Canada and lost, but Tucker dropped the suit before another trial took place.[38]

Douglas would later joke about the lawsuit when he addressed the Law Society of Saskatchewan. He had particular cause to be grateful to the profession, he told his audience, as two lawyers were all that stood between him and losing $200,000.[39] His address was largely about the difficulties that the division of powers created for national unity, but, alluding to the 1948 controversy, he said that new parties from outside the status quo might feel antagonism to lawyers and the judiciary as custodians of the law but would grow to value them. He quipped that it would help if the provinces could appoint judges. His tone suggested that the CCF's view had moderated to some degree.

Yet in 1951, Corman again introduced amendments to the court acts to eliminate judicial positions, one from the appeal court, and one from the trial court. With each court at full strength, the bills would only take effect when there was a death or retirement. Coming soon after the appointment of Culliton to the Court of Appeal, it seems inescapable that the provincial government was again protesting either the specific appointment, the lack of consultation, or both. The reaction to the amendments was muted. The opposition had little to say. Rather than polemics against the government, the *Leader-Post* published an editorial approving the reduction as a sound cost-saving measure.[40] It was as if everyone had decided to ignore the message, and the issue faded away for thirty years. The CCF reduced the number of District Court judges in 1958, but this was done on Justice Culliton's recommendation after a study of the court system.

Culliton's appointment in 1951 established the appellate bench of the 1950s, another long period of stability for the court. Interestingly, all four new appointees to the Martin court were born out of province. All were university educated, but Anderson and McNiven had done their law through articles while Procter and Culliton had law degrees. Culliton belonged to a younger generation than his brother judges. Aside from him, it was quite an elderly bench. Anderson was sixty-eight, Procter sixty-two, and McNiven sixty-one when they were appointed, all contemporaries of Gordon. Chief Justice Martin was only two years older than Anderson and had just turned seventy-five when Culliton was named to the bench. Culliton was only forty-five, the youngest appointee to the Court of Appeal since Martin in 1922. The four appointments were split between two "big-city" lawyers—Anderson and McNiven, who had both practised in Regina—and two small-town lawyers. The four were also split between trial judges and practising lawyers.

All four had served as Liberal MLAs, and two, Culliton and Procter, had been cabinet ministers, while McNiven had also served as a member of Parliament. It was the most overtly "political" bench in the court's history. The CCF's suspicions were not surprising, but the question was whether the decisions of the court, particularly regarding *The Trade Union Act* and Labour Relations Board, did indeed show a bias against the CCF and their progressive legislation.

THE POST-WAR COURT AT LAW

FROM THE CANADIAN perspective, the Second World War was a fight against totalitarianism and a defence of freedom. The conflict also saw a tremendous increase in state power, initially harnessed to the war effort, but in the post-war period, with memories of the Depression still fresh, many Canadians continued to welcome a greater role for government. Saskatchewan arguably led the way. A comparison province by province would likely show that the Douglas government was not that radical, that many of the policies followed, agencies and departments set up, and laws passed had equivalents elsewhere under a range of different political parties. But socialism had a lot of baggage, which became a much heavier burden with the start of the Cold War.

From its inception, Saskatchewan's Court of Appeal had been strongly deferential to the legislature and had accommodated legislative assaults on the common law with little comment, including laws that suspended and restricted debt actions. But even with Martin as chief justice, the post-war court was a different court. Douglas's radio address in 1948 raised the question of whether the court treated CCF legislation differently from the legislation of previous governments, and whether the premier was right and some degree of bias had crept into the court's deliberations. The decisions regarding *The Trade Union Act* were the obvious flashpoint and involved unionization and organized labour, which had historically faced an uphill battle in the Canadian polity and in Canadian courts.[41] The *John East Iron Works* decision would, at the Privy Council, establish fundamental elements of administrative law in Canada, but it was only one part of the Court's take on labour law.

PRACTICE AND PROCEDURE

THE MARTIN COURT made no breaks with the past in practice and procedure. The rules of court were revised in 1941, taking effect the following year, with a view towards reducing fees and increasing efficiency. As discussed previously, there had been no substantive changes. The light lists of the court meant there was little need to further modify its practices. As the nation focused on the war effort, legal business in the province was even slower than it had been during the Depression. Activity began to pick up again once the fighting was over. But while the trial courts were once again busy by the beginning of the 1950s, the appeal lists remained relatively light. When the CCF announced plans to cut judges in 1948, the profession was mostly concerned with the effect on the Court of King's Bench. Gardiner had noted that Martin had been away for a good part of 1949 working on the revisions to the *Criminal Code* and that the remaining judges had not felt overworked.[42] The consensus was that four judges could handle the court's workload but that an even number on the bench was very undesirable.

The Culliton Committee in 1957 recommended major changes for the District Court and the Court of Queen's Bench but had almost nothing to say about the Court of Appeal. The court did become busier as the decade went on. Along with the four scheduled sittings each year, there were numerous special sittings. Under the rules, counsel could request a special sitting by applying at the opening of court. This was usually to accommodate scheduling problems or to expedite appeals not yet on the lists. The practice of the court was to grant such applications unless unreasonable, with the result that the court sat nearly every month except during the summer vacation. Martin was quite proud of this tradition. "I think I can say without being boastful, that no Court in Canada is more considerate in meeting the requests of counsel and litigants than our Court of Appeal and this has resulted in a very happy relationship for all concerned," he wrote in a letter to the deputy attorney general.[43] Not all of Martin's colleagues agreed. Gordon, always the stickler for proper form, was displeased that the profession could not manage to get their appeals in for the regular sittings and was not hesitant in saying so.[44]

Martin wore the mantle of chief justice well. He was courteous and mild-mannered in hearings, but engaged and always well prepared. The bar had great respect for him. Emmett Hall, Saskatchewan's last appointment to the Supreme Court, rated Martin "a very fine judge." Martin's tenure was very nearly a short one: in 1944 he was sounded out to be lieutenant-governor.[45] Martin wrote frequently for the court right up to his retirement in 1961. Calvin Tallis, who later joined the court, started practising in the 1950s and witnessed Martin in action. Tallis recalled that towards the end of the decade the chief justice showed signs of aging, letting Gordon lead the hearings, but he still participated in discussions.[46] Martin considered retiring around 1956,[47] but he stayed on and finally left in 1961 with mandatory retirement, a much-admired public figure and held in high esteem by the bar, even if his best days were long behind him.

Chief Justice William Melville Martin, n.d. (Provincial Archives of Saskatchewan, R-D1750)

Percy Gordon was the major figure of the post-war court. He was a very hard worker and wrote more than any other judge, whether the lead judgment of the court, a dissent, or a concurring opinion. A model judge of the time, very mindful of appellate restraint, Gordon sometimes took "judicial notice" of prevailing social or economic conditions, often things that he clearly considered common sense. As previously discussed, he was the court's expert on procedure and invariably would write judgments on the subject. Gordon dominated hearings. He was opinionated and frequently crossed swords with counsel. As Tallis recounts, "He did not hesitate to intervene and indicate to counsel what his line of thinking on the issues was." This intimidated inexperienced counsel, but Tallis thought Gordon was not unreasonable. Senior counsel, such as Tallis's senior, renowned labour lawyer George Taylor, would squarely face Gordon. Tallis says Gordon "didn't mind at all" and relished the exchange. In Tallis's opinion, when Gordon interrupted counsel, it was often to keep them on point

Justice Percival Hector Gordon, c. 1950s. (Provincial Archives of Saskatchewan, R-D1751)

or to bring up issues he thought they were avoiding. Emmett Hall, on the other hand, thought Gordon had usually already made up his mind on an appeal before hearings and was a poor influence on the court.[48]

A stickler for proper form, Gordon was openly critical if he felt a lawyer was slipping into what he considered bad habits. He bemoaned the fact that lawyers frequently could not or would not draw up proper pleadings or asked for extensions for matters like filing appeal books.[49] To his mind, professionals were on top of these matters. Gordon fit into a mould of appellate judge very familiar to lawyers across Canada in that era: impatient, outspoken, even cranky, and irrepressible, sometimes crossing the line of propriety. In a 1956 hearing, Gordon was very critical of the province's labour legislation, the operation of the Labour Relations Board, and the competence of the board's chairman, Peter Makaroff. The *Leader-Post* quoted Gordon, saying, among other salty comments, that it was "no wonder that capital doesn't rush in to this province after it hears how the Labour Relations Board operates."[50]

For Premier Douglas, these remarks were fighting words. In the legislature a few days later, Douglas lambasted Gordon, accusing him of bias and overstepping the bounds of his office and casting aspersions on his fitness to be a judge: "If Mr. Justice Gordon wants to enter the arena of political controversy, he is perfectly at liberty to do so, but he ought to resign from the Bench, rather than use his exalted position to make political observations."[51] It was vintage Douglas. He had much more to say, none of it complementary to Gordon, and the outspoken judge wisely refrained from throwing more fuel on the fire.[52]

Procter and McNiven were not as controversial or as prolific as Gordon. In some years, each had one or two leading judgments in the reports and not many more concurring opinions. At times, McNiven and Procter wrote more dissents than anything else and appeared to put pen to paper mostly when they disagreed with the majority view. Like Gordon, Procter was sharp-tongued and lacked patience in hearings, and he shared much of the same outlook. McNiven was more gentlemanly and was remembered as being kindly and encouraging, but he didn't say much in hearings. McNiven drew heavily on his experience as a trial judge, as in one appeal of a child custody order:

> From experience as a trial judge I know how difficult it is to note and appraise every factor in a lengthy trial where the evidence covers a wide field. . . .
>
> . . . That evidence is undisputed—conceded by learned counsel for the wife. In the light of such evidence it is not the function of the court to speculate—to give legal effect to uncertainties, to probabilities, to possibilities. I would allow the appeal.

McNiven was a judge grounded in his experiences who preferred concrete problem solving over abstract principles.

Counsel who only remembered Ted Culliton as chief justice might be surprised that as a *puisne* judge, he was nearly silent. "He was the end judge" Calvin Tallis says, "and very seldom spoke up." This was in complete contrast to Culliton's style as chief justice, when he dominated hearings. The new judge from Gravelbourg did show early promise. He authored a reported decision for the court and a dissent in his first year, and wrote more and more as the decade wore on. His judgments were well organized and to the point. Culliton needed time to settle into his job, and according to Tallis worked very, very hard to learn his craft in his first years on the bench.

The arrival of Culliton changed decision-making dynamics. With the court usually short a judge or even two in the 1930s and 1940s, concurring opinions had become rare and dissents, never numerous, even rarer. In the 1950s, back up to full strength and usually sitting as a full court, the unanimity seen during Martin's early tenure noticeably declined and the proceedings were livelier if not necessarily more coherent. There were some clear differences of opinion and even a minor split on the court on negligence in motor vehicle accidents. The great increase in automobile use after the war produced many appeals, complicated by *The Contributory Negligence Act*, passed in 1944. The province had come late to this tort reform, which removed the all-or-nothing aspect of the common law defence of contributory negligence.[53] The judges were frequently drawn into debates over the degree of fault of the respective parties.

Gordon took a strong position on fault that put him at odds with his brother judges. He held, somewhat vehemently, that a driver with the right of way should have a presumption that they were not negligent or were much less negligent. He was irritated at the number of lawsuits where the plaintiff was the driver that did not have the right of way, and was further annoyed at trial judges apportioning blame equally when one driver had the right of way. His colleagues irritated him even more by upholding such judgments. As he stated in *Berry v Sparks*:

> My only reason for writing this short judgment is to emphasize that in my view, and I say it with every respect, when two vehicles collide at an intersection as the result of the negligence of both parties a greater degree of fault should be placed on the driver to the left if the facts are that he should have given way to the driver on the right.[54]

Apportioning negligence was generally a difficult exercise and was heavily dependent on the trial judge's fact findings. The judges often differed on their views on the trial evidence, and overall the court often interfered while protesting that deference should be shown to such findings.[55]

Matrimonial law was another developing field in Saskatchewan. Divorce was a federal responsibility, but Ottawa did not pass any laws on the subject until 1968. Until then, access to the courts for divorces depended on whether the 1857 English *Matrimonial Causes Act*, which had secularized divorce, applied in a province. A 1917 decision of the Privy Council had held that in Alberta and Saskatchewan it did.[56] After the war, the divorce rate jumped substantially, but the grounds for divorce were limited to adultery, free of any collusion or condonation, cruelty, or desertion.

Saskatchewan seemed to have more divorces than most provinces, something the court remarked upon. There was also an obvious divide between the Court of Appeal and the Court of King's Bench on the subject, with the former often allowing applications for divorce denied by the latter. Most divorces were granted for adultery, and several trial judges, particularly Justice George Taylor, were sticklers about collusion. The problem was that admitting to adultery, real or imagined, was the easiest and commonest way to procure a divorce. The judges on the appeal court took a more broad-minded view on what constituted adultery, cruelty, or desertion.

Gunn v Gunn demonstrated the divide and the reluctance on the trial court to grant divorces. The trial judge had refused to grant a decree of divorce, declaring the husband was not domiciled in the province, even though he had been transferred to Saskatchewan several years earlier. As the husband was likely to be transferred again, the judge decided the province was not his true domicile. This conclusion offended the appeal court's common sense and was absurdly out of step with the modern world. As Gordon wrote,

> A contrary view would result in an employee of any one of the chartered banks, the two trans-continental railway systems, the great oil companies, or the clergy of our churches, never acquiring a domicile of choice because every one would certainly admit that if he were offered promotion which entailed going to another province he would certainly accept it, apart from other rare considerations. It would mean, in fact, that if a Hollander emigrated to Canada with a young family, all of whom became naturalized with him, no member of his family who joined one of the above companies, could ever acquire a domicile of choice if he admitted that he would go to another province if offered promotion. His domicile would remain Holland.[57]

Gordon's decision illustrated that the court, although conservative, was not rigid and was willing to tackle a problem with a little judicial lawmaking when warranted.

The court indulged in some judicial lawmaking in cases involving oil and gas exploration and mineral rights, a relatively novel area of law in the province. There had been comparatively little oil exploration in

Saskatchewan until after the war. The 1947 Leduc strike in neighbouring Alberta created greater impetus, and it was not long before oil and gas litigation came to the Court of Appeal. In one early case, the court set its own direction in the definition of an oil and gas lease. In *Heier (Estate) (Re)*, the executors of an estate applied to the surrogate court for the approval of an oil and gas lease to the British American Petroleum Company, as section 15 of the provincial *Devolution of Real Property Act* required approval of any leases. The trial judge held that an oil and gas lease was not a lease in the usual sense but an agreement of sale for a severable portion of the land, and dismissed the application.

On appeal, the court split. The judges agreed that calling an agreement a lease did not necessarily make it a lease in a legal sense: this depended on the substance of the document. Martin and Procter followed the trial judge, arguing that there was ample authority for his conclusion from analogous mining leases. Like oil and gas leases, mining leases allowed the miner surface access, the right to build facilities for the extraction of the minerals, and the right to remove the minerals and sell them, with a royalty to the owner of the mineral rights. Gordon and McNiven disagreed, arguing that the agreement had many of the characteristics of a lease, such as a fixed term. Culliton sided with Procter and Martin. The court noted that there was considerable variance in judicial opinion on the point. And in the end, the Supreme Court of Canada settled the point by declaring that an oil and gas lease was a *profit-à-prendre*—literally, the right of taking—an interest in real property, which did not give possession but allowed one party to take natural resources from lands of another. For several years, however, the law in Saskatchewan was different.

The Trade Union Act, passed in 1944, was another novel statute which brought administrative law, a field that had been developing between the wars, under the court's scrutiny. Their deliberations in turn prompted the premier's accusation that the courts were biased against progressive legislation. *John East Iron Works* was one such decision, or more accurately series of decisions, that made clear the Court of Appeal's reservations about the CCF's legislation. Along with several other decisions both upheld and overruled at the Supreme Court and the Privy Council, *John East* helped create the principles governing appellate review of administrative boards and tribunals in Canada.[58]

ARTHUR THOMAS PROCTER

Arthur Procter was a Westerner, born in Oswald, Manitoba, in 1886. He was educated at St. JoÚ's College at the University of Manitoba and earned a law degree from the university in 1910.[4] He then decamped to Moosomin, that incubator of judges, and articled with Brown, Wylie and Mundell—Chief Justice Brown's law firm—staying with the firm after his call to the bar and becoming a partner.[5] Procter served as the district Crown prosecutor from 1914 to 1915. He enlisted in the army and served with the Fort Garry Horse. He was severely wounded in France, leaving him with permanent disabilities, but resumed his practice in Moosomin after the war. He was made a KC in 1926, two years before serving as assistant counsel to the Royal Grain Inquiry Commission, headed by Justice Turgeon.

Procter's political career overshadowed his legal accomplishments. He was defeated in his first tilt in the Moosomin riding in the Liberal's 1929 debacle but won a narrow victory in 1934. Re-elected in 1938, he was given the Highways and Transportation portfolio in the Patterson cabinet. He survived the 1944 election along with Patterson and was very prominent in opposition, leading the attacks on the Douglas government. Known for his quick wit and debating skills, Procter was well suited to the cut and thrust of legislative debate. His political career ended in 1948 with his appointment to the Court of Appeal.

Procter stepped down in 1961 at age seventy-five due to the institution of mandatory retirement. He died three years later after a lengthy illness.

Justice Arthur Thomas Procter, n.d. (Provincial Archives of Saskatchewan, R-D1748)

Saskatchewan Labour Relations Board meeting, c. 1954 or 1955. (Provincial Archives of Saskatchewan, R-B7078)

THE COURT OF APPEAL AND THE LABOUR RELATIONS BOARD

THE TRADE UNION *Act* was one of the novice CCF government's signature pieces of legislation. The statute was intended to support organized labour in the province, encourage unionization, and establish collective bargaining. The *Act* established a Labour Relations Board, made up of representatives of business, labour, and the public, to adjudicate disputes involving employers and employees over unionization and collective bargaining. Saskatchewan was the first province to enact legislation of this kind, although other provincial governments quickly followed suit. This reform was inspired by similar legislation that formed part of the New Deal in the United States and by wartime legislation passed to keep the peace between business and labour for the sake of the war effort.[59]

It was the dawning of a new age of industrial relations. Before the Second World War, Canada was not a friendly place for labour, even with unions legal since 1872.[60] Industrial unions had appeared by the twentieth century and grown with Canadian industry, but without a large industrial base until after the First World War, most union activity in Canada was restricted to the so-called craft unions, which were formed by workers in a skilled trade or occupation, such as carpenters. Unions had very little legal protection. Employers did not have to negotiate with them and could engage in union busting, with provincial governments often actively helping suppress strikes in the name of public order. In Saskatchewan, the 1931 Estevan coal mine strike was a recent, and brutal, example. Unions were also accused of being nests of communists and socialists. Undeniably, many labour activists, especially in the 1930s, were involved in radical politics, but it was also clear that there a great deal of "red baiting" to sway public opinion and undermine the labour movement.

Labour saw the courts as unfriendly and biased. Canadian courts consistently restricted the ability to strike through rulings declaring picketing illegal if it interfered with business activities or private property. Collective bargaining was a wholly foreign idea; judges viewed labour disputes through the lens of the common law as a matter of contract or master-and-servant relations. Provincial governments established labour boards to adjudicate labour disputes in part to avoid the courts: a tribunal with specialized knowledge could solve disputes in a faster and less expensive fashion. Labour legislation like Saskatchewan's *Trade Union Act* also represented the continued growth of the administrative state and the proliferation of boards and other tribunals, some of which had adjudicative roles not unlike the courts.

Outside of the coal mining regions, unions did not have a strong presence in agrarian Saskatchewan. Labour was one of the constituent parts of the CCF, however, and the Douglas government (the premier was trained as a printer and was a union member) was committed to protecting and encouraging unions. Like many other statutes that established a board with decision-making powers, such as the debt adjustment boards in the Depression, Saskatchewan's *Trade Union Act* also had a "privative" clause. Such clauses either restricted or eliminated any recourse to the courts and were intended by legislators to remove board decisions from judicial review. The justification was often that tribunals had specialized knowledge, experience, and expertise that judges did not, or broader aims than simply adjudicating disputes. It was also a handy way to keep the courts from interfering in an area where the government might be pursuing a certain policy. Privative clauses were initially not that effective. The courts regarded them with suspicion and often seemed determined to circumvent them.

A CCF lawyer from Ontario, F.A. Brewin, came to Saskatchewan to draft the *Trade Union Act*, likely with the assistance of Jack Corman and Morris Shumiatcher.[61] Shumiatcher would also play a major role in labour litigation, representing at different times the government, the board of review, and, once back in private practice, the unions. Another Ontario lawyer, W.K. Bryden, who had come to Saskatchewan to work on CCF legislation, was made the chair of the first Labour Relations Board created under *The Trade Union Act*. Bryden, Brewin, and Shumiatcher also represented "outside" experts of the sort that the CCF were heavily criticized for using, in part for importing new, bureaucratic ideas and policies to the province.

The major newspapers, who were no friends of the CCF and Douglas, took notice of the new legislation. The *Leader-Post* ran several editorials, noting that the statute, in setting up a board "with powers equivalent to those of a court," went further than any other labour legislation in the country. The newspaper criticized the legislation and the board in terms that were almost prescient of the fundamental issue that would emerge before the courts:

> Of the many objectionable features of the new Saskatchewan Trade(s) Union Act, the most objectionable and dangerous is that which confers upon the politically appointed board the powers of the courts and requires the courts to enforce the orders of the board without right of reviewing them or considering the foundation for their issuance. . . . There can be no resort to the courts.[62]

The newspaper warned that the statute was an "extreme departure from the basic principles of the British concept of law and justice" and that "the act is a major step towards authoritarianism." The writer also noted that the board "is not bound by any rules of evidence" and "can accept hearsay, rumours, idle chatter or malicious gossip." The writer feared that the board would be making decisions and issuing orders—enforced as a court order—without using "established rules of procedure or evidence." The paper predicted that the new legislation was the beginning of a system of unaccountable and politically appointed boards that "can be extended to almost every phase of human activity."

The newspaper's apprehension was a mild rebuke compared to the rhetoric of the CCF's opponents. The same day that the newspapers reported Douglas's attack on the courts, grocery wholesaler Abram Shelly of Saskatoon was telling the Canadian Retail Association that the province's *Trade Union Act* was the most radical in North America. He pronounced that "Mr. Molotov himself could not have written better legislation" and claimed that his firm had faced threats and intimidation from both unions and government officials, especially when the company threatened to challenge the constitutionality of the *Act* in the courts.[63] There were many other charges of this sort, from the press, the opposition benches, business groups, and so on. The spectre of authoritarianism was often invoked. With the Cold War in its early phases, the court undertook its deliberations on *The Trade Union Act* in a somewhat poisoned atmosphere.

THE PRELUDE TO *JOHN EAST IRON WORKS*

IT TOOK VERY little time before *The Trade Union Act* and the authority of the Labour Relations Board were challenged in court. The first significant appeal came before the court from a somewhat unusual source: the chief of the Regina City Police. The appeal was *Bruton v Regina City Policemen's Association*.

The rank and file of the Regina police force decided early in 1944 to unionize and approached the Trades and Labour Congress of Canada for assistance. Delegates from the congress tried to meet with Police Chief Martin Bruton as designated agents of the constables. Bruton refused to discuss the matter with anyone who was not a police officer. The newly formed policemen's association went to the Regina Board of Police Commissioners, who initially insisted on negotiating only with the police rank and file, but an agreement was eventually hammered out. The new union's relationship with the police chief remained rocky. Bruton continually refused to discuss grievances until finally the association applied to the Labour Relations Board for an order prohibiting the chief from engaging in unfair labour practices. The board agreed with the association's evidence and gave the order. Bruton then applied to the Court of Appeal for *certiorari* and the quashing of the board's order.

One of the wrinkles of the appeal was that the Trades and Labour Congress rep, P.W. Haffner, who was involved in the formation of the policemen's association, now sat on the Labour Relations Board. Like other provincial labour boards, Saskatchewan had a "tripartite" board, with representatives for labour and for employers and a "neutral" chairperson. Despite this, one of the grounds of the application was that the board was biased due to Haffner's presence. The other grounds were that the hearing was not public; that the board had exceeded its jurisdiction by making an error of law in finding that Chief Bruton was an employer or employer's agent as defined in *The Trade Union Act*; and that the statute was *ultra vires* because the powers of the board made it a judicial body analogous to a superior court, whose members the governor general had to appoint under section 96 of the *British North America Act*.

The court—with Martin, Gordon, and MacDonald writing opinions—granted the application and quashed the order, primarily on the ground that the Labour Relations Board had exceeded its jurisdiction. Martin held in a rather involved argument that the chief of police was not an employer or employer's agent even though he directly managed the force. Gordon also agreed that there was a "reasonable apprehension of bias" and that the *in camera* hearing violated procedural fairness. But more crucially, the *Bruton* decision established several important points that would guide the court for nearly a decade after the passing of *The Trade Union Act*.

The first was that the board was, if not a court, a tribunal that acted judicially. The powers and reach of the board's orders made this clear. As Martin wrote,

> It is essential however that the tribunal should be one which exercises judicial functions and which has the power to impose legal duties and obligations on the parties before it, similar to those which are usually decreed by Courts of Justice. In my opinion the Labour Relations Board is a body which is empowered by *The Trade Union Act, 1944* to exercise certain judicial functions in that it has power to determine questions affecting the rights of parties before it; and there can be no doubt that in making the order in question the board exercised a judicial function.[64]

Gordon rather neatly argued that because, under the *Act*, orders of the Labour Relations Board were enforceable as orders of the Court of King's Bench, ultimately such enforcement could result in imprisonment for contempt. This made it clear that the board exercised judicial powers.

As a judicial tribunal, the panel expected that the board should conduct itself to a large extent like a court, acting impartially and, if not with the same rigorous procedures of a court of law, with some reasonable approximation thereof. As MacDonald put it in a subsequent 1946 judgment:

> In my opinion the duty of the board is none the less to act faithfully to the best of their skill and knowledge, without fear or favour, bias or affection, to hold the scales of justice evenly between the litigant parties before it. To change the metaphor, when the board hews to the line it should be indifferent where the chips fall. It should also be indifferent as to their subsequent placement.[65]

The other conclusion followed hard after the first: that the rulings of the board, notwithstanding *The Trade Union Act*'s privative clause in section 15, were open to the review of a superior court through writs such as *certiorari*, *mandamus*, and prohibition. MacDonald in fact argued that the existence of the privative clause reinforced the status of the board as a judicial tribunal; otherwise, why the need for a clause denying superior court reviews? In *Bruton*, Martin and MacDonald held that there was ample precedent for this ruling wherever there was question of jurisdiction. The status of the police chief as "an employer or employer's agent" was a question of jurisdiction: if he did not fit the definition found in the *Act*, the statute did not apply to him.

With the *Bruton* appeal, the court had drawn a very definite line with their decision that the Labour Relations Board was a judicial body and thus had to act in various ways, and that the court was there to ensure it did, despite the presence of the privative clause. Morris Shumiatcher, as counsel for the board, tried in two early appeals to argue that the tribunal had an additional duty to further the aims of *The Trade Union Act*. He contended that this should be a factor in the board's decision-making. This line of argument fell on deaf ears; the court made it clear that in its view the board had no business combining policy-making with adjudicating.

JOHN EAST IRON WORKS

THE COURT DID not deal with the argument in *Bruton* that *The Trade Union Act* was *ultra vires* because the Labour Relations Board was acting as a superior court. It had not been necessary to decide the point, and the appeal court therefore declined to consider the argument, as was its practice. It was not long, however, before the idea was back in front of the court.

DONALD ALEXANDER MCNIVEN

Born in Walkerton, Ontario, in 1887, Don McNiven was still a baby when his parents settled in Virden, Manitoba. After school in Virden, McNiven went to Manitoba College, at that time part of the University of Manitoba and later a constituent of the University of Winnipeg.[6] One of his classmates was Jimmy Gardiner. After graduating with a degree in arts, McNiven taught school for two years and was the principal of a rural high school at Elkhorn, Manitoba.[7] He then went into law, beginning his articles in Virden at the firm of Chalmers and Brayfield.

Justice Donald Alexander McNiven, n.d. (Provincial Archives of Saskatchewan, R-LP-870)

McNiven came to Regina before finishing articles, entering the firm of Fish and Anderson, and was called to the bar in 1912. In 1919, he partnered with Douglas Fraser and was made a KC in 1927. McNiven served as president of the Regina Bar Association and was on the provincial executive of the Canadian Bar Association. He became deeply involved in Liberal politics both federally and provincially, first in the backroom and then as a candidate. He was the president of the Regina Liberal Association for seven years and was on the provincial executive for the party. Elected to the provincial legislature in 1925 as the member for Regina, McNiven went down to defeat four years later to his best friend, Conservative lawyer M.A. MacPherson.[8] He switched to federal politics a few years later and was elected in the Regina riding in 1935 and again in 1940.

McNiven was still an MP when he was offered a seat on the Court of King's Bench in 1944. He moved to the Court of Appeal five years later to replace Davis. Along with McNiven's judicial post came a stint as chairman of the regional war labour board and the Saskatchewan wartime Labour Relations Board. He was also the alternate chair of the National War Labour Board.[9]

Outside of his professional life, McNiven was very involved with the Community Chest, the forerunner of the United Way. As chairman in 1937, one of the darkest years of the

Depression, he managed to raise $40,000. McNiven remained involved once on the bench and was the chair of the local advisory board in 1958, when the Chest became the United Appeal. McNiven was a Mason and a member of the Assiniboia Club. Like most of his colleagues, he golfed, curled, and hunted.

As was strangely true of many members of the appeal court, McNiven was widowed relatively young and subsequently remarried. His health was also not the best. He had several heart attacks before succumbing in July 1961 at the age of seventy-four, just one year short of the new mandatory retirement age for federally appointed judges. McNiven was lauded for his industry and dedication but also as a helpful and accessible judge.

The John East Iron Works had been first established in 1910 in Saskatoon. The family business was strongly anti-union and had actively discouraged employees from forming or joining a union.[66] The company was brought in front of the Labour Relations Board after it fired six employees, five of whom had been active in unionizing their workplace. The United Steelworkers of America applied to the board to have the fired men reinstated and compensated for lost wages on the grounds that they had been dismissed for union activity, an unfair labour practice under the *Act*. The board duly found for the workers. The company then challenged the order by applying directly to the Court of Appeal for *certiorari*.

There were several grounds in the application, including the standard allegation of bias on the part of the board, but the main attack was that *The Trade Union Act* was *ultra vires*. The superior courts historically had exercised jurisdiction over enforcement of employment contracts and awarding damages for contractual breaches. Counsel for the company contended that section 5(e), which empowered the board to order the rehiring and compensation of fired employees, and sections 9 and 10, which made board orders enforceable as orders of the Court of King's Bench, essentially meant the province had set up a superior court and appointed its members. The board's jurisdiction and the power to enforce its orders made it analogous to such courts, and under section 96 of the BNA *Act*, only the federal government could appoint judges to the superior courts.

Although somewhat arcane to a layperson, it was a clever argument with supporting precedent, and it persuaded Chief Justice Martin, writing for the court. Other administrative tribunals had been challenged successfully on the same grounds in Ontario cases, some of which were upheld at the Judicial Committee of the Privy Council. If tribunals acted in an administrative or regulatory capacity, they generally remained within the competence of provincial legislatures; if tribunals determined matters that the courts had generally determined, they were taking on the character of courts and running afoul of the federal power over appointments. On this basis, Martin declared section 5 *ultra vires*, which almost completely undermined the Labour Relations Board as an adjudicator.

The court had ruled in favour of the company but was quick to grant the union, with support of the government, leave to appeal to the Judicial Committee of the Privy Council.[67] The hearing was instructive. Martin, for the court, agreed that the constitutionality of *The Trade Union Act* was a question of the "greatest public importance," which was a condition for leave to appeal in disputes where less than $4,000 was involved. Counsel for John East strenuously challenged the application. E.C. Leslie argued that since proceedings in front of the board could potentially end in fine or imprisonment, such proceedings were criminal law, and criminal appeals to the Judicial Committee had ended years before. Martin disagreed: in his view, there was no punitive aspect involved in the litigation, and he did not feel compelled to consider a hypothetical. The court concurred, but Gordon expressed "grave doubts" as to whether the Judicial Committee could hear the appeal.[68]

The Judicial Committee reversed the Court of Appeal and in doing so helped establish the modern administrative state in Canada.[69] Despite decisions barely a decade old that had supported Martin's conclusion, the committee's judgment took a different tack. Lord Simonds argued that the power of the board in section 5 was not analogous to a court enforcing employment contracts; it was for enforcing a new legal framework for deciding labour disputes through collective bargaining. This had not existed in 1867, when the BNA *Act* had provided the constitutional underpinnings of the judicial system, including giving the power of appointment to the federal government. In Simonds's view, the board was not exercising a jurisdiction similar to that of courts but something new. Furthermore, he thought it was clear that while the boards and tribunals might have some functions that were judicial, it was not conclusive that they operated as courts. In the case of the Labour Relations Board, he saw a "striking departure from the traditional conception of the court."[70] He noted that the judicial function of the board was calculated to advance the administrative policy of the statute. This alone made the board fundamentally different from a court.[71] "It is a common characteristic of so-called administrative tribunals," Simonds wrote, that "the ultimate decision may be determined not merely by application of legal principles . . . but by considerations of policy also."[72]

One authority has said that the Judicial Committee "in bold strokes declared the distinctiveness of the organs of the administrative state and described not only their differences from courts, but the grounds for deference to them."[73] The decision of the Judicial Committee may have established the legitimacy of administrative tribunals, but it was not the end of the John East litigation. The committee had noted that there had been other objections to the board's original order that the Court of Appeal had not found necessary to decide. The matter was sent back for the court to decide on the application for *certiorari*.[74]

If the Judicial Committee decision suggested that courts should approach administrative tribunals differently, the Court of Appeal did not appear to have got the message. MacDonald, writing for the court in the subsequent *John East* decision, struggled with the fact that the English law lords had not decided whether the board had been exercising a judicial power, as it was generally held that only proceedings of a judicial character were open to *certiorari*. His conclusion was that if the Judicial Committee had remitted the appeal without saying one way or another, he was justified in following the previous decisions of his own court regarding board orders that *certiorari* did apply.

That out of the way, MacDonald held that the board had no ability to determine the lost wages owed to the company employees. Lord Simonds had written that "the jurisdiction of the Board under s. 5(a), is not invoked by the employee for the enforcement of his contractual rights; those, whatever they may be, he can assert elsewhere." MacDonald took this to mean that while the board could order employees to be compensated, it could not determine the damages; this had to be done in the courts in accordance with the law for wrongful dismissal. In MacDonald's view, this was why the Judicial Committee had not ruled the board was analogous to a court, as the board was not exercising a jurisdiction of the courts. This almost entirely took the committee's comment out of context. What Simonds had more likely meant was that *The Trade Union Act* operated on its own terms, not the common law, around employment.[75] Orders of the board for reinstating an employee and compensating him were to enforce fair labour practices, not employment contracts. Employees might also have had alternative recourse under the accepted law of employment contracts, but this was not what the board was considering.

The Judicial Committee's decision in the first *John East* appeal had affirmed that the Labour Relations Board's powers were constitutional. In the second appeal, the Saskatchewan court affirmed its stance that the Labour Relations Board was a tribunal whose decisions were judicial in character, allowing for judicial review. MacDonald and the court seemed either to not understand or to disregard Lord Simonds's views as to the different character of a tribunal such as the Labour Relations Board, which admittedly did not make the court's position untenable. The court denied leave to appeal to the Supreme Court of Canada, and that august body also refused leave, leaving the court's decision final.

AFTER *JOHN EAST*

FOR SOME TIME after *John East*, the Court of Appeal stuck to its mantra that the Labour Relations Board was a judicial tribunal that must act judiciously. Procter aptly summed up the court's attitude:

> *The Trade Union Act, 1944* gives to the Labour Relations Board powers so extensive that rights usually regarded as fundamental in democratic states are severely curtailed, and in particular a citizen's right of access to the courts to protect him from injustice or hardship purports to be taken away. In such cases the Act must be strictly construed by the courts.[76]

Procter wrote this in the court's 1951 judgment *Sisters of Charity, Providence Hospital v Saskatchewan (Labour Relations Board)*, an appeal from Justice George Taylor's decision granting an application of *certiorari* and quashing an order of the Labour Relations Board. The hospital, run by a religious order, had fired three laundry employees. The Textile Workers Union applied to reinstate the employees, alleging the firing was due to their union activities, although the workers did not belong to the union.

The board did so, although counsel for the hospital argued that the union had no standing to bring the application, as it was not directly involved. Then five other employees of the hospital laundry applied for a rehearing, alleging the first three employees had been let go for cause, not union work, and that the rest of the staff would quit if they were reinstated. The application was dismissed, and finally the hospital applied for *certiorari*. The union then appealed Taylor's decision.

Procter upheld the quashing of the board's reinstatement order, ruling that the *Act* and regulations the board had passed under authority of the statute clearly stated applicants to the board had to have a direct interest in the proceedings. He also held that applicants had to make a *prima facie* case before the board with evidence of their allegations. Although Procter conceded that the board did not have to be as rigorous as a court of law in allowing such evidence, he also held that the proceedings of the tribunal had to record the basis of their decision. The point was once again that the Labour Relations Board as a judicial body had to conform to certain standards.

The Court of Appeal never once supported the Labour Relations Board in the ten years after it was established.[77] In every case, the court granted each application for relief, or upheld the granting, and seemed implacably critical of the board's orders. But in 1954, the court split, with Martin and Culliton dissenting. The F.W. Woolworth Company and an alleged majority of employees in their Weyburn store applied to the court for an order of *mandamus* to compel the board to carry out proceedings to decertify the union previously granted recognition as the bargaining agent for the store's employees. The board had refused to do so, holding that the employees' request was not legitimate but was company-sponsored. The board chair cited the troubled history of labour relations at the Weyburn store, including previous orders of the board, and held that there was evidence that the company was behind the employees' bid to decertify the union.

The majority of the court held for the company. Seemingly forgetting his many pronouncements on respecting fact findings in inferior courts or tribunals, Gordon reviewed the evidence cited in the board's decision and pronounced "that there was not a scintilla of evidence" that the company had put the employees up to applying for decertification.[78] He wrote, perhaps somewhat petulantly,

EDWARD MILTON CULLITON

Ted Culliton was beyond doubt a giant in the annals of the legal profession in Saskatchewan and another long-serving chief justice. He defined the court for twenty years in a fashion unprecedented in the province.

Justice Edward Milton Culliton as a major in the Canadian Army, c. 1944. (Provincial Archives of Saskatchewan, R-A2822)

Culliton was born in Grand Forks, Minnesota, in 1906, but his parents were Canadians of Irish stock.[10] His father was a CPR agent whose job had taken the family to the United States. Soon after Culliton was born, his father was transferred to Saskatchewan. Ted Culliton grew up in several small towns but had most of his schooling in the community of Elbow, on the banks of the South Saskatchewan River.[11] He went from high school in Elbow to the University of Saskatchewan to take an arts degree. He waited on tables in the residence dining hall and worked summers as a CPR section man to help pay for his education. A "big man on campus," Culliton played varsity hockey, worked on the student newspaper as business manager, and while in law school served as president of the student council.[12] He maintained a strong relationship with the university his whole life and was on the board of governors from 1956 to 1962, was chairman in 1961 and 1962, and served as chancellor from 1963 to 1969.[13]

After earning his bachelor's degree in 1926, Culliton went directly into law school and finished in 1928.[14] He was the first judge of the Court of Appeal to have a law degree from the university. He was fortunate to graduate and enter articles before the Depression began. Even so, he sold life insurance briefly while looking for articles, which brought him to Gravelbourg, a decidedly multicultural community southwest of Moose Jaw.[15] Culliton articled with Thomas Gallant, KC, a French-speaking Catholic who, when he was appointed to the District Court in 1930, handed over an excellent practice to his former student, barely a year at the bar. Like many practitioners in small towns dependent on agriculture, Culliton took his share of fees in kind. He had a general practice, including criminal law. He got acquittals for the accused in two sensational trials in the early 1930s, one for a bank robbery and the other on a charge of murder.[16]

Culliton entered politics shortly after getting established in Gravelbourg. Elected in 1935, he was the youngest member of the legislature. Like Procter, he was quickly moved into the Patterson cabinet with the portfolio of provincial secretary. Culliton had been in the army training corps during university and joined up in 1941.[17] Posted to the artillery, he commanded several units before he joined the Office of the Judge Advocate General in London. While on active service, he remained in cabinet as minister without portfolio and stood for re-election in 1944. Absent in England, he lost by only ninety-five votes.[18] After the war, Culliton returned to practice but contested the leadership of the provincial Liberal Party, losing to MP Walter Tucker. He returned to the legislature in 1948 and served as Tucker's finance critic. The Liberal leader would later say Culliton was his right hand and deeply regretted losing him to the bench.[19]

Culliton went straight to the Court of Appeal in 1951, replacing MacDonald as the Catholic judge, and served for thirty years. John Diefenbaker appointed him chief justice in 1962 after Emmett Hall was sent to the Supreme Court of Canada, a rare example of non-partisanship. While a *puisne* justice, Culliton headed the 1957 commission on the administration of justice in Saskatchewan, which led to major changes on the District Court. He was also deeply involved in the creation of the Canadian Judicial Council in 1971.

Among Culliton's many honours was a doctorate from the University of Saskatchewan in 1962 and being named a Companion of the Order of Canada in 1981. More unusual was a papal decree inducting him into the Vatican's Order of St. Gregory. Culliton stayed involved in the community as a judge, serving as chairman of the Saskatchewan golden jubilee committee in 1955 and the university's jubilee committee in 1959. He was on three hospital boards and worked with the Canadian Red Cross, the Canadian National Institute for the Blind, the United Appeal, and St. Thomas More College. When Culliton had time, he liked to curl and golf, and he went to Hawaii every year without fail. He remained busy in retirement with volunteer work and government commissions and died in Regina in 1991 at the age of eighty-five.

> Are we sitting in appeal from the board just because we look into the evidence to see whether there is a single line on which its conclusion can be based? I do not think so. Am I to banish from my consideration facts which are notorious, such as the difficulty of getting help in the towns and small cities of the province and the rapid turnover of such help? Why should girls, who are only taking a position for a few months, be forced to join a union at all? The duty of explaining this fact to new untrained help is on the employer. One of the orders made against this employer for "unfair practices" we are told was its failure to discharge an employee who would not join the union.[79]

Procter was more measured in his comments but also held that the evidence did not support the board's decision. Martin, with Culliton's concurrence, returned to the court's more traditional deference when dealing with the fact finding of an inferior tribunal. The chief justice argued that the board had the power to make the findings it did; that there was evidence that warranted its findings; and that the members of the board had the advantage of examining the evidence, including witness testimony, first-hand. Martin's ruling was only unusual in that he took this stance with a decision of the Labour Relations Board.

And within a year, the court upheld an order of the board in *Re: Marshall Wells Company*, and other affirmations followed.[80] *Marshall Wells* ushered in a more deferential approach. The court continued to claim the power to review board decisions, which was "an orthodox principle of administrative law" but became much more circumspect. Procter and Gordon never looked to be fully reconciled to the board, often dissenting, but the court seemed able to show some deference. After 1961, with Culliton as chief justice and four different *puisne* judges, the court exercised great restraint with appeals of board orders.[81] In part this reflected a different Labour Relations Board as well as a different court; Makaroff left in 1961 and the right-leaning Ross Thatcher Liberals appointed a new board several years later. But deference to administrative tribunals had also become a well-entrenched principle, and courts started to respect privative clauses much more.

DEFENDERS OF THE ESTABLISHMENT OR DEFENDERS OF FREEDOM?

WAS TOMMY DOUGLAS right that the courts had deeply held biases against progressive legislation like *The Trade Union Act*? There was certainly support for his view. In a 1952 article, Bora Laskin, one day to be chief justice of Canada but then a law professor in Toronto, analyzed the application of *certiorari* to the decisions of administrative tribunals and concluded that privative clauses were scarcely worth drafting. More than half of his case examples came from Saskatchewan.[82] For ten years after the passing of *The Trade Union Act*, the Court of Appeal was deeply suspicious of the Labour Relations Board and anxious to assert a supervisory role. Procter, McNiven, and Gordon were often harshly critical until Douglas finally called Gordon out in the legislature. There are stories that the entire court would turn in their chairs and face the wall when counsel rose to defend the unions or the board, although these may be apocryphal.[83] Gordon himself was cut exactly to measure for Douglas's insinuations: formerly a wealthy lawyer with many corporate clients, involved in Conservative Party politics.

Yet it was not clear whether Gordon was hostile towards the policy embodied in *The Trade Union Act* and the Labour Relations Board so much as he was concerned about the operation of boards and tribunal and what he saw as incompetence. Gordon had similar complaints about *the Farmers' Creditors Arrangement Act* boards of review. He had voiced misgivings about procedural fairness and argued the board of review should be held to the same standards as courts of law.[84] The court's position in *John East* and other labour appeals was consistent with its FCAA jurisprudence: that the board was a judicial body and should act judicially; that the statutory language of the *Act* had to be strictly construed as it affected previous existing rights; and that judicial review was available through *certiorari* and other writs irrespective of a privative clause. The court admittedly was more deferential in FCAA appeals, but this likely reflected that judges such as Brown and Martin headed the review boards, that the FCAA was written to deal with an economic disaster that severely affected the province, and that legislator-jurists of the calibre of Haultain, Turgeon, and Martin were on the court.

The court's stringent treatment of the Labour Relations Board was thus striking but not unprecedented. And it applied similar standards to yet other statutory boards. In another appeal, McNiven ruled that the Provincial Mediation Board was a quasi-judicial body and had to act fairly. "I have always regarded it as a fundamental principle of our jurisprudence," McNiven wrote, "that no subject should be deprived of his property or his constitutional rights without being given an opportunity to be heard unless opportunity were denied him in the most unequivocal language by competent legislative authority."[85]

McNiven's statement captured an important aspect of the court's outlook. The superior courts, in the British tradition, were protectors of constitutional liberties and civil rights within the constraints of prevailing doctrines of parliamentary supremacy. Supervising and holding tribunals and boards to certain standards was part of this tradition.

This does not mean that the judges of the court didn't carry some biases. Saskatchewan had a long tradition of progressive politics, but the CCF represented something different. *Socialism* was a freighted term, made worse by the Cold War, and strongly associated for many with organized labour and industrial unions. The judges were men of their time. It was somewhat telling that Frederick Cronkite, dean of law at the University of Saskatchewan, declared in an address that courts "should desist in the practice of committing 'judicial sabotage' on government statutes."[86] Cronkite used President Roosevelt and the Supreme Court of the United States as an example but surely had the recent tempest in Saskatchewan in mind. Cronkite spoke eloquently of the needs of the courts and judiciary to modernize not only procedure but also their approach to law and look to contemporary mores as well as precedent. This sounded very much like advocating consideration of policy and social needs in judicial decisions, something more characteristic of modern approaches to statute interpretation. He also doubted it would happen. Cronkite's comments captured what would become a growing frustration in the near future: the inability of the courts, trapped in narrow formalism, to adapt the law to a rapidly changing society and deal with injustices.

John East was one of the last important appeals from Saskatchewan to go to the Judicial Committee of the Privy Council. In 1949, appeals to that body from Canada were abolished as the last step to true nationhood. Appeals for litigation begun before that fateful day in 1949 could still be taken to the committee, however, and it was not until 1959 that the last Canadian appeal was finally heard. The severing of that connection was momentous. Canadian courts alone now charted the course of the law. And the Saskatchewan Court of Appeal was just one rung away from Canada's court of last resort.

Dean Frederick Cronkite, College of Law, University of Saskatchewan, c. 1950. (Provincial Archives of Saskatchewan, R-A5331)

CONCLUSION

IN 1939, WHEN the CCF was still a small if vocal opposition party and Tommy Davis had not yet joined the court, he complained to his friend Jimmy Gardiner about the proliferation of government boards and tribunals. Davis bemoaned the fact that these bodies were intruding into the jurisdiction of the courts and planned, as attorney general, to disband some of these bodies and let the courts assume their function. As Davis said, with fine rhetorical flourish, "The courts are the bulwark and last resort for protection of the citizen as against his fellow citizen and also against the unfair encroachments of the state against his rights."[87]

It was clear that the judges of the Martin court felt much the same way. The court had for years been deferential to such boards as they proliferated, but with the election of the CCF and the creation of the Labour Relations Board and others, a tipping point was reached. Tommy Douglas was likely right when he claimed the courts were biased. They were not necessarily biased against his government, however, but against the creation of bodies that could have great impact on people's lives and livelihood but were by design not answerable to the courts. The single-minded determination of the court to assert a supervisory role over the Labour Relations Board might not have been motivated so much by animus against the CCF or organized labour as by concern over the reach and power of unaccountable government bodies.

CHAPTER 6

DIEFENBAKER'S COURT

EMMETT HALL WAS NOT A MAN TO MINCE WORDS. LONG considered one of Saskatchewan's leading barristers, Hall had become the chief justice of the Court of Queen's Bench. He was also a trusted adviser to John Diefenbaker—his law school classmate and now prime minister of Canada—particularly about the judiciary. Writing Diefenbaker at the end of 1960, Hall had some harsh words about the province's Court of Appeal:

> The CofA situation causes me a great deal of concern. It was once a great court but has lost that prestige and fallen into the bad practice of more or less deciding the result before hearing the argument. Gordon is the real culprit but Culliton has become an apt pupil though without Gordon's at times unpleasant manner. McNiven cannot be counted on to make a contribution.[1]

Saskatchewan's was not the only appellate court in Canada in need of renewal. Diefenbaker was willing to make long-overdue changes to bring about that renewal, and in doing so he completely remade Saskatchewan's appeal court. It became a court that reflected Diefenbaker's own concerns with civil liberties and due-process rights, with first Emmett Hall and then Ted Culliton as chief justice of Saskatchewan. Culliton would succeed Hall in short order, and sitting with four Diefenbaker appointees he created a court that would be remembered for its robust contributions to the criminal law.

A CANADIAN REVOLUTION

IN 1957, JOHN G. Diefenbaker achieved his boyhood dream of becoming prime minister of Canada. With his election victory, Diefenbaker ended twenty-two consecutive years of Liberal government. It was practically a revolution. The following year, a snap election gave Diefenbaker what is still considered the largest parliamentary majority in Canadian history.[2]

Diefenbaker was very much a man of Saskatchewan, the first and so far only prime minister from the province.[3] The son of a schoolteacher, he was born in Ontario in 1895, and the family came west when he was eight. Educated in Saskatoon, Diefenbaker earned a master's degree at the University of Saskatchewan before enrolling in law. He practised briefly in the small town of Wadena before gravitating to Prince Albert. He rose to prominence as a criminal defence lawyer and developed a lifelong passion for civil liberties.

Diefenbaker was a master of the dramatic jury address. His thunderous oratory served him well in his relentless pursuit of political office, but it was not until 1940 that he was finally elected to Parliament. On the opposition benches as a decidedly Red Tory, Diefenbaker honed his message of an inclusive nationalism "without hyphenations," social progress in the form of an enhanced welfare state, and the protection of civil liberties. His government would introduce a bill of rights that anticipated and inspired the *Charter of Rights and Freedoms*.

Diefenbaker also greatly contributed to achieving universal medical care in Canada by appointing Emmett Hall head of the Royal Commission on Health Services in 1961. Hall's commission strongly recommended that the federal government help finance the provinces in establishing public health care. Hall went beyond the usual remit for an active judge on a commission and lobbied for his recommendations with public speeches as well as buttonholing government ministers.[4] In 1966, the Lester Pearson government implemented federal health-care funding.

Diefenbaker and Hall were following the path already blazed in Saskatchewan by Tommy Douglas. The introduction of universal medical care in the province was the CCF premier's crowning achievement.

Douglas had fought the 1960 election largely as a plebiscite on public health care.[5] Ironically, it was left to his successor, Woodrow Lloyd, to face down the province's doctors and implement the Saskatchewan Medical Insurance Bill. Douglas returned to Ottawa in 1961 to lead the national CCF, rebranded as the New Democratic Party.

Lloyd suffered the same fate as many who succeeded a long-standing and popular leader, losing the 1964 election. The absence of Douglas was one factor in the CCF's defeat. Another was the party's nearly twenty years in power. The opposition Liberals had found an effective leader, businessman Ross Thatcher of Moose Jaw, a disenchanted former CCF MP. Thatcher switched his allegiance in 1955 and became the Liberal Party leader in 1959. In an early debate with Douglas, Thatcher demonstrated he was a force to be reckoned with.[6] By framing the choice for voters as economic development fuelled by free enterprise versus inept CCF bureaucracy and high taxes, he consolidated anti-CCF sentiment under the Liberal banner.

Thatcher inherited a fiscally sound government, but the state of the province's economy had played into his hands during the election. While Saskatchewan was more prosperous than ever, in relative terms it had fallen behind the other Western provinces.[7] The population remained stuck at just under a million and economic growth in Alberta, British Columbia, and Manitoba had substantially exceeded Saskatchewan's. The stagnant population growth was in part due to migration: young residents were leaving for better opportunities elsewhere, often taking an excellent university education with them. Alberta and British Columbia benefited from an influx of Saskatchewan lawyers.[8]

Thatcher declared Saskatchewan "open for business," reducing government spending, lowering taxes, and selling some Crown businesses. Many senior bureaucrats anticipated being fired and moved on to Ottawa, establishing the "Saskatchewan Mafia," which was very influential under the federal Liberals.[9] For all his talk of small government, Thatcher did not radically downsize the civil service and left the CCF's popular social programs alone. Like his predecessors, he worked on diversifying the economy, primarily through encouraging foreign investment. He managed with great effort to get a pulp and paper mill built near Prince Albert to boost the timber industry. The potash industry benefited from Liberal policies, and Thatcher engineered a cross-border pro-rationing system with US jurisdictions to support prices.

The Liberals were easily re-elected in 1967, but Thatcher's second term was less successful. The premier introduced an austerity budget that took even members of his own government by surprise.[10] He particularly targeted university funding, seemingly motivated by suspicion of campus radicalism.[11] It was a wrong-headed policy when higher education was in great demand thanks to the baby boom generation and the needs of the modern economy. But it was the introduction of health-care user fees that put a real dent in Thatcher's popularity and led to his electoral defeat in 1971.[12]

Beyond politics, the post-war trends of Saskatchewan society continued. By the end the 1960s, a solid majority of residents lived in urban centres.[13] Agriculture was still a major part of Saskatchewan's identity but took on a nostalgic hue for more and more people. At the same time, farm life improved with modern amenities like indoor plumbing becoming unremarkable. Increasingly, people had post-secondary educations and white-collar jobs. The local arts scene flourished while American pop culture ruled. The advent of official multiculturalism was on the horizon, but the province's multiple ethnicities had largely melted together. A Ukrainian or Polish family name was no longer a barrier to advancement in business or the professions. And although large numbers of women had worked outside the home in the 1950s, the stirrings of feminism were also felt, and a growing number of women started to make a mark in traditionally male spheres such as the professions.

During the 1960s, female students became steadily more common at Saskatchewan's law school. The Saskatchewan bar was relatively progressive when it came to women and the law. There had been pioneers like Mary Cathcart, the first woman admitted to the Saskatchewan bar, in 1917, and Jean Ethel MacLachlan, who was made a juvenile court magistrate in the same year.[14] Dorothy Greensmith earned a law degree in 1925 while working in the Department of the Attorney General and was made a KC in 1948.[15]

Aspiring women lawyers in the 1960s had several prominent role models, such as Tillie Taylor, Marian Wedge, and Mary Batten. Taylor was the daughter of prominent Saskatoon lawyer J.M. Goldenberg.[16] She worked as a secretary while her husband, noted labour lawyer George Taylor, got his law degree, and, after raising two children, earned her own degree in 1956. She was appointed the province's first female provincial magistrate in 1960. Marian Wedge, Emmett Hall's daughter, entered law at the age of thirty-seven, graduating in 1961 while pregnant with her fifth child.[17] Wedge was later appointed to the Court of Queen's Bench, joining one of the profession's trailblazers, Mary Batten, who had been appointed to the District Court in 1964, the first woman to be appointed to a federal court in Saskatchewan and only the second in Canada.[18] Born Mary Fodchuk, Batten had graduated in 1944 and articled with Diefenbaker.[19] She was a Liberal MLA crucial to Ross Thatcher's leadership bid. Batten became chief justice of the Queen's Bench in 1983, the second woman in Canada to head a superior trial court. Through the 1960s, the number of women graduating in law gradually increased.

These young lawyers and their male colleagues started their careers under the mostly benign eye of Ted Culliton, the chief justice of Saskatchewan. He presided with a bench of Diefenbaker appointments, which would be Saskatchewan's appellate bench for nearly twenty years.

THE CULLITON (AND HALL) COURT

BY 1961, AS Emmett Hall had noted, the Court of Appeal was in need of renewal. Saskatchewan was plagued with a difficulty weighing on many Canadian appeal courts: old and cranky judges. The most recent appointment, Culliton, was a hale and hearty fifty-five, but his colleagues were older by twenty years or more. Chief Justice Martin was well into his eighties, and Gordon, Procter, and McNiven were all in their seventies, with McNiven in very weak health. Martin's hearing was poor; one counsel recalled the chief justice asking his brother judges what counsel had just said.[20] Martin was also suffering serious health problems and was hospitalized towards the end of 1960. Another Diefenbaker correspondent, John Hnatyshyn in the Senate, informed the prime minister of Martin's illness, adding, "In the meantime Judge Gordon is having the time of his life signing judgments as 'Acting Chief Justice for the Court of Appeal for the Province of Saskatchewan.'"[21]

Diefenbaker was quite familiar with elderly judges from his long years at the bar and was determined to succeed where R.B. Bennett had failed and institute mandatory retirement. The federal government had previously set seventy-five as the age of retirement for the Supreme Court and the Exchequer Court of Canada. But the provincial superior courts were different. Under section 99 of the BNA *Act*, the judges appointed to these

EMMETT MATTHEW HALL

Emmett Hall was one of the legal giants of Saskatchewan. His impact on the Court of Appeal was only minor due to his short tenure as chief justice, the shortest of any for the court. But in many other respects, he cast a long shadow in the history of the province. He is sometimes considered, along with Tommy Douglas, to be the father of universal public health care in Canada.

Hall was born in Saint-Colomban, Quebec, on November 9, 1898.[1] He was the fourth of eleven children. Hall and his siblings were the only English-speaking children at the local school, and he became fluent in French. His parents, James and Alice, were staunch Catholics of Irish descent and dairy farmers. They moved the family west in 1910 and settled on the outskirts of Saskatoon, attracted to the growing little city's temperance roots and the newly established university.[2]

After finishing high school at Saskatoon Collegiate Institute, Hall got a teaching job in Northern Saskatchewan thanks to his proficiency in French.[3] He had decided on the law, and in 1916, after a summer teaching, he entered articles with the firm of Murray and Munro as well as the college of law at the University of Saskatchewan. At the time, law students articled during office hours and took classes in the morning and evening. Hall graduated with a law degree but never took an undergraduate degree. Blind in one eye, he was declined for military service and threw himself instead into his studies. His 1919 university yearbook noted that "Emmett is the 'boy' graduate in law this year, but for all that he is recognized by all as a 'comer.' Predictions are odious, but when one possesses such abilities as he does, no heights are unsurmountable—in short, his future is assured."[4]

Hall began practice with the Saskatoon firm of Bence, Stevenson and McLorg and was hired away by E.S. Wilson of Humboldt on the strength of his experience handling Soldier Settlement Board clients, which had been part of the Bence firm's business.[5] He then worked with J. Harvey Hearn in Wadena and eventually bought Hearn's practice. After several years of trying to make a go of it, Hall accepted an invitation from Hearn to join him in Saskatoon. He soon made a mark as a litigator, making his first appearance at the Supreme Court of Canada in 1928, successfully arguing against a decision of Justice Lamont – who had just been appointed to the court – on the liability of farmers towards free ranging livestock.[6]

Hall was adept at civil litigation, but he was best known for his criminal defence work. Painstakingly thorough in preparation, he was aggressive in the courtroom, reflecting an absolute commitment to his clients. There was some concern when he was appointed to the bench that Hall was too combative to be a judge.[7] In 1935, he partnered with Percy Maguire and the following year received his KC. By the time of his appointment as chief justice of the Court of Queen's Bench, Hall was considered one of the leaders of the bar. He was a bencher of the Law Society from 1945 to 1957 and president in 1952, the first former bencher to be appointed to the court since Elwood.[8] Hall also served as the Saskatchewan vice-president of the Canadian Bar Association from 1943 to 1945. He taught at the University of Saskatchewan's law school from 1945 to 1958 and would later serve as chancellor of the university.

Politics was one arena where Hall did not enjoy success. Long a Liberal, he transferred his allegiance to the Progressive Conservatives and ran in the 1948 provincial election but lost. In 1957, he failed even to get the party's nomination.[9] Hall later joked that the voters did both him and themselves a favour. Aside from dabbling in politics, Hall threw himself into various community causes, propelled in part by his strong Catholic faith. He served on the Saskatoon Separate School Board for a dozen years, as its chair for nine, and was also chair of the Catholic School Trustees Association of Saskatchewan. His other major commitments were the board of St. Paul's Hospital, where he was the chair, and the national executive of the Red Cross.

Chief Justice Emmett Matthew Hall, c. 1961. (Provincial Archives of Saskatchewan, 61-842-01)

Hall joked that St. Paul's was the reason why Diefenbaker asked him to chair the Royal Commission on Health Services in 1961.[10] He undertook the task with customary thoroughness and boldness. Many were surprised that a Tory judge recommended such a far-reaching, comprehensive vision of national health care, and were even more surprised by his very public advocacy. Hall remained a passionate defender of public health care.

Hall's service on commissions and inquiries may have rivalled Turgeon's. While still a judge, he recommended a controversial restructuring of Ontario's education system. After retiring from the Supreme Court, he had a second career as a commissioner, working on university education in Saskatchewan, an overhaul of the provincial court system, a re-examination of public health care, and grain handling and rail transportation. This last inquiry brought him into direct conflict with Otto Lang, the minister of transport.[11] It was typical Hall: he thoroughly canvassed the issues and formulated his conclusions and then fearlessly defended them whatever the controversy or opposition that might follow.

Not surprisingly, Hall's singular contributions to Saskatchewan and Canada were well recognized. He was made a Companion of the Order of Canada, was given multiple honorary doctorates, and was a member of two different papal orders of knighthood, the Knights of Malta and the Order of St. Gregory.[12] He also served as the chancellor of the University of Guelph. For all his awards and honours, Hall kept his perspective on life and a sense of humour. When a law student asked Hall the source of his success, Hall replied, "I had the good fortune to sit beside John Diefenbaker in law school."[13]

courts had life tenure, and there was a question as to whether the Canadian Parliament had the power to unilaterally amend the constitution to establish a retirement age. The Justice Department determined that the Imperial Parliament—the British legislature acting in its larger capacity to legislate for colonial possessions and dominions—had to make the amendment. Diefenbaker's first justice minister, Davie Fulton, quietly negotiated with the provinces to secure their support. Their unanimous consent spoke volumes. Robert Walker, the attorney general of Saskatchewan, even suggested seventy rather than seventy-five for retirement.[22]

There was still controversy. The opposition questioned why, unlike in the United Kingdom in 1959, the amendment applied to sitting judges as well as to subsequently appointed judges.[23] Lester Pearson suggested that forcing retirement on judges with life appointments might be a violation of contract. He also raised the question of whether the amendment undermined judicial independence. Members of the judiciary made similar objections and more in submissions to the minister of justice. There was grumbling about court challenges. Diefenbaker and Fulton did not back down. The amendment was passed in London near the end of 1960, taking effect on March 1, 1961.

The amendment had major consequences for Saskatchewan's Court of Appeal. Martin and Gordon had to step down immediately and Procter three months later. McNiven died in July 1961. Only Culliton remained. Diefenbaker and his Progressive Conservative government made five appointments to the court, almost completely remaking it. Four of the five were entirely new to the judiciary and inexperienced.

Gordon did not go quietly. He was firmly opposed to mandatory retirement and took it as a personal affront. He said on retirement, "I would rather work on a lawsuit than anything else in the world." And true to his word, Gordon went back to the practise of law, but not in an advisory capacity as was usually the case. He had been a litigator, and a litigator he became again.

This was not unprecedented. Justice Roy Kellock of the Supreme Court of Canada famously did the same. There was no rule against it in Saskatchewan, just convention, and perhaps common sense. The propriety of a former judge of appeal appearing in front of his own court, which Gordon did, was suspect. Garrett Wilson, as a very young lawyer, had the dubious distinction of being opposing counsel at one of Gordon's first appearances at the court after his retirement.[24] He recalled that Gordon lectured the panel in a rather hectoring fashion. Gordon also won the appeal. He was quite irrepressible. He acted for the Saskatchewan doctors opposing public health care and aided Morris Shumiatcher in his fight against criminal conspiracy charges, dealt with below. The two became close friends, any friction from Shumiatcher's appearances at the Court of Appeal on behalf of the Labour Relations Board long forgotten.

Martin was also disappointed. After six decades of public service, he still felt he had something to offer. One Regina lawyer recalled seeing Martin interviewed on local television.[25] The chief justice complained that he was still vital and able to do his job and made a pointed comment about young and inexperienced judges taking over, perhaps forgetting that Culliton was sitting beside him during the interview.

The first order of business was a new chief justice. There was little doubt in Saskatchewan who it would be. Diefenbaker duly promoted Emmett Hall from the Court of Queen's Bench. Hall had briskly overhauled the trial court, which had become disorganized in the last days of Chief Justice Brown.[26] The Queen's Bench had its share of elderly judges and also benefited from mandatory retirement. Before his appointment as head of the Queen's Bench, Hall was considered a leading barrister of the province, with a particularly strong reputation as criminal counsel. He was an Irish fighter who loved an underdog. He had helped defend the Regina rioters without hesitation and in his youth had fearlessly taken on the Ku Klux Klan. He had the dubious distinction of being burned in effigy by the KKK. Hall later became the civil libertarian on the Supreme Court of Canada. Famously, he was the only dissenter on the Steven Truscott reference in 1967.

Hall also thought he was the obvious choice for chief justice of Saskatchewan. Writing Diefenbaker about potential appointments, Hall raised the possibility:

> I say truthfully that I am very happy in my present office and happy to remain here—I do not covet Martin's place.... However, with equal frankness and sincerity I want to say that if it should suit your plans and be your will to put me in Martin's place I would go gladly and be the more in your debt for the opportunity of being able to dedicate myself to rebuilding and restoring the CofA to the position it once held.[27]

Hall felt a strong background in criminal law was vital for the new chief justice. "Too many otherwise qualified judges are very deficient in this branch of the law and some are a complete loss in it," he told Diefenbaker.[28] He also emphasized the importance of the court in providing leadership to the judiciary: "A good C. of A. can set the standard for the other courts. A poor C. of A. can destroy or frustrate the work of the lower courts however good the judges of the lower court may be." He believed he had a responsibility to restore the court's prestige and excellence.

In truth, Hall was the best choice, especially when the need to satisfy party loyalists was taken into account. In opposition, Diefenbaker, along with others in his party, had decried the role of patronage in judicial appointments. Davie Fulton raised the question of patronage in the House in 1952, but the subsequent debate never really wrestled with the true issue: whether appointments were being made on the basis of party service over ability, causing the best candidates to be passed over in favour of party stalwarts.

Emmett Matthew Hall, 2013. (Artist: Jill Armstrong; photo: Mark Greschner. Court of Appeal.)

Diefenbaker, like R.B. Bennett before him, found it nearly impossible to avoid political imperatives. The Conservatives had been out of power since 1935, and there were many lawyers who expected that their time was at hand. But in Saskatchewan, lawyers of Conservative convictions and the requisite ability were in short supply. Many talented lawyers were too old for appointments in light of mandatory retirement.[29] E.C. Leslie, a brilliant civil litigator, was possibly the leading barrister in Saskatchewan. Hall still considered him a possible appointment as chief justice of the Court of Queen's Bench or the appellate court in 1961, but Leslie was sixty-nine and his time had passed. He had also angered Diefenbaker years earlier at a bar association dinner.[30]

There were some promising prospects for the future, but in the meantime Hall's pool of suitable candidates was quite small. He suggested Reginald Balfour from Regina, and Percy Maguire of Saskatoon, despite their relatively advanced age: respectively, sixty-three and sixty-one.[31] A.H. Bence of Regina was a younger candidate at fifty-two. Hall liked the idea of promoting a sitting Queen's Bench judge to the appeal court, because he thought appellate judges benefited from trial experience. He felt Russell Brownridge, a Moose Jaw lawyer who had gone to the bench in 1959, showed promise. For possible Queen's Bench appointments, there was Leslie; Bence; M.A. "Sandy" MacPherson of Regina; Roy Hall, Diefenbaker's former partner in Prince Albert; and Mervyn Woods, a Saskatoon lawyer who taught at the law school. One candidate, Ariel Sallows of North Battleford, flatly turned down the offer of the bench.[32]

Diefenbaker largely followed Hall's advice, although not without some misgivings. The first new appointments to the court were Hall as chief justice (with Alfred Bence replacing him as head of the Queen's Bench) and Merv Woods to replace Gordon. Other advisers had also recommended Woods. He had been a war hero, commander of a navy frigate in the Second World War, and had practised in Saskatoon for a decade before joining the faculty of the law school. Brownridge, who had articled with Diefenbaker, was tapped to replace Procter. McNiven's replacement was more difficult. Hall and others strongly suggested Percy Maguire, who was respected. "Quite impossible," read one terse Diefenbaker memo.[33] Aside from his age, Maguire had been Hall's partner and practised in Saskatoon, which would have made him the third appointment from that city, which was sure to raise the ire of the bar in Regina. A year later, the prime minister changed his mind. With three judges from Saskatoon, the new bench was reminiscent of the Prince Albert–dominated court of the 1920s.

Emmett Hall and Culliton seemed to get on well. An old politico, Culliton had no expectation for the leadership of the court, despite his seniority. He and Hall were in some ways alike: Irish Catholics with a strong social conscience and sympathy for the underdog. It did not escape notice that Diefenbaker had broken with convention by appointing a second Catholic to the court. Hall and Culliton, who had also done a fair amount of criminal work, had strong civil libertarian leanings and agreed on criminal justice matters. Hall was more combative, but Culliton was commanding and assertive. The two men also had their share of Irish charm. Hall leaned on Culliton's experience, and Culliton later said he learned a great deal from Hall, who was a true student of the law and was proving a broad-minded, creative judge of a new mould.[34]

The opening of the new Regina courthouse in 1961, one of Hall's first acts as chief justice, was symbolic of the renewal of the court. Given the number of commodious courthouses built throughout Saskatchewan in the 1920s, it was a little scandalous that the old territorial courthouse, built in 1894, was still in use, with the Court of Appeal and the Regina Queen's Bench and District Court judges shoehorned into the building. It was crowded and dingy, too hot in the summer and too cold in the winter. Hall had pushed hard for a new courthouse while on the Court of Queen's Bench and took pleasure in opening the building. He was curiously restrained at the event, which was put down to the presence of the attorney general, Robert Walker.[35] He and Hall had knocked heads over the government's District Court reforms, and Hall was not quite ready to forgive his adversary.

Emmett Hall had very little chance to put his stamp on the Court of Appeal. Shortly after becoming chief justice, he began his work on the health-care commission. And in only sixteen months, he was on the move again, this time to Ottawa. It was Saskatchewan's turn to fill a berth on the Supreme Court of Canada. The last Saskatchewan judge had been James Wilfred Estey, who had gone straight to the court from practice and politics in 1944. Once again, Diefenbaker turned to his old friend, appointing Hall in November 1962.

Chief Justice Emmett Hall (*left*) swearing in Justice Percy Maguire, 1962. (Saskatoon Public Library, B-11153(1))

CULLITON'S TIME

TED CULLITON WAS promoted to replace Emmett Hall. This was not a foregone conclusion. Hall's views on who should succeed him aren't known, but Diefenbaker consulted a number of supporters in Saskatchewan, and Culliton's name was not at the top of the list. Leslie was suggested again, and several of Diefenbaker's correspondents thought Maguire was a good choice. Brownridge was put forward as well. The prime minister inquired if Bence or D.C. Disbery, another recent Queen's Bench appointment, would consider moving to the Court of Appeal, likely with an eye towards being chief justice.[36] Finally, Merv Woods stepped in. According to Calvin

Opening ceremonies for the new Regina Courthouse, 1961. Honourable William Martin leaving the dais. (Provincial Archives of Saskatchewan, R-B4542-3)

Tallis, Woods told Diefenbaker he had to appoint Culliton as the only logical choice.[37] In Woods's view, Culliton had the respect of the bar and the experience necessary to lead the court.

Diefenbaker heeded the advice and reaped some political reward by making a prominent judicial appointment across party lines. Years later, he touted Culliton's appointment as an example of his willingness to put merit over partisanship.[38] Culliton wrote the prime minister a handsome letter to thank him for the opportunity.[39] Perhaps laying it on a bit thick, he ended by requesting an autographed photograph of the prime minister for his office, presumably as a reminder of his good fortune to have Diefenbaker as his benefactor.

This left the need of a replacement for the departing chief justice. The prime minister chose Roy Hall, a Prince Albert lawyer and Diefenbaker's former partner. Hall was young—only forty-two—and did not have an especially high profile, but several people, including Emmett Hall and

Bence, had nonetheless recommended him for a trial court appointment. Diefenbaker, aware that the optics were not the best, sent his former partner to the Court of Appeal. He was the most youthful appointment since Culliton. Brownridge was forty-eight, while Woods was fifty-two and Culliton was a seasoned fifty-six. Maguire had turned sixty-three. Four were Second World War veterans. Maguire had served in both wars, while his younger peers had served in combat units.

The judges all had law degrees from the University of Saskatchewan. Emmett Hall and Maguire had got their degrees under the old-fashioned system of combined articles and courses, but Culliton, Woods, Brownridge, and Roy Hall had earned academic degrees followed with short articles. The last three judges were born and raised in Saskatchewan, which became the norm for future appointments. Aside from Culliton, no one had held senior elected office, although Emmett Hall, Maguire, and Brownridge had run unsuccessfully and all had been involved in party organizing. Their legal careers were a mixed bag. Emmett Hall had been a star counsel and Maguire was well-respected. Wood had solid practice experience before teaching. Brownridge and Roy Hall had somewhat slender resumes. Brownridge did have some trial judge experience, which Emmett Hall thought good for the appellate bench. This was the Saskatchewan Court of Appeal for the next dozen years, a Diefenbaker legacy for the province.

THE COURT AT LAW: IN DEFENCE OF CIVIL LIBERTIES

JOHN DIEFENBAKER, EMMETT Hall, and Ted Culliton had something in common: a deeply held conviction that upholding civil liberties was important. This was at least in part derived from being criminal defence lawyers—Culliton was very proud that he never acted as a prosecutor.[40] They knew that the police sometimes performed sloppy work or got tunnel vision; that prosecutors did not have to disclose most of their case (although some did); and that judges at trial could be arbitrary and even biased. Hall told Diefenbaker that the appointment of judges who really knew and understood the criminal law was necessary, implying that some were not properly applying that law. Diefenbaker's government, meanwhile, passed the *Canadian Bill of Rights* in 1960 to define and protect civil liberties and human rights. Diefenbaker's friend Hall was outspoken about the

MERVYN JOHN WOODS

Born in Regina on June 8, 1909, Merv Woods was a genuine war hero, thrust into the midst of the Battle of the Atlantic and ending the war in command of the frigate HMCS *Longueuil*. He was made a Member of the Order of the British Empire in recognition for his meritorious service.[14]

Justice Mervyn John Woods, n.d. (USKUASC, A-8874)

Woods grew up and was educated in Regina; the village of Kincaid, near Grasslands National Park; and Moose Jaw, where he graduated from high school. He then enrolled in the teaching college in Moose Jaw and received his teaching certificate in 1929. For the next five years, Woods taught school in several small communities in the Mossbank area. In 1934, savings in hand, he enrolled in the law school in Saskatoon, graduating with distinction in 1937. He did a year of post-graduate work at New York University and then articled with the firm of McKercher, McCool and Francis in Saskatoon.

On September 1, 1939, the day after he was accepted to the bar, Britain and France declared war on Germany and Woods joined the navy. He was posted to British Columbia and served on small coastal vessels and then spent a year seconded to the Royal Navy, on trawlers pressed into military service in the North Sea. In 1941, Woods was posted to the corvette HMS *Convolvulus*, escorting convoys between Liverpool and Gibraltar. After two years of shore duty in Halifax, he was given command of HMCS *Longueuil* in 1944, with the rank of lieutenant commander.

After the war, Woods took up practice in Saskatoon as a founding partner of the firm Francis, Woods and Gauley. He was a generalist, adept at criminal law, civil litigation, and solicitor work. He made the headlines with a 1954 murder case in which his client was convicted on the lesser charge of manslaughter and served only three years. He was solicitor to many co-operatives and became an authority on co-operative law.[15]

After ten years of practice, Woods went to academia, accepting a full-time position at the law school in Saskatoon. Most of a generation of Saskatchewan lawyers learned property, commercial, and taxation law from Woods. While teaching, Woods earned a master's and then a doctorate from New York University.[16] Many students remembered his dry and sometimes cutting sense of humour, and he had facility for reciting poetry.[17]

Dr. Woods became Justice Woods in 1961, joining the appeal court to replace Gordon. Woods had been a stalwart in the Progressive Conservative Party and was provincial president in the 1950s.[18] He had also been active in service clubs and community groups, serving as a lieutenant-governor in the Kiwanis Club, as a director of the Saskatoon Industrial Exhibition, and as a governor of St. Andrew's College at the university.[19]

Woods remained interested in military and veterans' affairs. He commanded the University Naval Training Division until going to the bench and was later an honorary colonel of the Regina Rifles. He was both provincial and national president of the Royal Canadian Legion. While on the court, Woods headed a committee that reported to the minister of Veterans Affairs on pension reform for veterans. Woods could also take some credit for the establishment of medicare in Saskatchewan, as chair of the Royal Commission on Hospital Privileges. For this service, Queen Elizabeth inducted Woods into the Order of St. John. Woods retired from the Court of Appeal in 1984 and died in Regina in 1995.

judiciary's requirement to give efficacy to the *Bill of Rights*. Saskatchewan led the way, as the province had with health care.

As appellate judges, Hall and Culliton had the responsibility of ensuring fair trials but also of further defining and developing the criminal law. Hall made his greatest contribution at the Supreme Court of Canada, while Culliton had a unique approach to sentencing that has become part of the lore of the Court of Appeal. Other contributions the court made to the criminal law can be seen in two trials. The first was the tribulations—and trials—of Morris Shumiatcher, whose defence over the course of two trials and related proceedings produced numerous appellate decisions, some of which made some important statements of law in search and seizure, the preparation of indictments, and conspiracy. The second was the trial for murder of David Milgaard, who now symbolizes the dangers of wrongful conviction and why procedural rights are so important. In one of those terrible ironies, Culliton's decision in Milgaard's initial appeal defined an important procedure in the criminal law but also unknowingly missed a chance, albeit a slim one, to exonerate Milgaard.

PRACTICE AND PROCEDURE

IN HIS BRIEF tenure, Emmett Hall signed off on new rules of court. It was the second revision since separate appeal rules were promulgated in 1922. Saskatchewan had developed a laudable tradition of reviewing the rules every twenty years or so.[41] As with the first revision, in 1942, the changes were minor. The court's workload had not yet created pressure for changes in procedure.

The institution of sittings in Saskatoon in 1961 was the exception. The profession had agitated for regular Saskatoon sittings for decades, with the Saskatoon Bar Association and the Law Society of Saskatchewan periodically passing resolutions on the subject. Regina was some 260 kilometres away, and even in 1960 with a modern highway, it was a major inconvenience for a busy practitioner. The court gave priority to appeals of visiting counsel at hearings and would also grant special sittings, but a trip to Regina from Saskatoon, Prince Albert, or North Battleford usually required at least two days.

In 1960, Attorney General Robert Walker announced that legislation was in the works.[42] Walker was acting against the wishes of the court. Chief

Justice Martin was blunt in his opposition.[43] Speaking for the whole court, Martin pointed out that the judges would incur considerable expense in travelling to and staying in Saskatoon. He thought it would interfere with the court's ability to offer special sittings, which he contended cut down expense and inconvenience for litigants. This was especially true for counsel from other towns, who would often request a special sitting. Martin also anticipated that judges would not work on their reserved decisions while in Saskatoon; they would not have their library and would have many social obligations as visitors.

Martin's complaints were disingenuous. He was ignoring the fact that the Law Society and most of the bar wanted Saskatoon sittings. Diefenbaker, in correspondence on the subject, tartly observed that lawyers in Saskatoon and Prince Albert had complained for years about the trek to Regina.[44] He noted that neighbouring Alberta had managed to have sittings in Calgary and Edmonton. Walker was not cowed by the court's opposition. Although the amendment had already gone through the legislature, Walker consulted with the profession at the summer convocation of the Law Society. A group of Regina lawyers led by E.C. Leslie organized a resistance, but the members voted in favour.[45]

On October 3, 1961, Emmett Hall, Culliton, and Merv Woods opened the first sittings of the court to take place outside Regina.[46] More than one hundred people crammed into a courtroom designed for fifty in the new Saskatoon courthouse, which had opened in 1958. Diefenbaker's former partner J.M. Cuelenaere gave the welcome of the Law Society, followed by his brother, R.C. Cuelenaere, speaking as president of the Saskatoon Bar Association. There were just three appeals.

Three judges had gone to Saskatoon for the historic hearings. Under Culliton, the court started to sit in panels of three for nearly all appeals, sitting as a full court only for appeals with wide significance, such as constitutional matters. This was not Hall's doing; he was of the opinion that the court should always sit as a full bench.[47] Small panels were fast becoming standard practice in Canada. Ontario had been using them since the 1930s, British Columbia in the 1950s, and Alberta started around the same time as Saskatchewan. On the three other, larger, courts, panels could sit simultaneously and handle more appeals. In Saskatchewan, with only a five-judge court, sitting as a small panel did not offer quite the same benefits but allowed the non-sitting judges time for other duties, and the

The first appeal sittings, Saskatoon, October 1961. *From left:* Justice Edward Culliton, Chief Justice Emmett Hall, Justice Merv Woods. (Provincial Archives of Saskatchewan, *Star-Phoenix* Collection, S-SP-B16899-1)

flexibility helped when judges were seconded to commissions and avoided the even-numbered courts that often sat in the past.

CULLITON'S COURT

HALL DID NOT have the chance to put his stamp on the court, but the opposite was true for his successor. Culliton's dominance was unprecedented for Saskatchewan and unequalled anywhere in Canada. There were essentially two courts: Culliton and then his four colleagues. When Culliton was on a panel, the other judges often said nary a word. Culliton usually did not hear counsel out. He would listen for a few minutes and then interrupt to say, "Here's how I see it." Frequently, he would start a hearing by telling counsel his understanding of the important issues and direct the argument. On occasion—and it did not happen much—Culliton was not certain about an appeal, at which time there might be a more conventional presentation and the other members of the panel had a chance to weigh in.

The bar had many stories about Culliton's court. William Vancise recalled one typical incident that made the rounds:

> Gwen Randall was there acting for CUPE. I was acting for the city, as I was a switch hitter in those days. Gwen stood up and said, "My Lord, there are three grounds of appeal in this case." Culliton interrupted her and said, "And you aren't going to argue the first two, are you?" Gwen replied, "Well, I was until a minute ago."[48]

Emmett Hall had complained that Culliton had often made up his mind before the hearing. It took strong counsel to contradict the chief justice and insist on pursuing a different line of argument. Not all counsel minded his way of running appeals. Some liked the fact that they quickly knew where they stood. The rest lived with it.

It is a bit astonishing that Culliton could run the court this way, but the bar considered him to be a strong jurist and his court was quick and efficient. Culliton was very accommodating of the needs of counsel, a long-standing tradition of the court. Most courts, including in Saskatchewan, did not have fixed dates and times for hearings in the 1960s. The panel tackled appeals in the order filed, with out-of-town counsel or very urgent matters jumping the queue. In Alberta, the difficulty of predicting when an appeal might be heard was a point of great irritation for the bar, as counsel often had to wait around, sometimes for several days. In Saskatchewan, lawyers called the registrar who, on Culliton's instructions, gave them an estimate.

His brother judges did not seem to mind Culliton's imperious ways. This reflected in part their lack of judicial experience. There was no training for judicial appointments; as practising barristers they were reasonably familiar with the court's procedures, and the rest they learned on the job. As the experienced judge, Culliton took on a disproportionate amount of the work and then never relinquished it. The other judges accepted this, perhaps lacking confidence or assertiveness, or perhaps taking the path of least resistance.

Culliton's style anticipated a change in Canadian appellate practice in the 1980s towards much more advance preparation for appeals, known as the "hot" court. As discussed earlier, in the British tradition, panels had little advance knowledge of an appeal to ensure an open mind. American practice opted for written arguments in factums, which became increasingly

RUSSELL LAWRENCE BROWNRIDGE

Given the number of Saskatchewan Court of Appeal judges who had been premiers, cabinet ministers, members of Parliament, or in the provincial legislature, it was a little ironic that Russ Brownridge came out of law school in 1939 intent on a political career.[20] He did serve five years as an alderman in Moose Jaw, but this was his highest electoral office. More importantly for his future, Brownridge worked on Diefenbaker's 1938 campaign for leadership of the provincial Conservative Party.[21] He entered "The Chief's" law office in 1939, transferring his articles to William G. Ross in Moose Jaw when Diefenbaker was elected to Parliament in 1940. Brownridge remained in Moose Jaw, practising with Ross and later as Brownridge and Schollie until his appointment to the Court of Queen's Bench in 1959.[22]

Justice Russell Lawrence Brownridge, c. 1984. (Provincial Archives of Saskatchewan, 84-2125-007)

Born in Saskatoon on November 23, 1914, Brownridge grew up in Moose Jaw, where his family moved when he was four.[23] His father worked for the CPR. After graduating from Central Collegiate, Brownridge took a business course at the Moose Jaw Technical School and worked as a bookkeeper at the local YMCA until he could afford university, returning to his birthplace in 1935.[24] He continued to work part-time through his undergraduate and law degrees. Brownridge took advantage of the five-year combined arts and law program and finished in 1939 with a degree in economics and political science with distinction and his law degree. He was on the university debating team and was never defeated.[25]

Like many lawyers of his vintage, Brownridge had a general practice in Moose Jaw, acting as city solicitor, and received his QC in 1951. He remained active in politics as president of both the provincial and federal Conservative riding associations in Moose Jaw. He was also very involved in the community. He ran twice for mayor as well as serving as an alderman and was on the public library board for fourteen years. He was on the board of the YMCA, the chamber of commerce, and the Family Service Association, where he was also president. There seemed no part of community life in Moose Jaw that Brownridge did not participate in. He was the Kiwanis Club's district lieutenant-governor; president of the Canadian Club; an elder of St. Andrew's United Church; on the Moose Jaw Union Hospital board; and president of the Red Cross, Saskatchewan division, and the first person from Saskatchewan to serve as the Red Cross's national president.

Emmett Hall was a champion of Brownridge and was likely responsible for his appointment to the Queen's Bench. Brownridge was initially stationed in Moose Jaw but was moved a year later to Regina. Courteous, conscientious, and scrupulously fair-minded, he was well liked as a trial judge. Forty-six when first appointed a judge on to the Queen's Bench, Brownridge stepped down from the Court of Appeal in 1988 at mandatory retirement age. He died on November 3, 2005, in Regina, aged ninety-one.

comprehensive until, by the 1960s, many US courts considered limiting or even eliminating oral argument. Culliton was a one-man hot court. There were always some judges who mined an appeal before hearings: Gordon, known for his impatience, was one, and Emmett Hall thought Culliton emulated the older judge. As chief justice, Culliton went much further. He put in astonishing hours preparing for appeals as well as writing judgments. Factums were becoming more comprehensive, and Culliton would study the evidence and the law at length. His office light was often seen shining late into the night. The result was that he had a comprehensive grasp of appeals and a strong opinion on the outcome before hearings.

Stories also circulated about Culliton's informal case management. This took the form of friendly phone calls to counsel to advise them as to the wisdom of continuing an appeal. There was no suggestion that he coached counsel; the calls seemed aimed at winnowing out fruitless appeals and saving money for all the parties. Culliton would call Serge

Kujawa, appellate counsel for the attorney general's department, to run over the upcoming criminal appeals.[49] It would be considered outrageous now, but standards were different in that era. "Woodshedding" judges, who intervened before or during trials to force settlements or have hopeless suits withdrawn, were not uncommon. It was much more unusual for this to occur at the appellate level, but Culliton was in a class by himself.

The rest of the court suffered from being in Culliton's shadow. The chief justice invariably sat on any important appeal as well as nearly all the criminal panels, while the other judges tended to handle the more mundane civil cases. One counsel who appeared frequently at the court confessed that it was sometimes hard to remember the rest of the panel was there, and most lawyers pitched their arguments to the chief justice.

But Culliton could not be at every hearing. Reported judgments hinted at what might have been with a less domineering chief justice. Woods, Maguire, and Roy Hall all wrote frequently. Dissents and concurring opinions, while not numerous, showed the rest of the court was engaged. It was, however, a court of few words. Hall, Woods, and Maguire seem to have been in competition to be the most concise. Hall was probably the winner. His judgments were models of brevity and incisiveness. Hall also had a strong independent streak and didn't hesitate to dissent, even when Culliton was writing for the majority. Woods was restrained and pragmatic but was an insightful and intelligent judge. One counsel recalled that Woods was the most likely to ask questions of counsel when sitting with Culliton.[50]

Brownridge did not quite live up to Emmett Hall's expectations while sitting with Culliton and was widely thought to lack self-confidence in his role. His reported judgments were competent but not numerous. Several were noteworthy. Brownridge wrote one of the court's first decisions on the *Divorce Act* of 1968.[51] The Pierre Trudeau Liberals had finally passed legislation on divorce, an unfulfilled federal responsibility, replacing the 1857 *Matrimonial Causes Act*, which had served most of the country.[52] In *Austin v Austin*, the trial judge believed that he should be applying an "objective" standard for determining cruelty. Brownridge gently corrected him, stating that what constitutes cruelty must necessarily be determined from the context of the relationship. The judge does not apply a standard but does determine if there was cruelty. He also admonished the trial judge for interviewing the couple's fifteen-year-old son privately rather than having him testify in open court, agreeing with the female plaintiff's counsel that this was unnecessary and unsound practice. That counsel was Percy Gordon, now eighty and as sharp as ever.

Over his thirty-year career, Culliton's jurisprudence and judicial outlook evolved. This evolution reflected changes in the Canadian judiciary, a loosening of the formalism and its consequent black-letter approach to the law that had dominated Canadian courts. Emmett Hall was in many ways on the leading edge of this change. It was a development that flowered in the 1970s, and will be discussed further in the next chapter. In the 1960s, Hall and Culliton were part of another development, a burgeoning interest in the protection of civil liberties, especially due-process rights, and the principles of sentencing.

Justice Edward Milton Culliton, c. 1965. (Provincial Archives of Saskatchewan, R-A22811)

THE *BILL OF RIGHTS*

LONG BEFORE BECOMING prime minister, John Diefenbaker had advocated better protection for civil liberties. Many of these rights had a legal existence as part of the "unwritten constitution" inherited from England, a combination of tradition, common law, and statutes. One example was the writ of *habeas corpus*, an order of the court for authorities to produce someone detained in order to determine if the detention was legal. But under the doctrine of parliamentary supremacy, a simple statute could eliminate even the most ancient liberty. A bill of rights had been included in the US constitution to remedy this deficiency. In the wake of the horrors of the Second World War, human rights took centre stage. One of the first acts of the United Nations was to enact a universal charter of rights and freedoms. Through the 1940s and 1950s, academics and parliamentary committees alike debated the wisdom of creating a bill of rights for Canada.[53]

Tommy Douglas was inspired to pass the *Saskatchewan Bill of Rights* in 1947. The legislation was groundbreaking and far-reaching, anticipating the human rights codes common twenty years later.[54] The bill included fundamental freedoms such as freedom of expression, conscience and religion, and association and peaceful assembly; legal rights such as protection against arbitrary arrest and detention; and protection from discrimination in employment and accommodation. Douglas's *Bill of Rights* was curiously underutilized in the courts, with little significant jurisprudence.[55] In a 1950 decision, Gordon had given it his stamp of approval, writing,

> Such an Act as this endeavouring to guarantee to every one in the province certain basic rights should be given the widest possible interpretation. This Act gives rights which go to the very roots of our democratic institutions and ensures protection to persons who are endeavouring to carry out their own legal obligations.[56]

Surprisingly, Diefenbaker rarely, if ever, cited the Saskatchewan bill as inspiration,[57] although admittedly his interest in fundamental rights predated the statute. Diefenbaker was very proud of Canada's British heritage, including traditional rights and freedoms, but also well understood their fragility. As an experienced defence lawyer, he knew first-hand the failings of the police and courts. Like other civil libertarians of the era, he worried about the growing power of the state and railed against the Liberals' serial extensions of wartime emergency powers into the 1950s.[58] Once Diefenbaker had his majority government, he made a bill of rights a priority, and the *Act for the Recognition and Protection of Human Rights and Fundamental Freedoms* was passed on August 10, 1960.

The *Canadian Bill of Rights* was doomed to be ineffectual. Diefenbaker did not have the stomach for the political wrangling necessary for the bill to be entrenched in the constitution and apply to all jurisdictions, provincial and federal. Instead, the *Bill of Rights* was a simple statute of Parliament that applied only to federal laws. The bill also contained a "notwithstanding" clause that allowed the government to ignore its provisions when passing new legislation if it was deemed expedient, and the legislature could overturn the statute at any time. The courts completed the neutering of the *Bill of Rights*.[59] Judges were reluctant to give it authority and full expression when it was not a constitutional document, and its generalities did not accord well with their training and outlook. As

The Court of Appeal, c. 1965. *From left:* Justice Percy Maguire, Justice Mervyn Woods, Chief Justice Edward Culliton, Justice Russell Brownridge, Justice Roy Hall, and (*front*) registrar Frederick H. Sparling. (Provincial Archives of Saskatchewan, R-B3452)

one observer commented, "Common law judges, who commonly turn to literalism in interpreting written laws, are not accustomed to giving content to vague formulae."[60] There were few decisions where the courts properly interpreted and applied the *Bill of Rights*, even the due-process rights, which seemed relatively straightforward.

One of Emmett Hall's great frustrations was his difficulty convincing his brother judges on the Supreme Court of Canada to apply the bill.[61] Fully sympathetic to the statute's aim, Hall felt a duty to give broad expression to the *Bill of Rights*. One of his biographers has said that "the cause of the individual" was a fundamental part of Hall's social conscience.[62] Like many civil libertarians, he felt individual rights and the protection of individuals from the power of the state had a higher priority than maintenance of order. Like Diefenbaker, Hall had spent a great deal of time in the trenches of criminal law and had no illusions about police methods or the abilities of prosecutors and judges. His stinging lone dissent in the *Truscott* reference, where the Supreme Court reviewed the trial and conviction of Steven Truscott, a fourteen-year-old accused of murdering a young girl, demonstrated his commitment to civil liberties. Hall, along with justices Cartwright and Spence, formed a libertarian wing of the Supreme Court.

R v Morrissette and Culliton's Reappraisal of Sentencing

CULLITON INHERITED HALL'S mantle on the Saskatchewan Court of Appeal. He was not as overtly a civil libertarian as Hall was, but Culliton's criminal law decisions in in the 1960s and 1970s made clear his concern with procedural fairness and upholding due-process rights. Culliton's great concern, even obsession, was sentencing and the proper application of sentencing principles. Few, if any, appellate judges of his generation in Canada emphasized rehabilitation as much as Culliton did, or as consistently allowed appeals of sentences on the part of offenders.

The court had long taken the stance that it had the right and the duty to thoroughly review sentences on appeal and freely intervene. Martin, in *R v Finlay*, acknowledged the trial judge's advantages in the first instance but held the appellate court must carefully consider all the circumstances, including mitigating factors. The reported sentence appeals of the court—relatively rare until the end of the 1950s—demonstrated a tendency to leniency.

Culliton endorsed *Finlay* but went much further. He argued for an expanded role of appellate courts in sentencing, even if at the loss of some discretion for the trial judge. As he wrote in 1970 in *R v Morrissette*, his classic and influential sentencing judgment,

> A provincial Court of Appeal, being the final court in dealing with appeals in respect of sentences, has a duty to give some guidance to trial judges in this field. Upon the Court of Appeal rests the responsibility of stating the principles underlying the imposition of a sentence so that at least uniformity of approach to this problem may be achieved. Also, while there can be no such thing as uniform sentences, it is incumbent upon the appellate court to see that the disparity in sentences for the same or similar offences can be rationalized.[63]

To eliminate unduly harsh punishments had long been a general theme in Culliton's sentencing decisions. But Culliton went even further in justifying appellate intervention. He argued that the advantages of the trial judge in sentencing had become significantly eroded.[64] His court saw nearly all offenders in person at hearings, and Culliton was well known for insisting on questioning them directly. He contended that the additional materials filed at sentence appeals (this was before sentencing submissions at trials were common) even gave the court an advantage over the trial judge.

Culliton also made a strong case for putting an emphasis on rehabilitation in sentencing. He contended that the principles of sentencing had to be reappraised periodically to reflect changing attitudes of society towards punishment and crime.[65] In *Morrissette*, Culliton argued that such a reappraisal was underway. He agreed with other judges that retribution was no longer the aim of punishment but rather deterrence and the protection of the public. He also argued strongly that reformation and rehabilitation not only benefited the offender but served society by ultimately reducing crime. Culliton furthermore attacked the efficacy of long sentences for deterrence.[66] He was a progressive on the issue, reflecting ideas that were taking hold among the judiciary. And although no single proposition that Culliton advanced regarding appellate review or sentencing principles was especially controversial, taken together his views constituted a somewhat idiosyncratic approach that was the court's approach until the 1980s.

One striking example of Culliton's "dovishness" on sentencing was with narcotics cases. Street drugs, previously almost unknown in Saskatchewan, became widespread in Canada in the 1960s, particularly marijuana and LSD among young people. Initially, the courts cracked down heavily on marijuana offences, even simple possession, with jail time and relatively long sentences.[67] Many trial judges soon changed their approach. Faced with youthful offenders who were often university students and otherwise not engaged in criminal activity, many judges eased up on sentences for users. The Le Dain Commission, which recommended decriminalization of marijuana possession, found that appellate courts across Canada took a much less tolerant attitude, stressing deterrence over other factors in sentencing and frequently increasing sentences, even for simple possession.[68] Appeal courts eventually softened their stance, but in many cases not until well into the 1970s.

While acknowledging deterrence in narcotics cases was important, Culliton argued that it should not be overemphasized simply because drugs were involved; the principles of sentencing were the same for any offence.[69] He disagreed with decisions in other courts that held prison sentences were necessary, and continued to stress rehabilitation as an important goal. He felt that trial judges should have the full range of tools available, including suspended sentences. *R v Larre* was one such example. The accused was a university student who had brought back some joints from Mexico that he shared with friends. Culliton agreed with the trial judge that a charge of trafficking was ludicrous and that a custodial sentence over the Christmas break was quite sufficient for deterrence.[70] In a much more serious case of trafficking, he substantially reduced the sentence to keep the offender out of the federal penitentiary, noting the significant efforts of the accused to reform himself.[71] In dealing with drug offences, Culliton set a direction for the court that reflected the attitude of many trial judges on the front lines.

Not surprisingly, the Court of Appeal saw a lot sentence appeals, especially in the 1970s. Although laudable, Culliton's desire to give the convicted a fair shake probably went too far. Even around the mid-1970s, the court was clogged with sentencing matters, and Culliton's liberal stance was blamed for unnecessary appeals.[72] As one later judge of the court put it, sentence appeals became "almost automatic. Prisoners knew that they would get a trip to town, a little repartee with the chief justice, and a reduction in sentence."[73] Culliton's insistence that offenders be in court for their hearing meant a great deal of work and worry for the corrections service and the RCMP. In the 1970s, prisoners attending sentencing appeals were flown from Prince Albert—on "Con Air," as one judge called it. Amazingly, there was very little trouble with inmates and no escapes.

The sentence appeals also meant a fairly substantial and quite possibly unnecessary increase in the court's workload. And there was some question as to the utility and jurisprudential soundness of the endless hearings. Some viewed it as the worst sort of appellate tinkering, which trespassed on the discretion of trial judges. Culliton was very proud of the fact that he never increased a sentence, although some appeals were dismissed, which raises the question whether he was simply soft-hearted. His somewhat extreme approach may have been a corrective to overly harsh sentencing in the trial courts, but to examine that requires more study and analysis than is possible in this history.

Culliton made other notable contributions in the criminal law. Some of these can be seen in the many appeals resulting from the prosecution of Morris Shumiatcher, a unique epic in the annals of the criminal law in Saskatchewan.

IN THE EARLY 1960s, Morris Shumiatcher, once a star adviser to Tommy Douglas and then a prominent barrister in Regina, became ensnared in a tangled web of stock promotions and corporate transactions. It brought him to the Court of Appeal as an accused, convicted of conspiracy and sentenced to the penitentiary. Shumiatcher faced professional ruin as well as incarceration, but his five-year saga produced some important decisions on the criminal law.

Shumiatcher was a singular character. He was born in Calgary to Russian Jews who immigrated to Canada in the 1920s. His father, Abraham, had become a lawyer while working as a humble CPR clerk. Morris Shumiatcher had a brilliant academic record at the University of Alberta and then at the University of Toronto, where he earned the equivalent of a doctorate in law. After serving in the Second World War as an air gunner in the RCAF, Shumiatcher established himself in Vancouver, but he was soon recruited as a special adviser to Tommy Douglas. In 1948, he was made a KC, the youngest in Saskatchewan history, so he could argue in front of the Privy Council on the *John East* appeal. He quit the government in 1949 and went into practice in Regina. "Shumi," as he was known, initially did labour law but soon branched out and established a reputation as a fine litigator as well as doing some solicitor work. And it was in his work as a solicitor that his troubles started.

Resource development and mineral exploration in Western Canada in the 1950s were reminiscent of the Wild West. Land men fanned out across the Prairies to secure oil and gas rights and there were plenty of stories about fraud as well as many lawsuits. In Saskatchewan, numerous companies were formed to look for oil and gas, uranium, coal, and other riches. Many were not much more than stock promotions, some outright fraudulent. As an Ontario mining expert put it, some companies were formed to mine the public, not the ground.[74] By the late 1950s, the Saskatchewan government had become very concerned about fraudulent investment dealers, and the Saskatchewan Securities Commission cracked down.

Walter Luboff was a promoter in the resource field. He was president of the Western Bond and Share Corporation, which sold securities, primarily the stock of Columbia Metals Exploration. Luboff was general manager and a major shareholder in Columbia, formed in 1954 to develop uranium claims, and was also involved as an investor in other small firms. Western

The new Regina Courthouse, on Victoria Avenue, built in 1961 to replace the 1894 territorial building. (Provincial Archives of Saskatchewan, R-5585-6)

had a number of salesmen who flogged Columbia's stock to friends, family, and farmers. Luboff's sales manager was Edward Leier, who had also been involved in stock promotions for a number of years. Leier bought into Western but later had a falling-out with Luboff.

Shumiatcher's professional relationship with Luboff began innocently enough. He first met Luboff when his firm was retained to collect money from the promoter.[75] Luboff, Western, and Columbia then became clients of one of the juniors at Shumiatcher, Moss and Lavery. Shumiatcher himself took over Luboff's business late in 1955 at the promoter's personal request. Shumiatcher and his new client hit it off. Shumiatcher had some experience with the oil and gas industry, and they decided to form a new company, Continental Geological, to make investments in petroleum and potash. Luboff and Shumiatcher were the only shareholders, acting as president and secretary respectively. Over the next few years, several complex deals were struck between Columbia and Continental to explore for and produce oil, natural gas, and potash on various leases. Shumiatcher billed Columbia, Western Bond, Continental, and other related concerns for legal services while also having large holdings of Columbia stock and

Appeal courtroom in the new Regina Courthouse, 1961. (Provincial Archives of Saskatchewan, R-B5585-7)

making money through deals involving Continental. As Chief Justice Culliton later pointed out, there was no absolute proscription on a solicitor entering into business deals with a client while acting for them, but it was fraught with potential danger.[76] This certainly proved correct.

In the case of Shumiatcher, one of these dangers was being charged with counselling to commit fraud and criminal conspiracy. In 1958, the Saskatchewan Securities Commission investigated Western Bond and Share over allegations of misleading and fraudulent sales tactics. Over the course of several hearings, salesmen from Western initially denied using misleading information in their pitches to customers but then later changed their tune. They alleged that Luboff had coached them to make false claims about Columbia's financing, holdings, and uranium finds, and Shumiatcher had counselled them before the first Securities Commission hearing to lie to protect the company and Columbia's share value. Leier, Western's sales manager, and two other salesmen also claimed that Shumiatcher had further pressed them to sign false statements for a lawsuit of disgruntled shareholders. The Securities Commission turned the information over to the attorney general's office, which began an investigation.

Shumiatcher's prosecution featured a blizzard of applications and appeals; a trial that ended in a mostly hung jury; another series of applications and subsequent appeals; another trial; and finally the main event, his conviction. And to cap off the sordid tale, there was a Law Society disciplinary hearing and yet another appeal.

The first significant decision in the Shumiatcher affair arose from search of his office by the RCMP and Securities Commission investigators. Armed with a warrant, officers carried off large amounts of documents, including client files for Shumiatcher's partners. Shumiatcher's lawyer, Alan Embury, immediately challenged the legality of the warrant. While he did so, a Securities Commission officer obtained another warrant from a different magistrate, to be used by the investigators occupying Shumiatcher's office if the first warrant was quashed.

Emmett Hall, still chief justice of the Court of Queen's Bench, heard the applications and struck down both warrants. His outrage was palpable. He held that neither magistrate had acted judicially in granting the warrants, as the request was too vague and too broad, lacking particulars. Hall wrote,

> I can hardly conceive that in a law office such as that of Shumiatcher, Moss and Lavery, in which no suggestion of wrongdoing has been suggested against the partners Moss and Lavery or against Mrs. Shumiatcher, it would be possible for a peace officer executing the warrant to know just what to seize. I do not think it was ever contemplated by parliament that under the search warrant authorized by sec. 429 of the *Criminal Code* . . . those executing the warrant would have *carte blanche* to open and to read the private papers of clients and of partners in the hope of finding something therein that might in the sole judgment of those searching have evidentiary value relevant to the charges made against Shumiatcher.[77]

Hall called the second warrant an abuse of process of the court. Round one had gone to Shumiatcher.

Even with this setback for the prosecution, Shumiatcher was charged with seven counts of perjury for counselling the salesmen to give false testimony at the Securities Commission hearing, one count of perverting the course of justice, and three counts of counselling to make a false statement under oath. To prosecute, the Crown brought in Norman Matthews of Toronto, while Joe Sedgwick, one of Canada's leading criminal defence lawyers, defended Shumiatcher, assisted by Alan Embury. Shumiatcher's first trial started near the end of January 1961 with Justice Disbery and a jury. Disbery severed the charges, putting aside the first seven counts for another trial, dispensing with the eighth, and proceeding on the last three. The Saskatchewan papers followed the sensational trial closely through its five-week duration, one of the longest in the province.

The trial was highly technical, with the jury frequently out of the courtroom for *voir dire* hearings. The examination-in-chief and cross-examination of the three primary witnesses—Leier, the sales manager of Western; John Abbott, another salesman; and Herbert Gjosund, a vice-president of Columbia—took days and days. A little comic relief was interjected when Sedgwick questioned Leier about his involvement in schemes to find Incan and pirate treasure hoards in Peru and the Caribbean.[78] Even Justice Disbery joked about Leier's search for Captain Kidd's treasure. Sedgwick's point was that Leier had a history of dodgy schemes. Sedgwick hammered at the fact that the witnesses had previously perjured themselves, had unpaid Securities Commission fines, and, in Leier's case, a $100,000 lawsuit against Luboff and Shumiatcher, to suggest there was ample doubt they were telling the truth. With a sympathetic charge to the jury from Disbery, the jury acquitted Shumiatcher on one charge, but they could not agree on a verdict on the other two. It was almost back to square one.

More legal manoeuvring followed. Shumiatcher's team attempted to get the original indictments and committal for trial thrown out via an application for *certiorari*, arguing that the proceedings at the Securities Commission were not judicial proceedings and no criminal charges for perjury were possible. This ended up at the Court of Appeal, but Culliton dismissed the application for want of jurisdiction.[79] A similar gambit was tried at the Supreme Court of Canada with an application for *habeas corpus*.[80] This also went nowhere, even with the assistance of Percy Gordon,

PERCY HATHAWAY MAGUIRE

Percy Maguire was a veteran of both world wars. He joined the Royal Air Force in 1918, serving briefly before the end of the war. In the Second World War, he went to Ottawa to join the army's Office of the Judge Advocate General with the rank of major. Between the wars, he was a leading lawyer in Saskatoon and a partner of Emmett Hall for many years.

Justice Percy Hathaway Maguire, c. 1960. (USKUASC, A-10546)

Maguire was born in Elgin, Manitoba, on October 14, 1899. His family moved west to Saskatchewan in 1909, settling in Saskatoon, where Maguire attended Victoria and Albert Public School and Nutana Collegiate.[26] He was a noted athlete in high school, and at university he was on the football team, the track and field team, and the basketball team and later organized the University of Saskatchewan Grads, playing with them until 1929.[27] Maguire later became an avid golfer and was president of the Riverside Country Club in Saskatoon. He entered the University of Saskatchewan in 1917 but then joined the RAF. He earned his bachelor of arts in 1921 and his law degree in 1924. After joining the bar, he spent a year at Harvard Law School on a course of special studies.

Returning to Saskatoon in 1925, Maguire began practising with the firm later known as Carroll, Sheppard and Maguire. In 1935, he teamed up with his law school friend Emmett Hall to establish a firm known as Maguire, Wedge, McKercher, McKercher and Purdy when Maguire left for the bench. He was made a KC in 1937. Maguire served as president of the Saskatoon Bar Association and from 1959 to 1961 was the Saskatchewan vice-president of the Canadian Bar Association. He also put in his time in the political trenches, making two unsuccessful bids for the legislature, in 1944 and 1952, and was the president of the Saskatoon Progressive Conservative Association and on the party's provincial executive.[28]

Maguire was community minded. He was Kinsmen national president 1935 and president of the predecessor Saskatoon Eclectic Club. He was also a president of the Saskatoon Rotary Club. He ran the Community Chest campaign—the forerunner of the United Way—in 1954. He spent eleven years on the public school board and in 1946 was elected to the Saskatoon Technical Collegiate board and was its chair several times. A member of the congregation of Grace United Church, he served in various executive functions there. After moving to Regina and joining the appeal court in 1962, Maguire stayed active in the community. He served on the Court of Appeal until he retired in 1974, and he died on November 19, 1984.

Although reserved, even taciturn, Maguire was known for his kindly treatment of young lawyers, who he tried to put at ease. He had long taught a course at the law school. He was regarded as an excellent lawyer and a sound judge.

who appeared with Embury on behalf of Shumiatcher. Gordon assisted Shumiatcher's defence but wisely stayed out of the Saskatchewan courts.

Before the next trial, the prosecution changed tack. Instead of pursuing Shumiatcher on the perjury charges, the Crown brought a new charge of conspiracy to defraud the public against Luboff, Shumiatcher, and John Fawcett, a geologist who had taken over the field operations for Columbia and was made vice-president. The prosecution's argument was now that Shumiatcher's alleged counselling of perjury was part of a larger scheme of enrichment, to pump up Columbia's stock and sell it to the public. Shumiatcher immediately applied to quash the indictment on the grounds that it was too general. Culliton, writing for the court, agreed. The charge in his view did not properly meet the requirements of the *Criminal Code* to provide sufficient detail of the alleged offence so that the accused knew the case against them. Furthermore, he argued that the indictment had to state what "transaction," or conspiratorial acts, were at the heart of the charge. Neither condition had been met.

Hall concurred, but the prosecution's actions compelled him to add some comments. The chief justice could not understand why the Crown had put so little detail in the charge. He could only conclude that it was intentional, and he implied that the prosecution wanted to keep the accused in the dark about the case he faced. This deeply worried and offended Hall. To his mind, this was exactly why the recently passed *Bill of Rights* was necessary. As he wrote,

> It is a fundamental principle of criminal law that an accused person should be able to tell from the information or indictment the precise nature of the charge against him. That principle has been carried into the *Canadian Bill of Rights*. . . .
>
> . . . The prosecution, acting in the name of the sovereign, is, in my opinion, under a specific duty not to circumvent or negative this positive injunction of the parliament of Canada. The courts, too, must be vigilant in seeing that the provisions of the *Canadian Bill of Rights* are not breached, ignored or whittled away.[81]

Hall and Culliton had crafted an important judgment regarding the right of the accused to a specific and answerable indictment. But for all of Hall's appeal to fundamental rights, Shumiatcher's successful appeal was hollow victory. The Crown quickly charged him again, simply appending particulars of the alleged misdeeds of Shumiatcher and his co-conspirators that formed the basis of the conspiracy. His defence tried again to get the indictment quashed, but this time Culliton ruled that the charge was sufficient.[82]

Late in 1964, Shumiatcher and Fawcett finally went on trial. Luboff had died. The second trial lasted even longer than the 1961 trial, forty-four days. The prosecution examined in excruciating detail the history of Luboff with Columbia and other companies and the intricate transactions between them, as well as going over much of the same ground covered in the first trial. The judge's charge to the jury was long and complex. The jury had to interrupt their deliberations to ask the judge for additional directions. If Shumiatcher took any hope from the jury's lengthy huddle, it was soon dashed. He was found guilty and sentenced to three years in the penitentiary.

Shumiatcher returned to the Court of Appeal, facing potential ruin. Culliton admitted in his judgment that he wrestled with the appeal. He concluded, however, that the prosecution had made a fatal error the trial judge then exacerbated with his charge to the jury. The Crown had never described the agreement between the parties that lay at the heart of the conspiracy, which Culliton held was crucial to proving the charge. Instead, the jury was invited to infer a conspiracy, but not a specific conspiracy, and even possibly more than one conspiracy.

Conspiracy was often a difficult charge to prove. Direct evidence was often lacking, as was the case with Shumiatcher. As Culliton pointed out, the conspiracy must usually be inferred from the actions of the accused. This made it very important, in Culliton's view, for the prosecutor to present a clear picture of the alleged agreement that created the conspiracy for the jury. It was also vital that the evidence presented clearly supported the existence of the agreement alleged. Extraneous and non-relevant evidence confused the issue—and the jury. In Culliton's opinion, after extensively canvassing the evidence, the only scenario that matched the evidence was that Luboff and his salesmen defrauded the public with the misrepresentations about Columbia's stock, Shumiatcher subsequently counselled perjury, and finally Fawcett joined the conspiracy, covering up disappointing results of Columbia's uranium exploration.

This was not the conspiracy that the prosecution presented. In Culliton's view, the Crown tried to build a case that there was a conspiracy without explaining the nature of the conspiracy to the jury except in the general terms of the indictment. Matthews argued that this was proper in the law and that the Crown only had to prove the basis of a conspiracy, the nature of which the jury could infer. Culliton disagreed. This violated the same principle that Hall and Culliton had earlier elucidated: that an accused should face a definite charge and definite case. Another difficulty was that the original charge, while general, did not allow for multiple conspiracies. If there were multiple conspiracies, these should be described and alleged.

In Culliton's opinion, much of the evidence of the Crown was vague and did not prove anything. The Crown led a great deal of evidence regarding the complicated transactions between the companies in which Luboff and Shumiatcher were involved. The implication was that the transactions were improper, but the Crown never showed any proof of wrongdoing or unjust enrichment. In one instance, Matthews implied an arrangement between Luboff and Columbia was improper, even though the Securities Commission had sanctioned it. The Crown also put Shumiatcher's large

ROY NORMAN HALL

Roy Hall was a man of few words—his law school yearbook made mention of the fact—but several prominent counsel rated him the strongest judge on the Culliton court after the chief justice.[29] Hall was elevated to the Court of Appeal at forty-two, straight from Prince Albert, where he had practised with John Diefenbaker since 1946.

Hall was born in 1920 in Ponteix, Saskatchewan, south of Swift Current, and later attended high school in Shaunavon.[30] An athlete as a youth, Hall was a sports fanatic. He finished his law degree in Saskatoon in 1943 and enlisted in the RCAF. He was posted to the Pacific as a navigator and ended the war with the rank of flying officer. After the war, he articled with Diefenbaker and Cuelenaere and stayed on after his call to the bar in 1946. He was junior counsel to Diefenbaker on many files but also carved out his own niche in civil litigation. Hall became a partner in 1948, with the firm becoming Cuelenaere and Hall after Diefenbaker became prime minister. He was the president of the Prince Albert Bar

FACING PAGE: *From left*—John Cuelenaere, John G. Diefenbaker, and Justice Roy Norman Hall in Diefenbaker's Prince Albert law office, c. 1953. (USKUASC, JGD 336)

Association and the Prince Albert Cosmopolitan Club but was not particularly active in the community. Hall did a great deal of constituency work for Diefenbaker, although he was not on any party executive.

In 1962, as the story goes, Roy Hall found out about his appointment from his barber.[31] He had come in for a cut, and his barber offered congratulations. Hall asked what for and was informed he was now on the Court of Appeal. Diefenbaker had insisted on calling his former partner with the news but then forgot. This was apparently not uncommon with the prime minister, and the appointment was subsequently announced in the local paper without Hall's knowledge. He served twenty-seven years on the court, retiring in 1989 with the respect of the bar and his colleagues. He died on March 25, 2005, in Regina.

legal fees into evidence, again without showing that the fees were unwarranted or were fraudulent.

The jury charge exacerbated the confusion the prosecution's case created. Culliton acknowledged the difficult task facing the trial judge, but in the chief justice's view he had made several crucial mistakes. The primary error was that, like the prosecution, he had not defined the conspiracy beyond the indictment's generalities. Disbery also did not properly distinguish the difference between proving illegal acts and proving these acts were evidence of a conspiracy, another fatal flaw. There were other issues, but these two problems were enough to question the jury's verdict. Culliton, however, directed a new trial. He acknowledged there were good grounds for acquittal but in his view there was evidence that a properly instructed jury should weigh. In conclusion, Culliton put the blame for the debacle squarely on the Crown, Norman Matthews.

It was the end of the prosecution—some might say persecution—of Morris Shumiatcher. After two trials and many trips to the Court of Appeal, the attorney general's department finally gave up. The change of government in 1964 and a new minister may have played a hand, but it also seemed clear that the Crown had tried two different routes to convict Shumiatcher and had not been able to present a convincing case. The Crown stayed the charges and Shumiatcher was a free man.

DISCIPLINE BY THE LAW SOCIETY

SHUMIATCHER HAD BEEN spared jail, but his difficulties were not over. In 1965, the Law Society of Saskatchewan instituted disciplinary proceedings. The complaint charged Shumiatcher with unethical and unprofessional conduct in his dealings with Luboff, Columbian Metals, and other companies. The evidence against him came direct from his criminal trials. The discipline committee of the Law Society, after a two-day hearing, found Shumiatcher guilty of "unprofessional conduct or conduct unbecoming a barrister and solicitor." Shumiatcher was suspended for six months. *The Legal Profession Act* allowed for appeal from decisions of the committee direct to the Court of Appeal, and Shumiatcher was back in front of Culliton yet again.

The chief justice took a stern view of the proceedings. Quoting from case law, Culliton compared such professional discipline to facing criminal charges due to the powerful negative effect on the reputation of a practitioner and set a threshold for proving misconduct that came close to the standard of criminal law:

> The principles to be deduced from these authorities, in my opinion, are these: When a complaint is made against a solicitor which may result in his suspension or disbarment, effect should not be given thereto unless the grounds of the complaint are established by convincing evidence, and when the complaint involves a criminal act, by evidence establishing the grounds beyond a reasonable doubt. In the assessment of the evidence, the solicitor's explanation should be accepted if there is a reasonable probability of it being true.[83]

Culliton held that the deliberations of the discipline committee were judicial in nature and the members had to act in a judicial fashion assessing the evidence and making a decision.

Applying these principles, Culliton quickly allowed the appeal and dismissed the committee's findings. Reviewing the evidence, the chief justice could find no basis for their conclusion. Culliton saw no concealment or misrepresentation on Shumiatcher's part, no transactions detrimental to any of the companies or individuals involved, and nothing unlawful about contracts set up between Columbia, Continental, Luboff, and Shumiatcher, nor anything improper in the fees for legal services that Shumiatcher had charged. The only items that required some explanation were charges Shumiatcher had made to Columbia Metals regarding two potash leases. Shumiatcher testified that he had made a mistake in regard to the leases: he had inadvertently included the work on the leases in the narrative he had appended to his bill and had not actually charged for the services. Culliton applied the rule he had formulated and concluded that it was a reasonable explanation and Shumiatcher should be given the benefit of the doubt.

Culliton's judgment and its endorsement of Shumiatcher also made clear that the chief justice thought the criminal charges had been baseless. Shumiatcher thought that Culliton had ordered a new trial instead of an acquittal to get unanimity on the panel.[84] The exonerated lawyer fervently believed he had been the subject of a personal vendetta of the attorney general and that the head of the Securities Commission and Walker had been looking for "big fish" to fry. He and Luboff had fit the bill, Shumiatcher thought, especially after he repeatedly clashed with W.W. Cameron, the Securities Commission chair and criticized his suitability for his post. Shumiatcher thought the timing of the charges and raid on his office was very suspicious: he had been scheduled to meet with Premier Douglas regarding what Shumiatcher called the chairman's witch hunts. Despite not receiving an acquittal, Shumiatcher was able to rebuild his career and again took up the mantle of distinguished counsel. He and his wife were leading patrons of the arts in Saskatchewan for many years. In 1981, Shumiatcher was made an Officer in the Order of Canada and later was made a member of the Saskatchewan Order of Merit.

R V MILGAARD

THE NAME DAVID Milgaard has become synonymous with the wrongfully convicted. In 1969, Milgaard was tried and convicted of the rape and

Opening ceremonies for the new Saskatoon Courthouse, 1958. It replaced the courthouse built in 1908. (Provincial Archives of Saskatchewan, R-B12249)

murder of Saskatoon nursing student Gail Miller. Ted Culliton heard Milgaard's appeal. Milgaard's counsel, Calvin Tallis, was widely considered the best defence lawyer seen in Saskatoon since Emmett Hall. Yet his appeal was denied and the fact remained that he was completely innocent of the crime. In retrospect, the police investigation had faults, the trial judge made several mistakes, and Culliton made an error as well, but by the standards of the time Milgaard received a fair trial.[85] Without DNA analysis performed more than twenty years later, Milgaard might never have been fully exonerated. The story of Milgaard illustrates why the civil libertarianism of jurists such as Emmett Hall and Culliton was so timely yet ironically did not save him from a terrible ordeal.

Milgaard had come to Saskatoon from Winnipeg with two friends on an extended road trip to Vancouver to purchase drugs. The three were

The appeal courtroom in the new Saskatoon Courthouse, 1958. The austere modernist decor was not universally popular with judges and lawyers. (Provincial Archives of Saskatchewan, R-A11618-6)

right out of central casting: young, shiftless, involved in petty crime and drug use, perfectly representing the anxieties at the time of respectable society towards youth. Milgaard, Nichol John, and Ron Wilson were only sixteen. In Saskatoon, the trio intended to recruit Milgaard's friend Albert Cadrain for their trip. By terrible coincidence, they arrived in town not only at the very time that Miller was murdered but only two blocks from the scene of the crime. It was later revealed that the actual killer, serial rapist Larry Fisher, lived with his wife and daughter in a basement suite in Cadrain's house.

The Saskatoon police launched a massive investigation. Milgaard was not initially a suspect. He entered the picture when Cadrain came forward two weeks later and testified that Milgaard changed some bloodstained clothes the morning Miller was killed. When questioned, Wilson and

John contradicted Cadrain and claimed that Milgaard was with them at the time of the murder. The stories of Milgaard, John, and Wilson seemed vague and evasive to investigators. Under repeated questioning, Wilson and John later changed their story, revealing that Milgaard had a knife, that they had asked a women who might have been Miller for directions, and that their car had become stuck in an alley, at which point the trio had split up to find help and Milgaard had been alone for a short time. Other witnesses came forward to testify that at a Regina party several weeks later, in response to a question about the murder, Milgaard had grabbed a pillow and started stabbing it with his hand, yelling he had killed Miller.

Wilson and John were subjected to further questioning and polygraph tests in Calgary, which showed they were lying. They changed their stories, implicating Milgaard, and John made the sensational statement that she had actually seen Milgaard stab Miller. But critically, elated that they had finally got the truth, the police did not test the new statements with the polygraph. The John statement and later testimony, and how it was treated at trial, became one of the crucial links in Milgaard's conviction. At the preliminary inquiry, John changed her testimony again, saying that she had not seen Milgaard kill Miller.

Chief Justice Alfred Bence and a jury tried Milgaard. The evidence was damning but almost entirely circumstantial. At the appeal, Tallis raised four grounds, but the second, regarding how an application to cross-examine John was handled, became the crux. At the trial, the prosecutor, T.D.R. Caldwell, wanted to question John about the discrepancy between her statement that she saw Milgaard kill Miller and her testimony at the preliminary inquiry and at trial that she had not seen him do this. In common law, counsel cannot cross-examine and discredit the credibility of their own witness unless the witness had given a prior statement inconsistent with their testimony. Counsel could then challenge what the witness was saying in court with what they had said earlier.

This exception was codified as section 9 of the *Canada Evidence Act*, with a subsection added shortly before the Milgaard trial to include statements in writing, at the discretion of the trial judge. There had not yet been any pronouncements on the exact procedure if counsel invoked subsection 2. Caldwell and Tallis both advised Bence that he should determine if such cross-examination should be allowed with a *voir dire*, a hearing within the trial without the jury present, often used to determine the admissibility of evidence without exposing jurors to the evidence. Bence did not follow their submissions and allowed Caldwell to cross-examine John with the jury present, which meant they heard exactly what was in her earlier statement. John disavowed that statement and stuck to her more recent testimony. Bence then instructed the jury to disregard the statement, but the damage had been done. Caldwell was able to introduce into the jury's mind John's claim that she had seen Milgaard kill Miller. Tallis, meanwhile, could do nothing; further questioning John about the earlier statement meant, at the very least, that the jury would be reminded again of what John had said, without any guarantee that Tallis could somehow discredit the statement sufficiently to erase its impact.

Culliton gave judgment for the court. After considering the facts found at the trial in some detail, he proceeded to the issue of how John's statement was handled. Culliton took it as patently obvious that having the jury present while determining if a cross-examination should be allowed was unsound.[86] He outlined a seven-step procedure to handle such situations.[87] Counsel advised the court they wished to make an application under section 9(2). The court directed the jury to retire. Counsel informed the judge of the circumstances and the alleged statement. The judge read the statement and decided if there were, in fact, inconsistencies of importance. If yes, counsel then had to prove the statement came from the witness, either by their admission or by leading other evidence. Opposing counsel then had an opportunity to question the witness and lead other evidence as to the circumstances in which the statement was made and the alleged inconsistencies to show why a cross-examination might not be allowed. Finally, the judge decided if cross-examination should be allowed and brought the jury back in.

As Culliton noted, there was no case law about the interpretation and application of section 9(2) and his decision set the law, followed or approved in numerous subsequent decisions. It even became known as the "Milgaard procedure."[88] But it gave the accused no relief. Culliton held that while Bence should have held a *voir dire*, it was almost certain that he would have allowed the cross-examination. Culliton also concluded that even if Bence was mistaken, it would not have made a difference to the outcome of the trial, invoking a provision of section 592 of the *Criminal Code* that allowed appellate courts to overlook trial errors if there was no miscarriage of justice. Although he did not say so directly, Culliton obviously thought the case against Milgaard was so strong that Bence's procedural slip did

Calvin F. Tallis, counsel for Morris Shumiatcher and David Milgaard and future judge of the court, c. 1964. (Provincial Archives of Saskatchewan, *Star-Phoenix* Collection, S-SP-B5807-1)

not matter much. Leave to appeal to the Supreme Court of Canada was subsequently refused.

Milgaard was eventually exonerated after a long, tortuous process. After repeated applications for review, the federal justice minister sent a reference to the Supreme Court of Canada. The court held that a new trial was warranted but added there was still a strong possibility Milgaard was guilty. The Saskatchewan government charged Milgaard again but then stayed the charges, leaving him in legal limbo, free but not declared innocent. Finally, DNA testing cleared Milgaard and implicated Larry Fisher, who had emerged as a suspect. Milgaard was given financial compensation, and the government of Saskatchewan called an inquiry to investigate the circumstances of his conviction, especially charges of a cover-up on the part of police and prosecution.

The Milgaard Inquiry concluded that police and the prosecution had acted professionally and ethically and that Milgaard had received a fair trial, at least according to the standards of the time. Justice Edward MacCallum also pointed out several mistakes, some critical, that led to Milgaard's long incarceration. One of the mistakes was Culliton's ruling.[89] MacCallum speculated that using Culliton's seven-step procedure, Milgaard's defence would have had a chance to inquire much further into the police interrogation of John and Wilson and thrown serious doubt on their testimony, probably excluding any cross-examination of John on her prior statement. A new trial might have also brought Larry Fisher to police attention sooner as a possible suspect. He had been arrested for sexual assaults in Winnipeg in 1971 and quickly confessed to similar assaults in Saskatoon. With Milgaard's conviction, further police investigation into Miller's death ended. MacCallum's conclusions were speculative, but a small chance of a different outcome would have been better than no chance.

Milgaard's conviction illustrated the dangers of circumstantial evidence. Ironically, even an efficacious *Bill of Rights* would not necessarily have saved Milgaard. Wrongful convictions continued to occur after the *Charter of Rights and Freedoms* was put in place. The most sweeping conclusion of the Milgaard Inquiry was that the courts were not sufficient to protect against wrongful convictions and the procedure for reconsidering convictions was deeply flawed.[90] MacCallum strongly recommended an independent panel be established, as had been done in the United Kingdom. Canada has not followed suit. It is one of the sad ironies of history that Ted Culliton, who as a man and a judge had great concern for the rights of an accused and great empathy for the convicted, missed a chance to save Milgaard from a major injustice. In hindsight, Culliton made a mistake, but at the time it was a judgment call.

CONCLUSION

DAVID MILGAARD'S CONVICTION and long incarceration demonstrated the limits of appellate review. Yet Chief Justice Culliton made one of his many contributions to Canada's criminal law in his decision on Milgaard's appeal. Morris Shumiatcher was luckier: he benefited from the sharp-eyed review of Emmett Hall and Culliton and emerged remarkably unscathed from his ordeal. Hall and Culliton again made important statements of law in the many appeals involving Shumiatcher. These are just two examples of how Culliton and Hall, both in Saskatchewan and Ottawa, were two of the foremost judicial guardians of civil liberties and did much to judicially advance the protection of accused under the law at a time when it was needed. To this Culliton added his careful review of sentencing in his province, determined to ensure that the convicted got every advantage possible, an expression on his deep humanity.

Emmett Hall retired in 1973, although he continued to make many contributions to the nation. Ted Culliton was far from done as chief justice of Saskatchewan. He continued to forge an impressive record in the criminal law until his retirement in 1981. But the 1970s was also a time of turbulent provincial–federal relations, and Saskatchewan and its Court of Appeal would be at the forefront of new battles over the control of Canada's natural resources.

CHAPTER 7
CULLITON AGAINST THE SUPREME COURT OF CANADA

Chief Justice Ted Culliton had finally had enough. The court was in danger of grinding to a halt. He had spent months pleading for more clerical help. Meanwhile, the chief justice and his faithful assistant had been working non-stop to cover the administrative tasks necessary to keep the court running. But even a renowned workaholic reaches his breaking point, and in October 1976 Culliton fired off an angry letter to the attorney general.

> I must say that in carrying out my responsibilities as Chief Justice of Saskatchewan, and as Chief Justice of the Court of Appeal, I am reaching a state of complete frustration. That frustration is due to my apparent inability to convince provincial administrative officials of even the minimum staff requirements of the Court. This inability arises, not from my lack of knowledge of the requirements, but because of the total and complete lack of appreciation by the Budget Bureau and senior administrative officials of the necessity for the effective, efficient and expeditious administration of justice.[1]

Culliton's problems, while more severe than most faced by chief justices, were not unique. Courts across Canada struggled to deal with an impressive surge of litigation. The strain on the courts and their need for more resources raised questions about judicial administration that no one in Canada had really considered, such as who should call the shots with court management: the civil service or the judiciary.

This was just one of many issues and changes for provincial appellate courts in the 1970s. The decade also saw a broadening of judicial perspective, known as legal modernism, in response to demand, within the judiciary and outside it, for the law to be developed, interpreted, and applied in a more flexible and responsive way. The shift was driven in part by the fact that matters coming before the courts were ever more complex and the consequences of judicial decisions ever more critical, especially in the realm of public law. The court battles in the 1970s over federal and provincial powers, particularly regarding natural resources, threw the issues of Canadian federalism into stark relief. Saskatchewan and its Court of Appeal had a central role in the controversies of the era.

BY ANY OTHER NAME . . .

THE 1970S BEGAN in Saskatchewan with a change in government. The CCF had a new name, becoming the New Democratic Party (NDP) in 1968, and a new leader, civil servant turned politician Allan Blakeney, who succeeded Woodrow Lloyd in 1970. Originally from Nova Scotia, Blakeney was a Rhodes Scholar with a Dalhousie law degree who came to Saskatchewan to work in the Douglas government.[2] First elected in 1960, Blakeney was in Lloyd's cabinet and narrowly beat lawyer and MLA Roy Romanow for the party leadership. The low-key, reserved Blakeney was considered a pragmatic moderate and a technocrat,[3] not a backslapper, but he took his campaign to the people, criss-crossing the province in a bus. The revitalized NDP benefited greatly from the unpopularity of Ross Thatcher's Liberals and romped to victory in the 1971 election with forty-five seats to the Liberal's fifteen. Thatcher, suffering from diabetes, died three weeks later, his legacy as Saskatchewan's most enigmatic premier secure. Blakeney went on to win two more elections against a declining Liberal Party and a reviving provincial Progressive Conservative Party.

Blakeney had an ambitious agenda of pragmatic socialism, "A New Deal for the People" that the premier called a blueprint for the decade.[4] The government aggressively expanded its direct role in the economy with new Crown entities. There were measures for social justice, such as a human rights commission and comprehensive legal aid; and social welfare, with a provincial drug plan, free dental care for children, and an end to the hated Thatcher health-care user fees. A new university was established in Regina. The party continued to base their social policy ambitions on sound fiscal management; Clarence Fines, Tommy Douglas's long-time finance minister, had been a Blakeney mentor.[5] Aided by burgeoning natural-resource revenue, the NDP returned ten consecutive budget surpluses.[6] Critics grumbled about high taxes and the excessive bureaucracy of NDP big government.

Like previous governments, Blakeney's NDP tried to address the economic and social situation of the province's Indians and Métis. Their world was changing: the Aboriginal population of the province was growing rapidly and migrating to the cities in search of better living conditions and employment opportunities.[7] Indians and Métis became assertive, even militant, about their concerns. Blakeney backed away from the assimilationist policies of past governments and tried to be more consultative. A new Department of Northern Saskatchewan was formed to deliver services in a more efficient and equitable manner to residents, who were largely Aboriginal, and Blakeney made noises about more local government. The NDP was receptive to Indian control over education on reserves and even instituted some affirmative action programs for university admission and government hiring in the late 1970s.[8] The public backlash to this showed that racism towards Aboriginals was alive and well in the province.[9]

Blakeney had no more success than previous administrations reversing rural depopulation.[10] Crop failures in the Soviet Union and wheat exports to China gave farmers several years of good sales and high prices,[11] but the established Saskatchewan pattern was repeated: good wheat prices discouraged diversification on farms and increased wheat acreage; bumper crops drove down prices; big farms survived, small farms went under; and the barriers for aspiring young farmers became ever greater. Skyrocketing oil prices in the 1970s drove up fuel and fertilizer costs just as wheat prices softened. The NDP tried a new take on an old idea, buying the land of retiring farmers to lease to new farmers with an option to purchase, and establishing a Crown corporation, FarmStart, to provide grants and loans.[12] The strategy did little to reverse the prevailing trends.

Economic diversification, that other Saskatchewan perennial, was high on the NDP agenda. Blakeney revived the Crown corporation as a vehicle for investment and economic development.[13] FarmStart was one example, and others soon joined the Saskatchewan "family of Crowns." Several of these companies were intended to increase the public presence in the booming natural resources sector. The Saskatchewan Oil and Gas Corporation was set up in 1972 to allow direct government involvement in the industry. Next was the Saskatchewan Mining Development Corporation in 1974. The company was primarily intended for public investment to encourage expansion of the uranium industry. Much more controversially, in 1976 Blakeney partially "nationalized" the potash industry with the enforced purchase of several existing mines by the Potash Corporation of Saskatchewan, another Crown corporation established the year before. Like previous attempts to directly encourage diversification, the NDP had only limited success. Challenges presented by geography and population were difficult to overcome, and even successful Crowns didn't generally become catalysts for more development.

Blakeney's potash strategy was the result of conflict between the provincial government, the potash producers, and the federal government. The struggle in the West between the two levels of government over natural resources, primarily oil and gas, defined the 1970s. It was a touchy subject in the region at the best of times, and plenty of resentment still lingered after Ottawa's seizure of control over resources with provincial autonomy and Saskatchewan's long fight to get it back. The rapid rise of oil prices after the Organization of the Petroleum Exporting Countries (OPEC) oil embargo in 1973 created new strains. It was a tremendous boon for Alberta and Saskatchewan, which had the lion's share of the country's production. Royalty money poured into provincial treasuries. The rest of Canada had to contend with the combination of inflation and stagnant growth—"stagflation"—brought on largely by the rise in energy prices. As deficits ballooned, the federal government cast a covetous eye on Prairie oil and gas revenues and tried to control domestic energy prices to cushion consumers. The provinces cried foul, and Canadian federalism was threatened with Western alienation as well as Quebec separatism.

Blakeney's government raised royalty rates and added new taxes to cash in on the boom until oil and gas producers threatened to leave the province. Potash prices also rose in the early 1970s, and potash producers grew restive under the pro-rationing system the Thatcher government had put in place when oversupply sank prices. The provincial government was dissatisfied with the existing low royalty rates on potash and instituted a new tax that outraged producers. The battles between Ottawa, Regina, and the oil and gas and potash industries ended up in court, producing two of the most controversial constitutional rulings in Canadian history and leading to major amendments to Canada's proposed new constitution.

THE WINDS OF CHANGE

FOR CANADA'S JUDICIARY, the 1970s was a significant decade. The "arid formalism" of the past was largely supplanted with "legal modernism," a broader jurisprudential approach more responsive to changing social and economic realities. Judicial education, new federal appointment policies, law reform, better academic law schools, the influence of academic thought on the role and purpose of the law, and dissatisfaction among lawyers and segments of the public with cautious, parochial judges were factors. Bora Laskin, appointed chief justice of Canada in 1973, symbolized the change, which was an evolution, not a revolution, in keeping with the incrementalism of the common law.[14] Saskatchewan's Court of Appeal had just one new appointment over the decade and was somewhat insulated from the trends, but Chief Justice Culliton was not a parochial judge. He played a direct role in changes such as the development of judicial education.

The first efforts to establish judicial training and education in Canada came at the end of the 1960s. The results were modest, but before 1968 there had been absolutely nothing in the way of training for newly appointed judges.[15] As senior members of the bar and usually experienced barristers, appointees were expected to understand how to be a judge and, if they had questions, to turn to colleagues on the bench or members of the bar or educate themselves. The shortcomings of this approach were obvious, especially considering that some new judges had not done any active courtroom work for years or sat alone in districts far from helpful colleagues. Courtrooms were becoming more complex and more was expected of judges.

Judges in the United States addressed judicial training and education—looking at procedure, comportment, and basic judgment-writing skills—long before their counterparts in Canada or the United Kingdom. This was often done in conjunction with law schools. New York University established its famous summer seminar for appellate judges in 1956, and similar programs were started at other universities, such as Stanford.[16] Appeal judges gathered to discuss everything from effective opinion writing to trends in the law to judicial administration. Canadian judges started to attend the US seminar as early as 1965 and increasing numbers made the trek in the 1970s. In 1963, the National Judicial College was established in the United States to provide formal and increasingly comprehensive education for judges, and state-level programs proliferated.[17]

In Canada, judicial education initiatives started with the first annual conference of chief justices in 1964.[18] Four years later, the conference, with the support of the federal Department of Justice, sponsored a seminar for federally appointed judges, with two judges invited from every province. The Canadian Judicial Council (CJC), established in 1971, had judicial education as one of its primary goals. The council sponsored an annual seminar for superior court judges, featuring leading academics from across the common law world, and added a similar seminar for district and county court judges.[19] The CJC also established a short orientation program for new appointments, which was known as "Dumb Judge Week." This provided basic instruction in how to be a judge. The CJC passed responsibility for these modest efforts to the Canadian Institute for the Administration of Justice (CIAJ) in 1975. For nearly a decade, the orientation course was the main offering. Attendance was not mandatory. As late as 1986, a third of section 96 judges had never attended a training or education seminar.[20]

The baby steps were nonetheless important. Judges recognized that adjudicating required certain skills that they may not have acquired in practice. And the door was opened for more comprehensive education and training. Canadian judges realized there were forums where court administration, process, procedure, and theory and philosophy were discussed. Much of this was a little rarified for Canadian judges in the 1970s, but it had an impact in the following decade, particularly on Saskatchewan's appellate court. Ted Culliton was deeply involved in education, primarily through the CJC, but also in other efforts. In 1977, he went to England's Cambridge University with a group of Canadian judges and academics to start the Canadian Institute of Advanced Legal Studies. The Cambridge seminars were an opportunity, in the words of one judge, "to broaden horizons and deepen the appreciation of the law in a hallowed academic setting."[21]

Chief Justice Edward Milton Culliton, c. 1966. (Provincial Archives of Saskatchewan R-A25033)

The CJC itself was a watershed. Prior to the 1964 conference of chief justices, contact between judges from different provinces was generally informal and irregular. The Canadian Bar Association's annual meeting was one occasion when they met, and the judiciary had also lobbied collectively for pay raises and against mandatory retirement. By the 1960s, there was a growing sense that the judiciary should have a forum to share ideas and common concerns. In 1964, Professor John Edwards of the University Toronto organized the inaugural conference of chief justices, afterwards an annual event.[22] Ted Culliton was the conference's first chairman. Judges discussed the formation of a permanent council of chief justices, responsible for establishing seminars for judicial education and preserving and enhancing judicial independence. The drawn-out investigation of Ontario judge Leo Landreville, who eventually resigned rather than face dismissal, demonstrated the need for a body to investigate complaints of judicial misconduct and carry out disciplinary proceedings, and gave more impetus to the idea of a judicial council.

Culliton, Chief Justice George Gale of Ontario, and Chief Justice Wilbur Jackett of the Federal Court led the effort to establish a permanent council.[23] Federal justice minister John Turner was enthusiastic, and in 1971 the *Judges Act* was amended to create the CJC. Jackett, a Saskatchewan transplant, drew up the amendments. The CJC had a statutory duty to investigate complaints against judges and recommend disciplinary measures, including a dismissal hearing in Parliament. Judicial education was another major part of its mandate, and after it handed over direct organization of education to the CIAJ, the CJC continued to fund seminars and courses.

Culliton was vice-chairman from the CJC's inception and was often acting chair. It was a labour of love for Culliton. He put a great deal of value on the council as a forum to discuss judicial administration and the development of the law and foster a "united and unified" judiciary. Bora Laskin said at Culliton's retirement dinner in 1981 that his colleague "was the sheet anchor of our organization, a man of infinite wisdom whose counsel never failed me. He has given substance as well as style to our most anxious authority . . . the entertainment of complaints against alleged judicial misbehavior."[24]

A HISTORIC FIRST

THE EARLY 1970S were also noteworthy for reform to the appointment process for section 96 judges. The first step came in 1967, when Pierre Trudeau, then justice minister, undertook to consult the Canadian Bar Association over appointments.[25] The Bar Association set up a committee that reviewed the names the minister presented and advised whether each candidate was suitable and desirable. The government was not obligated to follow the recommendations, but consulting the profession directly and broadly was revolutionary. The next justice minister, John Turner, pledged more consultation and declared outstanding ability was the criterion for appointments. Turner submitted names to the Bar Association committee but also actively searched for candidates. He called up chief justices and judges, talked to law society presidents, bar association heads, and law school deans as well as the party faithful for suggestions and to vet possible appointments. Several high-profile Turner appointments crossed party lines, and he was praised for the quality of people he was putting on the bench.[26]

Otto Lang, Turner's successor, did more. From Handel, Saskatchewan, and an alumnus of the province's law school, the Oxford-educated Lang, a Rhodes Scholar, succeeded Frederick Cronkite as the University of Saskatchewan's dean of law in 1961. Scarcely older than his students, Lang infused new energy into an already progressive law school. He exchanged academia for politics in 1968 and went immediately into cabinet, succeeding Turner as justice minister in 1972. Critical of the quality of judicial appointments while a professor, Lang created the position of special judicial adviser to the minister and hired Edward Ratushny, a former student and teacher at the law school. Ratushny did what Turner had done, "bird-dogging" new candidates, checking the credentials of recommendations and sounding them out about taking an appointment. Lang had some definite ideas about who should be judge. He wanted people with the right kind of human qualities as well as legal ability.[27] Lang was also interested in a more diverse judiciary. Appointments across party lines continued in many—but not all—provinces, and Turner, Lang, and his successor, Ron Basford, appointed a number of women and judges from a wider range of ethnic and religious backgrounds. Patronage and partisanship in appointments did not end, but the emphasis on merit meant Canadian courts were better served.

The reforms were timely. The judiciary rapidly expanded in the 1970s: in the space of barely six years, Turner and Lang made 272 appointments.[28] Population growth, economic activity, rising crime rates, and what became known as the litigation explosion of the late 1970s and early 1980s, created long court lists, and every province expanded its courts.[29] The federal government also created the position of supernumerary judge in 1973. Members of the bench could elect to go to part-time status, either when their age and years of service equalled eighty, or at seventy if they had served ten years on the bench. The government was obliged to appoint a full-time judge to replace a supernumerary, which allowed for a further expansion of the judiciary.

Conservative-leaning lawyers in Saskatchewan were more than a little skeptical of the substance of the reforms. It seemed like business as usual in the province, with appointments in Saskatchewan in the 1970s all going to prominent Liberals. The election of the Progressive Conservatives in 1982 immediately led to a major confrontation over patronage in appointments, discussed in the next chapter.

There was only one appointment to Saskatchewan's Court of Appeal in the 1970s. Percy Maguire reached mandatory retirement age in 1974. His replacement was Edward Dmytro Bayda. Bayda was from tiny Alvena, Saskatchewan, a half-hour drive from Saskatoon. His Ukrainian father, a successful farmer, had started his own farm implement dealership. The future judge graduated with distinction from the law school in Saskatoon and started his career at MacPherson, Leslie and Tyerman, in Regina,

Justice Percy Maguire after retirement, c. 1983. (Provincial Archives of Saskatchewan, 83-1218-015)

the province's largest law firm. Bayda then joined Johnson, Bayda, Halvorson and Scheibel, as the firm was later known. He was appointed to the Queen's Bench in 1972, the first Ukrainian appointed to the court. Bayda then set another first when he joined the Court of Appeal. Considered an excellent lawyer, Bayda was also a warm and sympathetic man with the kind of human qualities Otto Lang wanted on the bench.

Bayda was not the first Ukrainian judge on a section 96 court in the province. Thanks to Jimmy Gardiner, judges of varied ethnicities were appointed to the District Court in the 1940s and 1950s, a result of political calculation rather than enlightened policy. An increasing number of lawyers in Saskatchewan were not Anglo-Scottish in background, but more importantly, the province's ethnic communities were fundamental to Liberal support and thus wielded political clout. Gardiner used the District Court as way to satisfy minorities and engineered the appointments of a German Catholic and a Ukrainian judge.[30] The first woman appointed to the District Court, Mary Batten, in 1964, also came from a Ukrainian family. Bayda's appointment was nevertheless very important: it signalled the arrival of Saskatchewan's old ethnic minorities at the top of the profession.

Bayda's appointment symbolized the new approach to appointments but ironically was as much a product of the old. Bayda, while never having run for office, was nevertheless deeply involved in the backrooms of the Liberal Party and a key supporter and personal friend of Pierre Trudeau. He had another trump card. Stuart Cameron, appointed to the court in 1981, recalled that he and Harold MacKay, another young Regina lawyer involved with the Liberals, decided that Bayda was the ideal candidate to fill a vacancy on the Queen's Bench. On their own initiative, they asked Otto Lang to a breakfast meeting in Regina at the Vagabond Motor Inn with the intent of lobbying for Bayda's appointment. Lang listened with interest, though he said little and made no assurances. Not long afterward, Lang made the appointment. As Cameron, who later served as Lang's chief of staff, recalled, "It then dawned on me, as I think it did on Harold, that the appointment was almost certainly in the works at the time of our meeting, meaning the minister was probably amused, particularly with our earnestness."[31] Bayda was a close friend of Otto Lang, dating back to their law school days. If he had been eyeing Maguire's spot, it was almost certainly his.

Stuart J. Cameron, Liberal Party MLA and future judge of the court, c. 1978. (Provincial Archives of Saskatchewan, R-R13628)

Bayda was swiftly promoted to the Court of Appeal. His early opinions were reminiscent of John Lamont and W.F.A. Turgeon. They stated the issues incisively and were meticulously logical, well argued, well structured, and well written, although no one would call him concise or economical. Bayda obviously loved the law, and his early judgments often contained small essays on the development of a particular legal principle. He also knew his own mind—one of his first reported decisions on the court was a dissent.

For all his ability, Bayda was not Culliton's first choice for the court. The chief justice was a big supporter of Ray MacDonald, a Regina lawyer and a judge on the Court of Queen's Bench since 1965. Stuart Cameron recalled that when he was Otto Lang's chief of staff, Ted Culliton aggressively lobbied the minister to appoint MacDonald.[32] Lang finally refused to take Culliton's calls and left it to Cameron to deal with the chief justice. Cameron also recalled a story Bayda told him about a run-in with Culliton before Bayda joined the court. As a trial judge, Bayda was wrestling with a problem and sought Culliton's advice. Bayda then decided contrary to the chief justice's view. When the decision was appealed, Culliton made sure he was on the panel and overruled Bayda, later informing him, "Well, I said you were wrong."[33]

That sort of thing was typical of Culliton, and Bayda thought the story was funny, but the two judges did not get off on the right foot. Short-handed, Culliton was not pleased when Bayda accepted the job of commissioner for the Vancouver Port Grain Handling Industrial Inquiry so soon after his appointment and then subsequently chaired the Cluff Lake Board of Inquiry.[34] Culliton's imperious way of running the court must have been hard for the younger judge to accept, although a friend of Bayda says, "Ed would have made a point of getting along with Culliton."[35] Bayda was seen as the most likely successor to Culliton, but it turned out that Culliton had other ideas.

FIGHTING WORDS

CULLITON NEEDED MORE than just a replacement for Maguire. By the mid-1970s, Saskatchewan's five-judge bench was no longer sufficient. The province had experienced little population growth since the end of 1950s, but the appeals lists had gradually lengthened until the court started to feel pressed. In 1973, the court had 105 civil appeals, 78 conviction appeals, and 414 sentence appeals, an increase of 30 percent on the civil side and an astounding 200 percent on the criminal side. The year ended with only two reserve judgments outstanding.[36] But covering this took superhuman efforts: Culliton was working non-stop and presumably the other judges were also busy.

It was not just the number of appeals that increased the workload. Litigation across Canada in the 1970s became more sophisticated and more complex, adding to the pressure on courts. The *Canadian Industrial Gas and Oil Ltd.* (CIGOL) and *Central Canada Potash* appeals discussed below, for example, were major constitutional decisions that required a great deal of work. Another problem was the use of the judiciary for commissions of inquiry. Culliton often had only three other judges at hand in the latter half of the 1970s. After his appointment, Bayda had been almost immediately seconded to the grain handling commission and was often away. Bayda had barely finished that commission before he was named to the Cluff Lake inquiry and was not finished there until 1978. It is no surprise that the Canadian Judicial Council circulated a resolution to provincial attorneys general and the minister of justice to insist that governments be required to consult with the provincial chief justices before naming a judge to a commission. For all his own service on commissions, Culliton almost certainly had a hand in the resolution.

Culliton requested two positions be added to the court in 1976.[37] Ron Basford, the federal minister of justice, had told the provinces that Ottawa was ready to make the necessary appointments to address backlogs.[38] In Saskatchewan, however, the NDP dragged its heels. Culliton repeated his demand several times, and Roy Romanow, Blakeney's attorney general, was always agreeable, but he made no official request even though Ottawa was encouraging more appointments.[39] The government finally passed the order-in-council to add positions, but on the eve of Culliton's retirement, Romanow decided to consult his replacement as to whether the expansion was really necessary.[40]

It was a reversal of the usual problem with appointments: eager provincial governments gnashing their teeth while Ottawa delayed and equivocated. But the foot-dragging was perhaps not surprising given the NDP government's astonishing niggardliness towards the court. Two more judges meant two more offices and another courtroom, as Culliton wanted to have two panels, as well as demands for more assistants, more office fixtures, and so on. As it was, the court, although small, had wholly inadequate support staff. In 1972, there were two, Culliton's secretary and a stenographer.[41] For several months, it was down to one. The stenographer transferred to a different department, and although the treasury board had approved the hiring of a second stenographer, neither position was filled for months. Marie Ryan, Culliton's dedicated assistant, worked alongside the chief justice seven days a week, including most evenings. When Culliton asked that Ryan be paid overtime, Romanow replied that her position in the civil service was not eligible for overtime and it was a bad precedent to make an exception.[42] Nothing Culliton said could change his mind.

Ross Thatcher had been notoriously cheap as well, and the NDP arguably were continuing a long-standing policy of keeping departments on tight budgets, but times had changed. Saskatchewan's judges were hearing nearly as many appeals a year as British Columbia's court, which had twice as many judges.[43] In neighbouring Alberta, the judges had a similar workload as their Saskatchewan counterparts but had far more support staff and still felt they had insufficient clerical help The staffing problem in Saskatchewan extended to the court's registry. Back in the 1920s, the court had a full-time registrar and several clerks in the registrar's office, who sometimes assisted the judges. By the 1970s, there was a part-time registrar, and his two clerks were barely able to cover the front counter and file the appeals, much less augment the tiny complement of judicial assistants.[44]

Culliton had to contend with myriad other irritations resulting from government economy measures. The public works department turned off the courthouse air conditioning after hours and on weekends, which Culliton, regularly working overtime with Ryan, found intolerable.[45] A typewriter broke and it was months before it was fixed. The court couldn't order more bookshelves for the library and had to stack books on the floor. Bayda had to bring a chair from home for his office: his was broken and court services could not get a replacement.

Part of the workload for Culliton and his assistant was due to adopting a fixed hearing schedule in the early 1970s. Rather than having a general list for upcoming hearings, with appeals heard in order as the court got to them, the judges now heard each appeal on a scheduled date. The change was inevitable, but scheduled hearings required that the court know approximately how much time each appeal required. Neighbouring Alberta required counsel to provide a time estimate, and the registrar drew up the list with a judge acting as list manager. Culliton, as was his penchant, was the list manager in Saskatchewan. He took a very laborious approach, examining each factum and other filed materials to estimate an appropriate hearing length and then scheduling the hearing, apparently without the input of counsel.[46] It gave the chief justice finely tuned control over hearings but was an onerous burden. Under Culliton's successor, the duty was handed over to the court registrar.[47]

Even if Culliton made more work for himself, it was clear that the court was outrageously understaffed. As his requests for more people fell on apparently deaf ears, Culliton grew angrier and angrier. His strenuous complaints were eventually heeded and the government hired two more people, bringing the complement of secretaries to four, but Culliton never seemed to have more than two people on hand. The jobs did not pay well, the workload was heavy, and there was a lot of turnover. Every time a stenographer quit or transferred, it was months before a replacement showed up and usually only after Culliton vociferously complained.

Culliton's patience finally ran out in the fall of 1976 and he wrote a blistering letter to Roy Romanow in which he took the attorney general to task for not adequately supporting the court and responding to his complaints. He had reached his wits' end, he told Romanow. The utter lack of co-operation from the government had made it impossible to manage the court. He criticized the "bureaucracy and dogmatism" of the civil service, and the treasury office in particular, and tartly informed Romanow that "the work load of the Court is not controllable, even by Budget Bureau or administrative staff."[48] Aside from the manifest personnel shortage, Culliton found it extremely irritating that his requests were going to lower-level functionaries who passed the buck. He wanted a court manager who reported directly to the deputy minister as a conduit for his requests. The chief justice was also incensed that in a previous letter Romanow had excused the lack of action because the treasury board had refused to allow expenditures, leading Culliton to ask if the treasury was running the government or the government running the treasury.

Romanow pushed back, outraged at the chief's suggestion that he did not support the courts. Culliton then threatened to cancel civil sittings until the backlog of paperwork facing the court was dealt with. The chief justice won the day. After their exchange of blunt letters, the two men met and made peace. Romanow agreed to hire a couple more people and approve some much-needed renovations in the courthouse in Regina.

It should be said that the Court of Queen's Bench and the District Court felt just as neglected as the Court of Appeal; at the Queen's Bench, only the chief justice had a secretary and the court had just a couple of other clerical staff in Regina, and at that court too at least one judge had to provide his own chair. The judges in the smaller centres were on their own, lucky if they could get a court reporter or a clerk in the court office to help with correspondence or typing up a judgment.

The government's parsimony was puzzling, considering the NDP's other court reforms. Upon his retirement, Emmett Hall was asked to head a commission on the province's court system and recommend changes. In the wake of Hall's report, the magistrate's court was completely overhauled, becoming the Provincial Court of Saskatchewan. Over the heads of the judiciary and the opposition of much of the profession, the government also decided to amalgamate the District Court and the Court of Queen's Bench, which took effect in 1981.[49] These were common initiatives across Canada.[50] Amalgamation was almost always controversial and was often pushed through against the opposition of the judiciary, especially on the senior superior court. Hall had not favoured amalgamation in his report.

He had little to say about the Court of Appeal. He recommended criminal sittings and special sittings for Saskatoon, responding to continued agitation from the city's bar.[51] He also suggested sitting the full court for most appeals instead of three-judge panels, a suggestion Culliton ignored.

Disagreements over court organization, funding, and administration heralded the arrival of a new issue: the administration of courts as an aspect of judicial independence. The problems for Saskatchewan's courts were not unique, although they were worse than most. Almost all Canadian superior courts were short-staffed and didn't have basic office equipment like electric typewriters, and almost without exception they had no control over their budgets or even the management of whatever staff they had.[52] Some complained of bureaucrats interfering with list management and workflow, which judges saw as their prerogative. Canadian judges began to talk about the need to manage court administration themselves, as many American courts did.

In 1979, the Canadian Judicial Council commissioned Justice Jules Deschênes of Quebec to do a study on the subject. Provocatively titled *Masters in Their Own House*, Deschênes's report concluded that notwithstanding that the judiciary and the executive had a good relationship in most provinces, administrative oversight of the courts by civil servants who did not answer to the judiciary was a threat to judicial independence.[53] It was an opening salvo in a confrontation between judges and governments that would heat up in the late 1980s and early 1990s.

If Culliton agreed with Deschênes's report, he had no chance to act upon it. He retired in 1981, the year it was published. Beefing up the court would be a matter for his successor. Meanwhile, Culliton and his colleagues soldiered on, sitting on creaking chairs in stifling offices, wondering when someone might type up a judgment for them or whether they should do it themselves—if they could find a working typewriter.

THE COURT AT LAW

BORA LASKIN WAS not born in Saskatchewan, he never lived there, and he never practised law or sat as a judge there. Yet Laskin had an outsize influence on Saskatchewan's court and the entire Canadian judiciary. Laskin, a law professor turned judge who became chief justice of the Supreme Court in 1973, is often credited with leading an important sea change in

Canadian jurisprudence which altered the way judges approached the law. This was the advent of legal modernism, also called legal realism or contextualism.[54] Laskin's court also became a constitutional battleground, pitting provincial rights against federal policies at a time when both levels of government were activist and interventionist, almost guaranteeing a clash. In Saskatchewan, it turned into a battle over the control of natural resources—a perennial source of anger in Western Canada—and two memorable court cases demonstrated the two opposing schools of thought on the division of powers and the nature of federalism: *CIGOL* and *Central Canada Potash*.

MORE GUSTY WINDS OF CHANGE

ON HIS APPOINTMENT to the courts, a great deal was expected of Bora Laskin. He joined the judiciary just as a sort of revolution was taking place in common law jurisprudence. In the 1950s and 1960s, Lord Denning had become something of a folk hero in England with his bold judgments. Denning took a much more flexible view of precedent and reasserted the common law tradition of judge-made law that reflected and responded to changes in society. In 1966, the House of Lords, after decades of explicitly and implicitly regarding precedent as unreviewable, stated that under exceptional circumstances a previous decision of the Lords might be re-examined and overturned. American courts had long before stopped rigidly applying precedent, or had never subscribed to an absolutist approach to *stare decisis*. The decision of the law lords was probably the more influential in Canada, given the still strong deference of Canadian judges to English law, but developments in American judicial philosophy had their impact, thanks in part to academics like Laskin.

The University of Toronto and Osgoode Hall law professor joined the Ontario Court of Appeal in 1965, the Supreme Court of Canada in 1970, and became chief justice of Canada in 1973. Laskin was, in the words of his biographer, a "legal modernist."[55] As an academic, Laskin had been a harsh critic of the formalism that had dominated Canadian courts for time immemorial.[56] He called on judges to rediscover their lawmaking role and become more responsive to the larger social context in which the law operated.[57] He attacked what he saw as the mechanistic and absolutist application of *stare decisis* and felt there was much more room for judicial creativity.[58] Laskin and the evolution of the Supreme Court may seem tangential to the history of Saskatchewan's Court of Appeal, except that the province's court and judges were inevitably exposed to the new currents in jurisprudence, and the question is how much this influenced Culliton and his brother judges.

Laskin argued that law should be interpreted and understood purposively, in terms of what the aims of law might be. He adopted the so-called modern rule of statutory interpretation, often called "purposive interpretation." Rather than limiting analysis of a statute strictly to the words as written, purposive interpretation allowed for a broader examination of the statute, inquiring into the legislative background and the problem the statute was intended to address. The purposive approach went hand in hand with considering a decision's policy implications—how decisions affected and reflected the real world. As a law professor, Laskin called for courts to consider "extrinsic evidence"—academic law articles, economic data, parliamentary debates—when necessary and available to decide an appeal. When Laskin joined the Supreme Court, it still followed an unofficial rule of not quoting living authors, presumably as they had not stood the test of time and become authorities. Laskin wanted judges to get out of their ivory tower and move with the times.

Even as an academic critic, Laskin seemed more radical than he really was. His calls for greater judicial creativity had an element of nostalgia for a time when common law judges more readily developed the law. An influential American text referred to this kind of judicial engagement with society, guiding the law to respond to social change, as the "grand tradition."[59] Laskin in fact adhered very much to the incrementalism and inherent conservatism of the common law, very apparent in his own judicial decisions. Despite his reputation as a judicial activist, he honoured the doctrine of parliamentary supremacy, and while touting the purposive approach he was quite prepared to concede that it was a tool for when the law was vague or contradictory and that it was usually not necessary to look behind the words of a clearly written statute. Laskin's view could probably be summed up as "Boldness is sometimes necessary but not necessarily boldness."

Laskin was not a lone prophet. His views reflected developments in legal thought in the United States to which he had been exposed as a student at Harvard in the 1930s.[60] Cecil Wright, the University of Toronto dean of law, was a mentor, and there were other progressive academics in

Canada, including Dean Cronkite in Saskatchewan. The province was always a leader in legal education, with one of the first full-time university law schools, and Cronkite had ambitions to do more. But only in the 1960s did Canada generally begin to catch up to the rich academic discourse found in American law schools. Even after university law programs were established in the 1920s and 1930s, most of the instructors were part-time, often members of the bar who taught a course on top of full-time practice. Emmett Hall and Percy Maguire were two notable examples. A law school like Saskatchewan's might have only three full-time professors, and even they spent little time on an academic analysis of law.[61]

In the 1960s and 1970s, the size and number of law schools in Canada exploded. The complement of full-time faculty expanded drastically at law schools new and established, and many of these instructors were young and academically oriented. Critical analysis of the law proliferated, and it encompassed the interaction of law and society. Despite its limitations, Saskatchewan's law school under Dean Cronkite had been known for its progressive teaching, and Otto Lang had built on this foundation in the 1960s. The law school started offering graduate courses, and in 1967 the school's law journal, the *Saskatchewan Bar Review*, was retitled the *Saskatchewan Law Review* and took on a much more academic tone. Many graduates were prominent in the federal civil service, part of the "Saskatchewan mafia," before becoming influential academics.[62] One academic later on the bench quipped that "judges had nothing to do with law professors and vice versa, and judges do not read law review articles,"[63] but the fact was that such articles had an impact. New generations of lawyers were leaving law school with a broader perspective.

The appearance of law reform committees and commissions also played a role. These often involved academics as well as leading members of the bar, the judiciary, and politicians. With an explicit mission to eliminate obsolete statutes and suggest reforms and new laws, these commissions were far-reaching compared to the committees governments had previously struck to revise statutes. Law reform advocacy in Canada started immediately after the war and proceeded in fits and starts. Saskatchewan established a law reform commission in 1958 that was very active for five years or so before fading into obscurity.[64] In 1973, the provincial government re-established the commission with an expansive mandate.[65] Nearly every other province had a reform commission or institute, sponsored by a combination of government, the law society, and a law faculty.

In this atmosphere, the Supreme Court of Canada and other courts became the target of criticism for being timid and parochial, "black letter" in the pejorative sense.[66] The court's cautious jurisprudence was contrasted, sometimes in the press, to the boldness of its American counterpart.[67] After the end of Privy Council appeals in 1949, Laskin had called for the "captive court" to assert a role of leadership in developing the law in Canada and cast off the last shackles of colonialism.[68] The Supreme Court of the 1950s had shown sparks of creativity, significantly expanding civil liberties and labour law, but had settled back into a slumber when certain key judges like Ivan Rand retired.[69] As Supreme Court justice Ian Binnie recalled, in the 1960s the court "generally wrote reasons without reference to each other and all of them generally focused on error correction"[70] One reason Pierre Trudeau appointed Laskin to the court and then made him chief justice—bypassing Ronald Martland, considered a strong judge and very much Laskin's senior—was his modernist, activist leanings. As chief justice, Laskin was central to a renewal of the Supreme Court of Canada.

The first and most important change was eliminating appeals by right and taking control of the Supreme Court's calendar. Civil matters valued at over $10,000 could still be appealed without leave, clogging the court's list with cases that had no significance outside of the interests of the parties. An amendment to the *Supreme Court Act* that took effect in 1975 required leave for all appeals except criminal convictions where there had been a dissent at the provincial appellate court. This allowed the court to address only those appeals that had some significant public dimension, which included private law appeals to settle an important point of law. Although the amendment had been passed ostensibly to deal with an unsustainable workload of the court, it allowed the court to focus on developing jurisprudence. One very important side effect of the amendment was that it made the decisions of provincial courts of appeal much more important. Only a handful of decisions were now likely to be heard in Ottawa, and provincial courts had the final say in the vast majority of appeals. This put new emphasis on their lawmaking role, something that became very apparent in the 1980s.

Laskin otherwise attempted to address the points on which he had criticized the court for many years. As part of developing jurisprudence, he tried to bring more consideration of the policy dimensions involved in the questions that came before the court, applying the "purposive" approach where appropriate. He encouraged more research before and after hearings, and more collaboration. He used the so-called "extrinsic" material that had been frowned on. Laskin was frequently in dissent even as chief justice, but his example slowly changed the culture of the court, as did new appointments like Brian Dickson, his eventual successor. Laskin the judge turned out to be much less radical than Laskin the scholar, but he still became an icon of a more progressive, broader approach to law that reverberated through Canada's legal system and arguably influenced other appellate courts starting in the 1970s but more certainly in the decades to come. Young judges like Edward Bayda adopted this progressive approach, as did many of his colleagues in the 1980s.

There were of course other judges in Canada restive under the "dry legalism" of the times. When Laskin went to the Supreme Court as a *puisne* justice, he had immediately found a kindred spirit: Emmett Hall. They often found themselves in the minority on the court, frequently with Justice Wishart Spence, a precursor to the famous "LSD" trio of Laskin, Spence, and Dickson. Hall was not a legal scholar of Laskin's calibre: he wrote mostly in criminal law and on negligence and liability, areas that reflected his years of practice experience.[71] But Hall had a strong sense of social justice and was impatient with the notion that judges should not consider social, economic, and political factors beyond the immediate letter of the law. His biographer said that Hall was mystified by the strict formal approach to law of his colleagues. "To be stymied by precedent, or *stare decisis*, was a long-festering irritant for Hall."[72] Hall was much more concerned with just outcomes: If the law was not addressing the problems of litigants or society, then what was the point of the law? He gave an address at Osgoode Hall in 1971 that was deeply critical of the way precedent was applied in Canadian courts and hailed the 1966 House of Lords practice statement on departing from precedent.[73] Hall was not afraid to say that judges should think more about the ultimate consequences of their decisions and that they should play a role in advancing the law in response to change.

This could be seen in Hall's minority opinion in the *Calder* case, one of the first significant rulings of the Supreme Court on Aboriginal land claims. At issue was whether the Nisga'a people in British Columbia, who had never signed a treaty, still had Aboriginal title to their traditional lands. The court agreed that under the Royal Proclamation of 1763 Aboriginal title had existed, but the majority, on narrow grounds, ruled that British

EDWARD DMYTRO BAYDA

Ed Bayda was a Saskatchewan farm boy who went on to great things. In this, he was an exemplar of the migration from country to city in the province and of the final integration of the province's Old World ethnic minorities, although his Ukrainian heritage still made his appointment as chief justice both historic and noteworthy.

Born on September 9, 1931, in the tiny hamlet of Alvena, near Saskatoon, Bayda was the grandson of Ukrainian homesteaders who arrived at the turn of the century.[1] His father, Dmytro, started a successful implement dealership and hardware store as well as running a substantial farm. Bayda grew up in Alvena and went to Saskatoon to finish high school at City Park Collegiate.[2] He entered the five-year combined law and arts program at the University of Saskatchewan, receiving a bachelor of arts degree in philosophy and political science in 1951, and graduating with distinction in law in 1953.

Bayda articled with M.A. MacPherson at MacPherson, Leslie and Tyerman in Regina. He practised for a short time in Yorkton before returning to Regina and joining the firm later known as Johnson, Bayda, Halvorson and Scheibel. Four members of the firm went to the bench, and his partner Fred Johnson became chief justice of the Court of Queen's Bench. Bayda established himself as a leading criminal and litigation counsel and took several cases to the Supreme Court of Canada. Made a QC in 1966, Bayda was a bencher of the Law Society, a president of the Regina Bar Association, and chairman of the civil justice section of the Canadian Bar Association. He was active in the community, serving as president of the Kinsmen Club and on the Knights of Columbus executive and volunteering with the United Way.[3]

Bayda was appointed to the Queen's Bench in September 1972, and just over two years later, in December 1974, to the Court of Appeal. He immediately served on the Vancouver Port Grain Handling Industrial Inquiry as commissioner from 1974 to 1975. As chairman of the Cluff Lake Board of Inquiry in 1977, Bayda produced a report that became a landmark in community consultation for resource development. He also served for three years on the Law Reform Commission of Saskatchewan.

A friend described Bayda as a man about town: he was a patron of the arts, a supporter of the Regina Symphony Orchestra, the Globe Theatre, and the MacKenzie Art Gallery.[4] Bayda was sociable and fun-loving, with an infectious laugh. At home with people from all walks of life, he never lost his down-to-earth quality. He had a cherished 1972 Lincoln Continental that he cared for meticulously, involving frequent weekend visits to Canadian Tire. According to family, he could be found there chatting with other customers like old friends. Married twice, with seven children, Bayda cherished his family, including his many nieces and nephews.

Bayda was the youngest-ever chief justice in Canada upon his appointment in 1981 as well as the first of Ukrainian descent.[5] He was head of the court through the crucial first decade of the *Charter of Rights and Freedoms* and substantially modernized the court's practice and procedure. He was the longest-serving chief justice of the Court of Appeal, retiring in 2006 after twenty-five years, and had the second longest tenure as chief justice of Saskatchewan after Frederick Haultain. Bayda loved the law and returned to practice in retirement, joining the firm of Kanuka Thuringer in Regina.[6] Both his alma mater and the University of Regina gave Bayda honorary doctorates, in 1989 and 2006 respectively. A keen traveller, Bayda died on vacation in Turkey on April 2, 2010, at seventy-eight. He was given a state funeral in Regina.

Justice Edward Dmytro Bayda, c. 1980. (Court of Appeal/Photographic Services Agency)

Columbia's entry into Confederation extinguished Native title. In his dissent, Hall thoroughly canvassed the history of colonial relations with Canada's Indigenous peoples and concluded that in common law a right such as title to lands must be expressly surrendered or extinguished.[74] Furthermore, he argued that it was the Crown, not the Nisga'a, who should have the burden to proof as to whether the Aboriginal title had been eliminated, and he did not think the Crown had adequately satisfied that burden. Hall's judgment combined an old common law principle with a nuanced analysis of the historical context to right a historic wrong. Laskin and Spence concurred. And although it was a dissent, Hall's judgment changed federal policy. Trudeau was supposedly so impressed with Hall's argument that he abandoned the notorious 1969 White Paper on Aboriginal policy in favour of more conciliatory policies, including negotiating land claims.[75]

As an academic, Laskin had also been one of Canada's leading experts in constitutional law. He had been very critical of the early Privy Council decisions in division of powers cases that diminished the power of the federal government. Somewhat radically, Laskin had long believed that the "peace, order and good government" preamble to the list of federal powers in section 91 of the BNA *Act* gave Ottawa a general lawmaking power.[76] The enumerated jurisdictions were specific examples of the power. Privy Council decisions had turned the so-called POGG clause into a residual power. Laskin and the Supreme Court turned to POGG in the 1976 *Anti-Inflation Act Reference* to justify federal wage and price controls that amounted to a major extension of federal powers.

The *Anti-Inflation Act Reference* confirmed for many people that Laskin had a federalist bent. Not surprisingly, at the time of Laskin's appointment and many times since, it has been said that Pierre Trudeau chose him to be chief justice of Canada in part because of his obvious federalist leanings. This suited Trudeau well as the 1970s emerged as a constitutional battleground, particularly over the control of natural resources. This reopened an old wound that had long festered in Western Canada. The Culliton-led court came into direct conflict with the Laskin-led court, not the last time that Saskatchewan's Court of Appeal would have a fundamental difference of views with the Supreme Court of Canada.

THE EVOLVING JUDGE

BORA LASKIN DID have some Saskatchewan connections. He was a close friend of Morris Shumiatcher, who had been his student. Laskin then became a friend of Culliton when they sat together on the Canadian Judicial Council. And Culliton had a hand in promoting judicial education and creating the council, two examples of an evolving judiciary. Culliton, like Emmett Hall, had a strong sense of justice, and he also had the sort of commanding personality that might readily take to more latitude in judicial decision-making. But Culliton had also spent his first decade as a judge—his apprenticeship—on a very traditional if sensible court. As a *puisne* judge, Culliton hewed mostly to the orthodoxies of the time, and certainly some of those orthodoxies remained with him throughout his career. But early on, he also showed signs of having a more flexible approach to precedent, and he later flirted with the "purposive" approach to law even if not fully adopting it.

Culliton's judicial philosophy can be summed up in his own words: "The basic question which faces the court is, what is necessary to see that justice is done?"[77] One of Culliton's earliest reported decisions, a dissent dealing with a procedural point, articulated the principle that courts should not be so bound by precedent or rules of court that justice could not be done. Through his career, he consistently called for the "broad and liberal" interpretations of both statute and case law if he felt it was the best way to ensure justice. Culliton never showed the same impatience with *stare decisis* as Emmett Hall did, but he was the dominant chief justice of an intermediate appeal court, not one liberal-minded judge on a conservative bench. He likely found precedent less of a hindrance to getting the outcome he thought was right. This is not to suggest Culliton arbitrarily bent the law to a desired end, but there was often a range of interpretation possible and Culliton was persuasive. Even before the Supreme Court made it necessary to be granted leave, relatively few cases from the provincial appellate courts were taken to Ottawa, which allowed considerable latitude.[78]

Culliton had some of the qualities that Laskin thought desirable in judges. The *Morrissette* sentencing decision was, within the statute-constrained field of criminal law, a prime example of judicial lawmaking. In *R v Morrissette*, Culliton made the case that sentencing principles had to be adjusted to accord for new thinking about criminality and punishment and about changing societal attitudes, and he did not wait for the legislature. Sentencing was an area of wide judicial discretion, and at the time of the *Morrissette* decision, sentencing principles were not codified, which provided a sound basis for judge-made law. Given Culliton's general proclivities regarding sentencing, it is not surprising he did not hesitate to render a somewhat activist and certainly policy-driven decision. This was an area where he also did not hesitate, in a general sense, to look much further into the issues. In *R v Hartridge*, an important 1967 decision that analyzed the distinctions between insanity, autonomism, and drunkenness, Culliton had used a number of academic articles to inform his analysis, declaring them very helpful.[79]

Yet even if Culliton was forward-thinking enough to unabashedly use law review articles at a time when most judges avoided such things, he did not necessarily embrace the use of other extrinsic material. In a notable 1958 decision, *Cairns Construction v Saskatchewan*, Culliton and Martin had both expounded the principle that the court should not allow evidence of economists regarding the real-world operation of a tax, stating that statutory interpretation should be limited to the words of the statute itself except in exceptional circumstances and limited ways. Twenty years later, in *Central Canada Potash Corp. v Saskatchewan*, discussed below, Culliton was prepared to allow more "contextual" evidence, but he took the trial judge to task for considering far too much evidence he deemed irrelevant, declaring that some well-known facts and the statute under consideration were sufficient for the constitutional argument.

In the constitutional cases of CIGOL and *Central Canada Potash*, Culliton argued for constitutional interpretation that was grounded in real-world consequences and, to use a judicial catchphrase, "a broad and liberal" interpretation of the statute under consideration. This sounds very much like what Laskin was looking for in judges and accorded with his own thought.[80] But it was also true that constitutional law was an area where Canadian judges had been historically less constrained in their decision-making. The "living tree" analogy used by Lord Sankey to describe the BNA *Act* in the Privy Council's decision in the famous Persons Case of 1929, in a sense allowed judges to take a wider approach to constitutional interpretation. Culliton was, in the tradition of the court, generally quite conservative in regards to interpreting and certainly making law but also quite willing to do more when the opportunity was open to him, guided by the principle that justice should be done.

FOR THE REST of the court, *Rathwell v Rathwell* in 1976 may have indicated an adoption of modern methods but it may simply have been a manifestation of Culliton's question "What is necessary to see that justice is done?" *Rathwell* was a celebrated Saskatchewan decision on the division of matrimonial property that followed in the wake of the notorious Supreme Court decision of *Murdoch v Murdoch*, which *Rathwell* subverted.

After the 1968 *Divorce Act* and with divorce rates rising, many cases came before the courts of women seeking a division of farm assets that the family had acquired during the course of marriage. These assets—land, machinery, and livestock—were nearly always in the name of the husband, and working farms and ranches were not easily divided. In *Murdoch*, an Alberta case, the wife in a bitter divorce presented a strong argument that money she had inherited and her labour had been instrumental in creating a substantial ranching operation. The judge at trial held that she had not proved unequivocally her funds were used in acquiring ranch lands and that her other contributions were no different from those of "any other farm wife."

The Supreme Court endorsed the trial judge's fact findings and ruled the wife had no claim on the assets of the ranch, a decision that outraged Canadian women and was roundly and loudly condemned. Bora Laskin dissented. He argued that the trial judge had erred in his findings of fact and that the doctrine of constructive trust should be applied in the situation. A doctrine of equity used in cases of unjust enrichment, a constructive trust did not require an explicit agreement or contract towards achieving an end but could be inferred from the circumstances. Laskin argued that the efforts of both parties in a marriage towards their family's economic success was a circumstance where a trust might be created. His dissent was an example of his progressive jurisprudence: he stated that a legislative approach was the best solution for the problem at hand but that it was not the only solution, and the court could creatively relieve the inequity through a constructive trust.[81] Implicit in his judgment was that women were being unfairly deprived and the court could do something about it. Justice Martland, in his majority opinion, was unequivocal that Laskin's solution was judicial legislating and invaded the prerogatives of the legislature. Martland's decision, although making a valid point, was an example of why the Supreme Court was criticized as being out of touch and regressive.

Murdoch was far from the last word on the subject. Other cases arose, including the celebrated *Rathwell*. The circumstances in *Rathwell* were essentially identical to *Murdoch*: a woman argued that money she put in a joint account early in her marriage contributed to the couple's purchase of their first farm lands and that her labour subsequently made the farm a success. The trial judge, Disbery, found that there was no connection between her deposit in the joint account and the purchase of land, no evidence that there was any common intent in building up the farm, and took up the "typical farm wife" line in regards to her other contributions. Disbery caused a great furor with his comments in his judgment and in court, which were breathtakingly sexist even for 1976.[82] This included the gem "Somebody has to defend the men from the present mode of the women's liberation movement."[83] Disbery's bias against the plaintiff was a ground of appeal.

Woods, Brownridge, and Roy Hall allowed the appeal, each writing reasons. The common conclusion was that there was a constructive trust that entitled the wife to an equal division of the property. Hall, for good measure, also ruled that the division of property did not disentitle the wife to alimony, as these were separate legal rights. Although *Murdoch* seemingly precluded the court declaring a constructive trust, Woods et al. used the time-honoured technique for getting out from under a precedent: they distinguished the facts of the case. Indeed, in a very Saskatchewan twist, given the court's statutory power to review fact findings, the panel substituted its own determinations for those of the trial judge. The panel held—"with the greatest respect"—that Disbery had misapprehended the evidence, and it concluded instead that the wife had made an initial financial contribution and also found in the testimony sufficient evidence that the husband and wife worked as a team with the common goal of having a successful farm. This allowed the panel to declare a constructive trust existed in favour of the wife, entitling her to a share of the property. Brownridge quoted with approval Laskin's *Murdoch* dissent.[84] Hall, in his analysis, concluded that the wife's contributions to the farm in *Rathwell* were actually rather less than had been the case in *Murdoch* yet still gave her claim to a trust.[85] It seemed a rather pointed criticism of *Murdoch*.

Rathwell was one of a number of decisions where lower courts looked for ways to circumvent *Murdoch*.[86] It was clear that the panel in

Saskatchewan, as elsewhere, thought *Murdoch* was unjust and out of step with the times and should not stand. The Supreme Court of Canada upheld the Saskatchewan decision five to four. Justice Dickson, writing for the majority, did his best to limit and circumvent *Murdoch*, coming about as close as possible to saying it had been wrongly decided without actually doing so.[87] Martland for the minority unrepentantly stuck to his earlier conclusions. At this point, the legislature stepped in. The outrage over *Murdoch* had led to a concentrated push for new legislation to govern the division of matrimonial property. The Saskatchewan government passed *The Matrimonial Property Act* in 1979, which addressed the problem at the heart of *Murdoch* and *Rathwell*.

The Court of Appeal's *Rathwell* decision arguably fit into a broader approach to law. The panel creatively circumvented a binding precedent and tackled an obvious legal and social problem. The judges then took the opportunity to apply a legal solution that was at hand, which, if not the law, had the imprimatur of a Supreme Court justice who was not afraid to judicially legislate. If the three Saskatchewan judges were squeamish about the policy dimension involved, they could argue that they were merely finding justice for the litigant before them. But it is hard to believe that Woods, Brownridge, and Hall did not realize that their decision was not traditional judging. And it is hard to imagine the court of even ten years earlier, with exactly the same judges, coming to the same decision. It was a preview of the more creative, less rigid jurisprudence that became the norm in Canada in the 1980s, and it was crucial to the success of the *Charter of Rights and Freedoms*.

FUELLING WESTERN ALIENATION: *CIGOL* AND *CENTRAL CANADA POTASH*

WHILE ALBERTA GARNERED the lion's share of public attention in debates over natural resources in the 1970s, Saskatchewan was by far the more important legal and constitutional battlefield. *Canadian Industrial Gas and Oil Ltd. v Saskatchewan* (usually known as CIGOL) and *Central Canada Potash Corp. v Saskatchewan* were decisions where the provincial conception of the separation of powers and control of natural resources clashed with a federalist conception. In both cases, the Supreme Court overruled Culliton and the Court of Appeal, significantly limiting the ability of provincial governments to tax their resources and extending the reach of the trade and commerce power of the federal government. In both cases, the Supreme Court decision was subsequently heavily criticized and even called "bad law."[88] The political fallout from CIGOL and *Central Canada Potash* led to a constitutional amendment that significantly increased the protection of provincial jurisdiction over resources.

Natural resources were a particular sore point in Saskatchewan and Alberta. When the two provinces were formed in 1905, in return for a direct financial subsidy Ottawa had kept control over resources, which under the BNA *Act* was a provincial jurisdiction. Twenty-five years later, after much onerous negotiation, Saskatchewan finally gained control. The next few decades saw relative peace, constitutionally speaking, between Ottawa and the provinces.[89] In terms of resource development, both levels of government were eager to exploit the nation's natural riches and there was generally more co-operation than conflict.[90] To help Western Canadian oil producers, the 1961 federal oil policy forced Ontario refiners (and consumers) to use Western oil instead of cheaper imported oil.

The 1973 OPEC oil embargo ended this period of peace. The price of oil doubled and doubled again in the space of a year and continued to climb. The governments of the producing provinces moved to capture some of the windfall profits. The federal government, meanwhile, confronting the economic headwinds created by high energy prices, coveted the oil and gas revenues going into provincial coffers but was also mindful of the effect on consumers of higher oil and gas prices and was apprehensive about security of supply. When Ottawa slapped an export tax on oil and gas and then imposed price ceilings for domestic sales, there were howls of protest from Alberta and Saskatchewan and applause from Ontario. The two Prairie provinces immediately tried to siphon off resource revenue before the federal government could tax it. The early sparring in retrospect looked like a tempest in a teapot when in 1980 the Trudeau government introduced the National Energy Program in the wake of another spike in oil prices. And while oil and gas were the primary bones of contention in the 1970s, other resources, like potash, were drawn into the fray.

There was also a larger constitutional struggle under way. The 1970s was a time of activist government, both provincially and federally, and inevitably there was overlap in legislative programs and intrusions into each government's spheres of responsibility. The Trudeau government was aggressively centralist. The prime minister believed that the regionalism of

Canadian federalism harmed the national interest. The 1976 *Anti-Inflation Act* reference was a watershed moment. The Supreme Court ruled that federal wage and price controls were *intra vires* both as an emergency measure and under the "peace, order and good government" clause of the BNA *Act*, taking precedence over provincial control of property and civil rights. The decision was generally viewed as an extension of federal power.[91] There were many other court challenges in the 1970s involving the division of powers, in areas such as prosecutorial authority, the reach of the criminal law power, and so on.[92]

CIGOL and *Central Canada Potash* both started as the challenges of private corporations to Saskatchewan laws that, in the former case, imposed punitive taxation and, in the latter case, instituted a pro-rationing scheme limiting potash production. The companies challenged the statutes on the basis of the division of powers, arguing the laws exceeded provincial jurisdiction. What began as producer challenges quickly drew in the federal government and, as intervenors at the Supreme Court of Canada, other provincial governments. The federal government's interest was not surprising. Almost all the oil and gas and potash produced in Saskatchewan was sold outside the province, either in other parts of Canada, the United States, or internationally, and interprovincial and international exports were an area of federal lawmaking under Ottawa's trade and commerce power. Another irritant for the federal government was new provincial taxes and royalty rate increases that effectively reduced the export taxes and corporate income taxes paid federally.[93] In the provinces, critics suspected the federal government was looking for a back door via the courts to control resources by disallowing provincial taxation and using federal trade and commerce power or potentially even the "peace, order and good government" clause.

CIGOL was the first case to go through the courts. In 1973, the Blakeney government in Saskatchewan enacted *The Oil and Gas Conservation, Stabilization and Development Act*, the centrepiece in a complex structure of statutes and regulations the whole of which became known colloquially as *Bill 42*.[94] There were three main aspects to the enactments. The first was the expropriation of freehold mineral rights. Existing leases were honoured and the previous owners of the rights were compensated. The mineral rights for freeholds under 1,280 acres were not expropriated, the so-called farmer's exemption, aimed at not penalizing small landowners receiving royalties. Any company ceasing production on the expropriated leases was subject to heavy penalties. The second element was the implementation of a "royalty surcharge" on all production from Crown lands, including the expropriated mineral rights. This was an additional payment on top of the royalty already set in the lease. The last part was a "mineral income tax" on the profits of all production not subject to the surcharge. Both the surcharge and new tax were defined as the excess over the "basic wellhead price," the price that producers had been receiving for their oil before the OPEC embargo. That price, around $3.50 a barrel before prices spiked, was now set by statute. To discourage companies from selling their production at a discount to subsidiaries or other companies in sweetheart deals to avoid the tax, the tax was calculated against the market price for oil rather than for what the producers sold their oil. The provincial government through the royalty surcharge and mineral income tax basically took all the extra profits the hike in oil prices created, leaving the producers with what they had been earning pre-crisis. It was a price freeze for producers.

The aim was to capture the "windfall" profits that the sudden rise of oil prices had created. Alberta instituted similar policies, though not as draconian and somewhat differently structured. Needless to say, oil and gas producers in both provinces were not pleased. Not only were companies in Saskatchewan not making any money out of the rise in oil prices, there was an onerous amount of paperwork: returns for each well had to be submitted monthly to the minister of natural resources giving the price for each barrel sold and a list of all entities that received income from the sale. Canadian Industrial Gas and Oil Ltd. was a mid-sized domestic company with substantial Saskatchewan interests. The company took the provincial government to court, attacking the royalty surcharge and mineral income tax as *ultra vires* as indirect taxation, and *Bill 42* generally as interfering with the federal power of trade and commerce by regulating oil exports.

Under the BNA *Act*, the provinces were restricted to direct taxation, while the federal government could resort to both direct and indirect taxation. The nineteenth-century political philosopher John Stuart Mill had famously defined the distinction between the two types of taxes: "A direct tax is one which is demanded from the very persons who, it is intended or desired, should pay it. Indirect taxes are those which are demanded from one person in the expectation and intention that he shall indemnify himself at the expense of another."[95]

Income taxes or property taxes were the classic examples of a direct tax, while import and export taxes or manufacturer's taxes were examples of indirect tax, because these costs were invariably passed on to the consumer in the sale price of a good or commodity. Mill's division of taxes was a legal concept rather than an economic one, as the actual effect of taxes was often quite complex; many "direct" taxes were to some extent passed on from the primary payer. The Mill's test was useful and in Canadian law was still the standard used in determining the nature of a tax.

Canadian Industrial Gas and Oil argued that the royalty surcharge was, in essence, a tax identical to the mineral income tax and that both were indirect taxes, because the oil companies did not directly bear the cost of the tax, the purchaser did. Its claim was dismissed at trial and the matter came before Culliton and the court in March 1975. Culliton saw that the stakes were high and sat the whole court for the appeal. The court's judgment was finally rendered on December 18, 1975, a very long reserve for the court at the time. For all the wait, Culliton's judgment was not very long, some twenty pages, over half of which was dedicated to describing the relevant legislative history, which was admittedly complicated. In Culliton's view, the actual issue in the appeal was not that complex and in fact did not require a long-winded analysis.

> Before concluding, I want to make this observation in explanation of the fact that I have not referred to the many authorities quoted by counsel. I approached the problem on the basis that the answers to the questions posed could best be found by an examination of the language used in the legislation and regulations, interpreted in the light of the relevant data in accordance with the well-established definition of direct and indirect taxes. In my view, the intent and purpose of the legislation and regulations, as well as their general tendency and nature, were clearly evident in the legislation and regulations, viewed in the light of their own facts. This approach simplified the problem and it is not an approach which, in my opinion, oversimplified those problems.[96]

Culliton did not see how the company's contention that the mineral income tax and royalty surcharge were indirect taxes could be correct. He held that the royalty surcharge was in fact a royalty, but even if it was a tax, he argued, this would not matter. Mill's test was clear: the cost of the tax had to be obviously passed on to make a tax indirect. In the case of both charges, there was no way of passing on the tax from producer to consumer. As Culliton put it, "As a matter of fact, the true situation is that the tax does not influence the price but, rather, the price determines the tax."[97] By this he meant that the tax would not change the price producers would charge for the oil. There was no point to doing so; to raise prices to pass on the tax to refiners and ultimately consumers would do nothing more than increase the amount of tax the company paid. Oil markets also did not allow for individual producers to pass on extra expenses or taxation—the price was the price. Since purchasers of the oil were paying the market price, Culliton could not see how this possibly meant they were paying for the tax. Clearly, the producer paid, and only paid when the oil was sold. "There is no doubt in my mind," Culliton stated, "that both the mineral income tax and the royalty surcharge were imposed for one purpose, and one purpose only—to drain off substantial benefits that would have accrued to the producers due to the sudden and unprecedented price of crude oil."

Culliton also could not see how the taxes interfered with the federal trade and commerce power. The price of the oil was unaffected; there was no extra cost to imported oil in the province nor any extra cost to the oil exported, as the taxes and royalties did not change the price of oil. The legislation made no direction about the sale of the oil except that it should be sold at fair market price and the ministry would calculate the tax based on that price if it deemed the oil had been sold for less. Culliton saw no interference with exports with this or any provision.

The other major point on the appeal was whether the province had the power to expropriate the leases. Culliton thought the answer to this was also simple: the powers of the provinces over property and civil rights were more than adequate. No federal power could be extended to interfere without being an unsupportable intrusion into provincial jurisdiction.

The Supreme Court of Canada agreed with Culliton on that point, but only that point. The court, with justices Brian Dickson and Louis-Philippe de Grandpré dissenting, ruled that the taxes were indirect and interfered with the federal trade power. Surprisingly, it was not Bora Laskin, the supposed arch-federalist, but Ronald Martland who wrote the majority decision.[98] Martland was the senior judge, an Albertan who had experience with oil and gas law in practice and was known for his narrow approach to law. The fact that the minister in Saskatchewan could determine and set the price of oil heavily influenced the majority decision:

Martland seemed to take this to mean that the ministry would do this rather than use the power as a last resort to prevent tax avoidance.[99] Setting the price on a product that was almost entirely exported in his view intruded on the federal power and also made the imposed taxes export taxes, borne by the purchasers of the oil.

Although Culliton's argument was stronger, there was logic to Martland's position. The question of who paid the tax was a brain twister, and neither Martland nor Culliton had fleshed out his argument particularly well, each clearly thinking his respective position was obviously correct. In his dissent, Dickson elegantly summed up the problem: the tax did not obviously fall either on consumer or producer. But Dickson noted that the legislation had exempted small acreage holders, which clearly indicated the producer was the intended payer of the tax.[100] Although not income taxes, the taxes were clearly direct, Dickson thought, as their structure left no room for them to be "passed on." Any effect on trade and commerce was incidental; the legislation showed no intention to regulate trade, and Dickson recognized that the ministerial powers to set prices were extraordinary remedies only implemented in cases of tax evasion. Dickson did a fine job of filling in the more precise arguments Culliton had not bothered with, showing the talent that eventually made him chief justice of Canada. Written in dissent, his decision was cold comfort for Saskatchewan.

The rules of court in Saskatchewan required that the federal government be notified of constitutional challenges and allowed to intervene, but there was still considerable anger at the aggressive intercession in CIGOL. The minister responsible, Otto Lang, was not sympathetic. His department had warned Saskatchewan that the law violated the BNA *Act* and would almost certainly be challenged.[101] Lang had considered using the federal government power of disallowance even before CIGOL but thought better of it. He instructed the government to intervene in CIGOL but defended this as the usual practice in constitutional challenges. But the federal government may have had a larger agenda.

CENTRAL CANADA POTASH CORP. V SASKATCHEWAN

NO SOONER HAD the Supreme Court undermined Saskatchewan's control over its oil than the court considered regulation of another of the province's natural resources, potash. In *Central Canada Potash Corp. v Saskatchewan*, the pro-rationing scheme that Premier Ross Thatcher created to keep the potash industry viable came under attack as an infringement on the federal trade and commerce power.

The development of the province's massive potash reserves had been a preoccupation of the provincial government since the first discoveries in the 1940s. The industry took off in the 1960s and grew in leaps and bounds, and in fact was too vigorous. Production increased a hundredfold to several million tons annually.[102] As the end of the decade approached, supply had far outstripped demand, and Saskatchewan's potash industry was in serious trouble. The US market was by far the industry's largest and most important, accounting for 67 percent of Saskatchewan sales. Producers in the small American potash industry in New Mexico complained that Canadians were dumping potash into the market, leading to a trade investigation, dumping duties, and the threat of import quotas and tariffs.

The Thatcher government leapt into action, directly negotiating a pact with New Mexico to ration production and set a minimum price for potash, controlling supply to drive up prices and make producers profitable again. The pact neatly bypassed Ottawa and Washington, with the feds turning a blind eye. The provincial government instituted *The Potash Conservation Regulations, 1969*, passed under the wide powers granted the minister under *The Mineral Resources Act, 1965* to "promote and encourage the discovery, development, management, utilization and conservation of the mineral resources of Saskatchewan."[103] The regulations established a minimum price for potash and set up a pro-rationing system based on the productive capacity of each mine, the estimated demand for the coming year, and the amount of potash necessary for reserves and working stock. Each mine was given an initial quota of 40 percent of capacity and could then apply for supplementary licences if there was excess demand.

In 1972, the department decided to simplify the system, and subsequent quotas were calculated on capacity and demand. This presented a problem for Central Canada Potash. The company was a joint venture of Noranda Mines and Illinois-based Central Farmers Fertilizer, a large farmer's co-operative. Central Canada Potash was set up to supply Central Farmers and was contracted to supply all of its needs, starting at 575,000 tons. By 1972, Central Canada Potash needed to produce over 744,000 tons for Central Farmers. Under the original pro-rationing scheme, the company had no difficulty obtaining the supplementary permits necessary to fulfill its obligations. Under the new system, it did not have enough allowed production to supply Central Farmers, and the ministry refused any supplementary permits, although nothing prevented Central Farmers or Central Canada Potash from buying potash on the open market.

Central Canada Potash turned to the courts, first making an application for an order of *mandamus* to force the ministry to provide a licence for sufficient production. This failed, so the company challenged the *Potash Conservation Regulations, 1969* as *ultra vires* for intruding on the federal trade and commerce power. The company was successful at trial. Justice Disbery of the Court of Queen's Bench concluded that the regulations were designed to restrict exports of potash abroad and within Canada and make such exports subject to the prices set by the minister. Along with declaring the regulations *ultra vires*, Disbery also gave the company $1.5 million in damages for the tort of intimidation, which the company had sued for based on the ministry's threat to rescind its production licence if it exceeded its quota.

Central Canada Potash, it should be added, was not the only litigant in the Queen's Bench action. The other party was not another potash producer; it was the federal government. While Saskatchewan's rules required that in a constitutional challenge the attorney general of the province and of Canada be notified so as to allow them to participate, the federal attorney general instead took the unusual step of joining the suit as a co-plaintiff. The move fed the view in the West that Ottawa was really making a grab for control over provincial resources.

On appeal, Chief Justice Culliton, writing for the full court, held that regulations were within the competence of the provincial legislature. Culliton argued that the pro-rationing scheme was in essence a scheme for the "development, management, utilization and conservation" of potash, as allowed in *The Mineral Resources Act*. The effect the regulations had on the export trade was incidental rather than the central purpose. This, Culliton contended, was clear from the face of the regulations but also was true of the "pith and substance," or true aim, of the regulations. "In my view," wrote Culliton, "the true intent and purpose of the pro-rationing and price stabilization programs were to protect the potash industry of Saskatchewan and to overcome the immediate economic problems which it faced for the purpose of preserving and conserving it as a viable industry in the province."[104]

Culliton noted that the industry, with the exception of Central Canada Potash, was supportive of the regulations. Central Canada Potash had not protested the rationing scheme until it was changed and the company could no longer fill its exclusive contract with Central Farmers Fertilizer. Another key fact in Culliton's estimation was that the pro-rationing and price setting schemes at no time created a shortage of potash on the market. Anticipated market demand was a factor in setting the rationing. Thus, market set the quotas, the quotas did not determine the market, and the statutory minimum price set had been lower than the market price.

Culliton thought that the trial judge had construed the powers of the minister to manage, utilize, and conserve too narrowly, as meaning only the immediate and physical. Looking at the totality of *The Mineral Resources Act* and regulations, Culliton argued that the intent was to prevent the collapse of the industry and put it on a sound footing, and this economic goal could be encompassed within the meaning of "manage" or "conserve." And in fact, by the time Disbery's judgment was appealed, the Saskatchewan government had amended the *Act* to broaden the definition of section 2, which laid out the ministerial powers to allow for such an interpretation.

The trial judge had also decided the potash conservation plan was a marketing scheme, similar to a number of statutes in other provinces that had imposed import and export quotas and set prices on agricultural products such as eggs, pork, and milk. In three of four decisions, the Supreme Court had ruled these statutes *ultra vires* as interference with trade and commerce. Culliton distinguished potash pro-rationing from the *ultra vires* schemes on the basis that in those instances the statutes controlled the commodities both imported and exported. The Saskatchewan regulations only affected potash while in the province, at time of production and purchase. Culliton took exception to the dicta of the Supreme Court in *Re Farm Products Marketing Act*—which had concerned eggs—that once a commodity entered the "flow of interprovincial or external trade" it was no longer a matter of local concern. To follow this literally, he contended, would make it impossible for a province to legislate regarding a product or commodity except in the most restricted sense. The same decision made clear, he felt, that the true nature or intent of the legislation was what counted. In addition, in the *Carnation Milk* decision, the Supreme Court had endorsed a Quebec law that set prices on milk produced in the province although much of the milk was exported, because the court did not feel that legislation was primarily intended to control trade. Culliton saw an exact analogy with the Saskatchewan law. In the case of the potash regulations, although their application might very well have substantial effects on exports, this was not primary purpose or goal of the regulations.

Culliton's decision ended with a plea for the direct consideration of the real-world effects of constitutional rulings.

> I also recognize that the constitution must be made to work and that the responsibility of assuring it does work rests in substantial measure upon the courts. In the discharge of their duty, courts must approach constitutional problems with a sense of realism and practicality; they must strive to attain that end which the legislation intended, viewed in the overall intent and purpose of the B.N.A. Act.[105]

Culliton argued that the "pith and substance" or "true nature and character" tests were doctrines adopted precisely because they were pragmatic and realistic, and this should govern how the tests were applied. This had become particularly important when dealing with disputes such as the appeal at hand, as any policy dealing with natural resources or other economic matters was likely to have broader effects. In decisions such as CIGOL and the appeal under consideration, Culliton saw a danger of a serious erosion of provincial legislative authority. "It follows, therefore," he wrote, "that over-emphasis on the effect of provincial legislation, in the determination of its validity, may lead to a denuding of provincial powers, a result which defeats the purposes intended by the B.N.A. Act."[106]

Dickson had written a similar warning in CIGOL. Culliton took the line of thought further. He posited that division of powers analysis was a zero-sum game. He contended that all areas of legislative activity were encompassed in the BNA *Act*: either provinces or the federal government had to be able to legislate on a matter. This being the case, if the province could not legislate a price for potash and limits on production, who could? Ottawa? This was clearly not the case, in his opinion, and therefore it was more likely that the regulations were within provincial competence. It was a nice rhetorical flourish.

Bora Laskin did not buy this argument. In his view, defining the limits of provincial jurisdiction implied nothing about the reach of federal legislation.[107] Laskin, writing for the whole court, declared the potash regulation *ultra vires*. He heartily agreed with Culliton as to how constitutional rulings should be made. Culliton was largely advocating for a purposive style analysis, which was congruent with the tradition in "broad and liberal" interpretation that was generally used in constitutional deliberations. This was music to Laskin's ears.

Laskin was not prepared, however, to view the effect of the potash regulations on trade and commerce as incidental. Laskin, like the trial judge, made much of the fact that the draft potash regulations had contemplated requiring a selling licence, although this had been dropped. To Laskin, this showed some intent to control exports. As with Martland in CIGOL and the court's agricultural product decisions, Laskin interpreted the price-fixing mechanism as being intrinsically a violation of trade and commerce because it might determine the price of the exported product, and he viewed rationing as having the same effect. The argument made sense with the potash regulations. In a literal way, pro-rationing determined how much potash was produced for export, and the scheme had been originally instituted to restrict supply to drive up prices and had put in place a minimum price. Although conditions were such that the regulations were not restricting overall supply, this was a possible outcome if prices dropped again with oversupply. It is perhaps telling that Brian Dickson, who had agreed with Culliton's logic in CIGOL, did not dissent in *Central Canada Potash*.

The Supreme Court decisions in CIGOL and *Central Canada Potash* have subsequently drawn considerable criticism: one academic writer bluntly called CIGOL "bad law."[108] The court was accused of ignoring its own previous case law and insufficiently explaining or justifying the majority's assertions regarding the effect and nature of Saskatchewan's legislation. *Central Canada Potash* was more complex: the provincial measures arguably were much more likely to directly affect potash exports, both in supply and price. Thus, even if the regulations were not primarily intended to control exports, their effect was hard to characterize as merely incidental, because the regulations did directly control supply.

Culliton had chosen the interpretation that left the provincial statutes intact and efficacious. His arguments were certainly defensible, but the decisions in *Central Canada Potash* and CIGOL also fit neatly into a larger pattern. Alberta's court of appeal also tended to strongly uphold the provincial position in the majority of division of powers cases from that province in the 1970s, and this was likely true in other jurisdictions.[109]

At the Supreme Court, the record was more mixed: there were usually dissents and the court frequently overturned laws with just a bare majority, and in some appeals declined to throw out provincial statutes. Laskin consistently supported the federalist interpretation. The cases that went to the final court of appeal were of course the difficult ones, but it is telling that, even with judges at both levels of court doing their best to weigh the arguments carefully and objectively, this pattern existed.

Edward Milton Culliton, 2013. (Artist: Jill Armstrong; photo: Mark Greschner. Court of Appeal.)

CIGOL left the government of Saskatchewan with a $500-million tab, the amount of tax the province had gathered and now had to pay back. The Blakeney government had already overhauled the royalty structure in 1976 to replace the surcharge and mineral income tax, and made other amendments to make clear that the minister's power to set prices was only in instances of tax avoidance. In 1978, new retroactive legislative allowed the province to keep the taxes it had collected before the new royalty regime. In the case of the potash industry, Blakeney responded to the Supreme Court decision as well as another legal fight with the producers over taxation with the Potash Corporation of Saskatchewan.[110]

CIGOL and *Central Canada Potash* also contributed to the enactment of section 92A of the *Constitution Act, 1982*. Premier Blakeney was outraged at the Supreme Court rulings and was so outspoken in his criticism that there was talk of charging the premier with contempt of court.[111] Blakeney had a close ally in Peter Lougheed, the premier of Alberta, who had also been openly feuding with Ottawa, and the other Western premiers. The protracted and at times bitter negotiations to bring Alberta's and Saskatchewan's natural resources under provincial control had not been forgotten, and the Supreme Court rulings seemed to take away that hard-fought-for authority. In the view of the Western provinces, these and other cases steadily extended federal powers at the expense of the provinces. The National Energy Program (NEP) in 1981 was the final straw. The legislation amounted to a massive federal intrusion into provincial control of oil and gas resources. The NEP affected Alberta and Saskatchewan most directly, but other provinces could see that in principle oil and gas were not necessarily different than gold, coal, iron ore, or lumber.

The repatriation of the constitution, Pierre Trudeau's great ambition, created some leverage for the provinces; Trudeau needed the support of the Western provinces for his constitutional project. Blakeney's price was an amendment that allowed the provinces to tax natural resources in whatever manner they chose—including indirect taxes—and wider latitude to legislate even when it affected trade in the resources. He recruited Ed Broadbent and the federal NDP to press for an amendment, and after much negotiation, some of it at the eleventh hour, section 92A was incorporated into the new constitution. Although somewhat watered down from Blakeney's original proposal, the amendment extended the provinces' ability to tax their natural resources, expanded the latitude of legislation aimed at conservation and management, and even allowed provincial legislation that affected interprovincial trade, although not international trade. Critics expressed doubt as to how well the amendment would really protect provincial legislation from judicial review.[112] Yet, after its enactment, there was a long period of peace between the federal and provincial governments over natural resources.

CONCLUSION

THE COURTS HAD made constitutional decisions before the 1970s that had been contentious and controversial and prompted further legislative action. *CIGOL* and *Central Canada Potash*, however, had arguably raised the stakes, resulting in major constitutional change. The controversy also put a new spotlight on the courts, their powers of review, and the potential impact of their decisions. It was no coincidence that this came at the same time that judges, and by extension courts, were rediscovering their role, even duty, as lawmakers. It also set the stage for a truly transformative moment for Canada, one that would thrust the judiciary into an even more prominent role in the nation's political life: the advent of the *Charter of Rights and Freedoms.*

Chief Justice Edward Culliton would not see this next revolution except from the sidelines. He turned seventy-five in 1981 and had to step down. It was truly the end of an era. For a generation of lawyers, Culliton had embodied the Court of Appeal for Saskatchewan, a unique judicial personality not only in the history of the province but in the history of Canada.

CHAPTER 8

THE *CHARTER* COURT

CHIEF JUSTICE CULLITON HAD QUITE THE SEND-OFF. A committee of judges and lawyers had been planning his retirement gala for months. Every chief justice and chief judge in the country was invited and nearly all came, as did almost the entire Saskatchewan judiciary. Bora Laskin was there as an honoured guest, along with three Supreme Court colleagues. Premier Blakeney and Roy Romanow attended, as well as the lieutenant-governor and members of Parliament and the Senate. Justice Minister Jean Chrétien sent his regrets after cancelling at the last minute. The Pope sent a special blessing via the Archbishop of Regina. Over five hundred people joined the glittering assemblage of the legal and political elite of province and nation. Along with the banquet that night of March 20, 1981, at the Hotel Saskatchewan, a $75,000 scholarship was established in Culliton's name. The chief justice humbly called it "the best night of my life." Culliton was not done with public service: he would lead several government commissions, including the province's electoral boundaries commission in 1988.

Culliton retired just as a revolution began. When the *Charter of Rights and Freedoms* became part of the law of Canada on April 17, 1982, judges and courts were handed new powers and new responsibilities and a much-expanded role in the political life of the nation. With the *Charter,* they were charged with the duty of safeguarding the new constitution and the rights and freedoms enshrined there. In Saskatchewan, a new chief justice and a nearly entirely new Court of Appeal faced this monumental task and tackled it with boldness and vision.

COMEBACKS AND SURPRISES

THE 1980S DAWNED with a political comeback. Pierre Trudeau had gone down in defeat in 1979 to Joe Clark, the young leader of the Progressive Conservative Party. It was also the last election for John Diefenbaker, who died several months later, still an MP (and a thorn in Clark's side). The inexperienced Clark lived up to Dief's worst expectations and was unable to finesse the delicate balancing act of running a minority government. Trudeau had resigned and his political career appeared over, but the Liberal Party was slow to select another leader. When Clark lost a confidence vote nine months into office, Trudeau moved swiftly to seize the reins of his party again and, after the ensuing federal election, was once more prime minister of Canada.

Trudeau returned with a renewed sense of purpose. While he still found time to anger Western Canadians with the NEP and other controversial policies, his obsession was the repatriation of the *British North America Act* to give Canada control over its constitution and end one of the last vestiges of colonialism. Reaching further still, Trudeau was determined to include the *Charter of Rights and Freedoms* in a repatriated constitution. Entrenched in the constitution as the supreme law of the land, the proposed *Charter* would have the teeth the *Bill of Rights* had lacked. Two years of conferences and controversy followed, including a politically charged Supreme Court decision on repatriation. Allan Blakeney and his attorney general, Roy Romanow, were particularly prominent players in the byzantine negotiations, securing important concessions for the provinces.[1] In the end, Trudeau was more or less successful. He failed to get Quebec's support—a ticking time bomb—but the constitution came home and the *Charter* was a reality.

Back in Saskatchewan, Blakeney and Romanow's preoccupation with the constitution contributed to the NDP's electoral undoing in 1982. Blakeney's government was distracted from retail politics in the province and missed some important signs. Obsessed with maintaining fiscal discipline as a recession loomed, Blakeney and his cabinet did not appreciate the impact of high interest rates on voters or their intense dislike of the provincial gas tax the NDP had instituted. When Blakeney went to the polls in April 1982, he made the same mistake Ross Thatcher did in 1971, running on the NDP's record as sound administrators but offering little that was new or addressed voter concerns.[2] After over a decade in power, the NDP was past its best-before date.

Blakeney had also benefited from facing a fading Liberal Party as opposition. After Thatcher, the party was unable to find a leader or a platform that resonated with voters. Stuart Cameron of the Court of Appeal, a Liberal MLA in the 1970s, recalled that the party had nothing to offer but criticism of the NDP.[3] An alternative emerged, but it took time to develop. Dick Collver, a Saskatoon financial adviser, took over the moribund Progressive Conservatives (PCs) in 1973. His tireless rebuilding saw the party get 28 percent of the vote and elect seven MLAs in 1975, and the PCs became the official opposition in 1978. Scandal involving his business dealings then claimed Collver. His replacement was Grant Devine, a farmer and agricultural economics professor at the University of Saskatchewan, a relative political neophyte who had never held office. It had looked like Blakeney might have another election in the bag.

No one told Devine and the Conservatives. They trounced the NDP, winning the largest majority in Saskatchewan history.[4] The folksy, enthusiastic Devine connected with voters, and anti-NDP sentiment coalesced around his party. The PC Party raised the banner of free enterprise and also exploited a growing rural–urban divide among voters. Devine effectively attacked the NDP over rural decline and lack of economic growth, undermining the government's fiscal record. He made bold, easy-to-understand campaign promises—repealing the gas tax, mortgage interest relief—that he then kept, despite the cost to the provincial treasury. During their first term, Devine's Progressive Conservatives spouted a lot of rhetoric about free enterprise replacing socialism, but they did not roll back social programs or sell off Crown corporations. The Devine government ran up increasingly large deficits to afford tax cuts while maintaining programs and instituting initiatives to help farmers, anticipating that a resurgent private sector would balance the province's books.

The 1986 election was a close-fought affair, with the NDP and PCs trying to outdo each other with expensive promises.[5] Devine prevailed but was confronted with a major recession and a crash in oil, grain, and potash prices that drove up unemployment and cut deeply into government revenues. His administration drastically cut program spending and ratcheted up taxes, reinstating the hated gas tax. Even so, deficits ballooned. The PCs aggressively pursued privatization, selling off Crown corporations such as the Saskatchewan Oil and Gas Corporation and the Potash Corporation of Saskatchewan. Unfortunately, Devine made the same mistake made by many provincial governments of the era and tried to encourage diversification and industrialization with tax breaks, loan guarantees, grants, and subsidies. These proved expensive and not very effective. One example was the heavy-oil upgrader at the Co-op Refinery Complex in Regina, which did not really give a good return on the investment.

Privatization was Devine's Waterloo. A plan to sell SaskEnergy swung public opinion against the premier, and the NDP took full advantage with a legislative boycott.[6] Devine was forced to cancel a planned sale of shares in the Crown corporation. Other factors affected Tory popularity. Devine had a near obsession with the rural economy, at a time when agriculture had declined to only 12 percent of the provincial economy. The rural population continued to drop. Saskatchewan briefly broke the million-person mark in 1986, but 40 percent lived in Regina and Saskatoon and 63 percent were considered urban dwellers. City residents, in line with trends since the war, were more educated, wealthier, and increasingly diverse, as immigrants headed for the cities, not farms and small towns. Regina and Saskatoon were union strongholds. The political divide between town and country sowed the seeds for Devine's defeat in 1991.[7] This was despite a change in electoral boundaries that arguably favoured the rural precincts of the province, which became a celebrated case in *Charter* jurisprudence.

The electoral boundary dispute—the question of whether there can be large disparities in population between ridings without unduly undermining the right to vote—was an example of the reach of the *Charter of Rights and Freedoms* and how it brought the courts squarely into basic questions of public policy. Section 3 of the *Charter* guaranteed every individual the right to vote in elections. But it was silent on specifics beyond this. The courts were expected to further define the rights and freedoms and how they would be applied. It was a brave new world for the Canadian judiciary, one which put great demands on their sagacity, a revolution which is still ongoing. In Saskatchewan, the Court of Appeal forged a reputation for progressive and bold *Charter* jurisprudence.

A NEW CHIEF JUSTICE

Chief Justice Edward Dmytro Bayda, n.d. (Court of Appeal/Photographic Services Agency)

CULLITON WAS GOING to be a tough act to follow. Justice Edward Bayda was the obvious candidate, with relative youth, vigour, and a reputation for striking jurisprudence. But according to the lore of the Saskatchewan bar, Culliton did not want Bayda to succeed him. Culliton had wanted Ray MacDonald to replace Percy Maguire in 1974 and had then been annoyed when Bayda had immediately accepted a commission of inquiry, taking him away from court for a number of months when he was needed. Culliton called anyone with influence and bent their ear, making clear his opposition. Perversely, Culliton suggested MacDonald as chief justice. MacDonald was a good trial judge and had sat ad hoc several times on the court, but at sixty-six he was too old. Culliton did succeed in getting MacDonald appointed to the court, but he filled the vacancy created with Bayda's elevation to chief justice. Bayda's promotion had been a foregone conclusion. Among other factors, Otto Lang was plumping for Bayda and still had a great deal of influence.

Two more appointments quickly followed. Merv Woods and Russell Brownridge took supernumerary status in July 1981, and Stuart Cameron and Calvin Tallis were appointed to replace them on October 13. Cameron was a Regina litigator with Balfour Moss. He had been prominent in the federal Liberal Party and had also sat for a term as a provincial MLA. Tallis had been a leading criminal and civil litigator in Saskatoon. He had taken an appointment to the Supreme Court of the Northwest Territories in 1976, relocating to Yellowknife, and now returned to his home province.

The priority for the new chief justice was securing more appointments to fill the two positions on the books. The court's workload was growing rapidly. The two supernumeraries gave Bayda some extra manpower, especially as Brownridge and Woods continued to work nearly full-time,[8] but it was not sufficient. Bayda desperately needed more full-time judges. And a new obstacle had emerged. The NDP had put the planned expansion of the court on hold when Culliton retired, prioritizing Queen's Bench appointments and taking a wait-and-see approach with his replacement.[9] The new Devine government and its first attorney general, Gary Lane, were in no mood to expand the court. A major fight was brewing over appointments.

The 1981 appointments to the Court of Appeal and two others to the Queen's Bench brought out long-festering dissatisfaction over the selection of judges. The Devine government was angry about the lack of any formal consultation with the province. The federal power of appointment under section 96 of the BNA *Act* was absolute, and there was no obligation to consult, but provincial governments disliked having no input over who sat on their superior courts. Over the previous decade, the federal justice ministers had informally consulted with their provincial counterparts, often via judicial advisers, but it was irregular, varying from province to province.[10]

Lane aimed to change that by using the strategy the CCF had employed in 1948, threatening to eliminate positions. He cancelled the existing order-in-council that authorized two more positions on the Court of Appeal.[11] Even more controversially, the government issued a new order-in-council that eliminated two vacant positions on the Court of Queen's Bench.[12] Then Ray MacDonald decided to go supernumerary in November 1983. He was replaced, literally overnight, by Bill Vancise, a Queen's Bench judge, formerly a litigator and labour lawyer at the Balfour Moss firm, and a prominent Liberal Party organizer. Lane was not consulted or even informed until after the fact. Another order-in-council followed, this time eliminating the next position that fell vacant on the Court of Appeal.[13] Lane's message to Ottawa and local Liberal Party circles was clear: there would be no more superior court appointments in the province for the foreseeable future.[14]

From Lane's perspective, the high-minded pronouncements of Otto Lang and other justice ministers about judicial appointments were so much hypocrisy, at least when it came to Saskatchewan. He claimed

RAYMOND ALEXANDER MACDONALD

Ray MacDonald was Ted Culliton's particular choice for the Court of Appeal, but he was appointed only after the chief justice retired, taking the berth opened with Edward Bayda's promotion. MacDonald was born in Saskatoon in 1915.[1] He attended the University of Saskatchewan, taking the combined arts and law degree and graduating from law in 1938. MacDonald had his articles with John A. Fraser of Regina and joined the bar at the end of 1939. He answered the call of his country and joined the army and was posted overseas to the Army Service Corps. He attained the rank of major and was made a Member of the British Empire for meritorious service.

Returning to Regina in 1946, MacDonald entered partnership with Fraser and also married Fraser's daughter Helen.[2] MacDonald and Fraser practised together until Fraser retired in 1960, at which point MacDonald became part of the firm of Nicol, Keith, Armstrong, MacDonald and Cruickshank. He was made a QC in 1964. MacDonald was involved in civil and community affairs, including politics. He took a tilt at elected office, unsuccessfully running in the 1958 federal election as a Liberal.[3] MacDonald's appointment to the Court of Queen's Bench followed in 1965. A respected trial judge, he was elevated to the appeal bench at sixty-six. The appointment was surprising only due to his age and reflected not only Culliton's support but also MacDonald's reputation as a jurist.

Justice Raymond Alexander MacDonald, c. 1983. (Provincial Archives of Saskatchewan, 83-1218-040)

MacDonald retired in 1984 at seventy and was immediately active in civil affairs, most prominently as the chair of the Board of Regents of Campion College at the University of Regina. He also served as the chair of the board for the Santa Maria Seniors Citizens Home. MacDonald died 1991 in Regina at the age seventy-six.

Gary Lane, attorney general, c. 1986. (Provincial Archives of Saskatchewan, 86-3600-603)

that a small clique of Liberal lawyers known as the "silver seven" had a stranglehold on appointments, to the extent that Lane heard complaints from other Liberals about being shut out. Bayda was one of the seven. Lane had a point: there were no appointments across party lines in Saskatchewan, unlike in other provinces. The Canadian Bar Association undertook a major study on judicial appointments in the 1980s, and Saskatchewan was identified as a jurisdiction where political factors had a strong influence. As with the previous CCF threats to shrink the courts, it was not clear exactly what the government wanted to accomplish beyond mounting a protest. In reply to this question in the Legislative Assembly, Lane declared that the province wanted some kind of formal or informal consultation on appointments, while acknowledging this would be a strictly voluntary arrangement.[15]

At a time when the court's burden was growing rapidly, the government's actions were pure brinkmanship. Bayda and the court were outraged at being held to ransom. By 1983, the lists had reached an all-time high. In the scramble to stay on top, the court had allowed a major backlog of reserve judgments to develop, but this had not prevented delays for hearing new appeals.[16] Bayda had written Lane early in 1983 to forcefully draw his attention to the problem, telling him that every judge was working flat out, including the supernumeraries. After the November order-in-council, relations between the court and the attorney general rapidly deteriorated. Bayda went over Lane's head to Premier Devine, which only added fuel to the fire. The exchange of letters got personal. Perhaps intemperately, Bayda referred to Lane's claim that he was proceeding in the interests of the administration of justice as "Orwellian" and bluntly observed that he was speaking to "someone whose experience as a counsel is limited and as a judge non-existent."[17] Lane was not cowed, retorting,

> I do wish to remind you I have more counsel experience than some recent appointees to the courts and I have had more solicitor experience than some appointees to the court. It is also abundantly clear that I have had more political experience . . . and accordingly I feel more than capable of responding to the concerns of the public as to the manner of appointments.[18]

The bad blood continued. The court was loath to break tradition and publicly criticize the government, but eventually, as the judges were blamed for delays, the frustration was too much. In a 1985 judgment, Cameron wrote,

> Had this appeal come on for hearing within a reasonable time—even within a year of the judgment having come down—the amendment would not have been passed and would not have featured in the determination of the appeal. The case did not come on earlier and could not have been heard until now largely as a result of the executive branch of the government of Saskatchewan having in May of 1982 reduced the size of this court, making it impossible to deal with this matter as expeditiously as it deserved.[19]

The tense relationship between Lane and Bayda was not improved when their exchange of correspondence was filed in court proceedings. The Saskatoon Criminal Defence Lawyers Association tried to have the orders-in-council declared *ultra vires*, arguing that *The Court of Appeal Act* set the bench at five and an executive order could not reduce the number. When the application came before Bayda at the Court of Appeal, the government tried to force him to recuse himself on the ground that he had a conflict of interest. The government's counsel filed some of the correspondence. Bayda then added the rest on his own initiative. He also refused to step aside, reasoning that as chief justice, he had two roles, judicial and administrative, and could separate the two.[20]

The application by the Criminal Defence Lawyers Association was eventually argued at the Court of Appeal, but the court never issued a judgment to decide the issue.[21] With no retirements, the order shrinking the court never took effect. And when the Progressive Conservatives came to power in Ottawa in 1984, Lane relented and the order-in-council

Justice William Vancise, Justice Raymond MacDonald, Justice Roy Hall, c. 1984. (Court of Appeal/ Photographic Services Agency, 84-2240-08)

was rescinded. The appeal had become moot and there was no reason to stir the pot further. John Crosbie, the new justice minister, announced that the federal government would consult with the provinces on judicial appointments.[22] He singled out the tiff in Saskatchewan. On November 14, a new provincial order-in-council rescinded the previous order eliminating a position and instead increased the court to seven.[23] In 2000, *The Court of Appeal Act* was amended to make it impossible to decrease the size of the court with an order-in-council. Two new judges, Thomas C. Wakeling and Marjorie Gerwing were appointed on December 13, 1984. Wakeling, a war veteran and Regina lawyer, had been president of the Law Society and practised for six years with MacPherson, Leslie and Tyerman before becoming a partner in McDougall, Ready, Wakeling in 1963. Gerwing was a Regina litigator and a partner at the MacPherson firm, which she had joined in 1968 as an articling student. The Mulroney government was quite progressive in advancing women in the judiciary, and Gerwing's appointment was a historic first for Saskatchewan.

Ray MacDonald's tenure on the court was short. He stepped down on November 13, 1984. A year later, Roy Hall decided to become supernumerary. His replacement was another first for the court. Nicholas Sherstobitoff, of Saskatoon, was of Doukhobor heritage and came from a firm with a large union clientele and strong links to the NDP. The Blakeney government had appointed him chair of the Labour Relations Board, and the Devine government had immediately fired him after taking office. By appointing Sherstobitoff, the Mulroney government—and Gary Lane—may have been making a point. None of the Mulroney appointments was very political. None had stood for office or played a prominent role in party politics.[24]

The judges appointed to the court in the 1980s shared many characteristics. All were born and raised in Saskatchewan and received their degrees from the province's law school. MacDonald and Wakeling were veterans while four belonged to the Depression generation. Gerwing, born in 1943, was almost the court's first baby boomer. The average age at appointment was just below fifty and ranged from forty-two to sixty-six. All were primarily barristers but had a range of practice experience. Tallis was the only outstanding criminal lawyer. There was an interesting split between the earlier "Liberal" and the later "Conservative" groups. The former had experience as trial judges while the latter came straight from practice. This likely reflected that further promotions from the trial courts would almost certainly be Liberals. In a break with the past, the appointees were all from Regina and Saskatoon. Lawyers from other centres became uncommon on the court, as legal talent was increasingly concentrated in the province's two main cities, whether in private practice, as academics, or as government lawyers.

THE HOT COURT AND OTHER REFORMS

BAYDA HAD HIGH ambitions to build a court of appeal second to none. The court was also facing rapidly expanding case lists and needed to address its workload. To reach both goals, the court carried out what can only be called a modernization of its practices. The judges embraced prehearing preparation and conferencing, judgment circulation, regular court meetings to consider jurisprudence and administration, and random panel assignments, all aimed at more efficiently processing appeals and improving the quality of jurisprudence. Many of the initiatives reflected developments in American appellate courts. The changes in court procedures were a companion to the broader approaches to jurisprudence that had gained momentum in the 1970s and reflected the outlook of a new generation of judges.

Becoming a "hot court" was fundamental and transformative. An American idea, hot courts practised extensive preparation before hearings. There had always been some degree of preparation on those Canadian courts that had used factums and appeal books, and some judges, like Gordon or Culliton, went further in their preparation, but it was not court policy. Hot courts went beyond reviewing factums with additional reading and research in the case law and legal literature as necessary. In Saskatchewan, panels conferenced before hearings, identifying the important issues and often forming preliminary opinions. The chief justice also "circled" a judge to lead each appeal. Every judge on a panel prepared, but the circled judge gave the appeal special attention and was expected to lead discussion in the hearing and in conference and write the judgment. The circled judge might prepare, before hearings, an outline or draft of a judgment in simple cases.

A hot court meant expedited appeals and focused hearings. The panel could immediately discuss the crucial points, seeking expansion and clarification. More oral decisions and fewer reserve decisions was the order of the day, as the court was frequently ready to give a judgment immediately after a hearing. The results were not dramatic but still significant: reserves overall dropped from 28 to 18 percent of appeals. For criminal appeals, the drop was from 25 to 8 percent. The other goal was to produce superior jurisprudence, as judges went into every appeal with a greater grasp of the issues and more productively interacted with counsel.

Saskatchewan was on the forefront of adopting the hot court in Canada. There were still judges and courts in Canada that did little advance preparation, believing, in the English tradition, that this ensured an open mind. Stuart Cameron recalls telling Darrel Heald, formerly the attorney general and then a judge on the Federal Court of Appeal, about the hot

The Court of Appeal, c. 1981. Calvin Tallis, Roy Hall, Mervyn Woods, Chief Justice Bayda, Russell Brownridge, Raymond MacDonald, and Stuart Cameron. (Court of Appeal/Photographic Service Agency)

court and Heald scoffing at the idea.[25] Surprisingly, despite years of arguing in front of the highly prepared Culliton, not all counsel liked the focused and dynamic hearings of the hot court. Panels rarely waited through a presentation to question counsel, and the lead judge often directed argument immediately, which threw some counsel off. Most adapted quickly, but there were lawyers who complained panels were too aggressive.

Circulation of reserve judgments was another important new policy, necessary on a larger court sitting three-judge panels. Decisions were usually reserved because the legal issues were complex and important, often precedents. It was critical that other judges knew what panels decided, to eliminate the possibility that different panels might decide differently a point of law. Divergent rulings had occurred in Nova Scotia and Ontario, and most Canadian appellate courts eventually adopted circulation to prevent the problem.[26] Ontario, the largest appellate court in the country, was an exception until relatively recently.[27] Circulation also provided input from judges not on the panel. Constructive critiques improved judgments and found errors, and the other judges could voice their opinion on legal questions. This took on new importance as the lawmaking role of intermediate appellate courts was enhanced in the late 1970s. Many courts used circulation to improve decisions with significant precedential weight and could claim that a circulated judgment represented the opinion of the court, not just one panel.

Commenting on drafts was a delicate exercise. Ultimately, the panel was independent and could disregard input from the rest of the court. Circulated reserves were discussed at the court meetings Bayda instituted to discuss issues facing the court. The meetings were useful in addressing the backlog of reserves, as their status was regularly reviewed, but the discussion of jurisprudence ultimately proved contentious and they were discontinued as counterproductive.[28] Saskatchewan was not the only court to try discussing reserves in this fashion and end with the same result.[29] Judges continued to comment on circulated judgments via memo or annotations.

The court also instituted randomized assignments. It has long been the duty of a chief justice to assign duties for the court. Before the adoption of small panels, this was largely irrelevant, as the judges sat as a full court. Culliton made assignments as he pleased and nearly always assigned himself to criminal panels or anything important. Perhaps in reaction, Bayda and the court instituted an arm's-length system. Every judge had the same number of sittings, with the panels constituted and the appeals assigned randomly. Random assignments spread the work evenly and exposed each judge to all areas of law, and each judge worked with all their colleagues. Counsel could not "judge-shop" for a preferred panel in hope of a better outcome. The main drawback to random panels was that a judge with strong expertise in an area of law might not sit on a particular appeal, but this also avoided having judges monopolize some types of appeals. Different courts had different approaches. Ontario tailored assignments in the 1980s, while in Alberta panels were mostly random but also tweaked for expertise.

To manage work flow better and address urgent matters, the court also set up five appeal "streams" with regular and expedited criminal and civil appeals and sentence appeals. This replaced the "special" sittings for urgent appeals, which were impractical with the volume of appeals. Chambers practice was regularized. Previously, there had been scheduled chambers, but Cameron recalls that many lawyers often just found a judge who wasn't busy and asked them to hear an application on the spot: "You might go into the library with Brownridge and sit at a table and he would hear you."[30] It was all a little casual and chaotic. Lawyers were now required to attend chambers set for two days every month. Judges also rigorously enforced leave requirements, especially for appeals of interlocutory orders—decisions on motions and application brought during trials. Interlocutory appeals slowed litigation and the issues were usually best considered in a full appeal, and the court wished to discourage them.

To notify the profession about changes to procedure, the court resorted to another innovation: practice directives. Traditionally, the rules of court were amended for new procedures. Bayda instituted directives as a much faster and more flexible way of instituting changes. Practice directives often involved quite substantive changes: the first one, in 1981, instituted factums for criminal conviction and sentence appeals.[31] Another directive established the new chamber days.[32] Directives allowed for experimentation without constant amendments to the rules.

With two additional judges and the changes to practice, the court tackled the backlog. A drop in appeals and the emphasis on making oral decisions helped a great deal. Appeals and applications rose from 569 in 1981 to a peak of 730 in 1983, and then dropped to 521 by 1986, still a very heavy workload.[33] The number of reserves declined from 183 in 1980 to 136 in 1985. That year, the court claimed that 93 and 71 percent of criminal and civil appeals respectively were disposed of within one week. But the reserve judgments remained a lingering problem. Between 1980 and 1985, the average time for reserves tripled for criminal cases and doubled for civil cases, from 55 to 165 days and from 125 to 240 days respectively.[34] This in part reflected that the press of business gave judges little time to tackle written decisions and the complex *Charter* cases that were now appearing.

It proved very hard to improve the statistics for reserves. Eight months for a major civil reserve was not terrible; six months was the goal for most appellate courts.[35] But eight months was the average. Some decisions took much longer. In 1985, there were six criminal and twelve civil reserves that

From left: Chief Justice Bayda, Justice Mervyn Woods, and Justice William Vancise, c. 1984. (Court of Appeal/ Photographic Services Agency, 84-0809-11)

had been outstanding for more than a year, and in 1987 there were two reserved criminal judgments still not done after four years. The court acquired a reputation for tardiness.[36] Justice officials thought that the judges were not tackling the reserves expeditiously due to organizational and management issues.[37] The court's reply was that the government had precipitated the backlog and more resources would help solve the problem.

THE POOR RELATIONS

THE JUSTICE MINISTRY'S criticism of the court's performance was not surprising. Government and the judiciary clashed in the 1980s and 1990s over court administration and judicial independence, spawning litigation that went to the Supreme Court. Culliton's fight with Romanow was a prelude to a much wider conflict. Provincial governments worried about court backlogs and delays, often as they cut budgets to fight deficits, while courts protested that more funding and more resources were required to deal with a surge of ever-more-complex litigation. The *Charter* also meant the courts were scrutinizing legislation in an unprecedented fashion, which frequently angered politicians.

Justice Mervyn John Woods, c. 1983. (Provincial Archives of Saskatchewan, 83-1218-071)

Gary Lane had caused a great deal of grief over appointments but otherwise was supportive of the courts. Lane moved portfolios after the 1986 election, however, and was replaced by Robert Andrew, a lawyer from Kindersley. As Stuart Cameron recalls, the relationship with the government took a turn for the worse.[38] The new attorney general had an adversarial bent and a crime-control agenda. He was impatient with some of *Charter* rulings coming out of the province's courts in criminal cases, and thought the Court of Appeal was too lenient with sentencing.[39] The Devine government had also started to slash expenses.

Bayda still wanted more full-time judges. The court was due to lose its supernumeraries by the end of the 1980s. Woods left in 1984, Brownridge in 1988, and Hall in 1989. They had been essential in meeting the court's workload, working nearly full-time for several years. In 1987, with Brownridge's retirement looming, Bayda requested two more positions. Aside from keeping abreast of the court's caseload, Bayda wanted the additional judges so that larger panels could sit more frequently for constitutional cases and to make it easier to have two panels sitting simultaneously.[40] His entreaties fell on deaf ears.

Justice William Vancise, Chief Justice Bayda, and Justice Nicholas Sherstobitoff, in the courtroom after its renovation giving it a more traditional appearance, c. late 1980s. (Court of Appeal/ Photographic Services Agency)

The Justice Department also failed to satisfy Bayda's frequent requests for more clerical assistance and more law clerks. The clerks were a sore point and an example of the strained relationship. One of Bayda's initiatives was to have students at law article at the courts, a practice that became common in Canada in the 1970s and 1980s. The students did research and briefed the law for the judges as they prepared for hearings and wrote their judgments, which the students might also proofread and critique. American appellate courts took this further and often had staff lawyers who assisted judges. The articling program in Saskatchewan started small, with just one student.

Bayda was very enthusiastic about the students and thought increasing the complement would greatly benefit the court, including the tantalizing prospect of moving appeals along faster. The Justice Department came to the same conclusion in 1985. The deputy attorney general had decided that two students was not sufficient and told his staff to see about increasing the number.[41] But when Bayda broached the idea a year or so later, the department turned down the request after conducting a study and looking at the court statistics. It was true that when asked, all but one of the judges had opined that clerks would not speed up appeals, but all had agreed that the assistance of clerks did improve the court's decisions.[42] The department's change of heart likely reflected deficit-cutting priorities.

Saskatoon sittings, a perennial sore point for the court, were another source of disagreement with Andrew. The bar in the north had started lobbying for sittings from the establishment of the court in 1918. The institution of a limited Saskatoon schedule in 1961 did not long appease lawyers from Saskatoon and Prince Albert. The bar had lobbied Emmett Hall, who in his 1974 report on the province's justice system recommended expanding the schedule and adding criminal sittings, but nothing was done. As soon as rumours surfaced that the Court of Appeal would expand, the Saskatoon bar jumped into action. At its 1981 annual meeting, the Law Society passed a Saskatoon Bar Association resolution calling on the government to split the court between Regina and Saskatoon[43] This was not unprecedented. British Columbia's court had once been split between Vancouver and Victoria; Alberta maintained half its judges in Edmonton and half in Calgary; and in Quebec, the court was split between Montreal and Quebec City.

Bayda was firmly against splitting his court. In his opinion, it would entail extra logistical and administrative hassle.[44] A decent library was required in Saskatoon, and he felt the collegiality and the cohesiveness of the court would be severely effected. Bayda was also opposed to adding more sittings of the court in Saskatoon; the civil case load was easily handled within the four scheduled sitting weeks, and he thought that there was no pressing reason for criminal sittings, which would require extra security. Bayda's opposition killed another attempt to force the issue of criminal sittings in 1987.[45] The attorney general was not pleased with the chief justice's intransigence. The deputy minister suggested that *The Court of Appeal Act* could be unilaterally amended to create more sittings—the government was not under any legal obligation to consult the judges—but cooler heads prevailed.

Despite his sometimes frosty relationship with Lane and Andrew, the chief justice did convince the government to carry out a much-needed renovation to the courthouse in the mid-1980s. The renovation was long overdue, and with the expansion of the court it had become imperative. Tom Wakeling and Marjorie Gerwing were in temporary offices, and the court had no meeting room aside from the cramped library. Stuart Cameron recalled that a great deal of diplomacy and persistence was required on Bayda's part.[46] The court gained more offices, a conference room, and a much-expanded library, while the appeal courtroom was given a more traditional look. Other renovations followed over the years, one of which necessitated the unenviable task, which fell to the chief justice, of convincing the Court of Queen's Bench to give up offices on the second floor to further accommodate the Court of Appeal.

Gary Lane returned as attorney general and minister of justice in 1989, and relations between the department and the court improved. Lane was keen on technology and included the court in a department-wide computerization drive. Lane also agreed to Bayda's request for more judges and moved relatively quickly to add two more positions to the court. As it turned out, he may have had an ulterior motive. In 1991, Lane joined the Court of Appeal, a story for the next chapter.

One factor adding to the court's workload, especially the reserved decisions, was the arrival of the *Charter of Rights and Freedoms*. The *Charter* inevitably created more litigation, especially in the realm of criminal law, but also imposed a new interpretative burden on the courts. It took judges into unfamiliar territory replete with policy considerations, but also required them to come to grips with the scope and meaning of the enumerated rights and freedoms and what limits were reasonable. In the formative years, there were no easy *Charter* decisions. Saskatchewan's Court of Appeal took this new duty seriously, determined to breathe life into the *Charter* and taking great pains to get it right.

THE COURT AT LAW AND THE *CHARTER*

THE CHARTER OF *Rights and Freedoms* was a watershed for Canada and for the Canadian judiciary, and to quickly summarize its significance is no easy task. The *Charter* was an integral part of the *Constitution Act, 1982*, now the supreme law of Canada.[47] Section 32 of the *Charter* spelled out its reach, applying to all legislatures and governments in Canada, meaning that statutes, regulations, even bylaws had to conform to the *Charter*, subject only to certain limits.[48] The *Charter* had, at least on paper, the reach and the bite that the *Bill of Rights* had lacked. The powers of review and remedy given to the Canadian judiciary under the *Charter* were extensive, but the question was whether Canadian judges would exercise their new influence or the *Charter* would be largely neutered like the *Bill of Rights*.

The enumerated rights and freedoms in the *Charter* covered much ground. There were the fundamental freedoms: of speech, of religion, of assembly, and of association. There were democratic rights to vote and run in elections. There were mobility rights. There were the legal rights: to life, liberty, and security of person; against unreasonable search and seizure; to be informed of the reasons of arrest; to retain and instruct counsel; to be presumed innocent; and so on. There were equality rights under section 15, to be equal before the law and have the protection of law without discrimination. Language and education rights for French and English were specifically protected, as was the country's multicultural heritage. After much lobbying by women's groups, gender equality received additional protection by way of section 28. The all-important section 24 gave recourse to the courts for any violation of the rights and freedoms guaranteed in the *Charter* and gave the courts the power to create remedies as seemed appropriate.

The *Charter* was not a document of absolutes. The framers of the *Charter* included several limits. Section 1 guaranteed the rights and freedoms of the *Charter* but subject "to such reasonable limits prescribed by law as can be demonstrably justified in a free and democratic society." This short phrase became central to *Charter* jurisprudence. There was also section 33, known as the "notwithstanding" clause or the override power. This allowed legislatures to pass a law that infringed the *Charter*, subject to a five-year reappraisal. Allan Blakeney had pushed for the notwithstanding clause in constitutional negotiations, and it was necessary to win over the provinces. The clause seemed like a good way to guarantee that the *Charter* would be irrelevant, but section 33 became the nuclear option, sometimes threatened but rarely used, except in Quebec.[49] Saskatchewan invoked the clause after the Court of Appeal struck down right-to-work legislation. Usually, politicians registered their disapproval of a court decision by threatening to apply section 33, but generally have not risked the potential controversy by doing so.

The task of interpreting the *Charter* fell to the judiciary. By 1982, Canadian judges were much better equipped to handle a bill of rights. The generation that had chafed under the black-letter judges and courts of the 1950s and 1960s and watched the *Bill of Rights* neutered now made up the judiciary and had tools such as purposive interpretation for *Charter* interpretation. Under Chief Justice Brian Dickson, the Supreme Court of Canada rose to the occasion. In the first significant *Charter* decisions, the court laid out the broad brushstrokes for interpreting and applying the document. The foundation was the "living tree" analogy used by Lord

Sankey in the 1929 Persons Case: that the constitution was a living, changing document. Another basic tenet was that constitutional documents should be interpreted broadly, liberally, and generously, avoiding "the austerity of tabulated legalism."[50] In other words, constitutional enactments were not to be interpreted narrowly.

From this basis, in cases such as *Hunter v Southam*, the Supreme Court created the interpretative framework for the *Charter*.[51] The document was to be interpreted purposively, which meant that the overall purpose of the *Charter*, to guarantee and protect rights and freedoms, was the guiding principle of *Charter* jurisprudence. The enumerated rights and freedoms were to be given broad and generous interpretations, with few limits in the definition of their scope and application. Restrictions on rights were better found with an application of section 1, inquiring whether an infringement of a right or freedom was a "reasonable limit," thus creating a two-step interpretation. The court created the *Oakes* test, known as the proportionality test, to govern section 1 analysis, which asked if an infringement was "demonstrably justified in a free and democratic society," was proportionate to the end sought, and was a minimal impingement on a right.[52] The Supreme Court also declared that *Bill of Rights* jurisprudence was not determinative of the *Charter* despite the similarity between the documents. The *Charter* was part of the constitution and the supreme law of Canada and not to be given the crabbed interpretation of the *Bill*.

Approached this way, the *Charter* created a greatly expanded power of review for the judiciary. Inevitably, as legislation was scrutinized for compliance with the *Charter*, this was going to involve questions of public policy. Concern about giving this sort of power to judges dated back to debates leading up to the *Bill of Rights*. Critics feared that with the power of review and the ability to strike down legislation, an unelected judiciary could impose its own biases and preferences on the law. Even when the constitutional debates were ongoing, some commentators were speaking of "activist judges" who would "make the law" instead of legislatures, a charge heard ever more frequently as *Charter* decisions proliferated. The notwithstanding clause was a manifestation of the fear of excessive judicial power.

Defenders of the judiciary argued that these concerns were a misunderstanding of the true dynamic created with the *Charter*. Legislators, by creating the *Charter*, ended the supremacy of the legislature and thrust a new duty on judges, which they tried to fulfill to the best of their ability. Far from running wild and imposing an agenda, the judiciary was limited to what was brought before it, the terms of the *Charter* itself, and the further review of higher courts. The judiciary is also not homogenous: in terms of jurisprudence, there are conservative judges, bold judges, and judges who are neither, and these categories do not necessarily correspond with a jurist's own private political and social convictions. And as the joke goes, any time a judge makes a *Charter* decision someone doesn't like, it is judicial activism. It is arguable, however, that the *Charter* has enabled "progressive" political and social changes and, in the words of one critic, "legalized" the political process.[53]

Judges in Canada for the most part embraced their new role. No one knew better the failings of the legal and legislative framework of the nation and the fragility of rights under the doctrine of parliamentary supremacy. Some judges may have felt the zeal of reformers, and many others the excitement of a new and meaningful challenge. There were good decisions, poor decisions, and decisions that changed society. As time passed, *Charter* cases became both easier and harder. Easier as a body of law and principles was created; harder as decisions increasingly involved balancing rights and difficult concepts such as substantive versus formal equality.

THE COURT OF APPEAL AND THE *CHARTER*

SASKATCHEWAN'S COURT OF Appeal forged an early reputation for bold and imaginative *Charter* jurisprudence.[54] Some of the earliest landmark *Charter* cases, particularly in criminal law, came from Saskatchewan, and the court was arguably more adventurous than the Supreme Court of Canada. The *Charter* was a challenge that energized a relatively new and progressive-minded bench. As one of those judges, Stuart Cameron, says, "On the whole, I'd say our court embraced the *Charter*, the work there, enthusiastically, had quite an open mind and was generous in the interpretation of it."[55]

Cameron was one of the chief architects of the Court of Appeal's early *Charter* jurisprudence. But nearly every judge contributed major decisions as part of the court's embrace of the *Charter*. The court in the 1980s was generally recognized as being very able. Professor Howard McConnell, of the law school, claimed it was one of the best courts the province had ever seen and singled out Bayda, Cameron, and Tallis as "a core of leadership displaying an infinite capacity for hard work and research."[56] Bayda told

CALVIN FORRESTER TALLIS

Cal Tallis was born in March 5, 1930, on the family farm near Borden, Saskatchewan, to Ernest and Beryl Tallis. His grandfather George had homesteaded after emigrating from Bournemouth, England, in 1904 with his seven brothers. Tallis attended a one-room school in the Halcyonia district before taking high school correspondence courses, finishing Grade 12 in the nearby village of Borden. His next stop was the provincial normal school and a teaching certificate. Tallis taught in rural schools from 1947 to 1949, earning money for university.

Justice Calvin Forrester Tallis, c. 1983. (Provincial Archives of Saskatchewan, 83-1218-46)

Tallis entered the combined arts and law program at the University of Saskatchewan in 1949. He earned his arts degree in 1952 and law degree in 1954, graduating top of his class. He took articles with the firm of Goldenberg and Taylor in Saskatoon. J.M. Goldenberg and his young partner, George Taylor, were the leading labour lawyers in Saskatchewan. As Taylor's student and then junior, Tallis participated in many of the labour cases that went before the courts in the 1950s. He quickly began forging his own reputation as a civil litigator and criminal defence lawyer. Tallis was counsel in a number of high-profile criminal cases, including David Milgaard. He was recognized as one of the pre-eminent trial lawyers in the province, known for his thorough preparation and grasp of courtroom tactics and strategy.

In 1976, Tallis accepted an unusual judicial appointment, becoming the next "judge of the North," replacing Justice Bill Morrow on the Supreme Court of the Northwest Territories. Tallis and his wife relocated to Yellowknife. He was the sole judge of the court. From his base, he went on circuit, travelling by plane and holding court in schools and community halls. By virtue of his appointment, Tallis was an *ex officio* judge of the Supreme Court of Yukon and the NWT and Yukon appeal courts, sitting with Alberta and BC judges who came north to hear appeals. Tallis sat in the North at a time when the local bar was growing and developing. There are now four full-time judges on the NWT Supreme Court and four on the Nunavut Court of Justice.

In 1981, Tallis was offered a berth on the Court of Appeal. He came to the court as a seasoned jurist both at trial and appeal and was considered one of the strongest judges of his era, writing key judgments for the court's *Charter* jurisprudence. Tallis served until mandatory retirement in 2005. He did not cut all ties to the North after returning to Saskatchewan, serving as a deputy judge for the Yukon, the NWT, and later Nunavut, and by special warrant as a justice of the NWT and then Nunavut appeal courts. Through his years of practice and on the bench, Tallis also managed the farm where he grew up. It was his refuge from a busy professional life.

reporters that his day almost never ended until late in the evening, and a briefcase of work usually accompanied him home on the weekend.[57] Cameron attests to the fact that he, Bayda, and Tallis were workaholics. The usual routine was working evenings except for Fridays and half days on weekends.

Bayda was every inch the chief justice in those years. Cameron recalled that Bayda was energetic and innovative, full of ideas, and led the charge to establish a superlative court. Most of the initiatives to improve the court's performance came from the chief justice. Bayda prepared for hearings and researched his decisions meticulously, quietly setting an example for his colleagues. Cameron praised Bayda's analytical skills and ability to focus on the crucial issues. The chief justice had a philosophical bent and usually started with fundamentals and first principles and then moved to the specifics of an appeal. His judgments often contained references to literature and philosophy. Counsel appearing in front of Bayda recall his delight in exploring all the different angles and issues in appeal, and nothing pleased him more than a spirited exchange over an interesting point.[58] He truly loved the law.

Bayda was also a perfectionist. He said in interviews that he might spend "an entire day fine-tuning one paragraph" and frequently put decisions through a dozen drafts.[59] This accounted for the fact, as some observers noted, that Bayda did not write that much despite his long hours and explains why he was sometimes slow with his judgments. But the responsibilities of a chief justice were also increasingly onerous in the 1980s, with administrative tasks and the requirements of the Canadian Judicial Council and other bodies. Most chiefs found it nearly impossible to sit and write full-time, although they were also expected to provide leadership in the court's jurisprudence.

Tallis was one of the court's leading judges. Like Bayda, he often looked for first principles upon which to build the specifics of a decision. Like most effective counsel, he had the ability to quickly find important issues in litigation. Tallis did thorough research and had an astounding memory for case law. More incisive than Bayda, he still had an appreciation for the larger historical and legal context. Stuart Cameron was also an extremely able judge, combining strong analysis and precise reasoning with excellent writing skills. Both he and Tallis had perhaps a more practical bent than Bayda. Bill Vancise was a strong analytical thinker but also imaginative and quite bold, and always ready to make new law.

Wakeling was much admired as an independent, intelligent, common-sense judge and a straight shooter. Bill Vancise says, "You always knew where you stood with him."[60] Wakeling was a conservative jurist, one of the many judges who still felt that their role was best confined to interpreting and applying the law in a strict fashion. Wakeling was the member of the court most likely to dissent and was a counterpoint to his more liberal colleagues with the *Charter*. Sherstobitoff offered succinct analysis and exposition and plenty of common sense, but he was also a bold, liberal-minded judge. It is somewhat more difficult to appraise Gerwing. She pulled her weight on panels and often gave short, blunt, well-reasoned oral judgments from the bench. Her intellectual quality was well known, and much was expected of her, but Gerwing produced relatively few reported decisions. This may have been due to a conviction that most decisions did not require a written judgment, but Gerwing might possibly have had an aversion to writing.

The Diefenbaker-era judges still contributed a great deal. Woods faded into the background after becoming supernumerary, but Brownridge got a second wind. After turning supernumerary in 1981, Brownridge wrote

The Court of Appeal, c. 1984. *Standing, from left:* Justice Thomas Wakeling, Justice William Vancise, Justice Marjorie Gerwing. *Seated, from left:* Justice Stuart Cameron, Justice Russell Brownridge, Chief Justice Bayda, Justice Calvin Tallis. *Foreground:* unknown, Fred Newis, registrar. (Court of Appeal/ Photographic Services Agency, 84-3428-10)

more than he ever had under Culliton and became much more engaged in hearings. Roy Hall's younger colleagues spoke very highly of Hall's ability. He was incisive in hearings and, as Cameron put it, "had a real ability to draw together the strands of argument into an excellent judgment in a very economical fashion."[61] Hall had abundant common sense but also easily grasped the larger dimensions of appeals.

The 1980s court had a great deal of discipline as well as boldness. While the chief justice enjoyed mining the issues in an appeal, overall the court was tightly focused. There was seldom *obiter* commentary, and the court rarely addressed matters unnecessary to the outcome of an appeal. Side issues or possible ramifications were noted but rarely explored. The younger judges, such as Cameron, Sherstobitoff, and Vancise, showed the influence of judicial education and changing practice with much more organization and structure in their decisions than seen in older judgments. Long-winded quotes from case law were fast becoming relics of a past age, with the emphasis now on clarity and brevity, particularly with time a scarce resource.

Bayda, Cameron, Sherstobitoff, Tallis, and Vancise emerged quickly as the core group in the court's *Charter* jurisprudence.[62] The five took an expansive approach to interpretation of the *Charter* but had some differences in the ways they came at it. Bayda's predilection to look for first principles made him quite well suited for *Charter* interpretation, but his sometimes lofty philosophical musings and the inspiration he drew from non-legal thought was somewhat idiosyncratic and not emulated by his colleagues.[63] It was not uncommon for other judges to write a concurring opinion taking a different tack from the chief justice. Tallis and Cameron were probably more influential. Both continually stressed the proper principles of *Charter* interpretation in their early decisions, perhaps to firmly establish these principles. Both also took a very generous approach to defining rights and freedoms and set the bar high for their infringement, particularly Tallis with legal rights. Vancise was bold and imaginative and quite willingly pushed the boundaries of rights under the *Charter*.

Tom Wakeling was the court's conservative voice on the *Charter*. He clearly showed reservations about its reach and effect, primarily in criminal cases. One appeal, *R v Mohl*, was something of *cause célèbre* after the attorney general publicly criticized the decision.[64] *Mohl* demonstrated Wakeling's and Vancise's different approaches. The appeal involved section 10(b) of the *Charter*, the "right to retain and instruct counsel without delay and be informed of that right." The police had informed the accused of his right to retain counsel, and he had not requested counsel, but it later emerged that he was so drunk that he did not understand. Vancise, writing for the majority, held that this was a violation of section 10(b). In his view, the police knew the accused was intoxicated and their caution was disingenuous and lacked substance. Wakeling came to a different conclusion, reasoning that the accused had voluntarily become severely drunk and should not have recourse to the *Charter* to avoid the consequences. As one commentator noted, Wakeling frequently invoked public confidence in the justice system as a factor in determining the reach of a *Charter* right.[65] *Mohl* was one of many appeals where the majority was expansive with *Charter* rights and Wakeling held for something more restrictive.

Brownridge was even less enthusiastic about the *Charter*. He wrote dissents in several of the province's celebrated cases. In nearly every instance, Brownridge supported a narrower interpretation of the enumerated rights and freedoms, in the spirit of *Bill of Rights* jurisprudence. In one *Charter* decision, *Therens*, Brownridge argued that previous *Bill of Rights* decisions should be followed as precedent. Like many of the older members of the judiciary in their new role, he was clearly more comfortable with a conservative approach to the *Charter*. Almost every court had judges with a similar outlook, including the Supreme Court. In another appeal, *RWDSU*, discussed below, Brownridge's dissent mirrored the majority decision of the Supreme Court, which was roundly criticized for a crabbed approach to freedom of association. Brownridge was not always on the conservative side of *Charter* interpretation; there were decisions where he agreed with his brother and sister judges' more expansive treatment, and he wrote three opinions for the court upholding the application of the *Charter*.

Brownridge's and Wakeling's more skeptical approach to the *Charter* was not uncommon, but the core of the Court of Appeal took a liberal approach, following the early *dicta* of the Supreme Court and striving to give each right a broad definition and scope. As several of the court's celebrated *Charter* decisions show, the Saskatchewan judges repeatedly and consistently stressed that limits on rights were best found in an application of section 1 rather than in their definitions. The general approach of the court has been called innovative and activist and calculated to boldly give life to the *Charter*.

THE *THATCHER* APPEAL

CHARTER JURISPRUDENCE WAS not the only important legal development in the 1980s. The *Mercure* appeal, discussed below, was an important constitutional decision. A new *Divorce Act* in 1985 and further amendments to Saskatchewan's *Matrimonial Property Act* produced many important decisions. The court also did important work in administrative law.[66] The *Young Offenders Act* in 1984 was a controversial statute that required interpretation. There were significant changes in Saskatchewan sentencing jurisprudence as the court moved beyond the somewhat idiosyncratic tradition of the Culliton years. But other decisions of the court were eclipsed with a tabloid-worthy story of wealth, intrigue, and murder.

It is pretty much impossible to discuss the province's justice system in the 1980s without talking about *Thatcher*. It was the trial of the century in Saskatchewan. Colin Thatcher, son of Premier Ross Thatcher, and a cabinet minister in the Devine government, was tried and convicted for the murder of his ex-wife, JoAnn Wilson. Appeals followed, right up to the Supreme Court of Canada. Thatcher went to jail but vehemently maintained his innocence. Even in prison, he never seemed far from notoriety, with every application to review his conviction and every parole hearing bringing the sordid tale back to light.

Colin Thatcher was called the "J.R. Ewing of Saskatchewan." He had built a successful cattle and horse ranch near Moose Jaw, and in 1975, following in his father's footsteps, he went into politics and was elected as a Liberal MLA. Two years later, he defected to the Conservatives and became minister of energy and mines in the Devine cabinet. Thatcher's marriage with his wife, JoAnn, deteriorated, and they divorced in 1979. The battle over custody of their three children was exceedingly bitter. JoAnn suffered months of harassment from Thatcher and anonymous threats before an unknown assailant shot and wounded her through her window. A year and a half later, on January 21, 1983, she was found dead in her garage, severely beaten and shot.

After a long investigation, police arrested and charged Thatcher. There was a strong circumstantial case, but investigators were not sure if Thatcher had committed the murder or hired a hit man. Thatcher had tried to hire a killer twice, and a witness saw a man running from the garage who did not resemble the accused, but there was also a great deal of evidence pointing at the former politician as the killer. Crown prosecutor Serge Kujawa pursued both theories, arguing that the evidence clearly showed that Thatcher wanted his ex-wife dead, and if he had not done it personally, he was responsible for her death, and left it to the jury to decide his guilt or innocence depending on which theory they accepted. Thatcher was found guilty.

Bayda sat a panel of five for the appeal: himself, Tallis, Brownridge, Hall, and Vancise. There were numerous grounds on appeal. Tallis, writing for the court, zeroed in on the crux: whether the trial judge had properly instructed the jury on section 21.1 of the *Criminal Code* and whether he should have directed that the jurors had to be unanimous in picking one of the Crown's theories. Section 21.1 defined a party to an offence as one who commits an offence, one who does or omits to do something for the purpose of aiding in its commission, or one who abets any person in committing the offence. The trial judge told the jury that they could convict Thatcher either if they believed he committed the murder or he aided in the commission, as section 21.1 made him equally culpable. Tallis saw nothing wrong in this, and the prosecution had been clear that two different theories were being pursued. He further held that there was no requirement for unanimity on which theory the jurors believed. Just as jurors could accept and ignore different bits of evidence, one juror could accept one theory and another juror the other theory. The other attacks on the jury charge he found to be without basis and dismissed the appeal.

Vancise could not agree and dissented.[67] He accepted that jurors could come to the same conclusion by different routes and did not have to be unanimous about which theory they believed. But the two theories required jurors either to accept or reject an alibi and meant that the trial judge had to be very careful in putting the evidence to the jury. In Vancise's view, the trial judge had not been sufficiently careful, particularly with the theory of the hit man. He thought that the evidence for the hit man theory was weak, particularly without a possible suspect named. Vancise argued that it was vital that the jury be instructed carefully about reasonable doubt on both theories and that the trial judge had not been careful enough. For good measure, Vancise also argued that the judge's charge summed up the evidence in a manner prejudicial to the defence and a new trial was required.

Vancise's dissent allowed further appeal to the Supreme Court. In a unanimous decision, the Supreme Court upheld the conviction. The trial judge, in the opinion of the court, had made no reviewable error and the justices agreed with Tallis's analysis of section 21. Thatcher continued to maintain his innocence and was released in 2006 on parole. It remains one of the most compelling and discussed crimes in the province's history.

Thatcher had not involved a *Charter* argument. Many criminal decisions in the 1980s did; the legal rights included in the *Charter* got a thorough working out in the first few years. Saskatchewan's court, as has been said, made a name for itself with bold *Charter* judgments that gave these legal

STUART JOHN CAMERON

Liberal Party politics were almost bred into Stuart Cameron. His father was Alexander Cameron, a long-serving Liberal member of the provincial Legislative Assembly and

Justice Stuart John Cameron, c. 1983. (Provincial Archives of Saskatchewan, 83-1218-054)

cabinet minister in the Thatcher government.[4] Cameron senior had been a school teacher who went into business in the small town of Richmound, near Maple Creek, with his brother-in-law and operated a garage and car and implement dealership. First elected in 1948, Alexander Cameron contested the Liberal leadership in 1960 and served as minister of mineral resources until his defeat in the 1971 election.

Stuart Cameron was born on May 15, 1939, in Maple Creek. After his initial schooling in Richmond, for high school Cameron attended Campion College, a Jesuit-run institution in Regina that later became part of the University of Regina. During summers, he worked a farm his father owned, saving money for university.[5] Cameron attended university in Saskatoon and entered the combined arts and law program, earning his bachelor of arts in 1961 and law degree in 1962.

Cameron articled with prominent litigator E.J. Moss in Regina, joining the bar in 1963. Moss and Ross Wimmer invited him into partnership the following year. At the time, Cameron was not especially interested in politics, but Wimmer ran for office and asked his young partner to help with the campaign. Cameron subsequently ran the campaign for another partner, Ken MacLeod, in 1971. He then became Otto Lang's chief of staff in Ottawa for two years. One of his responsibilities was assisting Edward Ratushny in finding and vetting judicial appointments. After returning to Regina and his law practice, Cameron was enlisted to run provincially and sat in the Legislative

Assembly from 1975 to 1978. He made a run for Parliament but was defeated. He returned to full-time practice, but was appointed to the Queen's Bench in 1980. Heavily involved in the community while a lawyer, Cameron served on the board of governors for the Regina General Hospital and as chair of the Regina Housing Authority. He was also on the board of the Saskatchewan branch of the John Howard Society and was president of the Regina Bar Association.

Cameron was soon moved to the Court of Appeal, appointed on October 13, 1981. He was reckoned one of the most able judges on the court, writing important and finely crafted judgments in nearly every area of law. Judicial education and training was one of his interests, and he was vice-president of the Canadian Institute for the Administration of Justice. He was one of the faculty of the bar admission course for many years. Cameron stepped down in 2014 upon reaching mandatory retirement age. In retirement, he composed a guide to appellate practice, published in 2015.

rights broad meaning and application. And one of the most influential of the court's criminal *Charter* judgments was also one of the earliest.

R v Therens

A SIMPLE DRUNK-DRIVING case and the proper definition of one word, *detention,* were the ingredients that produced Saskatchewan's first landmark *Charter* case. *Therens* was more than just a case that helped define how one legal right—section 10(b), the right to retain and instruct counsel without delay—should be applied. The decision also signalled how the Saskatchewan Court of Appeal would approach the *Charter.*

The 1968 law for impaired driving, which established the use of breathalyzers for enforcement, had created vast amounts of work for criminal lawyers, who used every conceivable angle to get clients acquitted. The *Bill of Rights* had been pressed into service, but the courts had used narrow definitions of the *Bill*'s provisions and done little to expand the rights of accused. Despite the similarity of many provisions of the *Charter* and the *Bill,* lawyers immediately used the *Charter* to challenge the breathalyzer laws. One of the things *Therens* did was differentiate the *Charter* from the *Bill of Rights.*

The facts in *Therens* were commonplace. The police responded to a single-vehicle accident and found the accused at the scene. The responding officer asked the accused, Paul Therens, to come with him to the nearest station for a breathalyzer test but did not put Therens under arrest. At no time did the officer inform Therens that he had the right to retain and instruct counsel. Therens blew over the limit and was charged. The trial judge threw out the breathalyzer evidence, holding that the accused had been detained within the meaning of section 10 of the *Charter* and his right to retain counsel without delay under section 10(b) had been violated. Invoking section 24(1) of the *Charter,* which allowed anyone whose *Charter* rights were violated to apply to the courts for relief, the trial judge threw the evidence out. This was a surprise, as section 24(2) of the *Charter* dealt specifically with impugned evidence in criminal proceedings, instructing judges not to allow such evidence if it "would bring the administration of justice into disrepute."

The Crown appealed by way of a stated case. The three questions were simple. Had the court erred in holding the accused had been detained? Had it erred in holding that 24(1) allowed for the exclusion of evidence without referring to the test in 24(2)? And was it appropriate to exclude the evidence? *Therens* was one of the first meaty *Charter* cases for the court, and Bayda sat a five-judge panel with himself, Brownridge, Hall, Tallis, and Cameron.

The Crown's position was that the accused had not been detained, arguing that detention required some form of compulsory restraint, following two *Bill of Rights* cases, *Chromiak* and *Dedman.* In *Chromiak,* the accused was asked to use a roadside screening device that determined if the police should perform a breathalyzer test. This was not deemed a detention, but *Chromiak* used a very narrow definition of detention that was essentially full arrest. Appellate courts were following *Chromiak* in the early *Charter* challenges to impaired driving convictions.[68] The Crown contended that to widen the concept of detention would mean that any police stop, such as spot checks and roadblocks, would engage section 10 of the *Charter* and make the job of the police impossible.

Tallis, writing for the court, thought this was nonsense. While cognizant that too broad a definition of detention might be unworkable, he did not see this in *Therens.* An important distinction from *Chromiak* was that a breathalyzer demand was far more serious than roadside screening.

Under section 235(1) of the *Criminal Code*, refusing to take a breathalyzer test without sufficient and reasonable excuse was a crime with the same punishment as a charge of driving over the legal limit. An accused had to make a critical decision—whether to refuse the test—which exposed them to criminal sanction. The average citizen, in the view of Tallis, required legal advice to make an informed choice.

Tallis used the average citizen's perspective further to argue for a broad definition of detention for section 10(b). In construing detention, Tallis thought that the common and ordinary meaning should be used, as this was what most people in such a situation would understand. Under this definition, the accused had been detained. As Tallis pointed out, while the accused had not been arrested and went voluntarily to get a test, it was a fiction to claim he was not detained. If he had refused to accompany the officer, he would have been arrested. The temporary restraint and compulsion would be apparent to most people. Furthermore, to define detention in a more narrow sense risked turning 10(b) into a nullity. People unfamiliar with criminal law, Tallis argued, might naively go with police and have no right to ask for counsel, while the uncooperative would be arrested and given access to counsel. A restrictive approach to the meaning of *detain*, in Tallis's words, "would be tantamount to saying that the law does not recognize rights under s. 10(b) as applying to an accused before arrest."[69] Narrow definitions of *Charter* rights, he contended, ran the risk of diminishing them to the point of uselessness.

> Our nation's constitutional ideals have been enshrined in the *Charter* and it will not be a "living" charter unless it is interpreted in a meaningful way from the standpoint of an average citizen who seldom has a brush with the law. The fundamental rights accorded to a citizen under s. 10(b) should be approached on the basis of giving the word "detention" its popular interpretation, in other words its natural or ordinary meaning. The implementation and application of the *Charter* should not be blunted or thwarted by technical or legalistic interpretations of ordinary words of the English language. Using this approach, our citizens will not be placed in a position of feeling that the statements in the *Charter* are only rights in theory. If these rights are to survive and be available on a day to day basis we must resist the temptation to opt in favour of a restrictive approach.[70]

This had been largely the fate of the *Bill of Rights*, and Tallis took the opportunity to explain why earlier jurisprudence was now irrelevant even if, as with *Therens*, the right in question was nearly identical in both documents. The *Bill of Rights* was, in Tallis's formulation, "a mere canon of construction for the interpretation of federal legislation."[71] The *Charter*, he contended, existed on "an entirely different basis" as a constitutional document establishing fundamental rights and freedoms. The *Charter* should not be interpreted like an ordinary statute but—following the much-quoted passage from *Fisher*, a Privy Council decision—given "a generous interpretation, avoiding . . . 'the austerity of tabulated legalism' suitable to give individuals the full measure of the fundamental rights and freedoms referred to."[72] The existing jurisprudence around the *Bill of Rights* was in the view of Tallis at best of "interpretative assistance," but in essence *Charter* interpretation started with a clean slate.

Turning to the question of remedy, Tallis agreed with the trial judge that section 24(1) could be used to exclude evidence as well as the more specific section 24(2). The Crown had argued that the latter clause was designed for the purpose of determining if impugned evidence should be excluded and that the onus was on the accused to show that its use would undermine the administration of justice. To Tallis, this approach was too restrictive and risked creating a useless remedy. It also took away a measure of flexibility and discretion in fashioning a remedy. Tallis adopted the trial judge's reasoning that section 24(1) was a general power and 24(2) one specific way of exercising the power that did restrict the former. Section 24(2) described a circumstance where the court had to exclude evidence rather than having broader discretion. This was a point that Bayda explored further in short concurring reasons to reinforce the argument that section 24(2) did not operate in an exclusionary fashion.

Brownridge's dissent took the other road. To his mind, the Supreme Court of Canada had already, in the *Bill of Rights* cases, "authoritatively interpreted" the meaning of *detention*.[73] He rejected the notion that the drafters of the *Charter* intended to depart from the law that previously existed. This was a common line of argument, placing the *Charter* within the evolution of the developed law but still subject to previous precedent. Not surprisingly, Brownridge also supported the more restricted view of section 24, saying, "It appears anomalous to me that the very power which is so circumscribed in s. 24(2) should be available under s. 24(1) without any restriction."[74] The gist of his dissent was that he did not see the *Charter* as a break with the past, which meant the same limited interpretation given to the *Bill of Rights*.

The Supreme Court followed much of Tallis's reasoning in *Therens*. Not only did the court agree with his analysis of the meaning of *detain* and *detention*, but Justice Gerald Le Dain took the opportunity to argue in no uncertain terms that there was indeed a break with the past with the *Charter*, in scope and content, and in the responsibility of the judiciary to develop the *Charter* and ensure the protection of rights and freedoms.[75] *Therens* would not be the end of litigation of section 10(b), as there seemed to be endless new angles involving the provision, but the decision laid an important foundation for interpreting that right as well as the proper approach to *Charter* interpretation. On the question of remedy, the Supreme Court took the more restrictive interpretation. The majority judgment did set the bar relatively low as to what might bring the administration of justice into disrepute: the violation in *Therens* was characterized as "flagrant," and the higher court decision strongly emphasized the importance of section 24 as an enforcement measure.[76] In the years after *Therens*, the application of the courts of section 24(2) has been criticized as unduly favouring the prosecution.[77] One can speculate about what might have been if the expansive definition favoured in Saskatchewan had been adopted.

RWDSU V SASKATCHEWAN

ONE OF THE boldest *Charter* decisions of the Saskatchewan Court of Appeal was *RWDSU v Saskatchewan*. The decision concerned one of the fundamental freedoms, section 2(d) of the *Charter*: freedom of association. The question was whether the freedom to associate included the activities and ends for which people might associate. Saskatchewan's court said yes. The Supreme Court of Canada said no, falling short of its own standards of *Charter* interpretation and in the view of some critics revealing a persistent bias against labour that not even the *Charter* altered. And twenty years later, the Supreme Court changed its mind.

The 1980s were not good years for organized labour in Canada.[78] Governments facing fiscal shortfalls and preoccupied with fighting inflation passed legislation to declare more and more public employees "essential" workers, removing their right to strike in favour of binding arbitration.[79]

WILLIAM JOHN VANCISE

A native of Regina, Bill Vancise was born in 1938. He attended public school in Regina and Grand Coulee before attending Luther College for high school. Like many lawyers of his generation, Vancise chose the combined arts and law program at the University of Saskatchewan, obtaining his bachelor of arts in 1958 and his law degree in 1960. He articled and began practice at the venerable partnership of Balfour and Balfour, becoming a partner in 1963, and remained with the firm as it evolved into Balfour Moss. Vancise was a litigator who specialized in resource, administrative, and labour law, acting both for unions and management. Vancise sat on several corporate boards, including Canadian National Railway from 1972 to 1982. He was a section chairman for the Canadian Bar Association and also served as a director for the YMCA. Vancise was also heavily involved in federal Liberal Party circles as an organizer and fundraiser but never ran for office.

Justice William John Vancise, c. 1983. (Court of Appeal/Photographic Service Agency)

In 1982, Vancise was named to the Court of Queen's Bench and a year later elevated to the Court of Appeal. He did not settle into the judiciary easily.[6] Vancise had not anticipated that he would be assigned as the resident Queen's Bench judge in Swift Current and almost resigned, but was able to persuade the attorney general to move him to Regina. In 1985, he considered returning to practice, going so far as to ask the Law Society to give a ruling on whether he could do so immediately, which caused some comment in Saskatchewan's legal community.

His resignation would have been a loss to the court. Vancise was another able judge, creative and something of a maverick. Some of his best-known decisions were dissents, such as the Colin Thatcher case, where Vancise held a new trial was necessary. Vancise also took a great interest in judicial education, working with the Canadian Institute for the Administration of Justice and the National Judicial Institute. He was also the founder and first president of the National Judicial Counselling Programme, which provided much-needed counselling services for the federal judiciary. In 2004, Vancise became chair of the Copyright Board of Canada in addition to his judicial duties at a time when technology was creating considerable new challenges.

Vancise became a supernumerary in 2007 and retired from the court in 2013 at seventy-five. In addition to his career as a lawyer and jurist, Vancise is a man of culture, a collector of art, and an opera buff, and he is known among the Saskatchewan bar as a fine raconteur.

The private sector followed suit, attempting to get their unionized employees to accept contracts that mandated arbitration. In the larger picture, unions felt with some justification that the courts continued to favour employers. Saskatchewan emerged as a battleground. The Devine government was no friend to unions. The members of the Labour Relations Board were replaced when the Devine government came in, and a new labour act was passed that unions thought tilted power to employers.[80] But an even greater conflict awaited.

In 1984, the Retail, Wholesale and Department Store Union (RWDSU) and other unions representing workers in the province's dairies organized a rotating strike as contract talks reached an impasse. The dairy companies, one a co-operative, responded with lockout notices, and a protracted strike looked likely. The Devine government stepped in with *The Dairy Workers (Maintenance of Operations) Act*. The statute declared dairy employees essential workers and outlawed any work stoppage, including strikes, slowdowns, work-to-rules, and lockouts, and sent the dispute to binding arbitration. To justify the measure, the province declared milk and other dairy products essential foodstuffs for consumers and claimed a prolonged strike would detrimentally affect the province's financially stressed dairy farmers. The unions immediately mounted a court challenge to *The Dairy Workers Act* but failed to get an order declaring the statute *ultra vires* for violating the *Charter of Rights and Freedoms*. They immediately appealed.

The union argued that *The Dairy Workers Act* violated section 2(d) of the *Charter*, freedom of association. In the union view, this freedom included the ends and objects of association, such as collective bargaining and its corollary, the ability to strike. The government position was that freedom of association protected the ability of people to form unions without interference but did not extend to the subsequent activities of the union. Alternatively, the law was justified under section 1 of the *Charter* as a reasonable limit. Chief Justice Bayda heard the appeal with Cameron and Brownridge. The majority allowed the appeal, holding that freedom of association encompassed striking and section 1 did not save the statute. Brownridge dissented.

Bayda's decision was as much an exercise in philosophy as law. As was his wont, he started at first principles, defining a freedom as opposed to a right. The latter was specific, he contended, with attendant duties, and the extent and reach was usually defined in law. A freedom was general and, most importantly, an area where the state had little or no say in what a citizen did or did not do. The law supported and defined a freedom primarily by providing safeguards but in some instances by also stating what might not be included, such as defamatory speech in freedom of speech. Bayda did argue that a freedom had some intrinsic limits:

> Every freedom has an inherent limit which determines what kind of acts are excluded from the sphere of activity within which the freedom reigns. Indeed, that every freedom has an inherent limit is axiomatic. A freedom without an inherent limit would lead to an absurdity, for a freedom by everyone to do everything is a freedom to do nothing.[81]

Bayda's formulation of freedom of association was very broad, encompassing any human action in concert, the only intrinsic limit being that, like individual action, it could not be directed with intent of harm. The action of striking passed this low threshold, and given that the law already recognized the legality of a strike, there was no reason for a strike to be precluded from freedom of association.

Turning to the concrete, Bayda analyzed the case law regarding freedom of association and collective action. A 1969 Privy Council decision,

Collymore, had decided almost the identical point in Trinidad, where the constitution included the protection of fundamental rights and freedoms. The Judicial Committee of the Privy Council held that freedom of association meant freedom to be in an association but did not extend necessarily to actions intended to bring about the object of association. Bayda thought the analysis was fundamentally flawed because the Judicial Committee's approach sought to define freedom of association by what was permitted and included, giving it a limited scope. Worse, Bayda found that law lords allowed the legislature to determine what was and was not included in the freedom under discussion, missing the point of giving constitutional protection.

Collymore had already influenced several Canadian appellate decisions on the issue. Nearly all denied that collective bargaining and striking was included in freedom of association, or that association included anything more than the bare freedom to be associated, or both. Bayda criticized these decisions as essentially attempts to define and limit the allowable acts of association, which had the effect of severely limiting the freedom without using section 1 of the *Charter*, in effect allowing legislatures to avoid full *Charter* scrutiny. This was antithetical to what Bayda argued was the proper approach to the question at hand and the *Charter* in general.

Addressing the question of whether *The Dairy Workers Act* could be justified under section 1, Bayda concluded it could not. He argued that finding a section 1 justification was a heavily fact-based enterprise, and it was the responsibility of the party—nearly always the government—seeking the limitation to provide the factual context of the argument with evidence to compel finding the limitation. This did not have to "be of such scope as to put the court in a position to resolve the very points of the conflict," but there had to be sufficient facts to allow a reasoned decision for finding a limitation.[82] He found the government case lacking in this regard.

Bayda's decision was probably one of his best-known pieces of work. His references to thinkers and writers as diverse as Thomas Aquinas, Alexis de Tocqueville, and Shakespeare, as well the usual gamut of legal theory and authorities, "generated widespread comment."[83] His philosophical inquiry was part and parcel of a powerful statement of how the *Charter* should be viewed and wielded, not just as law but as an expression of high ideals.

Cameron was more direct. His decision was also an exposition of principles, but explicitly directed towards the proper interpretation of the

Charter. He came to the same conclusions as Bayda. After dispensing with the background to the litigation, Cameron stated that "an interpretative framework for the *Charter* has been forming."[84] As the court had noted in *Therens*, the *Charter* should be approached as a living document, with rights and freedoms given broad and generous interpretations, and should be approached purposively.

In Cameron's view, *Charter* rights were subject to limitation in two ways: in their content and in their exercise. The judiciary was responsible for determining the content, using the principles for interpretation that had developed; and the legislature regulated the exercise of rights, but subject to section 1. This division allowed, in his opinion, for a "less timid" interpretation of the scope of a right or freedom. Consideration of public policy and competing rights was then addressed with a section 1 analysis. Cameron thought the benefit of this method was clear:

> These approaches have the long term advantage of anchoring the content of the rights and freedoms protected by the *Charter* against the ebb and flow of public opinion, while permitting their exercise to be reasonably limited on occasion, as may from time to time be "demonstrably justified in a free and democractic [sic] society," as provided for by Section 1. None of this is to say that the rights and freedoms of the *Charter* are to be the subject of extravagant or unnatural interpretation. It is only to say they may be interpreted generously, resolving ambiguities in their favour, with a view to giving them full recognition and effect—and without excessive concern for where this liberal construction may lead in the light of the power of the legislative branch to limit their exercise under s. 1, or, for that matter, to temporarily suspend them for up to five years under s. 33. These powers, often referred to in the literature of the *Charter* as the "double-override," afford the legislative branch extensive authority to restrict the exercise of the rights and freedoms in issue, a fact which I think has a place in determining the scope of those rights and freedoms.[85]

Turning to the case at hand, Cameron rejected the existing case law on section 2(d). The approach in *Collymore* seemed to him to put the cart before the horse. Allowing the legislature to have a say in what conduct might be part, or not part, of freedom of association removed much of the protection of the right. But more importantly, Cameron thought that not including the aims, ends, and activities for which one might associate as part of freedom of association made it a rather hollow right. Cameron argued that the point of forming a union was to act to better the position of its members, and without the ability to collectively bargain, the freedom to associate lost much of "its practical value."[86] Collective bargaining got much of its teeth from the possibility of a strike, and "without it there would be little if anything left of the freedom of employees to act as one in their dealing with their employer."[87] Essentially, freedom of association was close to meaningless if it was not defined more broadly. In Cameron's view, the interpretive framework he had sketched made this reasonable, as the "double-override"—section 1 and section 33, the notwithstanding clause—still allowed for the restriction of the broad right.

Turning to section 1, Cameron agreed that the fundamental flaw in the government's case was that it did not provide evidence for its assertions. Cameron opined that the dairy industry was not clearly an essential service such that the court could take judicial notice of the fact. That the proposed strikes might cripple the dairy industry and drive farmers out of business might be true, but the court required an evidentiary basis to conclude this and determine if these effects merited section 1 intervention.

Brownridge was having none of Bayda's philosophizing and Cameron's principles, and lined up squarely with the law lords in *Collymore* and the body of Canadian appellate opinion that followed that decision. As with *Therens*, he preferred a more restrictive approach to the definition of the right. The large number of decisions that had already held that freedom of association did not extend to the actions and goals of those associated—including collective bargaining and striking—were in his eyes more than sufficient authority. Having reached this conclusion, he had no reason to inquire as to the effect of section 1.

The Saskatchewan government was outraged with the appeal court decision. The Devine administration immediately drafted a new law which included the invocation of the notwithstanding clause of the *Charter* to protect it from judicial review. The provincial government also gained an unexpected ally in the Supreme Court of Canada. RWDSU was one of the "labour trilogy": three appeals decided in 1987 that declined to give a more expansive meaning to freedom of association. One opinion from the

MARJORIE ANNE GERWING

The Saskatchewan Court of Appeal had not just one opera fan but two. Marjorie Gerwing, appointed on December 14, 1984, was a devotee, regularly travelling to London and New York to see performances. She also has an impressive collection of opera and other recordings. Music was her refuge from the pressures of a career in law.

Justice Marjorie Anne Gerwing, c. 2005. (Photo by Trevor Hopkin, University of Regina Photographic Services)

Gerwing almost did not become a lawyer. She was originally a pre-med student and didn't switch paths until three years into university.[7] She was born in Humboldt in 1943, and grew up in the village of Lake Lenore, population 450. Her father owned the town's general store. The Ursuline Sisters taught Gerwing at the local Catholic elementary, and she boarded at an Ursuline convent from Grade 9 onwards. The nuns were strict disciplinarians, but Gerwing recounted that they encouraged academic excellence. Gerwing proceeded directly to university and after earning a bachelor's degree in 1964 entered law school, graduating in 1967.

Female lawyers and judges were not uncommon in Saskatchewan, but Gerwing was part of a new wave that entered into corporate law and civil litigation at major firms. She articled with David Tyerman at MacPherson, Leslie and Tyerman and stayed with the firm after joining the bar in 1968. She had planned to spend just a few years in private practice before returning to academia but was soon caught up in a fast-paced career.[8] Gerwing specialized in corporate litigation, acting for a number of mining companies, particularly the uranium industry, and other prominent clients, such as Regina steelmaker IPSCO. She was known as an aggressive litigator, always well prepared and with an ability to cut quickly to the key issues. A frequent visitor to the Court of Appeal, Gerwing also made appearances at the Supreme Court of Canada. In 1976, she was appointed to the Law Reform Commission of Saskatchewan.

She sat on a number of corporate boards, and in 1982 the new Devine government named Gerwing to the board of the Saskatchewan Transportation Company. The appointment was interesting, as Gerwing supposedly leaned Liberal in personal convictions but was essentially apolitical, focused on her career.[9] The MacPherson firm had strong ties to the federal Conservatives, but Gerwing's reputation in the courts made her an obvious choice to be the historic first female appointment to the Court of Appeal. Her colleagues on the court attested to her ability to quickly grasp the nub of an appeal and see the best result. Perhaps because of this, while an active judge in hearings, Gerwing did not write extensively; most of her judgments were given from the bench. She served for nearly twenty years, taking supernumerary status in 2007 and retiring in 2013 at the age of seventy.

trilogy held that collective bargaining and the right to strike were statutory and therefore not available as part of a fundamental freedom, while the majority opinion held again that freedom of association did not include the various things one might associate to do. The dissenting opinion of Brian Dickson and Bertha Wilson gave the more expansive meaning to section 2(d), but Dickson would have allowed a section 1 limiting of the right in RWDSU.

Nearly twenty years later, the Supreme Court had a change of heart. In *Saskatchewan Federation of Labour v Saskatchewan*, the court reversed its previous stance in the trilogy and included the right to strike in section 2(d) of the *Charter*.[88] In that case, it was argued in Saskatchewan's Court of Appeal that there had been a steady erosion of earlier jurisprudence and that it was open to the lower courts to ignore the Supreme Court precedent set by the trilogy.[89] The Court of Appeal deferred to the judges in Ottawa. And to bring things full circle, Premier Brad Wall of the Saskatchewan Party publicly mused about once again invoking the notwithstanding clause.

AMONG THE UNIVERSAL rights and freedoms and equality and gender guarantees, some might consider the *Charter*'s language and education rights somewhat anachronistic in the multicultural reality of 2018. Sections 16 to 23 honoured and strengthened the original compact between francophones and anglophones and the declaration that the nation was officially bilingual. In the wake of the first Quebec referendum, language rights were a crucial part of the constitutional debate leading to the *Charter*. Language had historically been a controversial subject in Saskatchewan, and *R v Mercure* was a major case in the 1980s. But *Mercure* was not a *Charter* case. The litigation started before the *Charter* and concerned the interpretation of section 110 of the *North-West Territories Act* and section 16 of *The Saskatchewan Act*. Like the *Manitoba Language Rights Reference*, the final result of *Mercure* made the laws of the province invalid for not being enacted in French as well as English, but there was an easy fix. But if the *Charter*'s language sections had been in force, would the outcome have been different?

Père André Mercure was an unlikely crusader. The Roman Catholic priest was originally from Quebec and had come to Saskatchewan in 1942 as a teacher. He later became a parish priest and was stationed in Battleford when the litigation began. He was also a proud francophone and a bit of an activist. When Mercure received a speeding ticket in December 1980 printed only in English, he decided to mount a constitutional challenge. At Provincial Court, he requested that French be used for the proceedings and the relevant statutes be made available in French. Mercure did not want translators; he wanted his trial in French. It was a test case, and in fact Mercure allegedly raced his car back and forth in front of the city police station until he got a ticket.[90]

Mercure argued that section 110 of the *North-West Territories Act* still applied in Saskatchewan. The statute had given francophones the right to use French in court proceedings and in the Territorial Assembly, mandated the journals of the Assembly be in both French and English and the laws of the Territories published in both languages. Section 110 had never been repealed, but the Territorial Assembly and the courts had increasingly ignored the measure. When the province was established, section 16 of *The Saskatchewan Act* mandated that "all laws and all orders and regulations" in place continued to apply unless inconsistent with the

Act or specifically repealed. *The Saskatchewan Act* made no pronouncement on language in the courts or Legislative Assembly, and Mercure argued that section 110 still applied. He should be able to have his trial in French and the province's statutes should be available in French. The Provincial Court judge held that Mercure did have the right to use French himself but not to have the trial conducted entirely in French, and that the requirement for bilingual statutes had not been carried forward. Père Mercure appealed by way of a stated case.

Bayda wrote the decision of the court, with Tallis, Cameron, Brownridge, and Hall joining him on the appeal. The two central issues were whether section 110 had become part of the laws of Saskatchewan, and if so, what was entailed in the use of French in the courtroom. In his usual style, Bayda set up an analytical structure with several criteria to determine whether the language provisions survived. Focusing on the provision for French in the courtroom, he concluded that it easily passed five of his criteria. It had been valid law when Saskatchewan became a province; it was consistent with *The Saskatchewan Act*; there was no provision replacing it; Parliament had not repealed or replaced the measure; and the province had not repealed or replaced it. The other criterion, derived from a 1906 decision of the Supreme Court of the North-West Territories, was whether the statute was a law of the Territories with general application or a "special" law that applied only to a specific territorial matter.

This was a crucial distinction. If a statute pertained to a territorial institution or matter that ended with the creation of the province, and essentially no longer existed, then the law was likely defunct. The government argued that when the provincial courts replaced the Supreme Court of the North-West Territories, the provision of section 110 became void. Bayda disagreed, examining the language used in *The Saskatchewan Act* regarding courts and comparing it to that regarding legislative assemblies. The critical difference was that section 110 spoke specifically of the Legislative Assembly of the Northwest Territories, while generically of the courts. The territorial Legislative Assembly was replaced with the Legislative Assembly of Saskatchewan, and in Bayda's view this made the provision for French in the Legislative Assembly of no effect. Section 16(2) of *The Saskatchewan Act* referred to the ability of the province to set up a new court but was generic, not specifying which court was being replaced and which court was replacing it. The actual statutes that set up the provincial courts in 1907 and afterward did not state the language of proceedings, so section 110 carried over. As Bayda put it, "This means that different courts can come and go but the law remains and applies irrespective of those comings and goings."[91]

The government further argued that an express repeal was not necessary and that the creation of an entirely new court system and rules of court essentially displaced any operation of section 110. Bayda was not impressed with the government's argument that section 110 was "abolished by implication." In his view, section 110 was a law about language that applied to the courts, not about the constitution or general operation of the courts, and thus the implication argument did not apply.

Bayda also rejected Mercure's argument that section 110 was constitutionally entrenched, like section 133 of the *Constitution Act, 1867*, which established French and English as languages of Parliament and the Quebec courts, or section 23 of *The Manitoba Act*, which had nearly identical provisions as section 110. The difference was obvious: section 133 and section 23 were part of constitutional documents and could not be unilaterally altered, while section 110 was not part of *The Saskatchewan Act*, it was part the "general law of the Territories." Section 110 was no different than laws for chattel mortgages, in Bayda's view. More importantly, section 16 of *The Saskatchewan Act* gave the province the right to change these laws like any other laws of Saskatchewan.

Bayda then turned to the second important question: What did using French in the courtroom entail? Did all the proceedings have to be in French? Or was the right more limited: that individuals could use French themselves but the proceedings would not necessarily be in French? In a complex analysis, Bayda canvassed the possible forms the right could take but thought the best interpretation was that it allowed for the use of French or English but did not compel participants to use one or the other. Bayda used the Territories' Legislative Assembly as an analogy. Members used either language in debates and speeches, but there was no translation of speeches, and members did not have to answer French with French or English with English. This was true of Parliament, and the Manitoba Court of Appeal had concluded the same for Manitoba. In Bayda's opinion, this was conclusive that the right did not mean all the proceedings had to be in French. Bayda then finished by quickly concluding that there was no longer a surviving duty to provide laws in both languages. In section 110, this was framed in terms of ordinances of the Northwest Territories. This made it a special rather than general law, and it had been extinguished.

Mercure's limited success meant further appeal was certain. Père Mercure died in 1986, but intervening francophone groups carried the appeal to the Supreme Court of Canada. The majority decision of Justice Gérard La Forest agreed with Bayda's conclusion on the use of French in the courtroom. But he decided differently about the duty to provide bilingual statutes. La Forest thought that section 14 of *The Saskatchewan Act*, which replaced the Territories' Legislative Assembly with the provincial assembly, had carried forward the laws for the constitution of the earlier assembly and applied them to the new assembly, including language. As in Manitoba, the entire body of provincial statute laws and regulations were void. But La Forest also gave Saskatchewan an out. *The Saskatchewan Act* expressly allowed the legislature to alter or eliminate previous territorial statutes. Unlike Manitoba, the language requirements were not constitutionally entrenched. The province could pass a law rescinding the French requirement and make it retroactive.

The Devine government eagerly seized the lifeline despite receiving heavy criticism, citing the cost of translating the provincial statutes. Ironically, Grant Devine was a strong supporter of the Meech Lake Accord and was favourably disposed towards official bilingualism, even claiming he wanted one day to see Saskatchewan bilingual.[92] Saskatchewan's *Language Act* removed the requirement for bilingual statutes—although the government could provide some statutes in French if it wanted—but maintained the right to use French in courtroom proceedings and mandated translating the rules of court. And although the Court of Appeal was not under any obligation to provide hearings entirely in French, the judges embraced French language training and several, including Georgina Jackson and Vancise, became sufficiently bilingual to hold hearings. The court has on several occasions held hearings in French, including a follow-up appeal to *Mercure*, when a "fransaskois" challenged the province's new language law on the basis of a speeding ticket.[93]

Could the *Charter* have made a difference in *Mercure*? The answer seemed to be no. The *Charter*'s language provisions only entrenched bilingualism federally and in New Brunswick. Howard McConnell, a Saskatchewan law professor, argued that Canada's broader constitutional tradition provided a basis for making bilingualism constitutional and criticized the Supreme Court for deciding *Mercure* on narrow statutory interpretation.[94] McConnell thought that "broad historical understandings" and "questions of bedrock principle" could be invoked to argue that

French had a constitutionally protected status in Saskatchewan. *Charter* protections were part of this mix, supporting the historical compromise on the French language. Whether even a bold Supreme Court would have approached the problem this way seems unlikely. Interestingly, Cameron in his concurrence raised the possibility that section 15 of the *Charter* might be relevant, but no one has pursued this avenue to date.

BOROWSKI V ATTORNEY GENERAL OF CANADA

OF ALL THE significant early *Charter* cases of the court, *Borowski* was one of the few times the court took a narrower and more restrictive approach. The subject matter of the appeal had something to do with that: *Borowski* involved abortion and the rights of the unborn. There is likely no single political issue more divisive than abortion. Opponents, calling themselves pro-life, see it as murder. Proponents, also called pro-choice, view access to abortion as necessary to allow women full autonomy and control over their bodies, and an imperfect but necessary option for unwanted pregnancies. Abortions are generally available throughout Canada, but the procedure exists in a legal vacuum. As of 2017, Canada does not have a law governing abortion, just regulations for access that vary from province to province. Most politicians want nothing to do with the "third rail" in Canadian political life.

Abortions have been illegal to some degree in common law nations for centuries and became a serious crime in the nineteenth century. Under the 1892 *Criminal Code*, performing or procuring an abortion was an offence with a potential life sentence, and it remained so until 1968. Following a liberalizing trend in much of the developed world, the Trudeau government introduced subsections 4 to 6 of section 250 of the *Code* as part of the *Criminal Code Amendment Act*. The new subsections allowed an abortion if a board of three doctors deemed it necessary for the physical or mental well-being of the mother and a medical practitioner performed the procedure in a hospital. The amendment was known as the therapeutic abortion provision.

The provision was controversial and garnered immediate opposition. Joseph Borowski was one such opponent and a singular character. Originally from Saskatchewan, Borowski was a miner in Thompson, Manitoba, when he went into politics in 1969 as a candidate for the provincial NDP. He was in Ed Shreyer's cabinet as minister of transportation and public works but soon split from the NDP. A social conservative, Borowski was incensed with the 1968 therapeutic provision and made abortion his crusade. He demonstrated, wrote letters, accosted politicians, and went to jail after refusing to pay his taxes because the money indirectly paid for abortions. Next was an eighty-day hunger strike. Borowski then turned to the courts.

In 1978, Borowski brought an action in the Saskatchewan Court of Queen's Bench to have the therapeutic provision declared invalid for violating the right of the unborn to life, liberty, and security of the person, section 1(1) under the *Canadian Bill of Rights*.[95] Borowski argued that a fetus was an "individual" and had the protection of the *Bill*. The Crown questioned both Borowski's standing to bring his application, as he had no direct interest in the abortion law, and the jurisdiction of the Queen's Bench, arguing the application should be adjudicated in Federal Court. The Court of Appeal held in Borowski's favour. The Crown appealed to the Supreme Court, where Borowski had the dubious distinction of being ejected from the hearing after berating the court regarding abortion. The majority held that Borowski as a concerned citizen did have an interest and could bring his action, a ruling that considerably widened standing in constitutional cases. Within a few years he was back in Ottawa.

To get there, Borowski returned to the courts in Saskatchewan. He could now turn to the *Charter*. He attacked section 250 of the *Criminal Code* as a violation of section 7 of the *Charter*—which guaranteed that "everyone has the right to life, liberty, and security of the person and the right not to be deprived thereof except in accordance with the principles of fundamental justice"—and as a violation of section 15(1), the right to equality before the law. Borowski argued that a fetus was included in the definition of "everyone" as used in the *Charter*. The real issue in Borowski's litigation was whether and when a fetus was a legal person. If, as Borowski maintained, life began at conception and the fetus had the status of a person from this point onward, then it followed that the therapeutic exemption sections of the *Code* violated the section 7 in the most fundamental way.

Justice W.R. Matheson of the Court of Queen's Bench heard Borowski's application, which included extensive expert testimony on fetal medicine, abortion procedures, and the application of the therapeutic exemptions as well as case law regarding the legal status and rights of the fetus.[96] The Crown called no expert testimony, arguing that the medical evidence was irrelevant to determining the issues. Section 15 of the *Charter*

THOMAS CLARKSON WAKELING

His colleagues on the court called Tom Wakeling a true gentleman. He was born in Saskatoon on May 19, 1924, to a legal family.[10] His father, Bertram Wakeling, was a long-serving provincial magistrate in Saskatoon who as a young man had emigrated from England in 1905. Bertram Wakeling worked as a farm labourer and office clerk before taking up law. Tom Wakeling graduated from Nutana Collegiate Institute in 1942 and immediately enlisted in the air force. He was discharged in 1945 with the rank of flying officer after serving as an elementary flight instructor. Wakeling joined the wave of veterans that swamped the university in Saskatoon and entered the combined arts and law program, graduating from law in 1949. He had articles with V.U. Miner, QC, the mayor of Lloydminster, and remained with Miner for his first years of practice.

Justice Thomas Clarkson Wakeling, c. 1986. (Provincial Archives of Saskatchewan, 86-0097-05)

In 1957, Wakeling relocated to Regina and joined MacPherson, Leslie and Tyerman. Six years later, he became a partner in McDougall, Ready and Wakeling. Made a QC in 1971, Wakeling served the profession as provincial president of the Canadian Bar Association from 1970 to 1972, a bencher of the Law Society from 1973 to 1978, and president of the Law Society from 1978 to 1979. Wakeling was also the chair of the Saskatchewan Police Commission from 1975 to 1984. A community-minded man, Wakeling was the president of the provincial Red Cross, the Regina YMCA, the Regina Kiwanis Club, and lieutenant-governor for the Kiwanis International western division. An avid runner and golfer, he was also president of the Wascana Country Club.

Wakeling was appointed with Marjorie Gerwing on December 13, 1984. A small *c* conservative in outlook, Wakeling had not been especially involved in politics. On the bench, he was known for his courtesy and as a common-sense judge, a frequent dissenter whose written decisions were readily understood by the layperson as well as the lawyer. After retiring in 1999, Wakeling sat on several arbitrations, including a wage settlement for the Regina Police Service. He died in Regina on November 19, 2005. His son Thomas W. Wakeling, practised law in Alberta and was appointed to the Alberta Court of Queen's Bench and subsequently the Alberta Court of Appeal, making it three generations of Wakeling on the bench.

was not yet in effect and was not considered. In a careful, well-researched judgment, Matheson concluded that in Canada the fetus had no legal existence or rights, and section 7 of the *Charter* did not give any protection to the unborn.

Justice Marjorie Gerwing, writing for the Court of Appeal, agreed with Matheson in an incisive judgment adopting much of his reasoning. Gerwing took a narrow approach in her analysis that focused on the historical status of the fetus in law, following Chief Justice Dickson's observation in *Big M Drug Mart* that history and tradition should be considered to understand the scope of a right. Gerwing examined the availability of abortion in the "Anglo-Canadian" common law tradition, whether there were fetal rights in other areas of common law, and also how abortion and the legal status of the fetus were viewed in other traditions. Until the nineteenth century, in common law, abortion had been viewed as a crime only after "quickening," the point at which there was fetal movement, around fourteen weeks. Abortion after this point was only a misdemeanor, not a felony. In 1803, abortion became a capital crime, and by 1929 only the preservation of a mother's life justified an abortion. American law mirrored English law. The first US abortion statute passed in 1821 and state laws became increasingly restrictive. From the historical background, Gerwing concluded that early-term abortion had been accepted in common law and was only restricted or prohibited by statute in the nineteenth and twentieth centuries.

Next, Gerwing examined the case law regarding fetal rights. It was limited, but Borowski had advanced cases in tort, property, and family law. In tort, there were cases where infants had successfully sued for damages incurred when they were still unborn. But Gerwing did not see how these helped Borowski's position, as in every case the child was born alive. This was also true in cases involving the inheritance of property, where rights to title were deemed to have vested in an infant while still in gestation, but again in every case the child had been birthed alive, and the same was true with maintenance and custody cases. She concluded that the apparent fetal rights were a legal fiction, applied retroactively when a living issue brought action as an adult or through a custodial adult. It fell far short, in her view, of proving any legal rights of the unborn.

Gerwing could also not find any recognition of fetal rights in European law, with one exception. The European Economic Community Court had considered an appeal from the United Kingdom that dealt with the same point that Borowski argued: that a fetus was included in the term "everyone" in the European Convention on Human Rights. That court concluded that in a first-trimester termination it was not. The only jurisdiction which did recognize a fetal right to life was Germany. The German courts had concluded such rights were implied because the drafters of the nation's constitution had discussed the concept although not explicitly including it. Gerwing did not find this example, acknowledged but not followed by the European court, to be sufficiently persuasive that such a right should be attributed to the *Charter*.

Gerwing also looked at *Bill of Rights* decisions dealing with the fetus, such as the 1976 *Morgentaler* decision, as usefully illustrative. An unreported Ontario decision, *Dehler*, dealt with the same contention Borowski put forward, and had rejected the argument but without reasons. Gerwing turned then to the interpretation of the *Charter*. She agreed with the trial judge's use of traditional interpretative techniques as an acceptable auxiliary to the purposive method, and argued that there was no direct evidence that the framers of the *Charter* had any intention to create rights for the unborn. As she wrote,

> An interpretation of the *Charter* which gave independent rights to a foetus would be a major departure from tradition. This is not of course to suggest that such a radical step in recognition of rights could not have been taken. However, since it is so novel, it

would suggest that clear and unambiguous wording should have been used to enshrine such rights.[97]

Gerwing had used a conservative, even crabbed, interpretation of the *Charter*. The trial judgment, which she had largely adopted, was criticized for having "in one fell swoop totally emasculated the *Canadian Charter of Rights and Freedom*."[98] This was a bit strong, but it was true that Gerwing did not make an expansive interpretation in the reach of the right in question and then search for limitations under section 1, the approach the Supreme Court and her colleagues advocated for the *Charter*. Instead, by creating a limit on the right rooted in history, past law, and traditional interpretative techniques, Gerwing's analysis was more akin to that used in *Bill of Rights* jurisprudence. But given the subject matter, a narrow interpretation may have been the best route, as extending the right to life to the unborn with the implications for the legality of abortion was something she likely thought had to be dealt with in the political realm instead of the courts. And ironically, by not being bold and expansive, Gerwing reinforced the ability of women to choose an abortion, a fundamental tenet for feminists and other progressives.

Gerwing was also arguably braver than the Supreme Court of Canada. She had at least decided that a fetus could not be considered a person in the sense of "everyone" in the *Charter* and "individual" in the *Bill of Rights*. The Supreme Court seemed determined to avoid the issue, and so it was with *Borowski*.

There was a parallel chain of litigation concerning abortion and another abortion crusader, Henry Morgentaler. Morgentaler also tried several times to get the same sections of the *Criminal Code* declared void, but as an unjustified restriction on abortion and the right of women to have the procedure. His challenge under the *Charter* reached the Supreme Court before *Borowski*. The court, in a landmark ruling, held that the therapeutic abortion provisions violated the rights of women under section 7 of the *Charter*. With the impugned sections of the *Criminal Code* declared void, the court subsequently held *Borowski* "moot," meaning the appeal was now irrelevant.[99] In another abortion case, *Daigle v Tremblay*, despite having the issue of the rights of the unborn in front of the court, the judges decided the appeal without addressing the point. In 1991, the Supreme Court finally concluded in *R v Sullivan* that the fetus had no legal rights until born alive—vindicating the Court of Appeal decision in *Borowski*.

Leaving abortion to Parliament also did not work out well. The Mulroney government tried to introduce a new abortion law, which looked a lot like the one struck down in *Morgentaler* but with changes to get past *Charter* scrutiny. Narrowly passed on a free vote in the Commons, Bill C-43 died in the Senate. The Conservatives had no appetite to try again. And thus abortion continues to exist in a legal limbo, not truly secure in law but also seemingly beyond the reach of opponents. It is a peculiarly Canadian compromise.

REFERENCE RE: ELECTORAL BOUNDARIES

THE RIGHT TO vote is fundamental to democracy and was included in the *Charter* as section 3, one of the so-called democratic rights. The right is so basic that it seems an unlikely subject for a major *Charter* challenge, but the historical realities of voting in Canada meant exactly the opposite. In a reference decision on Saskatchewan's electoral law, the Court of Appeal gave a powerful definition of the right that seemed unassailable—until it was reversed. Within the judgments of the Court of Appeal and the Supreme Court of Canada were two different conceptions of equality, even if not directly articulated, that would strongly influence *Charter* litigation for discrimination and equality issues.

Canadians generally assume that their vote has the same weight as the next person's, but historically this was not true in representative democracies like Canada, the United States, and Britain with "first past the post" electoral systems based on ridings or constituencies. The population of electoral districts varied wildly. Sometimes, the variation was intentional; its purpose was to skew elections. England had the "rotten boroughs" with very small populations easily swayed or bribed. In the United States, the term *gerrymander* was coined to describe altering constituency boundaries to create favourable electoral outcomes, which usually meant varying population to create unrepresentative results. Some state legislatures were controlled for decades by rural members elected in sparsely populated districts while burgeoning cities were massively under-represented. In the 1960s, the US Supreme Court mandated that congressional districts had to have mathematically equal populations, and other court challenges considerably reduced variation in state districts.[100]

In Canada, both federally and provincially, other factors competed with the ideal of one person, one vote, such as achieving adequate regional representation, geographical barriers and the scale of the country, and ensuring different communities had representation. Federally, representation by population was balanced with regional representation, and later with guarantees that no province would lose seats in a redistribution. Even at the time of the reference, the size of federal ridings within a province generally varied only within a small range, but between provinces the disparity in population could be great.[101] Still, in 1964 the first federal electoral boundary commission was established to reduce the very large disparities that had developed, and a subsequent law established a 25 percent rule with greater variations allowed in exceptional cases. By the 1970s, most provinces had followed suit, establishing commissions and often following the 25 percent rule, with some putting in stricter limits.

Saskatchewan had its own peculiarities. The NDP established the province's first independent boundary commission in 1971 in response to what the party claimed had been Liberal gerrymandering before the election.[102] (The Liberals claimed they were undoing previous CCF gerrymandering.)[103] The commission was permitted to allow a variation in population of up to 15 percent between constituencies with the exception of the two constituencies covering the far north of the province, which had a very sparse population. The constituency boundaries were redrawn to the commission's recommendations. In 1987, the Devine government passed *The Electoral Boundaries Commission Act* in preparation for once again updating boundaries. The new statute mandated a division of twenty-nine urban, thirty-five rural, and two northern constituencies, with the urban district boundaries consistent with municipal boundaries.[104] The number of constituencies for each major urban centre was also fixed. The maximum variance of population was set at 25 percent, with the two northern constituencies allowed much greater range due to their geographic size. The government appointed Ted Culliton to head the commission, and a new electoral map was produced in 1989.

Critics cried foul. Devine and the Conservatives had nearly swept the rural seats in the 1986 election, while NDP support was concentrated in the cities. Although the advantage to rural voters under the new map was not large—the countryside had 50 percent of the population and 53 percent of the seats, and urban areas 47 percent of the population and 43 percent of the seats, the two northern ridings making the difference—the

NICHOLAS W. SHERSTOBITOFF

Nick Sherstobitoff was that rarest of advocates to join the Court of Appeal: one thought to have strong NDP leanings. He was also the first Doukhobor to sit on the court. One of Sherstobitoff's early mentors and law partners, Peter Makaroff, possibly the world's first Doukhobor lawyer and heavily involved in the CCF, would have been pleased on both counts.

Justice Nicholas W. Sherstobitoff, c. 1986. (Provincial Archives of Saskatchewan, 86-0133-05)

Sherstobitoff was born in 1935 in the vicinity of Langham, about thirty-five kilometres northwest of Saskatoon. He grew up in Saskatoon, attending elementary and high school there. Like nearly every lawyer in his generation, Sherstobitoff did the five-year arts and law program offered at the University of Saskatchewan, receiving his bachelor of arts degree in 1956 and law degree in 1958, the gold medallist for his year.

Sherstobitoff articled at the firm of Makaroff, Carter and Carter, which had been originally founded by former law school dean Arthur Moxon and James Wilfred Estey, the second Saskatchewan appointment to the Supreme Court of Canada. The two Carters, Roger and Mary, were husband and wife. Roger Carter left the firm for academia in 1964, becoming dean of law at the University of Saskatchewan and establishing the school's Native law program, while Mary Carter was appointed to the provincial magistrate's court in 1960 and later served on the Court of Queen's Bench. Sherstobitoff joined the bar in 1960 and continued with the firm. He was primarily a litigator, although, as he recounted, specialization was still uncommon until near the end of his practice years and he also did solicitor work.[11] The firm had a substantial union clientele, and Sherstobitoff was frequently at the Labour Relations Board. He also handled what may have been the earliest cases of discrimination on the basis of sexual orientation in the province. In 1977, Sherstobitoff was named chair of the Labour Relations Board and served until 1982, when the incoming Devine government asked for his resignation. In addition, he chaired numerous consensual labour arbitration boards. He also served as chair of the Saskatchewan Safety Council.

Sherstobitoff was not politically active, but his background of acting for unions was unusual for a Court of Appeal appointment and welcomed as adding a new dimension to the court. One of his frequent opponents in court, Donald MacPherson, opined that the appointment was likely meant to showcase the Mulroney Conservatives' lack of partisanship.[12] Sherstobitoff replaced Roy Hall, who took supernumerary status. He was on the court for twenty-five years, retiring on September 28, 2010, after several years as a supernumerary.

government was accused of gerrymander.[105] Several groups protested, most prominently the Society for the Advancement of Voter Equality (SAVE), consisting largely of lawyers and university professors, including Howard McConnell of the law school. SAVE instituted an action in the Court of Queen's Bench challenging *The Electoral Boundaries Commission Act* and *The Representation Act*, which made the commission's recommendations law. With an election approaching, the government tested the validity of the laws with a reference to the Court of Appeal

A panel of five—Cameron, Tallis, Vancise, Gerwing, and Sherstobitoff—heard the reference. The opinion was written *per curiam*, with one voice, to give it the authority of a unanimous court. With the agreement of the attorney general, the court had appointed Roger Carter, QC, counsel for SAVE, to present the case against the statutes, with two other parties intervening. The reference asked two questions. The first was whether the variance in population between constituencies infringed the *Charter* and whether this was justified under section 1. The second was whether the mandated distribution of ridings as rural, urban, and northern violated the *Charter* and whether this was justified under section 1. The fundamental issue was whether section 3 of the *Charter* required an equal weighting of individual votes as a necessary part of the right to vote.

Section 3 of the *Charter* is brief. One of three sections dealing with democratic rights, it reads, "Every citizen of Canada has the right to vote in an election of members of the House of Commons or of a legislative assembly and to be qualified for membership therein."[106] Nothing was said about the relative population of constituencies. The court had to flesh out the definition of the right to vote. Examining the history of the franchise, the panel came to the obvious conclusion that the right had evolved over time and incrementally in England and Canada, noting that Aboriginals only gained the vote in 1960. Until the *Charter*, the right was also at the pleasure of the legislature. From this, the court concluded that it was vital that citizens have recourse to remedies to protect the right to vote and that a purposive and generous interpretation of the right had to avoid historical limits and definitions.

> This recognition of changing societal mores is especially significant when examining the historical political tradition of our society. The suppression of fundamental democratic values in earlier times ought not to lead us to a restricted view of the democratic rights enshrined in the *Charter*. Indeed, the practical political experience of the past is of limited value in passing upon the nature of such a basic democratic right as the right to vote . . . the *Charter* is not neutral. It does not seek to continue past abuses. On the contrary it vigorously champions and guarantees the rights and freedoms enshrined in it.[107]

In the view of the court, equality and democracy were "inextricably linked."[108] The ideal of equality was the fundamental underpinning of "one person, one vote," and the court concluded that equality should be the guiding principle for electoral distribution. The corollary was that a dilution of this equality undermined the right and could even render it meaningless, as had been seen in historical examples in the United States and United Kingdom. At the same time, the court acknowledged that strict equality, in the sense of mathematical equivalency between constituencies, was not practical; voters moved, populations grew, the day of election was not fixed. But the principle that gave, in the court's view, the proper expression of the right was clear: "While some deviation from the concept of equal representation is inherent, any such deviation must interfere as little as possible with the controlling principle of 'one person, one vote.'"[109] The starting point for any distribution should be substantially equal voter population.

The court concluded that the statutes infringed the *Charter*. The main problem was the mandated number of seats by category and urban centre and the strict use of municipal boundaries. In the view of the panel, these were arbitrary requirements that undermined the independence of the commission and in effect built in a variance in riding population that generally meant a higher, sometimes much higher, population in urban ridings and the reverse in rural ridings. The large variance—up to 25 percent—was also viewed as excessive. The panel contrasted the provincial constituency boundaries unfavourably with the work of the federal electoral boundaries commission for Saskatchewan, which had kept the variance between federal ridings to only 5 percent. While declining to state the allowable range, the court made it clear that variations should be very limited without good reason to increase them.

This raised the second question of the reference: Was Saskatchewan's electoral law justified under section 1 of the *Charter* as a "reasonable limit in a free and democratic society"? The court turned to the *Oakes* test, also called the proportionality test. Under the test, it had to be shown first that the impugned legislation or state action had an objective "of real and pressing concern in a free and democratic society." If so, the measures in question then had to fulfill three criteria of proportionality: they were rationally connected to the objective and achieved the objective; the right in question was impaired as little as possible; and the effects of the measure were proportional to the objective.

The main argument advanced on the part of the attorney general was that rural ridings were larger and more difficult to represent effectively. This was due to the distances between communities, which made it hard for a representative to meet constituents and required more time for travel. Overly large constituencies might also encompass a number of different and distinct communities with different needs, and it might be more difficult to represent them all. The court rejected this argument without compelling evidence. Noting that while this might have been true historically, the panel countered that modern transportation and communications infrastructure had greatly reduced the burden of travel. The panel also questioned whether the interests of rural and urban dwellers were so mutually exclusive as to require separate ridings, and suggested that the interests and needs of people were broad enough that distinct communities needing special consideration were hard to discern. The exception was the two northern constituencies. The court accepted that these areas did have special needs. But in sum, the court concluded that the impugned legislation did not meet the requirements of section 1 and the *Oakes* test.

The reference contributed to the Saskatchewan Court of Appeal's reputation as an activist court. There was little legislative deference in the decision. The court, taking its cues from the Supreme Court, had first defined the right in question in a broad and generous fashion, taking a philosophical rather than a historical view. The limitations that might apply to the right, such as a variable weighting of a vote, were then analyzed under section 1 and rejected.

Ironically, at the Supreme Court the majority decision of Justice Beverley McLachlin (as she then was) was criticized for not following the two-part *Charter* analysis and instead limiting the right while defining it, confusing the analysis of infringement and justification.[110] McLachlin, as chief justice of British Columbia's trial court, had previously written a decision striking down BC's electoral boundaries law, and the Saskatchewan decision had quoted her with approval. In that earlier judgment, McLachlin had made relative equality in voting weight the starting point but not in the strong terms of her Prairie colleagues.

McLachlin focused on "effective representation." Locating the right to vote in the Canadian tradition of balancing regional representation, community interests, geographical realities, and minority interests with the ideal of equality, she argued that what mattered was whether a voter's interests were effectively advanced. McLachlin claimed that mathematical equality could reduce effective representation by diminishing the role of other factors. The Saskatchewan decision was a classic example of formal equality while McLachlin's decision hinted at the more difficult concept of substantive equality. Arguments invoking substantive equality were commonly advanced in cases involving discrimination and the section 15 guarantee of equality. One critic was surprised that section 15 did not play a part in the boundaries litigation.[111] In analyzing the idea of "community of interest," McLachlin spoke of minority interests in a way that implied it might be necessary to consider the effective representation for different identifiable groups within society, particularly the marginalized or historically disadvantaged. Some commentators found the concept of "community of interests" to be vague and of dubious value.[112] The Court of Appeal's approach was praised as being principled, with the additional benefit of being straightforward and practical.[113]

CONCLUSION

THE *CHARTER* OF *Rights and Freedoms* changed Canada. It certainly changed the Canadian judiciary and thrust the courts into a much more prominent role in the nation's political life. The first years of the *Charter* were exciting ones, with the courts giving life and meaning to a grand endeavour. Saskatchewan's Court of Appeal garnered a reputation for boldness and was even out in front of the Supreme Court of Canada. The honeymoon wouldn't last. The *Charter* challenges grew more difficult; some decisions jumped ahead of political and public opinion; and strident criticism of "activist" judges began to take a toll, even while other critics castigated the judiciary for being too timid. The growing body of *Charter* decisions also established precedents that more and more constrained subsequent law. But there is no doubt that the first decade under the *Charter* were exciting and demanding times for the judges in Saskatchewan.

Saskatchewan's courts would continue to make important decisions on the *Charter*. But another controversy was brewing. This one was a clash over the proper extent of appellate review, which would pit the Court of Appeal against the Supreme Court of Canada. An unequal struggle, but one that the Court of Appeal fought tenaciously.

CHAPTER 9

THE STANDARDS OF REVIEW

The passage was not what one might expect in a judgment of the Court of Appeal for Saskatchewan. It is perhaps overly dramatic to say it was a statement of defiance towards the highest court of the land, but the judgment was guaranteed to raise controversy.

> There is a sense among members of the Bar of the Province that the role of the Court is on the wane, that the Court will not or cannot address appeals as robustly as it once did. The concern, which seems to have been mounting over the last several years, stems from what are nowadays referred to in increasingly comprehensive terms as the "standards of appellate review," a continually evolving set of uniform, national standards governing the determination of issues of fact and questions of law raised before the Court on appeal. It behoves us to recognize this concern and to address it.[1]

So wrote Justice Stuart Cameron in *Valley Beef Producers Co-operative Ltd. v Farm Credit Corp.*, a response to the Supreme Court of Canada judgment overturning the Court of Appeal in another appeal, *Housen v Nikolaisen*. Cameron believed that the Supreme Court had steadily eroded the powers of the provincial courts of appeal through dictates mandating excessive appellate restraint. In his view, the ability of the court to do justice was at stake.

Valley Beef was not the end. Cameron challenged the Supreme Court in another appeal, *H.L. v Canada*, which went to Ottawa for a final determination on the issues he raised. Cameron was not alone in his concern. Other judges, on other courts, expressed their dismay with the Supreme Court's dictates on the standards of review, but none in so public a forum. Academics wrote papers. The bar perhaps muttered post-hearing about neutered judges. The controversy did not attract public attention, and even for many in the legal profession it was a somewhat esoteric crusade. But the questions raised in a trio of Saskatchewan decisions—*Housen*, *Valley Beef*, and *H.L.*—went to the heart of the role of an intermediate appellate court.

SASKATCHEWAN AT THE END OF THE CENTURY

IN THE LAST decade of the twentieth century, Saskatchewan politics swung back to the left. Grant Devine's Progressive Conservative Party imploded in a dramatic fashion. First, there was a drubbing at the polls in 1991. Roy Romanow, now leader of the NDP, became premier in a landslide victory: fifty-five seats and more than half the popular vote.[2] The Conservatives were reduced to ten seats. A revived Liberal Party won more of the popular vote than the PCs did—25 percent compared to 18—but only one seat. A year later, a number of Conservative MLAs were facing jail. A party slush fund created with fictitious charges to legislators' communication allowances had come to light. Eleven former cabinet ministers were convicted of fraud.[3] The party would still go on to win five seats in the next election, but the end was nigh.

The new premier had grown up embedded in Saskatoon's sizeable Ukrainian community. Romanow barely spoke English when he started school.[4] Involved in CCF politics since university, he successfully ran for the legislature in 1967. He narrowly lost the 1968 leadership race to Allan Blakeney and then became Blakeney's right hand, serving as deputy premier, government house leader, and attorney general. Romanow was prominent on the national stage and an author of the famous "Kitchen Accord," which broke the federal–provincial impasse on the adoption of a new constitution. In the 1982 election, Romanow suffered a humiliating personal defeat when he lost his seat to a university student and part-time gas bar attendant by a razor-thin margin. After a brief time out of politics, he returned to the legislature in 1986. The obvious choice for the leadership after Blakeney resigned, Romanow capitalized on the unpopularity of privatization. The election had been his to lose.

Victory was something of poisoned chalice. The new government discovered that the province's financial situation was worse than Devine had let on. Bringing the deficit under control was Romanow's first priority. The premier and his tough finance minister, Janice MacKinnon, slashed spending. Romanow ended direct public investment in the economy, whether Crown corporations or subsidies and loans. NDP policy instead encouraged small business as an employment driver. To many Saskatchewan voters, it must have seemed like the Conservatives were still in power, and the premier's approach did not sit well with many in his caucus, who whispered that their leader was a strange sort of socialist. Early in his first term, Romanow threatened to call a new election to suppress opposition in his party to the austerity program.[5] Romanow's government, in its search for savings, undertook reforms with public health care and the provision of welfare. Critics muttered about "workfare" and bemoaned cutbacks in health services. The government defended the changes as innovative, stressing prevention over acute care and making the transition from social benefit payments to remunerative work easier.

The premier could also argue that he was returning to the old traditions of the CCF, establishing fiscal stability before tackling an ambitious social agenda. His strategy with the economy seemed to work, though good timing with the business cycle played a hand. By the mid-1990s, the province came out of recession and unemployment dropped rapidly. Within three years, the budget was balanced and the NDP started paying down the accumulated debt.

Romanow also tackled Aboriginal relations. By 1991, Indians and Métis made up over 8 percent of the province's population, and the number increased steadily with each census, with many now living in the cities.[6] There were two Aboriginal MLAs in the NDP caucus, representing the northern ridings. Romanow realized that the assimilationist policies of previous governments had to be abandoned. Despite the province's dire fiscal situation, Romanow honoured a major provincial commitment to fund the Treaty Land Entitlement, an initiative to allow bands to purchase promised treaty territory. With strong misgivings, Romanow also agreed to allow casino development by First Nations—with the province taking its cut.

There was also, in the wake of the *Charter*, a major reappraisal of Aboriginals in the justice system, especially sentencing. Saskatchewan pursued more culturally sensitive treatment of Aboriginal offenders, such as embracing sentencing circles. But to some extent, this was forced on the province. Horrific revelations surfaced regarding the Saskatoon Police Service's long practice of abandoning intoxicated Natives on the city outskirts, resulting in at least one death and eventually the convictions of two police officers. Aboriginal communities, especially on the remote reserves, still suffered from high unemployment, poverty, and lack of adequate services and opportunities. Saskatchewan seemed trapped in a legacy of a colonial past of racism and neglect. For every step forward for the Indians and Métis of the province, there seemed to be another step back.

Romanow had effectively sold deficit-fighting to the public, but there was still a political cost. The 1995 election saw the NDP returned with a still comfortable majority, but it was against a disorganized opposition. The Liberals, back from the grave under the charismatic Lynda Haverstock—Saskatchewan's first female party leader—won a respectable 35 percent of the vote and eleven seats but then succumbed to infighting. By the time of the 1999 election, a new player had emerged: the Saskatchewan Party, formed by right-leaning liberals and disenchanted conservatives and led by a former Reform Party MP, Elwin Hermanson. Fighting an uphill battle for a third term, Romanow barely scraped by with a victory and was forced to form a coalition government with the remnants of the Liberals.

The 1999 election and resulting minority NDP government led to a reordering of the political landscape. Left-leaning Liberals were pulled into the NDP orbit while many others joined the Saskatchewan Party. As one historian shrewdly observed, the rise of the new party also pushed the old Saskatchewan dichotomy of socialism versus free enterprise out of the spotlight and consolidated the rural–urban divide that had developed under Devine.[7] Rural NDP members in the legislature became a rarity. The divide was exacerbated with Romanow's deficit-cutting. Some of the cuts, such as hospital closures, fell heavily on rural areas. Continued rural depopulation made it impractical to maintain services to the same degree. Romanow even floated a plan to let some paved roads revert to gravel.[8] The family farm struggled on, often sustained with other employment, but rural communities continued to erode. The NDP had not much to offer farmers to deal with drought, price swings, and federal indifference.

After ten years as premier, Romanow stepped down in 2001. The NDP carried on under a new leader, Lorne Calvert. Even with the economy picking up steam, the NDP barely won a competitive election against the Saskatchewan Party in 2003. The latter got a new leader within a year, Brad Wall, who immediately moderated many Saskatchewan Party positions to undermine the NDP's characterization of the party as rebranded Tories. The new party was firmly established as the centre-right alternative to the centre-left NDP.

The new century had dawned optimistically for Saskatchewan, its fiscal house in order, with a more diversified economy and rising oil and gas prices about to ignite a decade-long boom. The 1990s had been a difficult decade, but the province entered the new century with renewed optimism. The decade had also had its challenges for the Court of Appeal. The court grappled with a difference of views on sentencing and with even more fundamental questions about its role in Canada's judicial hierarchy.

THE COURT EXPANDS

GARY LANE DID not suffer the ignominious fate of some of his cabinet colleagues in the Devine government. With the shrewdness that had made the attorney general a very successful politician, Lane left government two months before the 1991 election. Five days later, he was appointed to the Court of Appeal along with Regina lawyer Georgina Jackson, the court's second female judge.

The Lane and Jackson appointments were the first made to the court under the new vetting system put in place in 1988. *Charter* litigation had given fresh impetus to calls for reform. Judges making decisions with obvious social policy implications had many people questioning the appointment process.[9] Brian Mulroney had famously capitalized on public anger over patronage in the 1984 federal election but then followed up with judicial appointments. As a first step, Mulroney's first justice minister, John Crosbie, agreed to consult with the provincial attorneys general and said that more reforms would follow.

The Canadian Bar Association seized the moment with a comprehensive study of the judicial appointment process and presented a proposal to the government to set up independent selection committees in each province, composed of representatives of the profession, the judiciary, the

JOHN GARY LANE

Gary Lane was the last of a series of able politicians to become a judge of the court. Born in Saskatoon on May 2, 1942, Lane attended St. Paul's High School. He enrolled at the University of Saskatchewan, earning a bachelor's degree in history before entering law school in 1963. After graduating in 1966, he articled at the firm of Cuelenaere Beaubier in Saskatoon. Lane then joined the Department of the Attorney General as a Crown solicitor. From 1969 to 1971, he served as executive assistant to Darrel Heald, the attorney general under Ross Thatcher.

Justice John Gary Lane, c. 1992. (Court of Appeal/Photographic Service Agency)

Lane decided to try politics and was elected as a Liberal in Heald's former constituency of Lumsden (later Qu'Appelle-Lumsden) in 1971. He also entered private practice, first with Nicol, Keith, MacLean and Keith and then founding Gary Lane Law Offices in Regina in 1976. Lane was touted as a potential successor to Liberal Party leader David Steuart.[1] Astutely reading the political winds, he instead crossed the floor to join the Progressive Conservatives, which earned him lasting enmity in Liberal Party circles. Unlike many floor-crossers, Lane retained his seat in the next election and then joined the first Devine cabinet as attorney general.

Lane was one of the Progressive Conservative's most effective cabinet ministers and served in multiple portfolios, including provincial secretary, telephones, intergovernmental affairs, and finance, usually holding more than one portfolio at a time and sometimes up to three. The Department of the Attorney General became the expanded Ministry of Justice under Lane's watch. After his main portfolio switched to finance in 1985, Lane spearheaded the government's privatization program and oversaw the sale of the Potash Corporation of Saskatchewan. He switched back to justice in 1989. Among Lane's accomplishments was replacing rural party lines with full phone service, establishing the Saskatchewan Pension Plan, and leading an early push to adopt extensive information technology.

Lane resigned from government on September 5, 1991, and joined the Court of Appeal five days later. He was heavily involved in computerization of the court, particularly the eCourt project with Chief Justice John Klebuc. Lane was a long-standing member of the court technology committee of the Canadian Judicial Council as well as a director of the Canadian Superior Court Judges Association.

Justice Lane became a supernumerary judge in 2011 and retired in 2017. ❧

government, and also the public. The selection committees would also find candidates to recommend for judicial posts as well as vetting the suitability of candidates the justice minister submitted for consideration. Much more radically, the committees would create shortlists from which the minister would pick appointments.

Saskatchewan's Ray Hnatyshyn, minister of justice from 1986 to 1988, adopted a much-watered-down version of the Bar Association proposal. Candidates for the bench now submitted a formal application. The government established a five-person selection committee in each province and territory, with a representative of the law society, the local chapter of the Bar Association, the chief justice or his nominee, and provincial and federal government representatives. The committees were restricted to vetting names given to them by the judicial affairs commissioner, who took over from the special judicial assistants the Liberals had favoured. The committee could only rate the candidates qualified or unqualified, and the minister had complete discretion over who to appoint and still could appoint an individual not put to the committee. The committee made their recommendations based on the information provided in the candidate application forms and, with no staff to assist them, whatever legwork the members had time to do.

The Mulroney government announced the reforms with great fanfare, but there were skeptics about the amount of real change. A study on

Mulroney appointments concluded that patronage was alive and well.[10] The most disturbing conclusion was that promotions within the courts—from district to superior, from trial to appeal, from *puisne* to chief justice—still showed strong links to political affiliation. Mulroney avoided promoting judges who had been keen Liberals before going to the bench. One advantage of the new system was that it was now easier for a lawyer who was interested in the bench but had no political friends to make it known that they were interested in an appointment. Canada's method was compared, unfavourably, with the United Kingdom, where a well-staffed section of the Lord Chancellor's Department identified suitable candidates and direct political patronage had been expunged.[11]

There were some concrete advances. The Conservatives were proactive in appointing women to the judiciary. In the late 1980s, the pool of women with the requisite ten years of experience at the bar was relatively small; only 11 percent of women practising law in 1986 exceeded the minimal threshold. But almost 19 percent of judicial appointments were women.[12] The appointments were almost uniformly excellent, although often from a less traditional background, such as academia rather than private practice. One study concluded that weak candidates were usually men who relied on their networks to supplement less compelling resumes.[13] When Kim Campbell became justice minister in 1990, the pace of female appointments picked up, with Canada's first female provincial chief justice appointed as well as more trial court chief justices. Saskatchewan was a leader in this regard. The Liberals had made Mary Batten head of the Court of Queen's Bench in 1983, the second woman in the nation to be called chief justice.

The first two appointments to Saskatchewan's Court of Appeal under the new system seemed contrary to the spirit of Hnatyshyn's revamp. After the expansion in 1984, Edward Bayda felt strongly that a larger court was necessary. He started lobbying in 1986 for two more positions. In 1990, with Lane back as minister of justice, the government passed an order-in-council authorizing the expansion. Lane, meanwhile, had decided that he was ready to quit politics after nearly twenty years as an MLA. He decided that the judiciary was more appealing than returning to practice and applied. And he did not hesitate to let it be known through various channels that he was applying.[14]

Lane was duly appointed to fill one of the positions he had created. It was the third time an attorney general of the province had done this, and the fourth time one had gone straight from politics to the Court of

Appeal. Arguably, ten years in cabinet, six of them as attorney general, was relevant experience for the judiciary. Yet sensitivities were changing. One of the issues of judicial independence was the fact that government, which administered the courts and set their budgets, was also the single biggest litigator. Having the Crown's chief law officer move directly onto the courts, possibly rendering judgment on the acts of the government of which he had recently been part, had poor optics. Lane's appointment caused no public controversy, but some of the profession viewed it cynically given his earlier stand over patronage, and the court was not pleased when rumours surfaced that Lane was going to fill one of the new positions. Some judges were still angry over the standoff on appointments, especially as the court took the blame for the subsequent backlog of appeals. Bayda, with the agreement of the majority of the court, went so far as to contact the justice minister to express misgivings over the appointment.[15]

It was also well known that Lane had championed Georgina Jackson's appointment. Jackson had not been on the bar's radar for a judicial appointment. She was quite young at thirty-nine. Her involvement with the Canadian Bar Association had given her some profile with the profession at large, but she had primarily worked in the civil service and did not have extensive courtroom experience. An appointment of another woman was very much overdue. The court's gender balance was worse than the average for appeal courts. In the end, the court gained a good judge praised for her work.[16] Jackson was considered at least twice as a possible appointment to the Supreme Court of Canada. It also set something of a precedent for appointments of candidates who had forged their career within the Ministry of Justice.[17]

Jackson later became involved in judicial education, following in the footsteps of Cameron and Bayda. Training for judges made major strides in the 1990s.[18] The National Judicial Institute was founded in 1985, and, along with the Canadian Institute for the Administration of Justice, it greatly expanded educational programs. The Canadian Judicial Council instituted a study leave program for judges, allowing them to spend a sabbatical at a law school researching and writing. Another program allowed judges to sit on other courts; Jackson and Vancise both did a term on the Quebec Court of Appeal, which reinforced their French language training, another popular program. In 1991, the first Canadian appellate conference was held in Victoria, becoming a semi-annual event. Along with courses and seminars for the nuts and bolts of judging—writing decisions, time management, and so on—judicial education pushed into new frontiers, such as diversity training, in an effort to broaden the perspectives of a still very homogenous judiciary.

Lane and Jackson would be the only new blood on the court for thirteen years. The next appointment was in 2004. As Lane says, "That was a long time to be the junior judge."[19] Two more judges rather changed the court's situation. Saskatchewan now had the best judge-to-population ratio in the country, after decades of having had the worst.[20] Added to a smaller case load than the massive lists of the 1980s, the court was in a much better position.

INTERNAL AFFAIRS

DESPITE THE LIGHTER lists and the judges' overall success in eliminating the backlog, by the 1990s the court was coming under increasing criticism from the bar, and there was considerable speculation among the profession about its internal workings, particularly the relationships between the judges. Some of this was gossip, exaggerated in repetition, but there were more concrete issues, such as continuing problems with reserve judgments and a widening split over sentencing. Some members of the bar, and some judges on the lower courts, were concerned that internal disagreements were affecting the work of the Court of Appeal.

Other appellate courts in Canada have had troubles, sometimes quite public. In British Columbia, the rivalry in the early 1900s between Gordon Hunter and Archer Martin was so vicious that supposedly an appeal court was created to separate the two.[21] Martin took great pleasure in reversing Hunter's trial decisions. Martin then picked a fight with Hunter's successor as chief justice, who later named his dog after Martin.[22] It was not a compliment. In the 1920s, Alberta saw two judges locked in a court battle over who properly had the title of chief justice. In Ontario in the 1930s, judges insulted each other on the bench and were sometimes contrarian out of sheer spite.[23] The chief justice even called a *puisne* judge "insane." And in the 1990s, stories circulated about internal squabbling on the Alberta Court of Appeal. For much of its history, Saskatchewan's court gave gossips little entertainment, but this changed in the 1980s and 1990s.

The situation on Saskatchewan's court is not easy to analyze, and the judiciary generally feels that it is unseemly, even disrespectful, to discuss internal issues publicly. With one exception, the judges of that era do not want to discuss the topic on the record.[24] Off the record, there is considerable difference of opinion as to whether there were problems and the degree to which these mattered. As one judge pointed out, when a group of ambitious, intelligent, and driven individuals work closely together, there are bound to be disagreements. In some views, the interpersonal relationships of the judges of a court are irrelevant as long as the court's function is not impaired. The important question is whether this was the case, especially as appeal courts rely heavily on the sometimes intangible quality of collegiality.

Collegiality is important, even vital, for modern appellate courts. Collegiality—which is not camaraderie or friendship, although both can enhance it—is properly defined as the co-operative and respectful interaction of colleagues in pursuit of their duties. In the black-letter era, it was less important that judges saw eye to eye. Consensus was arguably not considered important to developing jurisprudence; the tradition was for each judge to give their opinion, even when there was substantial agreement. Although judicial independence remained paramount, by the 1980s most Canadian appellate courts strove for greater consensus to avoid ambiguity and uncertainty in jurisprudence. Many courts consciously aimed for one set of reasons and didn't issue concurring judgments unless there was a marked difference of opinion.[25] A high degree of collegiality also meant a more efficient, better functioning court. A landmark study of Canadian appellate courts found that the two qualities judges valued most in their colleagues were productivity and collegiality.[26]

Collegiality in the strict sense remained intact on Saskatchewan's court in the 1990s. The system of random sitting assignments never changed; every judge sat with every other judge, and they continued to work together. There was a high degree of consensus in the court's decisions. Analyses done in 1992 and repeated a decade later found that dissents were found in only about 5 percent of appeals. Separate concurring decisions were even more rare, only 2.5 percent.[27] One commentator on the court's jurisprudence was critical of the lack of dissension, fearing that judges were stifling creativity and not sufficiently exploring alternate reasoning in favour of consensus.[28]

There were some obvious issues, however. The problems with reserves started when the court was short-handed and overwhelmed, but it lasted longer than it might have. The court had taken the somewhat drastic measure of regularly reviewing the status of reserves at meetings as a form of peer pressure. Perhaps inevitably, this sometimes caused hard feelings. The court divided in the 1990s on the important jurisprudential issue of sentencing, and it exposed major philosophical differences among the judges, discussed in detail below. It was fundamentally a principled disagreement, but there were broader consequences. Frustration grew on both sides, and there was a hardening of positions. The court was unable to come to a consensus, prolonging an embarrassing situation and heightening tension between judges. Another issue was the effort to revise the rules of court, which, because of disagreements over specific changes, was drawn out far longer than necessary. Justice Thomas Wakeling, who had worked a great deal on the revision, became very frustrated with the difficulty in reaching consensus.[29] There was also a curious incident over amendments to *The Court of Appeal Act*. It was also true that regular meetings became infrequent by the end of the 1990s.

In the final analysis, it is difficult to assess the exact nature and extent of internal issues that might have arisen on the court. It is clear that some of the relationships between judges were strained at least some of the time. But not surprisingly, the judges from that era are not enthusiastic about discussing the subject. The bottom line was that the court continued to function tolerably well and still produced some excellent jurisprudence.

FIRST AMONG EQUALS

SOMEONE NOT FAMILIAR with appellate courts might ask why the chief justice did not step in to deal with any issues dividing the judges. The reality is that the authority of a chief justice is quite constrained and is almost entirely derived from convention and tradition rather than enshrined in statute.[30] A chief justice's leadership is exercised through a combination of mutual respect, diplomacy, consensus building, and often force of personality and ability. Every judge is absolutely independent and equal in the adjudicative sphere, and the principle of judicial independence informs the larger relationship of chief justices and *puisne* judges. The chief justice can't force a judge to finish a judgment and can only mediate between two judges if they are at loggerheads. As a rule, a chief justice can make few major decisions on administration without consulting the court and having a consensus. Judicial assignments are traditionally the one area where judges acknowledge the chief justice's authority. At the same time, the chief justice is accountable for the proper functioning of the court. It is a tightrope and demands a very united court or a strong but diplomatic individual as the chief justice, or both.

Edward Dmytro Bayda, 2006. (Artist: Zhong-Yang Huang; photo: Mark Greschner. Court of Appeal.)

This was demonstrated with the proposed 1990 amendments to *The Court of Appeal Act*. The original *Act*, proclaimed in 1918, had never been substantively revised. By the 1980s, both the court and the Department of Justice felt that the *Act* should be simplified and modernized, with archaic language removed and the statutory powers and jurisdiction of the court clarified. A revised act was drafted in 1986 but never implemented, likely due to the objections of the bar over some changes.[31] Several years later, the justice ministry, in consultation with Bayda, again put forward amendments to the statute.

Some of those latest amendments were specifically aimed at bolstering the chief justice's role as head of the court and improving administration and efficiency. The general administrative power of the chief justice was defined for the first time as the "general supervision of and direction over the sittings of the court and the assignment of the judicial duties of the court."[32] Several other amendments were proposed in initial drafts but dropped due to their potentially controversial nature. One measure, modelled on examples adopted in Ontario, aimed at giving the chief justice the ability to deal with late judgments.[33] The amendment created a time limit on reserve judgments. The chief justice could extend the deadline and, in the case of a failure to produce a decision, refer the matter to the

Canadian Judicial Council for possible disciplinary action. The bar had lobbied for the measure, but it was dropped.[34] There was also considerable discussion over creating the position of associate chief justice to assist with administration. Bayda thought this was unnecessary for a small court.[35] He did favour an amendment making the chief justice of the Court of Queen's Bench designated head of the court in his absence. By convention the senior *puisne* judge was usually considered the acting chief justice. This idea was also dropped, although a final amendment did give the sitting chief the power to designate who would be acting chief in his absence.

Bayda had not consulted the court about the amendments to the *Act*.[36] The other judges only realized amendments were on the table when the bill came up for passage in the Legislative Assembly. With Bayda away, other members of the court requested a meeting with the attorney general, Gary Lane, and asked that the bill be withdrawn. Nearly all the judges were alarmed at the lack of consultation and wanted to evaluate and discuss the amendments. The new act was shelved. The incident was unprecedented, and it demonstrated both the touchiness around judicial independence and the limits of the authority of a chief justice. It also raised intriguing questions about Chief Justice Bayda's relationship with his colleagues, but for the time being these questions remain unanswered.

ADMINISTRATIVE INNOVATIONS

NO ONE CONTESTS that Bayda was far-sighted and innovative. He had led the change to a hot court. And by the mid-1980s, Bayda had realized that administration was becoming sufficiently complex to require dedicated attention. Like many judges, he loved the law and wanted to minimize the time he spent on operations. Knowing that he was unlikely to persuade the government to hire a court manager to oversee staff and administration, he decided to create such a position on his own.

Bayda hired Marlene Rodie as an administrative assistant in 1986.[37] Her title was later changed to executive assistant to the chief justice. Rodie had been a paralegal at Bayda's old firm and had been highly recommended. According to Rodie, from the beginning Bayda wanted her to take on the role of court administrator, and he was able to get Rodie the requisite training and gradually expand her role. One of her first projects was overseeing the acquisition and installation of the court's first computers. Her job

Marlene Rodie, executive officer, and Chief Justice Bayda, c. 2006. (Court of Appeal)

eventually entailed a range of managerial functions, from human resources to budgeting. She was an ad hoc version of the professional management of court administration that other appellate courts established in the 1990s.

It was usually an uphill battle. Governments were often loath to give up direct supervision of court staff, invariably justice department employees, or control over even minor discretionary spending.[38] In Saskatchewan, the court had a good relationship with the justice ministry and a fair degree of autonomy. Rodie credited successive directors of court services with fostering a co-operative relationship. The court was able to hire administrative staff directly and was later given control over its budget. It was an unofficial, informal arrangement predicated on trust. Justice Georgina Jackson, once a civil servant, felt that the relationship reflected a co-operative culture peculiar to Saskatchewan.[39]

The harmony was maintained in part because the court's requests were reasonable. In the 1990s, the government was in austerity mode, and the court understood that money was tight. Rodie said that the court was very good at stretching its budget and getting the most out of the people and resources it had. As an example, as the court computerized, Marion Hingston, a judicial assistant hired by Rodie, demonstrated an interest with information technology. Rodie obtained training for Hingston and she became the court's de facto IT person. With patient lobbying, Rodie was then able to have Hingston reclassified, which gave the court a permanent IT position. When the court decided in 2007 to create a system of electronic filing for appeals, the mix of co-operation and autonomy was instrumental for the project's success, a topic for the next chapter. In 2010, Rodie was made the court's first executive officer, finally formalizing the position of court manager.

Another valuable Bayda innovation was hiring a professional librarian. The Court of Appeal had long maintained its own library for the convenience of the judges. Until a major renovation in the 1980s, the library was used for conferences and court meetings. But the library lacked a true librarian. In 2001, Bayda was able to secure funding for the position and the court hired Ann Marie Melvie, who had worked for a number of years at the Robertson Stromberg firm. With a master's degree in library science, Melvie proved invaluable in many capacities, maintaining and expanding the collection, doing extensive research for the judges, and also mentoring each year's batch of law clerks. The mentoring included giving a short course over the summer titled "Fun with Legislation." Melvie remains a fixture of the Court of Appeal.

In neighbouring Alberta and elsewhere, appeal courts made their registrar the court manager. In Saskatchewan, the registrar had been maintained as a quasi-judicial office separate from the rest of the court's administration and filled by a lawyer, although it became largely a sinecure, and the deputy registrar did the real work.[40] Fred Newis, who officially became registrar in 1985 after many years of running the office as deputy, was the only layperson to hold the position. When Newis retired in 1995, a lawyer once again was made registrar: Maurice Herauf, who would join the court as a judge in 2011. Newis had been a true fixture and highly respected by the bar, but litigation was increasingly complex and legal training was a distinct asset. Among the immediate challenges for Herauf was computerizing an office that was still almost entirely a paper environment.[41]

The revision of the rules of court was another compelling reason to have a lawyer as registrar. Unusually for an appellate court in Canada, the

Saskatchewan court retained control over the promulgation of its rules. In other jurisdictions, this had shifted to the government: the lieutenant-governor in council generally passed new rules, usually after a revision by a committee comprised of the judiciary, the bar, and the government. In Saskatchewan, it was entirely up to the judges to change the rules, although the court was very responsive to the other main stakeholder, the profession.

By the early 1990s, a revision of the rules had become a necessity. Nearly thirty years had passed since the last one, and the legal environment had changed a great deal. Practice directives had filled the gap, but after a decade the accretion of directives made a revision imperative.[42] Historically, the court had generally revised the rules every twenty years or so, and almost exactly on schedule started work in 1983, but the project had not proceeded quickly, despite a promising start. John Moss, QC, of Balfour Moss, had been commissioned to draft new civil rules,[43] and by 1987 had produced a draft, but then the revision languished until Justice Wakeling took charge around 1991. The court as a whole finished the rules in 1997. It had not been an easy process, marked by delays and some sharp disagreements.[44]

The new rules had an additional requirement for factums. Counsel now had to state the appropriate standard of review for the appeal.[45] The standard of review was essentially a test to determine whether appellate intervention was warranted in a specific appeal. Stating the standard of review in the factum focused counsel on ensuring their appeal met the standard. The inclusion of the appropriate standard demonstrated how previously looser rules for appellate deference had become formalized and applied as a filter for appeals coming to the court. There was much to recommend this approach but also disquiet as the Supreme Court pulled the door shut on a great deal of appellate review.

THE COURT AT LAW: JUSTICE AND APPELLATE RESTRAINT

IN THE 1990S, appellate judges often expressly invoked deferential standards of review when assessing appeals. Standards of review were nothing new. To a large extent, the standards were a formalizing of the traditions of appellate deference to trial judges and juries that had existed for over a century and have been referred to often in this history. These principles—largely the degree of deference that judges on appeal should show to the trial judge or jury—were essentially judge-made, owing their existence to the simple fact that appeals in the common law world were not a new trial but a review of the first trial. The original trier was deemed to have advantages in viewing and understanding the evidence before them, especially the testimony of witnesses, and disturbing the original trier's findings was not to be done lightly. Appellate judges certainly understood that this stance meant fewer successful appeals and would likely discourage some appeals. The right of appeal was thus subject to judicial policy to restrict that right.

For over a century, deference still allowed considerable latitude on appeals. The verdict of juries was always given a very high degree of deference, honouring the antiquity of the institution, but much less for judges sitting alone. In Saskatchewan, the original *Court of Appeal Act* gave the court the ability to intervene with any aspect of a trial judge's decision, including their view of the evidence, or, in other words, determination of the facts in a case. These powers carried over into *The Court of Appeal Act, 2000*, the most recent revision of the statute, and may even have been increased with the new wording. These statutory powers also apparently contradicted the much greater emphasis the Supreme Court of Canada placed on deferential standards of review. This trend had started in the 1980s, culminating with *Housen v Nikolaisen* in 2002, a decision that set the bar very high for appellate intervention except for questions of pure law. *Housen* raised the question of whether the application of deferential standards of review were too stringent, allowing obvious errors and injustice to persist in the interests of judicial efficiency, and in Saskatchewan, of whether the Court of Appeal's enabling statute superseded the Supreme Court's pronouncements.

The greater emphasis on deference extended to criminal sentencing. It was one factor that contributed to a jurisprudential split that emerged on the court over sentencing, with part of the court embracing new ideas of "restorative justice." This split preceded, but was exacerbated by, new amendments to the *Criminal Code* introduced in 1996. The amendments altered some sentencing verities and, as the Supreme Court ruled, also meant more deference. The difference in views over sentencing was not unique to Saskatchewan, but the degree to which it split the court was unusual. The two philosophical positions were very evident in the sentencing of Robert Latimer, one of the most controversial trials in Saskatchewan history. While perhaps not comparable to the controversy over standards of review, the different views on sentencing were another fascinating development in the Court of Appeal's jurisprudence.

A SENTENCING DIVIDE

CRIMINAL SENTENCING WAS an area of law that saw considerable change—and controversy—in the 1990s. This was largely due to Bill C-41, which came into effect in September 1996 and was considered the first major reform of sentencing in Canada since the *Criminal Code* was introduced in 1892. Comprehensive reform had been discussed since the late 1960s, and in 1984 the Canadian Sentencing Commission was established, producing a landmark report three years later. Another major parliamentary study followed in 1989. Both recommended major changes to sentencing. The result, a half decade later, was C-41.

Bill C-41 codified the principles of sentencing for the first time, in section 718 of the *Criminal Code*. The amendment enshrined proportionality as the basic underlying principle of sentencing: that punishment must be proportionate to the seriousness of the offence and the culpability of the offender. The other main principles enunciated were familiar from *Morrissette*, Ted Culliton's classic decision on sentencing—general and specific deterrence, safety of the public, rehabilitation—with important additions such as denunciation and parity. Other provisions indicated some rethinking of sentencing. Bill C-41 instructed judges to use the minimum sanction necessary and avoid incarceration if other lesser sanctions, such as probation, suspended sentences, restitution, or fines, were appropriate. Judges were also to give "particular attention to the circumstances of Aboriginal offenders." This addressed the fact that Aboriginals were disproportionately represented in the prison population, due to the social dislocation and marginalization they experienced.

The most controversial new measure was section 742.1, the conditional sentence, often thought of as house arrest. Non-violent offenders receiving a sentence of less than two years could now potentially serve their sentence in the community, subject to a range of conditions designed to restrict their liberty, such as electronic monitoring and being confined to their residence. As the Supreme Court observed in the 2000 *Proulx* decision, the legislative intent of the 1996 amendments was for less incarceration and to encourage a restorative approach to sentencing.[46]

Restorative justice had emerged by the 1990s as a fundamentally different approach to dealing with offenders. The restorative approach was in essence a form of mediation between offenders, victims, and their community that emphasized healing and restoring relationships. Restorative justice aimed to move beyond punishment, with offenders acknowledging their responsibility and desire to make amends, and with victims directly involved in the process of creating appropriate sanctions. Trial projects in different jurisdictions had shown promise: crime victims reported high satisfaction with restorative approaches, and recidivism rates for offenders were lower.[47] Restorative justice was based on traditional practices, some quite ancient, particularly those of indigenous cultures such as New Zealand's Maori people and Canada's First Nations. The use of sentencing circles for Aboriginal offenders in Canada is an example of putting restorative justice into effect.

The influence of restorative justice could be seen in C-41 with the greater acknowledgement of the victim, provisions for reparation of the harm to victims and community, and the promotion of acknowledgement of their responsibility by offenders, as well as the de-emphasis on incarceration. The restorative approach contrasted with the traditional approach to punishment, where the state, in the form of judges and corrections officials, decided on sanctions and which emphasized abstract concepts and goals of sentencing.

Proulx also made it clear that appeal courts should practise deference in sentencing, using a standard of "demonstrably unfit," confirming several previous Supreme Court decisions.[48] Thus deference was a live issue in the 1990s in criminal sentencing, exactly the same in principle to the deferential standards of review in civil law. When appeals of sentence were allowed in the 1920s, there was little statutory restriction on review, but appeal courts had soon held that the trial judge was owed deference because of their intimate knowledge of the case and the offender. Justice William Martin had acknowledged this advantage in the 1923 *Finlay* decision but had taken the position that, with the liberty of the subject at stake, the court's duty was to fully canvas a sentence appeal, establishing a tradition of appellate intervention. Subsequently, Culliton had declared that given the opportunity to hear from a convicted person, the appellate court was in as good a position to decide on sentence as the trial judge had been and sometimes better. As Justice Wakeling wrote, in Saskatchewan the court did not "give a high degree of deference to the sentence imposed by the trial judge."[49]

Culliton's *Morrissette* decision, which had established punishment, deterrence, protection of the public, and reformation and rehabilitation as the four chief considerations for a fit sentence, was considered a *locus classicus* and was still widely cited. But Culliton's handling of sentence appeals had verged on the absurd. His sympathies had leaned towards rehabilitation. Sentence reductions had become almost automatic, and the Crown rarely won a sentence appeal.[50] Culliton's approach also created a large number of appeals, not complex but still a burden for a busy court.

After Culliton retired, there was a strong consensus on the court for a more principled, nuanced, and balanced approach. Rehabilitation still received greater emphasis in Saskatchewan than in some jurisdictions, but denunciation, deterrence, public safety, and maintaining public confidence in the justice system were given more weight. The court usually gave first offenders, especially young offenders, a break except in the most egregious of circumstances. The court often kept these offenders out of the federal penitentiary system by reducing sentences to less than two years. But the court also took an activist stance towards violent crime, imposing tougher sentences as assaults and robberies involving weapons had a sharp uptick in the 1980s, and was hard-nosed with drug trafficking and crimes involving children. Bayda, who soon became a proponent of restorative justice, gave an interview in 1992 lauding the court's tough approach to crime and defending it as necessary to uphold confidence in the justice system.[51] It marked a major shift.

The court also emphasized reducing disparity in sentencing, eliminating large variations in sentences for similar crimes. This had long been a goal of appeal courts (Culliton discussed it in *Morrissette*), but some courts had begun stressing its importance in the 1980s.[52] One approach was starting points, where the appeal court established a typical sentence for a crime, which trial judges varied depending on mitigating or aggravating factors, and another was sentence ranges, where the trial judge applied mitigating or aggravating factors to set the sentence within the suggested range for an offence. Conceptually, both methods were intended to create a more uniform approach, promoting consistency and less disparity but preserving much of the trial judge's discretion. In Saskatchewan, the court published a sentencing digest to keep the trial courts up to speed. Another

Bayda initiative was to have provincial court judges attend sentencing appeals.[53] This was all aimed at controlling disparity.

The court's consensus ended in the 1990s as the bench divided on the proper appellate role but more fundamentally on the philosophy behind sentencing. Calvin Tallis, Stuart Cameron, Marjorie Gerwing, Nicholas Sherstobitoff, and Thomas Wakeling continued with robust appellate review and a focus on controlling disparity, crime control, deterrence, and maintaining public confidence. Edward Bayda, William Vancise, Georgina Jackson, and Gary Lane constituted a more liberal wing, interested in restorative justice, promoting sanctions without incarceration, and greater emphasis on rehabilitation. They were in sympathy with the goals of the 1996 sentencing amendments and—less so for Vancise—the increased deference that the Supreme Court mandated in *Shropshire* in 1995 and *McDonnell* in 1997.[54]

The addition of Lane and Jackson clearly changed the court's dynamic. Perhaps counter to some expectations because of his conservative politics, Lane was a progressive and liberal jurist. He took an expansive view of *Charter* rights, particularly due-process rights, and was very moderate on sentence. He was the quintessential common-sense judge. Jackson was a hard-working, productive judge; she or Cameron usually penned the most judgments. Jackson was independent, not hesitating to dissent or write a separate concurring decision. Like many women appointed to the courts in that era, she had a progressive sensibility, particularly with *Charter* rights, and more sympathy with section 15 claims, which posed a challenge for some older judges. Jackson was attuned to alternate views on sentencing, although she could also be tough, as could the other "dovish" judges.

R v McGinn in 1989 arguably foreshadowed the court's split and also showed that new ideas on sentencing were percolating long before C-41 was passed.[55] The trial judge had imposed a fine and probation in a minor drug trafficking case. Cameron for the majority allowed the Crown appeal, holding that it was well-developed law in Saskatchewan that a trafficking offence received a custodial sentence for specific and general deterrence. In Cameron's view, this maintained public confidence, although he carefully distinguished between reasonable and informed opinion and people who "constantly clamour for greater punishment no matter what the crime and what the circumstances."[56] The circumstances of the case, he argued, did not warrant stepping outside the generally accepted range for sentence.

Vancise in his dissent took a radical stance. He agreed that the trial judge had erred in not giving the accused jail time due to his record but questioned the presumption that incarceration was necessary. Vancise argued that despite its venerability, the concept of general deterrence was essentially bankrupt, with little evidence that it was effective, particularly with the small variations of sentence that often resulted from appeals. Vancise further questioned the general utility of custodial sentences in non-violent offences given the availability of other sanctions, such as community service, restitution, or fines. And while acknowledging the undesirability of disparity, Vancise argued that with sentencing in Canada, "the principle that each sentence be suited to the individual offender as opposed to the individual offense" was fundamental.[57]

In *McGinn*, Vancise and Cameron neatly expressed the two philosophical views of sentencing that would inform the debate in the court in the 1990s, which can be summarized as sentencing for the offence or sentencing for the offender. One observer characterized one group as preserving the basic and traditional principles of sentencing, with less appellate deference and extolling greater consistency and uniformity, and the other group as being interested in restorative justice concepts, minimizing incarceration, practising with more deference, and emphasizing the offender's individuality and the circumstances of their offence.[58] The two viewpoints are easily discerned in three of the court's major sentence decisions, one on sentencing circles and two on conditional sentences, new initiatives often seen as forms of restorative justice.

SQUARING THE CIRCLE: *R V MORIN*

EVEN BEFORE THE 1996 sentencing amendments and the 1999 Supreme Court *Gladue* decision, which mandated the consideration of an Aboriginal offender's circumstances, the Saskatchewan Court of Appeal considered the use of sentencing circles, an adaption of age-old traditional practice, to bring restorative justice into sentencing for Aboriginals. *R v Morin* clearly showed the philosophical division on the court in the contrasting views of the majority and minority. Both accepted sentencing circles, but one as a tool that augmented the usual approach to sentencing, the other as a more fundamental rethinking particularly appropriate to those of Aboriginal heritage but potentially for other offenders.

GEORGINA RUTH JACKSON

Born on September 9, 1952, Georgina Jackson was the court's first true baby boomer. Her parents were farmers near Yorkton, and both branches of her family had long-established roots in Saskatchewan. Justice Edward Wetmore signed the naturalization papers of Jackson's maternal grandfather, and her other grandfather worked in the Yorkton land office before turning to homesteading.

Justice Georgina Ruth Jackson, c. 1992. (Court of Appeal/Photographic Service Agency)

Jackson began her education in a one-room rural school house. She later attended the regional high school in Yorkton before finishing at the Sacred Heart Academy in the city. After graduation, she attended Campion College at the University of Regina, earning an undergraduate degree in English. Originally intending a career in journalism, Jackson wrote the LSAT on a whim and was accepted to the law school in Saskatoon. Graduating in 1976, she articled with the attorney general's department. She was hired as a Crown solicitor after articling and was initially responsible for prosecutions for the Department of Labour.

Jackson was then involved in the drafting and execution of the new *Personal Property Security Act*, which established an innovative electronic registry. She also wrote a manual of sheriffs' practice and an influential report on the reformation of mechanics' and builders' liens. In 1981, at the age of twenty-eight, she was made master of titles. Along with its quasi-judicial duties as master of titles, Jackson's position evolved to become executive director of the province's property registration system, and she oversaw the start of the full computerization of the real property registries. She also became involved with the Uniform Law Conference of Canada as the Saskatchewan secretary and from 1988 to 1990 served as president.

Jackson went into private practice in 1988 with the Regina firm of MacPherson, Leslie and Tyerman, where she had spent a month as part of her articles. Appointed Queen's Counsel in December 1990, she became a partner in 1991. Jackson was involved in the Canadian Bar Association, joining the executive of the Saskatchewan branch in 1984 and serving as the president from 1987 to 1988.

Jackson was named to the Court of Appeal on September 10, 1991, and was one of the youngest appointments in the court's history. She has been very active in judicial education and promoting judicial ethics. She was an associate director of the National Judicial Institute and a director and president of the Canadian Institute for the Administration of Justice, the foremost of a number of legal and judicial organizations where she has been a director or a member of the executive. Jackson taught an annual seminar at the Deutsche Richterakademie (German Judicial Academy) for ten years and created a training program on judicial ethics for judges-in-training in Morocco. Jackson has given speeches, talks, and seminars around the world on a wide variety of legal topics and is also heavily involved in organizing conferences, including the first national conference on Aboriginal peoples and the law. One of the court's fully bilingual judges, she spent three months with the Quebec Court of Appeal as part of a French immersion program.

Jackson has also found time for the community, as president of the parish council of the Holy Rosary Cathedral in Regina and a trustee and committee chair for the MacKenzie Art Gallery. Justice Jackson continues to serve on the Court of Appeal as a full-time judge.

Sentencing circles had first been used in Saskatchewan in 1992.[59] Modern circles, supervised by a trial judge, brought together offender, victim, and members of the community where the offence took place. The circle allowed the victim and the community to participate in sentencing and gave the offender a chance to acknowledge their responsibility and make amends. More importantly, a circle was a collaborative exercise to find suitable sanctions for an offender that would promote their rehabilitation while satisfying the community's need for redress. Practically, it meant less jail time and put emphasis on community-based rehabilitation, particularly appropriate given the role in criminal offences of substance abuse, frequently the result of the social ills that plagued many Aboriginal communities. Within two years, circles had been used almost one hundred times, nearly always in provincial court and in predominantly Aboriginal communities of the province. *Morin* was the first time a Queen's Bench judge had used a circle and was the court's first appeal on the subject. Due to the novelty and important issues, Bayda sat a panel of five, with Cameron, Tallis, Sherstobitoff, and Jackson joining him on the appeal.

The Métis offender in *Morin* had robbed a gas station in Saskatoon. Some participants in the circle—one of the victims of the robbery and assault, the gas station owner, the arresting officer, a psychologist—were not Aboriginal. One of the issues in the appeal was whether a sentencing circle was appropriate when an offence was committed in a community where the majority and the victims were not Aboriginal. The sentence for Ivan Morin was a short term of incarceration followed by house arrest, probation, and community service, as well as addiction treatment and counselling. The Crown appealed, arguing that the sentence did not reflect the seriousness of the crime and the record of the accused and did not consider deterrence and protection of the public, and that holding a circle for the offender in question was an error in law.

In Chief Justice Bayda's view, the important questions were determining when sentencing circles were appropriate and how they should be instituted. He laid out the four points to be addressed: whether a sentencing circle was recognized and accepted in law as a tool for determining a sentence; the circumstances that called for a circle; the proper way to establish and conduct a circle; and finally, the legal weight of the circle's conclusions. The answer to the first question was clearly yes, but the rest was still open to interpretation.

Bayda also had a larger issue in mind: how circles introduced a restorative approach to sentencing and how this might change the way a sentence was formulated and assessed as fit. The traditional healing circle, he noted, was used to repair relationships within the community that the wrongdoer had damaged and to address the underlying issues that led to the misbehaviour. Restoring harmony was the central purpose of the circle, not retribution. To use a circle in the proper spirit, Bayda believed that a fit sentence had to be defined differently.

> Is a fit sentence for *this* accused who has committed *this* offence better arrived at by using the restorative approach or the ordinary approach? In considering this question the judge will have to keep in mind that the sentence arrived at using the restorative approach will likely be quite different from the one arrived at using the ordinary approach. In the case of the restorative approach the incarceration component of a fit sentence will likely be less (or perhaps even non-existent) than the incarceration component of a fit sentence arrived at using the ordinary approach. The explanation is that the success of the healing component in a restorative approach is often contingent upon a minimal incarceration period or no incarceration at all. That may not always be true but often it will be. Accordingly, to assess the fitness of a restorative sentence by comparing its incarceration component with the incarceration component of a fit sentence using the ordinary approach is to engage in an exercise that is either flawed or irrelevant.[60]

In Bayda's view, the fitness of a sentence had to be considered primarily in restorative terms, not in terms of a traditional punitive sentence. Adopting the sentencing circle meant largely abandoning the preconceptions on sentencing in favour of a new paradigm. Not surprising, Bayda thought that only crimes with a mandatory minimum sentence precluded a sentencing circle for a particular offender. For any other offence, a circle was in theory possible.

Bayda's liberality extended to parity. He acknowledged that the restorative approach to a fit sentence, almost by definition, might violate the parity principle. The approach might also create two sentencing regimes, one for Aboriginals and one for non-Aboriginals. Bayda did not see any particular problem. He believed that disparity already existed for Aboriginal offenders, with an incarceration rate much higher than it was for mainstream society, and justified a major variation in sentencing. As he put it, there were already two systems of justice, and "sentencing circles have a role to play in breaking down that apparent anomaly."

Due to the departure from traditional sentencing, Bayda provided extensive criteria for the use of sentencing circles. The two basic requirements were simple: the willingness of an accused to participate and submit to the judgment of a circle, and the existence of a community willing to participate. The devil was in the details. Without being exhaustive, Bayda listed numerous and somewhat exacting prerequisites to properly fulfill the two main requirements. A community had to be well defined, through ethnicity, culture, and geography; it had to see the offender as a member of the community, with accountability to the community; it had to support the accused and accept their sincerity; and it had to be able to provide the required help for an accused. An accused had to see themselves as part of the community and accountable to the community; have taken responsibility for their wrongdoing, starting with a guilty plea; be prepared to accept the measures put forth in a circle; and have the sincerity and capacity to heal themselves and the breach with the community. Bayda allowed that not every factor had to be present and that there were other factors that might be relevant to the particular case. This was an area for trial judges to develop.

Bayda made one major concession to "ordinary" sentencing, as he termed it. The trial judge retained control over all the proceedings, from deciding to use a sentencing circle, to constituting it, overseeing it, and deciding to follow or vary the recommendations of the circle. Holding a sentencing circle did not bind the judge, and Bayda suggested that the trial judge should reassess the validity of the circle after hearing from accused and community. But to decide if a circle's recommendations should be followed, Bayda reiterated that judges should assess fitness with a restorative standard, not the conventional standard.

Bayda's judgment was far-reaching. It was also in dissent. Sherstobitoff wrote the majority judgment for the court and had a very different perspective. In Sherstobitoff's view, sentencing circles did not change the basic approach to sentencing, with the judge continuing to impose a fit sentence after applying the usual principles, including parity. The primary question was "how, and the extent to which, a meaningful use of sentencing circles may be integrated into this framework."[61] Sherstobitoff agreed that circles had obvious utility in the right circumstances but fit their use into usually accepted sentencing practices. He did acknowledge that circles required a modified approach to a sentence, one involving less incarceration and more sensitivity to Aboriginal needs and culture.

> The very purpose of sentencing circles seems to be to fashion sentences that will differ in some mix or measure from those which the courts have up to now imposed in order to take into

account aboriginal culture and traditions, and in order to permit and to take into account direct community participation in both imposition and administration of the sentence. It also seems implicit in all discussions of sentencing circles that they will in many cases, if not most of them, recommend sentences imposing lesser terms of incarceration than would have been imposed by a judge alone and to substitute alternative sanctions, usually involving the community in the administration of those sanctions.[62]

Sherstobitoff argued that this was still consistent with traditional sentencing. A trial judge could emphasize rehabilitation over others factors like deterrence and use a sentencing circle. He observed that sentencing disparity was implicit in circles but that the existing case law allowed some disparity if the circumstances warranted. But he held that the fitness of the sentence proposed in a circle was still determined with the application of the usual principles. This precluded a circle for any offence where the usual range of sentence was more than two years, as incarceration was almost certainly required and removed the judge's authority to impose other conditions.

Sherstobitoff did not see any factors in the appeal that justified making a substantial departure from the usual sentence for robbery with violence by putting rehabilitation before other sentencing principles. Rehabilitation was usually emphasized with young offenders, first-time offenders, and less serious offences. Morin's previous record, including frequent breaches of probation, indicated a lack of sincerity, as did his remarks in the sentencing circle. And while commending the local Métis community in Saskatoon for helping Morin, Sherstobitoff argued they were not the equivalent of the small, tightly knit, mostly Aboriginal communities where sentencing circles had been used successfully. In his view, the conditions in the sentence were unlikely to be effective in an urban environment. And while Sherstobitoff had not laid out specific guidelines, he noted that the criteria that provincial and Queen's Bench judges had already articulated for circles would preclude one for Morin.

Bayda would not have interfered with the trial judge's decision. He had similar misgivings, calling the appeal a borderline case. But he did not see any error in principle or such an unfit sentence, applying his new yardstick, that appellate intervention was required. Bayda applied the higher standard of deference that the Supreme Court soon mandated for all appeal courts.

Sherstobitoff was not hostile to the sentencing circle. He noted with approval that circles fit well with the recently introduced Bill C-41, particularly the requirement to consider the circumstances of Aboriginal offenders. But he placed circles within the usual sentencing framework, useful in some appropriate circumstances. Circles were essentially a tool for judges to craft sentences for less serious crimes rather than permission to introduce a new, non-punitive treatment of offenders. Bayda's dissent hinted at such a rethink. His enthusiasm for restorative justice extended past *Morin*. It was his subject for the 1997 Culliton Lecture, where he laid out the case for restorative justice.[63] Although he used the example of an Aboriginal offender, his argument extended to all sentencing. He made the same points as Vancise did in *McGinn*, questioning the efficaciousness of deterrence and the utility and long-term effects of incarceration, and posed the question of whether the restorative approach was the better way. As the court's jurisprudence on conditional sentences showed, some of his colleagues agreed, but others still held to the traditional verities of sentencing.

CONDITIONS ON CONDITIONALS

THERE WAS PROBABLY nothing in C-41 more contentious than conditional sentences. The public often didn't understand them, law-and-order types hated them, and judges were frequently unsure of how to apply them. Even after nearly twenty years, there are still disputes about the proper use of conditional sentences for crimes such as drug trafficking. Fundamental to the confusion and controversy was the common belief that the conditional sentence—where offenders served a sentence in the community subject to conditions instead of in an institution—was simply a lesser penalty than jail time. In Saskatchewan, conditional sentences also highlighted the clash of views on the Court of Appeal towards sentencing.

Conditional sentences were established in section 742 of the 1996 *Criminal Code* amendments. The new provision accompanied the requirement for judges to minimize incarceration. For offences with no minimum term of imprisonment and for which the judge imposed a sentence of less than two years, the sentence could potentially be served in the community if the judge was satisfied this would not endanger the public. This was the extent of the statutory directions for conditional sentences, which left much to the courts to fill in.

The first major decision in Saskatchewan on conditional sentences was *R v McDonald* in 1997.[64] It was a complex case. An Aboriginal woman had been convicted of criminal negligence causing death after running over another woman while badly impaired. She had apparently been trying to intimidate a rowdy crowd at a house party. The trial judge tried to hold a sentencing circle, but there was not enough community support and instead he held a sentencing hearing. He gave Donna McDonald a suspended sentence subject to a range of conditions, including nine months of electronically monitored house arrest, which allowed her to work but otherwise restricted her to a residence. The sentence split the community of Fond du Lac, and the Crown appealed it as unfit for the offence.

Vancise wrote a comprehensive analysis of the purpose of C-41 and the conditional sentence. Reviewing the history of punishment in Canada, he reiterated many of the points he made in *McGinn* and concluded that C-41 was a major reform intended to establish a new framework for sentencing, not simply codify the existing rationale behind sentences. Attempts to interpret the amendment in the latter fashion he termed reactionary and contrary to the liberal traditions of the court on sentencing established in *Finlay* and *Morrissette*. One of the most important elements of this new framework, in Vancise's view, was the instruction to employ incarceration as a last resort. Vancise acknowledged that judges to some degree had always exercised restraint, but he argued that there was a presumption of incarceration which was now reversed.

Turning to the conditional sentence, Vancise distinguished the new sanction from probation and suspended sentences, which sometimes imposed similar restrictions and obligations. In his view, conditionals were a "true alternative" to institutional incarceration but still a custodial sentence and not intended to replace other sanctions, like fines, restitution orders, or community service. To make this distinction clear, Vancise proposed a three-step approach to decide on a conditional sentence. The trial judge first determined, applying the usual principles, if a fit sentence required incarceration and the appropriate length of sentence. If the result allowed for a conditional sentence, only then did the judge determine if one was appropriate. Vancise was explicit that the principles of sentencing were used to decide on a custodial sentence but not subsequently to decide whether the custodial sentence could be in the form of a conditional sentence. This only had to be done once, as, in his view, the conditional sentence was incarceration, served in the community rather than prison. In Vancise's opinion, when the offender was not a threat to the community, any sentence under two years could be a conditional sentence, whatever the crime. To his mind, the goals of denunciation and deterrence were actually better served with the offender in the community as a reminder of the crime and the penalty.

Of Vancise's opinion, Sherstobitoff wrote, "I cannot agree with the result or with much of the foundation for it."[65] Sherstobitoff argued that the 1996 amendments were just what Vancise said they were not: a codification of the long-accepted principles of sentencing. This was even true of using imprisonment as a last resort. Sherstobitoff noted the qualifiers "appropriate" and "reasonable in the circumstances" and argued this was already the accepted approach in Saskatchewan. More fundamentally, he disagreed with Vancise's argument that a conditional sentence was not a lesser punishment and that the sentencing principles not be used to decide the fitness of a conditional sentence. In previous cases of criminal negligence causing death, the court imposed a jail sentence of over two years. In Sherstobitoff's view, there was nothing in the amendments suggesting the parity principle did not apply.

Ironically, Vancise and Sherstobitoff agreed that the actual sentence was not fit. But while both increased the sentence to just under the threshold mandating jail, Vancise kept the conditions intact and Sherstobitoff added a short term of incarceration. The third judge on the panel, Lane, supported Sherstobitoff in the result. He agreed with Vancise's analysis but felt that in the circumstances a sentence of two years was necessary and congruent with the court's previous jurisprudence. Sherstobitoff's disposition was the more suitable.

R V HORVATH

MCDONALD WAS NOT the last word on conditional sentences in Saskatchewan. *R v Horvath* demonstrated that with two opposing camps the law could potentially become increasingly incoherent. Bayda's judgment in *Horvath* strengthened the influence of the liberal group, but it also introduced to the debate the principle of increased deference to the trial judge.

Horvath concerned a pathological gambler who had defrauded her employer, a bank, and another financial institution to obtain funds to play video lottery terminals.[66] She had obtained funds in excess of $200,000. The accused was sentenced to two years less a day and given a conditional sentence, which included nine months of house arrest and electronic monitoring. The Crown appealed, arguing that the sentence was disproportionate to the offence and had not adequately considered deterrence and protection of the public.

Bayda adopted the reasoning of Vancise in *McDonald* regarding conditional sentences, including his view that the conditional sentence was not a lesser sentence but an equivalent alternative to institutional incarceration. He pointed out that ordinary jail sentences were largely served in the community through parole and early release, usually subject to restrictions and obligations similar to those in conditional sentences. The conditional sentence merely cut out the institutional incarceration. In his view, the conditional sentence gave judges some of the power exercised by corrections officials, allowing them greater creativity in crafting a sentence. In light of the subsequent amendment to section 742, Bayda did admit that a conditional sentence had to be consistent with basic sentencing principles, but he did not think this altered the Vancise approach. And he agreed that fundamentally the conditional sentence was something new.

> In summary, the enactment of s. 742.1 is, in my respectful view, an attempt by Parliament to blend certain goals of retributive justice (to use the current parlance) with certain goals of restorative justice. It is a parliamentary intention that the judiciary should do their utmost to bring to fruition.[67]

Bayda's judgment was most significant for his elaboration of deference in sentence appeals, essentially summarizing the Supreme Court's jurisprudence. Without an error in principle or a failure to consider and properly weigh a relevant factor, a sentence had to be "demonstrably unfit," or unreasonable, to merit appellate intervention. In the view of the Supreme Court, even in guilty pleas trial judges had major advantages in determining sentence due to their immediacy to the case and their first-hand experience with sentencing, including an understanding of the needs of the community as well as the individual offender. Parliament in Bill C-41 had also given trial judges wide discretion in sentencing. This discretion to a large degree trumped the parity principle. It was an endorsement of the view of Bayda, Vancise, and others on the court that sentencing was primarily aimed at the particular offender and particular offence, and was a profound shift for a court that had traditionally practised little deference on sentencing.

Bayda's decision in *Horvath* contradicted Sherstobitoff's in *McDonald*. Lane's agreement with Vancise's analysis, if not the disposition of the case, opened the door for Bayda to bypass the previous decision. It illustrated that the different views on sentencing meant that a panel might not follow previous decisions. This had occurred in *R v Taylor*, a sentencing circle appeal subsequent to *Morin*. The trial judge's sentence of banishment received most of the attention, but the majority had also ruled that a sentencing circle could be used although the crime in question would ordinarily attract a sentence of more than two years. This contradicted *Morin*. Cameron dissented on the point but came to the same result as the majority on other grounds. The Court of Appeal, like most intermediate appellate courts in Canada, considered previous decisions binding and only reconsidered earlier precedents in exceptional cases. While there was sometimes room for interpretation, the danger of incoherence and inconsistency was certainly present in the debate over sentencing. As one observer put it, "Counsel arguing sentencing appeals in 1997 faced a difficult task."[68]

The divide in the court on sentencing eventually started to narrow.[69] In part, this reflected the growing body of law on the sentencing amendments and conditional sentences. The Supreme Court in *Proulx* gave a broad and liberal interpretation of the conditional sentence provisions, coming to conclusions similar to Vancise's and Bayda's.[70] The liberal wing of the Saskatchewan court also seemed to lose some enthusiasm for conditional sentences and restorative justice. A harder line crept into decisions dealing with drugs, violent crime, and sexual offences. One commentator speculated this was perhaps due to a persistently high crime rate in Saskatchewan.[71] Ultimately, the passage of time healed the rift as new judges, including a new chief justice, joined the court.

Some of the split over sentencing on the court was informed by different attitudes towards deference. And deference was the central issue in a five-year running battle between the Court of Appeal and the Supreme Court of Canada over standards of review and appellate powers. Sentencing was also central to one of the most controversial cases that ever came before the Court of Appeal, the tragedy of the Latimer family.

R v Latimer: The Quality of Mercy

On October 24, 1993, Robert Latimer killed his severely disabled twelve-year-old daughter, Tracy. Everyone could agree on that, but the debate over whether it was murder or an act of mercy or both raged for years. The *Saskatchewan Law Review* dedicated an entire issue to the legal, moral, and ethical ramifications of the case. The disabled community was outraged at the killing, which Latimer justified as necessary to spare his daughter constant agony. Latimer ultimately was convicted of second-degree murder and served his full sentence. Many Canadians thought that this was an injustice. Many others felt that acquitting Latimer, or giving him a light sentence, set a dangerous precedent. Two trials, two appeals in Saskatchewan, and two further appeals to the Supreme Court did not suffice to answer the larger question of *Latimer*: Can murder be mercy, and if so, is it really murder?

Bob Latimer was a farmer near Wilkie, Saskatchewan. Tracy was his eldest daughter. She had been deprived of oxygen during a difficult birth and left with severe cerebral palsy. Tracy Latimer had limited mental awareness, was quadriplegic, and was unable to care for herself. She had regular seizures requiring powerful medication, suffered chronic and often intense pain, and had required several intrusive surgeries such the insertion of steel rods to straighten and immobilize her spine. The family decided not to take the option of institutionalizing Tracy and instead provided her care at home.

Latimer decided to kill his daughter when doctors recommended another major surgery to prevent Tracy's hip from constantly dislocating. While his wife and other children were at church, Latimer put Tracy into his truck and piped the exhaust into the cab. He then returned Tracy to her bed. Latimer claimed the death was natural, but an autopsy revealed carbon monoxide poisoning. He was arrested and confessed when questioned. Controversially, Latimer was charged with first-degree murder due to the premeditation.[72] At his first trial, Latimer was convicted of second-degree murder and given the statutory sentence of life imprisonment with no parole until ten years was served.

Bayda, Tallis, and Sherstobitoff heard the appeal of conviction and sentence. Unusually for a criminal appeal, there were intervenors, several groups representing the disabled, who Sherstobitoff gave leave to appear. The conviction appeal had little hope. The first two grounds were in legal terms almost pure rhetoric. Latimer claimed the trial judge had erred "in failing to allow the jury to decide the case on what they felt was just . . . requiring them to follow black letter law, irrespective of their conscience." He further asserted the judge should have given the jury the option of finding he had a legal right to decide on death for his daughter.[73] The substantive grounds were that Latimer had not been properly informed of his rights to counsel, specifically legal aid, violating sections 7, 9, and 10(a) and 10(b) of the *Charter*. The judge had also withdrawn the defence of necessity from the jury on the basis that there was no evidence to sustain it.

Tallis, writing for the court, carefully considered the trial judge decision but found little error. Despite a few irregularities, Latimer was properly arrested and had ample opportunity to retain counsel before making his confession. The defence of necessity clearly did not apply. Akin to self-defence, necessity excused culpable homicide when individuals had no reasonable way to avoid "imminent risk of peril" to themselves or another. This defence did not contemplate a mercy killing. Tracy's condition was miserable and perhaps unbearable, but her death was not the only option, and there was no impending peril intrinsic to the defence. As Tallis wrote,

> Applying these controlling principles to the jury instructions under review, we must reject this ground of appeal. The trial judge was correct in finding that there was no factual foundation for this defence. In this case the appellant's life was not in peril. He was concerned with Tracy's quality of life. The evidence clearly established the bleak future that faced this little girl. Although her scheduled surgery involved a long recovery period, there was the prospect of some pain alleviation.

Tallis made it very clear that in his view Tracy's death had disturbing implications. He agreed with the interveners on the appeal that characterizing the murder as a mercy killing carried with it an implied judgment on the worth of the life of the victim.

> This is not a case of withholding potentially life-prolonging treatment to a seriously disabled person. It deals with the deliberate decision to terminate another's life rather than continue with the scheduled medical treatment and care. In such circumstances it is no defence for a parent to say because of a severe handicap, a

> child's life has such diminished value that the child should not live any longer. It does not advance the interest of the state or society to treat such a child as a person of lesser status or dignity than others.[74]

Tallis addressed this again with the sentence appeal. The failure of the necessity defence made it very clear that, in the circumstances of the *Latimer* case, an accused had no real defence if the prosecution pursed a murder charge.

The only other hope for Latimer was a lesser penalty justified on the grounds that Tracy's death was a mercy killing. Latimer attacked his sentence as constituting "cruel and unusual punishment" under section 12 of the *Charter* due to the mandatory minimum of ten years before hope of parole. He argued that while the Supreme Court had held that minimum sentences did not violate section 12 generally, the specific circumstances of his case brought the *Charter* back into play. Unlike the vast majority of murders, he had killed his daughter as an act of compassion to end her suffering, and being subjected to the same punishment as other murderers was grossly disproportionate. The solution was a so-called constitutional exemption. Under section 24(1) of the *Charter* and the power to fashion a remedy, the court could make a special exception while continuing to hold the law valid.

Tallis did not accept this argument. "We are asked to treat the conviction as essentially the functional equivalent of manslaughter for the purpose of determining a fit sentence," he wrote. In his view, this trespassed on the prerogatives of the parliment. There was no allowance in the *Criminal Code* for acts that might be characterized as mercy killings, and it was not for the court to create this category. Fundamentally, murder was murder, and putatively altruistic motives did not change this. Tallis argued that the law was written to avoid exactly the situation in Latimer.

> Our law does not authorize such surrogate decision-making based on the assessments of the personal worth or social utility of another's life or the value of that life to the individual involved or to others. Our society, through its criminal law, may properly decline to make judgments about the quality of life that a particular individual may enjoy, and simply assert an unqualified interest in the preservation of human life. Surrogate decision-makers are

> not entitled to arrogate to themselves the life and death decisions under review in this case.[75]

Tallis did not question that the accused was sincere in his desire to alleviate Tracy's pain, but he questioned whether death was the only option. And more damning, he speculated that the fact that Tracy was severely handicapped played a role in Latimer's course of action.

> In this situation it is a fair inference that such a decision would never have been suggested or considered if Tracy were not handicapped and in extreme pain. This difference in approach between handicapped and non-handicapped children directly reflects a sense that the life of a handicapped child is of significantly less value than the life of a non-handicapped child in extreme pain. A pivotal question to be considered is, "If the child were not permanently disabled, but in extreme pain, would there be any question about making heroic efforts to sustain and maintain life?" If the answer is no, then the decision would appear to be clearly predicated upon the diminished value assigned to the life of a handicapped child. One would not be so inspired by love and compassion to take the life of the non-handicapped child.[76]

Tallis believed that the law in regards to murder was necessarily rigid. There was another avenue to plead for lesser penalty, which was executive clemency. Tallis thought this was a better course than a constitutional exemption from the courts.

Bayda took a very different view on the sentence. In his dissent, he chose mercy, which reflected his view that a sentence should fit the offender and the circumstances of the offence, not simply the offence. He approached the *Charter* argument from the perspective that the right not to be subjected to cruel and unusual punishment was an individual right, and it was the circumstances of that individual that should determine whether the *Charter* right was violated. In Latimer's circumstances, he argued, a sentence of murder became a cruel and unusual punishment because it was disproportionate and inequitable in treating someone who killed for compassionate reasons the same as people who committed other murders.

Bayda found support in four unreported cases of mercy killings. The circumstances of these cases were different from Latimer's but the common factor was that the prosecution had exercised discretion to avoid trying the accused for murder. In two cases, the charges were reduced to "administering a noxious substance," with minimum penalties. This illustrated, to Bayda's mind, that such cases were often treated differently than "conventional" murder due to the compassionate motives of the perpetrator. It also illustrated another fact: that the treatment of so-called compassionate killers was uneven and arbitrary. In some cases, they might essentially go free, in others to jail with long sentences.

When motive was considered, Bayda saw more disproportionality and inequality. The fact that someone in Latimer's situation was treated exactly the same as someone who had committed a murder for greed, jealously, or some other base motive was, in his view, inherently unfair. "The actor himself was not a murderous thug, devoid of conscience, whose life has been one of violence, greed, contempt for the law and total disrespect for human beings," he wrote. "On the contrary, the actor was a nurturing, caring, giving, respectful, law-abiding responsible parent of the victim."[77]

Another "disturbing comparison" was that defences such as provocation or drunkenness could reduce murder to manslaughter and lead to a much lesser sentence because the accused was deemed less culpable. It seemed inherently disproportionate to the chief justice that an individual "almost invariably motivated by anger, hate, jealousy or some similar vice" might hope for a lesser sentence than someone in Latimer's position.[78] Bayda argued that the strong public outrage over the sentence was further compelling evidence that the punishment was excessive and disproportionate. A number of letters to ministers of justice, the prime minister, MPs, and the governor general were admitted as fresh evidence at the appeal. A common theme of the correspondence was that Latimer should not be treated like other murderers. Bayda also questioned whether a long custodial sentence served any real purpose. The prosecution conceded specific deterrence, protection of the public, and rehabilitation did not apply to Latimer. He was almost certain to not reoffend.

Bayda concluded that a constitutional exemption was the proper course in the circumstances. He was mindful that the Supreme Court of Canada, although not making any binding statement of law, had shown considerable skepticism about granting exemptions, fearing that doing so instead of striking down a law might create "unpredictability and uncertainty." Bayda argued that the law was already uncertain in the treatment of compassionate killings. The public outrage over *Latimer* and the *Rodriguez* decision not long before, where the Supreme Court had not allowed an assisted suicide, demonstrated to Bayda that legislative change was likely coming. He noted that a recent Senate committee report on euthanasia recommended lesser penalties for compassionate killings. An exemption acknowledged the potential legislative change and did not subject Robert Latimer to a sentence that might soon be obsolete. And fundamentally, Bayda argued, the *Charter* existed to grant an individual relief from the actions and inaction of legislatures and executives. The role of the judge was to correct excess and injustice, not perpetuate it with "misguided deference."

Tallis and Bayda presented neatly opposed views on the appropriate punishment for Latimer. Tallis viewed the appeal primarily as a matter of properly upholding the law, with his sensitivity to the victim making it difficult for him to accept a lesser degree of culpability. Bayda presented a passionate argument for the plight of Latimer and posed powerful questions about crime and punishment, less founded on law and more in morality and a sense of justice. The two judgments reflected starkly the divide that became more and more obvious on the court regarding sentencing. Tallis dealt with sentence according to the crime and larger societal interests, Bayda according to the specific circumstances and nature of the offender.

Bayda was in the minority, but his dissent allowed appeal to the Supreme Court of Canada. Latimer's story took a strange turn at this point. The Crown prosecutor had been aggressive in his conduct of the trial, and a ground of appeal was that his address to the jury was unnecessarily inflammatory. Subsequently, it came to light that the prosecutor had prepared a questionnaire soliciting the views of prospective jurors on the issues in the case, such as euthanasia. The RCMP administered the questionnaire to some thirty people in the juror pool and had further interviews with them. Five served on the jury and the prosecutor did not disclose his contact with them. The Supreme Court ordered a new trial. At the second trial, Latimer was convicted of murder. The judge elected to give a constitutional exemption, sentencing Latimer to one year in jail and one year's probation.

Cameron, Vancise, and Wakeling upheld the conviction but allowed the Crown appeal of sentence. Despite the new trial, the pertinent questions regarding sentence were settled in the earlier judgment of the court and had not been overruled. The Supreme Court agreed. Latimer's applications for early parole were denied and he served the full ten years before being released in 2011. The Supreme Court has given several constitutional exemptions, but not in criminal sentencing.

Latimer has lasting relevance, particularly as societal attitudes towards assisted dying and euthanasia are shifting and selective abortion raises profound and disturbing questions about the worth and dignity of the disabled. The recent law allowing the terminally ill assisted death did not address the situation in *Latimer*. There has been no move to introduce a mercy killing amendment in the *Criminal Code*. The decision to pursue murder charges remains a matter of prosecutorial discretion, and in circumstances similar to the *Latimer* case is highly unlikely. This is no doubt cold comfort to those on either side of the debate.

FIGHTING THE GOOD FIGHT: *HOUSEN*, *VALLEY BEEF*, AND *H.L.*

THE LEADING CANADIAN textbook on standards of review said it all in 1994: "The governing principle for limiting review should be that the sole purpose of a standard of limited review is to avoid duplication of effort by judicial actors on issues if no commensurate improvement in the quality of justice occurs."[79] In other words, the principle for limiting review should be to prevent appeal court judges from unnecessarily reviewing and interfering in trial decisions particularly if their subsequent decision was really no better than the first. The application of formal and more rigorous deferential standards of review was not only dictated from above to intermediate appellate courts. Many judges, especially on very busy courts, welcomed standards of review, as did many counsel. Their use reduced the volume of cases, gave greater structure and certainty to appeals, and reduced the expense to litigants who might otherwise pursue pointless appeals. And many still think standards of appeal are invaluable. But with the formalization and widespread application of the standards, others felt some disquiet at the seeming triumph of process over the merits of an appeal.[80]

As stated earlier, the deferential standards of review were a formalizing of the principles of appellate restraint that courts had applied for over a century. Loosely speaking, the standards were rules governing when an appeal court should intervene in a trial or administrative decision and when it should show deference to the trial judge or administrative tribunal, primarily on determinations of fact and inferences from determined facts. The restraint reflected in part that appeal courts were latecomers in the common law and there remained great reverence for the primacy of the trial and the institution of the jury. It also reflected that appeals were not new trials, and deference went hand in hand with other restrictions appeal courts created, such as not permitting new evidence or hearing additional witnesses, and discouraging novel legal arguments at appeal. In Canada, the principles of deference formalized as deferential standards of review in the 1980s and early 1990s. The Supreme Court played a central role, looking askance at unnecessary interference by intermediate appellate courts and at inconsistency in when and how those courts showed deference.

Deferential standards of review had particular importance in administrative law, and their prevalence in that field almost certainly influenced the wider application of deferential standards. Legislatures, with privative clauses and other restrictions, limited judicial review of the decisions of statutory boards and tribunals, such as seen with the Labour Relations Board in the 1940s and 1950s. Often, administrative bodies were concerned with technical fields that courts were not well suited to review, and sometimes government simply wanted board decisions to be final. Aside from statutory restrictions, the case law promoted a large degree of deference towards administrative boards, panels, and tribunals. The application of the standards of review in administrative law had its own particular structure and nuances, but the emphasis on deference influenced the general use of standards. That excessive deference resulted in injustice—the Saskatchewan court's primary concern—was a criticism certainly heard in administrative law.

The basic standards of review in Canada were correctness, unreasonableness, and patent unreasonableness in the administrative law context and correctness and "palpable and overriding error" in the trial context. The least deferential standard was correctness and was applied primarily to questions of law: the trial judge's understanding and application of the relevant legal principles or statute. Appellate courts, with their responsibility to develop the law, owed no deference to a trial judge's interpretation of law and were free to decide whether it was right, wrong, or if there was a better one. Unreasonableness was a more deferential standard. An appellate court did not interfere if the conclusions of a judge or tribunal were reasonable, rational, and based on evidence, even if the appellate court did not agree with those conclusions. This was a standard often used in administrative law.

The standard of "palpable and overriding error"—stated as "patent unreasonableness" in administrative law—was very deferential. *Palpable* meant obvious and clear; *overriding* meant that the error affected the outcome. An appellate court only intervened if it was shown that the trial judge had made an obvious and important mistake in the determination and weighing of the evidence. The "demonstrably unfit" standard in sentencing was essentially the same. Palpable and overriding error was the standard, if not called such, historically applied to a judge's assessment of witness testimony. The controversy arose from the application of this standard to other findings of fact, inferences from established fact, and questions of mixed law and fact. This is what the Supreme Court did in *Housen v Nikolaisen.*

HOUSEN V NIKOLAISEN

THE DECISION THAT started the Saskatchewan resistance was *Housen v Nikolaisen*. It was innocuous enough litigation. Douglas Nikolaisen had been impaired when he lost control of his truck while negotiating a curve on a damp dirt road. The passenger in the truck, Paul Housen, had been rendered quadriplegic by the accident. The dirt road in question, known as a land access road, was primitive and not engineered to any specification, and there was no statutory requirement for standard signage. Local rural governments were required, under section 192 of *The Rural Municipality Act*, to maintain the roads and were potentially liable for hazards. At trial, a judge sitting alone found that Nikolaisen was 50 percent responsible, the rural municipality of Shellbrook 35 percent, and Housen 15 percent for accepting a ride with an intoxicated driver. The judge found that the municipality should have known the corner where the accident took place was potentially hazardous and posted a sign, holding that a motorist exercising ordinary care and prudence could come to grief.

The panel of Cameron, Gerwing, and Lane took issue with this last finding and allowed the appeal of the municipality. The appeal essentially concerned the trial judge's findings of fact and the evidence she chose to follow. Cameron, writing for the court, set out the appropriate standard of "palpable and overriding error," which he warned was "a formidable obstacle on the way to overcoming factual determinations at trial." Cameron agreed with the trial judge's analysis of the law and her finding that the municipality had a duty of care that might include putting up a warning sign. But he found her finding about the extent of the hazard to be flawed. It lacked an essential and explicit analysis of how a reasonably prudent driver would have driven on that road, and thus whether there was really a hazard. This lack of assessment, he asserted, amounted to an error of law.

There was conflicting expert opinion and witness testimony about how much of a hazard the corner represented and the appropriate speed for drivers. On Cameron's reading of the evidence, the two experts who the trial judge followed fundamentally misjudged the hazard, in part by assuming the road would be driven at relatively high speed. He concluded that the basic character of the road was such that a prudent driver, exercising reasonable care, would be unlikely to be driving quickly. The relative familiarity of Nikolaisen with the route threw additional doubt on whether the road was a factor in the accident, as did the fact that Nikolaisen was significantly impaired.

Likely Cameron and many others were more than a little surprised when the Supreme Court turned *Housen* into the leading judgment—cited thousands of times—to define the deferential standard of review for facts found at trial. The majority judgment of justices Frank Iacobucci and John Major took the position that while every jurist understood the standard of review was "palpable and overriding error," many did not really apply it, and that was the case in *Housen.* Although the Court of Appeal had putatively used this standard, in reality the panel had approached the judge's findings with less deference. The Supreme Court decision was aimed squarely at establishing and justifying a high bar for review of any fact finding, as part of an explicit definition of the proper role of an appellate court.

In the view of the majority, there were three basic principles behind a highly deferential standard of review. The first was to avoid overloading the judicial system: extensive appellate review of facts was "needless duplication of judicial proceedings." The second was to promote the "autonomy and integrity of the trial proceedings" by not eroding confidence in trial judges and recognizing their competence. The third was the recognition of the advantageous position of the trial judge in understanding and weighing evidence, particularly their understanding of the case as a whole.

In pursuit of these three principles, Iacobucci and Major greatly expanded the reach of the standard of "palpable and overriding error." It had long been recognized that trial judges had a great advantage in assessing witnesses. In a 1987 Saskatchewan case, *Lensen v Lensen*, the Supreme Court declared this was the standard for witness testimony, arguably the beginning of the mandate of more stringent standards. *Housen* made "palpable and overriding" the standard for all fact finding, including the trial judge's inferences of fact. Historically, appellate courts were considered as well placed as the trial court to make further inferences from established facts and did not show particular deference on such findings. *Housen* ended that practice. The majority also addressed questions of "mixed law and fact," where a legal test or standard is applied to the facts of the situation, such as a finding of negligence. While acknowledging that it is sometimes difficult to determine whether a trial judge's error was the application of the law as opposed to the conclusion drawn from the established facts, the majority stated that the stringent standard must be applied when fact findings were at issue or the facts could not be separated from the application of the law.

Essentially, the majority decision at the Supreme Court told appellate courts to stick to the law and leave the facts to the judge at trial unless there were obviously and clearly wrong conclusions that also clearly affected the outcome. This was a dictate that did not sit well with some judges on the intermediate appellate courts, particularly in Saskatchewan.

VALLEY BEEF PRODUCERS V FARM CREDIT CORPORATION

HOUSEN V NIKOLAISEN laid down the law, quite literally, on appellate review of fact findings, and there may not have seemed much room for argument. But the Supreme Court had not considered Saskatchewan's *Court of Appeal Act*. The statute establishing the province's appellate court contained several sections that appeared to lay out much broader powers of review than allowed under the standards. In *Valley Beef Producers Co-operative Ltd. v Farm Credit Corp.*, Justice Cameron set out to show that in Saskatchewan, the rules were a little different. His question was simple: Given that courts of appeal were creations of statute, should the statute not then be the authority as to its powers and jurisdiction?

The litigation in *Valley Beef* was an interesting legal problem. A cattle breeder with a breeder's agreement with the Valley Beef Producers Co-operative bought a number of cows. Under the agreement, the co-operative, which provided the funds for the purchase, got title to the cattle while the breeder had possession for breeding purposes and could sell them and their offspring on behalf of the co-operative, getting a share of the sale. The breeder in question had secured personal loans from the Farm Credit Corporation with the cattle. When she defaulted, the Farm Credit tried to seize the entire proceeds of the sale. The co-operative, which had also used the cattle as security for its own line of credit with the Bank of Montreal, claimed ownership and the funds. On an application from Farm Credit, the trial judge held that the co-operative was a secured party like the corporation and under the applicable statute law did not have priority, and the proceeds went to Farm Credit.

On appeal, the court unfurled the banner of robust appellate intervention. Cameron seized the opportunity to tackle the question of whether *The Court of Appeal Act, 2000* provided for a broader appellate review than the standards of review, and which took priority, statute or judge-made law. The restrictive application of the standards of review had bothered Cameron for some time. According to Cameron, the profession in Saskatchewan, which had been accustomed to an interventionist court, complained that after *Lensen* in 1987 the court was "*Lensen*-ing everything to death."[81] *Housen* went much further, in Cameron's view making it difficult for the court to see justice done for litigants in many appeals where the trial judge's conclusions, although founded on evidence, did not seem the best possible.

Cameron argued that fundamentally the powers and jurisdiction of all appellate courts are created and defined in their enabling statutes. The crucial sections of *The Court of Appeal Act, 2000* were sections 7, 12, 13, and 14. The crucial point in section 7 was that all decisions of the Court of Queen's Bench except interlocutory orders could be appealed without restriction or leave. Section 12 specified the powers of the court. Of particular importance were subsections 12(1)d and 12(1)f, which specified that the court "may make any decision that could have been made by the court or tribunal appealed from" and "make any additional decision it considers just."[82] Section 13 more specifically addressed facts and evidence at trial. It gave the litigant the right, in cases tried by judge alone, to "make objections against the sufficiency of the evidence, or the view of the evidence taken by the trial judge, that are allowed in cases of trial or assessment of damages by a jury."[83]

Section 14 was the most important in terms of the standards of review and seemed to give the court the power to review nearly anything:

> On an appeal from, or on a motion against, the decision of a trial judge or on any rehearing the court is not obliged . . . to adopt the view of the evidence taken by the trial judge, but the court shall act on its own view of what, in its judgment, the evidence proves, and the court may draw inferences of fact and pronounce the decision that, in its judgment, the trial judge ought to have pronounced.[84]

In Cameron's estimation, section 7 and section 13 conferred broad rights of appeal on the litigant, while section 12 and section 14 gave the court broad powers of review. All the pertinent points were found in the 1915 *Court of Appeal Act*, and in fact sections 13 and 14 were nearly identical to sections 8 and 9 in the original, which had spelled out the court's ability to review fact findings in a fashion unusual even at the time. The sections had remained through successive iterations of the *Act*. Justice Percy Gordon said in 1955 that the enactments in Saskatchewan provided "the widest powers given an appellate court in Canada."[85]

Cameron bolstered his argument by examining the historical origin of the powers in the *Act*. He found that the Saskatchewan statute was based on (some sections had nearly identical wording) the statutes and rules that established the powers of the English Court of Appeal. There had been some debate in the late nineteenth century about the proper extent of appellate review. English decisions had settled on significant deference to a trial judge's finding with witness testimony but little deference to other findings and to inferences of fact, and this was formalized in statute. Following the English precedents, which were binding, the Saskatchewan Supreme Court *en banc* had decided the same in *Coventry v Annable*, a decision later upheld at the Supreme Court of Canada. In fact, as other authors aside from Cameron had noted, this was the general position in Canada until the 1970s, when the Supreme Court started to insist on more deference.

Cameron drew two critical points from the history. As with the English appeal court, appeals in Saskatchewan took the form of a rehearing. This was not a retrial but a review of the case on its merits, considering the evidence, the arguments, and the conclusions of the trial judge in full.

This was in contrast to a review for error, which considered the record of the trial in a more limited fashion to find obvious error and which, in Cameron's view, was what the standards of review created. The second point was that the court's enabling statute had preserved the much wider power of review that had existed historically. This was the basis of the modern *Court of Appeal Act*, and there was no reason to think that the meaning of the relevant sections had changed.

In Cameron's view, the Supreme Court's dictates on the standard of review in *Housen* were plain and simply the court making policy to control the flow of appeals at the intermediate level. As he wrote in a subsequent decision, *H.L. v Canada*,

> This standard is founded in judicial policy notions, beginning with the notion that finality is an important aim of litigation. The deference to the findings of the trial judge that underlies this standard finds its judicial policy justification, generally, in the presumption that trial judges are as competent as appellate court judges to ensure that disputes are resolved justly. More particularly, it finds its judicial policy justification in the desirability of limiting the number and length of appeals; of promoting the autonomy and integrity of the trial proceedings; of fostering the confidence of litigants in those proceedings; of recognizing the competence of the trial judge; and of reducing needless duplication of judicial effort with no corresponding improvement in the quality of justice.[86]

Cameron's argument in *Valley Beef* (and in *H.L. v Canada*, discussed below) was that the Supreme Court made a policy choice counter to the policy choice of the Saskatchewan legislature, and he questioned the authority of the Supreme Court to do so. But he also questioned the soundness of the court's policy objective. To Cameron's mind, it missed the point.

> The principal object of *The Court of Appeal Act, 2000* is to confer and give effect to rights of appeal. These are substantive rights of major importance to persons who find themselves before the courts and tribunals of the Province. It is often said that a right without a remedy is no right at all, a point that underscores the importance of the relationship between the right of appeal and the remedial powers of the Court. As the effectiveness of those

> powers ebbs or flows, so too does the effectiveness of the right of appeal, for the right is no more effective than the capacity of the Court to act upon it. And above all it is the object of the right of appeal that should command our attention.[87]

Cameron took up the cause again in *H.L. v Canada (Attorney General)*, a residential school case. The plaintiff had sued for damages for his sexual abuse at the hands of the residence administrator, William Starr, of the residential school on the Gordon Reserve. Starr had run an extracurricular boxing club, to which the plaintiff, who lived on the reserve but attended an off-reserve school, belonged. The trial judge found the federal government vicariously liable, as Starr was deemed an employee and the boxing club was sufficiently connected to his duties. On top of direct damages for the abuse, the judge awarded the plaintiff a large sum for loss of past and future earnings, tracing the difficulties the plaintiff had with substance abuse, criminality, and maintaining employment to his abuse. The government appealed, denying liability and arguing that the evidence did not support the awarded damages.

Cameron upheld the trial judge's finding of vicarious liability but allowed the government's appeal for the damages on past and future earnings. As this required a review of the trial judge's fact findings, inferences of fact, and application of law to fact, Cameron again took up the cudgel on standards of review. His arguments in *H.L. v Canada* were more or less the same as in *Valley Beef*, if further refined and also more broadly applied. *Valley Beef* had not been appealed further, and Cameron's insurrection was largely unnoticed outside Saskatchewan. But that now changed. Under the Supreme Court's statute, provincial courts of appeal could grant leave in matters that had significant public importance, bypassing the Supreme Court's leave process. It was a power that was rarely used. The plaintiff's counsel asked for leave, seeking more damages. Bayda, writing for the court, made clear the importance of the appeal and where his sympathies lay:

> This Court cannot operate under a dilemmic cloud. It, and the litigants and counsel who appear before it in all future cases, need to know whether the Court is required to follow the unequivocal specific statutory dictates of its creator, the Saskatchewan legislature . . . as those dictates have now been interpreted and construed in the present case, or the jurisprudential generic

dictates of the majority of the Supreme Court of Canada laid down in *Housen*, or some hybrid of the two sets of dictates.[88]

Bayda boldly raised the possibility that *Housen* was wrongly decided because the Supreme Court had not considered Saskatchewan's *Court of Appeal Act*. The substantive arguments regarding damages, of crucial importance to the survivors of residential schools pursuing recompense from the government and the operators of the schools, were an additional reason to grant leave.

The Supreme Court did not give an inch on the standards of review. The majority decision of Justice Morris Fish was at times brusque. He did not agree that *The Court of Appeal Act* provided any special powers or wider jurisdiction in hearing appeals, nor did he agree with Cameron's contention that in Saskatchewan appeals took the form of a rehearing rather than a review for error. Fish argued that far from being unique, provisions similar to section 13 and section 14 could be found in the statutes of most provinces, albeit in more general terms. Although in principle the province could grant wider powers of review, in Fish's view much more explicit and direct statutory language was required. Fish felt that the terms of *The Court of Appeal Act* were not incompatible with the standard of "unreasonable and palpable error"; this was simply the threshold at which the Court of Appeal could then substitute its own view of the evidence. He also did not see in the jurisprudence of the court any departure from the standards of review the Supreme Court promulgated, and he thought Saskatchewan's court historically was, if anything, more rigorous than most in showing deference.

Cameron did find sympathy in Ottawa. Justice Michel Bastarache, writing for the minority, agreed with much of Cameron's argument. Bastarache had earlier been the minority writer in *Housen* and obviously had some of the same concerns about excessive deference as Cameron. He thought his colleague Fish had misconstrued Cameron's reference to rehearing to mean a hearing *de novo*, or completely afresh, but more fundamentally believed the Saskatchewan court was correct in applying a less rigorous standard of review to inferences of fact, a position he had also taken in *Housen*. And in the case at the bar, Bastarache thought that even applying the most rigorous standard, the Court of Appeal was correct in challenging the judge's factual inferences.

H.L. ultimately concerned a critical, but to the layperson esoteric, matter of law. The debate over standards of review and deference overshadowed the fact that the appeal was part of the ever-growing body of litigation arising from the residential schools. The Supreme Court's *H.L.* decision, by upholding the trial judge's analysis of the causal connection between sexual abuse followed by alcohol abuse and the further consequences of social dislocation, incarceration, and unemployment—and subsequent damages for loss of past and future earnings—served notice to the government and other defendants that the courts might look broadly at causation and also types of damages that flowed from the abuse. It has also been noted, however, that plaintiffs could see *H.L.* as a warning that the connections between residential school traumas and actual compensation would be scrutinized and that litigation was likely to be prolonged and uncertain.[89] Adversarial litigation was clearly not a very good mechanism to address both the specific traumas of survivors and the larger issue of cultural destruction.

CONCLUSION

THE SUPREME COURT'S decision was the last word on the subject of appellate deference in Saskatchewan. There was no move on the part of the provincial government to change *The Court of Appeal Act*. Outside of the court and the profession, it was an issue that engaged very few people. And even within the legal world, many judges and lawyers wondered what the fuss was about. Standards made their jobs simpler. Others did not worry about injustice, confident that in cases of manifest unfairness the standards would not prevent redress. Others continued to chafe under the yoke. But the debate was over. Or was it? Not long after *H.L.*, the Supreme Court seemed to take a step back on deference with its *Dunsmuir* decision. The pendulum was perhaps due to swing back.

The Court of Appeal for Saskatchewan, meanwhile, was on the verge of another renewal. Twenty-five years of Bayda's stewardship would soon come to an end and new faces begin to appear on the court in rapid succession. The court entered a period of transition with a nearly complete changing of the guard. Two successive chief justices would mould the court that would celebrate the centennial and begin its second century.

CHAPTER 10

THE *CHARTER'S* SECOND COMING

THE LEAFLET WAS NOT THE SORT OF THING MOST people would want to find in their mailbox. Many probably threw it away without giving it more than a glance. But others who paused to read the leaflet were disturbed. Some were appalled.

> It has come to the attention of the Christian Truth Activists that a committee on "Gay, Lesbian, Bisexual and Transgendered issues," set up by the Saskatoon Public School Board had recommended that information on homosexuality be included in their curriculum and school libraries. . . . Children at this age are more interested in playing Barbie & Ken rather than learning how wonderful it is for two men to sodomize each other. . . . Now the homosexuals want to share their filth and propaganda with Saskatchewan's children.[1]

Strong, offensive, hurtful words. But words that should be illegal as hate speech? That was the question that came to the Court of Appeal.

The *Charter of Rights of Freedoms* led to many advances in human rights in Canada. *Charter* jurisprudence gave greater life and efficacy to provincial human rights codes and pushed governments to amend legislation to account for rights and freedoms. Section 15 of the *Charter* was a particularly important tool against discrimination. But section 15 claims involving gay, lesbian, and transgender rights also started to engage other *Charter* protections, specifically freedom of expression and freedom of religion, as not everyone welcomed the extension of rights based on sexual orientation. While balancing *Charter* rights was not a new exercise, it took on some urgency in the twenty-first century. And with the *Charter* now over thirty years old, some early decisions were coming under reappraisal as the "living tree" of the constitution continued to grow. In several instances, old *Charter* precedents were abandoned, and in a key Saskatchewan decision questions about the reach of *stare decisis* in the modern age were decided.

SASKATCHEWAN'S CENTURY

IN 2005, SASKATCHEWAN turned one hundred. The province celebrated its centennial with an optimism that echoed that of 1905. The vista of endless possibilities visible at the dawn of the last century was absent, but a decade of retrenchment was over, and as the world came calling for Saskatchewan's wheat, oil, and potash, the province entered its second century with good prospects. With renewed prosperity, voters turned their backs on the NDP, and the pendulum of provincial politics swung back to the right with the rise of the Saskatchewan Party.

In the wake of another NDP election victory, in 1997 four Progressive Conservative and four Liberal MLAs abandoned their respective parties to found something new.[2] Not surprisingly, the new Saskatchewan Party leaned to the right. Premier Romanow liked to call them "Saskatories," merely the Progressive Conservatives rebranded.[3] This was not strictly true, but the party did quickly fill much the same space in Saskatchewan politics. It was predominantly rural, conservative, and a proponent of small government and free enterprise. As a political writer noted, "The more centrist values of the former Liberals who helped found the party were not evident in its policies and pronouncements."[4] Under the first leader, Elwin Hermanson, a former Reform Party MP, the party had a social conservative tone—advocating boot camp for young offenders, for example—while also pursuing familiar Saskatchewan themes such as privatization of Crown corporations and, more controversially in the birthplace of public health care, allowing private clinics. The party was immediately competitive, capturing twenty-five out of fifty-eight seats in 1999, nearly unseating the NDP, and twenty-eight in 2003.[5]

The Saskatchewan Party found a winning formula with a new leader, Brad Wall. Born and raised in Swift Current, Wall had earned a degree in public administration and developed a taste for politics at the University of Saskatchewan.[6] He was a political aide in Ottawa and then in the Devine government before returning to Swift Current, first to manage a country music museum but later becoming the city's economic development officer and starting an adventure travel company. Wall was elected as a Saskatchewan Party MLA in 1999 and as justice critic was marked as a rising star. After succeeding Hermanson as party leader in 2004, Wall immediately moved the party platform towards the centre, emphasizing economic growth and job creation, and was rewarded with electoral success in 2007.[7] In what was now the classic Saskatchewan pattern, after over fifteen years in power the NDP fell hard. Wall and the Saskatchewan Party took 50 percent of the vote and thirty-eight seats.[8]

Wall took power at a propitious time. The provincial economy had entered a sustained boom, propelled by the "super-cycle" in global commodities, with strong prices for oil, gas, potash, uranium, and farm products. Bulging government coffers allowed Wall to cut taxes deeply and increase spending in health care, infrastructure, and social services while keeping a balanced budget. In 2011, Wall and the Saskatchewan Party were returned to power with a record 64 percent of the popular vote.[9] Wall was prominent on the national scene, continuing a Saskatchewan tradition as a strong voice for provincial rights, and many saw him as the defender of Western Canadian interests. Under Wall, in 2016 the party broke through the two-term barrier that had previously limited right-of-centre governments. The Saskatchewan Party handily won the 2016 election even as oil and potash prices tumbled and a major recession was underway. A year later, Wall somewhat unexpectedly announced he was resigning, choosing to leave while at the top of his game, raising interesting questions about the future for his party and for the province.

The boom times stanched the flow of people from the province and even brought expats back from Alberta, British Columbia, and Ontario, as well as a larger share of new immigrants to Canada. Saskatchewan

JOHN KLEBUC

Saskatchewan's seventh chief justice was born in Meadow Lake on April 24, 1940. His grandfather had emigrated from Ukraine in 1928 and worked as an agricultural labourer, saving money to bring over his family and purchase a farm. Klebuc's father had been born before the family came to Canada, and Klebuc himself spoke primarily Ukrainian until he started grade school. Growing up in Meadow Lake, Klebuc was introduced to the law with a summer job in a local lawyer's office. His father, a CPR section hand, greatly admired the Canadian legal system and encouraged Klebuc to become a lawyer. When Klebuc had second thoughts about university, his father took him out on the railroad for a day, pounding spikes. Klebuc entered the combined art and law program in 1959, studying sociology before entering law school. He graduated in 1964.

Chief Justice John Klebuc, n.d. (Photo: Patricia Holdsworth. Court of Appeal.)

After articling with William Elliott, QC, at MacPherson, Leslie and Tyerman in Regina, Klebuc remained at the firm for his entire time in practice. He appeared as junior counsel with Elliott and the great E.C. Leslie on several major commercial litigation files and had a significant family law practice before shifting to corporate and commercial work. Made a partner in 1971, Klebuc focused on corporate transactions and led the firm's real-estate section. He also took an early interest in the application of information technology, initially computerizing the firm's accounting. Klebuc then led initiatives to further introduce computers into the workplace. Outside the firm, Klebuc was a sessional instructor at the University of Regina and was involved with the Canadian Bar Association. He was also active in the Progressive Conservative Party. In 1985, Klebuc was appointed a Queen's Counsel of Canada.

Klebuc was named to the Court of Queen's Bench in 1993, the last Mulroney appointee in Saskatchewan. Assigned to Saskatoon, he was part of the court's bankruptcy and insolvency group in the city. He was also responsible, at the behest of Chief Justice Donald MacPherson, for establishing a simplified procedure in the Court of Queen's Bench for civil litigation under $50,000. Klebuc was the trial judge in *H.L. v. Canada*, which gave a landmark settlement and established an important precedent in residential school litigation.

On September 18, 2006, Klebuc was appointed chief justice of Saskatchewan. He was the second Ukrainian Canadian to occupy the post after Edward Bayda. After seven years as chief justice, Klebuc decided to step down but remained a supernumerary judge, the first time the head of the court had elected to do so. He retired on his birthday in 2015 but remains active with arbitration and mediation work.

saw its strongest population growth in many years and vaulted back over the million mark to stand at just under 1,100,000 in 2016. Behind the prosperity of the decade-long boom there were still certain hard realities. The economy remained strongly dependent on cyclical natural-resource industries, and the end of the commodities rally—particularly the crash in oil prices—immediately put pressure on employment and government finances. The need for diversification was as critical as ever. Despite the province's iconic wheat and canola fields, agriculture was a minor part of its GDP, employing only 5 percent of the workforce and still vulnerable to price swings and variable harvests.[10] Rural depopulation and the decline of many small towns showed no signs of slowing, while Regina, Saskatoon, and a handful of other cities thrived.

Demographics were a factor in another challenge. The province's Indigenous population continued to grow and move to the cities—in 2011, almost 16 percent identified as either First Nations or Métis.[11] Nearly 25 percent of Prince Albert's population was Aboriginal. The province's Indians and Métis had seen material progress over the decades, but there was an array of issues—from economic development on reserves to honouring treaty rights to the continuing disproportionate rate of incarceration for Aboriginals—that needed to be addressed. More fundamentally, with

Indigenous peoples forecasted to become almost one-third of the province's population in coming decades, there was a pressing need to find an accommodation between so-called settler society and Aboriginals that respected the latter's culture and sovereignty while providing the benefits of the economic and political mainstream. Wall's government was the latest that did not come to grips with this reality.

In 2005, the Court of Appeal was not yet one hundred, although an important milestone was only two years away: the centennial of the founding of the Saskatchewan superior court system. A long-serving chief justice was just about to step down. Over the next decade, leading up to its true centennial, the Court of Appeal went through a period of transition and renewal that placed it, like the province, on a good footing for its second century.

A TALE OF TWO CHIEF JUSTICES

CHIEF JUSTICE BAYDA had the pleasure of greeting the provincial centennial while occupying his high office. The celebrations inaugurated his last year as chief justice. Bayda stepped down on September 9, 2006, his seventy-fifth birthday, after twenty-five years. He was the longest-serving head of the Court of Appeal proper, and the length of his tenure as chief justice of Saskatchewan was second only to Frederick Haultain's.[12] Bayda was an institution, as much as Culliton before him and Martin before him. His leave-taking was another glittering affair. Many lawyers missed his inquiring mind, the spirited courtroom exchanges, and his obvious love for the law. Bayda was not quite done; he joined the firm of Kanuka Thuringer as counsel and took great delight in mentoring the firm's young lawyers, just as he had with the law clerks at the court.

Court of Queen's Bench justice John Klebuc became the eighth chief justice of Saskatchewan. It was a surprise choice. Klebuc was a partner at MacPherson, Leslie and Tyerman before joining the Queen's Bench in 1993, assigned to Saskatoon. A corporate and commercial solicitor in practice, Klebuc was a member of the Queen's Bench bankruptcy and insolvency section, judges who gave special priority to complex and time-sensitive corporate bankruptcies. He was a well-known trial judge and known to have a keen interest in technology, but Klebuc was a dark horse for chief

Chief Justice John Klebuc leaving the Legislature Building after the installation of the Lieutenant Governor in 2012. (Court of Appeal)

justice, especially as it had become general practice in Canada to appoint a sitting judge on an appeal court.

Klebuc had an explanation for his choice.[13] He was a strong Conservative Party supporter before going to the bench. He had not been involved in partisan politics for years, but this background was a major advantage after more than a decade of Liberal appointments. Although the patronage aspect of judicial appointments had diminished, the newly elected Conservative government of Prime Minister Stephen Harper was naturally inclined to consider candidates with some party background. Judges on the Court of Queen's Bench were pushing to have trial judges promoted to the Court of Appeal, given that five of six appointments to the higher court preceding Klebuc were "off the street." Of the two strongest internal candidates for chief justice on the existing appeal bench, one was a recent appointment, and the other had been very active at one time in Liberal circles. Klebuc followed in the footsteps of Emmett Hall, the last appointment from outside the court, and from the Queen's Bench, direct to the chief's chair.

The change in leadership was part of the renewal of the appellate bench. The court had gone an astonishing fourteen years with no new appointments, and nearly all of the early 1980s alumni were still there in the early 2000s, although two had taken supernumerary status. But once started, change quickly gained pace. Between 2004 and 2017, there were eleven appointments to the court including two new chief justices. Among the full-time judges, there was a near complete turnover of personnel, although a large number of supernumeraries ensured continuity.

The first new appointment came in 2004 with Robert G. Richards. He was a leading appellate counsel in Saskatchewan and a very familiar face at the Court of Appeal and the Supreme Court of Canada. Justice Claire L'Heureux-Dubé, speaking for herself and her colleagues in Ottawa, called Richards "one of our favourites."[14] He was the director of constitutional law for the Saskatchewan government in the 1980s and then practised at MacPherson, Leslie and Tyerman, primarily in public law. Bayda had not been shy about asking Richards, who had never considered the bench, to apply for a position on the Court of Appeal.[15] Richards filled a long-standing vacancy created with Thomas Wakeling's 1999 retirement.

Richards was followed in 2005 by Justice Gene Anne Smith from the Court of Queen's Bench. She replaced Calvin Tallis, who retired that year. Smith had been a professor of law in Saskatoon for nearly two decades before going to the trial court in 1997. Smith was the Saskatchewan example of a trend seen across the country, where able women who had flourished teaching and writing in law schools were appointed to the bench. Smith had briefly been a philosophy professor before becoming a lawyer.

Two more appointments followed quickly in 2007 as four judges chose supernumerary status. Darla Hunter and Ysanne Wilkinson were both from the Queen's Bench, appointed there in 1990 and 1996 respectively. Hunter was another MacPherson, Leslie and Tyerman alumnus while Wilkinson had practised in Prince Albert. Both were on the appeal court for only a short period, with Wilkinson returning to the Queen's Bench in 2009 and Hunter retiring in 2010. They were replaced by Ralph Ottenbreit, another Queen's Bench judge, and formerly a Regina litigator, and Neal Caldwell, a corporate-commercial solicitor with the McDougall Gauley firm in Saskatoon.

With Hunter and Wilkinson, the court had also achieved a milestone: gender parity. For two years, four of the seven full-time judges were women. Including supernumeraries, the court had five women and six men in total. Saskatchewan had joined Alberta and British Columbia in achieving parity, but, given the vagaries of appointments, it did not last.

Justice Nicholas W. Sherstobitoff's last day in court, 2010. (Court of Appeal)

More judges would have been appointed had the court not shrunk in 2007 from nine to seven full-time judges. The court's large number of supernumeraries was a factor in this unexpected and unprecedented development. By the early years of the new century, the court's lists had shrunk considerably from the hectic period in the 1980s.[16] The first rush of *Charter* cases, which had taken up a considerable amount of judicial time, had abated. A larger trend was the greatly increased use of private arbitration and mediation for corporate and commercial disputes.[17] The institution in 1994 of mandatory mediation for civil cases at the Court of Queen's Bench was another factor.[18] This was very effective at diverting cases out of the litigation stream. After Wakeling retired, his position was not filled for several years at Bayda's request, as the court had no difficulty managing the workload.

When four judges—Bill Vancise, Stuart Cameron, Marjorie Gerwing, and Nick Sherstobitoff—went supernumerary in the space of two years, the court was suddenly in the position of potentially having too many judges. Bob Richards recalled that he was concerned about not having enough work, particularly the meaty appeals he liked, and in this he was not alone.[19] Chief Justice Klebuc remembered that one of his colleagues told him quite vehemently that it was embarrassing for the court to have some judges less than fully occupied.[20] Others on the court shared these sentiments. Despite the fact that the court had been overburdened in the

GENE ANNE SMITH

Justice Gene Anne Smith was originally an American, the first to serve on the Court of Appeal since Ted Culliton. But while the American-born Culliton had grown up in Saskatchewan, Smith first came to Canada as an adult, to teach philosophy at the University of Saskatchewan.

Justice Gene Anne Smith, c. 2005. (Photo: Patricia Holdsworth. Court of Appeal.)

Smith was born in Arkadelphia, Arkansas, on March 6, 1941. She earned a bachelor of arts degree in 1963 at Mary Baldwin College in Staunton, Virginia, and then started a doctorate in philosophy at Duke University in Durham, North Carolina. In 1967, her dissertation not yet complete, Smith accepted a position at the University of Saskatchewan. She found teaching undergraduate philosophy unrewarding and decided to try a career in law. She entered the law school in 1970 and graduated in 1974 as the gold medal winner.

Smith articled with Bob McKercher at the firm of McKercher, McKercher, Stack, Korchin and Laing and remained there as a litigation associate. McKercher was Saskatchewan counsel for the Canadian Medical Protective Association and Smith was his junior on medical malpractice litigation and also did significant amounts of labour law. In 1979, Smith was offered a position at the college of law and she returned to academia to teach for eighteen years. Legal theory, administrative law, and contracts were particular areas of interest, but she taught every subject over her academic career and was widely published.

Looking for a new challenge, Smith applied for the judiciary and in 1997 was appointed to the Court of Queen's Bench. She was promoted to the Court of Appeal in 2005, only the third woman on the court and the second appointment of a law professor after Merv Woods. She was an excellent judge, tough and practical, bringing great intelligence and academic sensibilities to decisions that dug into the law, and she was one of the court's prolific writers. Smith stepped down in 2012, several years short of mandatory retirement.

past, after a unanimous vote the judges asked the government to shrink the court. The decision may be unprecedented in Canada. Klebuc's letter to the provincial minister of justice made much of the savings for both levels of government, but still the bemused minister contacted Klebuc to make absolutely certain about the court's wishes. And so, after being twice threatened with losing positions, in the 1940s and the 1980s respectively, the judiciary reduced the court on their own initiative.

The elimination of two full-time judges seemed a good idea at the time, but two potential problems subsequently arose. By 2015, the supernumeraries were mostly gone and the court was much busier. And the federal government had allowed a backlog of appointments to form. As Richards said, "We are at the wrong end of the supernumerary cycle."[21] It was clear from the workload facing the judges that restoring at least one position was vital, but he large number of vacancies and insistent demands for more judges in jurisdictions across Canada made the prospects of success uncertain. With effective lobbying, Richards got the court increased to eight in 2018, although at the time of writing no one has yet been appointed.

The departure of Sherstobitoff, Smith, Vancise, Gerwing, and Cameron by 2014 still required several new appointments. Maurice Herauf, formerly the court's registrar and a Queen's Bench judge since 2007, replaced Sherstobitoff in 2011. Peter Whitmore, a Regina lawyer and former partner of Gary Lane, appointed to the Court of Queen's Bench in 2008, joined in 2013, along with another Queen's Bench colleague, Jacelyn Ryan-Froslie, originally from Swift Current. The round of appointments reduced the representation of women on the bench to only two. The last appointment at the time of writing, Justice Lian Schwann of the Queen's Bench, in 2017, has redressed the balance to some extent. Schwann was following in Herauf's footsteps: she had succeeded him as the court's registrar and then gone to the Queen's Bench in 2011.

Conferencing at Justice Vancise's last sitting, 2013. *From left:* Justice Richards, Justice Vancise, and Justice Caldwell. (Photo: Patricia Holdsworth. Court of Appeal.)

The upset in the gender balance threw a light on the appointment practices of the Harper Conservatives. The Mulroney Conservatives and subsequent Liberal governments had appointed many women to the bench—Hunter, Smith, Wilkinson, and Ryan-Froslie were all appointed to the Court of Queen's Bench during this time. The early Harper appointments were fairly gender-balanced, and many Liberal-era trial court appointments were promoted to appeal courts. Yet some observers claimed that there was a notable shift after the Harper Conservatives won a majority in 2011, after five years of forming minority governments.[22] In Saskatchewan, it was true that noticeably fewer women were appointed, and there was little progress in increasing the representation of visible minorities and Aboriginals even as the pool of eligible lawyers was expanding.

Harper also allegedly wanted appointments aligned with his government's priorities—more deferential, skeptical of rights claims, tough on crime—replacing party patronage with ideology. This culminated in the Marc Nadon controversy, where the government appointed a federal court judge to the Supreme Court likely because of previous decisions favourable to the government. But by then, the Conservatives had discovered that judges in Canada answered to a higher calling than partisan politics and their appointees could not be counted on to rule in a particular way. And whether the Conservatives were any different from previous Liberal governments in trying to align the judiciary to party ideology is debatable.

Justice William John Vancise on his retirement, 2013. (Photo: Patricia Holdsworth. Court of Appeal.)

Saskatchewan's new appointments demonstrated other changes in policy. The majority had trial experience: nine of the eleven appointments since 2004 had spent time on the Queen's Bench. Hunter, Wilkinson, and Ryan-Froslie had long tenures on the trial court before their elevation; Smith and Whitmore had shorter but still substantial service; while Ottenbreit, Herauf, and Schwann had less time but still two to four years. All were respected trial judges. Just Richards and Caldwell came from practice. This mix was typical for most appellate courts, the general principle being that most appointees should have a trial court background with a few straight from practice. It was quite a contrast to previous Saskatchewan courts. Interestingly, Justice Ottenbreit has pointed out that Richards and Caldwell are particularly strong appellate judges.[23]

The Regina bar dominated the appointments. Seven had practised or worked in Regina before their first judicial post, two in Saskatoon, and one each in Swift Current and Prince Albert. There was some range of background, but courtroom lawyers dominated, with six former litigators, one of whom became court registrar, three solicitors, a former registrar

DARLA CATHERINE HUNTER

Born on August 28, 1948, in Regina, Darla Hunter grew up on the family farm near Fillmore, Saskatchewan. She earned a teaching certificate from Regina Teachers College in 1967 at the age of only nineteen. She entered the University of Saskatchewan shortly afterwards and earned a bachelor of arts degree, with distinction, in 1972. Two years later, she entered the law school, graduating in 1977.

Justice Darla Catherine Hunter, n.d. (Photo: Patricia Holdsworth. Court of Appeal.)

After articles at the Queen's Bench and admission to the bar in 1978, Hunter became the director for the Court of Queen's Bench rules revision project and a sessional lecturer at the law school in Saskatoon. In 1981, she joined MacPherson, Leslie and Tyerman and practised as a civil litigator. While in practice, Hunter served on the board of inquiry for the controversial Rafferty-Alameda dam project. She was also a member of the Canadian Bar Association's Supreme Court of Canada liaison committee.

In 1990, Hunter was appointed to the Court of Queen's Bench in Regina. As a trial judge, she was thrust into the media spotlight when she conducted the "faint-hope" hearing for Colin Thatcher's application for early parole, in which a jury allowed his application to go forward. Hunter was appointed to the Court of Appeal on March 2, 2007, after seventeen years of service on the trial court. Her tenure as an appellate judge was short, as Hunter chose to retire on March 1, 2010.

and civil servant, and an academic.[24] Unlike most Canadian appellate courts, there is currently only one judge with much previous practice experience in criminal law: Ottenbreit, a senior, albeit part-time, federal drugs prosecutor. The age of appointments rose. Caldwell was young at forty-three; the average age at appointment was fifty-seven, in part due to the promotions from trial court. This was substantially older than the last big round of Saskatchewan appellate appointments, in the early 1980s, but it is not known if this was common to other courts and represents a change in policy. The greater age will limit supply of supernumerary judges in the future.[25] It was also the baby-boomer court, except for Klebuc and Smith, who were of a slightly older generation, and Caldwell, the sole Generation Xer and forerunner of the next generational shift.

THE KLEBUC YEARS

THE NEW CHIEF justice came to the court as an outsider, the first in forty-five years and something of a rarity for contemporary Canadian appeal courts. Promotions to the top job usually came from within. Klebuc's new colleagues were helpful and supportive as he settled into his new role, and Klebuc turned to the "old guard" and Cameron in particular for their assistance.[26]

Klebuc reinstituted regular meetings for the court. These had been erratic and infrequent during the last years of Bayda's tenure. The meetings addressed immediate issues and long-term plans. Other judges took a role in administration, continuing a tradition started under Bayda, supervising the student clerks, maintaining the library, liaising with the government on facility needs, sitting as a representative on all-court committees, and so on.

There were also some obvious projects to tackle, such as a revision of the criminal rules. The *Criminal Code* provided a basic procedural framework for appeals, but provinces supplemented with their own rules of court. For example, the *Code* was silent on matters such as factums and appeal books, and the provincial courts set other procedure as well. Saskatchewan had generally revised the civil rules on a twenty- to thirty-year cycle, but the criminal rules had been untouched since 1924, aside from some practice directives.[27] Klebuc recalled a judge from another province telling him that Saskatchewan's rules must be really good since no one ever updated them. Justice Georgina Jackson took on the task, assisted by

Justice Hunter, Justice Cameron, and Lian Schwann, the registrar. The court approved the new rules in November 2010.

Klebuc also instituted a casual Friday afternoon get-together for the judges, copying a tradition of end-of-week cocktails among the Saskatoon Queen's Bench judges. He also made a habit of dropping by the offices of individual judges for a coffee and a chat. Stuart Cameron recalled that Klebuc was a very congenial man and enthusiastic about enhancing collegiality. Klebuc had an ally in Bob Richards. On his first week at the court, after a hearing, Richards suggested lunch to his fellow panel members. This suggestion seemed to take them by surprise, as Richards recalled, but they accepted the invitation. Richards continued to ask colleagues to lunch, and the practice got traction among the judges. Klebuc's and Richards's efforts had an effect. The newly appointed judges readily joined in, and the veterans, too, appreciated the more social atmosphere.

Klebuc had inherited a relatively well-organized court. Aside from the criminal rules and some minor tweaking of the civil rules, the court's practice and procedure were sound and sufficiently efficient to move appeals along in a timely fashion. But Klebuc did see one major deficiency that he believed would only get worse as time went on: the lack of an electronic filing and document management option.

DO JUDGES DREAM OF ELECTRONIC APPEALS?

KLEBUC'S FOCUS AS chief justice was eCourt. In essence, eCourt was a system allowing electronic filing and document management for appeals, which in 2018 may seem quotidian. But superior courts in Canada had a tortured history with technology initiatives. Under Klebuc, Saskatchewan's Court of Appeal succeeded in installing a functional, cost-effective system where other, much richer courts had not.

Computers had inevitably made their way into courthouses. Some judges were interested in applying technology, particularly judges in the United States, where conferences on the subject appeared as early as the 1970s.[28] Starting from word processing and other basic computer use in the 1980s, in the next decade courts installed databases and internal networks, connected to the internet, and set up websites.[29] A tantalizing prospect for appellate courts was electronic filing and document management. At the end of the century, Canadian appellate courts were mostly still paper

The Court of Appeal, c. 2010. *From left:* Justice Darla Hunter, Justice Robert Richards, Justice Gary Lane, Justice Marjorie Gerwing, Justice Stuart Cameron, Chief Justice John Klebuc, Justice William Vancise, Justice Nicholas Sherstobitoff, Justice Georgina Jackson, Justice Gene Anne Smith, and Justice Ralph Ottenbreit. (Photo: Patricia Holdsworth. Court of Appeal.)

environments, with factums and appeal books filed in hard copy. Some courts had experimented with computer-searchable electronic appeal books, particularly useful in corporate civil litigation, where paper versions sometimes ran to multiple volumes. The next step was to file appeal materials in electronic form, over a secure internet portal, into an internal database for staff and judges.

The shared characteristic of nearly every attempt elsewhere in Canada to set up such a system was failure, either partial or complete. Alberta embarked on a very ambitious electronic filing and management project, which was launched in 2004 but proved something of a flop and was seldom used.[30] In its initial attempt, Ontario spent several million dollars on a system only to abandon it.[31] Technical limitations, resistance from the bar, or runaway costs hampered early attempts. Government bureaucracy was another culprit. Courts were not allowed to run their own projects, which were frequently subsumed into larger departmental information management projects.[32] As a journalist noted, governments at all levels "tend to have an unquenchable thirst for overelaborate bespoke systems, usually created at fantastic expense by outside consultants, and a habit of over-paying for substandard gear."[33]

Unlike some jurisdictions, the Saskatchewan government had been relatively quick to supply computers to the court, primarily for word processing and other office functions. Chief Justice Bayda was not personally versed in computers but recognized their utility and pushed for adequate resources for the court. Lane and Jackson were the first judges to use personal computers in their work. Calvin Tallis, despite his vintage, was another early adopter. Tallis created his own database for case law, which encompassed not just Saskatchewan decisions but a wide range of significant judgments of common law courts.[34] He was happy to let his colleagues use his database, but only through his computer; he initially refused to network his computer or connect to the internet due to privacy and security considerations.

Bayda shared Tallis's concerns about security and insisted that the court have its own separate server for internal networks and data storage.[35] He felt this was necessary to protect judicial independence, a live concern among the judiciary due to the potential access of the government to internal workings of the court. He had also established a permanent IT position to provide in-house support. Scott Polowyk filled the position in 2009 and was invaluable for the eCourt project. More importantly, Bayda had established an important precedent of independence for the court regarding technology.

Klebuc, with his keen interest in technology, was an early adopter. At his old firm, he had led the charge to computerization and even helped install hardware and software.[36] He had little chance to pursue technology initiatives on the Queen's Bench, but he kept abreast of developments and was very intrigued by electronic filing and document management, as was Justice Lane. Klebuc and Lane had both drawn inspiration from a seminar they had attended, Lane for the Court of Appeal and Klebuc for the Court of Queen's Bench.[37] The eCourt project was a collaboration between the two judges. They were quite aware of the difficulties encountered by other courts in obtaining a system that worked but were convinced the benefits made it worth pursuing.

The task absorbed much of Klebuc's and Lane's attention for three years. They canvassed other courts and drew the lesson that the project had to be court driven and directed. They took advantage of Lane's connections and convinced the justice ministry to provide funding and let the court run the project. The next step was finding the right consultants and software. Fortunate timing was part of Saskatchewan's success. By 2007, when the project began, there had been significant advances in software and American vendors had extensive experience with courts. The court hired Sandra Potter, an experienced Australian consultant, who spent weeks assessing the processes for appeals and developed a detailed project framework. For development, the court hired Sustain, an American firm with widely used customizable software. Sustain sent two developers to Regina for the development phase. The implementation required a year, with the online portal operating by January 10, 2011.[38]

Chief Justice John Klebuc, 2015. (Artist: Iris Hauser; photo: Mark Greschner. Court of Appeal.)

Klebuc was closely involved in the development phase, along with Marlene Rodie, Scott Polowyk, and Lian Schwann, the court registrar. In the early phases of planning and development, Klebuc was at nearly every meeting. Schwann took over for Klebuc as the project advanced. As Schwann recalls, her children thought it was funny she was working on an IT project given her rudimentary computer skills, but she was the "subject matter expert."[39] Polowyk worked with the Sustain development team and Rodie provided support. The court had taken the critical step of making electronic filing mandatory, which made it essential to train the profession on how to use the system. (It did, however, leave an exemption allowing paper filing for small offices and older lawyers who had no computer skills and no access to IT professionals.) Justice Lane led an intensive educational campaign, and from March to August 2012, Lane,

Rodie, and Polowyk held training seminars across the province, which were crucial to the success of eCourt.

The project was on budget and on time. Saskatchewan's Court of Appeal had succeeded where some much better resourced courts had failed. Klebuc saw eCourt, an affordable, if basic, system, as a first step which positioned the court for the realities of the twenty-first century.

A more prosaic adoption of technology was the introduction of video conferencing. The motivation was to eliminate prisoner travel for sentence appeals. The days of "Con Air" were long over; inmates at the federal penitentiary in Prince Albert faced a long, uncomfortable ride to Regina in a van called the "ice cream wagon." The travel seriously disrupted the inmates' routines: they lost their cell assignments, had their possessions put in storage, and faced a full physical exam on their return. And it was expensive. The solution was video conferencing. It had been pioneered in Quebec, allowed under an amendment to the *Criminal Code*. Video conferences worked well for sentence appeals and saved the corrections service and the RCMP a considerable sum.

The court also saw video conferencing as a means of access for lawyers outside of Regina and Saskatoon for other hearings. The option, added to the rules of court, allows busy practitioners to avoid time-consuming travel and expense. There has not been much uptake, but some appeals have been conducted from Prince Albert and North Battleford. The facilities exist, and the option to use them may be exercised more in the future. There are at the same time some limitations to the use of video conferencing, and whether it is appropriate for appeals of conviction is an open question.

CHIEF JUSTICE ROBERT G. RICHARDS

IN 2013, KLEBUC decided to step down as chief justice. Instead of simply leaving, he took advantage of a clause in the *Judges Act* that allowed a justice to stay on as a supernumerary. This appealed to him as a way to ease into retirement, and by taking this route he established a first for the court.

Justice Robert G. Richards became the eighth chief justice of Saskatchewan and the seventh chief justice of the Court of Appeal, appointed on June 30, 2013. He was the clear choice of bench and bar, including his predecessor, but as Richards says, nothing is a foregone conclusion with judicial appointments. The other judges praised Richards's qualities as

Conferencing for Justice John Klebuc's last sitting as chief justice, 2013. *From left:* Justice Jackson, Justice Klebuc, and Justice Caldwell. (Court of Appeal)

a jurist and called him "a mainstay of the court."[40] Stuart Cameron, the senior judge, declared, "We're very delighted with this, and that's true of all my colleagues." Richards was regarded as a fine writer with a superb grasp of the role of an intermediate appellate court, and a deep, principled thinker with a strong sense of justice, but he was also applauded for his pragmatism.[41]

Richards was a seasoned judge on top of twenty years as an appellate counsel and understood the court and its workings like few others. As a *puisne* judge, he had set about making the court a more accommodating forum for counsel and litigants. It previously had a reputation for curtness, which Richards thought was a result of the heavy workload the court once faced. In his own experience as a lawyer, panels took "the shortest line" in hearings. Richards quietly insisted that all litigants be fully heard, even when it was not really necessary to have argument from both sides. The court had also long been criticized for not providing reasons for many decisions.[42] This was another response to the lengthy case lists, with some simpler appeals allowed or dismissed with a short oral judgment from the bench. Richards argued that more writing was important, and observers soon noticed the increase in written judgments.[43] He gave full credit to his colleagues for meeting the challenge.

Richards assumed the office of chief justice with a clear vision for court. His first and most important priority was the core mandate: hearing appeals and in a timely fashion producing high-quality judgments that stated and developed the law clearly and carefully. With his colleagues, Richards worked at building and maintaining a corporate culture focused on excellent judicial decision-making. To this end, he pursued several initiatives to position the court to do the best work possible. There was a thorough review of all operations and procedure. The court brought in experts on judgment writing and started educational sessions. The sitting schedule was rebuilt to provide blocks of uninterrupted time for judgment writing. Richards secured another law clerk for the court. When Marlene Rodie retired, Richards decided that a lawyer was really required as the executive officer. He asked Joanne Colledge-Miller, who had once clerked at the court, to take the job on an interim basis. Colledge-Miller returned to private practice after a year and was replaced by Nadine Barnes, a highly regarded young lawyer with the Ministry of Justice.

Richards was also determined to be, as he puts it, the chief justice for all of Saskatchewan, not just Regina. Towards that end, he has worked on increasing the public's understanding of the court's function. He has toured the northern areas of the province with the justice minister and heads of the trial courts. He has attended local bar association functions across the province, from Prince Albert to Moose Jaw. Richards regularly lectures at the College of Law and for the bar admission course, and is a frequent presenter and panelist for the Law Society of Saskatchewan, the Canadian Bar Association, and the Saskatchewan Trial Lawyers Association. Whenever the opportunity presents, he also gives talks to lay audiences on the law and the judiciary's role and attends a full slate of charity events in addition to his duties as provincial administrator.

Under Richards, the court has initiated a number of measures to aid self-represented litigants, who have become an increasingly large group of appellants. The registry is the front line, and Richards praises the current

YSANNE G.K. WILKINSON

Justice Wilkinson was the only example in the court's history of an appointment from the trial court who later returned to the Court of Queen's Bench. While not unprecedented in Canada, it was a first in Saskatchewan.

Wilkinson was born on November 29, 1953, in Singapore. She attended high school in Prince Albert and entered the University of Saskatchewan in 1971, earning a bachelor of arts. She went straight into law school and graduated in 1977. She subsequently articled with James H.W. Sanderson in Prince Albert and joined the bar in 1978. Wilkinson continued in practice with Sanderson and in 1981 became a partner in the firm. She had a broad general practice, doing corporate and commercial work and civil litigation. Wilkinson served as the president of the Prince Albert Bar Association from 1987 to 1990 and was co-chair of the Law Society's annual convention in 1991. She was also a frequent lecturer and presenter for the Saskatchewan Trial Lawyers Association, the Saskatchewan branch of the Canadian Bar Association, and Saskatchewan Legal Education Society. Wilkinson served on the Provincial Planning Appeals Board from 1987 to 1990 and the appeal committee of the Saskatchewan Assistance Plan. She was also a director of the YWCA in Prince Albert.

In 1996, Wilkinson was appointed to the Court of Queen's Bench, Family Division, in Saskatoon. A highly respected judge, she developed particular expertise in child protection law while on the family division. She was appointed to the Court of Appeal in December 2007 to replace Marjorie Gerwing, who had elected supernumerary status. The appointment was widely perceived as bolstering the court's family law expertise. A clear and eloquent writer, Wilkinson showed great promise as an appellate judge but after two years elected to return to the Queen's Bench. She replaced Ralph Ottenbreit, who replaced her on the Court of Appeal.

Justice Ysanne G.K. Wilkinson, c. 2017. (Photo: Mark Greschner. Court of Appeal.)

Justice Stuart Cameron (*right*) swearing in Chief Justice Robert Richards, 2013. (Court of Appeal)

registrar, Melanie Baldwin, QC, and registry clerks for their patience and helpfulness. The registrar's office has a public service terminal for people to access forms with the assistance of the clerks. Baldwin has developed how-to guides that are available on the court website and in hard copy. The guides take self-represented litigants step by step through the process of preparing, filing, and arguing an appeal. The guides make clear the difference between trial and appeal, and also explain the standards of review.

Other initiatives include a plain language review of forms and correspondence to make them accessible to lay people. A recent addition is an orientation seminar introducing self-represented litigants to the appellate process, courtroom protocol and procedure, as well as the courtroom.

The Court of Appeal, c. 2013. *From left:* Justice Peter Whitmore, Justice Neal Caldwell, Justice John Klebuc, Justice Gary Lane, Chief Justice Robert Richards, Justice Georgina Jackson, Justice Ralph Ottenbreit, Justice Maurice Herauf, and Justice Jacelyn Ryan-Froslie. (Photo: Mark Greschner. Court of Appeal.)

Every hearing with the self-represented starts with the panel giving a short orientation on the appellate process. Saskatchewan's judges of appeal recognize, as does the judiciary in Canada generally, that self-represented litigants are a part of the landscape for the foreseeable future. They have worked hard at making the court a more welcoming place for laypeople trying to solve their problems through the law.

Even with all these initiatives, Richards remains one of the most prolific writers on the court.[44] The administrative and public duties of chief justices often meant they do not sit as often or write as much as *puisne*

ROBERT GERLING RICHARDS

Bob Richards was born on December 26, 1952, in Assiniboia, Saskatchewan, the fourth of six sons. Raised on the family farm, Richards attended school in nearby Assiniboia and was student council president in high school and an athlete. He attended the University of Saskatchewan, starting a combined commerce and law degree but then dropping law to pursue a graduate degree in agricultural economics. He changed back to law after one term. Entering the law program in 1976, he became a top student and earned several scholarships. After graduating in 1979, Richards clerked for Justice Ronald Martland at the Supreme Court of Canada. A year-long stint as a parliamentary intern followed, partly spent with Ray Hnatyshyn of Saskatchewan. Richards then went to Harvard University for a master's degree in law with an eye to potentially teaching. He finished in 1982 and returned to Ottawa to join the Gowling and Henderson firm as an associate. Richards was not involved in party politics, but Hnatyshyn asked him to become his chief of staff when the Mulroney government was elected in 1984.

Justice Robert Gerling Richards, c. 2005. (Photo: Patricia Holdsworth. Court of Appeal.)

Richards had declined a position with the constitutional law branch of the Saskatchewan attorney general's department in 1982. Three years later, he was offered the directorship of the branch in Regina. As director of constitutional law for five years, Richards appeared as lead counsel for the government in nearly every major constitutional case from Saskatchewan. He then joined the Regina law firm MacPherson, Leslie and Tyerman. He established what he described as a somewhat unique practice in public law and appellate advocacy, including many constitutional cases. He had a national reputation as an appellate counsel and appeared in over forty appeals to the Supreme Court of Canada as well as numerous cases at the Court of Appeal. He authored a number of peer-reviewed articles and presented widely. While in practice, Richards was a frequent lecturer at the University of Saskatchewan College of Law and for the bar admission course. He was the chair of the Canadian Bar Association's Supreme Court liaison committee and co-chair of the constitutional and human rights law section.

Richards was appointed from practice directly to the Court of Appeal on October 1, 2004. He was seen as a leading candidate for appointment to the Supreme Court of Canada in 2006 and again in 2015. He became the eighth chief justice of Saskatchewan on June 30, 2013.

judges do. Although he starts with a lighter load of scheduled sittings, Richards then takes on appeals as he can and ultimately ends up shouldering a full share of the writing duties. He often writes on the more complex appeals. It reflects his motivation in becoming a judge in the first place: to do interesting and exciting law.

THE SELF-REPRESENTED

THE SELF-REPRESENTED HAVE become a major challenge for Canadian courts. "Self-reps" were comparatively rare until the 1990s. There had always been a few litigants who, due to lack of funds or a conviction they could do a better job, did not have a lawyer. The latter were often "chronic" litigants who, for a variety of reasons, were frequently involved in lawsuits. Some were characters, and judges sometimes took a shine to them. Historically, by far the largest group of self-represented in Saskatchewan were coming before the court to appeal sentences, thanks largely to Chief Justice Culliton.

As the new century approached, the numbers of self-represented steadily climbed, and a growing proportion were ordinary citizens. This phenomenon was largely due to the changing economics of the legal profession. Lawyers simply became too expensive for many people to afford. Another common complaint was poor service from counsel.[45] Self-reps were often pursuing family law matters at both trial and appeal.[46] These litigants were not always easy to deal with, given the emotionally charged nature of many family law proceedings. Self-represented litigants presented other difficulties. They rarely understood protocol, procedure, or rules of evidence and on appeal would often focus on fact findings. Judges at both levels of court were in the awkward position of trying to guide the self-represented while maintaining impartiality. Some self-represented were excellent—they did their homework, prepared well, and knew their case better than a lawyer juggling many files. Most self-reps muddled through.

Among the self-represented was a small but problematic group who were soon labelled vexatious litigants. This diverse group included so-called sovereign citizens, "de-taxers," and chronic litigants, often mentally ill.[47] What every variety had in common was, in the words of one law professor, that they "persistently exploit and abuse the processes of the court in order to achieve some improper purpose or obtain some advantage."[48] Such litigants could be frightening: one group in Ontario harassed court officials, including judges. Although vexatious litigants made up only a small percentage of the self-represented,[49] they caused the most problems and most courts were forced to take measures. The Court of Queen's Bench and the Court of Appeal instituted rules in 2007 that allowed a judge on application, at his or her discretion, to dismiss litigation as vexatious and order a litigant not to institute proceedings without leave.[50] There was a danger, however, that the rule could cast too wide a net and be used unfairly against the self-represented.

In a 2015 costs decision, *Hope v Pylypow*, Richards made it clear that the court should give full consideration to self-reps and urged restraint in labelling them vexatious.[51] The case was an important statement on access to justice. Kevin and Fay Hope represented themselves in a suit against the municipal district of Parkdale over the misalignment of a roadway. The Saskatchewan Municipal Board had ruled in the Hopes' favour, but Parkdale did nothing, leading the Hopes to sue again for malfeasance in office but also defamation for comments a Parkdale councillor made in a meeting. A judge in chambers, on an application to dismiss the action, declared the proceedings vexatious and awarded solicitor-client costs against the Hopes.

Richards, writing for the court, allowed the Hopes' appeal. He found the Hopes had a cause of action on both grounds, that the proceedings were not vexatious, and that the punishing costs award was not appropriate. He also removed a long-standing inequality in awarding costs in which the self-represented could not recover more than their disbursements. In Richards's view, this meant a self-rep was in serious hazard of paying far more costs if they lost than they would ever receive if they won. The *Hope* decision updated the law and made it possible for self-reps to recover for the time and other expenses they spent on their litigation. Richards complimented the Hopes on their presentation, making his point that the proceedings were not spurious and the couple were rational litigants with a legitimate complaint, but also making a strong statement about how the courts should treat the self-represented.[52] It is characteristic of the court under Richards as chief justice.

THE COURT AT LAW—THE *CHARTER*'S SECOND COMING

THE ADVENT OF the *Charter of Rights and Freedoms* was a watershed for Canadian law and for the Canadian judiciary.[53] One can speak of the pre- and post-*Charter* legal landscapes. The expanded role of the courts as constitutional arbitrators, the explicit powers of judicial review and disallowance, the broad and contextual analysis of statutes, and the weighing of policy considerations required in *Charter* decisions greatly influenced the general approach to jurisprudence of Canadian judges.[54] This is not to say that the judiciary approached all decisions in the way they might deal with a *Charter* decision—far from it—but without question the advent of the *Charter* further enhanced the broadening of perspectives and techniques that had started in the 1970s. Due to the *Charter*, the courts took on an expanded role in Canadian society and over thirty-five years of decisions have shaped that society profoundly.

Charter jurisprudence has changed with the passage of time. Many of the landmark decisions of the 1980s, such as the Saskatchewan examples discussed earlier, were primarily concerned with giving full definition and articulation of the rights and freedoms enumerated in the *Charter* and how best to determine the limits of these rights. Judges had something of a blank slate. Even with more than one hundred years of *Bill of Rights* decisions in the United States and European human rights law for inspiration, *Charter* jurisprudence was essentially a Canadian enterprise. The famous decisions of the 1980s determined how the *Charter* was interpreted, defined the rights and freedoms, and found the limits of these rights through means such as the *Oakes* test for the application of section 1. It was heady

RALPH KURT OTTENBREIT

Born in Ludwigshafen, Germany, on February 9, 1953, Ralph Ottenbreit immigrated to Canada with his family in 1957, settling in Regina, where his great uncle had lived since the 1920s. The Ottenbreits were displaced Germans from Ukraine. Raised and educated in Regina, Ottenbreit started a combined degree in English literature and law at the Regina campus of the University of Saskatchewan before going to law school in Saskatoon. He graduated with distinction with an arts degree and law degree in 1975.

Justice Ralph Kurt Ottenbreit. (Photo: Mark Greschner. Court of Appeal.)

Ottenbreit articled at the Regina firm of Griffin, Beke and Thorson to James Griffin, QC, whom he cites as a role model. He stayed with the firm after his call to the bar and practised there until 1982. Initially, he was primarily a solicitor, working in commercial real estate and general corporate practice, but then gravitated towards litigation. Ottenbreit later became a senior drug prosecutor for the federal government, a contract position that allowed him to maintain his civil litigation practice. In 1982, he became a partner with Shirkey, Ulmer, Ottenbreit and Shirkey. He was appointed a Queen's Counsel in 1989. Two years later, the firm merged with Robertson Stromberg of Saskatoon, originally founded by J.W. Estey and Arthur Moxon and including Peter Makaroff, George Taylor, and Nick Sherstobitoff among its distinguished alumni. Ottenbreit remained in the Regina office of the firm, practising civil and criminal litigation and family law. He served as president of the Saskatchewan branch of the Canadian Bar Association and on the legislative audit committee of the Law Society. Outside of law, Ottenbreit was involved in politics as an organizer and fundraiser. He coached amateur sports and was director of the Globe Theatre in the 1980s.

Ottenbreit always had the judiciary in mind, and in 2007 he was appointed to Court of Queen's Bench in Saskatoon, but the position was immediately moved to Regina as a result of a reorganization of the court. Interested in the development of the law and with a strong academic bent, he joined the Court of Appeal in 2009, replacing Ysanne Wilkinson, who filled the spot he had vacated on the lower court. Ottenbreit is considered an independent judge, sometimes authoring dissents and concurring opinions.

stuff and a time of great judicial creativity. Not every decision was timeless, and some were probably wrong, one of which is discussed below. Later *Charter* decisions have been made with a large body of settled law. More recent decisions have not broken the same sort of jurisprudential ground, but they have frequently had profound social and economic implications.

Another major change for *Charter* jurisprudence was the political landscape. Decisions that affected deeply held convictions and made overt policy choices inevitably drew the attention of politicians and the public. The *Charter* has created a voluminous literature dedicated to the thesis that the powers granted to the judiciary in the *Constitution Act, 1982* allowed unelected judges to make profound policy choices that should be the realm of the legislature and, in some views, impose a particular "liberal" or "progressive" agenda.[55] Much of the criticism about judicial activism was simply a matter of people, especially politicians, not liking the decision rather than anything untoward in the decision-making. Sober critics, however, raised valid points about the suitability of the courts, with obvious limitations in the evidence at hand, for performing the job of balancing different societal interests. There are certainly cogent arguments that judges should avoid being drawn too far into policy and leave this to legislatures, and Canadian judges would likely agree wholeheartedly. On the other hand, there are also fears that relentless criticism, mostly from the political right, has made judges and the courts needlessly conservative.

Much of the political fire has arisen from the application of section 15 of the *Charter*. The equality provision in the *Charter* was meant to address discrimination and has been a powerful tool for minorities and the marginalized. The astonishingly quick change in the acceptance of the lesbian, gay, bisexual, and transgender (LGBT) community stems in part from judicial recognition of the historic discrimination faced by sexual minorities, the declaration of sexual orientation as a ground of discrimination analogous to race, religion, and gender, and the steady accrual of rights for same-sex relationships, including marriage.[56] But giving full expression to equality rights has often meant conflict with other rights, most often freedom of expression and freedom of religion. In the new century, this has become the frontier of *Charter* jurisprudence.[57] In 2002, Justice Frank Iacobucci of the Supreme Court of Canada stated, "The task of reconciling *Charter* rights is challenging, and there can be little doubt but that difficult cases are on the horizon."[58] There is probably no place where the conflict of rights was thrown into harsher relief than between the equality rights of lesbian, gay, bisexual, and transgender individuals and freedom of religion.[59]

As has often been the case, Saskatchewan was on the front line with two important decisions: *Whatcott v Saskatchewan* and *Re: Marriage Commissioners*. Although concerning a human rights code rather than strictly a *Charter* case, *Whatcott* involved an identical balancing of rights—freedom of expression and freedom of religion with equality rights—and was heavily informed by *Charter* jurisprudence and principles. In *Whatcott*, the Court of Appeal made a strong statement about the importance of freedom of expression. The Supreme Court would overturn *Whatcott* in part, but the two decisions contributed an important dimension to the clash of free speech and discrimination on the basis of sexual orientation. The *Marriage Commissioners* reference was not further appealed, but is destined to be a touchstone when the issue—the accommodation of religious belief in employment when it impacts on equality rights—inevitably comes before the Supreme Court of Canada.

Another aspect of later *Charter* jurisprudence is how early decisions have stood the test of time. *Saskatchewan Federation of Labour v Saskatchewan* revisited an early *Charter* decision, RWDSU *v Saskatchewan*, one of the "labour trilogy." While the Court of Appeal wrestled with the proper reach and effect of *stare decisis*, the application of precedent, in a time of contextual interpretation and procedures for reconsideration of past decisions, the Supreme Court made the decision that had been made in Saskatchewan thirty years previously.

Justice Stuart Cameron on the day of his last sitting, 2014. Cameron had been one of the judges on the RWDSU appeal. (Court of Appeal)

WHATCOTT V SASKATCHEWAN (HUMAN RIGHTS TRIBUNAL)

WHATCOTT V SASKATCHEWAN involved one of the most fundamental democratic rights, the right to free speech. The appeal revisited a difficult area of law: the determination of when free speech and expression devolved into hatemongering. It was not technically *Charter* jurisprudence; *Whatcott* instead tested the provisions of the *Saskatchewan Human Rights Code*. But the appeal involved exactly the same exercise in rights-balancing that commonly occurred with section 15 *Charter* jurisprudence, and the principles from this jurisprudence were largely determinative of the issues in *Whatcott*. The subsequent Supreme Court decision was a landmark for the application of human rights codes in protecting individuals from

NEAL WILLIAM CALDWELL

Neal Caldwell is the second member of the court from the northern community of Meadow Lake, after John Klebuc. Caldwell was born in North Battleford on October 16, 1966, but shortly afterward his family moved to Meadow Lake, where his father was a social worker and his mother taught piano. Caldwell started university in Saskatoon in 1984 at the age of seventeen. His undergraduate education was not continuous, alternating between studies and employment. In 1989, he went to work for George M. McLeod, the MLA for Meadow Lake, deputy premier, and minister of health. It was initially a summer job, but he remained three years, latterly in charge of the minister's media relations.

Justice Neal William Caldwell. (Photo: Mark Greschner. Court of Appeal.)

Returning to university in 1991, Caldwell had intended to study human geography and become an urban planner but instead wrote the LSAT at the suggestion of a friend. He earned a bachelor's degree in history in 1992 and enrolled at the college of law as a mature student on the basis of his employment history. As a law student, Caldwell excelled academically, earning a number of awards. He served as president of the law students' association in his third year and as an editor of the *Saskatchewan Law Review*. Graduating with distinction in 1995, he articled to Chief Justice D.K. MacPherson of the Court of Queen's Bench.

After joining the bar, given a poor job market for young associates in Saskatchewan, Caldwell moved to Vancouver and joined Clark Wilson. Three years later, he returned to Saskatchewan to join Gauley & Co. in Saskatoon, later McDougall Gauley, where he was a trademark agent and partner, practising in the areas of corporate governance, commercial transactions, intellectual property, regulatory compliance, and privacy.

In 2010, he was recognized by his national peers for his intellectual property practice. Caldwell wrote extensively for legal education seminars and was published in the *Saskatchewan Law Review*. He was also a sessional lecturer at the law school and a facilitator for the bar admission course. Caldwell had been active in the federal Progressive Conservative Party, but focused on provincial politics, serving in a number of roles for the Saskatchewan Party. He was on the executive of the Saskatchewan Police Commission, and his other community work included the boards of Habitat for Humanity and the Broadway Business Improvement District in Saskatoon.

Like several of his colleagues, Caldwell had an early interest in becoming a judge and applied after being encouraged by a Queen's Bench judge and mentor he knew from his articling days. He joined the court on April 23, 2010, at forty-three, the youngest appointment since Georgina Jackson and one of the few appointments with a background primarily as a solicitor.

discrimination and hate based on sexual orientation, but the *Whatcott* appeal also demonstrated the Court of Appeal's robust defence of free speech despite a very troubling intrusion on equality rights.

Bill Whatcott was a singular individual much like abortion crusader Joseph Borowski. He had been a street kid, involved in drugs and prostitution, and became a born-again Christian while serving time.[60] Whatcott turned his life around and became a licensed practical nurse. He was also a committed activist, campaigning against abortion and homosexuality. By one count, Whatcott was arrested twenty-seven times.[61] He had previously been at the Court of Appeal. In a 2008 case, the court overturned disciplinary action on the part of the Saskatchewan Association of Licensed Practical Nurses against Whatcott for his protests against Planned Parenthood.[62] In that case, the court ruled that if Whatcott's activities were on his free time and he did not involve the association, the body could not discipline him for his views.

One of Whatcott's preferred methods was distributing leaflets bearing the name of a group called Christian Truth Activists which used offensive, sometimes very offensive, language in concert with biblical quotations attacking same-sex rights. In 2001 and 2002, Whatcott distributed four different pamphlets to home mailboxes in Saskatoon and Regina that attacked a decision to teach about homosexuality in the public school system and an educational conference on the subject at the University of Saskatchewan. The message was clear—references to homosexuality had no place in the school curriculum and were "gay lifestyle propaganda"—but the language was inflammatory, including liberal use of the terms sodomy and sodomites and what appeared to be veiled references to pedophilia. One pamphlet reprinted personal ads from a gay magazine that Whatcott claimed showed men looking for boys. Four recipients of the pamphlets brought complaints to the Saskatchewan Human Rights Commission. A tribunal found that the pamphlets contained hate speech, contravening section 14 of the *Saskatchewan Human Rights Code*, which created limits on broadcasts and publications. Concluding that section 14(1)(b) did not violate Whatcott's *Charter* or *Code* rights to free expression and freedom of religion, the tribunal ordered Whatcott to pay damages to several of the complainants, and he appealed.

Saskatchewan had a proud history with human rights legislation. The 1947 provincial *Bill of Rights* was the first comprehensive human rights legislation passed in Canada and was far in advance of the time. The *Bill of Rights* protected fundamental rights and freedoms but also included far-reaching protection from discrimination and, both in the bill's original form and by later amendment, economic rights of the sort proposed for but never included in the *Charter*. It was no coincidence that Diefenbaker, who introduced the first federal human rights legislation, was from Saskatchewan. The NDP replaced the *Bill of Rights* in 1979 with the *Human Rights Code*. The new statute was more than just a renaming. In line with other provinces, the *Code* established the Saskatchewan Human Rights Commission to investigate complaints and the Human Rights Tribunal, a quasi-judicial body, to adjudicate alleged violations.

The rights and freedoms laid out in part 1 of the *Human Rights Code* were similar to those found in the *Charter*, but in place of the generalities of the *Charter*'s section 15, part 2 of the *Code* laid out specific prohibitions against discrimination and discriminatory practices. The key sections of the *Code* for the *Whatcott* appeal were section 5, on freedom of expression, and section 14, on prohibitions against publication. The first section read,

> Every person and every class of persons shall, under the law, enjoy the right to freedom of expression through all means of

> communication, including, without limiting the generality of the foregoing, the arts, speech, the press or radio, television or any other broadcasting device.[63]

Section 14 was rather longer:

> (1) No person shall publish or display, or cause or permit to be published or displayed, on any lands or premises or in a newspaper, through a television or radio broadcasting station or any other broadcasting device, or in any printed matter or publication or by means of any other medium that the person owns, controls, distributes or sells, any representation, including any notice, sign, symbol, emblem, article, statement or other representation:
>
> > (a) tending or likely to tend to deprive, abridge or otherwise restrict the enjoyment by any person or class of persons, on the basis of a prohibited ground, of any right to which that person or class of persons is entitled under law; or
> >
> > (b) that exposes or tends to expose to hatred, ridicules, belittles or otherwise affronts the dignity of any person or class of persons on the basis of prohibited ground.
>
> (2) Nothing in subsection (1) restricts the right to freedom of expression under the law upon any subject.

Applying section 14 of the *Code* raised an obvious question: When was it lawful to restrict speech because of its negative effects on other people?

Hunter wrote the decision of the court, with Smith adding concurring reasons. Hunter's careful decision was to the point and determined the appeal on relatively narrow grounds. There were several precedents that governed the appeal. One was a 1990 Supreme Court decision, *Taylor v Canada*.[64] Chief Justice Dickson had determined that section 13 of the *Canadian Human Rights Act*, which was very similar to section 14 in Saskatchewan's *Code*, was constitutionally valid as a limit on free speech. He had also adopted the definition of hate speech from *Keegstra*, the infamous decision involving a Holocaust denier and Jewish conspiracy theorist. Dickson held that speech had to be in extreme form, expressing

MAURICE J. HERAUF

The registrar and first media relations officer for the Court of Appeal from 1995 to 2007, Maurice Herauf joined the court on March 3, 2011. He has one of the more unusual backgrounds for a judge of the court. Born on January 27, 1952, in Regina, Herauf grew up on the family farm near Odessa, a small village not far from the capital. After finishing high school, he started work as a clerk in the attorney general's department in Regina. Gary Lane, then chief of staff for the attorney general, helped Herauf fill out his application form.

Justice Maurice J. Herauf. (Photo: Mark Greschner. Court of Appeal.)

After four years at the attorney general's office, Herauf was sent to Battleford as deputy sheriff and deputy registrar for the Court of Queen's Bench. He was then the first registrar of the Unified Family Court in Saskatoon from 1979 to 1982.

At this point, married with two preschoolers, Herauf took a five-year leave from the civil service and went to law school. Graduating in 1986, he articled at Mitchell, Taylor, Romanow and Ching. His principal was nominally Doug Kovatch, now of the Provincial Court, but he spent most of his articles assisting legendary labour lawyer George Taylor, QC. After joining the bar in 1987 with the Academic Excellence Award for highest overall marks in the Saskatchewan bar examinations, Herauf returned to the civil service as director of maintenance enforcement for the Saskatchewan Ministry of Justice and in 1993 became manager of the licensing administration branch of the Saskatchewan Liquor and Gaming Authority. As well as being registrar of the Court of Appeal, Herauf was also registrar in bankruptcy for the Court of Queen's Bench, and he authored numerous reported judgments in bankruptcy and insolvency law as well as articles in the *Saskatchewan Law Review*. He was appointed a QC in 2001.

Both Bayda and Klebuc had encouraged Herauf to apply for the judiciary. Herauf was appointed to the Queen's Bench in 2007, assigned to Swift Current. In 2009, he was reassigned to Moose Jaw. Two years later, he returned to Regina and the Court of Appeal.

"extreme feelings of opprobrium and enmity against a racial or religious group" and understood by a reasonable person to promote such feelings in others. It was a relatively high threshold for banning speech.

There were also two important Saskatchewan decisions on section 14 of the *Code*. In *Bell*, Sherstobitoff had considered whether an injunction preventing someone from selling stickers that had a "not permitted" symbol (a circle with diagonal line across it) over racial caricatures was valid.[65] He held that section 14(1)(b) was a reasonable limit on section 2(b) of the *Charter*, on freedom of expression, and adopted the definition of hatred in *Taylor*. He in effect "read down" section 14(1)(b) to conform with *Taylor*, interpreting "ridicules, belittles or otherwise affronts" to mean extreme speech. In *Owens*, Richards considered a newspaper advertisement that had anti-homosexual biblical quotations and the "not permitted" symbol over two stickmen holding hands.[66] Richards decided that *Bell* correctly interpreted section 14(1)(b) to mean extreme speech rather than hurt feelings. *Owens* also made clear, following Dickson's lead in *Taylor*, that an objective standard had to be used in determining if expression should be consider hateful: that of a dispassionate, reasonable person examining the full context and deciding if the speech in question would be understood as exposing a person to "hatred or as ridiculing, belittling or affronting their dignity within the restricted meaning of those terms as prescribed by *Bell*."[67] Richards ruled the advertisement was not hate speech and affirmed that in Saskatchewan the bar to restrict speech was set high.

In Hunter's view, the terms of the *Human Rights Code* required a balancing of the rights, freedoms, and protections that it contained, which was also congruent with *Charter* jurisprudence. She argued that it was clear the legislature intended a very strong protection of free speech and expression, giving the right specific protection in section 5 and also in section 14(2), which stated that the right to freedom of expression was not restricted by section 14(1). Hunter argued that this was consistent with general principles of statutory interpretation; the legislature was assumed to mean what a statute said, and the two sections together said free speech had high priority. Given the precedents that applied in the case, the only question was whether Whatcott's pamphlets passed the threshold for hate speech.

Hunter concluded that the tribunal and the Queen's Bench judge sitting on appeal had not applied the objective and contextual standard that was mandated in *Taylor* and *Owens*. This was particularly important in the appeal at hand. As Hunter wrote,

> Context is of particular importance when considering complaints based on sexual orientation and the impact on freedom of expression. Most often, underlying these complaints are issues relating to matters of morality. It is acceptable, in a democracy, for individuals to comment on the morality of another's behaviour. For this reason there will be a relatively high degree of tolerance for the language used in debates about moral issues, subject, of course, to limitations. Anything that limits debate on the morality of behaviour is an intrusion on the right to freedom of expression.[68]

Hunter analyzed the content of the pamphlets and concluded that the tribunal and the Queen's Bench judge had taken the more offensive phrases out of the total context of both the pamphlets' message and the general debate on teaching about homosexuality. The Queen's Bench judge in particular thought Whatcott's message was that homosexuals were pedophiles. To Hunter, it was clear that the pamphlets, when looked at as a whole, were part of a legitimate debate over teaching about homosexuality and same-sex relationships in public schools. While Hunter had no doubt that the language Whatcott used, including the biblical quotations, was crude and offensive, both standing alone and in context, in her view it fell short of the standard for hate speech. Smith agreed with Hunter's conclusions and disposition of the appeal, but wrote a concurring opinion to dig down a little deeper into the issues. "I would like to add some comments," she wrote, "as this seems to me to be an appropriate case to bring together some of the principles of interpretation of this troublesome provision."[69] Her elegant judgment bolstered the conclusion of the court that free speech in a democracy necessarily included offensive speech and that a high threshold was appropriate.

The Supreme Court overturned the Court of Appeal in *Whatcott* in what has become a key judgment involving freedom of expression, freedom of religion, and protection from discrimination and hate speech. Justice Marshall Rothstein, writing for the court, essentially split the difference between the Court of Appeal and the previous Court of Queen's Bench and tribunal decisions. Engaging in his own contextual analysis, he decided two of the pamphlets violated section 14(1) of the *Human Rights Code* but two did not. More importantly, he decided that section 14(1)(b) of the *Code*, which banned any publication and broadcast "that exposes or tends to expose to hatred, ridicules, belittles or otherwise affronts the dignity of any person or class of persons on the basis of prohibited ground," was overly broad and had to be severed from the statute. In the court's view, "ridicules, belittles or otherwise affronts the dignity" included too much expression that, while offensive, fell short of the definition of hate speech and had too much of a chilling effect on free speech. While perhaps casting a broader net as to what constituted hate speech, Rothstein upheld the principle that the threshold must be a high one in a democracy. Yet *Whatcott* is unlikely to be the final word. As Hunter observed, "There may never be an end to this debate as long as there are people who, as part of their belief or value system (whether religious or otherwise), disapprove of same-sex sexual practices."[70]

THE *MARRIAGE COMMISSIONERS* REFERENCE

FEW SOCIAL REVOLUTIONS have been as swift and as far-reaching as the growing acceptance of the LGBT community. As members of that community sought the right to marry, it was probably inevitable that there would be a clash of *Charter* rights. Many Canadian saw marriage as the bedrock of the social order, the linchpin of the family, and the institution was heavily freighted with religious significance. In Canada, marriage was also an area where the Fathers of Confederation had divided up responsibility between federal and provincial governments. Under section 91(26) of the *Constitution Act, 1867*, Parliament has legislative competence over capacity to marry, while under section 92(12) the provinces control the solemnization of marriage. In other words, Parliament says who

PETER ALEXANDER WHITMORE

Peter Whitmore is a fourth-generation Reginan. His great-grandfather had come to the North-West Territories around 1880 and was postmaster for Moose Jaw and later Regina. Whitmore's grandfather and father were prominent businessmen and real-estate developers in the city.

Justice Peter Alexander Whitmore. (Photo: Mark Greschner. Court of Appeal.)

Born on April 8, 1949, in Regina, Whitmore attended local schools until going to boarding school in Toronto in 1961. He subsequently earned a bachelor's of commerce at McGill University in Montreal in 1971. Deciding on law, he returned to Saskatchewan and college of law in Saskatoon, graduating in 1974. He articled at Balfour Moss (as the firm was later known) with John Moss and then started practice in 1975 with Armstrong and Associates, moving on after a year to become part of Wilson, Drummond and Whitmore. In 1977, he went into partnership with Gary Lane as Lane and Whitmore Law Offices. Initially a generalist, including litigation and criminal work, Whitmore became primarily a corporate and commercial practitioner, doing major corporate financings and transactions and commercial real-estate law. In 1984, Lane gave up practice upon his appointment to the provincial cabinet, and in 1985 the firm became Whitmore and Company after taking over the Armstrong firm, where Whitmore had first practised, upon Grant Armstrong's appointment to the Court of Queen's Bench. In 1989, Whitmore merged his firm with McKercher, McKercher, Stack, Korchin and Laing of Saskatoon, which was looking to expand to Regina. The firm became McKercher, McKercher Laing and Whitmore, with Whitmore heading the Regina office. Whitmore was appointed a QC in 1986.

After over thirty years of private practice, Whitmore decided that the bench would allow him to extend his career further and applied for a judicial appointment. He joined the Court of Queen's Bench at Regina in 2008. He then replaced Richards as a *puisne* justice of the Court of Appeal on June 30, 2013. Outside of the law, Whitmore was vice-chancellor and then chancellor of the Anglican Diocese of Qu'Appelle for almost thirty years and served as a member and as chair of the board of regents of Luther College in Regina. In 2004, Whitmore received a doctor of canon law from the University of Emmanuel College in Saskatoon. Justice Whitmore oversaw the Court of Appeal centennial celebrations, including this history.

can be married, legislatures say how. The federal government also had jurisdiction over divorce. In Saskatchewan, *The Marriage Act, 1995* governed.[71] The statute empowered different types of clergy, broadly defined, to conduct marriages. It also provided for marriage commissioners to hold civil ceremonies. Such ceremonies had by law a set form that was entirely secular in content.[72]

Starting in the 1990s, various jurisdictions around the world started introducing laws recognizing civil unions of same-sex couples.[73] Canada was not on the leading edge; in 1999, Parliament passed a Reform Party motion defining marriage as a heterosexual union. But shortly afterward, the Liberal government passed Bill C-23 to give same-sex couples the same "benefits and obligations" as opposite-gender couples. Within two years, the British Columbia and Ontario appeal courts ruled that by defining marriage in terms of heterosexuality, federal marriage law violated the rights of same-sex couples. The Paul Martin government responded by drafting the *Civil Marriage Act* and submitted the proposed statute to the Supreme Court of Canada for the court's opinion on its constitutionality. The proposed law changed the definition of marriage to a lawful union of two persons and allowed LGBT couples to have a civil marriage. The statute specifically exempted the clergy from an obligation to solemnize such marriages. The Supreme Court ruled that the statute was constitutional, and in 2004 same-sex civil marriages became legal in Canada.

In the wake of the Supreme Court same-sex reference, marriage commissioners or their equivalent across the country refused or threatened to refuse services to same-sex couples, almost invariably citing their religious beliefs that marriage was only between opposite genders.[74] Some provinces responded with informal measures to accommodate the religious scruples of commissioners and allow them to opt out of same-sex ceremonies. Prince Edward Island brought in legislation. The change had immediately created litigation in Saskatchewan. Shortly before the Supreme Court reference, a Queen's Bench decision had declared the existing definition of marriage unconstitutional, and the government instructed commissioners to conduct ceremonies for same-sex couples. Some marriage commissioners refused on the basis of their religious convictions, and three filed human rights complaints that their freedom of religion was being infringed, which were dismissed. The commissioners further instituted a lawsuit in the Court of Queen's Bench against the government, seeking a declaration that their religious rights were being breached and an order forcing the government to accommodate their beliefs. A human rights complaint was also filed against one of the marriage commissioners.

Saskatchewan initially declined to accommodate commissioners' religious scruples, but in 2009, in the wake of the litigation over the issue—and with a more socially conservative government in power—two possible amendments to *The Marriage Act* were drawn up. One was a grandfather clause, allowing marriage commissioners appointed before 2004 to opt out of providing services. The other was a general clause, simply allowing all commissioners the same accommodation. The government sent the proposed amendments to the Court of Appeal on a reference, asking the same two questions for both measures: Were the statutes consistent with the *Charter*, and if not, why, and to what extent?

Klebuc sat a panel of five for the reference, as was traditional, with Vancise, Richards, Smith, and Ottenbreit joining the chief justice. The court ruled that the amendments were unconstitutional. Richards wrote the majority decision, with Klebuc and Ottenbreit joining him. Smith wrote separate reasons with the same result but taking a different tack in her analysis. Vancise concurred with Smith.

Richards approached the reference as fundamentally an exercise in balancing rights. He started from the perspective that there was no hierarchy of *Charter* rights. Each instance where rights clashed had to be analyzed on its own merits and context. In line with long-held *Charter* principles, rights and freedoms should be given broad expression. Finding the limitations of the rights and freedoms, and the balancing of the rights, was best done in a section 1 analysis. For simplicity, and as there was, in Richards's view, little difference between the two amendments in the constitutional analysis, both were considered together. Richards also focused exclusively on the issue of same-sex marriages, as this was clearly the main issue driving the amendments.

It was abundantly clear in Richards's view that the amendments violated section 15 of the *Charter*. He thought it was easy to discern negative effects on the impacted group. The amendments made a distinction based on sexual orientation and allowed differential treatment due to the distinction. In Saskatchewan, couples approached marriage commissioners directly. In Richards's estimation, the amendments at the very least inconvenienced same-sex couples, who potentially might be required to contact several commissioners. Those in rural areas, with fewer commissioners to choose from, might have to incur travel expenses. It was quite possible that a significant number of commissioners might take advantage of the amendments to demur from solemnizing a marriage, making it quite difficult for a same-sex couple to find a commissioner. But much more important, in Richards's view, was the affront to the dignity and self-worth of homosexual individuals. It perpetuated the discrimination that the LGBT community had faced historically and continued to bear.

> The historical marginalization and mistreatment of gay and lesbian individuals is well known. . . . They have been able to recently claim the right to marry only after travelling a very difficult and contentious road. Accordingly, putting gays and lesbians in a situation where a marriage commissioner can refuse to provide his or her services solely because of their sexual orientation would clearly be a retrograde step—a step that would perpetuate disadvantage and involve stereotypes about the worthiness of same-sex unions.[75]

For Richards, the effect of the amendments clearly fell within the usual test for a section 15 violation. But he also held that the religious freedom of commissioners was impacted if they had to marry couples against their conscience. After establishing that the amendments violated section 15, he moved to the section 1 analysis to determine whether this violation was justified. Although not determinative, to fully understand the section 1 arguments, Richards thought it was necessary to understand the position of the commissioners under *The Marriage Act* without accommodation.

JACELYN ANN RYAN-FROSLIE

Jackie Ryan-Froslie was born February 10, 1954, in Saskatoon. She grew up on the family farm near Fielding, a small village which is no longer incorporated. Ryan-Froslie had her first six grades in a one-room schoolhouse in the village. She attended junior high and high school in the community of Radisson, where the family lived for several years after her father was injured. Entering the University of Saskatchewan immediately after high school, Ryan-Froslie originally intended to study journalism but had friends intent on law, and after two years of arts entered the combined program. She received a bachelor's degree in political science in 1976 and her law degree in 1977. While a law student, she clerked at the Provincial Court, worked for legal aid, and was a volunteer probation officer.

Justice Jacelyn Ann Ryan-Froslie. (Photo: Mark Greschner. Court of Appeal.)

Ryan-Froslie articled with the firm of Anderson Nimegeers in Swift Current, where she discovered she was the only woman entering practice in the southwest of the province. Her principal was Clifford Nimegeers. She remained with the firm, later known as Anderson and Company, after joining the bar in 1978. She practised primarily as a litigator and in family law, with some solicitor work, and had several appearances at the Court of Appeal. Ryan-Froslie was appointed a QC in 1999. An instructor for the bar admission course, she was local governor of the Saskatchewan Trial Lawyers Association and served as vice-chair of the Saskatchewan Police Commission.

Like all the current appeal judges, Ryan-Froslie was encouraged to apply for the judiciary. She was appointed in 2000 to the family law division of the Court of Queen's Bench. In 2009, she was made a deputy judge of the Supreme Court of Yukon, joining the corps of provincial judges who sit part-time in the territory. She continued to sit for the Yukon court after her appointment to the Court of Appeal in 2013. Ryan-Froslie took supernumerary status in 2017.

"More directly," he wrote, "the real issue is whether the s. 2(a) freedoms of a marriage commissioner would be curtailed if solemnizing a marriage would, in the words of the *Options*, 'be contrary to the marriage commissioner's religious beliefs.'"[76]

Freedom of religion had been broadly defined in *Charter* jurisprudence to include not being forced to take actions that might be contrary to sincerely held religious beliefs. Another test was whether the impact was trivial or inconsequential. Marriage commissioners faced the choice, in Richards's view, between their jobs and their conscience, not a trivial consequence. This meant that there was a clear violation of section 2(a) of the *Charter*, which guaranteed freedom of religion and conscience.

This analysis informed Richards's application of section 1, using the *Oakes* proportionality test. The first question in the *Oakes* test was whether the objective of the statute in question was of sufficient importance to potentially override a *Charter* right. Richards defined the objective of the amendments as the protection of the marriage commissioners' section 2(a) rights, specifically by accommodating their religious beliefs and not forcing them to undertake same-sex marriages. He disagreed with the argument that the objective was to deny same-sex couples certain rights, feeling this confused the effects of the amendments with their intent. Given the broad definition of freedom of religion and its importance as a *Charter* right in and of itself, he thought it obvious that the amendments had an important objective. "It seems clear enough," he wrote, "that a law aimed at preserving or accommodating a constitutionally guaranteed right or freedom must normally be taken to satisfy this aspect of the *Oakes* test even if the effect of the law in question is to impinge on other *Charter* interests."

While the objective of the statute was sufficiently pressing, in Richards's view the amendments did not pass the proportionality test in *Oakes*, which considered whether the means and ends of a statute were rationally connected, whether the statute was the least restrictive option, and the proportionality between the objective of the statute and its impact on the right in question. It was easy for Richards to imagine measures that had less impact on same-sex couples, such as a "single entry" system of commissioners, where people requested a marriage commissioner and were referred to one and religious scruples were handled "behind the scenes." There might still be a lack of access if too many commissioners declined to perform same-sex marriages, but there would be no direct affront to individuals. But while this fact alone was sufficient to declare the amendments unconstitutional, Richards felt it important to finish the proportionality analysis, as this was really the nub of the argument in terms of balancing freedom of religion with freedom from discrimination.

He found little proportionality between the benefits and harms stemming from the amendments. He argued that the core aspects of freedom of religion were not under any assault: marriage commissioners could hold beliefs and worship as they chose without impediment. It was only in the execution of their public duties that their religious beliefs were impacted. The harms were obvious: perpetuating discrimination and causing significant emotional distress to some same-sex couples. But the most significant negative effect was that the amendments allowed some individuals to impose their personal beliefs on their execution of their duties in a public office. Richards wrote that the two amendments would

> undermine a deeply entrenched and fundamentally important aspect of our system of government. In our tradition, the apparatus of the state serves everyone equally without providing better, poorer or different services to one individual compared to another by making distinctions on the basis of factors like race, religion or gender. The proud tradition of individual public officeholders is very much imbued with this notion. Persons who voluntarily choose to assume an office, like that of marriage commissioner, cannot expect to directly shape the office's intersection with the public so as to make it conform with their personal religious or other beliefs. Any idea of this sort would sit uneasily with the principle of the rule of law to the effect that "the law is supreme over officials of the government as well as private individuals, and thereby preclusive of the influence of arbitrary power."[77]

Unlike clergy and other religious office holders, Richards argued, marriage commissioners were public officials carrying out a public duty, and the amendments undercut the basic principle that government services should be provided in an impartial and non-discriminatory manner. No freedom or right under the *Charter* was absolute, and in this case the amendments were not justified. Richards's decision was typically elegant in simplicity and directness, yet fully canvassed the issues.

Smith arrived at the same result. She primarily disagreed with her colleague's proportionality analysis, in part because she wanted to emphasize

Justice Gene Anne Smith's last sitting, April 5, 2012. *From left:* Justice Robert Richards, Chief Justice John Klebuc, and Justice Gene Anne Smith. (Photo: Patricia Holdsworth. Court of Appeal.)

the degree of harm and the larger implications of the amendments, in part because Smith viewed the impairment of religious freedom addressed with the amendments as very minor. Given the general hostility of organized religions to homosexuality and same-sex marriage, Smith contended that a civil ceremony was the only option for many same-sex couples, magnifying the harm. While Smith and Richards were on the same page as to the effects of the law on the LGBT community, Smith went a step farther: the very existence of the amendments was, in her view, an affront to the dignity of homosexuals and perpetuated harmful discrimination and stereotypes. She saw an additional danger in that the amendments opened a door for similar laws accommodating the religious views of public officials and permitting discrimination in other contexts.

Smith and Richards parted ways in the determination of the first part of the *Oakes* test: whether a statute addressed a pressing and substantive concern. While Smith agreed that the benefit-versus-harm analysis was most relevant in the last part of the proportionality test, she argued that this analysis also helped determine whether the statute met the first criteria. She concluded it did not, and had several points of attack. Like

Richards, she identified the core of religious freedom as holding beliefs and engaging in religious practice. Actions that involved imposing religious beliefs on others were not part of that core, and acting on beliefs that resulted in discrimination was not protected. This meant that there was little basis for a law protecting the marriage commissioners' ability to act on their beliefs. Part of the difficulty, she felt, was that despite the clearly secular nature of civil marriage, the objecting commissioners continued to conflate civil with religious marriage. "The performance of a civil marriage by a marriage commissioner under the *Act* is not a religious rite or practice," she wrote. "Nor does the requirement to do so limit or restrict religious belief."[78]

The other argument put forward, that by performing civil ceremonies for same-sex couples commissioners were condoning or approving their unions and homosexual conduct, Smith felt was flawed. Performing the ceremony could be neutral, a legal obligation of the position of commissioner, but the refusal was clearly condemning and discriminatory. The sum of Smith's argument was that the imposition on religious freedom in the situation failed the first part of the *Oakes* test; it was secondary and really arose from commissioners inappropriately imposing their religious beliefs on a secular activity. Smith felt it was also important to state the objective of the law more precisely to reflect that fact. In her formulation, the amendments were intended "to permit marriage commissioners to refuse to perform same-sex marriages when they object, on religious grounds, to doing so."[79]

Smith also squeezed in some commentary into her *Oakes* analysis that was somewhat *obiter*: as she put it, "These points do not sit comfortably within the traditional analysis required in relation to the rational connection test."[80] One aspect of the amendments that both judges noted was that the statutes required a notwithstanding clause to make the *Saskatchewan Human Rights Code* of no effect. Smith saw this as a somewhat sinister background factor that informed the *Oakes* test. The clause was the only one of its kind within the province's statutes, which Smith called "not merely extraordinary. It is unprecedented." But her criticism went much deeper:

> Astonishingly, this clause would grant to a public official, charged with the delivery of a public service, an immunity to the anti-discrimination provisions of the *Code* not enjoyed by any other

From left: Justice Ralph Ottenbreit, Justice Neal Caldwell, and Justice Robert Richards, at the courthouse rear entrance, 2012. (Court of Appeal)

> person in this Province. Moreover, in practice, it would deny to gays and lesbians the protection from discrimination that the *Code* provides to others.[81]

The contrast between majority and minority judgments is instructive. Both Richards and Smith effectively canvassed all the issues involved, and most of the difference between them was a matter of emphasis, but one was more fundamental. Richards had carried out a classic *Charter* analysis and had been willing to give wider play to freedom of religion in balancing rights.[82] Smith had, as one commentator noted, taken an approach seen in jurisprudence on hate speech where some expression by its nature and content was given less value as free speech and less *Charter* protection. Smith's outrage at the amendments came across clearly, while Richards played his judgment more coolly. Richards's judgment also left some room for the possible accommodation of marriage commissioners; Smith's view strongly implied there was no need for accommodation, as the violation of freedom of religion was trivial.

The end result was the same, as was the message. Public servants had to provide services to the public without any discrimination, and religious convictions were not sufficient grounds for an official to refuse to do so. The principle seems uncontroversial, but the implications of the decision are profound for freedom of religion. Although Richards was clear that there is no hierarchy of rights under the *Charter*, the removal of conscience as a ground for a public servant to refuse to carry out their duties if this results in discrimination is a significant contraction of religious rights. In the view of some commentators, this was also discrimination that could be challenged on the basis of section 2(a) and section 15.[83] Such arguments, however, overlooked Smith's conclusions about the degree of the violation involved.

The issue has not come before the Supreme Court of Canada as yet, but it seems inevitable. Some provinces informally accommodate the religious beliefs of marriage commissioners, and one, Prince Edward Island, put in place legislation allowing commissioners the right to refuse. In the light of the Saskatchewan decision, it seems very likely that if challenged, both informal and legislative attempts to accommodate religious beliefs in this context would be declared unconstitutional. But as some commentators have noted, there is also a duty of government, as an employer, to accommodate religious beliefs and practices, and this too might be one day litigated. Both Richards and Smith articulated arguments that the Supreme Court of Canada may adopt.

The *Marriage Commissioners* reference also highlighted the growing tendency for politicians to use the courts as political cover, at least in the eyes of critics of the practice. Referring proposed legislation to the courts superficially seems a reasonable course of action, saving the time and money of potential litigation by having judges vet statutes ahead of time. But some commentators believe references are more useful to politicians as a public relations exercise, allowing them to appear to take action on controversial files in a fashion pleasing to their supporters while knowing full well that the courts will not approve the legislation. The courts then take the blame. There may be some truth to this view: governments surely have competent legal advice and must know when a statute is unlikely to pass review. This may not have been the case with the issues involved in the *Marriage Commissioners* reference, but it is true that the court's decision predictably drew public criticism, including from a Conservative Party MP.[84] The courts, making critical decisions that often involve complex legal reasoning and fine distinctions not easily reduced to sound bites, without sophisticated public relations experts spinning their decisions, and also maintaining a long tradition of having judgments speak for themselves, are uniquely vulnerable in the modern media age. And the stakes are high: the proper administration of justice and the confidence in the courts of the public at large are critical to the rule of law in a democracy.

Justice Gary Lane before retirement, 2017. (Photo: Mark Greschner. Court of Appeal.)

SASKATCHEWAN FEDERATION OF LABOUR V SASKATCHEWAN

IN THE SECOND decade of the twenty-first century, the Supreme Court of Canada has reconsidered and overruled several earlier *Charter* decisions, looking at earlier rulings on the legality of prostitution and assisted death, and also on the right to strike. In *Saskatchewan Federation of Labour v Saskatchewan*, the court reconsidered its infamous "labour trilogy," three decisions which had included RWDSU *v Saskatchewan*. In that appeal, the court had overruled the Court of Appeal, which had held that freedom of association had to protect the right to strike; otherwise, as Stuart Cameron had written, it would be an empty right. The issue arose again in Saskatchewan in 2013 when the provincial government introduced new labour legislation. At the Court of Appeal, the main issue was the force and effect of *stare decisis* in the *Charter* age, while the Supreme Court made a historic about-face that vindicated the Saskatchewan court's original ruling on freedom of association.

A new government with a different view on labour relations precipitated the litigation. In 2008, the Saskatchewan Party passed two statutes, *The Public Service Essential Services Act* and *The Trade Union Amendment Act*. The first introduced new restrictions on the ability of public service workers to strike. The second changed the rules for union certification, such as the use of secret ballots and allowing greater communication from employers to employees during a unionization drive. Mild compared to "right to work" legislation that had become common in the United States, the statute provoked howls of outrage in Saskatchewan, as did *The Essential Services Act*. A court challenge swiftly followed. The trial judge and the Court of Appeal agreed that *The Trade Union Amendment Act* made unionizing a workplace more difficult but not to a degree that violated the freedom to associate or other *Charter* rights. Most of the measures in the *Act* could be found in other Canadian labour legislation.

The trial judge came to a different conclusion with *The Public Service Essential Services Act*. He ruled that the statute violated section 2(d) of the *Charter*, on freedom of association, and was not saved under section 1. He did so on the basis that freedom of association had to include collective bargaining and the right to strike. This flew in the face of the Supreme Court of Canada's conclusions in its labour trilogy. The trial judge relied on the fact that the Supreme Court, in more recent decisions, had substantially changed its position on section 2(d) since the trilogy to include collective bargaining under freedom of association. He reasoned that as the Supreme Court was clearly gradually expanding the reach of the right and his analysis indicated that striking should be part of freedom of association, he did not have to follow a precedent he deemed outdated.

The trial judge was correct that the jurisprudence had changed significantly.[85] In the labour trilogy, the majority of the Supreme Court had elected to take a narrow reading of freedom of association that supported the right of the individual to associate but denied any protection to the ends for which individuals associated, regarding these as derivative rights, and thus avoided extending *Charter* protection to so-called group rights. The majority also argued that Canadian courts had historically paid great deference to the legislature and to labour tribunals, due to the complex balancing of rights and difficult policy choices involved in creating labour legislation and the very specialized nature of labour law. The dissenting opinion had taken the same view as Bayda and Cameron in RWDSU: that freedom of association had to include, at least to some extent, the objectives and actions that people associated together to accomplish, otherwise it was a limited right. The Saskatchewan decision had conformed better to the Supreme Court's own interpretative scheme for the *Charter*: the broad, contextual interpretation of rights and freedoms, with reasonable limits found within a section 1 analysis.

As time went on, a different Supreme Court agreed more and more with this view. In *Dunmore*, a 2001 decision regarding agricultural farm workers in Ontario, the majority of the court recognized that freedom of association had to recognize the importance of collective action. In a 2007 appeal, *Health Services*, a majority held that section 2(d) included collective bargaining, directly repudiating the labour trilogy but stopping short of saying the right to strike was also protected. The court's support of collective bargaining was still somewhat limited, with the majority judgment stating that not all violations of collective agreements or avoidance of collective bargaining necessarily violated the *Charter*. In *Fraser*, another decision on the protection of farm workers, the court also stepped back to declare that section 2(d) conveyed a general right to collective bargaining but not any specific model or method. But it was clear that the court's jurisprudence was developing in a direction that reduced the precedential authority of the labour trilogy.

Stare decisis, or precedent, is a central principle in the common law. At the time the Court of Appeal was founded, in 1918, Canadian courts observed *stare decisis* strictly—mechanistically in the view of later critics. But there was always some leeway with precedent. Part of the exercise of applying precedent was deciding if it applied to the facts of a case, and modifying or adopting a new rule when it did not, "distinguishing" one case from another. Judges also had different attitudes towards precedent, with some, such as Emmett Hall, chafing against its bonds and within ethical boundaries willing to bend, stretch, or dodge a precedent that gave an unjust result. Even in the age of strict observance of precedent, there was some awareness that a decision might be wrong and the precedent

LIAN MARGARET SCHWANN

The last appointment to the Court of Appeal before its centennial was Lian Schwann, a judge on the Court of Queen's Bench immediately prior to her appointment.

Justice Lian Margaret Schwann. (Photo: Mark Greschner. Court of Appeal.)

Schwann was born in Edmonton, Alberta, where her father attended dental school. The family returned to Regina, where Schwann went to public school. She attended Carroll College in Helena, Montana, graduating in 1976 with a bachelor of arts in social sciences. She then entered law school at the University of Saskatchewan, graduating in 1980. She articled in Regina with the firm then known as McDougall Ready and Wakeling. Tom Wakeling, who was subsequently appointed to the Court of Appeal in 1984, served as her principal. In 1984, Schwann joined the civil law division of the Department of Justice and Attorney General (now Ministry of Justice) as a Crown counsel. She appeared at all levels of court and before various boards and tribunals, practising predominantly in the areas of health, environmental, natural resource, privacy, and public law. She was appointed Queen's Council in 2007.

While in practice, Schwann was involved in various capacities with the Canadian Bar Association. She was chair of the Saskatchewan Crown Counsel Association and on the Justice Employment Equity Committee. Schwann was a frequent presenter at seminars and conferences. In 2002, she became a sessional instructor for the First Nations University of Canada at the University of Regina, teaching on environmental and public health law.

After twenty-three years in government, in 2007 Schwann assumed the joint position of Court of Appeal registrar and registrar in bankruptcy, following Justice Herauf's appointment to the Court of Queen's Bench.

As Court of Appeal registrar, she was heavily involved in the court's eCourt project and the revision of the criminal appeal rules. In March 2011, Schwann was appointed to the Queen's Bench as the resident judge for the Judicial Centre of Moose Jaw. In 2016, she was transferred to the court's general division in the Judicial Centre of Regina, where she sat until her elevation to the Court of Appeal on August 17, 2017. She replaced Justice Ryan-Froslie, who had elected supernumerary status.

abandoned. In Saskatchewan, Chief Justice Turgeon had decided in an obscure 1934 judgment that a previous decision of the court should not be subsequently followed. Although it was *prima facie* recognition that a decision may later be deemed incorrect, Turgeon's judgment did not lay down general principles or procedures for overturning past precedents.[86] The court continued to observe a fairly strict adherence to *stare decisis*. Even Culliton, with his fine sense of justice and imperious ways, was scrupulous about precedent.

In the 1970s, judges and court became somewhat less strict with precedent, just as the "modern rule" for statutory interpretation introduced a broader, more context-driven way to understand statutes. Famously, in 1966, the House of Lords announced it would reconsider and potentially overturn past precedents. The Supreme Court of Canada never made a definitive announcement and might have taken this stance as early as the 1950s, but after 1975 it was generally understood the court would reconsider a past decision.[87] By the 1980s, most appellate courts in Canada had instituted formal or informal policies to allow this. Saskatchewan did not have a formal reconsideration process, but the court would hear an argument against a past decision.[88] Circumstances had to be exceptional and a precedent clearly wrong or no longer applicable.

All this concerned what is sometimes called "horizontal precedent," a court abandoning or changing its own previous decision. Vertical precedent, the decision of a higher court, was another matter. Some trial judges had, at different times, argued that much-changed social conditions made a precedent obsolete and justified not following it.[89] This idea had always been slapped down on appeal. The trial judge in *Saskatchewan Federation of Labour* had done something different: he argued that the precedent in the labour trilogy was not just in error but that the Supreme Court was very likely to change it soon, and this justified contradicting the decisions.

As Richards wrote, "This line of argument self-evidently involves a novel view of the doctrine of *stare decisis*," and as he noted, "there is no authority . . . for this proposition."[90] Richards succinctly reviewed the general operation of precedent. Although he granted that there had been some academic approval of the idea of "anticipatory overruling," as he called it, this was hardly sufficient for such a radical departure from long-accepted and fundamental doctrine. But Richards chose to explore the trial judge's argument further. He argued that even if a lower court could pre-emptively abandon a precedent, it was not sufficiently certain that in the appeal at hand it would be justified.

In Richards's view, although the Supreme Court had changed its position on section 2(d) considerably from the labour trilogy, it was far from certain that the court would include the right to strike in freedom of association in a future decision. In the *Health Services* decision, the majority decision held that collective bargaining was not a modern right created in legislation, like the trilogy had decided, but rather a part of the fundamental freedom that had become incorporated into labour statutes. But the Supreme Court had also said that the right did not guarantee any particular outcome and also no particular model of labour relations. In *Fraser*, which had looked at the constitutionality of new Ontario legislation brought in after *Dunmore*, the majority further explicitly rejected the argument that striking was a necessary element of collective bargaining, envisioning various methods to make the process viable. To Richards's mind, this raised enough doubt as to how the Supreme Court would rule on the matter of striking to make the trial judge's ruling presumptuous. The court might rule that striking was just one possible mechanism to make collective bargaining work and not give it explicit protection. The Supreme Court might also look at striking as a stand-alone right, and again, to Richards, it was not obvious that the court would necessarily rule a particular way. More importantly, unlike cases where an appellate court reconsidered a previous decision, allowing lower courts to abandon precedents went too far in undermining the consistency and certainty that *stare decisis* instilled in judge-made law.

In Richards's view, this was the nub of the Saskatchewan Federation of Labour's appeal. Richards did consider a number of other *Charter* arguments the unions raised that attacked *The Public Service Essential Services*

Act and *The Trade Union Amendment Act* on the basis of section 2(b), on freedom of expression, section 7, on the right to life, liberty, and security of person, and section 15, on equality rights. He found these arguments unconvincing. On the first, he thought that the impact on freedom of expression was minor. Unions and employees could still express their views and even picket; they were only not allowed to walk off the job. It was clear in the jurisprudence that courts had decided that striking was best considered as part of freedom of association. On section 7, he could see no deprivation of life, liberty, and security of person aside from a rather far-fetched claim that employers could force ill or injured worker to stay on the job. And on the equality front, Richards did not think that being a public sector employee or unionized worker was analogous to prohibited grounds of discrimination like sex, race, or religion. The Supreme Court had made it clear already that choice of career was not the same as personal characteristics. The other argument, that reducing the effectiveness of unions affected historically marginalized groups, Richards found too remote.

It was ironic that on further appeal the Supreme Court of Canada chose to reverse the labour trilogy once and for all. Essentially adopting the reasoning from Chief Justice Dickson's dissents in the original judgments, the majority decision ruled that the right to strike had to be considered a part of freedom of association. The court did not address the notion that lower courts might see the way the jurisprudential winds were blowing and depart from a precedent likely to fall.[91] There was also a stinging dissent that argued the court had constitutionalized a particular labour relations scheme and did not see any compelling reason to depart from the majority reasons in the trilogy. The majority decision had come to the same conclusion that Chief Justice Bayda and Justice Cameron had arrived at almost thirty years earlier. And to close the circle completely, Premier Wall of Saskatchewan threatened to use the notwithstanding clause, just as the Devine government had done in the wake of the Court of Appeal's RWDSU decision in 1986.[92]

CONCLUSION

THE *CHARTER* AND human rights litigation that has come to the Court of Appeal in the past decade only made up a very small, if very significant, part of the 110 to 120 decisions the court issues every year. The court has also made important decisions on class action law suits, as Saskatchewan has one of the country's most active firms in this area. Another was Aboriginal sentencing, unfortunately a major issue with Saskatchewan's large Aboriginal population and disproportionate rate of incarceration. The court has wrestled, as have others, with *Gladue* principles in sentencing, which mandate that trial judges consider all the circumstances facing Aboriginal offenders in arriving at a proper sentence. And as always, many decisions of the court, while they may not have any larger resonance, break new ground, or become legal landmarks, have supreme importance in the lives of citizens of Saskatchewan. And it is for them that the judges of the court work tirelessly and bring their best efforts to every appeal. In this, they continue a tradition of service and excellence that has been characteristic of the court for over one hundred years.

CONCLUSION

In 2018, the Court of Appeal for Saskatchewan turned one hundred. A simple statement of a simple fact, but one that represents a century of hard effort and often hard decisions, soul searching, striving to provide justice while maintaining the coherence and clarity of the law, discipline, creativity, and sometimes brilliance. A centennial is an appropriate moment to take stock of the court's history and its contributions to the people of Saskatchewan, but it is only a pause in the story, and the briefest of pauses at that. The court will celebrate the centennial but then return to work the next day, hearing appeals of applications, orders, and judgments from the courts below, listening to the focused arguments of experienced counsel and the nervous presentations of young counsel, and helping the unsure and intimidated self-represented give voice to their appeal.

In Chief Justice Bob Richards, the court has a fine leader, widely praised as a judge and as an administrator. As one colleague has said, "He was tailor-made for the role." Richards speaks as highly of his colleagues as they speak of him, calling them devoted, collegial, good lawyers with abundant common sense. Georgina Jackson is deeply experienced, dedicated, and hardworking, a major contributor to the court's jurisprudence. Ralph Ottenbreit is an independent thinker whose analysis of legal problems

LEFT: Chief Justice Robert Gerling Richards.
(Photo: Mark Greschner. Court of Appeal.)

is informed with broad practice experience. Neal Caldwell is analytical and a strong writer whose broad commercial background is very useful. Maurice Herauf is pragmatic and practical, with an especially keen eye for the procedural side of appeals, as well as personable and pleasant. Peter Whitmore is a true gentleman, a model of collegiality, with a nose for the central issue of an appeal and, like Herauf, the practical dimension of a decision. Jackie Ryan-Froslie is a careful thinker and writer and exceptionally diligent, with great expertise in family law and an infectious laugh and positive outlook that brighten the court. Lian Schwann's dedication as registrar is well remembered, and she brings broad courtroom experience as a trial judge to her new position. All these judges attest to the excellent collegiality of the court, and many say that they feel their fellow judges are friends as well as colleagues. The judges also have nothing but praise for the dedication and ability of the court staff.

The bench of 2018 is one of the most diverse groups the court has ever seen. The fact that the court has two sitting judges who both once served as the registrar is a uniquely Saskatchewan twist. It is a small court, and not every practice background is presently represented, but the mix changes with new appointments. There are still some potential firsts to be had. No judge has ever been promoted from the Provincial Court all the way to the Court of Appeal. The court also still awaits a judge who is a visible minority. Justice McKay notwithstanding, a suitable candidate from Saskatchewan's Indigenous community is necessary in a province with a large Aboriginal population.

No judge is exactly like another, and in sum its complement of judges gives each court an identity. Saskatchewan has had its share of brilliant judges, good judges, and average judges, and perhaps one or two who were a little out of their depth but did their best. Some, as documented in this book, have been exceptional characters and part of the legal and political fabric of the province: Wetmore, Haultain, McKay, Turgeon, Martin, Gordon, Culliton, Bayda, the list goes on. Historically, the nexus between politics and law has been particularly strong in Saskatchewan, and the story of the court has been greatly informed by this reality. Like all institutions, courts are made up of individuals whose strengths, weaknesses, beliefs, and philosophy of the law influence not only particular decisions but the institution itself.

Like its judges, the jurisprudence of the court is also its identity, created in a certain context of time and place while fitting into the larger

Judges and staff of the Court of Appeal, 2018. *From left:* Justice Peter Whitmore, Allison Hahn, Becky Frisko, Daina Haniak, Ann Marie Melvie, Justice Jacelyn Ryan-Froslie, Amanda Haynes, Registrar Melanie Baldwin, Justice Maurice Herauf, Chief Justice Robert Richards, Justice Neal Caldwell, Lori Vollman, Justice Ralph Ottenbreit, Karen Smith, Justice Georgina Jackson, Samantha Leippi, Dawn Blaus, Executive Officer Nadine Barnes, Justice Lian Schwann, Scott Polowyk (Photo: Mark Greschner. Court of Appeal.)

picture of the development of law in Canada. Saskatchewan's court hewed closely to the predominant judicial norms of the time, from the black-letter orthodoxies of the early decades of the century to the gradual broadening of judicial perspectives after the Second World War, to the rise of legal modernism, and finally to the contextual, purposive style of modern courts. But within these larger developments, the Saskatchewan court had its own particular character in each era.

The court of Wetmore, Haultain, and Turgeon was disciplined, its judges resisting the impulse to interfere unnecessarily with their trial brethren, and demonstrated a fine understanding of the appellate role and a strong sense of justice. Decisions like *Quong Wing* or the reference on *The Grain Marketing Act* demonstrated the restraint, while *Finlay* and the court's jurisprudence on Prohibition showed the concern with justice. The judges of Martin's time resisted the limiting of the court's role in the review of state action, which informed their jurisprudence regarding administrative tribunals such as the Labour Relations Board. Culliton, with great humanity, sought, within the limits of his position, to help those who had transgressed against society in his sentencing decisions, including the widely cited *Morrissette*. The court of the Bayda years exemplified the

The Court of Appeal, 2018. *Standing, from left:* Justice Jacelyn Ryan-Froslie, Justice Maurice Herauf, Justice Neal Caldwell, Justice Peter Whitmore, Justice Lian Schwann. *Seated, from left:* Justice Georgina Jackson, Chief Justice Robert Richards, Justice Ralph Ottenbreit. (Photo: Mark Greschner. Court of Appeal.)

creativity of a generation of judges at a crucial juncture, the introduction of the *Charter of Rights and Freedoms*, with decisions like RWDSU. This court later ably defended the position that robust appellate intervention was necessary in the interest of justice. The current court combines rigour, pragmatism, and a profound concern for providing the best outcomes possible for those who come to the court.

The decisions of the court also tell a story of Saskatchewan, a timeless record of a changing and evolving society, and are a testament to the service and dedication of a small group of individuals to the province and to the administration of justice. The first one hundred years of the Court of Appeal for Saskatchewan laid a strong foundation for the next one hundred years and more.

COURT OF APPEAL CENTENARY DINNER

On March 2, 2018, the Court of Appeal celebrated its centennial with a banquet at the Hotel Saskatchewan in Regina. Over 360 members of the bench and bar attended the dinner, including the Right Honourable Beverley McLachlin, retired Chief Justice of Canada; the Honourable Ralph Goodale, Minister of Public Safety; the Honourable W. Thomas Molloy, QC, Lieutenant Governor of Saskatchewan designate; Deputy Premier Gordon Wyant, QC; and the heads of the trial courts, Chief Justice Martel Popescul and Chief Judge James Plemel. The keynote address was given by Mr. W. Brent Cotter, QC, of the College of Law at the University of Saskatchewan.

The following morning the court hosted a reunion for all former law clerks, the students at law who articled at the court.

Centennial Dinner in the Regency Ballroom, Hotel Saskatchewan, Regina, March 2, 2018. (Photo: Ali Lauren Creative Services.)

This page, clockwise from top left: The Right Honourable Beverley McLachlin, former Chief Justice of Canada; The Honourable Ralph Goodale, Minister of Public Safety and Emergency Preparedness; Justice Richard Danyliuk, Court of Queen's Bench; Justice Georgina Jackson, Court of Appeal; W. Brent Cotter, QC, College of Law, University of Saskatchewan; Justice Jacelyn Ryan-Froslie, Court of Appeal. (Photos: Ali Lauren Creative Services.)

This page, clockwise from top left: Chief Justice of Saskatchewan Robert Richards; Chief Justice Martel Popescul, Court of Queen's Bench; The Honourable Gordon Wyant, QC, Deputy Premier of Saskatchewan and Judge Gerald Morin, Provincial Court; Riva Farrell Racette; Chief Judge James Plemel, Provincial Court; Graeme Mitchell, QC. (Photos: Ali Lauren Creative Services.)

Attendees of Law Clerks Reunion, March 3, 2018. *Standing, from left:* Jessica Brockman, Melissa Wallace, Mark Prescott, Kelly Nicholson, Leah Howie, Rae Mitten, Greg Fingas, Lauren Wihak, Prasanna Ranganathan, William Lane, Paul Olfert, Andrea Argue, Pat Quaroni, Nicole O'Byrne, Peter Bergbusch, Murray Sawatzky, Christopher Triggs, Phillip Scheibel, Marianne "Chuck" Davies, Renée (Tulk) Moore, John Williams, Mark Gelowitz, Michelle Korpan, Brian Rolfes, Bradley Berg, Theo Litowski, Ryan Rempel, Heather Jensen, Allison Graham, Rashmi Goel, Nadine Barnes, Melanie Baldwin. *Middle row, seated, from left:* Patricia Farnese, Jaime Carlson, Eustathios "Stathy" Markatos, Erin Gagner, Justice Meghan McCreary, Joanne Colledge-Miller, Janelle Souter, Katelyn Sheehan, Laura Mazenc, Rob Martz, Jeremie Roussel, Kristy Pozniak, Meredith Hagel, Jenelle (Matsalla) Breker, Adryan Toth, Lauren Scharfstein, Wendy Kelley. *Front row, seated, from left:* Ann Marie Melvie, the Honourable Stuart Cameron, the Honourable CalvinTallis, Justice Schwann, Justice Herauf, Justice Ryan-Froslie, Justice Jackson, Chief Justice Richards, Justice Caldwell, Justice Ottenbreit, the Honourable John Klebuc, the Honourable William Vancise, Justice Whitmore, the Honourable Gene Anne Smith. (Photo: Ali Lauren Creative Services.)

Current and former judges of the Court of Appeal. *Standing, from left:* Justice Maurice Herauf, Justice Ralph Ottenbreit, Justice Lian Schwann, Justice Georgina Jackson, Justice Jacelyn Ryan-Froslie, Chief Justice Robert Richards, Justice Neal Caldwell, Justice Peter Whitmore. *Sitting, from left:* The Honourable Stuart Cameron, The Honourable Calvin Tallis, The Honourable Gene Anne Smith, The Honourable William Vancise, The Honourable Nicholas Sherstobitoff, Justice YsanneWilkinson. (Photo: Ali Lauren Creative Services.)

APPENDIX ONE:

JUSTICES OF THE COURT OF APPEAL FOR SASKATCHEWAN, 1918–2017

Frederick William Gordon Haultain,
March 2, 1918–November 1, 1938
Chief Justice of Saskatchewan, October 29, 1912–November 1, 1938

John Henderson Lamont, March 2, 1918–April 2, 1927
Supreme Court of Canada, 1927–1935

Henry William Newlands, March 2, 1918–February 17, 1921
Lieutenant-Governor of Saskatchewan, 1921–1931

Edward Lindsey Elwood, March 2, 1918–May 19, 1921

William Ferdinand Alphonse Turgeon,
March 14, 1921–September 25, 1941
Chief Justice of Saskatchewan, November 1, 1938–September 25, 1941

James McKay, October 12, 1921–December 1, 1932

William Melville Martin,
July 22, 1922–March 1, 1961
Chief Justice of Saskatchewan, September 25, 1941–March 1, 1961

Philip Edward Mackenzie, April 2, 1927–June 19, 1946

Percival Hector Gordon, August 10, 1935–March 1, 1961

Thomas Clayton Davis, June 29, 1939–January 13, 1948

Hector Y. MacDonald, September 25, 1941–February 1, 1951

Percy McCuaig Anderson, October 30, 1946–November 19, 1948

Arthur Thomas Procter, May 28, 1948–May 11, 1961

Donald Alexander McNiven, July 6, 1949–July 31, 1961

Edward Milton Culliton,
February 1, 1951–April 8, 1981
Chief Justice of Saskatchewan, November 23, 1962–April 8,1981

Emmett Matthew Hall,
March 1, 1961–November 23, 1962
Chief Justice of Saskatchewan, March 1, 1961–November 23, 1962
Supreme Court of Canada, 1962–1973

Mervyn John Woods, June 13, 1961–June 7, 1984
Supernumerary Judge, July 1, 1981–June 7, 1984

Russell Lawrence Brownridge, October 23, 1961–July 3, 1988
Supernumerary Judge, July 3, 1981–July 3, 1988

Percy Hathaway Maguire, July 16, 1962–October 14, 1974

Roy Norman Hall, December 13, 1962–January 1, 1990
Supernumerary Judge, October 24, 1985–January 1, 1990

Edward Dmytro Bayda,
December 20, 1974–September 9, 2006
Chief Justice of Saskatchewan, April 16, 1981–September 9, 2006

Raymond Alexander MacDonald, July 16, 1981–November 30, 1984
Supernumerary Judge, November 17, 1983–November 30, 1984

Stuart John Cameron, October 13, 1981–May 15, 2014
Supernumerary Judge, January 1, 2007–May 15, 2014

Calvin Forrester Tallis, November 12, 1981–March 5, 2005

William John Vancise, November 17, 1983–January 10, 2013
Supernumerary Judge, January 1, 2007–January 10, 2013

Thomas Clarkson Wakeling, December 12, 1984–May 19, 1999

Marjorie Anne Gerwing, December 12, 1984–January 31, 2013
Supernumerary Judge, April 10, 2007–January 31, 2013

Nicholas W. Sherstobitoff, December 3, 1985–September 28, 2010
Supernumerary Judge, January 1, 2007–September 28, 2010

John Gary Lane, September 10, 1991–May 2, 2017
Supernumerary Judge, January 1, 2011–May 2, 2017

Georgina Ruth Jackson, September 10, 1991–

Robert Gerling Richards,
October 1, 2004–
Chief Justice of Saskatchewan, June 30, 2013–

Gene Anne Smith, May 19, 2005–December 31, 2012

John Klebuc,
September 14, 2006–April 24, 2015
Chief Justice of Saskatchewan, September 14, 2006–June 30, 2013
Supernumerary Judge, June 30, 2013–April 24, 2015

Darla Catherine Hunter, March 2, 2007–March 1, 2010

Ysanne G.K. Wilkinson, June 1, 2007–June 19, 2009

Ralph Kurt Ottenbreit, June 19, 2009–

Neal William Caldwell, April 23, 2010–

Maurice J. Herauf, March 3, 2011–

Peter Alexander Whitmore, June 30, 2013–

Jacelyn Ann Ryan-Froslie, November 11, 2013–
Supernumerary Judge, May 5, 2017–

Lian Margaret Schwann, August 15, 2017–

APPENDIX TWO:

LAW CLERKS OF THE COURT OF APPEAL

1982–1983
Walter Kosteckyj—Chief Justice Bayda

1983–1984
John Williams—Chief Justice Bayda

1984–1985
Margaret Eckenfelder—Chief Justice Bayda

1985–1986
Ross Macnab—Chief Justice Bayda
Murray Sawatzky—Justices Tallis, Cameron

1986–1987
Mark Gelowitz—Chief Justice Bayda
Darcy McGovern—Justices Tallis, Cameron

1987–1988
Pat Quaroni—Chief Justice Bayda
Stefania Fortugno—Justices Vancise, Wakeling

1988–1989
James Nugent—Chief Justice Bayda
Gary Bainbridge—Justices Gerwing, Sherstobitoff

1989–1990
Kate Sutherland—Chief Justice Bayda
Kurt Sandstrom—Justices Tallis, Cameron, Gerwing

1990–1991
Ryan Rempel—Chief Justice Bayda
Melissa Wallace—Justices Vancise, Wakeling

1991–1992

Pablo Fernández-Dávila—Chief Justice Bayda
Wendy Kelley— Justices Tallis, Cameron
Phyllis Norrie—Justices Gerwing, Sherstobitoff

1992–1993

Brian Rolfes—Chief Justice Bayda
Dan Halyk— Justices Vancise, Wakeling, Sherstobitoff
Bettyann Cox—Justices Tallis, Cameron, Gerwing

1993–1994

Lana Finney—Chief Justice Bayda
Bradley Berg—Justices Wakeling, Gerwing, Sherstobitoff
Isa Gros Louis—Justices Tallis, Cameron
Rashmi Goel—Justices Vancise, Jackson, Lane

1994–1995

Madisun Browne—Chief Justice Bayda, Justices Jackson, Lane
Jan Cowie—Justices Wakeling, Vancise, Sherstobitoff
Elaine Lee—Justices Tallis, Cameron, Gerwing

1995–1996

Helen Yum—Chief Justice Bayda
Peter Bergbusch—Justices Tallis, Cameron, Gerwing
Eamon O'Keeffe—Justices Vancise, Wakeling, Sherstobitoff

1996–1997

Heather Heavin—Chief Justice Bayda
Rangi Jeerakathil—Justices Tallis, Cameron, Gerwing
Owen Griffiths—Justices Vancise, Wakeling, Sherstobitoff
Dawn Pritchard—Justices Lane, Jackson

1997–1998

Kelly Nicholson—Chief Justice Bayda
Phillip Scheibel—Justices Tallis, Cameron, Gerwing
Matthew Lewans—Justices Vancise, Sherstobitoff

1998–1999

Meghan McCreary—Chief Justice Bayda, Justice Wakeling
Eugene Okanee—Justices Sherstobitoff, Lane
R. Liam Mooney—Justices Tallis, Cameron, Gerwing
Erin (Rettie) Gagner—Justices Vancise, Jackson

1999–2000

Karen (Tereposky) Georgacacos—Chief Justice Bayda, Justice Jackson
Will Clements—Justices Tallis, Cameron, Gerwing
Hargo Mundi—Justices Vancise, Sherstobitoff, Lane

2000–2001

Michael Mysak—Chief Justice Bayda, Justice Gerwing
Neal Ross—Justices Tallis, Cameron
D. Mark Prescott—Justices Vancise, Sherstobitoff
H. Rae Mitten—Justices Lane, Jackson

2001–2002

Andrea Argue—Chief Justice Bayda, Justice Sherstobitoff
Nicole O'Byrne—Justices Tallis, Cameron, Gerwing
Patricia Farnese—Justices Vancise, Jackson, Lane

2002–2003

Eustathios "Stathy" Markatos—Chief Justice Bayda, Justice Sherstobitoff
Jaime Carlson—Justices Tallis, Cameron
Melanie Durette—Justices Vancise, Gerwing
Sonya Guiboche—Justices Lane, Jackson

2003–2004

Amanda Dodge—Chief Justice Bayda, Justice Lane
Mike Morris—Justices Tallis, Cameron, Gerwing
Lindsay Ferguson—Justices Vancise, Sherstobitoff, Jackson

2004–2005

Darren Reed—Chief Justice Bayda, Justice Sherstobitoff
Cherie Jarock—Justices Tallis, Cameron, Gerwing
Greg Fingas—Justices Lane, Jackson

2005–2006

Heather Jensen—Chief Justice Bayda, Justice Richards
Christopher Triggs—Justices Cameron, Gerwing
Prasanna Ranganathan—Justices Vancise, Lane
Angela Cousins—Justices Sherstobitoff, Jackson

2006–2007

Marianne (Chuck) Davies—Chief Justice Bayda, Justices Richards, Smith
Stephanie LeBlanc—Justices Cameron, Gerwing, Sherstobitoff
Kristy Pozniak—Justices Vancise, Lane, Jackson

2007–2008

Amanda Doucette—Chief Justice Klebuc, Justices Vancise, Lane
Jenelle (Matsalla) Breker—Justices Cameron, Gerwing, Sherstobitoff, Wilkinson
Meredith Hagel—Justices Jackson, Richards
Renée (Tulk) Moore—Justices Smith, Hunter

2008–2009

Leah Howie—Chief Justice Klebuc, Justices Vancise, Lane, Smith
Jill Chapin—Justices Cameron, Gerwing, Sherstobitoff, Richards
Lauren Wihak—Justices Jackson, Wilkinson, Hunter

2009–2010

Emily Luther—Chief Justice Klebuc, Vancise, Lane
Glen Rutland—Justices Cameron, Gerwing, Sherstobitoff
Sarah Burningham—Justices Jackson, Hunter, Ottenbreit
Laura Mazenc—Justices Richards, Smith

2010–2011

Jared Craig—Chief Justice Klebuc, Justices Lane, Gerwing
Rob Martz—Justices Cameron, Vancise, Richards, Caldwell
Megan (Vuksic) Savard—Justices Jackson, Smith, Ottenbreit

2011–2012

Jade Buchanan—Chief Justice Klebuc, Justices Lane, Gerwing, Herauf
Joanne Colledge-Miller—Justices Cameron, Vancise, Richards, Caldwell
Theo Litowski—Justices Jackson, Smith, Ottenbreit

2012–2013

Erin Smith—Chief Justice Klebuc, Justices Vancise, Lane, Herauf
Adryan Toth—Justices Cameron, Gerwing, Jackson, Caldwell
Kyle Ross—Justices Richards, Smith, Ottenbreit

2013–2014

Paul Olfert—Chief Justice Klebuc, Justices Caldwell, Herauf, Whitmore
Annie Alport—Justices Cameron, Richards, Ottenbreit, Whitmore
Michael Stevens—Justices Lane, Jackson

2014–2015

Michelle Biddulph—Chief Justice Richards, Justice Lane
Sarah-Jane Nussbaum—Justices Jackson, Ottenbreit
William Lane—Justices Caldwell, Herauf, Whitmore

2015–2016

Victoria Bae—Chief Justice Richards, Justices Lane, Ryan-Froslie
Katelyn Sheehan—Justices Jackson, Ottenbreit, Caldwell
Michael Adams—Justices Herauf, Whitmore

2016–2017

Janelle Souter—Chief Justice Richards, Justice Lane
Julia Kindrachuk—Justices Jackson, Ottenbreit
Jeremie Roussel—Justices Caldwell, Ryan-Froslie
Jon Ponath—Justices Herauf, Whitmore

2017–2018

Jessica Brockman—Chief Justice Richards, Justice Ottenbreit
Michelle Korpan—Justices Jackson, Ryan-Froslie
Lauren Scharfstein—Justices Caldwell, Herauf
Allison Graham—Justices Whitmore, Schwann

ACKNOWLEDGEMENTS

The author and the Court of Appeal for Saskatchewan would like to thank the members of the centennial book committee for helping make this history a reality: Dean Beth Bilson of the College of Law, University of Saskatchewan; the Honourable Stuart Cameron; Chief Justice Robert Richards; Dr. William Waiser, professor emeritus of history, University of Saskatchewan; and Justice Peter Whitmore. The committee members read drafts of the work and provided many invaluable comments and suggestions.

The following individuals agreed to be interviewed for the book, some very extensively, and are owed special gratitude: Justice Neal Caldwell, the Honourable Stuart Cameron, Gerry Gerrand, QC, Justice Maurice Herauf, Justice Georgina Jackson, the Honourable John Klebuc, the Honourable Gary Lane, Kenneth MacKay, QC, Fred Newis, Justice Ralph Ottenbreit, Chief Justice Robert Richards, Marlene Rodie, Justice Jacelyn Ryan-Froslie, Justice Lian Schwann, the Honourable Nicholas Sherstobitoff, the Honourable Gene Anne Smith, the Honourable Calvin Tallis, the Honourable William Vancise, Justice Peter Whitmore, and Garrett Wilson.

The following archives and libraries and their reference staff were critical to the history: the Provincial Archives of Saskatchewan at Regina and Saskatoon, with special thanks to Lisa Long, Tim Novak, Joe LeClair, Anna Stoszek, Catherine Holmes, Rob Phillipson, and Amanda Don; the University of Saskatchewan Archives and Special Collections, with special thanks to Cheryl Avery; the Saskatoon Public Library, Local History Collection; the Legislative Library of Saskatchewan; the Law Society of

Saskatchewan Library in Regina, with special thanks to Alan Kilpatrick; Library and Archives Canada; and the Legal Archives Society of Alberta.

At the Court of Appeal, Melanie Baldwin, Nadine Barnes, Joanne Colledge-Miller, and Ann Marie Melvie were of great assistance with numerous administrative and research tasks. No individual was more critical to the book's completion than Justice Peter Whitmore, who acted as project manager. Special thanks to Bruce Walsh, Alex Schultz, Duncan Campbell, Sean Prpick, and Kelly Laycock at the University of Regina Press, publishers of the centennial history.

The Court of Appeal acknowledges the financial contributions of the Saskatchewan Ministry of Justice and the Law Foundation of Saskatchewan that made this book possible.

Finally, the author owes a tremendous debt to the scholarship of the academics, lawyers, and judges who have written on the law in Saskatchewan and on legal history more generally, without which this history would not have been possible.

NOTES

CHAPTER 1: THE NORTH-WEST TERRITORIES

1 http://www.famous-trials.com/louisriel/879-sentence.

2 Hamar Foster, "Long Distance Justice: The Criminal Jurisdiction of Canadian Courts West of the Canadas, 1763–1859," *American Journal of Legal History*, vol. 34 (1990), 3; H. Robert Baker, "Creating Order in the Wilderness: Transplanting the English Law to Rupert's Land, 1835–1851," *Law and History Review*, volume 17, no. 2, 1999, 215. The following section is based on these two articles and is a necessary simplification of a very complex topic.

3 Baker, "Creating Order," 215; Louis Knafla, "From Law to Written Memory: The Common Law Tradition in Western Canada," *Law and Justice in a New Land*, ed. Louis Knafla (Calgary: Carswell, 1986), 85.

4 Wilbur F. Bowker, "Stipendiary Magistrates and Supreme Court of the North-West Territories, 1876–1907," *Alberta Law Review*, vol. 26, no. 2 (1988), 247–8.

5 Colwyn Williams, "Law and Institutions in the North West Territories, 1869–1905," *Saskatchewan Bar Review*, vol. 28, no. 3, 112.

6 *An Act respecting the Administration of Justice, and for the establishment of a Police Force in the North West Territories*, SC 1873, c 35.

7 Rod McLeod and Nancy Parker, "Justices of the Peace in Alberta," *Forging Alberta's Constitutional Framework*, eds. Richard Connors and John M. Law (Edmonton: University of Alberta Press, 2007), 278.

8 Bowker, "Stipendiary Magistrates," 256–8; McLeod and Parker, "Justices of the Peace," 278.

9 Bowker, "Stipendiary Magistrates," 253.

10 *An Ordinance respecting the Administration of Civil Justice*, Ordinances of the North-West Territories, No. 4, 1878, s 1. Qu'Appelle was renamed Assiniboia in 1882. The judicial districts did not correspond to the administrative districts of the Territories, which numbered four at one point and served as boundaries of federal electoral boundaries.

11 *The North-West Territories Act, 1875*, SC 1875, c 49, ss 58–63.

12 Bowker, "Stipendiary Magistrates," 262.

13 Ibid, 263.

14 *An Ordinance respecting the Administration of Civil Justice*, Ordinances of the North-West Territories, No. 4 of 1878, s 11; *The Administration of Civil Justice Ordinance, 1884*, Ordinances of the North-West Territories, No. 3 of 1884, s 3.

15 *An Ordinance to Amend Ordinance No. 3 of 1884, Known as "The Administration of Civil Justice Ordinance, 1884"*, Ordinances of the North-West Territories, No. 5 of 1885, s 1(1).

16 Glenbow Archives (GA), James F. Macleod Family fonds, M776-14a, series 1, 1881/03, 1883/29, 1886/07, James F. Macleod to Mary Macleod, June 8, 1881; December 29, 1883; November 23, 1886.
17 Sherrill Maclaren, *Braehead: Three Founding Families in Nineteenth Century Canada* (Toronto: McClelland & Stewart, 1986), 156.
18 Louis Knafla and Rick Klumpenhower, *Lords of the Western Bench* (Calgary: Legal Archives Society of Alberta, 1997), 160.
19 *Journals of the North-West Council*, 1885, 86. There are only a half-dozen reported appeal judgments before 1887, originally in the law reports for Manitoba and reprinted in the first volume of the *Territorial Law Reports*.
20 Shelley A.M. Gallivan, *Hunger, Horses and Government Men: Criminal Law on the Aboriginal Plains, 1870–1905*, (Vancouver: UBC Press and Osgoode Society, 2012), 44.
21 *R v Riel* (1885), 1 Terr LR 20.
22 W.A. Waiser, "The White Man Governs: The 1885 Indian Trials," and Bob Beal and Barry Wright, "Legal Responses to the 1885 Crisis," *Canadian State Trials, Vol. III: Political Trials and Security Measures, 1840–1914*, eds. Barry Wright and Susan Binnie (Toronto: University of Toronto Press and Osgoode Society, 2009). Waiser, Beal, and Wright make a strong case that Richardson was thoroughly out of his depth in the treason trials. Interestingly, while Waiser concludes that Rouleau in subsequent trials at Battleford acted more as prosecutor than judge, Beal and Wright feel that he would have been a far more competent choice than Richardson for the Riel trial.
23 Waiser, "The White Man Governs," 472.
24 Gallivan, *Hunger*, 44.
25 Ibid. Chapter 3 gives examples of the latter.
26 Ibid, 130.
27 Ibid, 124.
28 Colwyn Williams, "Law and Institutions in the North West Territories, 1869–1905," *Saskatchewan Bar Review*, vol. 31, no. 3, 150.
29 *Journals of the North-West Territories Council*, 1885, 86.
30 *An Act to further amend the law respecting the North-West Territories*, SC 1886, c 25.
31 Ibid, s 49.
32 *The Judicature Ordinance 1886*, Ordinances of the North-West Territories, No. 2 of 1886.
33 Vincent M. Del Buono, "The Right to Appeal in Indictable Cases: A Legislative History," *Alberta Law Review*, vol. 16, no. 2, 448.
34 Ibid, 42–453.
35 Ibid, 457.
36 J.E. Cote, "The Introduction of English Law Into Alberta," *Alberta Law Review*, vol. 3 (1964).
37 Ibid, 271–2.
38 See *Massey Manufacturing Co. v Hunt* (1895), 2 Terr LR 84, also *R v Tebo* (1889), 1 Terr LR 196, and *R v Mills* (1890), 1 Terr LR 292, where the trial judge concurred with allowing an appeal of his decision.

39 James H. Baker, *An Introduction to English Legal History* (London: Butterworths, 1979), 61. The following is based on chapter 9 of this work.
40 Ibid, 63.
41 Christopher Moore, *The Court of Appeal of Ontario: Defining the Right of Appeal, 1792–2013* (Toronto: Osgoode Society, 2014), 18, 41.
42 Bowker, "Stipendiary Magistrates," 280.
43 Robson, "McGuire," 139.
44 C.C. McCaul, "Precursors of the Bench and Bar" *Canadian Bar Review*, vol. 3, no.1, 39.
45 Robson, "Wetmore", 442.
46 Bowker, "Stipendiary Magistrates," 278.
47 Robson, "McGuire," 141.
48 *Emerson v Bannerman* (1903), 1 Terr LR 224, at 230.
49 McCaul, "Precursors," 39.
50 *Pacific Investments v Swan* (1898), 3 Terr LR 125 at 13.
51 This generalization is based on the reported judgments of the Territorial Law Reports for Rouleau's tenure.
52 McCaul, "Precursors," 38.
53 *R v Rondeau* (1903), 5 Terr LR 478.
54 Bowker, "Stipendiary Magistrates," 275, 277.
55 *West v Ames Holden and Co.* (1895), 3 Terr LR 17, at 25. Wetmore refers to the plaintiff's factum. Rules of Court dated 1900 and published in volume 4 of the *Territorial Law Reports* give specific requirements for factums and appeal books. None of the previous judicature ordinances, however, lists requirements for factum.
56 Robert J. Martineau, *Appellate Justice in England and the United States: A Comparative Analysis* (Buffalo: William S. Hein, 1990), 101–3.
57 Christopher Moore, *The British Columbia Court of Appeal: The First Hundred Years, 1910–2010* (Vancouver: UBC Press, 2010), 31.
58 J.E. Côté, "History of Factums," *Alberta Law Review*, vol. 51, no. 4 (2014), 78.
59 Ibid, 109.
60 GA, Macleod Family fonds, 1890/2, James Macleod to Mary Macleod, June 5, 1890.
61 Ibid, 1889/15, December 5, 1889.
62 Ibid, 1893/03 June 11, 1893.
63 Ibid, 1888/06, September 11, 1888.
64 *Allen v Pierce* (1895), 3 Terr LR 319, at 329.
65 Iain A. Mentiplay, *A Century of Integrity: The Law Society of Saskatchewan, 1907–2007* (Regina: Law Society of Saskatchewan, 2007), 205.
66 Provincial Archives of Saskatchewan (PAS), R-85, Richardson Papers, series II, file 2, Supreme Court *en banc*, Regina, June1–3, 1896, transcript, p. 1.
67 Ibid, 128.
68 GA, Macleod Family fonds, 1889/10, Macleod to Macleod, November 14, 1889.
69 Ibid, November 15, 1888.

70 Roderick Martin, "The Common Law and Justices of the Supreme Court of the North-West Territories," *Law and Societies of the Canadian Prairie West, 1670–1940*, eds. L.A. Knafla and J. Swainger (Vancouver: UBC Press, 2005), 226.
71 *Pacific Investments v Swan* (1898), 3 Terr LR 125.
72 Ibid, para. 10.
73 Ibid, para. 5.
74 Bruce Ziff, "Warm Reception in a Cold Climate: English Property Law and the Suppression of Canadian Legal Identity," *Despotic Dominion: Property Rights in British Settler Societies*, eds. J. McLaren et al. (Vancouver: UBC Press, 2005), 104.
75 *Wilkie v Jellet* (1898), 2 Terr LR 133.
76 Bowker, "Stipendiary Magistrates," 276.

Chapter 1 Sidebars

1 Thomas Flanagan, "Richardson, Hugh," *Dictionary of Canadian Biography*, vol. 14, http://www.biographi.ca/en/bio/richardson_hugh_1826_1913_14E.html.
2 R.C. Mcleod, "Macleod, James Farquharson," *Dictionary of Canadian Biography*, vol. 12, http://www.biographi.ca/en/bio/macleod_james_farquharson_12E.html.
3 Louis A. Knafla, "Rouleau, Charles-Borromée," *Dictionary of Canadian Biography*, vol. 13, http://www.biographi.ca/en/bio/rouleau_charles_borromee_13E.html.
4 Stanley D. Hanson, "Wetmore, Edward Ludlow," *Dictionary of Canadian Biography*, vol. 15, http://www.biographi.ca/en/bio/wetmore_edward_ludlow_15E.html.
5 H.A. Robson, "Edward Ludlow Wetmore," *Canadian Bar Review*, vol. 22, no. 5, 442.
6 Ibid, 446.
7 Knafla and Klumpenhower, *Lords of the Western Bench*, 123.
8 Robson, "Hon. Thomas Horace McGuire of Saskatchewan and the Yukon," *Canadian Bar Review*, vol. 23, no. 2, 139.
9 PAS, R-85, Richardson Papers, series II, file 1, McGuire to Richardson, Jan. 19, 1893.
10 Knafla and Klumpenhower, *Lords of the Western Bench*, 153.
11 Ibid, 152.
12 Louis A. Knafla, "Scott, David Lynch," *Dictionary of Canadian Biography*, vol. 15, http://www.biographi.ca/en/bio/scott_david_lynch_15E.html.

CHAPTER 2: THE SUPREME COURT OF SASKATCHEWAN

1 *Regina Leader*, October 10, 1907.
2 Ibid.
3 Gordon L. Barnhart, "Walter Scott," *Saskatchewan Premiers of the Twentieth Century*, ed. Gordon L. Barnhart (Regina: Canadian Plains Research Center, 2004), 7.
4 Census of Canada, 1911.

5 *An Act respecting the establishment of a Supreme Court in and for the Province of Saskatchewan*, SS 1907, c 8.

6 *An Act respecting the establishment of District Courts and the Practice and Procedure therein*, SS 1907, c 9.

7 Ibid, schedule A.

8 Provincial Archives of Saskatchewan (PAS), R244, Committee to Reform the Judiciary, Report, p. 7.

9 PAS, Walter Scott fonds, M1, series IV, file 26(1), 80853-4, letter, Scott to Aylesworth, August 19, 1907.

10 Ibid, file 26(1). The scandal with Judge Maclean is discussed in a number of letters.

11 *Regina Leader*, September 20, 1907.

12 PAS, Scott fonds, M1, series IV, file 26(1), 30846-50, correspondence, Scott to Aylesworth, Aylesworth to Scott, July 9–August 14, 1907.

13 Ibid, 30646.

14 *Regina Leader*, September 20, 1907.

15 PAS, Scott fonds, M1, series IV, file 26(2), 72971-5, letters, Scott to Hitchcock, March 5, 1905, Scott to Fitzpatrick, March 30, 1905, Fitzpatrick to Scott, March 31, 1905.

16 Ibid, series V, file 9, 73025, letter, Scott to Fitzpatrick, August 12, 1905. Scott did not specify the problem with Johnstone's appointment. He tended to be quite arch when discussing such matters in his correspondence.

17 Ibid, series IV, file 26(1), 30846, letter, Scott to Aylesworth, July 9, 1907.

18 Two very good articles exist: Philip Girard, "Politics, Promotion and Professionalism: Sir Wilfrid Laurier's Judicial Appointments," and Johnathan Swainger, "Judicial Scandal and the Culture of Patronage in Early Confederation 1867-78," *Essays in the History of Canadian Law: A Tribute to Peter N. Oliver*, vol. 10, eds. Jim Philips, John Saywell, Roy McMurty (Toronto: University of Toronto Press and Osgood Society, 2008). Peter Russell, *The Judiciary in Canada: The Third Branch of Government* (Toronto: McGraw-Hill Ryerson, 1987), 112–7, has a general discussion of patronage.

19 Swainger, "Judicial Scandal," 225.

20 James Snell and Frederick Vaughan, *The Supreme Court of Canada: History of the Institution* (Toronto: Osgoode Society, 1895), 84–85.

21 William H. Hurlburt, "Symposium on the Appointment, Discipline and Removal of Judges," *Alberta Law Review*, vol. 11 (1973), 289. The symposium was yet another Canadian Bar Association discussion on the subject!

22 Canadian Bar Association Committee, *The Appointment of Judges In Canada* (Ottawa: Canadian Bar Association, 1985).

23 *Regina Leader*, April 5, 1910.

24 PAS, Scott fonds, M1, series IV, file 26(2), 31007, letter, Martin to Scott, undated.

25 Ibid, 31010, letter, Turriff to Scott, March 1, 1910.

26 Ibid, 31006, Letter, Scott to Turriff, February 25, 1910. Telegrams between Turgeon and Scott were actually in code, and Martin, Turriff, Scott, and Turgeon never state clearly what the problem was with Brown or what hold he had over the administration to make not appointing him a mistake.

27 PAS, Scott fonds, M1, series IV, file 125, 50486, letter, Scott to Laurier, February 25, 1910.

28 *Regina Leader*, October 16, 1912.

29 *Regina Leader*, August 29, 1912.

30 H.A. Robson, "Edward Ludlow Wetmore," *Canadian Bar Review*, vol. 22, no. 5, 449.

31 *Regina Leader*, January 26, 1922.

32 Bill Waiser, *Saskatchewan: A New History* (Calgary: Fifth House, 2005), 98.

33 *Regina Leader*, October 25, 1912.

34 Ibid, August 29, 1912.

35 Ibid, October 25, 1912.

36 Ibid, October 30, 1912.

37 PAS, Turgeon fonds, M3, series I, file 1909-11 V-Z, 587–90, letter, Wetmore to Turgeon, January 3, 1911.

38 *Regina Leader*, January 6, 1913.

39 *Regina Leader*, September 20, 1913.

40 PAS, Turgeon fonds, M3, series I, file 1912-14 H, 381–4, letter, Haultain to Turgeon, December 19, 1913.

41 Ibid, 378–9, letter, Turgeon to Haultain, December 26, 1913.

42 Knafla and Klumpenhower, *Lords of the Western Bench*, 79, gives Johnstone's retirement date as November 28, 1913, although other sources say 1914. Haultain does not mention Johnstone's retirement in his December 1913 correspondence with Turgeon, but Johnstone does seems absent from the law reports after 1913.

43 At the time of this writing, some superior courts are so short-handed that serious criminal charges are being dismissed for want of prosecution. See *The Globe and Mail*, October 17, 2016.

44 Census of Canada, 1911. Alberta stood at 374,295 compared to Saskatchewan's 494,432.

45 PAS, Attorney General, R244, Committee to Study and Reform Judicial System, Report, 7.

46 *Regina Leader*, January 6, 1913.

47 Iain A. Mentiplay, *A Century of Integrity: The Law Society of Saskatchewan, 1907–2007* (Regina: Law Society of Saskatchewan, 2007), 31.

48 PAS, M3, series I, file 1909-11 V-Z, 587–90, letter, Wetmore to Turgeon, January 3, 1911.

49 *Regina Leader*, June 11, 1915.

50 Ibid, June 4, 1915.

51 *An Act respecting a Court of Appeal for Saskatchewan*, SS 1915, c 9.

52 Library and Archives Canada (LAC), R188-38-8-E, vol. 2154, file 1917-863, letter, Turgeon to Doherty, November 26, 1915. A copy of the Turgeon correspondence can also be found in PAS, Scott fonds, M1, series IV, file 26(2).

53 Ibid.

54 PAS, Turgeon fonds, M3, series I, file 1916-17 H-K, 44–5, letter, Halliday to Turgeon December 30, 1915.

55 Osgoode Hall was built in 1832 as the headquarters of the Law Society of Upper Canada. After 1846, the hall also housed the superior courts of Ontario. The law society held mandatory classes for articling students at the hall but only formally established a law school in 1889. Students at the law school still spent only mornings in classes and worked in law firms in the afternoon.

56 PAS, Scott fonds, M1, series IV, 30852-3, letters, Aylesworth to Scott, August 14, 1907, Scott to Aylesworth, August 19, 1907.

57 *Lee v Broley* (1909), 2 Sask LR 288 (CA), at para. 9.

58 J. David Murphy and Robert Rueter, *Stare Decisis in Commonwealth Courts* (Toronto: Butterworths, 1982), 3–4; Jim Evans, "Precedent in the Nineteenth Century," *Precedent in Law*, ed. Laurence Goldstein (Oxford: Oxford University Press, 1987), 64.

59 Evans, "Precedent," 64.

60 *Consolidated Orders and Rules of the Supreme Court of Saskatchewan* (Regina: King's Printer, 1911), 131.

61 Ibid, 136.

62 The evidence for this is the reported judgments. From 1912 to 1917, nearly all appeals from the District Court had three judge panels, but occasionally four judge panels were used.

63 This is implied in Haultain's letters to Turgeon.

64 *Lindsay v Davidson* (1911), 4 Sask LR 415 (CA), at para. 2. *Res ipsa loquitor* is a doctrine in torts where negligence is inferred from the nature of an accident or injury, because such cannot normally occur without negligence.

65 Garrett Wilson, *Outlier: Life, Law and Politics in the West* (Regina: Benchmark Press, 2016), 54–56. Wilson heard this story direct from Murray McIntyre.

66 *R v Schurman* (1914), 7 Sask LR 269, at para. 3. Haultain went on to say that believing the accused necessarily meant that the victim was a "woman of loose character" and a liar, which the defence counsel also objected to for its prejudicial effect on the jury.

67 PAS, Turgeon fonds, M3, series I, file 1916-17 M, letter, Murray to Turgeon, August 31, 1915. A Winnipeg barrister contacted Turgeon, the attorney general, about an outstanding judgment. The writer claimed that his Saskatchewan agent was in fact waiting for judgments in several cases, and that a colleague had also had a long delay—two years—on a trial judgment from the chief justice. Some years later, a country lawyer approached J.A. Cross, Haultain's former partner and now attorney general, about a decision that was four years outstanding. Cross agreed to intercede with the chief justice in his personal capacity. Two years later, the judgment still had not been given. See PAS, R996, Attorney General J.A. Cross Correspondence, series I, file 9g.

68 *Enkema v Cherry* (1911), 5 Sask LR 61 (CA), at para. 11.

69 McConnell, "Lamont, John Henderson."

70 McConnell, *Prairie Justice*, 207.

71 *Bellamy v Robertson* (1915), 8 WWR 305 (Sask CA), at para. 24.

72 *Lee v Broley* (1909), 2 Sask LR 288 (CA), at para. 8; *Regina Public School v Gratton Separate School* (1914), 7 Sask LR 451 (CA), at para. 1.

73 *Independent Lumber Co. v David and Hurlburt* (1911), 5 Sask LR 1 (CA), at para. 18.

74 *Lee v Broley*, at para. 6.

75 *Williams v Town of North Battleford* (1911), 4 Sask LR 75 (CA), at para. 9. After stating this, Wetmore decided that the trial judge had not made sufficient fact findings to have properly decided the matter and felt free to do so.

76 *Coventry v Annable* (1911), 4 Sask LR 425 (CA), at para. 10, quoting L.J. Holmes in 2 IR LR 1 *The Gairlock*.

77 *Davis v Burt* (1910), 3 Sask LR 446 (CA), see paras. 14–15.

78 *Gordon v Canadian Northern Railway* (1912), 5 Sask LR 169 (CA).

79 Ibid, at para. 1.

80 Ibid, at para. 1.

81 *An Act to Prevent the Employment of Female Labour in Certain Capacities*, SS 1912, c 17.

82 James W. Walker, *Race: Rights and the Law in the Supreme Court of Canada* (Waterloo: Osgoode Society and Wilfrid Laurier University Press, 1997), 53.

83 Lindsay Ferguson, "Constructing and Containing the Chinese Male: *Quong Wing v. the King* and the Saskatchewan *Act to Prevent the Employment of Female Labour*," *Saskatchewan Law Review*, vol. 65, no. 2 (2002), 555–6.

84 Constance Backhouse, "The White Women's Labour Law: Anti-Chinese Racism in Early Twentieth-Century Canada," *Law and History Review*, vol. 14, no. 2 (1996), 335. Both Backhouse and Ferguson in their excellent articles point out that *The Female Employment Act* was also profoundly sexist.

85 Ibid, 340.

86 Ibid, 320, note 15. The number comes from the 1911 census.

87 It should be noted that Willoughby, leader of the Conservative opposition and former political colleague of Haultain, had earlier spoken out in the Senate against the restrictions on the immigration of Chinese women, arguing that affording Chinese male residents in Canada the chance to marry and have families would have a salutary effect on the Chinese community. Lindsay Ferguson, "Constructing and Containing the Chinese Male," 558.

88 Barry Strayer, *The Constitution and the Courts: The Function and Scope of Judicial Review* (Toronto: Butterworths, 1988), 36.

89 *R v Quong Sing* (1913), 6 Sask LR 242 (CA).

90 Ibid, at para. 9.

91 Ibid, at para. 15.

92 Ibid, at para. 17.

93 Ibid, at para. 19.

94 Ibid, at para. 26.

95 Walter Tarnopolsky, *Discrimination and the Law in* Canada (Toronto: Richard de Boo, 1982), 15–17. Tarnopolsky analyzed the decisions in *Quong Wing* and held that *Bryden* was the better precedent.

96 See Walker, *Race*, 106–7, 119–20; Ferguson, "Constructing and Containing the Chinese Male," 570.

97 *Quong-Wing v the King* (1914), 49 SCR 440, 452.

98 David E. Smith, *Prairie Liberalism: The Liberal Party in Saskatchewan, 1905–1971* (Toronto: University of Toronto Press), 16.

99 Raymond Huel, "Pastor vs. Politician: The Reverend Murdoch MacKinnon and Premier Walter Scott's Amendment to the School Act," *Saskatchewan History*, vol. 32, no. 2 (1979), 62.

100 *Regina Public School v Gratton Separate School* (1914), 7 Sask LR 451 (CA), at para. 1.

101 Huel, "Pastor vs. Politician," 62.

102 *Regina Public School v Gratton Separate School*, at para. 1.

103 *Regina Public School District v Gratton Separate School District* (1915), 50 SCR 589.

104 Snell and Vaughan, *Supreme Court of Canada*, 34.

105 *Regina Leader*, Feb. 25, 1916.

106 Huel, "Pastor vs. Politician," 65-66.

107 *McCarthy v City of Regina* (1917), 10 Sask LR 14 (CA).

108 Ibid, at para. 10.

109 Ibid, at para. 10.

110 Ibid, at para. 72.

111 *The City of Regina and Others v J. McCarthy (Saskatchewan)*, 1918 UKPC 79.

112 Haultain's argument was that as there were no separate schools when the NWT first joined confederation in 1870, there were no separate education rights that applied in 1905 even though separate schools had been subsequently established in the Territories. See Smith, *Prairie Liberalism*, 17.

Chapter 2 Sidebars

1 Louis Knafla and Rick Klumpenhower, *Lords of the Western Bench* (Calgary: Legal Archives Society of Alberta, 1997), 137.

2 P.B. Waite, "Tupper, Sir Charles Hibbert," *Dictionary of Canadian Biography*, vol. 15, http://www.biographi.ca/en/bio/tupper_charles_hibbert_15F.html.

3 W.H. McConnell, *Prairie Justice* (Calgary: Burroughs, 1980), 40.

4 Knafla and Klumpenhower, *Lords of the Western Bench*, 137.

5 Holden Stoffel, "Newlands, Henry William," *Encyclopedia of Saskatchewan* (Regina: Canadian Plains Research Center, 2005), http://esask.uregina.ca/entry/newlands_henry_william_1862-_1954.html.

6 *Regina Leader*, March 21, 1921.

7 Howard McConnell, "Lamont, John Henderson," *Dictionary of Canadian Biography*, vol. 16, http://www.biographi.ca/en/bio/lamont_john_henderson_16E.html.

8 "John Henderson Lamont," unattributed and undated biography, Saskatchewan Law Library, Regina.

9 *Regina Leader-Post*, April 29, 1957.

10 McConnell, *Prairie Justice*, 207.

11 The Brown-Elwood Commission investigated sensational charges that members of the Scott government had taken bribes in regards to controversial liquor legislation passed in 1915. While the premier was cleared of any wrongdoing, several members of the legislature were charged with fraud and bribery. Gordon L. Barnhart, *Peace, Progress and Prosperity* (Regina: Canadian Plains Research Cneter, 2000), 138, 142.

12 *Regina Leader-Post*, April 29, 1957.

13 PAS, SHS 25, "Sir Frederick William Gordon Haultain," unattributed biography, 22.

14 *Regina Leader-Post*, January 30, 1942.

15 H.A. Robson, "Sir Frederick Haultain," *Canadian Bar Review*, vol. 22, no. 5, 643.

16 Ibid, 648.

17 Ibid, 649.

18 Lewis Thomas, "The Political and Private Life of F.W.G. Haultain," *Saskatchewan History*, vol. 23, no.2 (Spring 1970), 55–56.

19 *Morning Leader*, May 20, 1921.

20 Ibid.

21 Mentiplay, *Century of Integrity*, 36.

22 *Morning Leader*, May 20, 1921.

23 *Morning Leader*, May 23, 1921.

24 T.R. McCloy, "McKay, John," *Dictionary of Canadian Biography*, vol. 5, http://www.biographi.ca/en/bio/mckay_john_5E.html. Titameg and John Favell were the mother of Mary Favell, who married John McKay and was Justice McKay's great-grandmother.

25 *Regina Leader-Post*, December 1, 1931.

CHAPTER 3: THE COURT OF APPEAL FOR SASKATCHEWAN

1 *Regina Leader*, March 6, 1918.

2 BillWaiser, *Saskatchewan: A New History* (Calgary: Fifth House, 2005), 226.

3 Ibid.

4 Ibid, 217.

5 John H. Archer, *Saskatchewan: A History* (Saskatoon: Western Producer Prairie Books, 1981), 172.

6 Ted Regehr, "William M. Martin," *Saskatchewan Premiers of the Twentieth Century*, ed. Gordon L. Barnhart (Regina: Canadian Plains Research Center, 2004), 62–63.

7 Waiser, *Saskatchewan*, 265–6.

8 Ibid, 272.

9 Ibid, 282.

10 Provincial Archives of Saskatchewan (PAS), Martin fonds, M4, series I, file 1, 1211–2, correspondence, Bar Association and Martin, December 12, 21, 1917. Martin dryly noted he was at the meeting when the resolution was drawn up.

11 Library and Archives Canada (LAC), Department of Justice fonds, R188-38-8-E, volume 2154, file 1917-863, correspondence, Meighen and Edwards, April 20, 26, 27, 1917.

12 Ibid, telegram, Colclough to Newcombe, February 28, 1918, March 1, 1918; *Regina Leader*, February 28, 1918.

13 *An Act respecting a Court of Appeal for Saskatchewan*, SS 1915, c 9. The short title was *The Court of Appeal Act*.

14 Ibid, s. 10.

15 Ibid, s. 3(2).

16 Ibid, s. 7.

17 *Regina Leader*, June 7, 1915.

18 *Hallberg v CNR* (1955), 16 WWR (ns) 538 (Sask CA), at para. 17. This was the conclusion of Justice P.H. Gordon of the court after surveying establishing statutes of other Canadian courts of appeal.

19 See Chapter 9.

20 David Mittelstadt, *People, Principles, Progress: The Alberta Court of Appeal's First Century, 1914 to 2014* (Calgary: Legal Archives Society of Alberta, 2014), 85–102. The problem was largely Harvey's doing, as he attempted to draft the section in Alberta's act to force the federal government to make him head the appeal court. Due to protests from the Department of Justice that this interfered with the federal power of appointment, the section was later amended in such a way that Harvey ended up losing his title as chief justice of Alberta.

21 PAS, Turgeon fonds, M3, series I, file 1918 C, letter, Turgeon to Calder, January 23, 1918.

22 Ibid, letter, Turgeon to Calder, January 25, 1918.

23 LAC, R188-38-8-E, vol. 2154, file 1917-863, Calder to Doherty, February 6, 1918.

24 *Regina Leader*, February 28, 1918.

25 Ibid, February 19, 1921.

26 Ibid, March 8, 1921.

27 This was compiled from the CanLII database for the relevant year. The reported judgments would only have reflected part of the court's workload. While many decisions were shorter than those issued by modern courts, Stuart Cameron, a member of the court for twenty-three years, states this was an impressive output and a heavy load. Email communication with the author, August 10, 2016.

28 Ibid, March 14, 1921.

29 PAS, R6094-5, Turgeon interview, transcript, 26.

30 PAS, Attorney General James A. Cross Correspondence, R996, Series I, file 9a, letter, Haultain to Martin, January 27, 1922.

31 Christopher Moore, *The Court of Appeal for Ontario: Defining the Right of Appeal, 1792–2013* (Toronto: Osgoode Society, 2014), 42.

32 PAS, Attorney General James A. Cross Correspondence, R996, Series I, file 9a, letter, Haultain to Martin, January 27, 1922.

33 LAC, William Lyon Mackenzie King fonds, R10383-0-6-E, series J1, correspondence, 66104–05, letter, Martin to King, January 27, 1922.

34 Ibid, 66107, letter, King to Martin, February 4, 1922.

35 Ibid, 66120, telegram, King to Martin, May 24, 1922.

36 LAC, Arthur Meighen fonds, R14423-0-6-E, series 3, 066733–34, letter, Turnbull to Meighen, April 6, 1922.

37 Ibid, 066732, letter, Meighen to Turnbull, April 10, 1922.

38 *Regina Leader-Post*, February 1961.

39 *Saskatoon Phoenix*, April 5, 1927.

40 Leaving aside the judges coming from the Territorial Court, Brown and Ellwood were at Moosomin until shortly before their appointments, while McKay was from Prince Albert. Only Haultain had been practising in Regina for any length of time.

41 LAC, R188-38-8-E, vol. 2154, file 1917-863, Calder to Doherty, February 6, 1918.

42 PAS, R6094-5, Turgeon interview, 16.

43 Elizabeth Mensch, "The History of Mainstream Legal Thought," *The Politics of Law: A Progressive Critique*, 3rd ed., ed. David Kairys (New York: Basic Books, 1998), 32.

44 Vincent M. Del Buono, "The Right to Appeal in Indictable Cases: A Legislative History," *Alberta Law Review*, vol. 16, no. 2, 40.

45 *Schjaastad Estate, In re* (1919), 13 Sask LR 114 (CA). "A number of cases were cited on the argument, and I have had occasion to peruse several not cited on the argument but which I think have a bearing upon the subject."

46 *Great West Permanent Loan Co. v McEvers*, [1918] 2 WWR 396 (Sask CA).

47 See, for example, *Credit Foncier v Redekope* (1919), 12 Sask LR 83, and *Rimmer v Hannon*, [1921] 3 WWR 1 (Sask CA).

48 *Galvin Lumber Yards v Ensor* (1922), 15 Sask LR 349 (CA).

49 *Gutschenritter v Ball*, [1924] 2 WWR 128 (Sask CA).

50 University of Saskatchewan Archives, University Archives and Special Collection (USKUASC), MG319, Frederick Vaughan fonds, series 1, File—Emmett Hall interview by Prof. & Mrs. Colwyn Williams, 1971, transcript, p. 1.

51 Ibid.

52 See as example, *Wright v Canadian Pacific Railway Company* (1922), 16 Sask LR 367 (CA), at para. 17, where Turgeon comments, "Even the highest tribunals' efforts to draw any definite and consistent principles from the multitude of cases that have arisen have, so far, been unsuccessful."

53 *Kowelenko v Lewis and Lepine* (1921), 14 Sask LR 531 (CA).

54 *Wadgery v Fall*, [1926] 2 WWR 657 (Sask CA).

55 *Hogan v City of Regina* (1924), 18 Sask LR 423 (CA).

56 *Scott and Sheppard v Miller* (1922), 15 Sask LR 266 (CA), at para. 16.

57 *Miller v Foley and Sons* (1921), 59 DLR 664 (Sask CA), at para. 2.

58 *Gillett v Lawrence's Ltd.* (1922), 15 Sask LR 438 (CA), at para. 1.

59 *Municipality of Buckland v Donaldson and Horton* (1927), 22 Sask LR 326 (CA).

60 *Bloomaert v Dunlop* (1926), 21 Sask LR 63 (CA), at para. 29.

61 *Henke v Henke* (1928), 22 Sask LR 267 (CA).

62 See for example, *Robert Bell Engine and Threshing Co. Ltd. v Gagne* (1914), 7 WWR 62.

63 *Macdonald Estate, In re* (1928), 23 Sask LR 327 (CA), at para. 25.

64 *Hoy v Rural Municipality of Hillsboro*, [1923] 4 DLR 82 (Sask CA), at para. 2.

65 See Christopher Moore, *The British Columbia Court of Appeal: The First Hundred Years, 1910–2010* (Vancouver: UBC Press, 2010), 27, and Moore, *The Court of Appeal for Ontario*, 90, 109–10. The judges of the latter court seemed a particularly unpleasant lot.
66 Del Buono, "The Right to Appeal," 448.
67 Ibid, 459.
68 Ibid, 454.
69 *R v Finlay* (1924), 19 Sask LR 43 (CA).
70 Ibid, at para. 10.
71 See for example, *R v Whepdale* (1927), 22 Sask LR 148 (CA).
72 *Rex ex rel Mcleod v Boulding* (1920), 13 Sask LR 383 (CA), at para. 29.
73 James Gray, *Booze: When Whiskey Ruled the West* (Saskatoon: Fifth House, 1995), 75–83. This popular history is still the best account of Prohibition on the Prairies.
74 Ibid, 32–40.
75 Zhiqiu Lin, *Policing the Wild North-West: A Sociological Study of the Provincial Police in Alberta and Saskatchewan, 1905–1932* (Calgary: University of Calgary Press, 2007), 119–20.
76 Waiser, *Saskatchewan*, 202; Archer, *Saskatchewan*, 158.
77 Gray, *Booze*, 87–88; Gordon L. Barnhart, "Walter Scott," *Saskatchewan Premiers of the Twentieth Century*, ed. Gordon L. Barnhart (Regina: Canadian Plains Research Center, 2004), 22–23.
78 Zhiqiu Lin, *Policing*, 123–4.
79 Gray, *Booze*, 109–10; Zhiqiu Lin, *Policing*, 136–7.
80 Zhiqiu Lin, *Policing*, 131–2.
81 *An Act for Regulating the Sale of Liquor*, SS 1917, c 23, s 44–48.
82 *R v Ping Yuen* (1921), 14 Sask LR 475 (CA).
83 Ibid, at para. 30.
84 Ibid, at para. 36.
85 Ibid, at para. 2.
86 Ibid, at para. 24.
87 Ibid, at para. 25.
88 Ibid, at para. 26.
89 Barry L. Strayer, *The Canadian Constitution and the Courts: The Function and Scope of Judicial Review* (Toronto: Butterworths, 1988), 36. See also Walter S. Tarnopolsky, "The Historical and Constitutional Background of the Proposed Canadian Charter of Rights and freedoms," *Law and Contemporary Problems*, vol. 4, no. 3 (1981), 172.
90 *R v Busy Bee Wine & Spirit Importers of Saskatchewan Ltd.* (1921), 14 Sask LR 343 (CA).
91 Gray, *Booze*, 146.
92 *R v Regina Wine & Spirit Ltd. (No. 2)*, [1921] 2 WWR 1166 (Sask CA).
93 *R v Richardson*, [1924] 2 WWR 340 (Sask CA), at para. 5.
94 *R v Nat Bell Liquors*, [1922] 2 WWR 30 (UKJPC).
95 *Hudson's Bay Co. v Heffernan* (1917), 10 Sask LR 322 (CA).

96 *Canada Drugs Ltd. v Attorney General for Saskatchewan* (1922), 15 Sask LR 506 (CA).

97 *Murdoch v Minneapolis Threshing Machine Co.* (1921), 14 Sask LR 296 (CA), at para. 52.

98 Ibid, at para. 53.

99 Ibid, at para. 9.

100 Ibid, at para. 10.

101 Ibid, at para. 55.

102 *George White & Sons Co. Ltd. v Jashansky* (1917), 10 Sask LR 81 (QB).

103 See *Sumner v Squires* (1923), 17 Sask LR 98 (CA); *Dobson v Barr and Brinkworth* (1923), 17 Sask LR 111 (CA).

104 *Advance Rumely Thresher Co. v Yorga* (1925), 20 Sask LR 127 (CA).

105 Ibid, at para. 18.

106 Ibid, at para. 21.

Chapter 3 Sidebars

1 Regehr, "William M. Martin," 40.

2 Ibid.

3 Ibid.

4 *Regina Leader-Post*, September 4, 1961.

5 PAS, R6094-5, Turgeon interview, 1.

6 *Prince Albert Herald*, June 3, 1964.

7 PAS, R6094-5, Turgeon interview, 2.

8 Ibid, 9.

9 *Winnipeg Tribune*, November 3, 1938.

10 *Prince Albert Herald*, June 3, 1964.

11 *Saskatoon Phoenix*, April 5, 1927.

12 PAS, R996, series I, file 9a, letter, Brown to Cross, April 30, 1923, June 11, 1923. The correspondence on the topic shows this was a matter of some controversy for the Saskatoon bar, which in the end was successful at keeping Mackenzie in the city.

13 *Saskatoon Phoenix*, April 5, 1927.

CHAPTER 4: THE COURT OF APPEAL AND THE DEPRESSION

1 W.H. McConnell, *Prairie Justice* (Calgary: Burroughs, 1980), 114.

2 Barry Broadfoot, *Ten Lost Years* (Toronto: McClelland & Stewart, 1997).

3 John H. Archer, *Saskatchewan: A History* (Saskatoon: Western Producer Prairie Books, 1981), 216. Also see Bill Waiser, *Saskatchewan: A New History* (Calgary: Fifth House, 2005), 280–89, for a full account of the effect of the Depression on the provincial economy.

4 Waiser, *Saskatchewan*, 285.

5 Patrick Kyba, "J.T.M. Anderson," *Saskatchewan Premiers of the Twentieth Century*, ed. Gordon L. Barnhart (Regina: Canadian Plains Research Center, 2004), 121–22.

6 Ibid, 131.

7 *Farmers' Creditors Arrangement Act, 1934*, SC 1934, c 53, preamble.

8 Gerald Friesen, *The Canadian Prairies: A History* (Toronto: University of Toronto Press, 1987), 395.

9 Waiser, *Saskatchewan*, 320.

10 Beth Bilson, "William Patterson," *Saskatchewan Premiers of the Twentieth Century*, ed. Gordon L. Barnhart (Regina: Canadian Plains Research Center, 2004), 143–44.

11 Garrett and Kevin Wilson, *Diefenbaker for the Defence* (Toronto: James Lorimer, 1988), 153, 207.

12 McConnell, *Prairie Justice*, 225.

13 Ibid, 198.

14 Ibid, 97.

15 Ibid, 95.

16 Ibid, 95.

17 Ibid, 101.

18 Provincial Archives of Saskatchewan (PAS), R1022, Gardiner fonds, series VII.5, file T.C. Davis, 1938–42, 41373-4, letter, Davis to Gardiner, September 16, 1938.

19 PAS, R1022, Gardiner fonds, series VII.5, file T.C. Davis, 1938–42, 41434-6, letter, Davis to Lapointe, February 23, 1939. A similar decline was seen in the reported judgments of the court. The number of reported judgments was approximately half of all judgments, with a higher proportion of civil judgments reported than criminal.

20 Ibid.

21 James Gray, *R.B. Bennett: The Calgary Years* (Toronto: University of Toronto Press, 1991), 145.

22 William H. Angus, "Wanted: A New Method of Appointing Judges," *Chitty's Law Journal*, vol. 13, no. 9 (September 1965), 250.

23 *House of Common Debates*, May 17, 1932, 2999.

24 Angus, "Appointing Canadian Judges," *Journal of the American Judicature Society*, vol. 49, no. 11 (April 1966), 227.

25 PAS, R1022, Gardiner fonds, series VII.5, file T.C. Davis, 1938–42, 41417-8, letter, Davis to Gardiner, September 23, 1938.

26 Ibid, 41444-45, letter, MacPherson to Manion, March 15, 1939.

27 McConnell, *Prairie Justice*, 195.

28 PAS, R1022, Gardiner fonds, series VII.5, file T.C. Davis, 1938–42, 41418, letter, Davis to Gardiner, September 23, 1938

29 Ibid, letter, MacPherson to Manion, March 15, 1939, 41444-45.

30 *Regina Leader-Post*, June 17, 1936.

31 Christopher Moore, *The Court of Appeal for Ontario: Defining the Right of Appeal, 1792–2013* (Toronto: Osgoode Society, 2014), 90.

32 Ibid, 87.

33 Ibid, 86.

34 McConnell, *Prairie Justice*, 223.

35 Ibid, 199.

36 PAS, R6094-5, Turgeon interview, 14.
37 Grant MacEwan, *Frederick Haultain: Frontier Statesman of the Canadian Northwest* (Saskatoon: Western Producer Prairie Books, 1985), 177.
38 PAS, R1022, Gardiner fonds, series VII.5, file T.C. Davis, 1938–42, 41375-6, letter, Davis to Gardiner, September 16, 1938.
39 PAS, R1022, Gardiner fonds, series VII.4a, Judges, Sask, N–R, 34763, letter, Newlove to Gardiner, November 7, 1955.
40 The position was formally titled Envoy Extraordinary and Minister Plenipotentiary, which was not quite the rank of ambassador but was the highest rank for Canada as a dominion.
41 PAS, R1022, Gardiner fonds, series VII.5, file T.C. Davis, 1938–42, 41382, letter, Davis to Gardiner, September 22, 1938.
42 *Regina Leader-Post*, September 29, 1941.
43 PAS, R1022, Gardiner fonds, series VII.5, file T.C. Davis, 1938–42, 41382, letter, Davis to Gardiner, September 22, 1938.
44 Ibid, 41373-74, letter, Davis to Gardiner, September 16, 1938. Davis followed up soon after with another letter to urge his appointment when positions on the Court of Appeal and the King's Bench came open with Haultain's and Justice Knowles's upcoming resignations.
45 PAS, R1022, Gardiner fonds, series VII.5, file T.C. Davis, 1938–42, 41424, letter, Davis to Gardiner, February 15, 1939.
46 PAS, R1022, Gardiner fonds, series VII.4a, Judges, Sask, D–F, letter, Davis to Gardiner, December 11, 1947, 34030-2. This letter gives a complete account of Davis's career while nominally on the Court of Appeal.
47 Library and Archives Canada (LAC), William Lyon Mackenzie King fonds, R10383-0-6-E, series J1, correspondence, 262788-9, letter, Martin to King, October 5, 1941.
48 PAS, R1022, Gardiner fonds, series VII.4a, Judges, Sask, D–F, 34196, letter, Martin to Gardiner, September 4, 1941.
49 Ibid, Mac–Mc, 34679-8, letter, Gardiner to Mackenzie, December 13, 1955.
50 Ibid, D–F, 34185-6, letter, Demay to King, September 30, 1938.
51 Ibid, G–L, 34265-66, letter, Gardiner to Garson, September 12, 1952.
52 *Regina Leader-Post*, March 16, 1939.
53 *Hackworth v Baker*, [1936] 1 WWR 321 (Sask CA).
54 McConnell, *Prairie Justice*, 193.
55 *Saskatchewan Farm Loan Board v Tomlin*, [1940] 2 WWR 282 (Sask CA).
56 Ibid, at para. 10.
57 *Wolfe v Canadian National Railways*, [1934] 3 WWR 497 (Sask CA), at para. 27.
58 *R v Mandryk*, [1939] 2 WWR 300 (Sask CA).
59 Bill Waiser, *All Hell Can't Stop Us: The On-to-Ottawa Trek and Regina Riot* (Calgary: Fifth House, 2003).
60 McConnell, *Prairie Justice*, 76.
61 Waiser, *All Hell Can't Stop Us*, 250.
62 Ibid, 258.
63 *Regina Leader-Post*, June 15, 1936.
64 Ibid, June 16, 1936.

65 Ibid, June 17, 1936.
66 Ibid.
67 David Mittelstadt, *People, Principles, Progress: The Alberta Court of Appeal's First Century, 1914 to 2014* (Calgary: Legal Archives Society of Alberta, 2014), 127–33 This was certainly the case in Alberta, where reported decisions showed judges unsympathetic to demonstrators and their aims and greatly concerned with maintaining order. The court was mindful of the traditional protections of accused and in one case allowed an appeal on the basis that the wrong charge had been laid.
68 Friesen, *The Canadian Prairies*, 336–37.
69 *The Grain Marketing Act, 1931*, SS 1931, c 87, s 4–9.
70 *The Constitutional Questions Act*, RSS 1920, c 49. Alberta, in contrast, had provision for references in the Supreme Court Act.
71 *Regina Leader-Post*, April 9, 1931.
72 *Grain Marketing Act, In re* (1931), 25 Sask LR 272 (CA), at para. 8.
73 Ibid, at para. 58.
74 W.H. McConnell, "Judicial Review of Prime Minister Bennett's New Deal," *Osgoode Hall Law Journal*, vol.6, no.1, 46–47.
75 *Maley v Cadwell*, [1934] 1 WWR 51 (Sask CA), quote from trial judgment at para. 12.
76 Ibid, at para. 9.
77 Ibid, at para. 39.
78 Ibid, at para. 21.
79 Ibid, at para. 23.
80 *Farmers' Creditors Arrangement Act, 1934*, SC 1934, c 53.
81 McConnell, "Judicial Review," 45, 69, 74. *The Farmers' Creditors Arrangement Act* was passed a year before the slate of legislation passed by Bennett in the last few months of his mandate but was included in the references the King government sent to the SCC.
82 *Prudential Insurance Co. of America v Berg*, [1940] 2 WWR 381 (Sask CA), at para. 19.
83 *Carney (Re)*, [1941] 2 WWR 273 (Sask CA), at para. 6.
84 Ibid, at para. 22.
85 PAS, R1022, Gardiner fonds, series VII.5, file T.C. Davis, 1938–42, 41504-6, letter, Davis to Gardiner, November 27, 1940.
86 Ibid, series VII.5, file T.C. Davis, 1938–42, 41430, letter, Davis to Gardiner, February 23, 1939.

87 This statement contradicts the findings of David S. Cohen in "Law, Order and Democracy: An Analysis of the Judiciary in a Progressive State: The Saskatchewan Experience," *Saskatchewan Law Review*, vol. 56, no. 23 (1992). Cohen analyzed reported decisions from all levels of court involving statutes such as *The Debt Adjustment Act* and *The Farmers' Creditors Arrangement Act*. He found that for some statutes, decisions favoured creditors over debtors. However, Cohen also admits that several factors could account for this beyond any conscious or unconscious judicial bias against these laws. While I did not do a statistical analysis of the relevant court of appeal decisions, my impression was that there was no appreciably tilt toward either party.

Chapter 4 Sidebars

1 *Regina Leader-Post*, April 7, 1975.
2 McConnell, *Prairie Justice*, 191.
3 Ibid, 191–92.
4 Author interview with Garrett Wilson, June 22, 2016.
5 Author interview with Calvin Tallis, August 12, 2015.
6 *Regina Leader-Post*, February 10, 1961.
7 "Gordon, Percival H.," *Encyclopedia of Saskatchewan* (Regina: Canadian Plains Research Center, 2005), http://esask.uregina.ca/entry/gordon_percival_h_1884-1975.html.
8 Saskatoon Public Library, clipping file, "Clayton, Davis," unknown newspaper clipping, August 10, 1940.
9 David Green, ed. *The Saskatchewanians* (Regina: Saskatchewan Jubilee and Canadian Centennial Corporation, 1967), 45.
10 *Regina Leader-Post*, October 11, 1950.
11 McConnell, *Prairie Justice*, 80.
12 Ibid, 191.
13 Ibid, 45.

CHAPTER 5: TOMMY DOUGLAS VERSUS THE COURT OF APPEAL

1 *Regina Leader-Post*, January 29, 1948.
2 Thomas and Ian Mcleod, "T.C. Douglas," *Saskatchewan Premiers of the Twentieth Century*, ed. Gordon L. Barnhart (Regina: Canadian Plains Research Center, 2004), 176.
3 John H. Archer, *Saskatchewan: A History* (Saskatoon: Western Producer Prairie Books, 1981), 260.
4 Mcleod, "T.C. Douglas," 175.
5 BillWaiser, *Saskatchewan: A New History* (Calgary: Fifth House, 2005), 344.
6 Archer, *Saskatchewan*, 281.
7 Ibid, 260.
8 Waiser, *Saskatchewan*, 345.
9 Ibid, 365.
10 Ibid, 367.

11 Ibid, 369.

12 Ibid, 355.

13 Robert Allan, "Corman, John Wesley 'Jack,'" *Encyclopedia of Saskatchewan* (Regina: Canadian Plains Research Center, 2005), http://esask.uregina.ca/entry/corman_john_wesley_jack_1884-_1969.html. William Aberhart, the first Social Credit premier of Alberta, had to recruit a lawyer for his first cabinet as well. Aberhart later took over the portfolio himself, as did his successor, Ernest Manning. Corman, by contrast, was succeeded as attorney general by Robert Walker, QC.

14 Norman Ward, "The Politics of Patronage: James Gardiner and Federal Appointments in the West," *Canadian Historical Review*, vol. 58, no. 3 (September 1977), 301–3.

15 Provincial Archives of Saskatchewan (PAS), R1022, Gardiner fonds, series VII.4a, Judges, Sask, D–F, 34033, letter, Davis to Gardiner, December 11, 1947.

16 Ibid, 340562-3, letter, Turgeon to Gardiner, November 25, 1948; 34058-9, letter, Martin to Gardiner, December 16, 1948; 34065-67, letter, Martin to Gardiner, December 31, 1948.

17 This assertion is based on the number of reported judgments associated with each counsel as found in the Westlaw database. Anderson, the oldest, had 224, McNiven 76, Procter 28, and Culliton 3. While not definitive, these numbers are indicative.

18 PAS, R1022, Gardiner fonds, series VII.4a, Judges, Sask, D–F, 34026-7, letter, Gardiner to Davis, November 22, 1947.

19 When Culliton was under consideration for the chief justiceship in 1961, R.L. Hanbidge, QC, suggested Percy Maguire instead, saying, "I'm quite sure that Percy has had much more court experience than Culliton ever had." University of Saskatchewan Archives, University Archives and Special Collection (USKUASC), Diefenbaker Papers, MG01, series VI, file 28.1, Judges, Saskatchewan, 1961–62, letter, Hanbidge to Diefenbaker, November 20, 1962.

20 W.H. McConnell, "Chief Justice Edward M. Culliton, C.C. Politician and Jurist," *Saskatchewan History*, vol. XLIII, no. 1 (Winter 1991), 4.

21 *Regina Leader-Post*, February 10, 1049.

22 *Regina Leader-Post*, June 13, 1949.

23 *Edmonton Journal*, January 10, 1952.

24 William H. Angus, "Appointing Canadian Judges," *Journal of the American Judicature Society*, vol. 49, no. 11, (1965–66).

25 Ibid, January 19, 1948.

26 *Regina Leader-Post*, January 24, 1948.

27 *Saskatoon Star-Phoenix*, January 27, 1948.

28 Ed and Pemrose Whelan, *"Run It by Jack": Tommy Douglas' First Attorney General, J.W. Corman* (Regina: Whelan Publications, 2002), 52.

29 Ibid, 34.

30 James Snell and Frederick Vaughan, *The Supreme Court of Canada: History of the Institution* (Toronto: Osgoode Society, 1895), 214, 226; Christopher Moore, *The Court of Appeal for Ontario: Defining the Right of Appeal, 1792–2013* (Toronto: Osgoode Society, 2014), 145.

31 Whelan, *"Run It by Jack"*, 52.
32 *Regina Leader-Post*, January 23, 1948.
33 Ibid, February 24, 1948.
34 PAS, R1022, Gardiner fonds, series VII.4a, Judges, Sask, D–F, 34017, letter, Gardiner to Davis, August 18, 1947, and 34025, letter, Davis to Gardiner, September 23, 1947.
35 *Regina Leader-Post*, January 29, 1948.
36 PAS, R1022, Gardiner fonds, series VII.4a, Judges, Sask, Mac–Mc, 34471, letter, Davis to Gardiner, January 13, 1955.
37 Ibid, D–F, letter, Gardiner to Davis, February 6, 1948.
38 Mcleod, "T.C. Douglas," 192.
39 *Regina Leader-Post*, June 10, 1950.
40 Ibid, March 8, 1951.
41 See Judy Fudge and Eric Tucker, *Labour before the Law: The Regulation of Workers' Collective Action in Canada, 1900–1948* (Toronto: Osgoode Society and Oxford University Press, 2001).
42 PAS, R1022, Gardiner fonds, series VII.4a, Judges, Sask, N–R, 34804-5, letter, Gardiner to Pope, February 2, 1948.
43 USKUASC, MG01, series XII, A190, Diefenbaker Correspondence—Frank Bastedo, 004136-7, letter, Martin to Meldrum, January 22, 1960.
44 *Regina Leader-Post*, September 14, 1960.
45 PAS, R1022, Gardiner fonds, series VII.5, file T.C. Davis, 1943–46, 41783, letter, Davis to Gardiner, December 5, 1944.
46 Author interview with Calvin Tallis, August 12, 2015.
47 PAS, R1022, Gardiner fonds, series VII.4a, Judges, Sask, Mac–Mc, 34495, letter, Davis to Gardiner, March 8, 1956.
48 USKUASC, MG01, Diefenbaker Papers, series XII, file 28.1, Personal and Confidential Series, 1957–1979, Judges, Saskatchewan, 1960–62, letter, Hall to Diefenbaker, December 30, 1960.
49 See for example, Home Gas Limited v Streeter (1953), 8 WWR (ns) 689 (Sask CA), at para. 2.
50 *Regina Leader-Post*, March 29, 1956.
51 *Hansard*, Legislative Debates, 4th Session, 12th Legislature, April 2, 1956, 2, http://docs.legassembly.sk.ca/legdocs/Legislative%20Assembly/*Hansard*/12L4S/560402Debates.pdf.
52 *Regina Leader-Post*, April 3, 1956.
53 John C. Kleefeld, "The Contributory Negligence Act at Seventy," *Saskatchewan Law Review*, vol. 78, no. 1 (2015), 35.
54 *Berry v Sparks* (1955), 17 WWR (ns) 476 (Sask CA), at para. 19.
55 Kleefeld, "Contributory Negligence Act," 69.
56 *Board v Board*, [1919] AC 956 (UKJCPC).
57 *Gunn v Gunn* (1956), 18 WWR (ns) 85 (Sask CA), at para. 8.

58 I am greatly indebted to Beth Bilson, "John East Iron Works v. Saskatchewan Labour Relations Board: A Test for the Infant Administrative State," *Work on Trial: Canadian Labour Law Struggles*, eds. Judy Fudge and Eric Tucker (Toronto: Osgoode Society, 2010), and Gene Anne Smith, "The Judicial Review of Saskatchewan Labour Relations Board Proceedings," *Saskatchewan Law Review*, vol. 39, no. 1 (1974–75), for my account of the court and Labour Relations Board appeals.

59 Bilson, "John East Iron Works," 43–44, specifically the 1935 Wagner Act, which defined and made illegal unfair labour practices, guaranteed freedom of association for workers, and made collective bargaining mandatory when a union represented the majority of employees; and PC 1003, the Wartime Labour Relations Regulations, which established a labour relations board and instituted collective bargaining and arbitration proceedings, and protected employees who were engaged in labour organizing activities, but also restricted strike action while any negotiating or arbitration was in place.

60 Fudge and Tucker, Labour before the Law, gives an excellent account of the legal struggles of labour in Canada.

61 Bilson, "John East Iron Works," 45. Biographical material on Corman and Shumiatcher also credit them with drafting of the Act, and they may have assisted.

62 *Regina Leader-Post*, November 9, 1944.

63 *Saskatoon Star-Phoenix*, January 15, 1948.

64 *Bruton v Regina City Policemen's Association, Local No. 155*, [1945] 3 DLR 437 (Sask CA), at para. 16.

65 *Dominion Fire Brick & Clay Products Ltd. v Saskatchewan (Labour Relations Board)*, [1946] 3 WWR 459 (Sask CA), at para. 24.

66 Bilson, "John East Iron Works," 47–48.

67 *Saskatchewan (Labour Relations Board) v John East Iron Works Ltd. (No. 2)*, [1948] 1 WWR 247 (Sask CA).

68 Ibid, at para. 23.

69 Bilson, "John East Iron Works," 59.

70 Ibid.

71 Bilson, "John East Iron Works," 57.

72 *The Labour Relations Board of Saskatchewan v John East Iron Works Ltd.*, [1948] UKPC 75, 5.

73 Ibid, 59.

74 *John East Iron Works Ltd. v Labour Relations Board of Saskatchewan*, [1949] 3 DLR 62 (Sask CA).

75 Bilson, "John East Iron Works," 61.

76 *Sisters of Charity, Providence Hospital v Saskatchewan (Labour Relations Board)* (1951), 2 WWR (ns) 66 (Sask CA), at para. 27.

77 Smith, "Judicial Review," 2.

78 *F.W. Woolworth Co. v Saskatchewan (Labour Relations Board)*, [1954] 4 DLR 359 (Sask CA), at para. 29.

79 Ibid, at para. 53.

80 *MacCosham Storage and Distributing Co. (Saskatchewan) v Canadian Brotherhood of Railway Employees and Other Transport Workers, Division No. 189* (1958), 26 WWR (ns) 577 (Sask CA).

81 Smith, "Judicial Review," 2, 11–15. Smith points out that the context was somewhat different in what she termed the third period for the court regarding board orders, with more challenges coming from labour rather than business interests. Nonetheless, it seems clear that the Culliton court in the 1960s and 1970s gave the board much more deference. It should be noted that Makaroff also left the Labour Relations Board in 1961.

82 Bora Laskin, "Certiorari to Labour Boards: The Apparent Futility of Privative Clauses," *Canadian Bar Review*, vol. 30, no. 10 (December 1952), 993.

83 Author interviews with William Vancise, June 21, 2016, and Calvin Tallis, August 12, 2015. Vancise practised labour law in the 1960s and 1970s and related stories he had heard from older counsel. Calvin Tallis, however, often assisted George Taylor, a pre-eminent labour lawyer in the 1950s and 1960s and never saw this behaviour. He did recall that Gordon could be quite outspoken, as suggested. It should be noted that judges turning away from counsel was an old trick to indicate displeasure and is part of the lore of many courts. Two judges of the court were known to do it in the 1980s and 1990s.

84 *Carney (Re)*, [1941] 2 WWR 273 (Sask CA), as discussed in Chapter 4.

85 *Wing v Chang* (1954), 13 WWR (ns) 353 (Sask CA).

86 *Regina Leader-Post*, June 1, 1952.

87 PAS, R1022, Gardiner fonds, series VII.5, file T.C. Davis, 1938–42, 41433, letter, Davis to Gardiner, February 23, 1939.

Chapter 5 Sidebars

1 *Regina Leader-Post*, November 22, 1948.

2 Ibid, November 1, 1946.

3 Michael D. Stevenson, *Canada's Greatest Wartime Muddle: National Selective Service and the Mobilization of Human Resources During World War II* (Kingston and Montreal: McGill-Queen's University Press, 2001), 25–26.

4 While the Manitoba Law School was established in 1914, prior to that the university provided lectures to articling students that shortened articles and conferred a law degree but was not necessary to join the bar. See Wesley Pue, "'The Disquisitions of Learned Judges': Making Manitoba Lawyers, 1885–1931," *Essays in the History of Canadian Law: In Honour of R.C.B. Risk*, ed. David H. Flaherty (Toronto: Osgoode Society and University of Toronto Press, 1999), 514.

5 *Bench and Bar*, vol. 9, no. 1 (January 1939), 4.

6 *Regina Leader-Post*, July 31, 1961.

7 Ibid, July 9, 1949.

8 McConnell, *Prairie Justice*, 191.

9 *Leader Post*, July 31, 1961.

10 McConnell, "Culliton," 1.

11 *Regina Leader-Post*, March 20, 1981.

12 McConnell, "Culliton," 2.
13 *Regina Leader-Post* March 20, 1981.
14 McConnell, "Culliton," 1.
15 *Regina Leader-Post*, March 20, 1981.
16 McConnell, "Culliton," 2.
17 *Regina Leader-Post*, March 20, 1981.
18 McConnell, "Culliton," 3.
19 Ibid, 3.

CHAPTER 6: DIEFENBAKER'S COURT

1 University of Saskatchewan Archives and Special Collections (USKUASC), MG01, Diefenbaker Papers, series XII, file 28.1, Personal and Confidential Series, 1957–1979, Judges, Saskatchewan, 1960–62, letter, Hall to Diefenbaker, December 30, 1960.
2 Brian Mulroney won more seats in 1984, but Diefenbaker commanded a larger proportion in 1958.
3 Mackenzie King was the member for Prince Albert from 1926 to 1945, first elected in a by-election after losing his race in the 1926 election and continuing to run in this "safe seat," but no one thought of him as being from Saskatchewan. Laurier also briefly held the Prince Albert constituency. As a point of interest, Tommy Douglas held a British Columbia seat for years after losing the 1963 election for a Regina seat as new leader for the NDP.
4 Frederick Vaughan, "Emmett Matthew Hall: The Activist as Justice," *Osgoode Hall Law Journal*, vol. 10, no. 2 (1972), 416.
5 BillWaiser, *Saskatchewan: A New History* (Calgary: Fifth House, 2005), 384.
6 Dale Eisler, "W. Ross Thatcher," *Saskatchewan Premiers of the Twentieth Century*, ed. Gordon L. Barnhart (Regina: Canadian Plains Research Center, 2004), 247–48.
7 Waiser, *Saskatchewan*, 389.
8 The extent of this migration was such that in 2000 nearly a third of Alberta's appeal court were graduates of the University of Saskatchewan Law School. This included Elizabeth McFadyen, class of '66, and Constance Hunt, Keith Ritter, and Jack Watson, class of '72.
9 Waiser, *Saskatchewan*, 391.
10 Eisler, "W. Ross Thatcher," 264.
11 Ibid.
12 Waiser, *Saskatchewan*, 400.
13 Ibid, 406.
14 Iain A. Mentiplay, *A Century of Integrity: The Law Society of Saskatchewan, 1907–2007* (Regina: Law Society of Saskatchewan, 2007), 40.
15 Ann Leger-Anderson, "Greensmith, Dorothy," *Encyclopedia of Saskatchewan* (Regina: Canadian Plains Research Center, 2005), http://esask.uregina.ca/entry/greensmith_dorothy_ca_1890-_1951.html.
16 Mentiplay, *Century of Integrity*, 103.

17 *Vancouver Province*, September 24, 2016.

18 *Saskatoon Star-Phoenix*, June 2, 1964.

19 Brett Quirin, "Batten, Mary John," *Saskatchewan Politicians: Lives Past and Present*, ed. Brett Quiring (Regina: Canadian Plains Research Center, 2004), 13.

20 Author interview with William Vancise, June 21, 2016.

21 USKUASC, MG01, Diefenbaker Papers, series XII, file 28.1, Judges, Saskatchewan, 1960–62, letter, Hnatyshyn to Diefenbaker, November 28, 1960.

22 House of Commons Debates, 24th Parliament, 3rd Session, vol. 5, 4893.

23 Ibid, 4890.

24 Author interview with Garrett Wilson, June 22, 2016.

25 Author interview with Gerry Gerrand, November 2, 2016.

26 USKUASC, MG01, Diefenbaker Papers, series XII, file 28.1, Judges, Saskatchewan, 1960–62, letter, Hall to Diefenbaker, December 30, 1960.

27 Ibid, letter, Hall to Diefenbaker, December 30, 1960.

28 Ibid, memo, Hall to Diefenbaker, February 27, 1961.

29 Ibid, file A-531, Judgeships, 1957–58, letter, Bastedo to Diefenbaker, April 26, 1958.

30 Wilson, *Diefenbaker*, prologue, i.

31 USKUASC, MG01, Diefenbaker Papers, series XII, file 28.1, Judges, Saskatchewan, 1960–62, letter, Hall to Diefenbaker, December 30, 1960.

32 Ibid, file memo, Diefenbaker, December 17, 1960.

33 Ibid, file memo, Diefenbaker, September 23, 1961.

34 Frederick Vaughan, *Aggressive in Pursuit: The Life of Justice Emmett Hall* (Toronto: University of Toronto Press for the Osgoode Society for Canadian Legal History, 2004), 173. See also Emmett Hall, "Law Reform and the Judiciary's Role," *Osgoode Hall Law Journal*, vol. 10, no. 2 (1972).

35 Vaughan, *Aggressive in Pursuit*, 96, 101.

36 USKUASC, MG01, Diefenbaker Papers, series XII, file 28.1, Judges, Saskatchewan, 1960–62, file memo, Diefenbaker, November 22, 1962.

37 Author interview with Calvin Tallis, August 12, 2015.

38 John G. Diefenbaker, *The Years of Achievement*, vol. 2 of *One Canada: Memoirs of the Right Honourable John G. Diefenbaker* (Toronto: Macmillan of Canada, 1976), 56.

39 USKUASC, MG01, MG01, Diefenbaker Papers, series XII, file 345, The Judiciary Judges, 1957–63, letter, Culliton to Diefenbaker, November 26, 1962.

40 Provincial Archives of Saskatchewan (PAS), F14 Culliton fonds, R8351-53, interview, n.d. It was common for lawyers doing criminal work in that era to act both as defence and as crowns (on contract), "working both sides of the street."

41 In Alberta, the court rules were revised far less, with only two revisions in over one hundred years.

42 *Regina Leader-Post*, March 15, 1960.

43 USKUASC, MG011, series XII, file A190, Diefenbaker Correspondence—Frank Bastedo, letter, Martin to Meldrum, January 22, 1960.

44 Ibid, letter, Diefenbaker to Fulton, March 18, 1960.

45 *Saskatoon Star-Phoenix*, June 27, 1960.

46 Ibid, October 3, 1961.

47 USKUASC, MG70SI, Hall fonds, series VI F. Commissions Committees of Enquiry, file Sask Court Structure Report, 1974, Summary, 7.

48 Author interview with William Vancise, June 21, 2016.

49 Author interview with Garrett Wilson, June 22, 2016. Wilson says he actually witnessed one of these conversations.

50 Author interview with Calvin Tallis, August 12, 2015.

51 *Austin v Austin* (1970), 73 WWR (ns) 289 (Sask CA).

52 Under the BNA *Act*, marriage and divorce had been put in the federal column of powers, but the central government declined to introduce a statute. In some provinces, including Saskatchewan, The Matrimonial Causes Act was part of their received law. But in other provinces, including Ontario, an act of Parliament was necessary.

53 Christopher MacLennan, *Towards the Charter: Canadians and the Demand for a National Bill of Rights 1929–1960* (Montreal and Kingston: McGill-Queen's University Press, 2003), gives a comprehensive account of the efforts to create a bill of rights in Canada.

54 Ken Norman, "Saskatchewan Bill of Rights," *Encyclopedia of Saskatchewan* (Regina: Canadian Plains Research Center, 2005), http://esask.uregina.ca/entry/saskatchewan_bill_of_rights.html.

55 Ian Greene, *The Charter of Rights* (Toronto: James Lorimer, 1989), 23. This is clear from a review of the Court of Appeal's reported judgments.

56 *Smart v Livett* (1950), 1 WWR (ns) 49 (SK CA), at para. 59. Ironically, Gordon was quite happy to give this interpretation to the Bill, as the case on appeal involved one union suing another union for preventing their members from working.

57 MacLennan, *Toward the Charter*, 133.

58 Denis Smith, *Rogue Tory: The Life and Legend of John G. Diefenbaker* (Toronto: Macfarlane Walter & Ross, 1995), 158–61.

59 W.S. Tarnopolsky, "The Canadian Bill of Rights from Diefenbaker to Drybones," *McGill Law Journal*, vol. 17, no. 3 (1971), 442–43.

60 Peter Brett, "Reflections on the Canadian Bill of Rights," *Alberta Law Review*, vol. 7, no. 2 (1969), 307.

61 Vaughan, "Emmett Matthew Hall," 423.

62 Ibid, 420.

63 *R v Morrissette* (1970), 75 WWR (ns) 644 (Sask CA), at para. 13.

64 Ibid, at paras. 16–18.

65 Ibid, at paras. 6–7.

66 Ibid, at para. 10.

67 Marcell Martel, *Not This Time: Canadian Public Policy and the Marijuana Question, 1961–1975* (Toronto: University of Toronto Press, 2006), 10–11.

68 Gerald Le Dain, *Cannabis: A Report of the Commission of Inquiry into the Non-Medical Use of Drugs* (Ottawa: Royal Commission of Inquiry, 1969), 247–48.

69 *R v Larre* (1969), 69 WWR (ns) 561 (Sask CA), at para. 3.

70 Ibid, at para. 9.

71 *R v Potie* (1970), 74 WWR (ns) 235 (Sask CA).

72 USKUASC, MG70SI, Hall fonds, series VI F, Commissions Committees of Enquiry, file Jan–Sept, 1974, letter, Davis to Hall, January 4, 1974.

73 Author interview with Garrett Wilson, June 22, 2016.

74 *Regina Leader-Post*, February 12, 1961.

75 PAS, F3 Shumiatcher fonds, file 14.13, Memorandum, Concerning Salesmen Western Bond and Share.

76 *Shumiatcher v Law Society of Saskatchewan* (1966), 58 WWR (ns) 465 (SK CA), at para. 23.

77 *Shumiatcher v Saskatchewan (Attorney General)* (1960), 33 WWR (ns) 134 (SKQB), at para. 5.

78 *Regina Leader-Post*, February 3, 1961.

79 *Shumiatcher v Elliott* (1961), 36 WWR (ns) 301 (Sask CA).

80 *Shumiatcher, Re* (1961), [1962] SCR 38.

81 *Shumiatcher v Saskatchewan (Attorney General)* (1962), 39 WWR (ns) 577 (Sask CA), at para. 5.

82 *Shumiatcher v Saskatchewan (Attorney General)* (1963), 42 WWR (ns) 94 (Sask CA).

83 *Shumiatcher v Law Society of Saskatchewan* (1966), 58 WWR (ns) 465 (Sask CA), at para. 31.

84 PAS, F3 Shumiatcher fonds, box 28, file 14-21, letter, Shumiatcher to Laskin, July 19, 1965.

85 Edward P. MacCallum, *Report of the Inquiry into the Wrongful Conviction of David Milgaard*, vol. 1 (Regina: Queen's Printer, 2008), 300–301, 303. My summary of the police investigation and also the subsequent efforts to exonerate Milgaard is derived from MacCallum's report.

86 *R v Milgaard*, [1971] 2 WWR 266 (Sask CA), at para. 54.

87 Ibid, at para. 55.

88 J.C. Thomas, "Impeachment of Party's Own Witness by a Prior Inconsistent Statement," *University of British Columbia Law Review*, vol. 16, no.1, 58, n. 73. Justice Martland of the Supreme Court might have been the first to call it the Milgaard procedure.

89 MacCallum, *Report*, 405, 574–73.

90 Ibid, 411.

Chapter 6 Sidebars

1 Vaughn, *Aggressive in Pursuit*, 3.

2 Ibid, 6.

3 Ibid, 10.

4 *The Sheaf*, 1919, 218.

5 Vaughan, *Aggressive in Pursuit*, 19.

6 Ibid, 19.

7 Ibid, 92.

8 *Saskatoon Star-Phoenix*, November 14, 1995.

9 *Western People*, no. 223, February 9, 1984, 3.

10 Ibid.
11 Ibid, 4.
12 *Saskatoon Star-Phoenix*, November 14, 1995.
13 Author interview with William Vancise, June 21, 2016.
14 *Saskatoon Star-Phoenix*, June 15, 1961.
15 USKUASC, MG0I, series XII, file 28.1, Judges, Saskatchewan, 1960–62, biographical notes, Mr. Justice Mervyn John Woods, MBE.
16 *Regina Leader-Post*, March 25, 1995.
17 Roy Romanow, "My Experience in the Medicare Battle and the Woods Commission," *Canadian Bulletin of Medical History*, vol. 26, no. 2, 539; Author interview with Calvin Tallis, August 12, 2015. Romanow mentioned Woods's humour and poetry reciting. Tallis also recalled Woods's dry wit.
18 W.H. McConnell, *Prairie Justice* (Calgary: Burroughs, 1980), 211.
19 *Regina Leader-Post*, March 25, 1995.
20 McConnell, *Prairie Justice*, 211.
21 Ibid.
22 Ibid, 212.
23 *Regina Leader-Post*, July 7, 1959.
24 McConnell, *Prairie Justice*, 211.
25 *Regina Leader-Post*, July 7, 1959.
26 *Saskatoon Star-Phoenix*, July 5, 1962, and November 4, 1984. The date the Maguires came to Saskatchewan is given variously as 1909 and 1910 in different sources.
27 *Saskatoon Star-Phoenix*, November 21, 1984.
28 *Saskatoon Star-Phoenix*, July 5, 1962.
29 See author interviews with William Vancise, Gerry Gerrand, Stuart Cameron, and Calvin Tallis.
30 *Regina Leader-Post*, December 15, 1962.
31 Author interview with William Vancise, June 2016.

CHAPTER 7: CULLITON AGAINST THE SUPREME COURT OF CANADA

1 Provincial Archives of Saskatchewan (PAS), R-900, Roy Romanow fonds, series V, file 73d, letter, Culliton to Romanow, October 19, 1976.
2 Dennis Gruending, "Allan Blakeney," *Saskatchewan Premiers of the Twentieth Century*, ed. Gordon L. Barnhart (Regina: Canadian Plains Research Center, 2004), 273–74.
3 Ibid, 279.
4 BillWaiser, *Saskatchewan: A New History* (Calgary: Fifth House, 2005), 406.
5 Gruending, "Blakeney," 274.
6 Ibid, 311.
7 Ibid, 294.
8 Waiser, *Saskatchewan*, 415; Gruending, "Blakeney," 294, 312.
9 Gruending, "Blakeney," 311.

10 Waiser, *Saskatchewan*, 406, 413; Gruending, "Blakeney," 290.
11 Waiser, *Saskatchewan*, 413–14.
12 Ibid, 413; Gruending, "Blakeney" 290-91.
13 Gruending, "Blakeney," 296.
14 Christopher Moore, *The Court of Appeal of Ontario: Defining the Right of Appeal, 1792–2013* (Toronto: Osgoode Society, 2014), 145.
15 Ibid, 139. A judge appointed in Ontario in 1960 found it odd there was no training and sought out courses in the United States.
16 Delmar Karlen, "Judicial Education," *American Bar Association Journal*, vol. 52, no. 11 (November 1966), 1049.
17 Livingston Armytage, *Educating Judges: Towards Improving Justice, A Survey of Global Practices*, (Leiden: Brill, 2015), 13.
18 Martin L. Friedland, *A Place Apart*: Judicial Independence and Accountability in Canada (Ottawa: Canadian Judicial Council, 1995), 88.
19 David Roberts, "The Canadian Judicial Council," *The Advocate*, vol. 36 (1978), 119.
20 William A. Stevenson, *Towards the Creation of a National Judicial Education Service for Canada* (Ottawa: Canadian Judicial Centre Project, 1986), 6–8.
21 Stuart Cameron, private communication with the author, April 21, 2017.
22 Friedland, *A Place Apart*, 88.
23 Roberts, "The Canadian Judicial Council."
24 W.H. McConnell, "Chief Justice Edward M. Culliton, C.C. Politician and Jurist," *Saskatchewan History*, vol. XLIII, no. 1 (Winter 1991), 14.
25 Ed Ratushny, "Judicial Appointments: The Lang Legacy," *The Canadian Judiciary*, ed. Allen Linden (Toronto: Osgoode Hall Law School, York University, 1976), 34.
26 Ibid, 35.
27 Ibid.
28 Ibid, 33.
29 Perry S. Millar and Carl Baar, *Judicial Administration in Canada* (Kingston and Montreal: McGill-Queen's University Press, Institute of Public Administration of Canada, 1981), 3–4.
30 Anthony Gerein of Humbolt and Michael Stechishin of Yorkton, appointed in 1955 and 1940 respectively. Judge Gerein was the father of Chief Justice W. Frank Gerein of the Court of Queen's Bench.
31 Author interview with Stuart Cameron, November 1, 2016.
32 Ibid.
33 Ibid.
34 Ibid.
35 Author interview with Gerry Gerrand, November 2, 2016.
36 University of Saskatchewan Archives and Special Collections (UskUASC), MG70S1, Hall papers, series VI, file F, letter, Culliton to Hall, March 25, 1974.
37 PAS, R-900, Roy Romanow fonds, series V, file 73d, letter, Culliton to Romanow, November 12, 1976.
38 Ibid, file 170, memo, Romanow to Blakeney, November 22, 1976.
39 Ibid, file 73d, December 21, 1977. Culliton raised the matter again several times.

40 Ibid, file 171, telex, Romanow to Chrétien, July 7, 1981.

41 Ibid, file 73d, letter, Culliton to Romanow, June 20, 1972.

42 Ibid, letter, Culliton to Romanow, August 1, 1972, and reply.

43 Ibid, spreadsheet, October 27, 1976.

44 Ibid, memo, Bonneville to Romanow, November 9, 1976.

45 Ibid, memo, Huggett to Romanow, October 27, 1976, and letter, Culliton to Romanow, October 19, 1976.

46 Ibid, letter, Culliton to Romanow, October 19, 1976; author interview with Fred Newis, January 31, 2017.

47 Author interview with Fred Newis, January 31, 2017. Newis, who was the Court of Appeal registrar from 1985 to 1995 but had been the acting registrar for many years previously, recalled that his two immediate predecessors as registrar were essentially registrars in name only. He says he was somewhat mystified as to what they actually did, as he had been supervising the Court of Appeal and Court of Queen's Bench counter staff for many years as the acting deputy registrar. Newis recalled that he set the lists in the manner described above but did not say that Culliton had done it personally before he took over the task.

48 PAS, R-900, Roy Romanow fonds, series V, file 73d, letter, Culliton to Romanow, October 19, 1976.

49 *Regina Leader-Post*, July 3, 1981. See also *The Queen's Bench Consequential Amendment Act*, SS 1981 c. 75, which seems to be the only statute applying to the merger.

50 Peter H. Russell, *The Judiciary in Canada: The Third Branch of Government* (Scarborough, ON: McGraw-Hill Ryerson, 1987), 270.

51 USKUASC, MG70SI, Hall papers, series VI, file F, Report on the Administration of Justice, 47.

52 Jules Deschênes and Carl Baar, *Masters in Their Own House: A Study on the Independent Judicial Administration of the Courts* (Ottawa: Canadian Judicial Council, 1981), 19, 21–22, 37–38; Perry S. Millar and Carl Baar, *Judicial Administration in Canada* (Montreal and Kingston: McGill-Queen's University Press, 1981), 5–6.

53 Deschênes and Barr, *Masters in Their Own House*, 86–87.

54 Moore, *Court of Appeal of Ontario*, 146–48, makes this claim as well, arguing that Laskin was both a leader and a symbol of the change.

55 Philip Girard, *Bora Laskin,: Bringing the Law to Life* (Toronto: Osgoode Society and University of Toronto Press, 2005), 97–98.

56 Peter Hogg, "Laskin's Impact on the Supreme Court," *The Laskin Legacy: Essays in Commemoration of Chief Justice Bora Laskin*, eds. Neil Finkelstein and Constance Backhouse (Toronto: Irwin Law, 2007), 67.

57 Denise Réaume, "The Judicial Philosophy of Bora Laskin," *University of Toronto Law Journal*, vol. 35, no. 4 (1985), 446–48. Réaume identifies Laskin's outlook as "functionalism" rather than realism or modernism.

58 Ibid, 448–49.

59 Karl Llewellyn, *The Common Law Tradition: Deciding Appeals* (Boston: Little, Brown, 1960).

60 Réaume, "Bora Laskin," 440.

61 Paul Horwitz, "Bora Laskin and the Legal Process School," *Saskatchewan Law Review*, vol. 59 (1995), 95.

62 This included Barry Strayer, Walter Tarnopolsky, Edward Tollefson, Edward Ratushny, W.R. Lederman, and others.

63 Sydney N. Lederman, "Personal Reflections on Judicial Education in Canada," *University of British Columbia Law Review*, vol. 38, no. 2 (2005), 561.

64 Gavin Murphy, *Law Reform Agencies* (Ottawa: Department of Justice Canada, 2004), 2.

65 William Hurlburt, *Law Reform Commissions in the United Kingdom, Australia and Canada* (Edmonton: Juriliber, 1986), 241.

66 Hogg, "Laskin's Impact," 67–72, sums up the changes on the court very pithily.

67 Girard, *Bora Laskin*, 317, 367.

68 Bora Laskin, "The Supreme Court of Canada: A Final Court of and for Canadians," *Canadian Bar Review*, vol. 29, no. 10 (1951), 1057, 1075.

69 Girard, *Bora Laskin*,, 366–67. Interestingly, Rand's biographer William Kaplan states that Rand was incredibly bigoted but nonetheless struck down restrictive covenants on Jews and people of colour.

70 Ian Binnie, "Laskin's Legacy to the Supreme Court," *The Laskin Legacy: Essays in Commemoration of Chief Justice Bora Laskin*, eds. Neil Finkelstein and Constance Backhouse (Toronto: Irwin Law, 2007), 54.

71 Frederick Vaughan, *Aggressive in Pursuit: The Life of Justice Emmett Hall* (Toronto: University of Toronto Press for the Osgoode Society for Canadian Legal History, 2004).

72 Ibid, 172.

73 Emmett Hall, "Law Reform and the Judiciary's Role," *Osgoode Hall Law Journal*, vol. 10, no. 2 (1972). 400–401.

74 Ibid, 226.

75 Ibid, 227.

76 Katherine Swinton, "Bora Laskin and Federalism," *University of Toronto Law Journal*, vol. 35, no. 4 (1985), 356.

77 *Simpson v Saskatchewan Government Insurance Office* (1967), 3 DLR 51 (Sask CA), at para. 26.

78 This is speculative, but Justice John Major, once of the Supreme Court of Canada, told the author that in his experience at practice, judges on intermediate appellate courts had various ways to avoid inconvenient precedents, including sometimes not providing reasons of judgment to make it hard to appeal to the SCC!

79 *R v Hartridge* (1966), 57 DLR (2d) 332 (Sask CA), at para. 84.

80 Katherine Swinton, "Bora Laskin," 356–57; Horwitz, "Bora Laskin," 92.

81 Girard, *Bora Laskin*,, 400.

82 Leonard J. Pollock, "Matrimonial Property and Trusts: The Situation from Murdoch to Rathwell," *Alberta Law Review*, vol. 16, no. 3, 366.

83 Rathwell v Rathwell, [1976] 5 WWR 148 (Sask CA), at para. 51.

84 Ibid, at para. 58.

85 Ibid, at para. 76.

86 Pollock, "Matrimonial Property," 360, 366.

87 Ibid, 369.

88 W.D. Moull, "Natural Resources: The Other Crisis in Canadian Federalism," *Osgoode Hall Law Journal*, vol. 18, no. 1 (March 1980), 25.

89 W.D. Moull, "Natural Resources and Canadian Federalism: Reflections on a Turbulent Decade," *Osgoode Hall Law Journal*, vol. 25, no. 2, 414.

90 R.D. Cairns, M.A. Chandler, and W.D. Moull, "The Resource Amendment (Section 92A) and the Political Economy of Canadian Federalism," *Osgoode Hall Law Journal*, vol. 23, no. 2 (1985), 254–56.

91 Swinton, "Bora Laskin," 374.

92 Ibid, 354–55.

93 Moull, "Natural Resources: The Other Crisis," 15.

94 Ibid, 12.

95 John Stuart Mill, *Principles of Political Economy* (London: Longmans, Green, 1909), book 5, chapter 3.

96 *Canadian Industrial Gas and Oil Ltd. v Saskatchewan*, [1976] 2 WWR 356 (Sask CA), at para. 88.

97 Ibid, at para. 83.

98 *Canadian Industrial Gas and Oil Ltd. v Government of Saskatchewan*, [1978] 2 SCR 545.

99 Moull, "Natural Resources: The Other Crisis," 24.

100 Ibid, 18.

101 *Saskatoon Star-Phoenix*, November 25, 1977.

102 *Central Canada Potash Co. v Saskatchewan*, [1977] 1 WWR 487 (Sask CA), at para. 7.

103 *The Mineral Resources Act*, 1965, RSS 1965, c 50, s 3(a).

104 *Central Canada Potash Co. v Saskatchewan*, [1977] 1 WWR 487 (Sask CA), at para. 77.

105 Ibid, at para. 101.

106 Ibid, at para. 102.

107 *Central Canada Potash Co. Ltd. v Government of Saskatchewan*, [1979] 1 SCR 42, at para. 75.

108 Moull, "Natural Resources: The Other Crisis," 25.

109 David Mittelstadt, *People, Principles, Progress: The Alberta Court of Appeal's First Century, 1914 to 2014* (Calgary: Legal Archives Society of Alberta, 2014), 266.

110 Waiser, *Saskatchewan*, 422–23.

111 McConnell, "Chief Justice," 8.

112 W.D. Moull, "Section 92A of the Constitution Act, 1982," *Canadian Bar Review*, vol. 61, no. 4 (1983), provides a comprehensive analysis of the then new amendment, including a speculative look at how CIGOL and Central Canada might have been decided with the amendment in place. He concludes that the amendment provided less protection of provincial legislation than might be expected.

Chapter 7 Sidebars

1 PAS, R-900, Roy Romanow fonds, Series V, file 73d, "Biographical Sketch of Mr. Justice E.D. Bayda"; Harold H. MacKay, "Edward Bayda: A Life of Service," *Canadian Lawyer*, http://www.canadianlawyermag.com/902/Edward-Bayda-A-Life-of-Service.html.

2 *Regina Leader-Post*, April 21, 1981.

3 Ibid.

4 MacKay, "Edward Bayda"; "The Honourable Edward D. Bayda, Q.C., LL.D.," http://www.gov.sk.ca/adx/aspx/adxGetMedia.aspx?mediaId=654&PN=Shared.

5 There have been younger appointments since then. Interestingly, Mary Batten was not only the second woman appointed as chief justice of a superior trial court but also the first Ukrainian; she had been born Mary Fodchuk.

6 *Regina Leader-Post*, April 28, 2007.

CHAPTER 8: THE *CHARTER* COURT

1 Dennis Gruending, "Allan Blakeney," *Saskatchewan Premiers of the Twentieth Century*, ed. Gordon L. Barnhart (Regina: Canadian Plains Research Center, 2004), 309–10.

2 Ibid, 312.

3 Author interview with Stuart Cameron, November 1, 2016.

4 James M. Pitsula, "Grant Devine," *Saskatchewan Premiers of the Twentieth Century*, ed. Gordon L. Barnhart (Regina: Canadian Plains Research Center, 2004), 323.

5 Ibid, 327.

6 Ibid, 333.

7 BillWaiser, *Saskatchewan: A New History* (Calgary: Fifth House, 2005), 448.

8 Provincial Archives of Saskatchewan (PAS), R-900, Roy Romanow fonds, series V, file 73d, letter, Bayda to Gosse, February 5, 1982.

9 Ibid, box 2290, file Judges Act Federal, 1979–1985, memo, Richard Gosse to Romanow, October 30, 1980.

10 Canadian Bar Association Committee Report, *The Appointment of Judges in Canada* (Ottawa: Canadian Bar Association, 1985) 9.

11 *Regina Leader-Post*, May 14, 1982

12 Author interview with Justice Gary Lane, March 23, 2017.

13 *Regina Leader-Post*, November 30, 1983

14 Lane Interview, March 23, 2017.

15 Saskatchewan, Legislative Assembly, *Official Report of Debates (Hansard)*, 20th Legislature, 2nd Session, March 7, 1983, 2501–2.

16 Court of Appeal, court file, hearing transcript, September 20, 1984, letter, Bayda to Lane, February 23, 1983.

17 Ibid, letter, Bayda to Lane, January 11, 1984.

18 Ibid, letter, Lane to Bayda, February 27, 1984.

19 *Zadvorny v Saskatchewan Government Insurance* (1985), 38 Sask R 59 (CA), at para. 7. See also *Tekarra Properties Ltd. v Saskatoon Drug and Stationery Co. Ltd.* (1985), 37 Sask R 286 (CA), at para. 1.

20 Court of Appeal, court file, hearing transcript, September 20, 1984.

21 Author interview with William Vancise, June 21, 2016. See also author interview with Marlene Rodie, May 23, 2017.

22 *The Globe and Mail*, December 28, 1984.

23 *Saskatchewan Gazette*, OC 1291/84, November 14, 1984.

24 *Regina Leader-Post*, December 14, 1984. Lane defended the appointment of Wakeling and Gerwing on this basis.

25 Author interview with Stuart Cameron, November 1, 2016.

26 Jean Côté, *Well-Run Appeals* (Ottawa: Canadian Judicial Council, 2006), 139.

27 Ian Greene et al., *Final Appeal: Decision-Making in Canadian Courts of Appeal* (Toronto: James Lorimer, 1998), 79.

28 Author interview with William Vancise, June 21, 2016; see also author interview with Stuart Cameron, February 1, 2017.

29 David Mittelstadt, *People, Principles, Progress: The Alberta Court of Appeal's First Century, 1914 to 2014* (Calgary: Legal Archives Society of Alberta, 2014), 354. In Alberta in the early 1990s, a new chief justice started discussing circulating judgments at court meetings, but the practice was discontinued after several years, as it only seemed to exacerbate interpersonal issues.

30 Author interview with Stuart Cameron, February 1, 2017.

31 Court of Appeal, memo, "Court of Appeal Practice Directives," June 4, 2012, Practice Directive #1, 1981.

32 Ibid, Practice Directive #2, October 22, 1981.

33 Ministry of Justice (MOJ), box 53, file 104.2-13, Court Services, Court of Appeal, Court of Appeal: Law Clerk Study, 1986. See also Ministry of Justice and Attorney General, *Annual Reports*, 1981–1986.

34 Ibid.

35 Alberta Court of Appeal Administrative Records, box 2193, file Court Meetings, Minutes, 1988.

36 Author interview with Gerry Gerrand, November 2, 2016; author interview with Garret Wilson, June 22, 2016.

37 MOJ, Deputy Minister Files, box 53, file 104.2-13, Court Services, Court of Appeal, memo, Richards to Barrington-Foote, February 24, 1987, and meeting notes, January 28, 1987.

38 Author interview with Stuart Cameron, February 1, 2017.

39 M. Kim Anderson et al., "The Saskatchewan Court of Appeal and the Charter," *Saskatchewan Law Review*, vol. 52, no. 2 (1988), 219, note 158.

40 MOJ, Deputy Minister Files, box 53, file 104.2-13 Court Services, Court of Appeal, letter, Bayda to Lane, March 27, 1990.

41 MOJ, Deputy Minister Files, box 53, file 104.2-13, Court Services, Court of Appeal, memo, Taylor to Gary Brandt, director court services, August 13, 1985.

42 Ibid, memo, Richards to Barrington-Foote, February 24, 1987.

43 PAS, R-900, Roy Romanow fonds, series V, file 171, letter, Romanow to Bayda, June 4, 1981.

44 PAS, F-429, Bob Andrews fonds, series IX I.6, file (7.07e), Court of Appeals memo, Barrington-Foote to Holizki, June 8, 1987.
45 MOJ, Deputy Minister Files, Box 53, File 104.2-13, Court Services, Court of Appeal, memo, Zarzeczny to Barrington-Foote, May 1, 1987.
46 Email communication with the author, November 2, 2017.
47 Roger Tasse, "Application of *the Canadian Charter of Rights and Freedoms*, (Sections 30–33 and 52)," *The Canadian Charter of Rights and Freedoms*, 108.
48 Ibid, 69.
49 Ibid, 105, 107.
50 *Minister of Home Affairs v Fisher*, [1979] UKPC 21, at 5.
51 William F. Pentley, "Interpreting the Charter: General Principles," *The Canadian Charter of Rights and Freedoms*, eds. Gerald A. Beaudoin and Ed Ratushny (Ottawa: Human Rights Research and Education Centre, University of Ottawa, 1989), 22.
52 Ian Greene, *The Charter of Rights* (Toronto: James Lorimer, 1989), 55.
53 Michael Mandel, *The Charter of Rights and the Legalization of Politics in Canada* (Toronto: Wall and Thompson, 1989), 62–63.
54 Anderson et al., "Saskatchewan Court of Appeal and the Charter," 239.
55 Author interview with Stuart Cameron, February 1, 2017.
56 *Regina Leader-Post*, July 12, 1985.
57 *Saskatoon Star-Phoenix*, July 2, 1988.
58 Author interview Bob Richards, May 25, 2017.
59 *Regina Leader-Post*, July 12, 1985.
60 Author interview with William Vancise, June 31, 2016.
61 Author interview with Stuart Cameron, November 1, 2016.
62 Anderson et al., "The Saskatchewan Court of Appeal and the Charter," 240.
63 Ibid, 241.
64 *R v Mohl* (1987), 55 Sask R 22 (CA).
65 Ibid, 240.
66 Stuart Cameron in personal communication with the author, July 18, 2017. See also Beth Bilson, "Judicial Review of the Decisions of Labour Tribunals in the Bayda Court," *Saskatchewan Law Review*, vol. 70, no. 2 (2007).
67 Interestingly, Vancise says that he believed he was writing the majority decision of the court and that it turned into a dissent when other members of the panel later changed their minds. Author interview with William Vancise, June 21, 2016.
68 Kate Welsh, "Breathalyzer, Detention and the Right to Counsel: *R v Therens*," *Alberta Law Review*, vol. 23, no. 3 (1985), 529.
69 *R v Therens* (1983), 23 Sask R 81 (CA), at para. 11.
70 Ibid, at para. 10.
71 Ibid, at para. 9.
72 Ibid, at para. 9.
73 Ibid, at para. 37.
74 Ibid, at para. 40.
75 Welsh, "Breathalyzer," 535.
76 Ibid, 536.

77 David M. Paciocco, "Section 24(2) Lottery or Law: The Appreciable Limits of Purposive Reasoning," *Criminal Law Quarterly*, vol. 58, no. 1 (2011), summarizes many of the developments around section 24(2).

78 Judy Fudge, "Labour, the New Constitution, and Old-Style Liberalism," *Queen's Law Journal*, vol. 13, no. 2 (1988), 61.

79 Ibid, 62.

80 Jim Warren and Kathleen Carlisle, *On the Side of the People: A History of Labour in Saskatchewan* (Regina: Coteau Books, 2005), 239–40.

81 RWDSU *Local 544 v Saskatchewan* (1985), 39 Sask R 193 (CA), Bayda, at para. 12.

82 Ibid, at para. 29.

83 Anderson et al., "The Saskatchewan Court of Appeal and the Charter," 241.

84 *RWDSU*, Cameron, at para. 4.

85 Ibid, at para. 8.

86 Ibid, at para. 19.

87 Ibid.

88 *Saskatchewan Federation of Labour v Saskatchewan*, 2015 SCC 4, [2015] 1 SCR 245.

89 Janelle Souter, "Clearly the Arc Bends: *Stare Decisis* and *Saskatchewan Federation of Labour v. Saskatchewan*," *Saskatchewan Law Review*, vol. 78 (2015), gives a full account.

90 W. Howard McConnell, "Bilingualism on the Prairies: The Constitutional Status of French in Saskatchewan," *Saskatchewan Law Review*, vol. 53, no. 1 (1989), 143, note 5.

91 *Mercure v Saskatchewan* (1985), 44 Sask R 22 (CA), at para. 15.

92 Thomson Irvine, "Language Rights in Saskatchewan," *Saskatchewan Law Review*, vol. 79, no. 2 (2016), 158.

93 Ibid, 170.

94 McConnell, "Bilingualism on the Prairies," 149.

95 Morris C. Shumiatcher, "'I Set Before You Life and Death' (Abortion, Borowski and the Constitution)," *University of Western Ontario Law Review*, vol. 1 (1986–87), 2.

96 Tom Campbell, "An Analysis of Borowski v. The Attorney General of Canada and the Minister of Finance of Canada," *Saskatchewan Law Review*, vol. 49, no. 2 (1985), 359.

97 *Borowski v Canada* (Attorney General), [1989] 1 SCR 342, at 52.

98 Campbell, "An Analysis of Borowski," 364.

99 Beverly Baines, "Abortion, Judicial Activism and Constitutional Crossroads," *University of New Brunswick Law Journal*, vol. 157 (2004), 169.

100 F.L. Morton and Rainer Knopff, "Does the Charter Mandate One Person, One Vote," *Alberta Law Review*, vol. 30, no. 2 (1992), 679.

101 Morton and Knopff, "One Person, One Vote," 675.

102 Ronald E. Fritz, "Challenging Electoral Boundaries under the Charter: Judicial Deference and Burden of Proof," *Review of Constitutional Studies*, vol. 5, no. 1, 4.

103 Garrett Wilson, *Outlier: Life, Law and Politics in the West* (Regina: Benchmark Press, 2016), 186.

104 Duff Spafford, "'Effective Representation': Reference Re: Provincial Electoral Boundaries," *Saskatchewan Law Review*, vol. 56 (1992), 200.
105 Ibid.
106 *Canadian Charter of Rights and Freedoms*, s 2, Part I of the *Constitution Act, 1982*, being schedule B to the *Canada Act 1982* (UK), 1982, c 11.
107 *Reference Re Provincial Electoral Boundaries* (Sask.) (1991), 90 Sask R 174 (CA), at para. 28.
108 Ibid, at para. 33.
109 Ibid, at para. 47.
110 Fritz, "Challenging Electoral Boundaries," 8–9, 11; Ken Roach, "Surprising and Disturbing? The Saskatchewan Boundaries Decisions," *Constitutional Forum*, vol. 3, 29, also notes McLachlin's move away from section 1 limitation to a more constrained definitional approach.
111 Roach, "Surprising and Disturbing?" 30.
112 Fritz, "Challenging Electoral Boundaries," 10–12; David Johnson, "Canadian Electoral Boundaries and the Courts: Practices, Principles, Problems," *McGill Law Journal*, vol. 39 (1994), 237–39.
113 Johnson, "Canadian Electoral Boundaries," 246.

Chapter 8 Sidebars

1 *Regina Leader-Post*, July 18, 1981.
2 James K. McDonell and Robert B. Campbell, *Lords of the North* (Renfrew, ON: General Store Publishing, 1997).
3 PAS, Saskatchewan Sessions of the Legislative Assembly and Their Duration, n.d.
4 MaryAnne Cotcher, "Cameron, Alexander C.," *Saskatchewan Politicians: Lives Past and Present*, ed. Brett Quiring (Regina: Canadian Plains Research Center, 2004), 40.
5 Author interview with Stuart Cameron, November 1, 2016.
6 Author interview with William Vancise, June 21, 1985.
7 *Regina Leader-Post*, April 15, 1985.
8 Ibid.
9 Ibid.
10 *Regina Leader-Post*, November 21, 2005.
11 Author interview with Nicholas Sherstobitoff, October 31, 2016.
12 *Regina Leader-Post*, December 5, 1985.

CHAPTER 9: THE STANDARDS OF REVIEW

1 *Valley Beef Producers Co-operative Ltd. v Farm Credit Corp.*, 2002 SKCA 100, 218 DLR (4th) 86.
2 Bill Waiser, *Saskatchewan: A New History* (Calgary: Fifth House, 2005), 454.
3 Ibid, 455.

4 Gregory P. Marchildon, "Roy Romanow," *Saskatchewan Premiers of the Twentieth Century*, ed. Gordon L. Barnhart (Regina: Canadian Plains Research Center, 2004), 354.
5 Waiser, *Saskatchewan*, 459.
6 Ibid, 463.
7 Ibid, 473.
8 Ibid, 469.
9 Peter H. Russell and Jacob S. Ziegel, "Federal Judicial Appointments," *University of Toronto Law Journal*, vol. 41 (1991), 6.
10 Ibid, 19.
11 Ibid, 6.
12 Ibid, 12.
13 Ibid, 14.
14 Author interview with Gary Lane, March 23, 2017.
15 Provincial Archives of Saskatchewan (PAS), Bayda fonds, acc. 2009-646, box 76, series C.1, file 1.0, memo, March 7, 1991, and meeting notes, March 5, 1991.
16 Dwight Newman, "A Study of the Judgments of the Saskatchewan Court of Appeal, 2003," *Saskatchewan Law Review*, vol. 68 (2005), 82.
17 See Chapter 10. Maurice Herauf, one of the sitting judges, also spent much of his career in the civil service, although he was the registrar of the court and the registrar in bankruptcy for over ten years, both of which are quasi-judicial positions. The most recent appointment, Lian Schwann, was also employed by the ministry but as a Crown counsel before replacing Herauf as registrar.
18 Sidney N. Lederman, "Personal Reflections on Judicial Education in Canada," *University of British Columbia Law Review*, vol. 38, no. 2, 566–67.
19 Author interview with Gary Lane, March 23, 2017.
20 Ministry of Justice (MOJ), Deputy Minister's Files, box DMO-07, file 104.2-08, table with comparative statistics, c. 1995.
21 Christopher Moore, *The British Columbia Court of Appeal: The First Hundred Years, 1910–2010* (Vancouver: UBC Press, 2010), 16.
22 Ibid, 27.
23 Christopher Moore, *The Court of Appeal for Ontario: Defining the Right of Appeal, 1792–2013* (Toronto: Osgoode Society, 2014), 89.
24 With apologies to Bill Vancise, who was forthcoming about the court's internal problems. In the absence of other on-record accounts or documentary corroboration, I felt I could not use his version except in very general terms.
25 Ian Greene et al.., *Final Appeal: Decision-Making in Canadian Courts of Appeal* (Toronto: James Lorimer, 1998), 138.
26 Ibid, 29–30.
27 Dwight Newman, "A Study of the Judgments of the Saskatchewan Court of Appeal, 2000," *Saskatchewan Law Review*, vol. 65 (2002), 111–12.
28 Ibid, 112.
29 PAS, Bayda fonds, acc. 2009-646, series C7, file C7/7.3, memo, Wakeling to Bayda, November 1, 1996.

30 Peter McCormick and Ian Greene, *Judges and Judging* (Toronto: James Lorimer, 1990), 184–86. See also Peter Hogg, "The Role of the Chief Justice in Canada," *Queen's Law Journal*, vol. 19, no. 1 (1993).

31 MOJ, Deputy Minister's Files, box DMO-07, file 104.2.08, memo, Irvine to Seale, August 13, 1999, 11.

32 Ibid, box 53, file 104/2-13, Court Services—Court of Appeal, request for Cabinet decision, Lane to Cabinet, February 7, 1990.

33 Ibid, memo, "Detailed Analysis of the Court of Appeal Amendment Act, 1990," n.d.

34 Ibid, memo, Barrington-Foote to Moen, May 22, 1990,

35 Ibid, box 53, file 104/2-13, Court Services—Court of Appeal, memo, McGillivray to Barrington-Foote, March 27, 1990.

36 Stuart Cameron, personal communication with the author, July 19, 2017.

37 Author interview with Marlene Rodie, May 23, 2017.

38 Hogg, "Chief Justice," 251.

39 Author interview with Georgina Jackson, May 24, 2017.

40 Author interview with Fred Newis, January 31, 2017. Newis was deputy registrar and later Queen's Bench registrar when Byron Horner was Court of Appeal registrar and was not certain what his counterpart did.

41 Author interview with Maurice Herauf, May 25, 2017.

42 Ibid.

43 PAS, Bayda fonds, acc. 2009-646, series C7, file C7/7.2, letter, Bayda to Arscott, June 17, 1991.

44 Ibid, file C7/7.3, memo, Wakeling to Bayda, November 1, 1996.

45 Court of Appeal, Rules of Court, 1997, Rule 28(1), 12.

46 *R v Proulx*, 2000 SCC 5, [2000] 1 SCR 61, at paras. 15, 127.

47 Andrew Woolford, *The Politics of Restorative Justice: A Critical Introduction* (Black Point, NS: Fernwood Publishing, 2009), 78.

48 *R v Shropshire*, [1995] 4 SCR 227. This was the first of several SCC decisions on the subject.

49 *R v Manjanatha* (1995), 131 Sask R 316 (CA), at para. 2.

50 *R v Kennedy*, [1972] 2 WWR 547 (Sask CA), was one of these rare cases. Culliton increased a sentence for manslaughter from 2 years to 3.5 years.

51 MOJ, Deputy Minister's Correspondence, box 53, file Court Services 104.2-12-01 Judges Act, transcript, CBC Interview, Sept. 25, 1992.

52 Canadian Sentencing Commission, *Sentencing Reform: A Canadian Approach—Report of the Canadian Sentencing Commission* (Ottawa: Ministry of Supply and Services Canada, 1986), 79, 85.

53 Author interview with Stuart Cameron, February 1, 2017.

54 *R v Shropshire; R v McDonnell*, [1997] 1 SCR 948.

55 *R v McGinn* (1989), 75 Sask R 161 (CA). My thanks to Justice Georgina Jackson for drawing my attention to this case.

56 Ibid, at para. 9, quoting his own decision in *R v Cope* (1987), 59 Sask R 161 (CA).

57 Ibid, at para. 81.

58 Ryan Rempel, "1999 Survey of Saskatchewan Jurisprudence," *Saskatchewan Law Review*, vol. 64 (2001), 254.

59 *R v Morin* (1995), 134 Sask R 120 (CA), at para. 6.
60 Ibid, at para. 89.
61 Ibid, at para. 20.
62 Ibid, at para. 27.
63 E.D. Bayda, "The Theory and Practice of Sentencing: Are They on the Same Wavelength," *Saskatchewan Law Review*, vol. 60 (1996).
64 *R v McDonald* (1997), 152 Sask R 81 (CA).
65 Ibid, at para. 103.
66 *R v Horvath* (1997), 152 Sask R 277 (CA).
67 Ibid, at para. 33.
68 Ryan Rempel, "1997 Survey of Decisions of the Saskatchewan Court of Appeal," *Saskatchewan Law Review*, vol. 62 (1999), 277.
69 Dwight Newman, "A Study of the Judgments of the Court of Appeal, 2002," *Saskatchewan Law Review*, vol. 67 (2004), 20.
70 Robin McKay, *Conditional Sentences* (Ottawa: Library of Parliament, Law and Government Division, 2005). See also Julian Roberts and Patrick Healy, "The Future of Conditional Sentencing," *Criminal Law Quarterly*, vol. 44, (2000–2001), 311–12.
71 Newman, "Study of the Judgments of the Court of Appeal," 25.
72 Graeme G. Mitchell, "'No Joy in This for Anyone': Reflections on the Exercise of Prosecutorial Discretion in *R v Latimer*," *Saskatchewan Law Review*, vol. 64 (2001), 492–93.
73 *R v Latimer* (1995), 134 Sask R 1 (CA), at para. 19.
74 Ibid, at para.55.
75 Ibid, at para. 78.
76 Ibid, at para. 77.
77 Ibid, at para. 121.
78 Ibid, at para. 161.
79 Roger P. Kerans, *Standards of Review Employed by Appellate Courts* (Edmonton: Juriliber, 1994), 28.
80 Daniel Jutras, "The Narrowing Scope of Appellate Review: Has the Pendulum Swung Too Far?" *Manitoba Law Journal*, vol. 32, no. 1, 67.
81 Author interview with Stuart Cameron, November 1, 2016.
82 *The Court of Appeal Act, 2000*, SS 2000, c C-42.1, s 7.
83 Ibid, s. 13.
84 Ibid, s. 14.
85 *Hallberg v Canadian National Railway Co.* (1955), 16 WWR (ns) 538 (Sask CA), at para. 17.
86 *H.L. v Canada (Attorney General)*, 2003 SKCA 78, 230 DLR (4th) 735, at para. 94.
87 *Valley Beef Producers Co-operative Ltd. v Farm Credit Corp.*, 2002 SKCA 100, 218 DLR (4th) 86, at para. 45.
88 *H.L. v Canada (Attorney General)*, at para. 12.
89 Zoë Oxaal, "'Removing That Which Was Indian from the Plaintiff': Tort Recovery for Loss of Culture and Language in Residential Schools Litigation," *Saskatchewan Law Review*, vol. 68, no. 2 (2005), 370.

Chapter 9 Sidebars

1 Dana Turgeon, "Lane, John Gary," *Saskatchewan Politicians: Lives Past and Present*, ed. Brett Quiring (Regina: Canadian Plains Research Center, 2004), 133.

CHAPTER 10: THE *CHARTER'S* SECOND COMING

1 *Whatcott v Saskatchewan (Human Rights Tribunal)*, 2010 SKCA 26, 317 DLR (4th) 69, at para. 5.
2 BillWaiser, *Saskatchewan: A New History* (Calgary: Fifth House, 2005), 473.
3 Raymond Blake, "The Saskatchewan Party and the Politics of Branding," *Saskatchewan Politics: Crowding the Centre*, ed. Howard Leeson (Regina: Canadian Plains Research Center, 2008), 170.
4 Richard Foot, "Saskatchewan Party," *The Canadian Encyclopedia*, http://www.thecanadianencyclopedia.ca/en/article/saskatchewan-party.
5 Waiser, *Saskatchewan*, 473–74.
6 Holden Stoffel, "Wall, Brad," *Encyclopedia of Saskatchewan* (Regina: Canadian Plains Research Center, 2005), http://esask.uregina.ca/entry/wall_brad_1965-.html.
7 Blake, "The Saskatchewan Party," 175.
8 Ibid, 181.
9 http://www.cbc.ca/news2/canada/skvotes2011/.
10 Waiser, *Saskatchewan*, 482; www.saskatchewan.ca/business/invest-and-economic-development/economic-overview.
11 http://www.stats.gov.sk.ca/stats/pop/2011Aboriginal%20People.pdf.
12 Haultain was chief justice of Saskatchewan from October 31, 1912, to October 31, 1938, a span of twenty-six years.
13 Author interview with John Klebuc, August 10, 2017.
14 Robert Leuer, QC, introductory remarks, Richards swearing-in ceremony, July 2, 2013, courtesy Chief Justice Richards.
15 Author interview with Robert Richards, May 25, 2017.
16 Dwight Newman, "A Study of the Judgments of the Saskatchewan Court of Appeal, 2001" *Saskatchewan Law Review*, vol. 66 (2003), 23. These annual survey articles took into account all judgments of the court, reported and unreported. For the first decade of the new century, appeals heard averaged between 110 and 120 per year, less than a third of average 1980s levels.
17 Marc Galanter, "The Vanishing Trial: What the Numbers Tell Us, What the Numbers Mean," and Thomas J. Stipanowich, "ADR and the Vanishing Trial," *Dispute Resolution Magazine*, vol. 10, no. 4 (2004), 3, 8–9. These articles give American statistics and analysis, but the situation is generally the same in Canada.
18 Julie Macfarlane and Michaela Keet, "Civil Justice Reform and Mandatory Civil Mediation: Lessons from a Maturing Program," *Alberta Law Review*, vol. 42, no. 3 (2005), 682.
19 Author interview with Robert Richards, August 23, 2017.

20 Author interview with John Klebuc, August 10, 2017.
21 Author interview with Robert Richards, August 23, 2017.
22 Sean Fine, *The Globe and Mail*, July 24, 2015, https://beta.theglobeandmail.com/news/politics/stephen-harpers-courts-how-the-judiciary-has-been-remade/article25661306/?ref=http://www.theglobeandmail.com&.
23 Author interview with Ralph Ottenbreit, July 27, 2017.
24 Schwann was also a registrar but spent most of her career as an in-house litigator with the government.
25 The rule of eighty (age plus years of judicial service) determines when a judge may request to become supernumerary. Whitmore, for example, was appointed to the Queen's Bench in 2008 at the age of fifty-eight and can become supernumerary at sixty-nine.
26 Author interview with John Klebuc, August 10, 2017.
27 Ibid.
28 Robert A. Hanson, "American State Appellate Court Technology Diffusion," *Journal of Appellate Practice and Process*, vol. 7 (2005), 264.
29 Ibid, 263–64, 267–68.
30 David Mittelstadt, *People, Principles, Progress: The Alberta Court of Appeal's First Century, 1914 to 2014* (Calgary: Legal Archives Society of Alberta, 2014), 394.
31 Author interview with John Klebuc, August 11, 2017.
32 Mittelstadt, *People, Principles, Progress*, 394. This is exactly what happened in Alberta, and John Klebuc confirms that he heard much the same story from other jurisdictions as part of his research. Author interview with John Klebuc, August 11, 2017.
33 *The Globe and Mail*, August 29, 2017.
34 Tallis, personal communication with author, September 13, 2017.
35 Author interview with Marlene Rodie, May 23, 2017.
36 Ibid.
37 Ibid.
38 Court of Appeal, memo, "Detailed Accounting of the Process," n.d.
39 Author interview with Lian Schwann, July 28, 2017.
40 *Canadian Lawyer Magazine*, June 29, 2013, http://www.canadianlawyermag.com/legalfeeds/1554/colleagues-delighted-as-richards-becomes-saskatchewans-chief-justice.html.
41 Dwight Newman, "The Judgments of the Saskatchewan Court of Appeal, 2006," *Saskatchewan Law Review*, vol. 70 (2007), 346.
42 Dwight Newman, "A Study of the Judgments of the Saskatchewan Court of Appeal, 2000," *Saskatchewan Law Review*, vol. 65 (2002), 109.
43 Dwight Newman, "The Judgments of the Saskatchewan Court of Appeal, 2005," *Saskatchewan Law Review*, vol. 69 (2006), 346.
44 Sarah Burningham and Keir Vallance, "The Judgments of the Saskatchewan Court of Appeal, 2014," *Saskatchewan Law Review*, vol. 78 (2015), 294. For the last year statistics were compiled in the law review survey articles, Richards and Jackson tied for second place in the number of judgments, at twenty-one. Richards confirmed that he continued to rank second or third for decisions.

45 Julie McFarlane, "Time to Shatter the Stereotype of Self-Represented Litigants," *Dispute Resolution Magazine*, vol. 20 (Fall 2013), 14.

46 Ibid.

47 Donald J. Netolitzky, "The History of the Organized Pseudolegal Commercial Argument Phenomenon in Canada," *Alberta Law Review*, vol. 53, no. 3 (2016). This article gives a comprehensive overlook of these litigants.

48 *O'Neill v Deacons*, 2007 ABQB 754, 441 AR 60.

49 McFarlane, "Time to Shatter the Stereotype," 15.

50 *Saskatchewan Gazette*, vol. 103, no. 46, pt. 1, 1322.

51 *Hope v Pylypow*, 2015 SKCA 26, 384 DLR (4th) 255.

52 *Hope v Pylypow*, at para. 66.

53 Robert J. Sharpe and Kent Roach, *The Charter of Rights and Freedoms* (Toronto: Irwin Law, 2017), 2.

54 Frank Iacobucci, "The Charter Twenty Years Later," *Windsor Yearbook of Access to Justice*, vol. 21 (2002), discusses the extra dimensions the *Charter* has added to jurisprudence.

55 The literature is indeed voluminous, with Peter Hogg, Christopher Manfredi, Peter Russell, Ted Morton, Rainier Knopf being just a few of the prominent writers on the topic. Kent Roach, *The Supreme Court on Trial: Judicial Activism or Democratic Dialogue*, rev. ed. (Toronto: Irwin Law, 2016), is one of the best overviews of the debate on activism.

56 Brenda Cossman, "Lesbians, Gay Men, and *the Canadian Charter of Rights and Freedoms*," *Osgoode Hall Law Journal*, vol. 40 (2002), 223.

57 Jena McGill, "'Now It's My Rights versus Yours': Equality in Tension with Religious Freedoms," *Alberta Law Review*, vol. 53, no. 3 (2016), 583.

58 Frank Iacobucci, "The Charter: Twenty Years Later," *Windsor Yearbook of Access to Justice*, vol. 21 (2002), 31.

59 McGill, "'Now It's My Rights,'" 584–85.

60 *Saskatoon Star-Phoenix*, June 1, 2002.

61 Peter Bowal and Colin McKay, "The Whatcott Case: Balancing Free Speech and Social Harmony," *LawNow*, http://www.lawnow.org/whatcott-case-balancing-free-speech-social-harmony/.

62 *Whatcott v Saskatchewan Association of Licensed Practical Nurses*, 2008 SKCA 6.

63 *The Saskatchewan Human Rights Code*, SS 1979, c S-24.1.

64 *Canada (Human Rights Commission) v Taylor*, [1990] 3 SCR 892.

65 *Saskatchewan (Human Rights Commission) v Bell* (1994), 120 Sask R 122 (CA).

66 *Owens v Saskatchewan (Human Rights Commission)*, 2006 SKCA 41, 267 DLR (4th) 733.

67 Ibid, at para. 60.

68 *Whatcott v Saskatchewan (Human Rights Tribunal)*, 2010 SKCA 26, 317 DLR (4th) 69, at para. 60.

69 Ibid, at para. 90.

70 Ibid, at para. 64.

71 *The Marriage Act, 1995*, SS 1995, c M-4.1.

72 Ibid, s. 31.

73 Jamie Gardner, "Same-Sex Marriage: A Worldwide Trend," *Law in Context: A Socio-Legal Journal*, vol. 28, no. 1 (2010), 94–100.

74 Bruce MacDougall, "Refusing to Officiate at Same-Sex Civil Marriages," *Saskatchewan Law Review*, vol. 69, 2006, 353–54.

75 *Marriage Commissioners Appointed Under The Marriage Act (Re)*, 2011 SKCA 3, 327 DLR (4th) 669, at para. 45.

76 Ibid, at para. 62.

77 Ibid, at para. 97.

78 Ibid, at para. 147.

79 Ibid, at para. 115.

80 Ibid, at para. 159.

81 Ibid, at para. 158.

82 Jared Epp, "Justified Coercion: A Case Comment on the Marriage Commissioner Reference," *Saskatchewan Law Review*, vol. 75 (2012), 104.

83 Geoffrey Trotter, "The Right to Decline Performance of Same-Sex Civil Marriages: The Duty to Accommodate Public Servants," *Saskatchewan Law Review*, vol. 70 (2007), 365; Lorraine Lafferty, "Religion, Sexual Orientation and the State: Can Public Officials Refuse to Perform Same-Sex Marriage?" *Canadian Bar Review*, vol. 85 (2006), 309–15.

84 *Toronto Sun*, January 11, 2011.

85 Janelle Souter, "Clearly the Arc Bends: *Stare Decisis* and *Saskatchewan Federation of Labour v. Saskatchewan*," *Saskatchewan Law Review*, vol. 78 (2015), 400–401.

86 *Wolfe v Canadian National Railway*, [1934] 3 WWR 497 (Sask CA), at para. 26–27. Turgeon felt the precedent in question, *Mills v Sherwood Stores Ltd.*, [1918] 2 WWR 1030 (Sask CA), was an anomaly that did not itself conform to earlier decisions, and also subsequent decisions, and should be abandoned.

87 David J. Murphy and Robert Rueter, *Stare Decisis in Commonwealth Courts* (Toronto: Butterworths, 1982), 21; Debra Parkes, "Precedent Unbound: Contemporary Approaches to Precedent in Canada," *Manitoba Law Journal*, vol. 32, no. 1 (2006), 150.

88 *Tekarra Properties Ltd. v Saskatoon Drug and Stationery Co. Ltd.* (1985), 37 Sask R 286 (CA), at para. 8.

89 See for example, *R v Big M. Drug Mart*, [1984] 1 WWR 625 (Alta CA), which discusses the trial judgment and this argument.

90 *R v Saskatchewan Federation of Labour*, 2013 SKCA 43, 361 DLR (4th) 132, at para. 48.

91 Souter, "Clearly the Arc Bends," 409, discusses whether the court endorsed the concept. Souter sees some sign of this but is unconvincing.

92 *Regina Leader-Post*, February 5, 2015.

INDEX

Page numbers in *italics* refer to photographs.

A

D

E

F

G

K

L

M

N

O

S

T

U

Y